EDWIGE THIBAUT

THE SS ORDER
Ethics & Ideology

EDWIGE THIBAUT

THE SS ORDER
Ethics & Ideology

L'ORDRE SS
Éthique & idéologie
First edition - Avalon - Paris - 1991

Translated from French and published by
Omnia Veritas Ltd

www.omnia-veritas.com

© Copyright Omnia Veritas Limited - 2023
ISBN 978-1-80540-091-2

Heinrich Himmler in 1937, driven by the idea of a new aristocracy.

PREFACE BY LÉON DEGRELLE

Volksführer
Commander of the Walloon Legion
Knight of the Iron Cross

To tell the truth, when I received the enormous mass of pages that make up this book on the SS Order, I was rather stunned: eight hundred pages of tight text! My normal life is very full. But to read this kind of encyclopaedia would take me dozens of hours! In order to get an idea of the interest or otherwise of this unusual compilation, I first leafed through the first few paragraphs. Three days later, I reached the last page.

I had found there an extraordinary amount of knowledge presented in an introduction of one hundred pages which constitute a book in themselves, supported thereafter, with a perfect knowledge of the subject, by hundreds of quotations, both simple and striking, forming an enormous anthology of texts, written at the time without seeking to astonish the reader, but rather to inform and convince him. Politically, it was the entire panorama of the SS reconstructed by direct witnesses who had not even thought of being historians but who had, according to the staggered years, exposed the doctrine, the objectives, the methods, the mystique of the movement which was undoubtedly, along with Leninism, the most important political phenomenon of the 20th century.

* * *

Who had raised the money? A famous chronicler? No. A young, almost unknown woman, Edwige Thibaut, a fantastically hard worker who, for years, had read thousands of pages written about the SS by hundreds of analysts, philosophers and technicians. They belonged to the most diverse circles: young people, old people, intellectuals, grassroots observers. Edwige Thibaut had patiently sorted through these multitudinous works and then classified them in an intelligent order. She wanted, first of all, to satisfy her joy of discovery, but then, if the opportunity arose, to communicate this joy to the curious minds that try, here and there, to reach the Truth.

For such is the characteristic of this work: this young woman invents nothing, imagines nothing; she comments, of course, but she contributes one hundred texts written by others, published at the very time of their creation, written by numerous observers who expressed themselves in scattered publications. This recapitulation and unification, which had not even been imagined at the time, was carried out by Edwige Thibaut herself in the course of a work that would have earned her, had she been wearing a monk's habit instead of a skirt, the tenfold qualification of "Benedictine"!

* * *

Today's crowd reads in haste. But here it is a question of devoting dozens of hours of assiduous and arduous reading to scrutinising texts that demand a powerful application! But the subject is crucial. Who was this SS and, more specifically, the Waffen-SS? What do we know about it? What can we know about it? Such is the mission that Edwige Thibaut, braving the lightness of the century, had the energy to face. This veritable encyclopaedia of the SS could have remained in a drawer forever. Now a daring publisher is risking publication, despite the enormity of its contents.

In reality, until now, despite having been the subject of thousands of books, the SS is little known, poorly known, and has often been disfigured by summary accusations, bordering on the ridiculous or odious. The Waffen-SS, its most famous emanation, was the most extraordinary political-military formation that humanity has ever known. During the Second World War, the Waffen-SS had a million volunteers from twenty-eight different countries. All these boys had come of their own accord to offer their lives (402,000 died in combat) for a cause that had taken every ounce of their physical life and will.

All this did not happen by itself. The SS were only a handful at the beginning of Hitlerism. It took an enormous amount of faith to take hold of them and then to consume them so that this absolute gift, this free, total discipline, and the sovereign conviction that they were bringing a new type of man to the world, could blossom.

Who was this new man? What was his message? Where can we find the testimonies, transcribed at the very moment, of this will to create a universe (the Weltanschauung), where everything would be recreated, regenerated? This book provides the answer. Thanks to it, we will finally know what the SS was and what it could have given to man and the world if its victorious runes had definitively marked the universe.

* * *

In the cathedral that is this work by Edwige Thibaut, there is everything. After studying this encyclopaedia, one knows what the spiritual guides of the SS—brilliant minds as well as modest brains—had to say every day for years. Edwige Thibaut has taken up, page by page, the essence of their work, conceived in the heat and light of events.

Certainly, some of the problems to be solved have changed in scope. Certain conceptions have been modified along the way. In particular, the notion, sometimes too summary, of the spiritual life of man. The religious impulse has a thousand secret detours. Hitler, the first, knew that we all— and the universe—were dominated by the *Almighty*. The sometimes provocative intransigence of some SS men would soon be overtaken. I myself was an ardent Christian, which did not prevent Hitler from saying that if he had had a son, he would have wanted him to be like me! In the *Walloon* division of the Waffen-SS, we had our chaplains, sharing all our trials on the Eastern Front. In the SS *Charlemagne* division, a magnificent prelate, Monsignor Mayol de Luppé, led thousands of young French heroes into battle and sacrifice. Here too, the balance would be struck between a historical paganism that some wanted to resurrect and the mystical life, that secret vibration of the conscience.

The tremendous influence of the SS was not a dictatorship of the mind, but an adhesion of the whole being, freely and flexibly brought to bear. This immense wealth, which the SS carried before it as the ancient gods carried lightning, could have been lost, unravelled in the mists of time. Thanks to Edwige Thibaut, it has been reconstructed, honestly and completely.

Half a century has passed. Those who lived through this epic will feel their youthful ardour as they rediscover the milestones. I myself am the last living commander of a Waffen-SS division and the last *Volksführer*: in my eyes this reconstruction is a resurrection. But it is above all the young people that I am thinking of, the young people from whom the richness of the truth had been so hatefully hidden. Here it is. They are going to know, finally! in all its abundance and complexity, what the SS was. And, more particularly, its right arm, the Waffen-SS.

Who knows? Not only knowledge, but the voice, perhaps one day, reincarnated by them, will rebuild the new world that our brains and our weapons had wanted to create.

Léon Degrelle, Malaga, I June 1990

INTRODUCTION

In ancient times, people who were constantly fighting for survival in a hostile world had the right to life and death over the defeated. The natural right of the strongest prevailed; however, the adversary faced could keep the respect of the other party, which emphasised the greatness of the combatants involved. Men went to war for existential reasons, not ideological ones. The conquest of a territory justified warlike expeditions and the notion of honour or shame determined the value of each individual. What did an unknown moral right mean in the face of the sense of honour that guided every action, physical strength and agility, intellectual ingenuity, and above all the need to survive?

If we look critically at the course and conclusion of the war in 1945, we see the culmination of a long process that began with the emergence of the biblical religions, namely that morality and the notion of sin have replaced the sense of honour and politics. The worthy adversary was transformed into an absolute enemy, the bearer of all the vices that oppose 'civilisation' and must be converted or eliminated at all costs. After the wars of religion, the hunt for heretics and witches, came the imperialist wars of colonisation by religious missionaries. Now a *planetary* war was being waged not only between peoples, but between different conceptions of the world, some based on the rights and equality of all men, universalist and nomadic individualism, and others on the mystique of race, the valorisation of the heroic attitude overcoming the divisions of time, and community value. Considering that there are laws that are superior to those of states, the notion of crime, once exclusively individual, was broadened into "crimes against humanity" and applied to a system, an ideology and even an entire nation. The legality and specificity of system-specific state actions were supplanted by the legality of a universal humanistic right. For the first time in history, this particular moral right, directly derived from the spirit of the French Revolution, allowed men representing nations that had committed the crimes of Hiroshima, Dresden and Katyn to judge a political system that refused the levelling mould of a globalist order. The principle of retribution thus reached its climax. The American Nathan Kaufmann, in his pamphlet *Germany Must Perish* published in 1941, cynically expressed this state of affairs: "The present war is not a war against Adolf Hitler. Nor is it a war against the Nazis. It is a war of peoples against other peoples, of civilised peoples bearing light, against uncivilised barbarians who love darkness. This planetarisation of morality could only herald other wars against possible infringements of 'international law' which, under the guise of justice, impose a unilateral moral model on peoples and states.

The outcome of the trial left no doubt. The totalitarianism of this war could only mercilessly crush the defeated. The guilt of an ideology, National Socialism, and its defenders, modern devils, was recognised. A 'chosen people' was naturally confronted with a 'fallen people', eternally cursed. The SS was in the forefront of the attacks in this context too. The SS was in the front line of the attacks, represented by a number of generals and senior officers, since its leaders, Hitler and Himmler, had preferred to remain masters of their own destiny by killing themselves. What were they accused of? That it had been the implacable political instrument of National Socialism in achieving its objectives.

Since 1947, the media and the tabloid press have taken over from the international tribunal, but on a more extensive level. Countless books have been published on the subject of National Socialism, the SS and the concentration camps, demonstrating that the "forbidden and the unmentionable" still exert a fascination on a well-trained public. The production of "fascistoid" films such as *Rambo, Conan the Barbarian* or *Mad Max* are striking examples. However, the studies and scientific works of 'reputable' historians remain silent in the face of many questions asked by critical minds.

French literature likes to present the SS as a man with a whip as scathing as his words, listening piously to Beethoven and exterminating millions of people without a tear. Such a stereotypical and uniform image of the cruel and stupid camp guard seems profoundly restrictive in the face of the reality of the scientific researchers, artists, writers or soldiers who each embodied one of the many faces of the SS. Are they even comparable, when one knows the oppositions that may have arisen within the Order, despite the desire for ideological centralisation? It is certain that no society is spared the presence of dubious or criminal individuals in its midst. The human character always has weaknesses that are difficult to overcome and which sometimes manifest themselves. But can we conceive that it would be right to systematise such a phenomenon simply because we are dealing with enemies, or supposed enemies, whether they be literary, scientific or artistic? How could millions of men, including a large number of Europeans, commit their own lives to such a system that was supposed to deny all human dignity? A careful examination of the facts can provide the answer.

All those who study the tragic events of the Second World War will wonder about the motivations of these men, who are so little mentioned in history books. We French will be able to ask ourselves all the more, since 40,000 Frenchmen took part in the fighting under a uniform that had become European, and at least 10,000 of them became "political soldiers" of the SS. National Socialism belongs to history. It was born and died with Adolf Hitler. Many people who did not live through that time now wonder who those men were who went so far away to find death in a foreign land. Let us leave aside partisan passion which can only distort their history in one direction or the other. After the healing of obvious wounds, it is now time to de-dramatise passions, to analyse historical and political events with the same serenity as when dealing with the religious wars, the crusades or Plato's thought. It would be a cruel irony of fate to resemble those who are condemned by the use of censorship and intellectual repression. The purpose of this book is therefore to enable the reader to understand what may have led individuals who apparently had no predisposition to join the National Socialist side.

Dealing with the political ideas of the SS is a vast, difficult, surprising and confusing undertaking. To speak of the SS is first and foremost to study its "political ideas", which will certainly surprise those who conceived of the SS only as a repressive police body. It is therefore to speak more accurately of its "world view", its history, its goals, its aspirations, but also its errors and internal divergences. The National Socialist dialectic will be deciphered, allowing for a better understanding of the meaning of terms often misused today.

As explained in the first chapter of *The SS Order, History and Principles*, the SS originated in Adolf Hitler's personal security guard. Composed of hand-picked men, totally convinced ideologically, it was to take on a new dimension with the arrival of Heinrich Himmler at its head. Indeed, until 1929, the date of his appointment, the SS was nothing more than a super SA, obedient, free of any ideological initiative, a pure executive body, but already underpinned by the elitist idea. Working patiently in the shadows, Himmler had won Hitler's confidence and won over his vision of a new SS as a fighting ideological order, the foundation of a future society. It was no longer a mere security organisation; it became the active and principal instrument of National Socialism, having to protect the Reich but above all to produce the future elite of Europe and to educate the people in the National Socialist spirit. It was also an extraordinary field of experimentation, a "laboratory of ideas" that allowed the most diverse talents to flourish, encouraging permanent innovation without ever cutting itself off from a traditional value system. From Hitler's guard, the SS had experienced a new birth as the guard and spearhead of the National Socialist movement. Now it was totally committed to an idea, even to the point of being a vanguard movement.

The remarkable speed of its development from a certain period onwards demonstrates the new destiny assumed by the SS. From a low of 200–300 men spread over the whole of Germany since its creation in 1923, it rapidly increased to 1000 in 1929, 14,964 in 1931, stabilised between 209,000 in 1933 and 238,159 in 1938, and reached almost one million men in 1945. But this rapid growth should not be misleading. The SS was a selective organisation based, unlike the SA and the Party, on a *strictly voluntary* commitment. Since it did not force anyone to join, the selection was always very strict, as Himmler explained in a speech in 1937, when he excluded

60,000 SS men between 1933 and 1935 who were 'not absolutely enthusiastic or idealistic', while the other Party organisations opened up widely to their base.

This sudden but controlled expansion of the SS was a response to the extension of its tasks due to its new management and also to the new perspectives offered by the National Socialist takeover in Germany. It was to be divided into three main branches: the Allgemeine SS (general, or civilian, SS, from which the other two branches emerged), the SS-Totenkopfverbände (skull and crossbones units dealing with the external administration of the concentration camps and certain police tasks) and the SS-Verfügungstruppe (SS troops at the disposal of the SS, or paramilitary troops, which later gave birth to the Waffen-SS). While the Wehrmacht was responsible for the external security of the country, the SS was responsible for the internal security of the nation by policing the 'enemies within', as it called them, and above all for spreading the National Socialist world view.

The SS were thus educated in this sense, which gave them the status of cadres and encouraged them to achieve the highest results in all fields, be they civil or military, intellectual or sporting. They were to embody and teach a revolutionary and traditional faith, worldview and life. However, from the point of view of the SS, the revolutionary and traditional characters are not contradictory. The former represents a direct attack on the existing Judeo-Christian social and moral system, while the latter advocates a commitment to unchanging traditional values derived from the racial essence of the people. Through voluntary commitment to its ranks, it appealed to the militant spirit and the sense of responsibility and loyalty that are inseparable from the state of being a free man. The SS also acquired the character of a society within a society through the special internal rules and ethics it had established for itself. It was already realising within itself what was to become the future of Europe, and later of the world, in the eyes of the National Socialists.

It is understandable that the achievement of such objectives required the creation of appropriate departments. In 1929, the first SS office, the Central Management Office, was created, followed in 1931 by the Rasse-und Siedlungsamt (Race and Settlement Office) headed by Walther Darré, and the Sicherheitsamt (Security Office) for internal police and political surveillance headed by Reinhard Heydrich, which became higher offices (Hauptamt) in January 1935 as part of a general reorganisation. In the 1938 book on the organisation of the NSDAP, the tasks of the RuSHA were defined as follows: "It provides the SS, a community of clans selected according to Nordic racial views, with the instruments that make it capable of realising the idea of Blood and Soil through characteristic leadership. It consisted of different offices:

I. Ordnungs-und Verwaltungsamt (Administrative and Organization Office): It creates the basis for organization, personnel and materials to facilitate the work of the other offices.

II. Rasseamt (Race Bureau): The task of this office is to demonstrate and exploit the idea that blood alone determines history, civilisation, law and economy.

III. Schulungsamt (Educational Office): The purpose of the educational office is to instruct the SS ideologically. The aim is to bring every SS man to an absolute view of the National Socialist world view and thus to create a solid ideological bloc among the people.

IV. Sippenamt (Clan Office): This office is responsible for examining the heredity and origin of SS officers and non-commissioned officers already in the organisation, as well as newly admitted members.

V. Siedlungsamt (Settlement Office): It realises the idea of Blood and Soil through the sedentarisation of SS families as part of the policy of recreating the German peasantry and re-rooting the homes.

The SS-Hauptamt, as the Reichsführer SS's superior decision-making centre, had the task of training, instructing and committing the three parts of the Protection Troop to their respective tasks: the Allgemeine SS, the SS-Verfügungstruppen and the SS-Totenkopfverbartde. From 1940 onwards it was led by Gottlob Berger, the architect of the European Waffen-SS.

It included the following offices:

I. Führungsamt (Steering Committee): The steering committee is responsible for all matters relating to the training and organisation of the three SS branches.

II. Personalamt (Personnel Office): part of the 'Personnel Chancellery', authorised to deal with all personnel matters, especially those of SS officers and NCOs in charge of officer positions.

In addition, this area includes the convocation of officer cadets and the supervision of officer cadets from the SS Junker School.

III. Verwaltungsamt (Administrative Office): deals with all administrative and budgetary matters of the three higher offices.

As the only person mandated by the Reichsführer SS, he also directed relations in these areas with other services outside the SS.

The head of the administrative office is the sole proxy to the Reich Treasurer for the entire SS.

An institution was created to strengthen the means for the building and operation of the SS service in the administrative office. Non-SS Aryans became *"supporting members"* if they undertook to pay a monthly sum of money, which they set themselves, on a regular and voluntary basis.

IV. Sanitätsamt (Sanitary Office): The head of the Sanitary Office is responsible for all matters concerning the sanitary character of the SS. He is also responsible to the Reichsführer SS for the sanitary tasks of the SS by virtue of his qualification as "SS doctor".

V. Ergartzungsamt (Recruiting Office): deals with all new admissions of non-commissioned officers and enlisted men, as well as readmissions, suspensions, discharges, transfers and resignations. In addition, it deals with the carding and registration of all SS members, the calculation and evaluation of all SS forces.

VI. Amt für Sicherungsaufgaben (Office for Security Tasks): deals with all measures concerning SS activity at NSDAP events. It also collaborated with the Ministry of the Interior in all matters concerning the military service of SS members.

VII. Beschaffungsamt (Supply Office): The area of the supply office includes the provision of equipment for the entire SS.

VIII. Amt für Leibesübungen (Sports Exercise Office): prepares and implements all measures of SS sports activity in all sports and supervises SS sports training.

IX. Amt für Nachrichtenverbindungen (Office for Information Communications): deals with all matters concerning all SS news.

X. Versorgungs-und Fürsorgeamt SS (SS Supply and Welfare Office): deals with all matters of SS welfare, in close cooperation with the competent national and communal offices (labour offices, etc.) as well as with all matters concerning special donations.

(We list here only the offices of the two most important offices, those dealing with instruction and racial selection. The other offices will be dealt with at a later date in another book dealing more specifically with the history and development of the SS).

The Schulungsamt was therefore responsible for the educational work of the troops carried out by chief instructors. They were responsible for conducting instruction in the form of occasional lectures for the officer corps and in the form of regular education in basic principles for the troops. From 1934 onwards, they began to carry out their work, which also included everything that could be used to exert an indirect ideological influence, such as the organisation of troop bookshops, the supply of newspapers and magazines to the units, the design of internal troop celebrations and ceremonies, as well as other forms of cultural entertainment and soldier support. They also took part in the examination to decide on the final admission of the SS candidate to the Order. Before 1937, there was no military character to the training, which was the responsibility of the commanders and unit officers, etc. The leadership of the units was therefore divided between the commanders and unit officers. The leadership of the units was thus divided in two ways: militarily it was the responsibility of the commanders and ideologically it was the responsibility of the heads of training.

Such dualism naturally belied the traditional principles of military authority, as troop leaders were responsible for the minds and attitudes of soldiers as well as their military qualifications. The contrast is all the more striking in that the chief instructors saw their task unrestrictedly as ideological training work. For example, the chief instructor of the Leibstandarte Adolf Hitler stipulated in a memorandum in 1937 that the tasks and skills of his guild should be based on the example of the political commissar of the Red Army. The symptomatic nature of such an attitude demonstrates the divergence that can exist between SS ideology and the conservative spirit of the Wehrmacht military. However, this apparent dualism in education was by no means a consequence of the principles of SS ideology. Rather, it was the fusion of military and political power that was encouraged, and this was resented by the senior officers of the Waffen SS. It can therefore be assumed that this was the result of immediate ideological necessity. The members of the SS military units had for the most part already received the old military training which omitted or neglected political instruction. The SS leadership therefore wished to entrust the role of ideological instruction to a circle of specially selected men who would guarantee the faithful orientation of the young SS units.

From the end of 1937 onwards, this principle of distributing educational responsibilities gradually disappeared without, however, making the slightest concession on the ideological level or adapting to the customs in force in the Wehrmacht. Ideological instruction was gradually delegated to company commanders and also—with reservations—to battalion commanders. The chief instructors, now renamed 'Weltanschauliche Erziehung' (WE), continued their work at a high regimental level but were now limited to relieving the company commanders of part of the ideological education. This redistribution of roles remained as it was until the end of the war. It should also be noted that these WE leaders were given new duties, such as assisting families, maintaining graves and, above all, supporting the German volunteers of the SS. The reasons for the gradual disappearance of the separation of military and ideological competences were dictated by practical considerations. The increasing number of tasks that the SS was taking away from state and ideological needs ultimately threatened the very unity of the order. The SS leadership had to bridge the widening gaps between the Allgemeine SS, the police, the Totenkopfverblinde (TV) and the Verfügungstruppen (VT) at all costs. Himmler also pointed out that the obvious danger lies in the fact that the commander and the troop leader hand over to someone else the most important part of their function, namely educating their men themselves, because they have no interest in it. This may lead to a certain conflict in command. The militarisation of the skull and crossbones units and the Allgemeine, as well as the politicisation of the military branch of the SS, prevented this danger. The guiding principle of the "political soldier" contained this fusion within itself. In this spirit, a true SS officer could only be a troop officer if he was also the ideological instructor of his men. We shall see later how difficult this principle was to implement.

A study of the ideological work carried out long before the war reveals that it followed different stages in its conception and organisation. According to the lectures given by the first head of the Schulungsamt Cäsar (whose articles will be found in this book, and who was replaced in 1942 by Ludwig Eckstein, who is also represented by his articles) at a meeting of the SS Gruppenführer in 1939, the first educational phase dealt with the essential questions of SS racial policy. However, the men became weary of 'natalist policy', 'hereditary health issues', 'racology' and 'marital choice'. In a second stage, therefore, education was expanded to include the study of the "foundations of the National Socialist worldview". In the third stage, when 'this programme … no longer met the requirements', 'the historical themes from which the National Socialist position on all questions of political life is derived' were increasingly studied. Standartenführer Julius Cäsar summed up the development of education in the SS perfectly. The reorganisation of education even shows that the tasks of the SS have been expanded and changed to an even greater extent than is apparent from these statements. As early as March 1938, the SS Reichsführer had commissioned him to draw up "a multi-subject plan, valid for all times and also for future centuries, which would include in a logical sequence the birth of the world and thus the fields of science and astronomy, biology, and Hörbiger's doctrine of 'world ice'. It would also include the birth of our planets, the Earth and also the fields of geology, mineralogy, botany, zoology and all other related sciences. The origin of man, the marvellous art with which God organised and created him, as well as all the branches of knowledge related to man, whether it be the miracle of the birth of a new life or linguistics, anatomy or the knowledge of the complexity of the brain, as well as raciology, will also be studied… At the end of each year, a general summary must be made in a global presentation. The SS of today, in 1938, as well as those of the year 2000 and much later—I hope—… will be familiar with the history of our people, of all Aryans, of the Earth—its greatness and beauty—as well as that of the whole world and will become aware of the greatness and omnipotence of God. These considerations by Himmler are not innocent. They illustrate perfectly the gradual and organised evolution of the instruction carried out in the SS, as well as the extension of the role assigned to the SS.

On Himmler's orders, the Schulungsamt developed a whole range of means and tools for this task. The most important educational instrument was certainly the "SS-Leithefte" published from 1935. These 'guide books' conveyed the ideological package for the SS in the form of short articles (2–4 pages on average), aphorisms and poems from the works of great men. Emphasis was also placed on the illustrative aspect, considering that a photo speaks louder than a thousand words and has a stamp of authenticity that cannot be arbitrarily changed. These formative magazines sought quality in both ideological and iconographic terms and, even during the war, never allowed the slightest room for caricature or pin-up photographs, which were considered to present a degrading image of the human being. They were initially divided into two parts: "The first part contains the theme taught according to the order of the Reichsführer SS and is intended for monthly instruction (four passages from *Mein Kampf,* four stories, four examples from the work of the genealogical office. In addition, it contains the principles for calling up units. The editorial in this part, in which it is explained why and how the training on the theme of the month should be carried out, is only intended for SS officers, chief instructors and in general should not be taught to the troops.

"The second part ["for the personal training of SS officers and chief instructors"] is not intended to be taught. It is intended to enable SS officers and chief instructors to broaden their knowledge. They may exploit the subject as they see fit. *It would be a fundamental mistake to study the various articles one after the other in front of the troops.* This would lead to fatigue and intellectual overload which would be harmful to the men. The second part should also serve as supplementary material for the instruction of the SS-VTs, etc.' (Extract from a March 1936 guidebook).

In an issue from October 1937, the following statement is indicative of the changes made: "The words Distribution and reproduction prohibited! Only for service" is deleted in future: in its place is the statement "Only loan to others permitted! Reproduction is only permitted with the publisher's permission".

"The aim of the new regulation is first and foremost to make the guidelines accessible to all SS and their family members.

The officers of the units are thus given essential support in their educational work.

"The framework of the guidebook is also expanded. Until now it was intended to serve as an ideological instruction. This objective will be retained in the future. But the task of the guidebooks is being extended by the fact that they must also deal with *the overall training* of the SS.

"Thus, in a new section "We and the Service", practical instructions and suggestions are provided for military training (internal and external), sports, equestrian and technical training, and for the conduct of the SS in everyday life.

"Another part will show the effect of our worldview in all areas of life (family, morals, education, culture, economy, politics, sports, etc.). By means of constant presentations, the ultimate goal of our revolution will be indicated: the creation of a New Man who will once again embody a unity of mind-body-soul, blood-spirit-will-action.

"Another section must constantly keep the character of the National Socialist fighter alive and develop.

"In order to arouse the political instincts of the SS and to draw his attention to important political events, the "political situation" will be dealt with continuously in the future.

The "Guiding principles for troop calls" will now be deleted. Otherwise, the principles governing the two main parts are retained, namely the four articles following the different themes."

Various covers of SS magazines.

Other SS magazine covers.
The purity of the lines and the simplicity of the images are the secret of the aesthetics of the SS publications.

The SS notebooks were a constant concern for the Schulungsamt. This was even more the case when the Schulungsamt was transferred from the RuSHA to the SS-Hauptamt in 1938, which also reflected the reorganisation of the SS structures. Was it because of the conflicts between Heinrich Himmler and Walther Darré, due to the latter's lack of realism and practicality? In any case, the education office was now under the jurisdiction of the SS-Hauptamt, a service that belonged to Himmler's direct management. The proofs of the notebooks were therefore regularly submitted to him, and he corrected them with the utmost care. Until the last moments of the war, Himmler always attached great importance to ideological training. As early as 1937, he had sent a circular to all SS commanders and officers, telling them that they should 'adhere strictly to the sources indicated in the Leithefte'. In his speech to the propaganda chiefs on 28 January 1944, he further defined the purpose of his SS Leithefte: Each chapter must emphasise the concepts of the perpetual struggle on this earth, of tenacity, that only the strong survive in the end in the struggle—be it in plants, animals, small living creatures or humans. There is never peace, only struggle. In June 1944, in another speech, he said that the SS notebooks did not yet fully correspond to his wishes, but that they would improve with time.

Any SS man with writing skills and a solid knowledge of various fields was also invited to participate in the writing of the director's notebooks, as stated in the 1938 article "Which of you has a good pen? The Reichsführer

SS attaches the greatest importance to the cooperation of comrades in the troop with the SS-Leithefte, especially those who can write in such a way that they can be understood by any SS man.

"The troopers who attend ideological courses in the evenings after their work are not prepared to read complicated background articles and treatises that are difficult to understand. He wants to have typical stories and descriptions that touch his sensibility. Articles, narratives, short stories and discussions of this kind on the various aspects of life are retained in the SS notebooks. But the most important thing is that the content and form of these articles should provide the SS with important knowledge and teaching for the present.

"For example, in the stories of German history, it is not a matter of describing any event. People must *learn German history* and learn from it for the present struggle through descriptions showing them typical German characters manifesting themselves through virtues and weaknesses. It is essential to constantly repeat to people: "Look into the past of our people! The Germans have always made many mistakes and have had to pay dearly for them. We must therefore avoid them in the future. And also: The Germans have stifled the qualities and strengths present in our people. You must nurture them in order to be prepared for the fight to preserve the German character and its right to life, which each generation will have to take up again. It is likewise necessary to awaken national pride in people through heroic examples from German history.

"Studies and discussions of a scientific nature must be written in a simple way so that everyone can understand them. Their purpose is to give the SS a sense of the divine order of the world:

"The stories that describe the pernicious actions of the opponents of our worldview must show and make clear their tactics as they are seen in action, precisely because they must be teachable.

"Characteristic stories dealing with blood issues should show the SS the dangers of miscegenation and educate him to unite with an equally valuable mate. They should also awaken in him a taste for and love of genealogy...".

In practice, the SS notebooks were sent to the officers and heads of training who used them during the educational 'Sturmabende' or 'troop evenings' held twice a week in the evening after work. These courses were held for ten months, one month being free and two weeks devoted to various festivals. It was during these evenings that the ideological education of the SS was carried out, which was to fulfil two essential purposes: to enable the SS to *master the knowledge of* certain basic facts, and to teach them to acquire a *process of reflection* that *was independent of* external events and rooted in the world view. This education took two forms: 1. a *basic education which* provided the SS man with familiar notions from his long service and which were not contained in the SS books; 2. a *supplementary education* which served to broaden the ideological vision in depth to the cosmic, biological and political fields which we have seen, and which the SS books presented in the form of stories, addressing not only the men's intelligence, but also their emotional faculty. The two types of education were to be interwoven for better effect. Basic education had an extremely pedagogical function, serving particularly to pre-train the SS postulant, carried out in a strict, even military, manner. Further education was carried out in the form of a lecture by the instructor ensuring mutual participation of the men, in the more flexible form of a question and answer game. Troops and officers would meet in the evening in the troop mess to study and discuss the various topics presented the previous evening. Each evening was governed by a guiding idea called the 'troop call' and summarised in one sentence, for example: 'Be the enemy of gossip! Don't talk—act', 'Death for the fatherland deserves eternal veneration', 'The fame of the deeds of the dead lives forever'. Attendance at the troop's parties was based on voluntary participation. Each unit was thus almost entirely represented and only serious cases were excused, such as illness or death in the family. Virtues such as a sense of honour, bravery and manly courage were particularly emphasised. The young SS men were also taught to cultivate comradeship, to avoid quarrels and to always strive to convince fellow citizens with differing views but of value as Aryans through frank discussion. Struggles and oppositions had constantly caused the misfortune of Europe, ending most of the time in real fratricidal wars. The SS instruction tried to put an end to this!

As an example, plans for an evening of troupe and basic education can be provided for the months of November/December, January, February and March 1938.

Regular evening education course:
1. Singing.
2. Basic education: lessons and exercises (half an hour).
3. Break (ten minutes).
4. Words of Adolf Hitler.
5. Complementary education according to the SS booklets (three quarters of an hour—one hour).
6. New songs.

Work plan for 1938/39:
A. November: The NSDAP programme and its implementation (citizenship, work, morality, economy, youth, authority).
B. December: Customs during the year (SS festivals: naming, marriage, birth, burial; the Christmas festival and its realization; the meaning of: summer games, solstices, fire, the Jul candlestick).
C. January: The idea of blood (races in Germany, the Blood Protection Act, Germans abroad).
D. February: International Enemies (Judaism, the Press, Freemasonry, Bolshevism, Christianity and the Political Churches).

E. March: SS laws and SS selection principles (SS selection principles, SS laws on the SS clan community, marriage law, Lebensbom, widows and orphans, laws on combat rules, law of honour, sanctity of property, savings).

Since courses alone could not be absolutely effective, they found their logical continuation in the 'camaraderie evenings' in which SS wives, family members, friends and young people from the Hitlerjugend or the BDM could take part. The training extended its scope to include family and circles of friends and relatives. These evenings were held once a month. Ideological education could thus be pursued through discussions, relaxed conversations that encouraged reflection. Every moment of the service, be it leave, breaks during marches or exercises, guard duty or free quarters, was conducive to this education. It gradually lost its formal character, which was encouraged by troop commanders who encouraged their officers to seek personal dialogue and thus a rewarding human relationship rather than lectures and lessons. They could also choose aspects of the service or the private lives of their subordinates as a starting point for educational action. In this way, ideological influence took on a global dimension, affecting the SS not only politically, but also in terms of character and emotional and spiritual attitudes.

However, the arrival of the war brought about significant changes. The conditions associated with the war soon made it impossible to organise these troop parties. The unit commanders were given free rein to instruct their men ideologically. Ideology soon took a back seat to military matters. On the other hand, the extension of the participation in the struggle to foreign groups, especially Germanic ones, allowed the creation of new notebooks of the SS, the "Germanische Leithefte" which, at the end of the war, had editions in seven different languages, domiciled in particular in: The Hague (Holland), Antwerp (Flanders), Brussels (Wallonia), Copenhagen (Denmark), Berlin (Germany), Oslo (Norway), Reval (Estonia), Paris (France). There were also special editions, such as the magazine "Vormingsbladen" for the Dutch, and various weeklies like "De SS Man", "Storm SS", "L'assaut", "SS Germaneren", "Avanguardia", etc. The educational principle was considerably enriched: Going beyond the purely German dimension, the volunteer's attention was drawn to the meaning of the fight for a new united Europe, to European culture and to his character as a "political soldier" who had to spread his world view among his people.

The evolution of the number of published SS booklets also shows the new direction taken by the leadership: April 1937: SS-VT = 51, SS-TV= 165. January 1939: SS-VT = 1452, SS-TV= 719. April 1943: Waffen-SS = over 400,000. From the beginning of the war, the notebooks were widely distributed among the troops and a new format was adopted for them. From then on, a monthly guiding idea directed their content, such as: loyalty, order, comradeship, respect, risk and responsibility, etc. The division into two parts, the articles from the work of the Sippenamt, the studies of *Mein Kampf* were removed. Priority was given to general history articles, testimonies of soldiers at the front, informative stories written in an entertaining form, studies of nature life, etc. Now the notebook took on the dimension of a soldier's war companion, bringing him the comfort of the fatherland and supporting him in his political struggle. It is remarkable that despite the terrible wartime situation, the SS leadership took it to heart to open the minds of the SS fighters to natural beauty, to sharpen their sense of reflection and to elevate their souls through poems or aphorisms of great men. Discussions about love or the beauty of flowers and landscapes would seem to have little place in a world war! But National Socialism considered that war is also a matter of culture! All areas of life were to be taught. The use of aesthetics and mysticism in politics was its most important work, which had a profound effect on people's minds and thus gained many supporters. It was also expected that the knowledge of the beauty, value and importance of what the SS was fighting for would inspire him to the greatest military exploits.

Naturally, ideological instruction was given a prominent place in the military training schools (Junkerschulen) for officer cadets such as those in Bad Tölz or Brunswick created in 1934 and 1935 or the various officer schools for the police, the SD, the Leibstandarte, etc. It was given the highest coefficient, equal to the tactical courses. It had the highest coefficient, on a par with the tactical courses. The programme taught remained in line with the general spirit we have seen above. According to a carefully planned course, the volunteers underwent intensive sports training during the first three months, and then decreased, with the aim not of creating Olympic champions but men of will and character. Through military education, the officer cadets not only acquired the knowledge of how to lead units, but also an almost instinctive sense of decision making in a variety of situations. The training was not intended to impart academic knowledge but to create the precise ideological attitude and behaviour expected of an officer. The objectives of the SS military schools were to develop physical strength, attacking spirit and willpower, to strengthen esprit de corps and discipline, to provide instinctive self-confidence and a sense of responsibility, and to create an ideological attitude. As soon as the first foreign units were set up, the selected officer candidates were trained there in the same way as their German comrades.

As a logical outcome of the SS clan order idea, a special service was created in 1942, which is rarely mentioned in history books: the SS Women's Intelligence Corps, a "cell of an order of German women and girls" at the beginning, and then Germanic at the end of the war, this specifically female branch of the SS followed the same laws and was based on the same ideology as the male branch. The aim was not, of course, to train soldiers, but an elite of women who were aware of their political and moral responsibilities and their role in society. The girls were trained for professional life but also for life in the SS Order. Their main task was to become radio operators, teleprinter operators and telephone operators, to relieve the soldiers at the front. The training included physical training, instruction in military and intelligence matters, ideological instruction and home life tasks. The qualities required for admission were: intellectual alertness, reliability and discretion.

The ideological training, assisted by the SS workbooks, for women who reached the rank of non-commissioned officer or officer included the following topics:

1. Basic historical data

We studied the important periods and their repercussions, geography, geopolitics.

2. Raciology

Topics included general knowledge, marriage procedures, the character traits of the Nordic race, the SS, women in Germanic countries. The female volunteers were taught the nature of authority, i.e. training by example, the difference between educating and criticising, the phenomena of sympathy and antipathy, the notions of motherhood, children, breastfeeding, the duties of a leader and a wife, as a mother and as a member of a community, the principles of domestic work and also notions of gardening, care of domestic animals, etc.

3. Art and science in the service of the people

concerned the study of reading, how to read, the influence of reading on opinion, the study of the different types of press, music and song, their judicious use and their value for the home.

4. The party setup

The influence of the festivals was studied to increase vitality, conscious living, artistic feeling, controlled joy, spiritual impulse and humour.

5. Political education

dealt with the history of the NSDAP, occupational choice, legal issues concerning women, their role as a conservative force, guardian of loyalty and faith, and traditions.

6. The SS as the core of the Empire

The European tasks of the SS, its nature as a clan community, its laws and type of leadership, the place and role of the female officer and NCO within the SS female volunteer corps were studied.

The male creative force was thus harmoniously combined with the female conservative force to form the clan community of the SS.

THE SS AS AN ORDER

The idea of the Order is not new. It runs through German history and was familiar to Germans who were steeped in the spirit of student duelling associations, an old survival of chivalric jousting. In its elitist principle, the SS was therefore not a new phenomenon. It was part of an ancient tradition that was still alive. Its conception of the Order, however, took on a completely original form and dimension. The SS was certainly the first organisation in European history to question the validity of a 2000-year-old value system and to propose a redefinition of ethics and human destiny. This questioning in no way implied a rejection of a number of traditions and values that have made European civilisation great, but rather a distinction between what is particularly peculiar to the Indo-European soul and race, and what comes from a foreign contribution. By studying German and European history, he was able to identify the errors and mistakes that had been made due to the lack of a global view of the world and to synthesise ideas that had been separated until then. The idea of the Order of the SS was rooted in the examples of medieval chivalric orders as well as those of Frederick II's hussars. However, it differed from some of their Judeo-Christian principles and set as its goal the preservation and enhancement of the best hereditary characteristics of families and clans (see the article 'The Clan Order'). The SS defined itself as a "clan order", rejecting the chastity rule followed by religious orders, innovating against the traditionally individualistic and class-oriented army. In this way it sought to achieve an unchanging biological and spiritual continuity hitherto denied to temporal organisations. For to create a purely intellectual elite without taking into account biological and racial realities, as had been practised in the past, would have meant extinction in the more or less long term. Women and children were naturally given a place in this Order and were subject to the same rules of selection as men. It would have been pointless to select racially valuable men if they could be united with lesser women. In this, the SS followed the old philosophical saying "if you want to create a better world, you have to start with human beings". The idea of order also implied the idea of ethics and morality, following the old Germanic conception of right and law (see the articles 'German-German authority' and 'The honour of the Germanic woman'). The three virtues cultivated in priority were fidelity, thus reviving the ancient Germanic practice, obedience, without which no one can be master of himself, and comradeship, which is natural between men of the same community.

The SS differed from previous organisations in its trifunctional character. For the first time in history, an organisation tried to synthesise the three functions of Indo-European civilisation—spiritual, warlike and productive—within itself. The body was no longer dissociated from the spirit and soul, forming that harmonious unity defined by Rosenberg: 'The race is the soul seen from the outside and the soul is the race seen from the inside'. Eli professed an absolute recognition of the fundamental and indissoluble link between the different aspects of life and sought to give a tangible and homogeneous reality to a set of philosophical, scientific or religious concepts. It combined military character with faith, art with science, industry with peasantry in a supreme alchemy of the "new man". This term "new man" is opposed to the preconceived and generally peddled idea of "people of lords" or "supermen". Never in any text have these false and meaningless expressions been found, which are the fruit of Americanised and complexed mentalities. The 'superman' or 'superhero', a product of American fantasies, is totally alien to his environment and endowed with superhuman faculties denied to ordinary mortals who envy him. His superiority is in no way the work of his own hands and therefore deserves no admiration. Instead of the term 'lord', which implied class and arbitrariness, the National Socialists preferred the term 'hero', i.e. the man who was rooted in his community, who was responsible, who set an example by his ability to surpass himself, and who was capable of recreating the primordial human type from his own values.

This emphasis on ideological training, even in the worst moments of the war, stemmed from the desire to achieve a total identification of the SS with the Order, its principles, its values, resulting in an absolute attitude to life. The SS's victories were ultimately those of the Order, as were its failures. Such a conception, based on a sense of honour that was both individual and communal, led to the elevation of the concept of duty. Fulfilling one's duty meant being faithful to oneself, to one's word, to one's clan and to one's race. This identification transformed the SS into an active, goal-oriented element, encouraging him to overcome individualistic bourgeois egoism. He rediscovered the meaning and value of 'serving', whether it was the ideal or the Order. He became the indispensable element of an organic community in the noblest sense of the term. This was expressed in the symptomatic wearing of the uniform (see the article "Why we wear a uniform"), which became the symbol not only of an Order, but of a world view.

THE SS AS A RACIAL ORGANISATION

The SS concept of order took on its totally unique dimension through what formed the axis of National Socialist thought, i.e. the 'racial idea'. This concept became a revolutionary instrument and was the basis for the majority of the most important SS laws.

The examination of European and world history had led the National Socialists to the view that there were races, Aryan or not, which possessed civilisational aptitudes that were the result of thousands of years of evolution and specialisation. These civilisations were reflected in the development of intellectual, artistic and material incentives, the cultivation of a sense of beauty and the ability to shape their environment. Since these factors are intimately linked to the homogeneity of each race, the destruction of these factors through interbreeding leads in the long run to the disappearance of the civilising supremacy of that race. The racial unity of a people is part of its spiritual unity, thus indicating the indissoluble link between the mental and the physical, the latter being the external representation (see the article "From the racial body to the racial soul"). From these studies arose a science that reached a high degree of development, mainly in Germany, known as "raciology" and championed by researchers such as Hans F. K. Günther or Ferdinand Clauß. France was certainly at the origin of this phenomenon, with precursors such as the Count of Gobineau or Vacher de Lapouge.

The increasing globalization of trade, travel and relations had given rise to an exacerbated awareness of identity, fearing a future ethnic chaos. This feeling, hitherto diffuse, instinctive and often confused with nationalism due to ignorance of genetics, became the most revolutionary weapon of National Socialism. At a time when, as never before, the European peoples as a whole were faced with the danger of losing their identity, National Socialism offered them radically new solutions.

Within Europe, raciology distinguishes between several 'races' that make up the great Indo-European branch—the Nordic, Westphalian, Dinaric, Baltic-Eastern, Eastern and Mediterranean races, which are distributed differently in different countries (see the article 'What is the race?'). The distinguishing criteria are mainly based on the cephalic index, the general physiognomy and the character. These races are present to a greater or lesser degree in all European peoples, but the National Socialists emphasised the importance of the Nordic race as the unifying link between all Europeans, making its mark on European history. Special attention was also given to the Nordic race because of its constantly decreasing birth rate, which threatened it with extinction. Every effort was therefore made to encourage its growth by all means. But the 'Nordic' type should not be equated with a geographical fact or an archetype. It was called Nordic because individuals with these characteristics are most frequently found in Nordic countries. They are, however, found all over the world. The tall, blond Viking is a caricature of the Nordic, as the Nordic is rather a synthetic type of man, medium to tall, with light brown to blond hair, grey, green and blue eyes. The colour of the hair and eyes cannot be the only determining factor; some Slavs and Jews have light hair and eyes without belonging to the Nordic race. The Nordic ideal was certainly best defined by Greek art, of which the magnificent statues are a perfect example.

The SS gave priority to the selection of an elite that could only logically become European according to this Nordic physical and spiritual ideal that went far beyond the national framework. Candidates were therefore selected according to their racial characteristics that most closely resembled this ideal, bearing in mind, however, that the majority of Europeans no longer had the pure characteristics of one race or another; all these qualities combined to constitute the European genius. In addition to the Nordic type, the Westphalian and Dinaric types were also accepted. In fact, most of the SS, especially the leaders, distanced themselves from this caricatured post-war image.

Racial selection did not exclude women, as we have already said. The training attached particular importance to orienting the 'marital tastes' of the SS according to the Nordic model. Care was also taken to avoid marriages with individuals showing hereditary defects in order to achieve a gradual increase in the general value of the Order, since the SS also presented itself as an organisation with eugenic aims aimed at the gradual disappearance of hereditary diseases.

Many myths contribute to the idea of this selection. One of the main ones is certainly the "Aryan myth" equating Aryanness with northernness. As we have seen, the great Aryan family is divided into different subspecies and it would be a fundamental error to confuse the whole with the particular. The term Aryan was rarely used, often in the context of studies of Indian civilisation, contrary to what has been stated in many history books. The more explicit term Nordic was preferred.

The notion of 'Pangermanism' has also been very confusing. Pangermanism was equated with a term that could be translated into French as 'Allemanism' (Deutschtum), i.e. a radical, dusty and conservative German nationalism. It is true that in its early days, National Socialism, as a political party within the democratic system, was primarily aimed at Germans. More than one short-sighted party official saw it only in this light. However, the supra-national and supra-historical aspect of its world view was soon to be emphasised by the outbreak of war and the possibility of European participation in the struggle. The Germans would not have understood that Hitler was talking about Europe first, before settling internal political problems. He therefore left the initiative in this area to the SS, a vanguard organisation, as opposed to the NSDAP, a strictly political organisation. In a speech in 1944, Himmler lamented the fact that in 1935 too few people were able to understand the European and Germanic dimension of National Socialism, and that this had considerably hampered future work.

As an encouraging response, in many European countries there were also parties that openly claimed to be based on National Socialist philosophy, such as the French National Socialist Party, Leon Degrelle's Rex Party or Vidkund Quisling's movement in Norway.

A revolutionary concept for European unification was born as an extension of the racial idea: Germanness. It was still in its infancy before the war, confused by the National Socialists themselves with the synonymous terms "German blood", "German-German", "German-Nordic", "Nordic-German", in an apparent terminological imprecision. It was necessary to find a representative common factor at the ideological and biological level uniting all European peoples, and it was Germanness, the holder of the Nordic blood, that prevailed. In SS terminology, the German was more than just a member of a historical tribe. As a man from the North, an original Hyperborean, he was the 'germ' (from the Latin 'germen') from which the main European peoples had sprung. The use of the term 'Indo-German' in the texts is revealing, which was replaced after the war by 'Indo-European', much more 'suitable' for democratic ears. Léon Degrelle also spoke of "West Germans" when addressing Belgians or French.

The idea of Germanism, even Germanness (Germanentum), served above all to break down the old barriers of narrow nationalism, to put an end at last to the stupid quarrels that had torn Europe apart for the benefit of interests that were foreign to it. It made possible the unity of Europe, indeed of the Aryan world as a whole, with the Germanic core as its centre. It was not an attempt at uniformity comparable to the 'American myth', which tried to merge communities of very different origins, often with nothing in common, into a block. Americanism and cosmopolitanism were widely denounced as corrupting and anti-cultural, and as an enemy of the Aryan genius (see the article "America in Europe"). The SS ideology also put an end to the divisions between Celtic and Germanic brethren, artificially created by the Romans for political purposes. The Celts, Latins, Scandinavians and Indo-European Slavs, as multiple branches of the same tree, would be given their place in the future Europe as federated groups retaining their particularities. This project found its appropriate framework in the concept of an "Empire" (Reich), which lost its "Third" designation in 1939 on Hitler's orders. The overly German "Third" Reich was replaced by the European Empire, demonstrating once again the European commitment of the National Socialist leaders long before the war. The great European German Empire, a myth that had been a constant feature of European history but had never been realised, was to be created at last through National Socialism and serve as a structure for European unity. However, this Empire would have been limited to the historical living space of the Europeans (see the article "Heinrich I"), reconquering former lost territories in the East without making the historical mistake of going beyond them. The 'colonialist' mentality of past centuries has been strongly criticised.

Significantly, even well before the war, the SS appointed to positions of responsibility convinced supporters of the European idea, such as the Swiss Franz Riedweg, head of the "German section" of the SS as early as 1937, and Gottlob Berger, head of the recruitment office of the SS-Hauptamt as early as 1938 and promoter of the European Waffen SS. The SS had admitted into its ranks European groups, Swiss, Flemish, Dutch, Norwegian,

Finnish, then later, Walloons, French, Cossacks, Italians, Bosnians, in all about thirty nationalities, thus testifying to this awareness. Each European unit of the SS kept its language (German was used only as a command language in order to avoid general anarchy since the military cadres were German), and each custom or religious particularity was respected. In a speech in April 1942 to the SS Germanic Notebook Support Circle, Gottlob Berger said: " … we do not want to 'Germanise' or Germanise in the wrong sense of the word. We must strengthen our Germanic brothers in their love for their identity, for the preservation of their language, their customs. Without love for the fatherland, there can be no love for the Great German Empire. The merits of former adversaries were even praised when they had proved to be champions of an elitist philosophy (see the article 'Maxims on War'). Even European Muslim volunteers, admitted not as Muslims but as Europeans, were allowed to continue abstaining from pork and alcohol! Awareness of the racial idea went beyond the European framework, since, as early as 1939, Aryan Americans were invited to find their roots and to participate in the great struggle for the preservation of white identity (see the article "Racial issues in the United States").

THE SS AS A RELIGIOUS AND CULTURAL ORGANISATION

This statement, which at first sight is puzzling, is hardly surprising after all that has just been said. While the NSDAP was a political organisation that did not interfere much in religious matters, mainly for diplomatic reasons, the SS, as an ideological order, also made demands in this area. The return to a properly Aryan mental universe could not leave aside that which connects man to the absolute higher principle, i.e. religion. The denunciation of the inherent allogeneity of Judeo-Christianity, which had permeated the European mindset for centuries, was perhaps more virulent than that of Judaism. Christianity, which derived from Jewish philosophy, was not forgiven for having conveyed a globalist ideology and for having systematically erased and denigrated everything that might remind one of the ancient Germanic culture. As proof of this, let us take Cardinal Faulhaber's sermon on New Year's Eve in 1933: "One cannot speak of a Germanic culture per se dating from pre-Christian times on the basis of Tacitus. The Germans only became a people with a civilisation in the full sense of the word through Christianity. The hardest task for Christian missionaries was to get the Germans to melt their swords into ploughshares. Christianity, protector of the weak and sick, teaching sin and shame of the body, contempt for animals and women, stigmatising joy and pride, denigrating racial realities, was considered by the National Socialists as a "disease of the soul".

This was certainly the first questioning in history of the validity of Judeo-Christian philosophy as a whole. However, judgements remained nuanced according to its different aspects. There was relative sympathy for Protestantism only insofar as it expressed a revolt against the Roman papist spirit (see the article "The German University in the Counter-Reformation"), but it was rejected for its dogmatic biblical side (see the article "The Witchcraft"). In 1937, Himmler even sent a letter to all heads of instruction forbidding them to attack the person of Christ, no doubt believing that such an attitude would have offended the convictions of the majority of the SS still attached to the old religion and that a study of customs in a positive sense could only exert the most persuasive action.

The gradual disappearance of Christianity was therefore to be replaced by a return to the founding spirit of Europe that had animated the pagan religion of the ancestors. The SS proposed to rediscover the principle of a properly Aryan religious attitude towards life and the world, which had been stifled and disguised under Christian coverings but was still present, particularly in the peasantry (see the articles 'Harvest Customs' and 'Sacred Bread'). Religion was restored to its primordial meaning by placing it in the visible natural framework, a reflection of the invisible higher order. Man became aware that he was only a part of the natural order, subject to its law like every other living being. He could therefore only realise his full potential in this world by leading an existence that developed and nurtured the qualities of body, character and mind. To despise the physical and material aspect, as well as the living world in general, was to despise the sensitive mode of expression of the divine. In his respect for differences and his opposition to the unifying mixture, man was thus following the great commandments of sovereign nature. This piety, deeply faithful to the world of eternal natural laws, distanced itself as much from atheism, considered as a product of decadence, as from the outdated practices of pseudo-pagan groups (see the article "The Spiritual Crisis"). It also moved away from that form of idolatry which consisted in giving a material appearance (Christ the 'son' of God and the immaculate Virgin Mary) to a divine principle which was supra-material.

Through this fidelity to natural laws, the SS came to adopt an attitude that would nowadays be described as 'ecological', advocating a return to a healthy peasant life, the use of natural products (see the article 'Why a Sudeten Spring') and respect for nature (see the articles 'The Eternal Laws of Life', 'Comrade SS on my Side', 'The Forest as a Community of Life', 'Eternal Cycle'). This understanding of life was in stark contrast to the Christian tradition, which was hostile to all natural expression and taught the fear of God. The vanity of biblical man, believing himself superior to nature, can therefore only trigger the worst catastrophes, such as those looming on the horizon of the third millennium (disappearance of numerous animal species, deforestation, pollution, destruction of the ozone layer, etc.).

The SS always avoided criticising the religious views of individuals as a strictly personal matter. It primarily attacked church philosophy and institutions in the context of the study of the National Socialist world view, which may seem paradoxical. The sense of sacredness and piety in every individual, Christian or otherwise, remained absolute. Freedom of belief was respected. On the application forms, it was asked whether the applicant was a "Catholic, Protestant or ... believer" (gottglaubig), i.e. "pagan". The "religious revolution" was carried out gradually in order to gain decisive power. An attempt was made to turn the Christians into pagans by impressing them with the pomp and depth of religious ceremonies and by studying and emphasising the original, truly Aryan spiritual world. Only voluntary acceptance, not coercion, made the cleansing of the religious sense effective.

This 'new' yet immemorial religion had its own rites and ceremonies. It was also the task of the Schulungsamt to restore the original pagan meaning of festivals and ceremonies relating to the most important events in a person's life, such as baptism (reformulated as naming), engagement, marriage (see the article 'The Admission of Women to the SS Clan Community'), funerals, etc. Only the heads of training were authorised to design the spirit and form of the celebrations, with the exception of the practical applications, which were left to the heads of units. The SS did not want to create a new dogmatic clergy by granting prerogatives to the heads of instruction. The unit commanders performed certain ceremonies only where their men were directly concerned, thus excluding the risk of a sectarian transmission of religious power. Only the religious framework was maintained in which the personal sensitivity of each individual was freely expressed.

The festivals were conceived with the intention of restoring man's privileged relationship with nature as an expression of divine creation. It was also a question of removing the Judeo-Christian reorientation imposed on traditional festivals such as Jul (Christmas), Ostara (Easter), Summer Solstice (or St John's Day). In this respect, the peasant world was a perfect example of a society that had managed to preserve the meaning of its ancient traditions through its attachment to and loyalty to nature. Does the term "pagan" not come from "paganus", the peasant, whom the Christians never managed to convert completely? Thus, man once again felt himself to be the indispensable and responsible link in the long chain of the clan, passing on life and traditions in an unchanging manner. The pride of the bodies and the faces with sparkling eyes turned towards the Sun testify to the joy of the creation that God has given to man, who thanks Him through the festivals.

This spiritual revolution also took place in the context of writing history in a Germanic sense. The Germans were truly discovering a part of history that had hitherto been ignored or despised, that of their Germanic ancestors. The Enlightenment had taken Greek civilisation as its model, looking to it for aesthetic and philosophical roots. Germany was particularly affected by this phenomenon, and some even saw National Socialism as its heir. The plasticity of German neoclassical statues and architecture could betray this affiliation. However, a parallel and long-standing trend (German Romanticism) was to become more and more prevalent, that of a return to Germanness. The philosophy of the 'Germanists', especially those promoted by the SS, sought to bring the culture of Germany's direct ancestors out of oblivion and contempt, thus demonstrating that German morality, poetry and art were not inferior to others. The work already undertaken by other researchers such as the Grimm brothers or Gustav Kossinna was continued on a larger scale. The purpose of such historical interest, apart from re-establishing the truth, was also to provide legitimacy to the SS Order, which drew references from the teachings of the great historical warriors, politicians and artists. Frederick II of Prussia, Dürer, Nietzsche, Wagner, Bismarck or René Quinton all testified to the permanence of a certain attitude specific to the Aryan race. Were they not examples of the creative genius that overcame time and fashion and which the SS tried to synthesise? Did they not always have a message to convey, being forerunners in their own way? Let us mention just a few of the ideas from which the SS drew inspiration: the Carolingian idea of empire, the creation of values in a Nietzschean sense, Wagnerian spirituality, Prussian military virtue and medieval chivalric mysticism.

The admiration aroused by René Quinton, although he was an enemy of Germany in his time (1914), also reveals the overcoming of political or nationalist divisions. It confirms that any heroic philosophy could not but resonate with National Socialism (see the article "Maxims on War"). Sometimes the qualities of foreign peoples were even praised (see the articles "Yamato" and "The Empire of Ataturk"). The personality of Charlemagne did not leave the SS indifferent either. Some historians complacently spread the rumour after the war that he was called the "executioner of the Saxons". While not ignoring his troubled role in the Verden massacre, the SS saw him as the first architect of European unity and the creator of the principle of a Germanic Empire (see the articles "Charlemagne, Founder of a State" and "The Birth of Germanic Europe around 500 AD"). Charlemagne was a historical figure for both the Germans and the French and thus embodied the link between these two peoples of common origin.

LEGITIMATE QUESTIONS

Considering this ideology and these goals, one may ask to what extent the SS was able to achieve them and what obstacles it encountered. As we have seen, the SS was divided into three different branches which, over time, became increasingly different from each other in spirit. Despite the many efforts of the central leadership to maintain the cohesion and unity of the Order, various tendencies emerged which hindered the work of general edification. The military branch of the Waffen SS was linked to the great tradition of the Prussian army of Frederick II through leaders such as Paul Hausser and Sepp Dietrich, who gave it this impetus. For men trained at the old school, deeply marked by their traditional education, ideological instruction and religious questions remained "fuzzy" abstractions that they left to ideologists like Himmler or Darré who used the notebooks of the SS to spread these ideas, which were often considered utopian. Senior officers like Felix Steiner even deliberately neglected political courses, considering that the priorities of the war were to train combatants rather than political soldiers. On the other hand, the freshly minted privates were much more receptive and often understood the magnitude of the political issues better than their generals.

The Allgemeine SS and the Totenkopfverbande, the older 'political' branches, saw their role as that of revolutionary units that carried the National Socialist ideology. Some of their leaders, such as Theodor Eicke, even had a relative contempt for the Waffen SS, which was considered too traditionalist and 'militaristic'. The fact that rank designations were similar between all branches only made matters worse, as the Waffen SS found it difficult to accept that 'civilians' could be generals or colonels without having served at the front. It is fair to point out, in this regard, that SS ranks were only relatively equivalent to military ranks, and unlike them, were not preceded by 'sir' (German terminology), but rather corresponded to an individual's value per se. Civilians, as well as soldiers, were considered to be combatants in the cause of National Socialism. As a result, men in their thirties were promoted to the rank of general and talented 'civilians' such as Werner von Braun and Professor Porsche became 'officers' in the SS.

Moreover, during the war the Waffen SS received their military directives from the Wehrmacht, not from the central SS leadership, which provided supplies, created units and oversaw training. A certain sense of autonomy from the SS in Berlin thus emerged, but not to the extent of open opposition, as it reflected a divergence of experience rather than ideological opposition, especially as the Waffen SS never had to deal with the police tasks entrusted to particular SS units.

In view of these facts, a careful observer might say that reducing the history and concepts of the SS to the study of the guidebooks would not be in keeping with historical reality. The SS guidebooks presented ideas, characters or situations taken from reality and considered as exemplary or instructive. In this way, they reflected what National Socialist ideology considered to be essential virtues and qualities, which were points of reference for every SS member, even if reality and the necessities of life did not always allow for their application. But the SS publications allow us to judge this worldview precisely in its abstraction, which is more representative of a state of mind than of actions limited in space and time. In this respect, the SS Notebooks show us the SS Order's ideal vision of life and society and what it was aiming for.

However, the SS phenomenon must be seen in the context of National Socialism, which was a multifaceted ideology. The SS movement, although the most significant, was not itself always unitary and came up against other trends. Conflicts with the party over people and ideas made it even more difficult to achieve a homogeneous programme. The 'Allemanist' tendency in the party had difficulty with the creation of a federated Europe under SS supervision, and the twelve years of National Socialism were insufficient to bring about a radical change in mentality. They only served to lay the foundations. The generation of the Hitlerjugend and the younger SS classes would certainly have achieved this goal, but history did not allow them to do so. History did not give them the time. A former French volunteer once told me: "The National Socialists were like gardeners. They planted seeds, but they didn't have time to see the result. The appalling turmoil of the war brought this great adventure to an end.

With its rigour, discipline and spirit, the SS was able to claim to have created the beginnings of a new type of man who had been through the forge of leadership schools and the test of fire. Despite all these obstacles, it demonstrated this time and again on many fronts, both internal and external. Independent of the army, it created a new "fighting attitude", distinct from the Party, a new "ideological attitude" and distant from the Church, a new fundamental "spiritual attitude". If for Goethe action was the "celebration of the authentic man", then so was the SS. The revolution of the body was to be followed by a revolution of the spirit. But the time had not yet come.

* * *

As a warning, the author would like to make it clear that this book is intended to be a historical and scientific work that should not make us forget all the suffering that millions of men underwent during the last war. It cannot therefore be considered as apologetic. It studies certain ideas defended by a given political system and raw facts placed in a precise historical context. It strives to provide material that allows the reader to form an opinion in complete freedom, in relation to what has already been published on the subject. This should be the work of every authentic historian. It is therefore in this spirit that one should read the articles concerning the Jews or religious questions. The reader is the sole judge of the ideas presented in this book.

For further information, please contact the author via the publishing house.

Paris, 7 October 1990

CHAPTER I

I. THE SS ORDER, HISTORY AND PRINCIPLES

JOURNAL "BELIEVE AND FIGHT". FOR THE SS OF THE POPULAR GROUPS IN THE SOUTH EAST.

THE SS, HISTORY

On your belt buckle you wear the words: *"My honour is called loyalty"*. On your collar tabs are the two victory runes of the SS. You have therefore consciously joined a community that has been given special duties among the people. Are you clearly aware that you have to take on a specific part of these duties?

Have you ever thought about the nature of the particular duties of a SS? Do you know what the law of loyalty means to you as an individual? Do you know what the SS has achieved in the period of its conquest of power and in the new Germany?

In order to be able to answer these questions, you need to learn the essential features of the history of the SS, its tasks and its goals.

The history of the Black Corps began in *the early days of the National Socialist Movement*. In March 1923 the cell of the future SS—*the staff guard*—was formed from specially selected and absolutely reliable party comrades. These men already wore the skull and crossbones on their caps and the black-bordered armband.

In May of the same year, the staff guard became the *Hitler shock troop*—under the leadership of Josef Berchtold. This small unit, resolute to the last man, brought together Adolf Hitler's most loyal comrades in arms. Charged with tasks comparable to those later entrusted to the SS, the shock troop made history and fought relentlessly and uncompromisingly until it fell victim to the bullets of a treacherous and reactionary system on 9 November 1923.

THE FIRST EIGHT...

After the reorganisation of the Party in 1925, the Führer ordered in the same year the establishment of a new, small, highly mobile organisation, which was to be modelled on the 'Hitler shock troop' and was firstly charged with guaranteeing him absolute protection during his demonstrations and election trips, if necessary at the cost of men's lives. Secondly, it was to provide internal *security* for the party in the same way as the police do for the state itself.

At first no more than *eight men* were chosen for this great mission requiring total commitment. Their leader was Julius Schreck. It was he who laid down the first principles for the building of the Black Corps. On May 16, 1936, death cut short the career of this loyal and tried-and-tested comrade of Adolf Hitler, but by order of the Führer, the first unit in Munich bears the name "Julius Schreck" today and in the future.

The first eight SS were given the uniform of the former Hitler shock troop, only the anorak was replaced by the brown shirt with the black armband, and the ski cap by the black SS cap.

On 16 April 1925, this Protection Troop made its first public appearance in Munich. It was a sad occasion: the funeral of Pohner, the Führer's old comrade in arms from the 9th of November. Four SS men carrying torches walked on either side of the coffin and accompanied the dead fighter for the last time.

It was clear that, because of the difficulty of the action, only a few men chosen according to special points of view could be admitted to the Protection Troop. They therefore had to fit in perfectly with what was required of them. Unconditional loyalty, total commitment of the individual, iron discipline—who else but *soldiers at the front* would have been able to fulfil these conditions?

Those who risked their lives hundreds of times formed the core of the young group.

But the requirements were even higher: only Party comrades could be members of the Protection Troop, and each of them had to be able to present two sponsors, one of whom was a leader of the local group into which the young SS applicant was being introduced. In addition, each member had to be between 23 and 35 years of age, of sound constitution and absolutely healthy.

Naturally, the *weak* and the *whiny* with vices were rejected. The best were more than enough for the young formation! It was therefore an extreme distinction for any Party comrade to be able to serve in the Protection Troop. Absolute comradeship was to be counted among all the virtues and qualities, which prescribed:

All for one and one for all.

THE SELECTION PRINCIPLE

Thus, the number of followers grew to a small unit, a troop, which was not a military or mass organisation, but only wanted to be that perfect instrument on which the Führer could absolutely rely at any time

This first SS force spread terror among all the meeting disruptors and weaklings, all the Reds and all the other cliques. It ensured the smooth running of National Socialist events—wherever the Führer ordered! It was to the *credit of the first death fighters that these demonstrations were always successful and that the Movement grew every day.*

It was clear that in the long run the young unit could no longer recruit only from the generation of front-line fighters. Consequently, the conditions of admission also changed over time, but without losing their severity. But from the very beginning the following principle was established: numerical limitation and extreme selection!

The Munich leadership never sought to assemble as many men as possible, but emphasised the excellent quality of the men to be selected, which alone guaranteed the unconditional execution of all orders.

ONE LEADER FOR TEN MEN

It was therefore prescribed that in each locality, a troop could only have one leader and ten men; this was the ten. Their leaders (leaders of tens) wore a silver star in the middle of the swastika as the only outward sign of their rank. In fact, even a large city like Berlin had an SS with only two leaders and twenty men.

Soon the same picture was repeated everywhere. In every town and city, the SS, that small fighting unit, became the collecting pool of all genuine political fanatics, of all revolutionaries fighting against impotence and slavery, of all those who had nothing but their faith in Germany.

In 1925 and 1926, the young Movement carried out all the recruitment campaigns with these small units and the red underworld of Saxony and Thuringia learned what the SS spirit is!

BENEFACTOR MEMBER GROUPS (M.B.)

It is certain that even the best organisation with the greatest spirit of sacrifice cannot do without a sound financial basis—and that means money! —This requirement was as imperative for the establishment of the SS as it was for the Party itself. But since the party was still in the process of structuring itself and could not provide financial support for the Troop, the SS (the only party association in this case) was given the right by the Führer to seek *benefactor members* (M.B.). *Adolf Hitler* himself was *the first to* join this group of M.B.

Thus, an ideal solution had indeed been found to enable *the* organisation's *financial base. There were* still many Party comrades (because of their public position, economic situation or other important reasons) who did not have the opportunity to become active in the ranks of the Movement. In fact, as benefactor members, they rendered an unforgettable service to the Troop…

THE SS AS AN ACTIVIST

The Protection Troop developed and gradually, alongside the first task of protecting the Führer, a second task was added, that of militant! But the men with the skulls were not burdened with manuals on the "art of speech". It was known that each of them had the ability to convince citizens who were confused by false speeches.

In those days, every SS man was thus constantly a *militant* wherever he was: in the street, at home, at any time the service allowed. How many disconcerted, excited and betrayed men and women were won over by these preachers, unknown to the fighting and creative element of the young Movement! They are counted by the hundreds, by the thousands. They began by commenting on a Party *pamphlet*, they exposed the lies to the sceptics through the *Party press*, and they brought out the absolute weapon, the Führer's "Mein Kampf", thus sweeping away the last doubts.

A new elite was born, of which the Allgemeine SS represented the ideological core. Its leader, Heinrich Himmler (top), was also the creator of the 'SS spirit'.

From the "black" SS came the "green" SS, or Waffen-SS, a military troop that became famous throughout Europe.

THE BLOOD FLAG

In 1926, the ban on the SA was lifted, and the Protection Troop became more and more of an afterthought.

But that same year also represented a historic climax for the Black Corps. At the Reichsparteitag in Weimar, the second of the NSDAP, the Führer entrusted the Movement's most sacred symbol—the Blood Flag of November 9—to the custody of the SS.

Reichsführer SS Heinrich Himmler

With the appointment of Heinrich Himmler as Reichsführer SS by Adolf Hitler, a new milestone in the history of the SS began. This was on 6 January 1929.

Two hundred and seventy men throughout the Reich formed the core of the Protection Troop, which Heinrich Himmler took over at that time when he received the Führer's order to form an absolutely safe troop from this organisation—*the Party's elite formation.*

"Every one of us is an SS man, whether he is a rankless man or a Reichsführer," Heinrich Himmler said, and during the long years of struggle for power he and his men did indeed merge into an inseparable whole. He made the Black Corps what it is today: the troop that fights most for the Führer, our blood and the Empire.

The order to expand the organisation was given. And for the Reichsführer, whose personality marked this great mission, it was clear that the new, enlarged Protection Troop could only carry out its work if, as the supreme requirement and basis for its creation, the guidelines given by the leader of the Movement were unquestionable.

The four cardinal virtues

Only noble blood, only a genuine race, can achieve great things in the long run. Heinrich Himmler began his work with this major profession of faith when he issued his first order on 20 January 1929 as Reichsführer SS:

"By superior decision of our Führer, on January 6, 1929, I received the leadership of the SS of the NSDAP!"

So the former soldier and fellow fighter began his severe and methodical selection after surrounding himself with the men the nation had available and whom he knew to be truly the best in blood and character. Four cardinal guidelines and virtues determined their choice.

I. Race and clan

"Like the *farmer* who, starting from an old seed of varying quality which he has to sort out, first goes into the field to select the shoots, we rejected in the first place those men whom we believed outwardly could not be used for the building up of the Protection Troop.

"The nature of the selection focuses on choosing those who physically come closest to the ideal, Nordic type of man. Distinguishing marks such as height or racial appearance were and are important!

This was the expression of the Reichsführer, who had the extreme merit of having followed this path with courage and persuasion, for at that time, even in the ranks of the Movement, the racial question was still a totally obscure concept and the theoretical knowledge of the young Movement in the midst of reorganisation found its concretisation.

For the first time, the racial question was placed at the centre of concern and even became the object of concern, largely differentiated from the natural but negative hatred of the Jew. The Führer's most revolutionary idea was taking shape.

It is clear that as experience in this area accumulated, the selective provisions became more stringent each year, always striving to achieve the ideal.

"The terms and conditions must be set by our successors in a hundred years or more for more and more to be demanded of the individual, as is the case now. In the same way, we know that the very first principle of selection into the Protection Troop must be the appreciation of outward appearance, that a process of selection into the Protection Troop throughout the years must be a continuation of this, and that selection made on the basis of character, will, heart and even blood must not take second place to ability!"

These were the words of the Reichsführer, who fought with the greatest energy against self-sufficiency and vanity. He also made it clear that what has been achieved so far is only a rough draft, and that the creation of a human elite must be constant and limitless.

Because there is no standard SS!

Each generation of SS will have to be better than the last.

"By the laws we have given ourselves, we want to ensure In the future that not every son of an SS family listed in the SS ancestor book can apply for membership or again have the right to be an SSman. But we want to see to it that only a part of the sons of these families are admitted to us and are thus considered SS; that through permanent selection the stream of the best German blood present in the whole people may enter the Protection Troop!"

But racial selection and the building of a unit of men alone could not ensure the success of this great work. No, all these measures would remain ineffective if *the wives* of the selected men, their families and their future clans were not also considered.

Our history is rich enough in mistakes made by the soldiers' leagues and the Männerbunde in the past, which forgot to pass on the message of pure blood. After a while they disappeared into nothingness—centuries ago.

For the Reichsführer said:

"Only the generation that knows how to situate itself between its ancestors and its descendants, grasps inwardly the exact degree of the greatness of its tasks and obligations, and the smallness of its own ephemeral significance.

"He who is aware of this will remain *simple* in the noblest sense of the word. Times of great success will not blur his vision and times of great misfortune will not drive him to despair. He will accept success and misfortune without complacency, without presumption, without fatalism—but neither will he fall victim to a sense of mediocrity and desperate folly. He will remain master of his own happiness and misfortune with equal calm.

"Therefore we teach the SS that all our struggle, the death of two million men in the Great War, the political struggle of our last fifteen years, the building of our defence force to protect our borders would be in vain and useless if the victory of the German spirit were not followed by the victory of the German child.

(The Reichsführer SS)

For this reason, the Reichsführer SS issued one of the most radical and important laws of the SS on 31 December 1931: "The Marriage Order

At that time, it was a bombshell in Germany. In a system based on liberal principles, it seemed completely incomprehensible to many people who lived in the ephemeral and were intoxicated by pleasure.

It proved to be an extremely brutal intrusion into *so-called personal freedom*. Naturally, the Jewish and demagogic press emphasised this view with the necessary emphasis. But the scorn and derision that was spread about this order at the time did not affect the Troop. The Reichsführer had foreseen this and said in point 10 of his order:

"The SS is aware that it has taken a step of great importance with this order; mockery, irony and misunderstandings do not affect us; the future is ours!

2. Will to freedom and fighting spirit

The second virtue and the second guideline is the will to fight and the indomitable thirst for freedom: for this, according to unwritten laws, the SS had to be as much as possible everywhere the best—in the fight, in the street, in the gym, later in the biggest of all liberation wars. The bigger the opponent, the better for the Troop! For only if the SS was really the best troop could the title of an elite formation be justified.

Thus, during the founding years, the Reichsführer always considered *sporting values* as a principle and a duty. Every year, the SS had to participate in very difficult sporting events. The officer corps was particularly put to the test. Every promotion also depended on the acquisition of the SA or Reich sports badge.

Thus a great danger was a priori averted, that of weakening. The cause of the disappearance of so many *Mannerbünde,* which was *social affluence, did not* a priori threaten the ranks of the Black Corps. The comfortable existence of the bourgeoisie, which may be beautiful and attractive for some men, could never win over the SS.

3. Loyalty and honour

"As we teach the SS, many things can be forgiven on this earth, except one, infidelity. He who violates fidelity excludes himself from our society. For fidelity is a matter of the heart, never of the mind. This is sometimes detrimental, but never irreversible. But the heart must always beat constantly, and if it stops, the man dies, just like a people if fidelity is violated. We are thinking here of the various loyalties, loyalty to the Führer as well as to the Germanic people, to its conscience and its essence, loyalty to blood, to our ancestors and descendants, loyalty to our clans, loyalty to comrades and loyalty to the immutable laws of propriety, dignity and chivalry. A man does not only sin against loyalty and honour if he allows his own and the Protection Troop's to be violated, but above all if he despises the honour of others, mocks the things that are sacred to them, or if he does not stand up in a dignified and courageous way for the absent, the weak and the unprotected.

This is how the Reichsführer defined loyalty, the third virtue that influences the nature of the Protection Troop.

SS men go to the first large SS rally in August 1933 in Berlin.

On the cover, a drawing of the famous skull and crossbones ring, which symbolises the link with the SS sworn community.

4. Unconditional obedience

Obedience is the fourth and final directive.

This is a particularly difficult obedience to observe because it must come from *pure spontaneity* and requires all that a man can sacrifice in personal pride, external honours and many other things that are dear to him.

It requires "unconditional commitment" without the slightest hesitation and the fulfilment of every order of the Führer, even if the individual believes that he cannot overcome it internally.

But this obedience ultimately requires an extreme level of *mastery* and *dominance,* a burning desire for freedom, and impassivity to the enemy if ordered.

The old SS man knows perfectly well what this last point means. He has never forgotten the years of fighting, standing still and waiting, when the will of every comrade was supported only by a boundless hatred: Down with the damned system!

The men were always asking, "Why doesn't it start?

Why don't we strike? Now is our chance! Why does the Führer hesitate?" They thought: "We are strong, we have beaten the Commune wherever we met it. We have taken the Reichstag—down with the puppets of this rotten system! We want to deal with them!" But the Führer's order did not come. Consequently, they kept silent and *waited*.

During all these years, the SS is proud to have seen only him, to have obeyed only him and believed unconditionally in his victory. It has been as absolutely obedient as any formation before it.

THE SS IN ACTION AT THE TIME OF THE TAKEOVER

In the years leading up to the seizure of power, the SS was always the most active in protecting National Socialist ideas and demands, both *outside* and *inside* the country. They fought in countless meeting room brawls, they broke the enemy's terror in comradeship with the SA. They were the *nucleus* that the Movement always engaged on the red and black front. They stood in front of *all-communist enterprises and factories* with leaflets in their hands and collected the valid ones. They used the same methods in the *big grey housing estates* and also brought the truth to the *poorest slums*.

They protected the speakers of the Movement thousands of times. With their chinstraps under their chins and their hands on their belts, they stood from one end of the year to the other on either side of the speaker's lectern—in the Palais des Sports as well as in the smallest community hall. They were quiet and unmoving, but observed everything in the room keenly.

They were often hungry, as most of them were out of work. But they were always there when needed. And they were dying for their faith!

They were cowardly murdered, stabbed, shot in the back in the dark streets and beaten unconscious. But they endured everything despite the superiority of the enemy. The SS had *many victims in* this way. They still carried one of their best comrades into the ground, but they left the cemetery even more fierce, even more fanatical.

We must not forget the *heroes of Austria* who, as SS men, were the courageous victims hanging from the *gallows* of a brutal system and who, through their sacrifice, made possible the great reunification of Austria with the Reich.

But *internal security* was not forgotten either. More than once the Troop fought against the enemies of the Movement, against the break-up and betrayal of the Führer. At such times of crisis, which were so dangerous for the existence of the Movement, the Führer could make use of this solid instrument which was constantly and unconditionally at his side.

Thus Adolf Hitler gave his most loyal men the phrase which, since 9 November 1931, has been written on every belt buckle: "SS man, your honour is called loyalty!

THE CAREER OF THE SS

On 9 November 1935, the following was enacted by order of the Reichsführer:

"Every SS member is SS in the sense of the SS Order, who, after a period of one and a half years as a candidate, after taking the SS oath to the Führer, as well as after honourable fulfilment of his duty in the Labour Service and his military obligations, is given the weapon, the SS dagger, and is thus admitted to the SS Order as a genuine SS man.

"Each one of us is an SS man, whether he is an ordinary officer or a Reichsführer.

The art of riding…

… and the art of fencing are practised at the SS, which thus perpetuates the chivalrlc tradition.

After a thorough examination by SS commissions of his SS skills and worthiness, the 18-year-old Hitlerjugend boy first became an SS *postulant.* At the Parteitag of the same year, he joined the SS as an SS *candidate* and on 9 November, after a brief probationary period, he took the oath to the Führer. During the first year of service, the young candidate had to acquire his *sports badge* and *the bronze Reich sports badge.* Immediately afterwards, he went to the *Labour Service,* the *Wehrmacht* and then back to the SS. On the following 9 November, after a thorough and repeated ideological education, the SS candidate was finally accepted into the SS as an *SSman.* From that day on, he was simultaneously given the right to carry the SS dagger and promised that he and his clan would always follow the basic laws of the SS.

He remained in the general SS (Allgemeine SS) until he was 35 years old. After that, he was accepted into the reserve SS at his request, and after more than 45 years, into the mother SS section.

THE LAW OF HONOUR

The same order prescribes that every SS man has the right and duty to defend his honour with *his weapon in his hand.*

This law is of fundamental importance and commits every man in two ways:

He knows that he can be held responsible for every word and deed, regardless of his rank and position; therefore, let the community watch if he commits a dishonourable act or word and thus sins against the spirit of the people.

Secondly, he is asked to respect his own honour as well as that of others in order to serve the life of the community as a political soldier in an impeccable manner.

When the day of the takeover finally arrived, there were 51,000 SS men in full support of the greatest of all revolutions, ready to carry out every mission.

In the following months, the number of people joining our formations became so great that on 10 July 1933 a *ban on joining the* SS was imposed, which was only temporarily lifted in September 1934. For the Reichsführer always placed no value on a mass organisation, and he demanded the most severe examination of all new arrivals in order to incorporate into the ranks of the Black Corps only the really most valuable and healthy forces.

> *He who does his duty is above the criticism*
> *to which all men are subject.*

Prince Eugene

"THE SOLDIER'S FRIEND. ALMANAC OF 1944. EDITION D: THE WAFFEN SS.

I. THE SS AS AN ORDER

As can be seen from this brief overview, over the years the tasks of the SS became more diverse and their fulfilment was only possible through the unification of the entire Protection Troop.

Until 1929, the SS was a tried and tested troop for the protection of leaders and speakers. The Reichsführer made it *an Order of Honour, Loyalty, Service and Combat for the Führer and the Reich.*

The SS is a *Nordic* Order. Adolf Hitler based his world view on the unchanging essence of the Nordic species. The people and the Empire must be the structural future of this Nordic nature. As the leader of the Germanic peoples, the German people have the predestined task of being the first to lead the fight for the rebirth of Germanism. The Nordic race is also the major source of the Nordic blood heritage. The first objective of National Socialism must therefore be to pursue a sound racial policy. This requires a purification of the German people from all foreign influences in blood and character.

The SS therefore selects its members according to the ideal of the Nordic race in order to form a free Germanic type. Since the value of a man's soul cannot be judged at first sight, the selection is made according to the physical ideal of the Nordic race and according to his height. Experience has shown that a man's worth and ability are mainly determined by what his racial appearance suggests.

The selection criteria of the SS thus became ever stricter. The racial policy of the Reich encouraged the Nordicisation of the entire population. The closer one gets to this goal, the stricter the racial criteria of the SS become.

The SS does not aspire to acquire a privileged position among the people. It is an order which, through its combat action, serves to carry out a racial selection of the community and realizes the principles of racial politics as a distant goal for the community. In this way, the SS applies a fundamental law of our socialist scale of values, according to which each person receives his or her place according to the value of the result achieved within the popular community.

The SS sees clearly that it must be *more than just a Mannerbund*. It builds its ideas of the Order on *the community of clans*. It wants to be *an Order of clans* which will produce men of the best Nordic kind to serve the Reich. Thus, selection will increasingly judge not the individual, but the worth of an entire clan.

Absolute clarity and consensus are needed in the ideological questions concerning this principle of a Nordic racial clan community. This is the necessary condition for the strength of the SS and gives it its assurance.

With the *basic laws of the SS,* the Reichsführer gave each SS member guidelines for action.

The first of these fundamental laws is *the Order on Engagement and Marriage of* 31 December. This order introduces a "marriage licence" for all unmarried members of the SS, considering that the future of our people lies in the selection and preservation of hereditarily healthy racial blood. Therefore, this marriage licence, which every SS member must obtain before marriage, is granted only and solely on the basis of racial and hereditary considerations.

This order was necessarily the result of the desire to create a community of clans. Because a biological selection will only be successful if the choice of spouses and the offspring of the selected individuals are controlled. The SS must marry a woman of at least equal value. The man and the woman must be racially and conjugally valid. Such a law is not a constraint, but a link to a God-given order. It is natural that individuals of the Nordic species value those of their own kind.

It is not only the value of the hereditary heritage that determines the strength of a people. In the struggle for a living space and the right to life, the fertility of a people, the number of children, is decisive. An order such as the SS must therefore create a broad biological selection ground for itself. There must always be a large number of offspring. According to the best marital choice, the most worthy must always provide the Order with a rich progeny.

"The Golden Age is where there are children. Children are the greatest happiness of the SS. He himself, his will and his desires, his feeling and his thought live in them. What he receives from the chain of generations he gives to his children and thus confers eternal life on the people and the Reich of fighting men and faithful women, the guardians of the species and of civilisation.

The SS also takes care of the single mother. Love and procreation are the eternal laws of life that will always break down the barriers of custom and law. Here, too, the SS is closely linked to life. It knows no false morality and also deals with the illegitimate child of good blood. Thus, the racially and hereditarily healthy man can follow his destiny in the community and the people benefit from the strength, the value of a whole generation and thus from a future hereditarily healthy offspring.

As an Order, the SS has inscribed on its flag the preservation and perpetuation of the Nordic race, and is also leading a frontline fight for biological victory. Only the victory of the cradles gives the soldier's victory a historically lasting character.

After the outbreak of the present war, the Reichsführer SS once again summarised these fundamental views of racial policy with a particular reference to the bloodshed that the present war entails. He said in this order: "The old wisdom that only he who has sons and children can die in peace must again become the watchword for the Protection Troop in this war. He can die in peace who knows that his clan, that all that he and his ancestors strived for and wanted, finds its continuation in the children. The greatest gift to the widow of a dead fighter is always the child of the man she loved.

In the *Widow and Orphan Assistance* Act of 1937, the Reichsführer stipulates that the SS community must take responsibility for the care of the widow and child in the event that a member should give his or her life in the fight for the Führer and the people. The unit commanders are personally responsible for the support of all clans in their district.

The *"Lebensborn"* (source of life) also ensures the preservation and increase of pure blood. The dedication of the entire SS ensures that this requirement is met. Pure-blooded children were brought into the world in maternity homes and raised in the Lebensborn nurseries.

The racial idea also determines the importance given by the SS to *physical exercises*. Every SS member had to be able to perform well in sports. The Reichsführer ordered sport in the SS, not to achieve individual feats but to ensure general physical fitness.

The internal unity of the Protection Troop is also expressed in a *law of honour* determined by the Reichsführer. A special *law* on the *sanctity of property* teaches the troop an exemplary conception of property, honour and probity.

II. THE WAFFEN SS

With the practical knowledge of National Socialist selection, leadership and education, the Waffen SS (SS in arms) was created on the basis of the Allgemeine SS by setting up the SS-Verfügungstruppen (SS troops at disposal) and the SS-Totenkopfverbande (skull and crossbones units) after the takeover. It subsequently evolved into its present form.

It has already been said that it was created by the Führer to give the SS acting inside the country the possibility of having a force for action outside, in case of danger.

Units of the Waffen SS regiments, the Leibstandarte SS "Adolf Hitler", the Standarten "Deutschland" and "Germania" as well as parts of the former Totenkopfverbande faced the enemy with the German army when the Polish borders were crossed in September 1939 in a rapid offensive.

These regiments became organised *divisions*, built and run under the Protection Troop's own responsibility, thanks to the Führer's trust.

Even today, it is impossible to estimate the level of development of the Waffen SS achieved during the war. With all its divisions together, it consists only of volunteers selected according to the basic laws of the Protection Troop. It was only after the war that the German people became aware of the enormous amount of work that had been done by the SS-Hauptamt (SS High Office) to enable *the* constant *recruitment* of new units. It is a result that has taken a special place in the history of the German war. The task of the SS-Führungshauptamt (SS higher leadership office) was to set up, equip and train the units.

The harsh winter of 1941/42 demonstrated the importance of the Waffen SS in the conduct of the war. From Karelia to the Sea of Azov, Waffen SS divisions were in the *thick of the fighting* everywhere. Thanks to them, the Reichsführer SS gave the Führer units of steel which, even during that winter, did not reach their limits.

This winter, which tested the mettle of the German people so mercilessly, also tested this Waffen SS. It was up to the task.

When, in front of the Reichstag on 26 April 1942, the Führer made clear to the German people what that winter had really meant, he praised the Waffen SS, touching every one of our brave comrades.

"Speaking of this infantry, I would like to emphasize for the first time the consistent and exemplary bravery and toughness of my brave SS divisions and SS police units. From the very beginning I have regarded them as an unshakable, obedient, faithful and courageous troop in war, as they have promised to be during peace.

The fight of the Waffen SS was part of the proud tradition of the National Socialist Protection Troop. Here, too, the principle of selection, the temperament of a type of man and the consciousness of representing an idea proved effective.

III. GERMAN VOLUNTEERS AND THE GERMAN SS

The Führer's order to establish the 'Nordland' and 'Westland' units within the Waffen SS at the beginning of 1941 was fundamentally new in its nature and scope. A clear understanding of the implications of this order is essential to understanding the principles of the new European order planned by Germany and the development of the Empire in a National Socialist spirit. *The establishment of the volunteer units* was not the reparation of an oversight and a mark of generosity, but *a political act*. The enemies of National Socialism saw this immediately. It was a clear decision on the question of the formation of the future political order and the principle of German organisation in the living space conquered by hard fighting.

The fact that this order of the Führer found such an echo among German youth proves how much the meaning of our struggle was understood in all circles. It also reveals a strong desire to participate in this struggle. At the same time, it is a great proof of the esteem in which the Waffen SS, still so young, is held after the first confrontation, and of the trust placed in the SS in general regarding its vanguard position. Countless young comrades from German-speaking countries found their destiny in its ranks.

When the first volunteers joined the Waffen SS, the front was mainly against England. But the situation changed completely *with the entry into the war against Bolshevism*. In the last few years, the hostility provoked by the Bolshevist system in almost all European countries prompted Germany to consider participating in the struggle on a much larger scale. This was an opportunity to set up *homogeneous units in each country*. Naturally, the contribution to this movement in the German-speaking world was particularly high. The Norwegian and Dutch legions, the Flanders legion, the 'Denmark' free corps and the Finnish volunteer battalion came into being. These units also fought as part of the Waffen SS. Their struggle meant more than a pragmatic stand; it also represented a legal commitment of national forces to the power available for combat.

The conditions for admission to the Waffen SS were *the same* for all countries as *for the Reich*. Entry into the legion depended on character and suitability for service. Assistance and support in accordance with the provisions in force were regulated in the broadest sense for German volunteers, including family support. Particular support might be necessary for young National Socialists whose families were exposed to economic or political coercive measures in their homeland as a result of this voluntary commitment.

A special *German section* was created within the SS-Hauptamt to assist the volunteers. Together with its branches it was responsible for planning all political work in the German-speaking area. A strong Germanic Protection Troop was being created in Flanders, the Netherlands and Norway. In addition, there were also the recruitment commandos of the Waffen SS as well as the newly formed units and the entire complement of the legions, all of which depended on the German Volunteer Section.

Already during the war, the SS considered it its task to bring together the forces of the individual German-speaking countries with its own resources and to lay the foundations for close, joint work in the future.

IV. THE SS AND THE POLICE

Already long before the war the Reichsführer SS wanted to create a new German police force whose officers and men would meet the criteria of the SS and also be members of the Protection Troop. The present situation was therefore a development of the organisation. The nature of police work also changed under the influence of the National Socialist world view. Today, its primary function is educational: rather than punishing offences, it is more important *to prevent* wrongdoing, *to* protect the people and the state from acts that are harmful or dangerous to the community. Today, the SS not only ensures political security but also protects the people from the actions of anti-social elements. It has therefore created a specific institution for this purpose, the *concentration camps*. Under the old system, these elements had become the focus of professional criminality and caused great harm to the people. By the maxim above the entrance gate "work makes you free", these men are exhorted to productive work in these large educational centres because they are not yet lost to the community. They can regain their freedom through a strict education and their being brought to their senses.

An intelligence apparatus had to be created to support the preventive work of the police. As there was a lack of examples at the national level, one could only refer to the security service of the SS Reichsführer, which, under the leadership of SS-Obergruppenführer Heydrich, had already been created by the SS as a party organisation. The joining of the security police and the security service represented a particular fusion of state and movement forces in an extremely important area.

In contrast to the *secret state police* (Gestapo), which represented the political executive, *the criminal police* (Kripo) generally took care of the non-political executive, and was wrongly compared to the old criminal police, i.e. the one before 1933. But this is not true. A people's community that demands that its members follow a certain worldview, a type of state that is penetrated to the extreme by this ideology, must, of course, have a helpful criminal police force that views its tasks in terms of this. Exactly as in the field of the political executive, the absolute rule of the criminal executive requires: the *prevention, and* therefore the neutralisation of all elements that can harm the public good through their actions on the popular and economic force.

Fighting crime therefore means recognising and arresting the criminal, the anti-social element, before further crimes are committed or an anti-social existence is led. Preventive action against criminals is nowadays a generally accepted and approved measure.

The work of *the security service* provides the spiritual basis for the work of the security police. The work of the security service is not about the security police or the state, but about the simple reporting of a situation from material findings to the scientific examination of specific events and phenomena.

Similarly, from the time of the seizure of power until the beginning of the war, the overall work of the regular police, the security police and the SD contributed considerably to creating favourable conditions for the conduct of this great war among the German people. It also gave rise to new, more extensive and important tasks. Units and commandos of the order police, the security police and the SD entered all conquered territories with the victorious armies of our proud German Wehrmacht to take measures as quickly as possible—following the example of peacetime—firstly to create conditions that would restore calm to the rear of the fighting troops and, secondly, to establish civil or military administrative centres to facilitate the administrative work of the troops.

The events that followed the battles of the past months in the greatest winter war in history forced many police regiments and battalions to intervene at the front. In this battle, the men of the regular police proved their military valour, bravery and tenacity side by side with their comrades of the army and the Waffen SS. In this battle they showed that the German regular police perform their duty seriously wherever they are. The police battalions fought remarkably well. Neither the incessant Soviet attacks nor the relentless and deadly cold could overcome their tenacity and courage.

Even today, police units are still engaged in many hot spots on the Eastern Front. Their successful testing in tough battles is ultimately the result of the basic training of officers and men.

V. NATION BUILDING

Germany's new colonising work in the East found its rightful leader in the Führer's order of 7 October 1939, by which the Reichsführer SS was appointed Reich Commissioner for the Consolidation of the German Nation. Throughout the great periods of its history, the German people have always looked to the East for the deployment of their creative talent. But this history also teaches us that military victory alone is not enough to conquer a country. The tragic aspect of German eastern policy in the past centuries is that the movements of the people towards the East did not have a homogeneous objective and thus could not distribute their forces in an organised and planned way.

Thus, the *Eastern mission* is above all a mission of ethnic politics. The ethnic damage caused by the random individual emigration of the past centuries was corrected by *the repatriation of the Volksdeutsche and Reichsdeutsche from abroad to the Reich*. At the same time, *the harmful influence of* certain foreign population groups that posed a danger to the German community was stopped. *The creation of new areas of German settlement,* above all through the immigration and settlement of Volksdeutsche and Reichsdeutsche from abroad, is the third and most important task which the Führer has entrusted to the SS Reichsführer by his order. It includes the reparation of the historical mistake made by the Germans, which caused the popular forces to dry up through lack of comprehensive management of the national destiny.

An appropriate and effective apparatus was at the Führer's disposal to carry out this ethnic policy work immediately. As a doctrinaire who tirelessly taught the idea of the natural link between race and colonisation, the SS Reichsführer gave his *Protection Troop* a basic National Socialist conception and thus provided it with an executive body to carry out extensive constructive work. The idea of the peasant-soldier which this educational work gave rise to implied, in contrast to the 'colonies' of past centuries, that a settlement area had to be created in accordance with the racial character of the men who settled there. Through conscious selection, the SS forms a community in which the best strengths of our people can best flourish creatively. In order to achieve its final reattachment, the Eastern space needs men selected according to criteria of character and worth. This selection, which nature itself makes in groups of men struggling to survive and which future generations need, is guaranteed by the vanguard struggle of the SS.

VI. THE POLITICAL SOLDIER

We have only been able to deal here with the most important practical tasks of the SS. But the spirit of the SS is not limited to the fulfilment of these tasks, and—it must again be stressed—it sees its ultimate justification in the creation, education and selection of a new type of men and leaders capable of mastering all the great tasks of the future. For them, the concept of 'political soldiers' was used. But when the SS speaks of political soldiers, it is not only thinking of a revolution of the political by the military, but also of a revolution of the military by the political. *It is not only the "political fighter" who must be selected and educated, but also*—in the narrowest sense—the *"political fighter"*! In view of the war period, this task must be mentioned again in conclusion.

Historical development has taken its course since the French Revolution and the Prussian uprising of 1813 made the people the principle of military potential in war. More than ever before, ideology marches side by side and among the people on the battlefields. The racial idea clarifies the fronts.

The racial idea melts people and ideology into a solid whole and fights globalist ideologies of all kinds.

But *the war also became an ideological war*. The combination of the political idea and the conduct of war was achieved by a revolution in the art of warfare.

The predominance of worldview over politics makes any war with an enemy worldview a matter of survival. The fundamental law of ideological warfare is victory or defeat.

The historical situation of war demands of the *soldier the utmost firmness and dedication*. Each individual must strengthen himself in the idea of triumphing or dying. To consider that the military character is independent of the political and ideological form of life of the people is already a mortal threat and represents, from the start, a weakness in relation to the adversary.

Contrary to what many people think, there is no such thing as a good military type as a world view. The military character includes a whole series of virtues: courage, firmness, boldness, obedience, fulfilment of duty, dignity. The world view is the field where all these virtues are best expressed.

Arms, equipment and training are not essentially different in modern armed forces. Discipline and duty alone do not win an ideological war either. It is the one who, beyond the fulfilment of duty and obedience, surpasses the opponent by the harshness of the action and the audacity of the risk.

The foundation of the best military spirit is not only the fulfilment of moral duty, but above all the constancy of faith. For it is faith that ensures the stability of moral action in the first place.

To develop this constancy of faith is the supreme task of the SS. With this faith we will be able to build the future faithfully, in the words of the Reichsführer SS:

"Thus we approach and follow the path to a more distant future according to immutable laws as a National Socialist and military order of Nordic men and as a community sworn to its lineages. We wish and believe that we are not only the descendants who have done this best, but above all the ancestors of future generations who are indispensable for the eternal life of the Germanic people.

Power is only justified when it implies an obligation to serve.

Darré

THE HOUSE OF THE SS TROOP SPECIAL. 1942.
BETWEEN TWO MILESTONES

WORK REPORT 1941-42

What we want to be:

1.   A military order of politically and scientifically trained SS men, with keen instincts and a tough physique.

2.   An order of men from the Protection Troop and leaders who by their value, dignity, integrity, outward attitude want to win and keep the trust of others.

3.   An Order that asserts itself in life by its constant natural commitment.

4.   An ideologically frank Order, which cannot be affected by any of life's injustices in its uncompromising path, which instinctively manifests its ideological frankness in all its actions.

5.   An Order of scientifically trained soldiers who see clearly that every new promotion is not a promotion of lords. One can only judge by what one knows-and perform one's profession by vocation, giving it one's best.

6.   An order of soldiers who *only* express themselves on what they know in a rigorous way. We must express ourselves little, but well. It is an Order of men who know that having a name implies a duty.

7.   An Order of soldiers whose ambition is to have names that mean something and not to be anonymous title holders.

8.   An Order of soldiers who have the courage to recognise the value of the great men of their people, the work of others selflessly and who are fully aware of what they are capable of. Qualification and achievement must come first, not decorations and acquired titles.

9. An order of soldiers who, by their performance and dignified attitude, do not need to be consumed by ambition and jealousy of another for anything.

10. An Order of soldiers who, because of their personal simplicity, can adapt to any situation. It is an Order of men who see money only as a tool for the cultured, and who are determined to keep out the upstarts.

11. An order of soldiers in which the racial genotype determines membership in the organisation. Race and blood are our class consciousness, our title of nobility.

12. An order of soldiers who regard the Führer as the supreme authority, wanting to be a model of loyalty, obedience, action, dignified attitude and personal commitment to the Führer and his idea. In accordance with the order of the Reichsführer SS, they serve the German Reich as men and officers of the Protection Troop who are always conscious of their duty.

13. An Order of scientifically trained soldiers in a Nordic-type clan community of racially and biologically healthy women and children—the ancestors of future generations.

Ax.

SS Booklet No. 6. 1936.

Precepts for the Call of the Troop

1 week
a) "One does not die for trade, but only for an ideal. Never yet has a state been founded by a pacifist economy, but always by the instinct to preserve the species. This heroic virtue produces precisely civilised and hard-working states, while cunning is the origin of colonies of Jewish parasites.

b) "Never forget, SS man, that a new economic order built on racial knowledge cannot be created in a few months or even in a few years, but only gradually, and that therefore difficulties cannot be avoided during that time.

2 week
a) "A man who is willing to fight for a cause will never and cannot be a hypocrite and a spineless sycophant.

b) "SS man, acting as a National Socialist who wishes to be an example in the field of loyalty, obedience and discipline, but who considers it his duty to fight injustice and solve problems."

3 week
a) "Political parties are prone to compromise, a world view never."

b) "SS man, constantly believes that the National Socialist world view requires the total man, united with our people, and cannot tolerate to be in contact with any other world view in any field.

4 week

a) "A supporter of a Movement is one who agrees with its aims, a member of a Movement is one who fights for them. To be a supporter implies recognition, to be a member implies the courage to represent the idea oneself and to propagate it.

b) "SS man, be a constant fighter for our National Socialist idea, have above all the goal of realising our world view.

SS BOOKLET NO. 10. 1937.

WHY WE WEAR A UNIFORM

Uniforms were once a sign of recognition. In ancient times, uniforms were given to men in the same way as their thinking was influenced. They were 'stuffed' into them, and this expression already carries the bitter taste of constraint.

Today, it is worn as a sign of spiritual attitude. The only thing that counts is the will and the action of the men wearing the jacket, not the look or the fashion. For this reason, the simple feldgrau uniform is more valuable than the gold-laden dolman of a hussar.

The heroic struggle of our soldiers against an enemy world gave the feldgrau jacket its letters of nobility. It symbolises forever the memory of the misery and death that befell millions of Germany's finest fighters under rolling fire and in tank battles, on the silt fields of Flanders and on the icy expanses of Russia, on the grey "no man's land". They were men ready to accept death, united in victory and comradeship, heroic loners standing by their last machine gun.

Every man who wears the jacket has a duty to this tradition. It thus became the expression of the soldiers at the front, of the will of national defence. Adolf Hitler, the corporal of the Great War, made it the honorary garment of the new national army.

Similarly, the brown shirt will always be the honorary garment of the National Socialist fighter—a constant reminder of the sacrificial spirit of all the anonymous men and women who followed the Führer with sacred loyalty, driven by one constant idea: Germany! Germany, you must live, even if we must die. This spirit of sacrifice and loyalty, of comradeship and desire for freedom, firmly unites every wearer of the brown shirt. We recognize that we wear the brown shirt and the black jacket in the same spirit as these fighters.

The uniform implies a disciplined attitude.

It is no longer necessary to tell a National Socialist today that we make no distinction between service and private life. We are constantly in the service of our people. A National Socialist must therefore never let himself go. The SS must also, in civilian life, act as if he were on duty, as if he were wearing the black uniform, the honorary garment of his Führer.

The uniform therefore implies a duty. It must also be worn with the deepest conviction that it will become an honourable distinction for its wearer.

But the uniform also implies physical qualities. It should be worn by healthy men and not by weaklings. That is why in all units that wear a uniform, physical exercise is cultivated. Under the uniform, the man without attitude becomes the caricature of the soldier and thus makes the troop ridiculous.

The notions of soldier, defence and activity are linked to the uniform. Being a soldier implies the notion of duty. The uniform demands that the wearer is always aware that he or she has great duties to fulfil. Wearing a uniform requires the ability to fight with conviction for the idea that made us put it on. It is an expression of comradeship, perseverance and loyalty. He who thinks like this when he wears it and hangs his way of thinking with his jacket on his hanger is not only endangering his personal appearance. He harms the group to which he belongs. For the individual is nothing—perhaps a name that is forgotten three days later. The uniform wearer, on the other hand, symbolises an idea, even if his name is unknown.

The uniform demands from its wearer a total refusal to compromise. It tolerates no hesitation. It demands action'.

The wearer of the uniform is the focus of all eyes. When unforeseen events occur, the masses will turn to him, feeling that he knows what needs to be done. The civilian can afford to fail: no one will draw general conclusions. The soldier who fails undermines the respect of all those who wear the same jacket. He who wears the uniform is always placed at a higher level of responsibility, he is in any case a leader, an elected official. Our education must therefore aim to ensure that one day our young people wear the uniform out of conviction, and are not simply "stuck" in it. Young people must be aware that the uniform, in National Socialist Germany, has become the expression of all those who come together because they are of the same species. The grey jacket of the People's Army, the brown shirt and the black uniform are the honorary garments of men who are ready to fight for the National Socialist Reich and an eternal Germany.

So that's why we wear the uniform. A lot of people probably respected the black jacket at first because it looks good. They took pride in it and were satisfied. But gradually they realised that it also imposed duties, which we accepted voluntarily and out of conviction. One can perhaps follow the rules of an association, even devoting oneself twice a week to its objectives, but certainly not a world view. The black jacket implies that the wearer must act every day and every hour as a soldier of National Socialism. Every action on our part will therefore be observed, compared and judged. The value of an idea represented by the wearer of the uniform is judged by his behaviour

We must win the confidence of our fellow citizens by our thoughtfulness, for we do not want to impose our world view on the people, but to persuade them of its rightness. He who wears the uniform experiences National Socialism in advance. And our task is to spread our world view ever more widely in the community until it is understood.

We want to be respected and to judge the value of National Socialism by our attitude.

That's why we wear a uniform.

V.J. Schuster

The worst path one can choose is to choose none.

Frederick the Great

SS NOTEBOOK NO. 2. 1943.

THE ORDER OF CLANS

The word "order" is familiar to us from the monastic orders and orders of chivalry of the Christian Middle Ages. When we think of these orders, we think of the mighty, rebellious feudal castles and the long, windowed facades of monastic buildings. In the past, the former were inhabited by monk-knights wearing the cross of the Order on their doublets and cloaks. In the latter, we imagine men in sandals and frocks walking silently through the corridors and cells. In both cases, we already have an outward impression of the spirit of the Order.

An order is a community that follows an "ordina", i.e. a statute, a freely sworn rule of life. The characteristic of an order is that it serves a high ideal. For example, there has never been an "order of merchants", but at most, associations of merchants.

The spirit of the order plays an exceptional role wherever professions of faith, ideals and the defence of these values are concerned. This is how the most eminent monastic religious orders came into being at a time when extremely pious men wanted to pull the Church out of an ever-increasing "secularisation". The German orders of chivalry came into being when the Christian faith had to be taken to the "holy land" or to the East Slavic countries. The Jesuit Order developed when the Roman Church had to defend itself once again against the popular Nordic Protestant movement.

Regardless of the fact that these Christian orders were based on an alien conception and a mistaken ideology, that they degenerated and partly disappeared, we must nevertheless recognise that in these communities lived men who wanted to dedicate their lives to a high ideal. This ideal, this will, this profession of faith in private life was so heavy with consequences that it could only be the lot of a few, not of all. Moreover, for these idealists, it was necessary to build a community of life with the certainty that each one would be ready to demand the maximum of himself in the service of an idea. This certainty gave strength to the individual and the group. So we see that an order is, within an ideology, that restricted community whose members give absolute precedence in their existence to that ideology and freely commit themselves to following its laws. The stricter these laws are, the stronger the will to respect them, the greater the selflessness required, the more limited the number of members of the order, and the more powerful the order will be in pursuing its objectives.

An order is defined by its objective or programme. This, in turn, is determined by the ideology to which the order is attached.

The Christian monks had as their objective the elevation of the soul to a life in the afterlife. Since this, according to the Christian conception, can only be achieved by withdrawing from this world of sin and mortifying the sinful body, the monk took a vow of complete poverty (removal of all worldly goods), humble obedience (abandonment of all personal wills and rights), and chastity (refusal of all "desires" except for "God's", which is the most physically demanding). We call this attitude "asceticism". Despite justified indignation, we bow with respect to the high degree of idealism of these Germans, these Germans, accepting this personal sacrifice in the name of "God" and an "idea of perfection". The minority who made such commitments were undoubtedly largely elite in character.

The knight-monks of the orders of chivalry represent a more sympathetic image for us. The profession of Christian faith was combined with the chivalric way of life. In this respect, a more virile, more temporal, more active aspect follows. While the monk believed that he could only achieve his goal by self-destruction, the Teutonic knight had made it his mission to expand the kingdom with his warrior's body and sword.

The SS Clan Order, on the other hand, is founded within the National Socialist Movement on a completely new basis. The roots of its beliefs are different, and each of its specific laws and values are different. The most striking characteristic of Christian orders in the past, whether "contemplative", "active" or warrior, was the obligation to renounce women, marriage and children. The essential criterion of our Order is the obligation to get engaged and married! The guiding idea of medieval Christian orders was the elevation of the soul, the "deliverance from the body" to unite the soul with a god in the afterlife. Our credo is that the fulfilment, the "incarnation" and thus the proper destiny of the god of life, is through the evolutionary pathways of species and races; we see mate choice and permanent selection as the means to improve life (body and soul). We no longer need to be ascetics, for we do not want a god in the afterlife. Our god asks us to be "temporal", because the world, as we know, is his field of action, his "body". Thus the SS, as the pagan order of National Socialist ideology in the 20th century, is a temporal order in the highest sense of the word. The time for mistakes has passed. We are now experiencing a powerful advance in our knowledge, and the centuries to come will prove that it will have far-reaching consequences. To recognise the presence of God in nature (as the present state of science knows it) means to note its unity, yes, even its uniqueness with our destiny, subject to the hereditary law that he applies!

The SS began as a troop, but it knew from the start that this troop should not be an end in itself. We do not live to perpetuate a Menerbund, but we are men gathered together with our families, our clans, our people, our blood children, all the children of our people and a living future in mind. For us, "organisation" is only a means to serve "the organism". The organism is the people.

We see today that all the peoples of Europe, including our German people, have undergone a constant racial, and therefore psychic and spiritual, degradation over the last two thousand years, and this as a result of the mixture of blood (the microbes of Judaism and Christianity, its successor). We know that it is neither famine nor the destructive rage of the people that has caused the tragic wars and disorders of European history, but the corruption of the popular substance, the disregard of the divine will of love and marriage between equals by birth, of selection, of incitement to selection, as well as a vice that accompanies it: the reversal of the relations of authority in the popular bodies. We affirm that each one of us collaborates in the great political and historical human creations if, in the course of our lives, we do not deviate "one inch from the ways of God", if we are faithful and remain faithful to those who have chosen the same faith.

We men of the SS recognise that the words "people", "Reich", "honour" and "freedom" mean nothing if one does not have the will to bring to life the spirit that governs these concepts. The importance attached to this spirit must be placed in the order of the laws of nature. National Socialism is a biological ideology which asserts that the demands of nature are political demands. Nature has defined the rule of life which the races of good men must follow:

1. The individual aspiration for marriage between healthy and equal partners by birth.
2. On this basis, the development of the family as "the smallest, but most valuable unit within the whole organised structure of the state".
3. Life is built according to natural laws from the fertile branch of the family. The clan is rooted in the family, a living entity, a reality of the

Order that a biological as well as a political will has dreamed and desired.

It is only in the clan that the individual can develop his or her personality and qualities.

The best order is the one whose laws are none other than the divine laws of nature. From that moment on, the SS began to transform itself from a male association into an association of clans. The SS clans are thus animated by the spirit of the Order and tend to unite. The Order, however, lives through each clan and derives its own value from it.

The fear that anarchic particularism will develop in the clan with regard to the wholeness of the Order and its goal, "the Empire", and the opposite fear that the demands of the Order will prejudice the natural freedoms of the clan, are unfounded and without reason as long as the spirit of the Order and the spirit of the clan do not deviate from the natural divine laws of life.

The Order thus places a permanent obligation on all its members. Each member must therefore strive to keep the spirit of the whole intact. The SS member knows that it is a matter of natural law that an individual or another should fail in his duty, but he also knows that this must not take away his faith and loyalty. To maintain this unshakeable firmness is to be a true SS man, to prove the value of his blood.

History teaches us that organisations perish in the course of time through weakening of the spirit, alienation or torpor, when selfish and materialistic intruders take over, pushing aside bold, vivacious, creative personalities who, therefore, no longer feel attracted to the organisation. Our Order must therefore avoid allowing its basic spiritual idea to be perverted. We must also prevent it from favouring appearances and material forms to the detriment of its good men. Let us also keep our community free from those who do not give us disinterested faith and pure idealism, but selfishness, lust for power and bourgeois enjoyment. For—an Order is judged by impartial History according to the same laws as a people: according to the living qualities of its flesh and blood.

Once a millennium, people have the opportunity to look back on their mistakes and, enriched by painful trials and equipped with new creative forces, to regain awareness of the divine meaning of their lives.

The door to a great future is opening again. We are aware of the responsibility which, in history, always rests on the decisive minority. Thus we, the members of the SS and the SS clan, stand before the divine Creator with the motto which the Führer gave us: "My honour is called loyalty".

Mayerhofer

SS NOTEBOOK No. 5. 1944.

That's Why Our Cabinets Don't Have Locks

A young SS comrade, a cheerful blond, had chosen a splendid and unusual bookmark; a brand new two-mark note. It was certainly the result of a whim. Perhaps the little brown paper with the proud 'Two' reminded him of Giselle, or perhaps it was the eight-digit red number that had particularly interested him. Who could say why this young SS man had taken these two marks out of circulation? This new note had spent many happy hours going through the pages of his book! Now it was gone! A bad joke had replaced it with two old one-mark notes. At first Hans Jürgen gave a few rude words of resignation, but one evening an older comrade came back to the matter. Young man," he said, "one of our poets once spoke of a deceitful soul. He meets it in those young girls who paint their nails red, smear their lips with oil, in short look like a cabaret poster. But the beardless faces of boys can also harbour the same soul. Some of them, feeling targeted, smiled embarrassedly. A Hamburg man thought, "Let's not get carried away...". At that, the old man who was being apostrophised took the ball and said: "That's what I'm getting at! In life, it's all about not getting carried away. For big things as well as for small ones. We consider the bookmark exchange to be a joke. However, it already reveals an attitude towards the intangibility of other people's property which leads to the conclusion that there is a loss of a sense of justice. In all such cases, I tell you, we behave like Jewish flatfoots. If we want to be the best, an elite that creates an exemplary life and race, then we must also conform to the behaviour of our ancestors in our rules of life. They considered the property of others to be sacred and inviolable. Let us remember that in the earliest Germanic law, unlawful infringement of private property was unknown and, when it occurred, was punished as a crime unworthy of a free man.

—Come on, come on," says Gert, "we're not going to make a big deal out of a joke!

—I'm not talking about all that any more," replied the old comrade, "but about the basic law of the Reichsführer SS, that property is sacred. Perhaps one or other of you is not aware that the Reichsführer, in his order of 25 November 1937, considers "pilfering" to be a serious infringement of property, which affects honour. I do not even want to talk about serious violations of private property. Anyone who steals, embezzles or misappropriates knows what awaits him. I only want to state once again that "pilfering", i.e. the illegal appropriation of equipment or clothing belonging to the SS, which is called "grappling", will not be regarded as a harmless misdeed or a good deed, but that the guilty parties must expect to be held responsible. The superior takes the necessary measures for the benefit of the fighting troops, but actions on his own behalf are a condemnable business. You are proud that your cupboards have no locks," concluded the comrade, "so keep that attitude.

But Gert did not want to leave it at that after this call to sensible behaviour, and with an allusion to Hans Jürgen whose lost bookmark, he thought, had earned him this sanctimonious sermon, he remarked, "And all because of you, dearest Gisèle!"

With that, Hans Jürgen climbed onto his bed, took the two dirty one-mark notes and solemnly announced that he was offering this bad joke several barrels of lager.

Be fair
And fear no one.
An honest man is in my eyes of the highest nobility and value, for his virtue
shines through in everything he does.

Frederick the Great

SS Notebook No. 1. 1944.

Two cautionary examples

Whoever lives as a parasite during the war is caught!
There is nothing more shameful than unfaithfulness to oneself and one's people. The longer the war goes on, the harder the demands and sacrifices become, the stricter and clearer must be the attitude of all those who have to manage property, and who can therefore harm the community. Let us cite the following case as a warning example from legal experience: In 1940, SS officer X. was ordered to found and run an economic centre solely for SS troops. He was given full powers because of the trust placed in him. However, he abused these powers in a criminal and unrestrained manner to enrich himself. He exceeded his rights by improperly requisitioning belongings, food and the entire stock of fabrics, suits and clothes for trafficking with criminal and obscure elements with whom he had close relations. He used large sums of administrative money for speculative purposes in which they took part, and gave his accomplices full powers which they then used in the same criminal way. The damage his actions caused to the people and the Reich is inexcusable. He was sentenced to death for harming the people. The sentence was confirmed by the Führer himself and executed shortly afterwards.

Everyone can see, therefore, that every misdeed, even the most insignificant, is judged and must be judged inflexibly and ruthlessly. Every soldier and SS officer must realise that he is liable to the death penalty if he does not respect the things for which the comrade at the front is fighting, and that he must provide his fellow countrymen with the bare minimum of life. No one will be able to take advantage of his position or his services, however old and esteemed he may be.

Protection of life in the embryo

One of the most important principles of the SS is the conviction that the victory of arms can only be complete through the victory of the cradles. Whoever threatens life in the embryonic stage is harming the vitality of the people. Here is another example from practice:

The SS officer A., who had been married since 1935 and had no children, had a relationship with the young office worker B. that was not without consequences. As he feared that the illegitimate birth of a child might harm his situation, he encouraged B. to perform an abortion on her, which however was unsuccessful. When his own efforts had failed, he contacted a man through various intermediaries who had once been involved in an abortion case and who was now willing—after initially refusing—to perform the procedure. The accused even picked him up in a company car and gave him several pairs of shoes worth RM75 as payment for his efforts, in addition to reimbursement of expenses. However, the trials remained unsuccessful.

In contrast to the usual judgement, which sentenced the mother and the professional abortionist to three to eight months in prison and the other participants to up to six weeks in prison, the police and SS court handed down a considerably harsher sentence of one and a half years in prison. In particular, it considered that the accused had shown incomprehensible cowardice and irresponsibility for an SS officer, had unscrupulously endangered the life and health of the mother and had damaged the reputation of the SS. A harsher sentence was not passed because the accused was prone to heart weakness, was superficial in his behaviour, was in a constant state of depression and was dizzy. The Reichsführer himself confirmed the judgment and rejected a request for a pardon, as various circumstances spoke in favour of granting it, among them the accused's membership of the NSDAP before the seizure of power.

This extremely severe punishment is the result of the fact that offences committed against the ideological principles of the Order's community deserve a particularly strict judgement.

Extract from the SS Justice Office's communiqués

He who is not master of himself is not free.

Claudius

SS NOTEBOOK NO. 11. 1944.

TELL ME WHO YOU'RE SEEING...

Extract from the practice of the Superior Office of Justice SS

Karl and Hein were old comrades. They had often met death together and had honoured the runes of victory in many battles.

On the occasion of a joint holiday, Karl invited his comrade to visit him at his home. As the trip would only last a few hours, Hein agreed. Naturally, there was a lot of joy and Karl's parents had a hotel at the station, so the reunion was a lot of fun.

But all joy must come to an end, and 22-year-old Hein also had to return to his home. A friendly blonde-haired maid approached him there, he thought nothing of it, and while the maid was tidying up the room for the night, he made small, harmless conversation. At this the girl left with a friendly laugh.

Naturally, Hein told Karl about the nice girl. He couldn't even imagine that this blonde head was Karl's mistress. He only found out a year later. The girl had given birth to a child and declared Karl as the father. Instead of Karl decently siding with the young mother and acknowledging her child, he considered how he could avoid his duty. So one day he asked Hein not to abandon him and to help him out of this embarrassing situation. When he was caught, he would only have to declare that the employee had offered her services to him on the night of the visit, or rather, that she had made a commitment to him.

Then Karl told the friend that nothing could happen to him if he stuck to this statement. He also promised Hein a sum of money and a new invitation. Despite the fact that he might get into trouble with these lies, Hein gave his testimony and confirmed it with his oath.

K. was locked up in a reformatory for two years for incitement to false oath and H. for one and a half years for false oath. In addition, they were both expelled from the SS.

Perjury is one of the most vile and shameful crimes. In this case, it is particularly infamous because it was committed by the SS, of whom the German people have a particularly high opinion of the honour and responsibility of providing a child with the sustenance that is his due. This case shows how far misunderstood comradeship can lead. A 'comrade' of this kind is, strictly speaking, no longer a comrade but a truly unconscious corrupter.

SS Notebook No. 10. 1944.

PRESERVE THE MYSTERY OF LOVE!

"I know French, Russian and Italian girls, a German girl has nothing to offer me", says Rottenführer Hinterhuber, looking around provocatively. His round, 19-year-old face betrays this narrow-mindedness, which is equal parts stupidity and immaturity. He certainly commands a certain amount of admiration among his peers around him. In their eyes, he is a very experienced fellow who "knows women"—yes, it is possible to be that lucky in love! Such immature boasting could be ignored if it were not so typical of the attitude of some of the men in our ranks.

How did he acquire his knowledge and experience of women? It was certainly something very distant, without exaltation or romanticism. He wanted to know about love and found some dubious specimens of the female sex who occasionally went with him because he was there at the right time. What he considered a conquest was nothing more than the result of blind chance. For if it had not been him, the next man would have done just as well. So he did not need to look for long. Excited or venal, she left him. And he called it love! During his young life he was only a soldier. The war took him all over Europe. He brought back in his luggage the memory of vulgar French actresses, as well as the carefree primitiveness of Russian female nature. But those he loved were mediocre, second-rate—he did not discover the human richness of these peoples. Nationalist consciousness and a strong instinct raised countless barriers in the other camp.

What does this boy know about the real nature of women? He probably did not grow up in a real family community, did not feel the unattainable pride of the fiercely protected mother or sisters. For him, during the years when he became a man, women did not represent anything wonderful. He was not given time to think about it. He did not read Tacitus' texts on the veneration of the Germanic woman as the divine giver of life, nor did he read Werther. His literature on the subject remained the three-cent novels. And when he first felt a great inner restlessness, troubled, inconceivable and yet compelling, the war took him along for the ride and hardened his childlike senses to the point of transforming passionate exaltation into a cold, almost harsh realism.

It is a fact that some boys have not experienced the uniqueness and incomparability of first love. Life frustrated them with one of its most beautiful and ardent gifts. They had to give up what was a fundamental experience for previous generations. So they suddenly become 'men' and discover a mystery they never understood as such. Their first love was not sacred, passionate and enthusiastic, but cold. Their relationship with women was not one of adoration; they saw nothing divine in them, for they knew nothing of the sort in them, dealing only with the evil side of the other sex, the corrupted prostitute, and so came to regard everyone else in the same light. A contemptuous laugh greeted the possible exception.

This state of mind is dangerous. This war too will end one day, leaving room for normal life. We will have to heal the serious wounds that have been inflicted on our pool of men this year. At the forefront is the family, the will to have a child, otherwise a won war is meaningless. Today and in the future we must fulfil a racial and family programme according to the Führer's will. We are an Order of clans and, as such, charged with the enormous task of creating an extremely valuable blood supply in the hearts of millions of our people. This task demands of us an absolutely unreserved stance towards woman. For the moment we marry her, being the future mother of our children, she becomes a member of the SS like every other male comrade!

The war is infinitely hard. Only the strong will survive. But this strong and brave character does not have the soulless cruelty that can be observed precisely in our enemies. They, the representatives of Judeo-Bolshevist, liberal and anarchist ideas, appreciate love only as an unbridled intoxication, ignoring the slightest trace of ethics. All that matters is the moment and what it brings them. They always violate the noble soul, not going beyond the level of the most vulgar impulse. We have long since come to know the Bolshevist human animal. We are not ignorant of the horrors committed by the Americans on the women of Sicily. Between us and them there is not the slightest ideological or political trace of a compromise, but only the naked, brutal fact: Us or them! Do we want to put ourselves on the same level as their unbridled liberalism? Even in the things of everyday life, in our most intimate relations with the other sex, we do not want to follow their unclean example.

In the past, we were said to be the people of poets and thinkers. We were proud of this—the others, however, laughed silently, regarded us as children in politics and despised us.

While a Bach or a Goethe revealed to them, the scoffers, a sky of beauty, they shared the earthly riches and we remained poor before their golden doors. After centuries of backwardness, we have matured politically, we have been awakened by the great teaching of the Führer, worthy of political power at last. We had to face the hatred of the whole world and at the same time defend the new doctrine with arms. We were the best soldiers. The gates of the Reich opened, hundreds of thousands of soldiers marched across Europe in an unparalleled triumphal march. They winked at foreign countries and the particularities of other peoples. The last barriers of petty-bourgeois ways of thinking fell away and the bounded horizon expanded to the dimensions of the world.

But now we know the danger that remains attached to this rapid development. We have seen that more than one boy's mind was disturbed because the hardships of combat, the grandeur of the feeling of power, were too strong for his still immature character and unfit for wise discernment. The danger of a soldier's life drove him to seek passionately enjoyment, experience and adventure. And they became rough and shallow. They, the descendants of those ingenuous dreamers, fell into the other extreme. Today, there is no longer a Werther among us, and that is good, but a ruthless tyrant is just as reprehensible. He must disappear. We must educate him wherever possible. The married people among us have a great example to set here. Having learned about true love, they must cooperate in this work of education condemning obscenity and sexual ostentation. We are not angels, we all know the violent call of blood and senses. But here too we must be political soldiers. Let us draw them out of this poor, primitive and sensual unconsciousness, let us open their eyes to the real beauty which is also present in a thousand forms in the landscape and art of the enemy country around us. Even the most hardened still know how to dream, far from the war with its inflexibility and harshness.

Boys caught up in the whirlpools of carelessness and levity must be able to experience true love. A pure and healthy German woman will be able to give it to them, if Providence so wishes, so that they can pass on their lives to children. The children they have wanted with a beloved woman will be the living testimony of a love that includes both the physical and the spiritual.

In such hard times as those which have been imposed on us Germans, men need women at their side who can combine the originality of their nature and the warmth of their hearts with a frank and thoughtful broadmindedness. We need women who can form the healthy new generation we hope for, who from the very beginning teach their children to be members of their people and know that the future of this people and its spiritual mission determine its destiny and its history.

Gertrud Scholtz-Klink

SS NOTEBOOK NO. 3.1942.

LOYALTY

Today's war provides daily proof of daring and singular heroism. But there are no more small, anonymous heroisms of German soldiers. It is the silent, tenacious proof of loyalty and resistance. It was the loyalty of spirit that kept every unit of our army and our Waffen SS going for three months despite the encirclement and the blockade of normal supplies, and gave the Eastern Front the firmness and toughness that alone prevented a catastrophe in this cold and massive assault by the enemy. Only those who are familiar with the forms of fighting in the East know what this means. When the enemy tries to imitate our strategy, he always fails. General Rommel said it well: "Encirclement battles such as those being fought in the present war can only be fought by German soldiers.

What has been confirmed here will also be demonstrated in the future. Loyalty is a German virtue. There is no such thing as loyalty without content. It has nothing to do with that stubbornness which opponents like to possess. Nor is it obstinacy or firmness alone, although they are necessary companions. Fidelity, faith and honour are like three bark around the same precious core. But it is the soul of our people that constitutes the centre, that singular inner realm from which artistic strength arises, surprising the world with new creative manifestations that represent our greatest good. Individuals are more or less aware of this wealth. There are no Germans without an ideal. Loyalty is nothing other than a recognition of inner worth, personal vocation and destiny. In essence, the acts of loyalty that one encounters in times of distress are regarded as religious acts. Men who know these moments—they are not frequent in life—can speak of them and one can, so to speak, trace the inner vocation that gripped them. Political soldiers, thinkers and inventors have felt it. SS comrades also experienced it, persevering in their loyalty to the Führer and the Fatherland despite letters visibly lost in the ice and snow.

For the Germans, fidelity implies that one considers one's mission as an order from heaven. It is always in close connection with God and only a sceptical and superficial individual can doubt this. Loyalty to the Fatherland, the Movement and the Führer is rooted in the strength of the soul. He who is poor inwardly cannot be completely faithful either. Loyalty is the silent language of inner wealth.

Loyalty is demonstrated by action. In times of distress and misfortune, the German people have always shown themselves to be the most loyal, even the fighting part of them, i.e. the part that suffered and bore the brunt of this misery. These were the soldiers in the trenches of the last world war. They were the Führer's first comrades-in-arms. In this war, the front once again bears the main burden on its shoulders; but the fatherland also provides daily proof of the deepest loyalty through deprivation and self-denial.

Perseverance is also a component of loyalty. It would be absurd to think that we can change our homeland or our people. Our life will have found its meaning when we have remained faithful to ourselves. Everything is linked. Loyalty is in truth indivisible. Fidelity to the Führer, to the fatherland, to one's wife and children, that is the meaning of fidelity.

The SS is an order of loyalty. Loyalty to the Führer, to the comrades, to the fatherland and to the family is the fire that drives us. We know our people. We know from its fatal history that its credulity and ingenuity have often been abused by tempters. The SS must be a bulwark around our most sacred jewel, around the inner wealth of the German people. A deep faith in the divine mission of our people and its leader fills us. It enriches us. It makes us strong and unyielding. It gives us the strength to be faithful in times of maximum effort.

Gd

Getting through enemy lines is not easy!

SS NOTEBOOK NO. 6B.1941.

MEN, COMRADES, EXAMPLES

The man decides

SS-PK. The Soviets do not have the hitherto usual excuse of having been defeated by the superiority of German war material. They really had enough! However, we are used to facing a multitude of trials and only shook our heads when we saw the endless rows of destroyed tanks and guns along the offensive routes…

No, in the East, it's the man who decides! It is the German soldier, who has better nerves, a better constitution, who has, above all, a stronger faith. And therein lies the certainty of our victory, because these men are in our companies. They don't stand out much, they do their duty. They are soldiers with that self-evident character that perhaps only the German has. So we must talk about them!

I think of Rottenführer-SS H. I met him in an outpost of an SS cavalry brigade. I saw him for the first time in an engagement near L. He dug his anti-tank hole under heavy enemy fire, without haste, almost calmly as if he had been used to doing this work for years. Later—at that time we were cut off from all contact with our troops, with the Soviets at our backs—he hesitantly told me about him.

I was hardly surprised when he mentioned Spain. For two years he fought the Bolshevists there as a volunteer. He really had a lot of adventures behind him, but he joined the Waffen SS as a soldier the moment he returned to the Reich. For him, this was a natural thing to do.

I think silently ... this man has been living in the war for years now. And he has not become a "lansquenet". That same evening he tells me fervently about his wife. During a brief leave of absence, he settled as a craftsman in the General Government. And after the war—but he stopped with his plans ... the Bolshevists had to be liquidated first. They were getting weaker. He had already experienced this, once, when he was hunting them down in Catalonia.

This is how he is, the Rottenführer-SS H. He has never been particularly conspicuous. More than one of his comrades and superiors knows nothing about these things. He did his duty. He is a soldier only.

But the power of Bolshevism breaks on such men, the victory is theirs!

SS War Correspondent T. Kriegbaum

Missing artillery service—no!

SS-PK. Our outpost has spotted enemy armour, lightning fast, we dismount and take up positions on either side of the road. While we buried ourselves and the guns in anti-tank holes, our tank hunters placed their guns fifteen metres in front of us. When, ten minutes later, our pioneers return after laying mines, they stretch the camouflage net over the protective shield. Only the gun stretches its black mouth menacingly towards the road. We wait.

The platoon leader with the anti-tank gun looks around with his binoculars and suddenly sees the first tank. Three hundred metres ahead of us, its dome rises above the top of the cornfield. Its first shot thunders and a light green streak of light passes us by. A heavy engine screams on the other side, the colossus starts moving and crawls towards us. Now we see two more. No sooner do we recognise them than two shells tear through the air whistling and explode around our Pak gun. "Fire at will". This order devours the shells. Case after case is emptied. The artillery men work unimpressed by the explosions in the vicinity. After the first shots, the lead tank was already in flames. But an anti-tank gun is still facing four heavily armed tanks!

Worried, we look at our brave tank hunters. We can only see them for a short time as shell after shell falls beside them. Smoke and powder hide them from our view. But they are still firing. They know that our fate also depends on theirs. They see, they feel even more now what the section leader orders and read the movement of his powder-blackened lips. When will the enemy fire cease for good...? Then came the shot at the goal. It was only a flash.

We, the gunners, see only a small flame in a cloud of black smoke. The gun is enveloped in an impenetrable cloud of black-brown smoke. We hear:

"Missing artillery service, the Pak is not firing". We knew it! What happens now?

Yet, no, suddenly a voice shouts: "No, the company commander is alive and still firing…"! !" How is this possible? Yes, a stroke of luck! Another one! In the meantime the smoke cloud has dissipated. We now see that the company commander is charging, aiming and firing … and again charging, aiming, firing, all by himself.

Then, the lead tank changes its trajectory to the left and goes on the road! We are laughing hard because we know what is waiting for him there: a sure end. A few more metres and the staggering of our mines begins… Another ten metres … there in front of the small ford must be the first … now … an explosion and three, four jets of flame, the Soviet tank has fallen victim to our pioneers.

In the meantime, four gunners have jumped out and are hurrying to reinforce the company commander with the Pak gun. The third of these five Soviet tanks is also neutralised. Three shots in the tracks and it shows us its flank. The company commander fires well. The dome of the tank rises, two trembling hands grasping the edges: the last survivor surrenders. The occupants of the two tanks still intact give up the fight. Hands raised, they stand beside their colossus, ready to follow the path of captivity.

Then the artillery company commander plants the death runes on the three fresh graves of his comrades. "My honour is called fidelity' is written above. He then salutes them for the last time.

SS War Correspondent Ernst Gugl

Waiting for the first contact…

... which occurs explosively!

The distance is estimated...

... and the response is immediate!

SS BOOKLET NO. 10. 1939.

THE ELDERS

It was during the days of great unrest in the Sudetenland. The SS call-up orders rang out in the mess hall. The Wehrmacht had younger reserves: but an opportunity was offered to send men who were not physically inferior to them and whose spirit of sacrifice was equal to their own. What is a minimum age of 45 today? The SS called and all came. There were men of about 50 years of age who gladly welcomed such a mission—although it was usually related to commercial problems. All the districts sent their 'elders'. They were men from Hamburg, Berlin, Mecklenburg, Pomerania, Silesia who followed their vocation in Oranienburg and were happy to perform a task in the community camp of the 'old warriors' in Sachsenhausen.

The centuries are assembled. The first problem is that the feldgrau clothing of the slender men of the Totenkopf unit, which is engaged on the borders, does not fit. In the same row, without rank insignia, there are old officers from the front next to warrant officers and old soldiers. The tone of the language becomes warm, nostalgic when one of them talks about Verdun, another about Munkacz or Turkey. They take turns to take out their buckles with emotion and many iron crosses of the class decorate the chests. Everyone knows their duties in the SS camp, everyone knows how absolutely essential its action is to ensure the internal peace of the Reich.

Never in my life would I want to forget those weeks when I analysed a huge educational problem in all clarity, and which were spent in cordial camaraderie. This means, therefore, in the case of a difficult service, in an inflexible and persevering way; the duties seem less today, measured in the course of time.

Do you remember comrade?" one always asks when one meets, and one recalls the lines of the outposts, the company, the lights in the forest. You think of the sun, the grey fog and also of the days when it rained so hard that not even the canvas of the tent offered any protection.

I walk through the lines of the outposts of my column. On my way is one of the oldest who is over 60 years old. One step to the right, one step to the left. The rain is constantly pouring down on the canvas and enlarging the puddles in which even the best boots fail to fight the humidity … for hours … one step to the right … one step to the left. And I admire the old comrade who did not want to compromise and refused to take the easy way out. His head is white as snow.

Rarely has a community been as close-knit as this one. You can see in its eyes the same desire for the others. Every task is carried out 'voluntarily'.

Then the battle ends. The last pay is given and the commander pronounces cordial words of farewell.

I see the white-haired comrade in my column. He is again wearing the black garment of the SS. On his chest now shines the golden badge of the Party.

My respect, which was already very great, became total. To stand out at that age with silver hair and the gold pin of honour, and yet to have performed a difficult service in all simplicity, was for me a shining example of true National Socialist camaraderie.

Today, this eternally young ideological fighter holds in his hand a portrait of the SS Reichsführer which reads:

"To my brave, old SS men, who helped the Führer and the Fatherland in difficult times by doing their duty.

SS-Ustuf. Max Hanig, O.A. North Staff.

Total self-sacrifice is the source from which all abilities flow. It teaches us to put good name before material advantages, before a sense of dignity, and to prefer fairness to unbridled greed and covetousness, to put the benefit of the people and the state before our own and our family's; to consider the good and survival of the country as superior to our own security, property, health, and life.

It almost makes us citizens of a higher world.

Frederick the Great

SS BOOKLET NO. 6. 1942.

THE WILL OF AN SS

This is the will of SS Heinz H., who fell on the Eastern Front on 28 March 1942. He was newly married and did not yet know whether he would have a child

My will:

"If fate would have it that I should not return from this great war, I wish:

1. Let this event not be seen as anything other than what it is: a necessary sacrifice that I willingly make for Germany's victory by fulfilling my life as a soldier.

2. May my dear wife and my beloved parents overcome their grief, may they too willingly offer this sacrifice on the altar of the fatherland.

3. That in the death notice there is not a word about a divine decree, God, great pain, deep mourning etc. As a caption I would like the following sentence: For the victory of Germany we are ready to give everything. In mourning, in pride …;

4. No armbands or other signs of mourning should be worn.

5. May I not be taken back to my country, but may I rest with my comrades.

6. That if I should not have a son, my brother G. should be aware that he will then bear our name alone.

7. May my wife not remain a widow; may she, as a healthy woman, not forget the duty she must perform for the eternity of our Reich.

8. That if I should have a son, he should always bear my name, that he should be brought up to be a sound, honest, dignified, self-deprecating and courageous man, believing in Germany with unshakeable faith.

9. If I had a daughter, let her be brought up to be a proud German woman, aware of her duties to Germany.

A letter to his wife was attached to the will. We extract the following sentences from it:

"You have been a good comrade to me, a loving wife who has cared for me and will, I hope, be the mother of my child. Raise him in the same spirit as I would have done: Give him to believe early on in our Reich, in our eternal Germany.

Do not remain a widow. You are too good to spend your life in mourning, so healthy and so young. The important thing is not our life, but that of Germany. We shall win because we must. We have no other choice.

Then, in a letter to his brother:

"You are here now for both of us. Do not consider this a burden but a natural obligation. We do not live to go one day to a land of milk and honey called heaven, nor to amass material wealth, but to take our share in the eternity of Germany. This alone is the reason for a German's life. Never forget that!

In the part of the will devoted to material things, it was foreseen, in case his household had no children, that the savings account would be transferred to the national political institution of Köslin (Napola).

"Napola de Köslin! For three years I spent the most beautiful years of my life within your walls. You clearly shaped my idealism. You taught me to believe in the eternal German Reich. You gave my life a meaning. You were my second home. Anyone who has been a student of yours can never forget you. You inspired us all to work tirelessly for Germany. I will never forget your words: "Believe, Obey, Fight! They are an inexhaustible source of strength for me. As long as you instil these meaningful words into the hearts of your students, you will remain what you should be.

In case I don't have any children, I would like to leave you a few hundred marks in my postal account.

The best students in all classes should receive a book award. Please do not mention my name. It is not necessary. In the faith of victory and the continued existence of the Reich, your former pupil greets you.

Ten thousand such men have fallen in a blossoming of unparalleled warrior virtues, which would not be humanly conceivable were it not for a strength to move mountains, on the battlefield and in their souls.

Those who seek to express the meaning of the German heroic death are on the right track when they always return to the words: "Fallen for the Führer and the people, in faith in the permanence of the Reich.

BECOMING NO. 2. MARCH 1944.

ABOVE YOUR ADVANTAGE IS THE TEAM'S VICTORY

The above words are taken from the regulations for SS sports competitions issued by the SS Reichsführer in the spring of 1937. Nothing more striking can characterise the entire sports education of the SS.

When the SS was expanded and built up after the National Socialist takeover of Germany, the Reichsführer placed physical education at the forefront of all studies, alongside general intellectual education.

Well-known sportsmen and women in the ranks of the SS began to train their comrades.

The young teams of the SS met in many competitions with excellent opponents and they proved time and again on the sports fields their possibilities and energy.

Many masters in all fields of sport have emerged from their ranks and have given the SS a special reputation in this respect too.

In sports events, the SS has never considered individual effort; it has always demanded sportsmanship and camaraderie from the community on the stadium. The team effort dominates everything.

When the SS Reichsführer recently presented the sports badge he had created to almost one hundred SS leaders and men in Holland for the first time, he spoke again of the common sporting effort, saying:

—The SS Badge should be a proof of the efforts made and the means of education placed on the common path to win men, by a common struggle, for a common ideal.

And a little further on:

—This badge should be a testimony of some kind of collective effort.

Thus the meaning of sports education in the SS is verified. This sports rune is not only a spur to physical culture and military education, but it is also a symbol of collective effort.

The wearer of the SS badge must not only fulfil duties and tasks on the sports field, but also always refer to the eternal words of our new age: "Above your personal advantage is the victory of the Team.

This fundamental sentence remains, beyond the sporting effort of the SS, as an exhortation and a constant obligation.

One of the principles of the SS is to go beyond one's own limits.

Promoted by National Socialism, sport is a music of the body whose major chords are strength, grace and purity.

SS NOTEBOOK NO. 11B.1941.

WHY A SUDETEN SOURCE?

… and why the health service is in favour of mineral water

In the past, a fellow student might be extremely shocked that when he came back from sport or a walk, he could only quench his thirst by taking either an expensive mineral water or an alcoholic drink like beer. And he usually preferred beer because it was cheaper than mineral drinks. So more than one fellow student took to alcohol when he didn't want to.

The return of the Sudetenland to the Reich put an end to this abuse. Immediately after the occupation, the Sudeten *mineral water springs*, which were famous for their curative effect and good taste, became the property of the SS, together with the regional leadership. As prescribed by an order of the SS Reichsführer dated 15 September 1939, the old alcoholic beverages were to be replaced by the previously neglected natural waters which were owned and administered by the SS.

The spring is located in Grün-Neudorf, near the well-known health resort of Marienbad. It is tapped as it gushes out of the rocks under the high fir trees in the Kaiserwald. Thanks to a modern hygienic bottling process, the "Sudeten Spring" retains its original and special composition—crystal clear and sparkling—without any additives. The SS found the springs abandoned when they were taken over, due to the many changes of ownership and the increasingly negative influence of Czech rule.

In the meantime, numerous improvements in the technical use of the water by the staff were introduced in the interests of social hygiene. The springs were reopened because the men of the Waffen SS and the Wehrmacht in enemy territory consumed a lot of the mineral water. An adequate supply of good drinking water is not always possible, but this was made possible by the reopening of the springs and the Three Eight system.

Our mineral water plays a very big role in the new territories in the East, especially in Warsaw where the Wehrmacht depended almost exclusively on our SS Sudeten mineral water. It was known that in Poland there was great danger of epidemics, so no water could be used. Since water was in short supply, Sudeten mineral water was used for many purposes, even for washing and shaving.

The particularly cheap price of the drink is noteworthy. Immediately after the new operation, the prices, which until then had been much higher than those of beer, were drastically reduced. This gave everyone the opportunity to experience the beneficial effects of this good mineral water. The aim is to replace alcoholic beverages and artificial products that are harmful to people's health with these inexpensive, naturally pure table waters.

The mineral water from the "Sudeten Spring" is free of artificial additives such as carbon dioxide and other substances. In 1 litre of solution there are 5,679 millilitres of minerals. The mineral water, which is also radioactive, stimulates the appetite, strengthens the stomach, gently purges, dissolves stones, regulates the kidneys and fixes fat. There are also completely new mineral waters with the addition of natural fruit juices (such as lemon), which were very successful because of their vitamin content. The healing power of crystal-clear spring water is complemented by the effect of pure fruit juices.

So, comrade, if you suffer from thirst, take a "Sudeten spring"! Ask for it in the canteen! You are not only quenching your thirst in an advantageous way, you are also serving your health!

SS Notebook No. 2a.1941.

Spring—and yet tired!

Vitamins from SS Institutes

"It is May—however, spring brings me no joy! I am tired from morning to night. Yet I am prescribed vitamins. This is the main reason for my spring fatigue."

Two SS men stand in front of their shelter in the General Government. This winter, too, the service was difficult and the tasks immense. The countries will only be conquered after the victory. Yes, the first vegetables are already growing there. But here in the East—at the border ... and the other one laughs.

—It's spring fatigue, Karl! The poets have found the right word. Perhaps Schiller? I'm thinking of taking a long rest. I'm running out of fresh vegetables, that's all.

—You amuse me. Here, fresh vegetables? We are not there yet.

—That's right. But we do have vitamin supplements. I have to take them. The products provided help with spring fatigue, scurvy, cold sores and nostalgia.

—So you can go to hell with your medicine and your pills! I've never taken a pill in my life and I've always stayed well. Swallow a pill! Let's destroy the pills and be healthy like we used to be. Every pill-popper is a crybaby in my eyes.

—You are absolutely right...

—But I know what you're going to say now: "Pills are worthless, only my pills are worth gold.

—So how do you explain our spring fatigue?

—That's weakness, nothing else! And maybe you are missing some vegetables too?

—So what is in vegetables? I mean, what particular substance are we missing? We even get extra vitamins. For the equivalent of a head of lettuce, a pill, for a plate of spinach, a pill! No, you can't persuade me. Bad magic, young friend!

—Now I need to get some fresh air again! —Have you heard of the polar explorers and circumnavigators who fought scurvy on their ships? It was hard to understand why scurvy always broke out at sea. The sailors were sturdy fellows who set off in good health for a long voyage, ate the best meat, bread, the most fortifying food and yet! The longer the journey lasted, the more morose and miserable they became. They began to feel nostalgic, then weary, having no zeal for work and always terribly tired. The illness would start like this and end with the teeth falling out and then death.

But when the ship returned to port, the sailors went ashore and ate fresh vegetables, the scurvy disappeared as well as the tiredness, longing and languor.

—Why weren't the sailors given your famous pills?

—They were not known at the time. Nor were the causes of scurvy known. The disease was rife for centuries. Until the beginning of the 19th century, scurvy, phthisis, stroke and deaths were recorded in the death records. Doctors eventually discovered that scurvy was a dietary disease. Yes, the Vikings were aware of this because they constantly took barrels of sauerkraut with them on their ships when they went on long voyages.

In 1534, a physician reported that he achieved results in the fight against the disease as soon as he gave the patients pine needle juice.

Centuries passed before the mysterious substance that our bodies require was discovered.

In 1912, two German researchers, Holst and Fröhlich, carried out experiments on animals. Scurvy was shown to be a dietary disease when it was proven that the cause of the problem was due to a deficiency.

In our food, especially in fresh vegetables and fruit, apart from oils, there are carbohydrates and egg white vitamins without which man cannot live. Vitamin C was discovered. And these vitamins are precisely our supplements.

—Good grief! Now tell me, great scientist, approximately how many vitamins does man use?

—Our daily requirement is around 50 milligrams. This is already enough to ensure our well-being. But what the body contains in excess of C is unfortunately eliminated.

—What, so we have to run to the nurses for vitamins all our lives?

—No, nature gives us vitamin C, but not always enough In winter and spring, when we lack fresh vegetables and the fruit is not yet ripe, we all suffer from a lack of C and are tired. Our laziness is a vitamin C disease. However, the chemists have gone to work and made us a vitamin C preparation so that all the bad excuses disappear.

—Well, come on, let's go see the nurse. You converted me and I became a vitamin swallower. What kind of things you can learn in the East!

Not everyone knows that the German experimental laboratory in Dachau, an institution of the SS Reichsführer, also produced vitamins from fresh plants which proved their worth in the second year of the war, when they were distributed to SS units in the field, mainly in the East and in Norway. The vitamin is administered to the troops in the form of an herbal powder which also improves the taste of food. Our humorous description makes the meaning and value of these vitamin supplements clear.

Experimental and medicinal herbology in Dachau.

"Letter from the front", drawing by C. Schneider.

To the ultimate limit, drawing by war correspondent SS Petersen.

II. THE CLAN

SS BOOKLET NO. 5. 1938.

THE SEED OF THE PEOPLE

It is often said that the family is the "seed of the people". The comparison is well chosen. Every living thing, whether animal or plant, is made up of tiny elements that are alive: the cells. They form small microscopic organisms that can usually live on their own. These are called single-celled animals or plants. In higher animal and plant species, however, they are more or less numerous, with various tasks. They form a cell state, so to speak. In this cell state, one cell cannot live without the others, but neither can the whole live if each cell does not have a healthy life. If the latter interrupts its vital function in the cell state, then the cell state, the animal, the plant, the human being, and soon the whole living organism, becomes ill, and if the cells die, the cell state also dies.

The interdependence between the group and the individual, and vice versa, easily finds its analogy in the vital relations of the great popular organism. The life and health of a people are conditioned by those of its smallest individual cells. And the latter exist only if the whole is completely healthy and well.

But the individual can also live independently. A solitary Robinson can, if he has sufficient means, live alone for a lifetime. When he dies, this single man-people disappears on the island, because, unlike a single-celled animal, an isolated man does not even have the possibility of growing by division and constantly giving birth to a new life. In higher beings, two individuals of different sexes are needed.

Thus, individuals cannot be considered as cells living in the popular organism, but only that small unit capable of procreating continuously. This is constituted by the union of two beings of different sexes: This is the couple. These two beings uniting are alive, they are the constituent element of the people, the popular organism ensuring its life.

But if the family constitutes the cell that ensures the existence of the people, only the union of two spouses creating a new life can be considered a family. Marriage alone does not yet constitute a seed of the people, but only the marriage consecrated by children or only a young couple who wish to have children. For a marriage without children is as unimportant to the survival of the people as if these two people were alone and had not married.

We do not speak of a germ without reason. The nature of the germ lies in the fact that it is ready to germinate and can germinate. A cell that cannot germinate is a contradiction in terms and is sooner or later doomed to die.

Through its state, the people promote marriage, protect it and encourage it with many material benefits. They have even established the moral content of marriage through a new matrimonial law. But all this was done in the hope that a child would come. If it does not come about for some reason, this imperfect marriage is of less interest to the people and the new matrimonial law prescribes that such marriages can be annulled.

In this, the National Socialist conception of the people as a living organism differs from the liberal conception, which saw the people, or rather the state, only as an association of economic interests between individuals, as it were, a giant limited liability company. It did not matter to the liberal state whether a marriage produced children or not. It left this to the 'free will' of the spouses. Or it made sure that those who had many children were publicly mocked and called fools in comparison to the intelligent people who remained childless to enjoy the comforts of life. In his eyes, marriage was merely a paper contract between two economic partners, entered into first to enjoy sexual pleasures 'legally', and then to be able to support each other economically by dividing the work.

If many marriages in the National Socialist people's community are childless, it is only natural that we should regard them as unions entered into liberally by self-interested partners and not as that "family" representing the "seed of the people" which deserves respect or even protection. In the National Socialist state, anyone who marries with the conscious aim of enjoying "comfort" and leaving the task of having children to others, thus demonstrates that his conception of the people and the family is no different from that of the bygone liberal era. He therefore only entered into a partnership with an economic partner in order to legally enjoy the joys of marriage and to savour the material benefits of such a union.

This fact is confirmed every day by the "marriage market" in the bourgeois newspapers, where gentlemen covered with titles and honours seek rich women with the aim of concluding a marriage, where destitute ladies look for a spouse who can provide them with a pension and an assured standard of living, and to whom they would provide the joys of marriage in exchange.

Such unions are also called "marriage" and "family", and cannot be opposed because the registrar cannot know the real intention of the "engaged couple"—unless their age betrays them. Faced with the people, they are nothing more than worthless sham marriages. As the new moral concept has permeated the whole nation, we have come to hold these "spouses" in the same contempt as a swindler who claims undeserved titles or dignity.

Certainly, engaged couples cannot know in advance whether their marriage will be successful—they are therefore subject to the strict selective rules of SS. Older couples, if they married on a whim and still have no children in spite of themselves, can make up for this delay in a natural way. These faithful couples cannot be told that they should separate. But if they are infertile, they can be asked to at least cooperate in encouraging the fertility of others. He who helps an orphan or another child thus ensures that the life procreated by others will be preserved and will one day benefit the people.

But in any case the "seed of the people" must be fertile, encourage life, be procreative and life-protecting as much as we wish, for the greater good of the whole nation. He who does not cooperate in the survival of the people thus shows his lack of interest in them and their future.

A selection of healthy men and women must be based on race.

National Socialism had always celebrated the family as the lifeblood of the people. The SS went further by defining itself as an 'order of clans' who were to nurture their qualities in large families.

SS BOOKLET NO. 5. 1938

THE BLESSING THAT IS LIFE.

At harvest time, nature introduces us again to the process of growth that we can follow every year. Naturally, we extrapolate this to our community of people. Each century brings forth individuals in all peoples who, through their particular gifts, are of great value to their community.

The history of our people has seen the birth, in every era, of members of these large families who have become precursors of the spirit and of art, great creators of culture and of laws.

When, in the Middle Ages, the hammer sounded on the door of the castle church in Wittenberg, it was the son of a miner in a family of seven children who fought for the freedom of souls (Luther). Gottfried *Leibniz*, the great philosopher and academy professor, was also born into a large family circle. In the classical era of our poetry, *Klopstock*, the poet of the Messiah, came from a family of seventeen children. The Nestor of German poetry, *Goethe*, had six brothers and sisters. The instigator of the liberation struggle against Napoleonic domination, Fichte, had nine brothers. *Fichte*, had nine more siblings. The parents of the orientalist and poet *Rückert* had eight children. The great historian *Ranke* had eight brothers and sisters. The unforgettable composer *Bruckner* had ten siblings, Wilhelm *Busch* six.

The second child in a family of seven *Handel*, *Schiller* five, *Beethoven* five, *Novalis* ten, V. *Eichendorff* six and Justus *Liebig* nine siblings.

Albrecht *Dürer* was the third child in a family with eight children, Ulrich *Zwingli* with eight, *Lessing* with twelve, *Haydn* with twelve, *Arndt* with ten, Heinrich v. *Kleist* with seven, Robert *Koch* with thirteen, Carl Ludwig *Schleich* with six and Erich *Ludendorff* with six children

The fourth child was *Frederick the Great*, from a family of fourteen children, *Kant* of nine (*Napoleon* also of twelve), *Bismarck* of six, Werner *von Siemens* of fourteen, the war aviator *Boelcke* of six siblings.

Among the elite Germans who were the fifth children were Friedemann *Bach* from a family of six children, *Gellert* from thirteen, Baron *von Münchhausen* from eight, Baron *vom Stein* from seven, Carl *Runge* from eight siblings.

Among the seventh were Field Marshal *von Blücher*, *Mozart*, *Mörike* and *Geibel*.

The eighth child born to German families was Jost Amman, Prince *Eugene*, Johann Sebastian Bach, Count *von Platen*, Heinrich v. *Stephan*, the settler Karl *Peters*, Otto *Weddingen*.

Among the ninth born we count *Runge*, *Weber*, Richard *Wagner*, Friedrich *Siemens*.

And how poor German music would be without the eleventh child, Franz *Schubert*, without the twelfth, Karl *Lowe*.

When one progresses in history and does systematic research from these points of view, one becomes certain that the vitality of a people only bears fruit in the greatest spiritual and cultural achievements if the people have remained young and strong, and if they live exactly in accordance with nature.

Hannes Schalfuß

SS Booklet No. 1.1939.
What do people die of?

I. The German birth rate

Looking at the present time, we must ask ourselves whether Germany will last forever?

Answering "yes" depends on our will to make our people eternal, but also on the stream of blood that has been flowing for millennia. This is the chain of generations of which we are the links and which has never been broken in the course of the millennia, despite the wars and times of misery in German history, and which must not be broken in the future! If the German people were to disappear because they were too cowardly to fight for a healthy birth rate, then the work, the struggle and the worries of the past centuries would prove to be of no importance.

In an age of general expansion, when millions of flags and banners reflect the power and splendour of the Reich, the individual is easily led to see only the greatness of the present and to rejoice in it. He then forgets that it is not only in the present that the armed forces must be ready, nor that the planes must take off, nor that the farmers must work on their crops and the workers in their workshops, if Germany is to remain eternal. If the number of those who can be mobilised should one day decrease and more young people than ourselves should grow up in other countries, a terrible danger will arise for the German people and the Reich.

Germany may die despite its present power and splendour. History teaches us that people can disappear because since they exist they are responsible for themselves and their survival.

Until ten years ago, people, even among our own people, believed in the inevitable demise of the nation. Oswald Spengler's prophecy that the West would inevitably perish was accepted by the weak and the cowardly who had lost faith in life. They did not see the flaws and errors in Spengler's reasoning when he announced the fateful demise of all the peoples of Europe. Spengler said: "According to an internal law, every people and its culture must die one day after having experienced their youth and maturity! Just as a tree or a man grows old and then necessarily dies, so a people must grow old and disappear.

But the comparison between the people and the destiny of the tree or the individual is wrong. For every organism is born with new life and life force. This is the miracle of life, the marvellous secret of procreation and birth, that through reproduction eternal youth and renewal of life are conferred.

The existence of the individual is limited, he grows old and must die. The isolated tree grows and dies, yet the forests are eternal. The isolated man also lives and must die, and yet, the peoples are eternal!

Peoples do not have to die like the man or the isolated tree, but they are in danger of dying.

There are three natural causes of the death of a people. The past teaches us this as well as the present. An unfathomable fate was not the cause of the disappearance of the civilised peoples of antiquity; they violated the divine laws of life.

The Führer once said: "Man must never make the mistake of believing that he is promoted to the rank of lord and master of nature. He must try to understand and grasp the fundamental necessity of the rule of nature, and that his very existence is subordinated to these constant and eugenic laws of combat. He will then feel that in a world where suns and stars travel, where moons revolve around planets, where strength is always the master of weakness and makes it its obedient servant or breaks it, there can be no exception for men. The eternal principles of this wisdom are equally valid for him. He may try to understand them, but he can never ignore them."

Life requires the constant victory of the strong and healthy over the weak and sick. Nature's wisdom has enacted three fundamental laws accordingly:

1. The living must always procreate in large numbers.
2. In the struggle for life only the strongest survive. The permanent selection of the strong eliminates the weak or worthless.
3. In the natural world as a whole, species remain true to themselves. A species frequents only its own.

The peoples who have disappeared throughout history are those who have disregarded the wisdom and laws of nature. The natural causes of their weakening and disappearance are therefore these:

1. Failure to conserve the species.
2. Infringement of the law of natural selection.
3. Non-compliance with the requirement to maintain the purity of the species and the blood.

An examination of the numerical and qualitative development of the German people over the last hundred years shows that they too have recklessly and irresponsibly transgressed the iron laws of life.

In the mid-1970s, between 1870 and 1875, 40 children were born per 1000 inhabitants. Since 1900, only 36.5 per 1000, in 1913 only 27.5. Since the end of the war, when all sense of responsibility was lost, Germany has dropped to a dangerous low of 14.7 births per 1000 citizens.

The vitality of our people, which should be made up of innumerable young people, has therefore fallen in one generation, in percentage terms, from 40% to 14%. In addition, during the five years of the war, 3.5 million fewer children were born. Far more important than the losses on the battlefields was the loss of children who were neither procreated nor born because their potential parents were at the front. The permanent decline in births in Germany, from 2 million in 1900 to 900,000 in 1933, meant a steady decline and weakening of the armed power of the German people. The number of German children completing primary school was:

1,272,000 in 1925
1,125,000 in 1929
754,000 in 1930
606,000 in 1932

Assuming that half of the school leavers were boys, this meant that the number of possible mobilisables fell from 606,000 to 303,000, a figure from which those who disappeared before being called up for service had not yet been deducted.

If Germany does not by all means stop this decline in births as shown by the figures up to the year 1933, there will be only about 250,000 men available per year for military service in a few decades, while Russia, for example, had 1,750,000 mobilisable twenty-year-olds in 1930.

The age pyramid of the German people

If the German people had grown in the past decades, if the number of births had not constantly decreased since the beginning of the century, our people would have a natural and healthy age pyramid. This pyramid, in the popular mind, is determined by the proportional share of the annual generations in the whole nation. In a healthy pyramid the children under one year of age form the largest part of the population, each succeeding generation being, through natural death or accident, somewhat smaller in number.

If we represent this pyramid by drawing a line of length proportional to the number of citizens and superimpose it on the line of that generation for each year, we obtain the age pyramid of the people.

For example, that of the German people in 1910 is natural and healthy. But the one in 1975 is dangerous and shows us that our people can die.

In 1910, there were few old people and many young people in Germany:
Over 65s: 2.8 million = 5%.
Under 15s: 19.6m =34%.

The age pyramid for the year 1975 represents the population of the German people according to statistical forecasts, from which it necessarily follows that if during the reign of the swastika no decisive turning point is taken regarding a birth policy, the pyramid clearly shows us that the fall in the birth rate will cause the extinction of the people. The pyramid becomes a funeral urn.

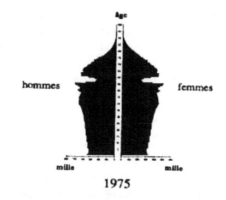

1975

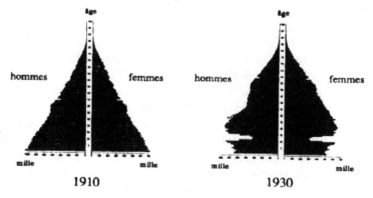

1910   1930

In Germany in 1975 there would be :
9.2 million people over 65
10.1 million under 15 years old
In 1975, there would be almost as many old people as children, whereas in 1910 the number of children was seven times that of the elderly.

The causes of the birth rate

When asked about the causes of the low birth rate, it is clear that:

The attitude of men, their conception of life and of the world, are the causes which led to the violation of the duty to ensure the numerical survival of the people. Economic misery was never the main reason, it only contributed to it, especially after the war. For while Germany's prosperity increased after the creation of the Empire in 1870/71, the number of births fell year by year from the beginning of the century until the outbreak of the war. And nowadays poor families almost always have more children than rich ones. So it was not misery and worry that prevented births, but the love of comfort, selfish reasoning and cowardice in the face of the struggle for existence or the fear of having to cut back on amenities and luxuries. The illusion of education was also important. A family with only one or two children can give them a better education than a large number of children. But the exaggerated concern to educate the child well has the consequence of producing a softened generation, which the parents remove from the beginning from the trials of life and which, therefore, does not fight.

The great personalities of German history *very often came,* not coincidentally, from *large families.* Great people are often the latest in a long line of brothers and sisters.

Apart from the liberal doctrine of individual happiness on earth, the churches were also pernicious with their sermons of happiness in the afterlife, their doctrine of hereditary sin and the promise of heavenly reward. During the Christian era, countless children were lost to the German people because priests and nuns denied the law of life in their search for heavenly happiness and voluntarily renounced becoming fathers and mothers of children.

The desire to have a child, or rather to have many children, must be a matter of course for each of us SS, because the German people must not die, but must be eternal.

SS-Ustuf. Dr Gerhart Schinke

SS BOOKLET NO. 3.1939.
WHAT DO PEOPLE DIE OF?

II. SELECTION AND COUNTER-SELECTION

In the first issue of the New Year's edition of the SS Notebooks, the causes of the death of a people were examined and it was shown that for several decades the German people had failed in their national duty of *numerical* preservation. It was shown how the population figure had continuously fallen from 1870 to 1932, so that the danger arose that our people would not only grow old, but die for lack of new youth.

We will demonstrate below that our people, too, have failed in their duty of survival and have contravened the *natural law of selection*.

The value of a man or woman to the continued existence of the German people lies in the purity of his or her blood, his or her hereditary qualities and his or her value to the existence of his or her people.

Neglecting to encourage the maintenance of blood purity

The doctrine of the equality of men, taught to all peoples by the Churches as well as by the apostles of Bolshevism, has tried to overcome the original idea of race and to remove the natural barriers between peoples which are the result of the laws of life and evolution. The Church brought together in religious communities men who were separated and different by race. And, according to the sermon of the pastors, a baptized Catholic Negro was closer to a Catholic German girl than to a non-Catholic German related by the same blood. The Church spoke of mixed marriages and included under this term a marriage of Germans when one of them had in his youth learned and sung Lutheran psalms and the other hymns to Mary. Ministers of religion refused to allow marriages between Germans of different faiths, but would bless without hesitation, often with a certain inner satisfaction, a marriage between a baptized Jew or Negro and a baptized German Christian girl.

While the Church encouraged people to determine their marital choice on the basis of religious considerations, liberal society tried to get its members to choose their partner only on the basis of his or her social standing, so that hereditary and racial value were mostly neglected. The choice of marriage partner was therefore not determined by the man's vigour, the woman's charm and joie de vivre, but by whether he belonged to the same community of ideas or by the amount of the dowry.

And men, forgetting the selection of the species, united with impure foreign blood and thus destroyed their hereditary heritage.

Bolshevism, which, like religious thought, originated in a Jewish conception, finally abolished all natural barriers between races and peoples. For centuries the Churches had taught that the ideal end of evolution was one shepherd and one flock; Bolshevism likewise demanded the chaos of the races as its ultimate goal.

When elements of our people began to mix with men of a different species, their vitality diminished as a result of this racial interbreeding. The species, which the Roman Tacitus once said "resembled only itself", mixed and became impure. In place of the beautiful and healthy statures of our race, with their harmonious attitudes and behaviour, there appeared species whose state of mind was unstable. Outwardly disharmonious, they also had many souls in their hearts, their character was no longer strong or homogeneous; they were inwardly torn in their thoughts and values. When our countrymen lost their unity of race and character, they soon no longer understood each other.

Men of the same race behave in the same way in the face of destiny because they have the same soul and the same value of character, the same sense of life and the same purpose. Men of the same blood and hereditary heritage not only have the same conception of honour, freedom and fidelity; they have the same spirit of decision in battle and in the face of danger, and they conceive God in the same way. A people whose elements share the same hereditary character presents a living unity, strong in itself, clear in all its decisions. A people is a representation of God and the representation of God is always clear.

Men of different races think differently about the value of character, love and marriage, right and wrong. They behave differently towards friends and enemies and act differently in times of distress.

If a people is racially mixed, it lacks bodily and spiritual unity. It has no common thought, no unitary will, no common belief or conception of life.

Thus our German people, as a result of racial interbreeding, have drifted away from the ancient ideal of the beautiful and heroic man. Sick creatures and miserable saints have been presented to them as ideal figures of life, whereas their hero and model was once Siegfried. Such a development has always led to the demise of a people.

We are aware of the profound truth contained in the Führer's words: "The hereditary sin against blood and race is the one great sin of this world and the end of the people who commit it.

Failure to comply with the law of natural selection

In nature, which has always organised itself according to divine laws, the law of natural selection reigns mercilessly. The perpetual struggle for existence destroys everything that is not viable, even in its embryonic state. The strong and the brave can face the thousand dangers that nature presents; in the forests and the seas no inferior or hereditarily sickly life can survive. Natural selection works in such a way that only the strong and healthy survive by fighting and multiply by procreation, but that everything that is sickly withers and dies.

The strongest and best fulfil their destiny in selection according to the divine laws, and thereby the maintenance of the value of the species constituting the eternal meaning of the perpetual struggle for existence, for its improvement and elevation is assured.

Our Germanic ancestors followed the laws of selection like all healthy peoples whose intelligence and sensitivity were not yet contaminated by false doctrines of pity.

The Church's false conception of God denied the divine laws of nature. Church teaching deliberately opposed the will of nature.

Once the people were preached that God died crucified out of pity for the weak and sick, the sinners and the poor, the unnatural teaching of pity and a false humanitarianism could promote the preservation of the congenitally ill. Yes, it was considered a moral duty to care for and favour mainly the sickly, the burdened and the poor in spirit.

Thus, the congenitally ill could multiply unhindered and the community of healthy people had to bear the burden of caring for these hereditarily diseased elements.

The large number of hereditary patients caused an almost unbearable financial burden on the state and local budgets. A backward schoolboy costs the state two to three times more than a normal child. A hereditary patient in a specialised home, a mental patient or an epileptic receives on average five times more from the state each year than a healthy social security recipient after a lifetime of work. Millions were squandered every year on madhouses, while healthy working families often lacked the bare necessities.

The hereditary heritage of the German people is also impoverished by the undifferentiated reproduction of racially diverse citizens. The structure of a people remains homogeneous when all its elements marry at the same age and produce many children in each union. There is a necessary and natural increase in the branch of the population whose members married early and have a greater number of descendants. In Germany, late marriages and a lack of children were the lot of the valuable people and thus of the valuable inheritance for decades, which led to a significant decrease in the most valuable part of the nation. Already in the years before the Great War, an undifferentiated reproduction was observed in the German people.

In 1912, there were on average 2 children in the marriages of senior and very senior officials, 2.5 children in the marriages of employees and professionals, 2.9 children in the marriages of educated workers and craftsmen, 4.1 children in the marriages of labourers and office workers, and 5.2 children among agricultural workers.

In recent years, families with higher education had an average of 1.9 children, families of well-to-do employees and craftsmen 2.2, and educated workers 2.9. Asocials, criminals and fathers of backward children had on average a large number of children.

Thus, the number of hereditary sick and insane people increased among the German people, while the number of healthy and valuable people decreased.

More than 700,000 patients with severe hereditary defects are treated in specialised institutions. The total number of hereditary patients is probably in the millions.

This shocking state of affairs is the consequence of doctrines of pity that are contrary to the laws of life; it results from the glorification of the incapable, the weak and the poor in spirit. All these hereditarily unhealthy individuals, if they were to take charge of themselves, would not be able to assert themselves and triumph with their energy in the struggle for life. In this God-ordained struggle they are necessarily defeated, for nature in her holy wisdom advocates the elimination of the weak and the sick.

Consequently, while in nature the law of selection reigns, the mismanagement of the nation by the state and the disruption of life that it has brought about in the people, have brought about precisely a counter-selection. As a result of counter-selection, the non-value multiplies at the expense of the value, the weak at the expense of the strong, and this because of the assistance and care provided by civilisation.

Many large cities are also a source of counter-selection. The big city has always attracted people who wanted to show themselves off and prove their competence, but they inevitably disappeared there in the second generation. Entire clans died in the big cities. If Berlin, for example, received no immigrants, according to Burgdörfer, based on the current number of births, in 150 years only 100,000 descendants would remain out of the 4,000,000 souls counted today.

Modern warfare is particularly effective in the sense of counter-selection. Men of good physical and spiritual health are almost exclusively called up, so that only those with a valuable hereditary heritage fall in the war. The battlefields thus swallow up the blood of the best sons of the people whose hereditary heritage is irreparably lost. Certainly, their death is a sacred sacrifice for the honour and freedom of the people.

Similarly, several hundred brave young Germans fall victim to sport or competition every year, in ice wrestling, in the snow, in car races or in aeroplanes.

No people on Earth died because of war, crop failure or political recession.

Peoples have only disappeared when the living substance ensuring their historical life, their blood, their race, has been exhausted. They therefore only die in the following cases:

1. When the number of births fell as a result of the regression of popular strength and the possibility was thus offered to a numerically and qualitatively stronger people to crush its weaker neighbour.

2. By a racial crossbreeding that has robbed an originally healthy people of their inner harmony.

3. By disregarding the laws of selection, which causes a reduction in the valuable hereditary heritage and leads to a reduction in abilities and qualities in the population.

The death of a people is thus based on a wrong conception of life, and is due to the non-observance of the eternal laws of the Earth. Man has learned to despise the laws of life because he has lost his connection with nature and life.

The Churches frustrated millions of us with the Germanic belief in earthly immortality, so that countless men and women gave up, in the name of an unreal heavenly will, on producing healthy children. The churches called the sacred earth a vale of tears and taught that procreation and birth were sinful and wrong. When the essential source of life, the will to live, was replaced by the pursuit of material or otherworldly happiness, the establishment of egoism and eventually of Bolshevism was possible, the latter of which has only the weakening and decadence of peoples as its aim.

National Socialism, teaching the eternal life of a people, leads men back to respect the divine laws of life. The Führer says: "The great revolution of National Socialism is that it has opened the door to the knowledge that all the faults and errors of men are due to certain circumstances and are therefore reparable, except for one: to despise the importance of preserving one's blood, one's kind and thereby the state of mind and character which God has bestowed upon them. We humans need not wonder why Providence created the races; we need only note that it punishes those who despise its creation."

"For the first time, perhaps, since there has been a human history, attention has been drawn in Germany to the fact that the first of all the tasks which devolve upon us, the noblest and therefore the most sacred to men, is that of preserving the blood and the species, as God created them.

As SS we are aware of our national duty and we want, under the sign of reborn life, of the holy swastika, to become fathers, and for love of the thrice-consecrated land which is the homeland of our ancestors and ours, to give eternal life to the German people.

The words of our SS comrade Lothar Stengel von Rutkowski in *Kingdom of this World* are our own:

You are a grandson
To victories and worries
From your ancestors
You owe your existence.
As a grandfather
You hold in your hands
Happiness and unhappiness
From the most distant generations.

SS-Ustuf. Dr Gerhart Schinke

Does a state have the right to practice eugenics to prevent unfortunate people from being affected by hereditary defects?
National Socialism answered in the affirmative.
On the right, a home for children from the Lebensborn association.

Positive" selection encouraged people of the same hereditary value to join forces.

People have two weapons in their struggle for life: their ability to defend themselves and their natural fertility. Let us never forget that the ability to defend oneself alone cannot ensure the survival of a people in the distant future, but that the inexhaustible source of its fertility is necessary.

Let us see clearly and act so that the victory of the German weapons is followed by the victory of the German child.

Heinrich Himmler

SS Booklet No. 4. 1938.

THE NEW MATRIMONIAL LAW OF GREATER GERMANY

The outdated provisions on matrimonial jurisdiction and divorce, as well as the return of the Austrian people to the German Reich, necessitated an accelerated transformation of the regulations concerning this important aspect of family law. With these laws, the first step towards the creation of German matrimonial and family law was taken. The National Socialist state's conception of the nature of marriage determined the institution of the new law. Rigid religious dogmatic ties in Austria, as defined by the creation of the law, had led to abuses in this vital area; beyond the framework of mere families, they threatened to poison public life and therefore had to be abolished. Throughout the Reich, marriage law had already brought about a great change in a National Socialist spirit through the fundamental changes to the German Blood Protection Act, the Matrimonial Health Act and the Law on the Protection of Marriage from Abuse.

The new law deliberately rejects the individualistic view of marriage as a kind of contract influenced by the personal interests of those involved. Similarly, it also moves away from the religious view that derives the sanctity of marriage from religious ties. Instead, the new law prescribes the sanctity and dignity of marriage which, as a cell of community life and the heart of the family, ensures the continuity of national life and creates the conditions for a sound and rigorous upbringing of offspring.

Every SS should be aware of the most important provisions of this law. They should be presented in a few points.

I.

1. A marriage can only be concluded by a registrar. In Austria, only a nuptial blessing has been sufficient until now.

2. A priori a marriage can be considered void, i.e. as never having been celebrated. It is null and void in the cases set out in the Nuremberg Laws and the Matrimonial Health Act.

Moreover, it is also:

—when it did not take place in the prescribed form before the registrar,

—when one of the spouses was incapable of entering into a contract or of exercising free judgment,

—when a marriage is concluded without the motive of living together,

—when one of the spouses was already married,

—when it was forbidden because of too close a relationship or as a result of adultery.

II.

1. A child of a marriage considered void under the Nuremberg Matrimonial Health Laws is illegitimate.

2. A child of a marriage that is void for other reasons mentioned is considered legitimate. Such children shall not suffer from the faults of the parents.

III.

In the past, a marriage could be contested in specific cases. If it was declared null and void, it was deemed never to have taken place a priori. This has now been abolished. A marriage can be "annulled" in certain specific cases. It is then broken off by the authority of the court.

The reasons for the cancellation are as follows:

—Lack of consent from the legal representative,

—unfounded marriage,

—poor physical condition relating to the person of the other spouse (e.g. infertility at the time the marriage was concluded),

—deception or threats of varying degrees of seriousness.

The reasons for cancellation correspond to the old dispute clauses.

IV.

A marriage can be "broken":

—when one of the spouses has stopped living together,

—when a spouse refuses without good reason to procreate or to accept offspring.

—when one of the spouses has so profoundly disturbed the harmony of the marriage by violating the conjugal duties that there is no reasonable hope of returning to the common life,

—when the other spouse is alienated,

—when the other spouse suffers from a highly contagious or repulsive disease,

—when the other spouse has become prematurely sterile after the union. (However, in this case, divorce is avoided when the spouses have legitimate offspring or an adopted and hereditarily healthy child).

In the case of totally destroyed marriages where the spouses have frequently lived apart for years and have not been able to divorce until now, the new law provides that either spouse may apply for a divorce if life together has ceased for three years and cannot be re-established.

V.
With regard to the question of the duty to assist.

A new settlement corresponding to modern conceptions can no longer take into account the standard of living of the beneficiary. It must be determined by the amount considered appropriate to the standard of living of both spouses.

VI.
The fate of the child after the divorce.

Since the National Socialist state was particularly concerned with the protection of young people, the question of who was to be entrusted with the child depended above all on the ability of the parents to give the child a proper upbringing. In this case, it was not the fault of the parents but the good of the child that was decisive.

VII.

In Austria, the situation was particularly unpleasant. A marriage between Catholics could not be annulled. In the past, the Austrian administrative authorities granted the so-called dispensation in such cases. If the spouse concerned then entered into a new marriage with dispensation, he or she had to state that the latter was not recognised by the courts. The children of this second marriage were therefore illegitimate. This terrible confusion is removed by the new law.

A marriage that is invalid according to the old laws can be considered valid as long as the spouses were still living together on 1 April 1938. Dispensatory marriages" are also valid from the beginning if the spouses were living together on 1 April 1938.

The new law came into force on 1 August 1938.

SS-Ostuf. Dr Schmidt-Klevenow

THE PATTERN OF CELEBRATIONS THROUGHOUT THE YEAR AND IN THE LIFE OF THE SS FAMILY.

MARRIAGE AND THE ADMISSION OF WOMEN INTO THE SS CLAN COMMUNITY

Marriage or engagement is carried out by the registry office. Until the beginning of the Second Reich, religious marriage was the only form of marriage which, afterwards, when Bismarck's law of 1875 entrusted the state with the legislation of marriage, was considered by most people to be indispensable, indeed by far the most important ceremony. This view was supported by the fact that the authorities regarded marriage as an official affair in poor areas.

The Third Reich took a different position on marriage. In contrast to the old regime and the Church, people wishing to marry were advised to prove that they fulfilled all the prerequisites for a union and that they were in good hereditary health. The state takes care of families, takes care of them, remedies material difficulties as far as possible and always gives priority to the importance of the family. In future, the civil form of marriage must also take account of this importance. Some municipalities provide a particularly beautiful room for the bride and groom. The employees perform the wedding ceremony in a dignified and solemn manner. The necessary decrees from the Reich Ministry of the Interior exist for this purpose. Recently, a Reich order has been implemented which gives the registry offices the status of clan offices and provides for official dress for the officials. It is possible that the necessary instruction to implement these decrees is often lacking.

In such cases, the Chief of Post, Clan Care, Unit Leader or Chief of Training may intervene in a qualified manner to perform the SS engagement. It must be ensured that the exchange of rings during the ceremony is done with mutual consent.

Marriage within the framework of civil status confers on the man and the woman the status of a couple. An SS ceremony in which a kind of 'marriage blessing' is performed with a question-and-answer game, fake altars, dagger handing, flaming basins and similar imitations of the Christian ritual should be banned.

We SS men must still proceed with the admission of the woman into the SS clan community. She should preferably be received during the wedding feast or, better still, before it begins.

The importance of the feast at the naming ceremony has already been mentioned, as well as at the ceremonies for the admission of the child into the Jungvolk, etc. The banquet is a very old custom, indissolubly linked to the family celebration! Special attention must therefore be paid to the preparation and execution of the wedding banquet. The feast must be able to take place, even if the means are modest! The room in which it takes place should be chosen according to the respective conditions. However, if possible, it should be in the home itself, otherwise in an inn. The table should be solemnly set and decorated with flowers or green fir branches. Emphasis may be placed on decorating the couple's seats. The unit leader or a comrade who is particularly close to the couple receiving the woman into the SS community sits in front of the couple. He addresses the newlyweds before the meal begins or during the meal between courses. In his speech, he should emphasise the value of marriage for the preservation of the people and the SS clan community. He must speak of the motto "My honour is called fidelity", which is also imperative for women, since they are now subject to SS laws. He should also emphasise that the SS man and the SS woman, who must be faithful to each other, are valuable members of our community and will always be safe within it. The speaker welcomes the woman into the SS clan and solemnly warns her to always think of her high mission as a woman and future mother, respecting the SS laws and living by them. A gift relating to the marriage or to the wife and mother is then presented in accordance with this welcome. In this regard, a particularly well-chosen book with a dedication or illustration is recommended. There is also a beautiful custom of presenting a wooden plate with salt and bread and two porcelain or earthenware cups. This gift symbolises the simple lifestyle that we should never forget.

The speaker's words should conclude with a "Sieg Heil" to the Führer and the young couple.

The rest of the wedding meal should be spent in good spirits. If there is an opportunity to dance, then this should be done.

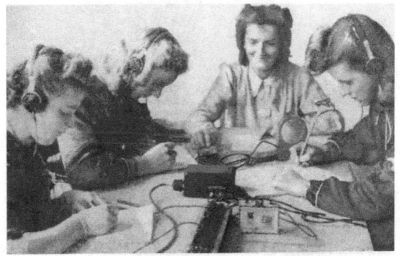

The SS, a "clan order", admitted women into its ranks. Above, volunteers take lessons in Morse code.

On the left, the best part of the day. On the right, a pin intended to be given to every mother of a first child in an SS family.

A rare example of a 'naming ceremony' in the years 1936-37.

The bride's costume should be solemn. Bridal crowns and veils should be avoided, however, as these are oriental ornaments. Apart from the form depicted above, the admission of the woman into the SS clan community is comparable to the celebration of marriage by the civil registry office, but in the form of an intimate ceremony. The room must be chosen with particular care. If there is no suitable room in the local SS department, the women's section, the Hitlerjugend or the town administration will assist. The performance of the ceremony requires careful preparation. Above all, it requires a musical atmosphere. If the members of an SS music unit or SS comrades' circles are unable to do so, the Hitlerjugend, the BDM, the women's section or others may help. A foreword, a poem or a piece of prose, a word from the Führer or Reichsführer should serve as an introduction to the speech given by the SS comrade. The words of the SS comrade should follow the thread of the ideas mentioned above. Since the circle of SS comrades is enlarged at this ceremony, the song of loyalty should be sung at the end. The room should be decorated simply. In the background is the flag with the runes of victory, in addition, a floral decoration is in order, but without palms and laurel but with oak, green fir, holly and ivy. Chairs should be provided for the bride and groom and the majority of the participants. Let us add once again by way of conclusion: The more the comrade who welcomes the woman into the community of SS clans knows about the future spouses, the more he will be able to speak with conviction. For this reason, the intervention of a unit leader or even a senior officer would be a big mistake, because the latter would mostly make a general speech, while the comrade will adapt his words to the sentimental evolution that the young couple will follow in the future, and perhaps also to their possible conflicts. This is the first condition in our community.

> *There is no greater nobility for a woman than to be the mother of the sons and daughters of a people. All this youth that we see today, so beautiful, on the roads, faces beaming, eyes sparkling, where would it be if there had not been women to give it life?*

Adolf Hitler
(Speech of the Führer at the Women's Congress, Parteitag of 1935).

"WITH A SWORD AND WITH A CUT, GUNTHER D'ALQUEN. 1937.

A WORD ON DIVORCE

All civil codes have always had to deal with one of the most controversial issues in the presence of divorce. Until now, ideological oppositions within parliaments always found a homogeneous solution. Justified solutions were only found when a state or a movement followed a clear ideology.

Thus, the Catholic Church supports the view of the indissolubility of marriage on the grounds that it was entered into by God. This obliges us to take a position on this worldview in the context of these applications. Moreover, our position is clear enough. But we state at once that the attitude of the Catholic Church on this point has not always been simple and uniform. The development of religious matrimonial law in modern times rather shows a tendency in this direction.

Liberalism, on the other hand, takes a completely opposite view of marriage—as the example of Soviet Russia teaches us. It regards it as a private legal contract that can be terminated at any time. This termination requires even only the request of one spouse.

This interpretation must also be rejected as it is based on a misunderstanding and disregard of the value of the family.

Our position must be directly inspired by Adolf Hitler's *Mein Kampf.* The Führer defined for the first time that marriage is not just a state—it is a mission.

The Family Law Committee of the Academy for German Law also takes this view when it currently provides a legal definition for a new divorce law. It provides for the following version:

"Marriage is considered to be that which is suitable for the community of people, a community of life based on mutual fidelity, love and esteem. Hereditarily healthy persons of different sexes have the purpose of safeguarding and maintaining the common good by close cooperation and for the procreation of hereditarily healthy children of the same race, with a view to making them true citizens."

It is clear that the National Socialist state, despite the importance it attributes directly to marriage, must also grant permission for separation. It has legally defined the prohibition of marriages that carry the seeds of degeneration (e.g. hereditary diseases). From the outset, therefore, it has prevented the persons concerned from getting into a divorce sooner or later.

But despite all preventive measures, there will always be marriages in which the conditions for living together are permanently disrupted. This is due to ignorance of human nature. As long as we are not able to understand the inner nature of man, to foresee the future, nothing will change.

However, since the National Socialist state attaches great importance to marriage—particularly in view of the danger of the family and thus the community breaking up—it must also provide for the possibility of divorce. It could not simply adopt the formulas of the Civil Code, but had to revise this law according to its world view.

Above all, we must again be aware of the importance of dignity.

It is a fact that in all divorce applications, compelling reasons lead to a desired conclusion in the short term. Adultery is the most common reason given. A statistic from 1933 tells us that one third of all divorces were based on this reason. It is therefore easy to see that many spouses tended to use this as a pretext for obtaining a divorce. However, this cannot be proven, and there are still known cases where adultery has been fabricated in order to obtain a divorce more quickly.

It would generally be desirable that before entering into a marriage, the sentimental preconditions and prophylactics should be taken into consideration, as the SS requires of its men and women. But we cannot avoid situations that exist: there are fake marriages where the spouses live together. They are simply forced to find reasons to divorce in order to escape from this situation which has become totally unbearable for them and of no value to the community. Although in our case the human elements prevail, a justified external reason must be found. According to the law in force today, separation must also be punished.

It is not necessary to show that such a procedure is incompatible with the National Socialist attitude. The Family Law Committee of the German Academy of Law therefore dealt with this point in particular detail when the divorce court was established. It also examined the proposal for a so-called "divorce by mutual consent ", i.e. a divorce with the mutual consent of both spouses.

The question here is whether a divorce should only be considered on the basis that, although no reason can be found for the separation, the two spouses have virtually nothing in common morally and emotionally. The separation is therefore justified.

From the National Socialist point of view, such a settlement would always be preferable to using the false pretext of adultery or any other reason.

The Family Law Committee has two main reasons for opposing "divorce by mutual consent". Firstly, it shows the danger of hasty decisions due to temporary anger which can break up an otherwise viable marriage. On the other hand, he believes that it can undermine the respect for marriage because of this mutual consent.

We had the opportunity to ask the opinion of a practical man, a Berlin judge. He told us that he fully approves of a separation made by mutual request. The objection of a hasty decision can be overcome by proposing a specific period of reflection before it is taken—about six months—to determine whether the two spouses have acted hastily or whether the marriage is indeed not viable.

The judge also points out that if both parties jointly request a divorce, it is because an insurmountable problem is destroying the marriage. The reasons for this should not be sought.

Naturally, in such cases, the intervention of a judge cannot be limited to receiving the proposals of the two spouses and pronouncing on the validity of their divorce—even after a waiting period. On the contrary, his task should be to be well aware of the fragility of the marriage, by understanding the situation (in some cases by asking for a medical consultation). It is clear to everyone that a marriage law drafted in this way places a greater responsibility on the judge and obliges him or her to have an attitude of a higher spiritual and moral nature than is the case with the present legislation.

We do not consider the pretext that the consideration of marriage could be affected by a regulation of this kind to be sufficiently valid, especially when one takes into account the German mentality in relation to other peoples.

Such fears were quite legitimate in the post-war years. But today, marriages are concluded under completely different conditions. A man who observes the National Socialist conception will certainly not conclude a marriage so quickly because he knows that the divorce law allows him a proper separation. If a National Socialist marries today, he is fully aware of his responsibility, but it cannot be said that this will be the case in twenty or thirty years for every German.

The remark that some individuals are shallow or light in character (there will always be such individuals in a popular community) does not seem to us to be valid, for the laws are not made for a numerically insignificant minority, and these groups would be capable of experiencing a "free union" which does not impose on them the obligatory duties of a conjugal life.

Adolf Hitler said that the struggle did not end in 1933. National Socialism is a doctrine of national education, and therefore an education in itself, which teaches adaptation, consideration, and mutual help, which, from generation to generation, raises and vivifies the community of the future!

We certainly believe that the more the National Socialist idea permeates the inner nature of our people, the fewer cases of divorce there will be. And so we need have no fear of an attack on the respect of marriage.

However, there will always be cases of divorce that no educational measure can prevent; they are not predictable, as has been said, and do not involve a notion of guilt. Therefore, it must be possible to prevent these pseudo-marriages without resorting to more or less valid pretexts, especially because until now the poor person has always been at a disadvantage compared to the rich one, as the intervention of specialists is usually quite expensive.

Ultimately, the state itself can find no interest in the continued existence of such marriages. On the contrary, it should proceed directly to the annulment of a marriage that is often sterile, and thus give both spouses the opportunity to get to know another partner in a harmonious way that serves the interests of the state. In such cases, there is always the possibility of new, happy marriages.

However, the issue becomes difficult when it comes to children. The judge who was questioned always insisted on the harmful influence that a divorce has on the development of the children. The danger of an exclusive education for the psychological growth of children is extraordinarily greater during a separation. Moreover, the judge cited many cases where the children had a direct influence on the marriage. The parents are finally forced to get along because of them.

In many cases—as the practitioner also pointed out—various personal relationships will have a role to play. Of course, we cannot forget the failures and not think of those unfortunate children who have grown up in a home where, from their earliest childhood, they have suffered this unhappy union. We can imagine that in many cases separation would be desirable in the interests of the child. There can be no standard here, but we can only insist that the state never asks too much of the judge in terms of human qualities, whether in terms of character or knowledge.

As a matter of principle, we do not want to support the idea of an easier separation, because the example of the Soviet Union has shown us what such situations can lead to. On the contrary, we are of the opinion that the great importance of marriage in the National Socialist state leads to a limitation of the possibilities of divorce, provided that selfish reasons or cowardice in the face of duties motivate it.

But if a marriage cannot be realised in the National Socialist spirit, we must be open and honest enough to follow a path to find a solution.

"WITH A SWORD AND WITH A CUT, GUNTHER D'ALQUEN. 1937.

THE ILLEGITIMATE CHILD

In some quarters, illegitimate children are still too readily regarded as a "faux pas". Clearly, we cannot agree with this. It is mainly the clerical circles that pronounce censorious judgements on "sinners" with a tone of conviction. Naturally, they base their judgements on the doctrine of the afterlife, which regards the body as something sinful in principle. In Catholic regions, it is well known how much customs and traditions contradict such a narrow-minded view.

In general, a farmer is far from delighted when his unmarried daughter announces the arrival of a child, something that causes a very legitimate surprise in the family; however, in rural areas, a healthy way of thinking means that, in most cases, this kind of thing is resolved much more quickly than in the towns, for example. In various valleys in the Tirol, this goes so far that girls who have no illegitimate children find it difficult to find a suitor, as they are assumed to be victims of sterility.

In the city, things are much more complicated… We will not review here all the cases in which low-level mothers—often drunkards—prostitutes, nymphomaniacs and the like, trade with men and give birth to fruits that end up in asylums; this testifies in favour of the need for racial hygiene. The danger to posterity from sexual relations of this kind, even if legitimate, is therefore far greater for the good of the people in general. No one will dare to equate the distressing products of such marriages with healthy yet illegitimate children.

This leads to the conclusion that on a purely biological and hereditary level, children from a legally concluded marriage cannot be considered superior to illegitimate children.

It is not only the illegitimate child who is despised by more than one class; it is above all the illegitimate mother who is the victim of the disgust of the narrow-minded ordinary man. Those women who profess their illegitimate relationships and those others in whom OR assumes the same thing never get pregnant because they have the technique and experience to avoid it. These kinds of women have no right to be considered more highly because they do not have children than a young woman who gives birth to a child, perhaps as a result of genuine love and ignorance of "various means".

The problem of the big cities is particularly obvious, with hundreds of thousands of people living in small spaces.

The issue of illegitimate births is above all a social problem. As the history of the past teaches us, not all political systems had the possibility of solving the social problem, and so National Socialism also had the task of giving the illegitimate child its rightful place in the popular community without devaluing marriage.

Until now, not all social reforms have been able to unite the 'classes' into a community; on the contrary, before 1933, the socialists and democrats took advantage of the creation of extreme antagonisms between the social classes. The term 'déclassé', which is applied to the illegitimate child, also comes from this period.

This intolerable situation cannot be maintained in our people's community; for the future existence of the people is the most important thing, and in spite of the present increase in births, it is not certain that we could do without illegitimate children in number.

We are not advocating illegitimate relationships and their consequences; but it is certain that with the elevation of the social position of the illegitimate child, a very great step has been taken to limit the many offences committed against the regulations concerning abortion, which made the people gain from births and reduced the number of cases of female diseases.

Illegitimate children are often accused of playing a considerable role in police statistics. In almost all cases, this is because illegitimate mothers have a profession and cannot devote themselves, for material reasons, to the upbringing of their children. Now the mother devotes herself to her child Neither the woman's parents, nor the man's parents, nor the physical father himself replace the mother. Even when the grandparents take care of the child, in 90% of cases the child is spoiled, pampered and in the end still sees the mother as a woman who does not give in for pedagogical reasons and is therefore "strict". The same criticism is rightly levelled at the absence of the father.

Whichever way one looks at it, we have no moral right to deny respect to the illegitimate child and the mother and to allocate to them a secondary role in the popular community.

The aim of our efforts must be to facilitate the conclusion of marriages as widely as possible through financial assistance. Adoption is the second solution for educating the illegitimate child and making him or her a valid member of the national community. But this will only happen if the mother freely agrees to leave her child in good hands because she knows that she cannot raise it herself.

SS BOOKLET NO. 2. 1938.

WHY DO WE ALWAYS TALK ABOUT A "FAMILY TREE"?

The instructor entered the section office. No sooner had he released the latch on the door than the nearest comrade turned to him: "Franz, I brought you my family tree, do you want to see it?

This term "family tree" obsesses the genealogist. He hears about it from acquaintances, on the street, in his workplace, from his superiors and in his circle of friends. Within a few years it has become a widespread concept in Germany. But in most cases it is *not* used *properly*!

All our comrades probably use it in this inaccurate way when they want to provide proof of their origin. The proof of origin that is required is carried out by listing and recording all direct ancestors. As the term "ancestors" is also used to refer to ascendants, the incorrect term "family tree" must therefore be interpreted correctly to mean *"ancestral certificate"*. This certificate, which includes the applicant, his two parents, the four grandparents etc., is represented in the form of a summary table, which is called an "ancestor table". It has *nothing to do* with the family tree.

If the table of ancestors is that of the candidate, i.e. the procreator, then the family tree shows the descendants of a specific procreator, the forefather. The forefather begets children, these in turn beget grandchildren and other descendants, which are generally called "lineage", since they all pass on the same name as the forefather. A "family tree" (starting from the oldest at the bottom) shows a lineage over centuries with all its branches. When we imagine the arrangement of the members of this line in the form of a precise table (starting from the oldest at the top), we get the "family tree".

The ancestor chart and the genealogical chart are types of representation of two different kinds of genealogical consideration, to which was later added the chart of relatives and descendants. The "family tree" is nothing more than an inverted "family chart", which is, however, conceived and designed with a strong emphasis on aesthetics.

Why is it precisely the 'family tree' that (wrongly) refers to so many different genealogical representations in the mouths of all people? Perhaps a brief study of its history can help us explain this fact.

There are some old "genealogists" who have raised the question of whether the family tree is of "German", "Roman Catholic" or "Eastern" origin. This question goes to the heart of the matter as we see it in terms of the racial consideration of history. Let us first ask ourselves where it first appeared in the form of a representation of genealogical relationships. The answer to this question is that the first examples of "family trees" were found in Central European manuscripts from the 11th and 12th centuries. These miniatures—pen-and-ink drawings or paintings—have different genealogical contents, initially in the form of a sketch of a family tree, which will develop further into a tree.

Inbreeding table
Modena, ecclesiastical library. I, 17.

Most of these 'trees' are not family trees in the true sense of the word, i.e. figurative representations of historically defined lineages with details for each branch. They are mostly advanced types of 'consanguinity tables', i.e. dry, schematic general views drawn up by Roman Catholic lawyers for questions of inheritance and marriage law. Figure I shows one of these tables of consanguinity, i.e. an "overview of biological kinship" from a ninth-century manuscript in Modena, Northern Italy. The diagram goes from the centre downwards: children, uncles, great uncles, etc.; with all relatives in collateral line on the paternal and maternal side. In this way the degree of relationship can be determined.

Even so, this drawing does not conform to the spirit of a 'family tree' with the oldest member of the line at the bottom; however, we can easily imagine that a superb tree has emerged from this sketch, as shown in illustration 2.

We see the same tradition influencing this evolution of the representation of 'trees', just as we also see its influence on the current denomination of the various genealogical tables and forms as 'family trees'.

Apart from these 'false' trees, there are also—from around 1100 onwards—trees that conform to the current concept of a family tree. As an excellent example, we can point to the family tree of the old Guelph house which, although still somewhat confused, is nevertheless a tree worthy of the name. This drawing is the archetype for all subsequent family trees. Most of the family trees of this period represent the line of Isaiah, whose most famous member was Jesus Christ of Nazareth. The various representations of the "Branch of Isaiah" explained to the barely Christianised German tribes of that time that Christ, the religious founder, came from an old and famous lineage to which kings, prophets, etc. belonged. These efforts to show that the new god is a pure-blooded person are reminiscent of the "Heliand" (saviour) stories that tried to get the apparently unenthusiastic Germanic peoples to accept Christ as German king. An example is a Salzburg manuscript (ca. 1130) on the "Branch of Isaiah".

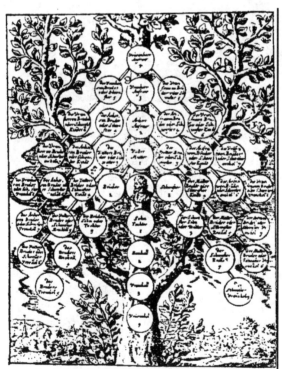

*Family tree from the legal regulations of Jül-Berg.
Düsseldorf 1696.*

The "Branch of Isaiah" and the few surviving trees from the 12th century are genuine family trees in the true sense of the word; however, the table of consanguinity already mentioned shows that the graphic representation of the tree also reflects other relationships of this type. As early as the 12th century, various concepts are represented in the form of a tree, the content of which is completely different and only comes close to it in terms of kinship. However, the form of the tree is in no way adapted to the nature of these representations. In fact, it is often completely contrary to them. Germany and its neighbouring countries have therefore had a particular preference for the tree symbolising degrees of kinship. This preference, which marks the ancient Germanic past, involves considerable research work which, as in other fields, is compounded by the absence of sources which have mostly disappeared. The perfectly recognisable form of expression that expresses certain degrees of lineage, symbolised by the image of the tree, draws our attention directly to the importance that the tree had for the Germans, which is also revealed by other testimonies. The popularity of the term 'family tree' is still alive today, due to the general awareness of the importance of these biological relationships.

The Branch of Isaiah. Antiphonary of St Peter, Salzburg, folio383, from Lind's publication, Vienna 1870, table 18.

SS NOTEBOOK No. 5. 1944.

HOW MY FAMILY BOOK WAS BORN

I think back to the number of years I spent making my family book. When it started, I was still in school. It was in the middle of the First World War.

Perhaps an old farmer, sharpening his quill pen, filled in an old pigskin folio he had inherited with clumsy handwriting, and thus gave birth to a book written in the form of a chronicle. Twenty-five years passed before I acquired this book. I mentioned this to show that a family book, a family chronicle, is a slow process, that it cannot be created suddenly and that it will look different every time. No two family chronicles will be alike, and if I sketch out the structure of this book, it is only a working plan, a presentation of how my family book came into being.

At the beginning of every family book is the ancestor book. It provides a framework of names and dates, plus some professional data. This framework must then be brought to life.

One person will start collecting titles, texts and letters, supplemented by portraits. Another will build up a set of ancestor cards, regularly adding whatever they can gradually learn about their ancestors. A third writes a book and notes down the results of her investigations in a jumble. Others will have a different approach, but they all have the same objective: to preserve what they find and pass it on to their children and grandchildren. Many readers of these lines will already have opted for one or other of these methods.

As far as the birth of my family book is concerned, I have to admit that I no longer remember the past, but only the history of my family. I saw—unconsciously at first but with increasing clarity—the family only as a branch of the nation, and my aspiration was to *reflect the people through the family history*. If I could have foreseen the difficulties that this task represented, I don't know if I would have had the courage to undertake it.

As anyone else would have done, I began by collecting the simplest dates and names. But I also tried to follow the traces of the oral traditions of the past that had come down to me, and I went from surprise to surprise; no doubt these first results encouraged my motivation. But no one should be discouraged if they don't find anything yet; it often takes time to get them, and then they flow in all the more abundantly.

I was interested first in the paternal and then the maternal branch of names. Then I filled in the gaps. I collected all the letters I could find, wrote down stories and anecdotes (annoying more than one elder in the family circle with my requests). Slowly the whole thing grew and took shape. Old administrative records appeared in the archives, all sorts of details from the parish registers revealed personal traits. I visited the places where the ancestors had lived, the churches they had prayed in, the farms they had owned; I took photographs of all these places. In a small village cemetery I found six gravestones with almost illegible inscriptions; but near them grew the most beautiful lime trees I had ever seen, and as it was June they bloomed steadily, enveloped in the fragrant exhalation and buzzing of bees in a marvellous parable of life being stronger than what is perishable. And so the years passed. My desk drawers filled up with material. I could hardly get a general idea of the research that was always bringing me new information (genealogical research, as we know, never ends). But I still lacked the *form* that would circumscribe this substance.

Who has never heard of the old family chronicles passed down from generation to generation? First I had to rewrite a chronicle of all the experiences made by the ancestors, and leave the possibility of constantly adding new details to it. This was the major difficulty: a chronicle is never finished. There is always an event that occurs, either because someone wants to give a testimony or because later on children and grandchildren want to do so. It was harder for me to find the right solution than to do all this research during those long years.

Then I explained why I wanted to write this chronicle. I wanted to introduce my children to their ancestors and their country, the homeland and its life. And I suddenly knew what I had to do: *I had to keep it simple.*

So I started. But where to start? Thinking of the old sagas, I started with the ancient times. I began to tell the story of the collapsing ice giants and the appearance of the country, rising from the glistening water of the North and Baltic Seas. I described the waves of the glaciers being swallowed up by the valleys and the birth of a beautiful patch of land in the middle of it all: the homeland of the ancestors. I evoked prehistory until the appearance of the latter. The country and the people came to life through their tales and legends, which I recounted. The accounts filled with details about specific ancestors or groups of ancestors always ended with illustrations of the homeland, such as: "My father speaks of Peter Pück", or "Grandmother J. and the story of the thousand thalers", or "the old house and the devil's gate of St Marien". And on the title page I put these words:

Book of the house and ancestors of the Metelmann children
Stories and portraits of the lives of their ancestors, accompanied by new tales and legends of the homeland.

To be read aloud to their mother by their father

So now I had found the shape. What *was* missing was *the* final *outward appearance.* But that followed logically: I had a binder made for myself containing the neatly written sheets, the carefully glued portraits and finally a summarised family tree in list form. The pages are not numbered so that other chapters or new stories can be inserted. The whole is perfect and beautiful. To see and read it is a joy for all. Two years ago, the "Book of Home and Ancestors" lay under the Christmas tree: we can't count the number of times it has been given to children to read. And God willing, many generations will still have the joy of leafing through it and even writing their lives and those of their families in it, thus remaining true to the spirit of our great German homeland.

SS Notebook No. 7. 1944.

What should our child be called?

Already weeks before the birth of a son or daughter, parents are preoccupied with what names they should give them. Until now, the task of choosing a name was taken so lightly that the mother-to-be looked at a Christian calendar and chose a few boys' and girls' names that she liked. She made sure that these names were in use in the area and in the family, and the following were listed on the ballot: Fritz, Hans, Klaus, Karl-Heinz, Peter for a boy and Ursel, Gisela, Annemarie, Bärbel or Gerda for a girl. She would then consult with the father. He would look at the calendar again and add his choice, and then they would agree on two or three names depending on the characteristics, hair colour of the expected children or the family "look". The remaining names were not discarded but only kept in reserve.

The parents did indeed think about it and yet they thought little. They did not know that all first names have a historical origin and a particular meaning.

In the mother's file we are talking about, there are some commonly used names, but they all have different meanings. Fritz is a shortened form of Frederick, an old German name, and is formed from two Germanic syllables 'frid' and 'richi'. Frid is related to "froh" (joyful) and "frei" (free). "Fro" is the old designation for the free man, the lord; "Frowe" meant the free woman, the ruler. "Frederick" is a man who is rich in peace-giving power. The fact that our ancestors created such magnificent names in pre-Christian times proves that they had a great natural ethic.

When our parents consciously decided to give a son the name Frederick, they were giving him a name: a name charged with meaning, a name that would distinguish a particular spirit, a particular quality that would follow the child. Ernst Wasserzieher wrote in his little book *Hans and Grete:* "Since the time of the Hohenstaufen, the name Frederick has been extraordinarily popular because of the memory of the legendary figures of Frederick Barbarossa and Frederick II, and it has been revived since Frederick the Great, Old Fritz.

But when the German name Fritz is given today, we do not think about its origin and meaning, as we do with the name Hans and others. It is clear that "Hans" is only a shortened and "Germanised" form of the Hebrew "John". John means "Jehovah is merciful". All the biblical names beginning with "J" and "Jo", such as Jeremiah, Joachim, Job, Jonah, Joseph, contain the two names of the Jewish god Jehovah and Jehovah abbreviated in these syllables. Where does Klaus come from? Klaus is the shortened form of Nicholas, whose origin is not Germanic but Greek. Karl-Heinz? Both Karl (Charles) and Heinz (Henry) are very old German names. Charles characterises a "Kerl" (able individual), the free man of non-chivalrous class, the free peasant on his hereditary estate. Henri comes from Hagenrich (the rich enclosure), the lord of an estate surrounded by hedges.

Peter is a widely used Christian name that is even more frequently found in choruses. Peter comes from Petrus, the rock, a Roman name, which is added to that of the apostle Simon as the first pope.

The Hebrew name Michael seems to be particularly common. Many citizens believe that they are naming their son after the 'invincibly strong' archangel, thus giving him a particularly modern name. But giving children foreign names can only be harmful today, as they grow up in an age of trying to find their origins and will later ask their parents with difficulty: In 1944, eleven years after the National Socialist Revolution, how could you still give us Jewish names?

Let's explain what the five names chosen by the mother mean: Ursula is Latin and means "the little bear". This name has become fashionable because of its harmonious sound. Bärbel, a sweet form of Barbara, is of Greek origin and means "the foreigner" (the barbarian). Annemarie is Jewish in both its components. There are so many beautiful Germanic names that we do not need to show our ignorance by giving the girls of our people such names and hundreds of fashionable nicknames as Mieke, Mia, Maja, Ria, Mimi, Miezl, Anke, Anne, Antpe, Annchen, etc. The same applies to the names of the girls of our country. The same applies to common oriental names such as Margarete and its abbreviated forms Marga and Grete.

So out of ten names, our mother chose six foreign names, mostly Jewish and only four Germanic.

Having criticised this irresponsible choice, as there have been (and always will be), we must now present the following characteristics for choosing names that correspond to our race and species:

1. First names or customary forms define a particular racial and national type; they express a hope and a desire related to the destiny of future generations. They express knowledge of the value of character, awareness of the identity of the clan, the people and God.

2. It is our duty to give our children characteristic names and to put an end to the tradition that still persists here and there of choosing foreign names.

3. Each name has its own specific ethnic origin and meaning. We mainly differentiate between North Germanic (Harald, Sigurd, Astrid, Thora), German (Albert, Heinrich, Gertrud, Irmgard), Roman (Anton-ius; Martin-us, Pet [e] r-us, Agnes, Klara), Greek (Georg, Eugen, Lydia, Monika) and Jewish (Jakob, Joachim, Johann, Joseph, Mathias, Michael, Thomas, Anna, Elisabeth, Eva, Edith, Gabriele, Magdalena, Martha, Maria, Suzanne).

4. The first name must match all the names of the parents' homeland. In Friesland other names are preferred than in Bavaria. The name should express the ethnicity. It is therefore important to find out what the name

means before giving it to your child. (A special issue of "Characteristic Names" has been published by the SS-Hauptamt. Circles and teachers from various regions provide information).

5. The first name must be in harmony with the family name to form an organic whole with it. But this is not always possible, as many surnames have little meaning. Consonance also plays a role.

6. The custom of giving children the first names of their ancestors (grandparents and great-grandparents) is healthy. The first name is an ancestral duty for the child, the heir of the ancestor. When the father and son have the same first name, confusion is easily possible. But the son will proudly bear the name of the deceased father. Choosing names from collateral lines expresses the desire for a classic family relationship, whereas family or clan names express the closest blood relationship, which is expressed in the form of a homogeneous community. The first name makes it possible to influence the future, and thus to determine how the biological heritage will develop. This is the major difficulty in choosing a first name. This implies knowledge of the hereditary characteristics of the clan, which can also enable us to create new names if we do not want the delivery of names to be no longer adapted to the evolution of life.

7. Instead of the abbreviated forms that have become customary, full first names should be used in future, apart from the nicknames used in family circles.

8. Double names (Karl Heinz, Ernst Dieter) only make sense if they refer to the degree of relationship with the godfather. Children should be made aware of these issues on their future birthdays. If there are compound names with Bauer, Müller, Schmidt, etc., the use of several first names is desirable. However, the transcription of several first names in a single form (Karlheinz or similar) should be avoided.

Now that we are living in an era where people are becoming aware of their racial origins, the choice of a first name is no longer an arbitrary matter. Through the giving of the first name, our world view expresses that the individual represents a link in the chain of generations of his clan and a branch of the tree of life constituted by his people. The first name forms both a vow in this sense and a biological link. The handing over of the first name is a step in the gradual awakening of the people, and when all Germans again bear German names, it can be concluded that the choice of marriage and the protection of the family have regained their priority and their right to consideration.

Let the name be the expression of the species!

SS NOTEBOOK No. 3. 1944.

THE GARDEN CEMETERY

Behind us are the endless, exhausting expanses of Russia, before us the cramped landscape of the fatherland. In the leave train from the front, the letters find mingled within them the memories of the often superhuman efforts made in battles undertaken to safeguard German land in the east, the simple family life, the green village, the lone tree on the country lane, the murmur of the stream winding through the meadows, the quivering forest and the hedge full of flowers and birds in their nests. Hans from Brandenburg received a letter from his wife saying that the cherry tree to the left of the bedroom window seemed to be covered in frost as it bloomed so much; Toni Wieser learned that a fruity '43 vintage required a lot of effort and work in the vineyard; Schulte's son from the Red Earth told him that he is diligent and helps to feed the cattle; Draxler from Tannensteig could be happy; his mother informed him that the house is shining and that she is looking forward to his coming! I love the March and I wouldn't want to frustrate you for anything, you who love your Swabian country more than anything else, or you who feel really at home in Silesia. Each of us breathes life into the region in which we were born, not only in a physical sense, but also in a spiritual sense. The previous generations of our family shaped our country and marked this piece of land with their character and strength. This radiates today, enriches our being and contributes to the magnificent development of all our qualities.

When we arrive at the house, we look around to see if everything is still as we left it. "Why did you cut down the big tree up there? Why is the fruit so worm-eaten? I distinctly remember biting into a ruddy-cheeked apple from the tree behind the barn. Who built this bare cemetery, with no trees or bushes, no birds chirping, no walls, but bare and open, exposed to all eyes, with only a fence to protect it from profane intruders? However, it is a good thing that you have put nests there behind the big lime tree! The birds will be able to nest again and help destroy the vermin. The woman has had a lot of work, yet the boy and girl have worked hard because the father who fights so bravely for us in the distance must be fully satisfied and happy.

—Tell me, woman, does it bother me who arranged the cemetery in such a tasteless way? You know, I have seen many comrades fall and I promised them all a place in my heart, as they enjoyed their lives. However, the village does not seem to hear their request: "Do not turn us into grave shadows, leave us the sweet fragrance of serenity that hovered over our youth like a brilliant glow! You the living, give your dead the right to return, so that we may remain among you in good times and bad. Do not mourn us so that every friend must be afraid to gossip and laugh about us. Do you know that the garden cemetery should be so beautiful that one likes to be with the dead. Any place can be suitable for this kind of cemetery, up by the big lime tree, or the mound over there on the way out of the village, or over there on the old steep river bed: but it should, where it is, be in a special relationship with the village and become a part of the regional beauty, like the old burial mounds or some of the little chapels. I compare this to Walter Flex's description in "Traveller Between Two Worlds": "On the height of Lemno Lake I decorate a hero's grave. Two lime trees above it like quiet guardians, the near rustle of the forests and the distant glitter of the lake protected it. The sun and the summer flowers bloomed in abundance in the peasant gardens around. The cheerful, sunny boy should have a grave made of Sun and flowers. For, you see, our duty is not just to bury the deceased who bequeathed us this beautiful village; we must also honour them with pride. People who are constantly apathetic and stingy with their time are not allowed to have a say in the selection of the sites, but only those like this old mother whom I met on a crowded omnibus. She was not afraid of the fatigue and the journey and had come from East Prussia to visit her son in the hospital in Innsbrück. The garden cemetery with its plots must fit into the vast natural expanse where you can feel the breath of eternity. With the children quickly put to bed, I will now talk about my motives and what should concern us all.

—We must come to terms with the fact that there will be duties in the community which we can no longer defer to a 'professional' who profits from them. We all constantly have sacred duties—which each individual must perform seriously, with love and equal warmth and which cannot be left to anyone else. The maintenance and care of this cemetery for our dead and fallen is that sacred duty. You see, we must all come together in the future in the village to carry out this cemetery.

—I think you must have often felt different emotions depending on the nature of the spaces you were in. A fellow architect explained this to me in so many words of peace: "Certain ratios of proportion already arouse different states of mind in us humans: profane feeling or solemnity. A longer or higher space evokes in us more solemn emotions than a theatre, even if it is overloaded with scenery, because an equilateral space gives rise to a feeling of tranquillity and pleasantness, and therefore more often incites to rest than to movement. But the present, the past and the future play an essential role in the great celebration of life. With his thoughts, man returns from the present to the past and rushes into the future. He finds himself in motion. Physically and morally man is set in motion in a long space like a peristyle or the nave of a great church. The height and length of a space can produce a state of recollection in men in everyday life, according to the following ratio of proportion: 2/3 for the cemetery-garden in which the present and the infinite meet.

—As the comrade had many other interesting things to say about the cemetery in our village, I will tell you everything he told me: The content and form of the garden cemetery are determined by the smallest formal unit, the grave, which must never have the shape of a triangle or circle.

Rhombuses, stars and crosses have a particularly powerful effect on the drawing board, but in nature they shape spaces in an absurd way. They are not experienced by man in the desired form because he does not walk in the clouds, but on Earth.

In the future, the appearance of cemeteries and memorials should be designed in a spirit of extreme simplicity. The signs created by human hands should fit ingeniously into the characterful surrounding nature. A place of remembrance for the dead of a village.

—The garden cemetery contains man, tree and eternity. The tree forms an intermediary between the latter and the generation. It becomes the tree of the ancestors in the field or the village cemetery when its branches watch over a lineage. Side by side, men are in close community, without difference, under the grass. The burial mound should rise ten centimetres above ground level. The best location for an individual, as long as it is not made compulsory, is not determined by wealth but only by the fame and respectability of a family or an individual. The municipality bears the costs for a period of at least 25 years and for the period in which the descendants participate in the maintenance of the grave. You see, this is how our garden cemetery will come into being, where the rank and value of the grave is of no importance, but only the plant and its care, because a garden without flowers is not a garden. Flowers specific to the country should delight us with their beauty and diversity of colour and form. The large number of greenhouse plants piled up in flowerbeds frightens the eye, which had hoped to see a meadow of flowers in the cemetery, albeit of many species, but intimately selected. In a place where people's sense of smell is more important than their sense of sight, colourful flower species are supposed to calm their hearts with their captivating scent.

Sketches by Klaus Stärtzenbach for new tombstones.

The stele in the middle of these flower-filled meadows symbolises man.

The grave holds the memory of hundreds of moments of a life and erases all quarrels.

It represents man in his final fulfilment. It evokes the past perspective of the man who could reach middle age, as well as that of the individual who was to live for many more years. With a simple chisel, each of us can carve signs of life, solar motifs such as the sun wheel and the cross of St. Andrew, without great expense. The tree of life teaches us that life, even if it dies out, always draws new strength from the old lineage. The tomb is not addressed to the world, but to one, two, three, four, five or six people who are in close physical or moral relationship with the dead person, for the inscription is no longer a simple text, but a dialogue. Thus, the calm that reigns in this cemetery-garden becomes a sort of perfect movement in itself, where the symbols rub shoulders in a tangible form; none is superior to the other, just as man is no longer different from his neighbour.

The wooden stele will always be taller than it is wide. The narrower it is, the closer it is to the shape of the tree reaching for the light. Stone, on the other hand, is heavy, layered, and is closely related to the earth and must be in keeping with its character. The funeral monument will be wider than it is high. The iron worked by the blacksmith in the round, square or flat must be struck or twisted, split, bent and riveted so that the wind and the sun can pass through freely, as through a spider's web. Influenced by our free and joyful spirit, form and essence unite in such a way that essence begets form, as the tree is born from the earth and the sound from the flute.

I am already looking forward to the time when all the peasants will gather to build the cemetery-garden together according to this beautiful project, with the conviction that every people is next to another people of immortals whose existence was indispensable because they represent our roots without which we could not move forward.

Klaus Stärtzenbach

SS BOOKLET NO. 6. 1944.

OF THE CHILD

Is there any greater joy than seeing a child? — Do you know one? — I don't! — It is a joy of the eyes. It is a joy of hearing. It is a joy for your hands that caress him. It is a blessing for your heart. You experience it with all your being but no words can express it. It is true that a child also requires constant care that takes many forms.

There are many concerns.

The child you have had, who develops, grows according to his inner self, is a part of you and yet follows his own destiny. You feel responsible for him, but you can do nothing for his good or his evil. You extend yourself into him, but it is his will that guides him. Is there no greater concern?

Celan' never stops. Before he is born, you wonder if he lives, if he is healthy. You worry about his health, his missteps, his results. You worry about his choices, his own questions. Your attachment to your child is so deep, so total.

But you are really fulfilled through your child. Your fulfilment in your efforts for your child is your secret value, your anonymous living value. Your value is your silent happiness. Then you are reassured at last: he lives, and thousands of little lives blossom in him as on a tree in springtime; his beauty shines like the morning moisture of the day. Your silent joy finds its crowning glory in its physical radiance. The healthy character of your child seems to light up your joy. His coming fills you with a glowing pride—can there be any deeper joy?

They also tell you that this child is a burden, the product of carelessness. But others express more sane and upright ideas, say that it is a matter of opinion, and certainly the most irrefutable, that it is a duty to the people, a responsible act, a proof of trust.

But the wisest word I will say to you is that there is no other reason for your desire to have a child than love. You love him for no other reason than joy.

III. RACIAL ISSUES

JOURNAL "BELIEVE AND FIGHT", FOR THE SS OF THE SOUTH EAST GERMAN FOLK GROUPS.

WHAT IS RACE?

"What is not of good breed in this world is worthless.

(Adolf Hitler, *Mein Kampf*)

Within the mass of living beings, groups can be discerned that are more or less similar to each other and have similar physical characteristics. They possess the same essence. We call these groups of living beings "species".

Humanity, which is alive today, forms a "species" because the individuals are mutually fertile. But when one considers and compares a white person, a Negro or a Mongolian, it becomes clear that one cannot speak unrestrictedly only of the species "man", one has to make a new sub-classification in order to make an accurate judgement. This leads to the concept of human races.

We can distinguish each race by the differences it possesses due to the particularity of its hereditary, psycho-intellectual and physical characteristics, dispositions and qualities. Each race has certain qualities and characteristics that are *unique to* it. These *racial characteristics* are transmitted hereditarily to the descendants.

The race is thus a group of living beings distinguished by the common possession of certain hereditary characteristics. It always produces similar beings. Or, to summarise: The race is a community of inherited dispositions (Stengel v. Rutkowski).

As long as a race remains pure, its hereditary heritage is passed on intact from one generation to the next. It is therefore necessary for men of the same race to have a heightened racial awareness and to recognise the dangers leading to interbreeding, transformation, degeneration and thus the decline of the race concerned. Each people has evolved from specific races into a homogeneous community of life. The overall race defines the ethnic characteristic and is immutably externalised through its hereditary heritage. Like all Germanic peoples, the dominant Nordic race also marks the German people with its specificity.

What is a people?

Each people represents an outwardly visible community. The same blood, the same land, the same language, the same customs, the same culture and the same history form an inseparable bond. Both race and history and culture are necessary for peoplehood. The people are both a community of hereditary dispositions and a community of environment. Each generation is only one link in the chain that begins with the oldest ancestors and continues into the future with future generations. Together they form the people's community. The existence of the individual therefore has a purpose when it is intimately connected with the people as a whole.

Every living blood holder in this community has a responsibility to give life to future generations.

Each people has its own ethnic characteristic. The racial composition of the people determines this characteristic.

The people are a community of origin and destiny. As a community of hereditary dispositions, it is capable of creating and largely shaping its environment.

The importance of races

The common hereditary mass conditions the physical and spiritual aptitude for creation that is proper to a race. Race" as a working concept not only refers to the particular vitality living and expressing in us, but also becomes the essential value, the ideological reference point.

There are races that can produce great civilisations and others that will never rise on their own. There are races with heroic attitudes and others without combative courage. Cultural creations are exclusively the work of races of great value. Humanity evolves or declines because of the preservation of the purity and strength of the civilisation-creating races.

The racial structure of a people is unique. Its modification always leads to a transformation of its character and civilisation. Any racial mixture means for the race worthy of the name a decrease in its value.

Related—foreign—same strain—different strain

Mankind has strongly separated racial groups within it. Broadly speaking, we distinguish between: whites, blacks and yellows. Each of these groups in turn comprises a number of sub-races that have certain traits in common. In this case, we speak of kinship or, briefly, of related races. Peoples who, in their racial composition, have the same components as the German people, are related to us. The majority of European peoples are in this case.

Since the essential racial substance often varies considerably among our relatives, the quantitative aspect of the racial components must be taken into account. The Germanic peoples have a predominance of Nordic blood in their racial mix. Their relationship to the German people is therefore defined as "of the same stock". Other peoples who also have weak Nordic racial components, but are not Nordic in substance, we say are 'of foreign stock'.

The favourable racial mixture present in the German people is based on the confluence of related races and the superior and predominant share of Nordic blood.

The origin of the Nordic breed

The central sphere of the Nordic breed includes the regions of Southern Scandinavia, Jutland, the North Sea, the Baltic Sea and extends into the heart of Germany.

From early on, the Nordic man was a sedentary farmer. He invented the plough, which was later adopted by other peoples, grew cereals and raised domestic animals. The enormous increase in population of this Nordic mankind prompted them to acquire new territories and caused wave after wave to flow into neighbouring lands: into the European area and into large parts of Asia. The original settled population was marked by the Nordic way of life, even if often only temporarily.

The statement that "light comes from the East", as science once claimed, is false. It should rather be said "strength comes from the North!

The importance of the Nordic race for humanity

The Führer says in *Mein Kampf*:

"All that we admire on this earth today, science and art, technology and inventions, are the creative product of a few peoples and perhaps, originally, *of a* race.

The great civilisations created by the Indo-Germans in India, Persia, Greece and Rome bear impeccable witness to the Nordic creative spirit. They also disappeared with the decline of the Nordic ruling class. Even today, we are aware of the kinship with these cultures, which have the same origin.

However, we are not so presumptuous as to believe that all culture, even that of ancient times, can be attributed to the Nordic race alone. People of other racial composition have also created civilisations. But we feel differently when we try to understand the cultures of ancient China, Babylon or the old Indian cultures of the Aztecs (in present-day Mexico) and the Incas (in present-day Peru). It is undeniable that these were also great civilisations; however, we feel the mark of an undeniably foreign nature in their contact. They are not related to us, but alien in race. Another spirit speaks in them. Never have these cultures of another kind reached a level comparable to that which has been influenced by the Nordic spirit.

Today's technical development has also been the product of Nordic men. This is the case, for example, with the new Turkey, the rise of North America or the progress of the Far East, on an equivalent level.

In places of mixing with neighbouring races, the influence of the Nordic race has consistently proved to be extremely innovative and has involved active developmental tendencies, giving rise to the highest cultural creations.

The German people and the Nordic race

In spite of the often high mixture and intermingling of breeds in various parts of the Reich, we find in the different parts of Germany distinct breeds that are more strongly typed.

There are regions where a tall stature, narrow face and light hair, eye and skin colours dominate (the physical appearance of the Nordic race). Closely related to the Nordic man, often referred to as a 'subspecies' of the Nordic man, the Westphalian man turns out to be taller, broader and more massive.

In many parts of the Reich, on the other hand, we find tall, short-headed men with a narrow face, a large nose, brown eyes and black hair (the physical appearance of the Dinaric race).

In some parts, small, slender and agile men with dark eyes and skin colour (the physical appearance of the Western or Mediterranean race) live.

In other regions, the following characteristics predominate: medium-sized, stocky bodies, short heads, broad faces with prominent cheekbones, blond hair and light eyes (physical aspect of the Baltic-Eastern breed).

Finally, in some parts of the Reich, one encounters stocky, round-headed men with broad faces, brown eyes, brown to black hair and dark skin colour (physical appearance of the oriental race).

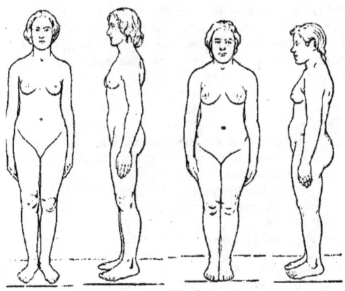

Nordic type—Baltic-Eastern type

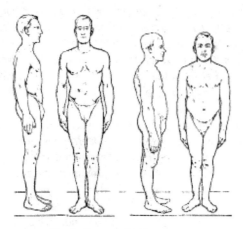

Nordic type—Baltic-Eastern type

The *Nordic race* is more or less strongly represented in all parts of the Reich, whether in the north or south, west or east. Many of our people cannot be exactly identified with one race. With the exception of those representatives who appear to be purebred, each race is found among all peoples in a more or less strongly mixed form.

The Nordic hereditary heritage predominates in the German people. The Nordic race is not only the *predominant race*, but its *blood is present in almost all Germans*. The concepts of "Blood and Soil" are not an empty concept, but constitute our destiny. The aim of the selection of the German people has therefore also been defined. It is carried out in accordance with the vital law of its creative race.

The share of Nordic blood in the hereditary mass of the German people amounts to about 50%. Apart from that, genealogy teaches us that *every German has Nordic blood*.

Thus the German people are a racial community in the truest sense of the word. History interpreted according to a racial principle has long since shown that the Nordic race produces a far greater number of outstanding men than other races. The Nordic race is above all the holder of the genius of the German people. Great achievements in all fields have made them the leading race of mankind. No other human race has produced so many outstanding spiritual leaders, army leaders and statesmen.

In the course of bold expeditions, the Nordic man conquered vast territories, founded states and created civilisations. Already around the year 1000, the Vikings had landed in America. The Nordic spirit realised the development of large areas of land.

One of the most striking qualities of the Nordic race is its self-control. Nordic boldness has inspired warlike conquests. Probity and strength of will, combined with self-confidence, powerfully reinforce the feeling of independence. These qualities certainly diminish intuition, and the Nordic man is in great danger of losing and wasting himself. The Nordic man has a great predilection for sport and combat—he loves risk. He is therefore more likely than other men to be found in occupations that involve danger. But it must be said that the character of the individual is more decisive than the colour of the hair. The individual essentially belongs to a race whose virtues he professes through action.

When we examine each country of Europe in its racial composition, we notice that in almost all the states the same races are found. We find the Nordic race outside Germany, in the Scandinavian countries, in England and the Netherlands, as well as in Russia, Italy, France, Spain, etc. But we also find, for example, men of the Oriental type in the various European countries. The important thing, in the end, is not to make a general racial judgement about a people. It is rather to study the *predominant elements of each race* in the people concerned. And it can be seen that on a purely numerical level, the Reich is already ahead of the other peoples in terms of the proportion of Nordic blood.

Germany can legitimately claim to lead the German-Nordic peoples.

SS NOTEBOOK NO. 7. 1942.

THE BIOLOGICAL MEANING OF SELECTION

Since Darwin, like Linnaeus, was no longer satisfied with defining a system of species, but also questioned their origin and tried to find an answer, the idea of selection has gained new momentum. In the past decades, efforts were already being made to apply it to humans. Today, the idea of selection is one of the key elements of the National Socialist worldview. Since its victorious eruption, the public domain has also taken a keen interest in it. Added to this is the fact that all the questions concerning the selection and orientation of men, their type of function and the distribution of tasks are particularly bright today.

Races and species are created through selection and elimination

Two fundamentally opposed answers have been given to the causes of the origin of the species and races on Earth. One looks for driving factors in external impulses, in the environment, in the "milieu". The other, on the other hand, speaks of the laws of hereditary transmission, and locates the basis of the origin, conservation and consolidation of the characteristic traits of the species at the heart of the living plasma itself. We feel closer to the second answer than to the first. We know, for example, that the loss of a limb due to freezing or the environment does not result in the disappearance of that limb in the offspring. Nor would this be the case if the cooling were to be repeated over several generations. Despite this, there are deep interrelationships between the origin of species and habitat conditions that we cannot consider from the point of view of any superficial theory of the environment. Homogeneous human groups, i.e. entire racial groups as well as specific races, only acquire the homogeneous characteristic of their own physical and psychic features in the course of ten to one hundred thousand years in harmonious connection with a living area appropriate to the species in question. Under the effect of all its geological, climatic and biological conditions, the area of life gradually brings about the consolidation and internal harmonisation of a perfectly determined hereditary trait. This was not the result of "the hereditary transmission of acquired qualities", but of selection in a positive sense and elimination in a negative sense.

The habitat produces a specific type of selection

The selection and elimination carried out in a territory specific to a given species means that only those that have grown up under the conditions of that particular area reproduce in the long term. Conversely, those that do not overcome these conditions disappear. An example: As the researcher v. Eickstedt has done, let us assume that the light-skinned Europoid Nordic mankind was particularly marked by the uniform and isolated North Eurasian (Siberian) habitat of the Ice Age. We can easily imagine the consequences of natural selection and elimination in this area. Only those who had been subjected to the harshest conditions could survive and perpetuate themselves over the following millennia. Reproduction and growth were given only to those who ultimately proved superior to this climate and inhospitable aspect of the earth, those who were ultimately stronger than nature through their inflexibility and hardness. Only those qualities that enabled the victorious man to overcome nature were perpetuated and consolidated through hereditary transmission. During the war in the East, the winter gave us a foretaste and a vivid illustration of what it means for people who are living beings not only to be subject to an all-powerful nature but to defy it victoriously.

Overcoming nature means more than having two specific qualities. Muscular strength or insensitivity to cold are not enough. Overcoming nature and the environment refers to the general character traits of body and soul. Nature must be overcome by physical toughness and an inflexible will to live. It must also be overcome by spiritual strength and great zeal. Already in our earliest ancestors, it fostered those qualities that we still feel in our souls today as the highest: defiance of external obstacles, toughness towards ourselves, an insatiable will to live, depth and belief in the victory of the soul, as well as all our higher qualities and strengths.

The origin of species is not the result of an easy adaptation process

We can never regard the triumph over stingy nature and the harshness of its living conditions as the result of easy adaptation. It is obvious that man also adapts and follows the path of least resistance, as far as he is allowed to do so. But escaping from the environment circumscribed by the ice age and surrounded by powerful natural barriers was often impossible or only to a limited extent during long periods of evolution. When the natural barriers gradually disappeared and could be overcome, the conquest of more favourable living spaces, then as now, was only possible by confronting other human groups already established there.

The birth of a species is not the product of an easy adaptation to an environment and to a "milieu". Rather, it is a gradual crystallisation and accentuation of all the qualities that make it possible to face the harsh conditions of life victoriously. Only the heaviest sacrifice makes this possible. The being who cannot stand the test delivered by elemental nature disappears and is ruthlessly eliminated. We therefore feel a deep respect for this process, which encourages us to be responsible for the preservation and reproduction of the humans of our species.

The progress of civilisation facilitates the conditions of existence and thus also modifies the original biological laws of selection

The more a human group succeeds in mastering and transforming the conditions of its living area through the establishment of a culture faithful to the law of life, the more easily the individual succeeds in preserving himself and avoiding elimination. The laws of selection and elimination, which are severe at the beginning, gradually disappear and become less severe. The older a culture gets and the later it reaches the stage of civilising eras, the more it loses its vigour. It even produces the opposite process. Weak and sick individuals can also survive and reproduce; different racial types mix. The law creating the species no longer seems to act.

When culture develops its own spiritual evolution and at the same time produces greatly facilitated conditions of existence, the spirit and nature of selection are greatly compromised. The preservation of purity, further education and the evolution of the species developing over millennia are gradually called into question.

Cultural selection replaces biological selection

Species and races were the magnificent result of natural biological selection. The civilisation that evolves as a result of the change in its conditions of existence imposes a certain form of selection on its side. This kind of selection results from the conditions of existence, the necessities and the fundamental ideas of the dominant culture and its spirit. The objective of selection pursued by a culture may have a different relationship to the original biological natural selection. This relationship determines our assessment of the value of cultural selection and its justification. It does not matter by what means it is carried out. It is of secondary importance whether it requires certain skills, a minimum degree of education, places the preservation of life at the top of its values, or uses the means of modern science to get to know man.

Different forms of cultural selection

The most favourable case of the relationship between cultural selection and the original biological natural selection is when the objective of the latter is pursued by the former. Thanks to a keen sense of the law governing the origin of their species, peoples such as the Spartans resorted in their selection to the same principles of inflexible severity originally prescribed by nature, even after their arrival on more hospitable territories. Other peoples of the Nordic race, such as our Germanic ancestors, naturally obeyed the biological laws governing the creation of their species.

On the other hand, we know that other forms of natural selection are totally contrary to the biological laws of species origin, or even hostile to them. This is mainly the case when the civilising spirit comes from outside and is not the product of the species itself. The acceptance, as well as the forcible establishment, of an alien culture of mind produces other types of selection and ultimately leads to the denial and destruction of the original and specific character of the species. The intrusion of Christianity into the culture of our Germanic ancestors gave rise to a form of selection which, from the very beginning, proved hostile to our species and its laws of evolution. The Christian priestly elite selects suitable and usable men for their purposes, but forbids them the perpetuation and preservation of the best racial heritage by forcing them into celibacy. A form alien to the principles of cultural selection, it makes advantageous use of the consequences of natural biological selection hundreds of thousands of years old. It makes use of the rich treasure of physical-spiritual talents of our race, but consciously and instinctively refuses to let them be preserved and renewed. For centuries it has lived on this capital, a process the full extent of which we are only now realising. We see that this capital of talent is already under threat and is by no means inexhaustible.

The spirit behind the forms of cultural selection of our time

The current forms of cultural selection are closely related to the cultural level itself.

Insofar as culture already has the characteristics of a late civilising action, "selection" has already turned into a frightening counter-selection. This is the result of protecting the sick and inferior as a result of the misguided "interest" in the value of the individual alone. Moral depravity, welfare, decadence of feeling and loss of all natural instincts are the cause. Our view of all this is clear and needs no explanation.

Apart from this automatically resulting civilising counter-selection, there are many attempts to practice conscious and methodical cultural selection. Its aim and intention is always "to put the right man in the right place". No one will dispute the practicality of such efforts. All the important institutions and organisations in our cultural life are now concerned to provide their offspring with a sufficient number of qualities. The great historical tasks which fate has assigned to our people no longer allow for the development of existing gifts. It is therefore all the more necessary to put the right man in the right place.

The problematic biological character of our cultural selection

In order to assess the significance of the attempts at selection made by our time, we cannot only start by looking at its undoubted immediate success. We must constantly ask ourselves whether they are consistent with the biological laws of species conservation. We must examine whether they both promote and prosper the millennial species, or at least conserve it, apart from their momentary practical effect. When we take this necessity into account, we find that our forms of cultural selection have lost sight of the original biological meaning of all selection. In some cases, we even come to a total unconsciousness or indifference, sometimes even to an instinctive and manifest hostility. This last case particularly concerns all forms of "purely spiritual" selection.

From a practical point of view, cultural selection is mainly carried out on superior individuals adapted to particular cultural purposes. *The original biological meaning of selection, i.e. that good men should be favoured in their reproduction*, is mostly not taken into account, or even intentionally denied. Many culturally conditioned forms of life and organisations prevent their members from reproducing through the establishment of multiple economic or moral barriers. For example, the incentive to follow excessively long training courses makes it economically and practically impossible to start a family. The number of children is limited because education requires enormous sacrifices. Other cultural organisations, which naturally claim the right to choose the best, erect moral barriers instead. A class morality, for example, in which the sense of biological duty is not well regarded, which condemns early marriage as vulgar as well as many children or young parents, betrays the original meaning of biological selection. The classes that express their "distinguished" cavalier morality by the formula: "Fall in love often, get engaged rarely, never marry", therefore have no moral right to participate in the selection within our race.

Cultural selection also has the opposite effect at the biological level when the best are chosen whose existence is endangered because they have to risk their lives to accomplish their tasks. The current war is a clear example of this, where the best of us are prevented from reproducing fully by death.

When we look at the big picture, cultural selection is still carried out today, in the most varied fields despite different reasons, in a biological way that is totally similar to the selection of the Church, which is constantly feeding on the capital of talent. While it rightly, yet deceptively, strives to put the right man in the right place, it often fails to realise the original meaning of any selection because of its narrow historical-temporal, ideological and moral horizon. And not infrequently, it even believes that it must disdainfully reject biological viewpoints on 'spiritual' grounds. It thus becomes a form of counter-selection that is frightening at the practical level because it is perfectly concealed. Added to this is the soundness and correctness of its partly highly developed selective procedures.

We cannot forgo the immediate result of good cultural selection in the gigantic struggle for the existence of our people. But this must not be achieved at the cost of an *impoverishment of our popular and racial substance rich in talent*, accelerated by the most refined means. That would be short-sighted politics. What civilising counter-selection gradually produces, i.e. the extinction and drying up of the good and even the best blood by the simultaneous increase of all that is mediocre, would then be accelerated by conscious processes. What, left to itself, would be a process spread over centuries, would take place in a few decades: a cultured race would see its final concentrated and exalted forces disappear all the more rapidly and dramatically! This would be tragic heroism in the Spenserian sense! Seeing this danger means fighting it by all means.

The reproduction of good people is more important than any cultural selection

Our point of view is clear: Any cultural selection—no matter what means it employs—must be exculpated and justified in the face of the millennial history of our race. In the light of the God-given principles governing our species, it has no reason to exist insofar as it opposes biological laws in a hostile, indifferent or unconscious manner. Voluntarily or not, it encourages the destructive exploitation of the highest and most eminent works of creation. Nature and the creator then apply the only sanction, namely the disappearance, the death of the species. Any conscious selection with its immediate successes, which may be assessed over years and decades, must be able to take place over centuries, millennia and hundreds of millennia. Otherwise it loses all credit with the history of our species and ultimately with its divine creator.

Our right to selection

National Socialism can only conceive of its demand for selection with the aim of bringing it into line with the biological laws of the origin of the species. It must therefore ensure that the idea of selection is defended and applied only in terms of *the entire* National Socialist world view. All its partial and rational applications produce the opposite effect. So far, the SS has become its most suitable instrument. Its laws of order and its institutions are animated by the spirit of biological duty. As early as 1931, the Reichsführer SS promulgated the order on engagement and marriage in this spirit. The SS order of 28 October 1939, concerning the entire SS and police, emanates from the same sense of duty to the race, of submission to the Creator, and for this reason it has been misunderstood and misinterpreted by those who do not think biologically.

Ludwig Eckstein

(Author's note: the order of 28 October stipulates that assistance and support must be given indiscriminately to the children, legitimate or not, of SS personnel who died at the front. The religious and reactionary camps saw this as an intolerable moral violation).

ANNALS No. 2. 1944.
EDITION OF THE SS WALLOON BRIGADE.

FROM RACIAL BODY TO RACIAL SOUL

It is not only because the Nordic man's body shape has certain dimensions in height, width and length, or because it is often characterised by blond hair and blue eyes, that we attach importance to it.

This is not why we value our Nordic heritage either.

Of course, the indications provided by the shape of the Nordic man's body are nonetheless the very basis of our ideal of beauty. This has always been the case in Western history, and for proof of this we need only look at the panorama of works of art produced over the centuries by all the civilisations and "cultures" that have succeeded one another on European soil. No matter how far back in time one goes, one can always find in sculptural figures and paintings evoking an ideal of beauty, the characteristic forms of Nordic man. Even in some Eastern civilisations we find the same phenomenon. While the deities are represented with distinctly Nordic features, the figures of demons or those representing inferior or dark powers have features characteristic of other human races. In India and even in Far Asia, Buddhas are often found with distinctly Nordic features.

That the Nordic racial body represents for us the ideal of beauty is only natural. But all this acquires its real and profound meaning only because we find in it the expression and symbol of the Nordic soul. Without this Nordic soul, the Nordic body would be nothing more than an object of study for the natural sciences, like the physical form of any other human or animal race.

Just as the Nordic body has become precious and pleasing to us as the perfect carrier and expression of the Nordic soul, so we are repulsed by certain Jewish racial cues because they are the direct symbol and sure indication of a Jewish soul that is totally alien to us.

Scholars on the subject tell us that a certain racial physical form and a certain racial soul necessarily go together and that they are, after all, expressions of one and the same thing. However, nothing seems more difficult to us than to demonstrate scientifically or by other means the correctness of this homogeneity between the racial body and the racial soul.

We believe that we must be extremely cautious in this area. In the normal state of things, there is obviously homogeneity and interpenetration between these two aspects of human reality. And it seems to us very difficult to push the dogma of the differentiation of the body and the soul to its logical extremes. The most authoritative representatives of this particular doctrine do not fall into this extreme.

Racial impurity is nevertheless marked, as we can see every day, by inner contradictions between the racial body and the racial soul. There are individuals who undoubtedly possess many of the physical characteristics of the Nordic race and yet do not possess the Nordic soul at all.

However, the essential question is to consider such a situation as absolutely abnormal and even monstrous.

And it seems to us that the transparency between the Nordic racial body and the Nordic racial soul is the true goal of all racial politics and morality.

SS NOTEBOOK NO. 6B. 1941.

TWINS AND HEREDITY

The twins prove the correctness of our racial doctrine

This time the SS Notebooks present an illustration that seems to be considerably out of the ordinary: These are pairs of twins taking part in a "competition for the most identical twins" held in California in 1931. One wonders what such an image, such an expression of the stupid American predilection for sensationalism, has to do with the SS notebooks. The vast majority of the girls shown are not even pretty!

Without question, these girls cannot be said to be at least cute. They were only chosen to entertain a niai audience, and yet this image is extremely interesting, striking and demonstrative.

Why? Because the photographer, with his photograph, has *provided unconscious and very impressive proof of the correctness of the racial doctrine of National Socialism*

At first sight, this statement seems bold. If we study it, we will see the picture in a different light. It shows six pairs of twins that belong to different breeds. The middle pair on the left seems to be of Nordic-Westphalian type; they are girls who are certainly of Germanic origin. The girls on the upper left appear to be Western (Mediterranean). It is also obvious that the other two on the bottom left are of Israelite origin. The three pairs on the right are mixed race, the one in the middle has dominant Indian blood, the upper and lower one mostly Negro blood.

So we see that the six pairs of twins are extremely different as a whole, which gives us a clear idea of the racial chaos in the United States. What is even more surprising is that the two sisters of the same pair are exactly the same every time! They could be switched without difficulty. There is no more difference than if the same person had been photographed twice. An example: they have exactly the same smile each time, which shows the same spiritual and moral character. To distinguish these twins, the mother had to put little red and blue ribbons on them as babies so as not to confuse them.

To us "ordinary" people, the difference between people is so obvious that we can tell them apart without difficulty. But if you meet twins in life like the ones in the illustration, you have the remarkably disconcerting feeling that you can't tell them apart. Meeting this twin brother would then give rise to the following thought: "When I saw you coming, I thought at first that it was your brother. Then I thought it was you. But now I can see that it was your brother.

But there are exceptions: Not all twins are as similar as the ones in the illustration. Let's just think of the ones we can know. *There are two kinds of twins.* In the first kind, the partners have equivalent similarities and differences, like ordinary brothers and sisters. These twins can also be of different sexes. Their origin can easily be explained: every higher living being is the product of the union of an egg cell and a sperm cell. The nuclei of these two cells contain the hereditary heritage. The fertilised egg cell thus has the hereditary heritage of the paternal and maternal sides, which produces a new living being. During a menstrual cycle, the woman normally only releases one egg from her egg supply, which can then be fertilised. In exceptional cases, however, two eggs may be released, each of which is fertilised by a sperm cell and then grows. In this way, twins are born who differ from the usual siblings only in that they grow together in the mother's body. These are "bivitelline" twins.

The creation of exactly similar twins takes place in a very different way. These account for about a quarter of the twins born. For them, they are born from a single egg that is fertilised by a sperm cell. But for unknown reasons, this cell divides at a very early stage of evolution. The two halves each produce a separate individual. Each is the product of a single fertilised egg, and with each cell division, the hereditary heritage is distributed completely equally between the two halves. These twins born in this way have exactly the same capital of hereditary characteristics. They are univitelline twins and therefore, because of their origin, entirely similar human beings from the hereditary point of view. Their frankly ridiculous resemblance is due to their hereditary similarity.

Binocular competition in California, USA.

*In the Third Reich there were no such "contests" expressing a penchant for "sensationalism".
Instead, unadorned and natural femininity was exemplified through such illustrations.*

Ridiculously similar and surprisingly similar fates

The similarity of identical twins can be seen in the smallest details. Two very real examples: A teacher had twins in her class that she could not tell apart. Finally, she was pleased to have found a sign of recognition in the freckles that had recently appeared on the tip of one girl's nose. Soon after, the other girl had exactly the same number of freckles in the same place. It was done again! Diseases (of course only of the hereditary type) can appear and develop in a completely similar way in twins with the same heredity, even if the two individuals have different lives. In the past there were two twin brothers, one of whom became a high ranking civil servant. He lived unmarried in the capital. His brother got married and lived in the countryside as a landowner. Despite these great differences in their living conditions, they both fell ill at the age of sixty. These once serene and healthy natures fell victim to a violent diabetes that caused great mental irritability and later gait disorders. In the course of the illness, both brothers suffered from retinitis and an open abscess on one of their toes, and both died within a few weeks of their illness.

The story of criminally inclined fraternal twins often follows a surprisingly similar course. These twins are sentenced at the same age, commit the same kind of crimes and behave in a similar way down to the smallest detail. For example, after the First World War there were two twins who were known to be swindlers of great style. One of them claimed to have made an invention of unbelievable importance. With his brilliant personality and persuasive eloquence, he was able to interest many people in his invention and to get money from them. However, the device never worked perfectly. He used the money to live a luxurious life. Eventually he was arrested. While he was in prison, his twin brother built the same kind of device, also found gullible people and gullible moneylenders until he was also imprisoned for fraud. In court, they both adopted the same attitude. With astonishing skill, they were able to express themselves and partly convince the jury. They also behaved in the same way in prison and managed to gain a lot of advantages.

There are countless amusing stories about twins. One of the two Piccard brothers, later famous stratosphere pilots, went to the barber as a student, got a shave and declared that he was suffering from extremely rapid beard growth. The barber promises to shave him again for free in case he needs it again that night. An hour later, the same student returns, actually the twin brother, completely unshaven. The barber was astonished to see such a beard growth. He had to shave him for free, as he had promised.

Two sisters used to regularly trick their music teacher when one of them wanted to take a day off. They had their lessons at different times and one of the girls would sacrifice two hours on the same day while her sister had fun in between.

Is hereditary inheritance predominant?

Despite the disconcerting and often fatal resemblance of some twins, it would certainly be a mistake to say that man is solely the product of his hereditary heritage. There are far more than two major groups of causes which determine the nature of man: his hereditary character and the environmental influences acting upon him. Univitelline twins are not completely alike in all respects. Their hereditary characteristics are similar, and the differences they show are attributed to environmental influences. But an interesting and important fact remains: in these univitelline twins who have grown up in a different environment, it is possible to determine the strength and limit of the environment's influences. The extent and degree of environmental influences can be seen. They may give rise to specific differences. But the overwhelming impression that emerges from twin research is that heredity is much more powerful than environment. Now let us return to our illustration. What is the main point of this picture, once we have gained some knowledge of the processes at work in hereditarily similar twins? It shows people who are indistinguishable because they have the same hereditary heritage. Yet pairs of different races show extraordinarily large differences. And now, to conclude:

If the physical and spiritual similarity of these women comes from the similarity of their hereditary heritage, the inequality of individuals and the difference of the human biological groups that we call races come from the inequality of their hereditary heritage. This is precisely the great fundamental idea of our racial doctrine.

Races differ psychically and physically because they have different hereditary characteristics. Their diversity, like that of the individual, does not come from the action of a different climate, different living conditions, different spiritual influence, in short from their environment, but from their different hereditary heritage. In the beginning is the blood. It is thanks to its hereditary heritage that a racially homogeneous people builds its own environment, marks its living space, creates its culture. Equality and difference are thus based on the natural and fundamental process of hereditary transmission. In the rare case of the total equality of men as manifested in univitelline twins, we can formally prove that their concordance is based on the equality of hereditary heritage. But it is also shown that the difference between men and races is based on the difference in hereditary heritage.

We therefore draw the following lesson from this: The hereditary heritage, the race, determines the external manifestations such as thought, feeling and action, the psychic attitude of each individual as well as of each people.

Does the soul escape the influence of hereditary laws?

Many people consider that only the *body is* the object of hereditary transmission, but the soul seems to them to be a supernatural entity conferred directly on the embryo by the Creator. Univitelline twins also provide irrefutable evidence to the contrary. What do they show? We see the same attitude, the same smile, the same crying, the same language, the same coquetry, the same qualities and defects in both twins. When the embryo is split, not only hearts but also souls are split.

The very human feeling that emanates from these univitelline twins seems extremely strong. We have the feeling that we are here in a place where nature lets us contemplate its mysteries in a deep and clear way. It is as if, through the univitelline twins, she wanted to show that she could also create identical men if she wanted to. These rare exceptions make it clear that she wants *inequality,* not equality. Through this inequality of its essence, nature maintains life in potential, pushing it forward.

The men of Roosevelt's country, which is a mortal enemy of the new Germany and of the Führer's doctrine, should see themselves in the face and not with the eyes of people hungry for sensations! The truth also exists there: the truth about the eternal law of blood.

SS BOOKLET NO. 3. 1939.

BLOOD TYPES AND RACES

In the light of the discovery of blood groups, which we briefly discussed in the last issue, their importance for racial science has been greatly overestimated. Thus, it is commonly believed that blood directly determines an individual's racial affiliation. But, as is well known, there are many more than four to six races on Earth. It is therefore quite obvious that the four to six blood types are not sufficient to associate one of the many races with a particular blood type. In fact, the four classic groups A, B, AB, O occur in *all* peoples and races. Blood types are therefore not able to determine whether an *individual* belongs to a race! Classifying people according to *a* particularity—in this case the blood group—leads nowhere. If, for example, one wanted to judge peoples and races *solely* on the basis of the cephalic index, Nordics and Negroes would be related, because both races are dolichocephalic! It is understandable that the importance of the blood characteristic in racial research has been overestimated, as this characteristic at least deserves special consideration. However, in the determination of blood groups, raciology is no less—but not more— present than the first biological procedure, which is qualified to richly complement those which, up to now, are almost solely descriptive and used to measure bodies. Moreover, the blood group of an individual remains constant throughout his or her life and, unlike other bodily characteristics, is completely independent of any action of the outside world.

Although no precise race can be assigned to the four to six blood groups, the discovery of these groups nevertheless provides valuable information for establishing the history of races and the discovery of peoples. It could be proved that the four groups A, B, AB, O are found everywhere on Earth, but that the *frequency of their appearance* is different according to the people and the races. A familiar example will shed light on the problem: If we compare the percentage distribution of blood groups in the German people, taking into account every survey published to date, with that of the 1000 Jews examined, we obtain the following table (rounded figures):

Blood types	O	A	B	AB	
Germans	36	50	10	4	
Jews		33	37	21	9

We find that the values for B and AB are twice as high among Jews as among Germans. The distribution of O's is roughly equal, whereas A is significantly more common among Germans than among Jews.

It is clear that such percentages give a more accurate picture the larger the number of individuals examined. If one were to examine only one hundred men of the SS, one would surely obtain a different picture of the distribution of groups than the one given above for the Germans. An examination of the entire SS would, however, give approximate figures. Data on the distribution of groups within specific countries is therefore very uncertain, because very few nationals of these countries are examined and the choice of those examined influences the results. In any case, *a picture of the distribution of blood groups among different peoples and national entities* can already be drawn today, taking into account the results of previous findings:

An overview shows *a significant preponderance of A-blood in northwestern Europe and B-blood in central and eastern Asia.* However, A-blood and the Nordic breed should not be confused, despite the geographical data known to date, as the examination of a group of East German populations with a majority of A-blood has revealed. In the Europe-Asia area, group A decreases steadily from west to east. It is striking that in *European Russia* there are fewer A's than in the Near East among the formerly northern *Iranians* and *Persians.* This is a clear indication of the push of the Indo-Germanic Nordic peoples towards Asia. As far as B is concerned, there is a preponderance of distribution in *north-eastern Europe* compared to the regions of south-eastern Europe and the Near East. Prehistory and history show that racial elements migrated from Asia to Europe. Regarding the distribution of A in other parts of the world, we find: the preponderance of A outside Europe is found in *Australia, Polynesia,* the Pacific and Japan as well as among the peoples of North Africa. The Australians and Polynesians show some analogy in their physical characteristics with the European parent stock, so that the high preponderance of A in these peoples is not so surprising. Among the *Japanese,* the preponderance of A blood stops after the Ainu, that ancient population of the Japanese islands which also shows a predominance of A, and is related to the European peoples by other physical characteristics. Among the peoples *of North Africa,* the predominance of A blood is consistent with the fact that this region belongs to the Mediterranean and therefore European racial sphere, a membership that may also be partly due to the Empire of the Germanic Vandals, who stayed in North Africa for over a hundred years. As far as B is concerned, outside the Europe-Asia continent, its presence is rather limited in the Pacific and its total absence in Australia. The O blood group *is* so preponderant (90%) among the *Eskimos* and the *North American Indians* who are related to them, that the non-O individuals could only have received their blood group from a foreign influence. There is, so to speak, no AB among them. A and B are so rare that their penetration into the primitive

North American population could be explained by the mixture of races following colonisation. Initially, the Eskimos and the North American Indians seemed to have possessed only O blood. They would thus be the only "pure race" in terms of blood type that we know of so far on Earth.

Since the Indians have such a clearly differentiated blood group, it can be clearly shown here how mixing with other peoples and races changes the original blood structure of a people. This can be seen in the following table:

Blood types	O	A	B	AB (%)
Purebred Indians	91,3	37,7	1,0	0,0
Métis Indians	64,8	25,6	7,1	2,4
American White	45,0	41,0	10,1	4.0

As was to be expected after the mixing of their race, the Indian half-bloods in percentage terms have an intermediate position between the pure Indians and the whites. Where mixing has occurred, intermediate figures are found in the averages. The figures for Eastern Russia suggest a wide mixture between Russians and Finno-Ugric and Mongolian peoples.

Conversely, with the help of blood types, it can be demonstrated whether a people maintains the purity of its blood or not. As it has been proven so far that the gender distribution remains stable over three generations, it must also be assumed that the blood group distribution of a people remains the same century after century, as long as there is no mixing of blood with people of different groups. In fact, it could now be argued that, for example, the "Transylvanian Saxons" who left Germany seven hundred years ago still have the same group distribution as the Germans in Germany, different from that of their Romanian or Hungarian neighbours! The Negroes in America have a group distribution comparable to that of their African brothers. The Dutch, too, in South Africa and the East Indies, have retained the same typology as their brothers in the mother country; the same is true of the English in Canada and Australia. Correspondingly, the distribution is also very striking among the Gypsies—the real Gypsies—who should not be confused with the vagabonds who have blended in here and there with these nomads. The distribution of groups among the Gypsies has nothing to do with that of the European peoples but rather with that of the Hindus. However, the Gypsy language is made up of bits and pieces of all the languages of the countries they pass through, and some words indicate that the Gypsies originated in India. Blood research has proven the validity of this view as the following comparisons show:

Blood types	O	A	B	AB (%)
Gypsies	27-36	21-29	29-39	6-9
Hindus	30-32	20-25	37-42	6-9

This astonishing example shows us how little the blood typology of the Gypsy people has changed, although there is evidence that they have dispersed since the XIII century into countless hordes across Europe, where they have lived their lives as parasites.

Like other hereditary characteristics, individuals within a people can naturally be differentiated by blood group. Thus, West and South Germans differ from East and Central Germans. However, the differences are not as great as between Russians and Germans or between Poles and Dutch. Nevertheless, within certain borders, one can speak of certain permanent figures that are characteristic of the Germans as a whole. Apart from a few local deviations, *all people, as far as the distribution of blood groups is concerned, are homogeneous within certain regions and this homogeneity is also surprisingly constant.*

We see, therefore, that it is quite possible to explain certain racial and national processes with the help of the blood group test.

The study of the properties of the recently discovered similar blood groups M, N, P, S, G, which have not yet been tested in racial experiments, may in the future provide us with a new method of explaining the interdependence between blood group and race.

Paul Erich Büttner

SS Booklet No. 3. 1936.

FOURTH EXAMPLE FROM THE WORK OF SIPPENAMT

This can be added to the third example from the work of the Sippenamt (Clan Office) in SS Notebook 2:

In various parts of Bavaria it is still possible to find the father of an illegitimate child. A man who marries a woman with a natural child often accepts the child as his own. In the 'single parentage contract', which is kept in the state archives, the father of the child is often indicated, together with the date and place of birth.

1 week from 26 April to 2 May 1936

When building a family tree, most SS men reach a "dead end" and cannot go any further. An example will be given of how this situation can sometimes be overcome.

An SS man found that his great-grandmother was born in Lüneburg in 1820. The great-great-grandfather was an owner of the local salt works. In order to be able to go back to 1800, the baptismal certificates and marriage certificates of the great-great-grandparents were still needed. But these were neither baptised nor married in Lüneburg.

The following steps were then taken:

First the death record was sought. But it turned out that the great-great-grandfather had died on 27 September 1865 at the age of 82 years, 3 months, 10 days; thus the approximate day of birth, 17 June 1783, was given, but not the place of birth. A search for the death records of the great-great-grandparents yielded no results.

As the date of death was around 1865, the place of birth was first enquired at the registration office, but the lists did not start until 1868.

The parish priest was then asked to look at the register of baptised people. In this register, next to the note indicating the baptism of an old sister of the great-grandmother, it was written that this sister was born in 1815 in Neusalzwerk, near Minden. This means that the great-great-grandparents probably moved from Neusalzwerk to Lüneburg between 1815 and 1820.

A letter was written to the parish priest in Neusalzwerk near Minden. But the letter was sent back as impossible to deliver.

What could be done, then?

All local registers were searched, but no place with the name 'Neusalzwerk' could be found. As a last resort one could write to the administration of the community of Minden to ask whether this place existed and to which parish it belonged.

It turned out that the present-day spa of Oeynhausen was formerly called Neusalzwerk.

The marriage certificate and the baptismal certificates could therefore be drawn up by the competent parish priest. The date was around 1800.

2 week of 3–9 May 1936

Why hereditary health formulas?

When discussing with SS people how to fill in the hereditary health forms, one often gets the impression that most of them have not understood at all the immense importance of scrupulously providing the required references. What then is hereditary health? Here we come to the familiar notion of health, i.e. the care of diseases, and something totally new, namely the treatment of predispositions for serious hereditary defects. Many will now ask what is inherited? In short, one can say everything that makes up a man physically, spiritually and psychically. His abilities come from his forefathers and he passes them on to his children. It was already known empirically that in every family striking physical characteristics reappear in the course of generations, for example the particular shape of the lower lip in the house of Habsburg, or the great musical talent of certain families. Many illnesses are passed on along with physical characteristics and spiritual abilities. The tragic world of today's insane and crippled asylums is due almost exclusively to these hereditary diseases. Every thinking and responsible man clearly and naturally demands that the most serious hereditary defects be reduced.

The difficulty begins when children and hereditary patients of the same blood have to be diagnosed. Frequently, these are outwardly healthy men who, according to the laws of atavism, may have a predisposition for one of these diseases in their hereditary heritage. The non-expert will not be able to understand at all that an apparently totally healthy man, who has no one in his immediate family with a hereditary defect and who may not know at all that a grandfather was already ill generations ago, can carry this defect in him. And if his spouse also carries the same predisposition, the disease will manifest itself in him or in the child. It is therefore the duty of every individual, out of responsibility to himself and his descendants, to seek advice from a doctor experienced in these matters. To make this task easier for the SS, the hereditary health formulas were created, with which the SS examining doctor advises his fellow soldiers. By means of specific examples, it will be shown that it is impossible for the layman to distinguish between the essential and the accessory in hereditary matters when judging his hereditary health. It is his duty to tell the examining physician openly and faithfully all that he has found out about his closest relatives. The latter can then tell him with the greatest probability whether the children and grandchildren will be healthy. He who omits to mention to the advising authorities the illnesses, deaths and particular events of his ancestors, not only acts criminally towards his future wife, into whose healthy family he brings the disease, but he burdens not only her, but his children and himself with a taint.

Contrary to what many comrades think, the requirements set by the RuSHA are not superfluous. They often result in benign data, but sometimes they also reveal hereditary defects that the individual did not even suspect. Only a qualified doctor can diagnose whether the applicant is a victim of a defect.

3 week of 10–16 May 1936

Many comrades in the country who are trying to get permission to marry will have already railed against the RuSHA many times in their hearts or even openly.

For example, such a person would like to get married quickly. So he sends in his papers and wants the matter to be settled as quickly as possible. To speed it up, he may even have already provided a lot of detailed information, such as a specialist doctor's report on the minor defects in his fiancée's eyes or a certificate of a required dental treatment. Believing that he has really done everything, he confidently awaits further developments in the case.

He is totally reassured, because everything is almost settled and there is no singularity in either family. A "no" answers all the questions in the health questionnaires; there is a question mark only for one uncle; because at the parents' house, it is known that this uncle appeared in court because of an arson attack; but he was not convicted and died shortly after.

So this case is obviously benign. And when, indeed, a letter from the RuSHA arrives, he opens it with a joyful heart because it should contain the hoped-for marriage authorisation. But then he is disappointed: "For the thorough study of your request, the RuSHA needs :

1. a certificate on the fatal accident of your fiancée's grandmother;
2. Further information on your uncle who appeared in court because of a fire. Name, date and place of birth, as well as the court of law; in addition, criminal records may be required.

First of all, there is a lot of irritation with this letter and its obviously secondary demands. One almost feels like sending a strongly worded letter and saying everything one thinks. But in the end, the matter is urgent and the data required is gathered willy-nilly. The findings are interesting and surprising for the SS inexperienced in medical questions of hereditary biology, and even more important for the RuSHA medical specialists.

The grandmother, whom the fiancée had only heard about from her parents, was not the victim of an accident, but in fact committed suicide. She had always been a peculiar and individualistic person, the parents reported on this occasion.

And the surprising thing is that his own family members, when asked about the uncle, tell him something completely similar. They say that he was an original who could not be trusted, and who often did incomprehensible things which he himself could not explain.

Thus, the apparently minor research reveals a fact that surprises the fellow student himself, but which the RuSHA advisers know the full significance of. From these indications it can already be assumed that in both cases, in the grandmother of the fiancée and the uncle of the applicant, the symptoms of the same hereditary mental illness are present. This assumption is confirmed by the criminal records produced. It appears from the forensic report that the uncle was not convicted because he was insane. He was not transferred to an insane asylum as planned because he died earlier of pneumonia.

Thus, it can be seen that the blood relatives of both future spouses have the same hereditary disease. Thus, because of the hereditary transmission of these diseases, it is very likely that both intended spouses carry the predisposition for this disease within them. Even if nothing is detected in them, there is a great danger that in the common children, the internal pathological predispositions of both parents add up and the disease reappears.

What comes out of this? Both fiancés should be advised against marrying because the danger to their children would be too great. However, it can be agreed that each of them should marry another healthy person in whose family the disease is not present. The child thus no longer runs the risk of receiving the same pathological predisposition which, through such a repetition, would cause the disease. Other hereditary diseases also have other types of transmission that must be taken into account when diagnosing a possible danger to children. It is therefore important to have precise data on the diseases of the clan members so that the doctor can form an accurate picture.

4 week of 17–23 May 1936

During the investigation of a marriage application it was discovered that an uncle of the applicant was deaf and dumb. Further information revealed that this uncle was hereditarily deaf. As the deafness affected an uncle, this defect is not very serious for the applicant. Further research also revealed that the bride's mother was deaf. A refusal should have closed the case if a repeated search had not revealed that the bride's mother had suffered from scarlet fever in her early youth; the doctor treating her in hospital reported that she had lost her hearing as a result of a scarlet fever injury to the middle ear. This was not a hereditary deafness but the consequence of an infectious disease. This changed things completely. The application could be approved because the defect was only on one side and not on the other. The children of this marriage will have the highest probability of being healthy.

Nature creates species, it does not create beings. The species is the end; the being is only the servant of this end. It is characteristic of the individual to deceive himself about his destiny and to believe that he was born for himself.

René Quinton

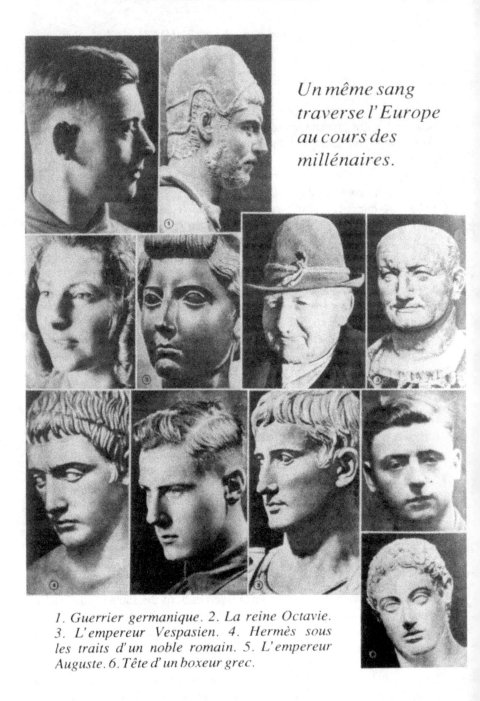

Un même sang traverse l'Europe au cours des millénaires.

1. Guerrier germanique. 2. La reine Octavie. 3. L'empereur Vespasien. 4. Hermès sous les traits d'un noble romain. 5. L'empereur Auguste. 6. Tête d'un boxeur grec.

SS Notebook No. 3. 1944.

Untitled

In front of you stands a horse. Do you like the animal? —I would like to think so. It's not just any horse either. It is particularly beautiful, noble and distinguished and belongs to the Lipizan breed whose family tree goes back to classical antiquity.

Why do you like this animal so much? Why are you happy to meet it? Why does its sight enrich your soul?

Strange questions, you may think; you don't need to ask yourself why you like a horse, such a magnificent creature. Why do I like him? Simply because he is beautiful; because he is harmonious in size; because everything about him is in harmony, the trunk, the head and the legs; because his coat is plain, his colour elegant, his movement supple and his gait proud.

All this is true, but I want you to speak to me in a different way, to tell me not the reasons for your satisfaction at the sight of these horses, but those that remain deep inside you.

What makes you able to feel the beauty of a horse? What qualities in you allow it? I know you can answer this question easily too—you say it's your sense of beauty, your instinct? Right, but more precisely? —So your sense of breed!

You see, it's not so easy to realise the obvious; I had to ask many "silly questions" to finally get the most relevant answer. This is often the case with the simplest things. The rest seems so obvious and easy. Such simple solutions are called eggs of Columbus. The solution to the race question is also an egg of Columbus. Today, it is hard to imagine that our ancestors could have occupied themselves for centuries with the cultivation of plants and the breeding of animals, albeit with sacred zeal, while completely forgetting the obvious, i.e. the cultivation and preservation of the purity of their own race. Although one may be persuaded daily to the contrary, the erroneous doctrine of the equality of all men peddled by an alien faith was held to be true for centuries. It is fortunate that our people were strong enough that the majority of men and women chose spouses of equal value. Otherwise we would have long since fallen back to the stage of the French promoting the mixing of races in a totally irresponsible manner. It was the Führer who first brought the divine necessity of a racial order back into the consciousness of the people.—in the moment of the greatest tragedy, in the ultimate moment. We must always remember this. Let us never forget these facts: the Führer had to impose his doctrine in the face of a hostile world; a Hans Günther was covered with scorn and sarcasm because of his racial doctrine. And isn't the present war mainly due to the fact that the opposing world, still living under the domination of the ideologies we defeated, fears the disturbing force that this knowledge reveals and provides us with?

Now you see the splendid horse again, comparing the two points of view. SS man, SS woman, rejoice in creation; drink in the beauty of this world with all your senses. But always be aware of the questions that God asks you through his manifestations. For there you will always find the fundamental answer that must determine your life. Questioning and finding answers is the characteristic of those who live on the threshold. We see behind us the centuries when those who had a strong hold on souls gave false answers and forbade questioning.

Our hard destiny is to provide the ultimate answer with the blood of the best, so that after us a generation will grow up that knows how to follow the right path without questioning the reasons for victory or defeat. Success depends only on each of us, on our lives and struggles,—and above all—on our recognition of the reasons, the necessities and our faith rooted in the awareness of serving the most sacred mission.

H. KI.

Lipizan horse.

SS NOTEBOOK No. 6. 1944.

THE SOLDIER'S ATTITUDE TOWARDS FOREIGN WOMEN

You are an SS, which means that you are not a mercenary. The latter was recruited for pay to fight for something that did not concern him. As an SS man you defend your people and your blood. You are also defending the SS, a community, an order within your people, which has made it its special task to keep the blood pure and to raise the value of the race. Therefore, when you find yourself in a foreign country, with a weapon in your hand, your duty is twofold: you must defend your people and the SS with dignity.

Yet you behave without dignity when, in the uniform of an officer wearing the insignia of the Reich and the SS, you stroll through the cafés and bars with those girls and women who don't care about the grief and pain of their people because they have no heart. You are right to think that they are not honest girls and women. For these girls whose brothers, these women whose husbands have been defeated by you and your comrades, will certainly not jump at your neck with joy. You must therefore be perfectly aware of what this flighty company will bring you.

What right do you have to rigour if you let yourself go? How can you maintain sound judgement and proper posture if you lose self-respect? During this war, many of you have the opportunity to take on more responsibility than you could have in peacetime. You will have to prove yourself worthy of those responsibilities. We know that you are brave in battle. That you all want to learn to be proud, disciplined and sober, even when you are not in line for battle, is what we all hope for the future of our people.

I will also tell you what you should do when you have read this. You have a keen eye, a brave heart and you understand what that means. You may also know that one or other of your comrades does not behave as he or she should. Until now, you have turned your head away and thought it was none of your business. Believe me, it is your business, it is our business. Try the path of true fellowship first: take your friend aside and talk to him sensibly. Tell him what it's all about. Tell him that the hour of destiny has come for all our people. Remind him that the Führer needs all his men.

Always think that you will remember for the rest of your life the months and years when you wore the SS runes on your jacket. For a German, these years are the most decisive in his life. Not only because the young SS volunteer becomes a man, his chest expands, his step becomes stronger, his eyes open to the outside world, but also because his mind is formed and he learns in the SS community what he will always carry with him: order, discipline, probity, punctuality, sacrifice and solidarity. Do not spoil this memory by thinking that you are not failing in your duties as your people expect you to do. If you neglect these things, you are doing yourself the most harm.

There was a time when people proclaimed "the right to dispose of one's own body". It was a time when the marriage of a black man and a white woman, the union of a German and a Jew, was blessed, and when those who killed a child in the womb if its birth bothered the parents were protected.

But the champions of that era, whom we defeated in Germany thanks to the Führer's fight, are now facing us tenaciously on all fronts.

When you let your body and your blood do what your desires dictate, then you are helping the opponents of our people and our ideology. When you dominate yourself, you will be in the truth because you will find the strength and pride to live according to the laws of your people, of your SS and of those you defend.

He who corrupts his blood, corrupts his people.

SS Booklet No. 2. 1938.

Racial Issues in the United States

The conquest and colonisation of the United States of America represents a migration of peoples that far surpasses any that has been carried out to date. Just as the colonisation of South America was carried out by the Romance peoples, the colonisation of the northern continent was the work of Germanic groups. The English and Germans were the main pioneers in this young country. The French portion should not be underestimated, but it is of a purely historical character and remains without influence on the development, culture and racial physiognomy of the country.

According to the record of colonisation itself, after the new state had gained its independence from the mother country, the influx from the Old World increased. Between 1820 and 1935, thirty-two and a half million people emigrated from Europe, five and a half million from other countries. Here too, the Germanic element predominated. The British led with about nine million, the Germans followed with six million. At that time, the predominantly Nordic peoples accounted for a total of approximately two thirds of European immigrants.

It is worth remembering these facts when we speak of a northern America. We think of our own blood flowing in this nation and the blood of other peoples who are of the same race as we are. We cannot therefore remain indifferent to the evolution of North America, and to the question of whether the racial heritage is being preserved or squandered.

The great Nordic peoples of America are the most threatened, first of all by the coloured races they have welcomed into their midst; in addition to this, the role played by the peoples of Eastern and Western Europe is one that has increased extraordinarily over the past decades and contributes to the transformation of the original racial image.

It is well known today that the Negro question is the crucial problem for the United States. Twelve million Negroes and half-breeds of Negroes make up a total population of about one hundred and twenty-three million (1930 figures). This is one-tenth of the population. Half-breeds were also considered "Negroes" in the 1930 census, including those with only a small amount of Negro blood, the "near whites", as well as half-breeds of

Negroes and Indians; unless Indian blood predominates, in which case they are generally considered Indians. According to reliable estimates, half-breeds account for about three-quarters of the total negroid population, and only one-quarter are pure-bred negroes. It is precisely this large number of half-breeds that endangers the existence of the whites, for it is primarily to them that the white race transmits a lasting hereditary heritage and not to the pure negroes. They also bring coloured blood into the white people.

In 1619, twenty Negro slaves from the West Coast of Africa were brought to Virginia for the first time. North America thus followed the example of the South, which had already made use of this cheap labour force in the plantations and mines 100 years earlier, as the Indians were too weak as beasts of burden. This is how the mixing of the white and black races began in the South. The Dutch ruled in Guiana—they also behaved in a similar way in the Dutch East Indies and South Africa—and the French in Haiti. The white servants, who at first outnumbered the slaves and were mostly hired on an indentured basis to work for years or to pay for the crossings with labour, first had affairs with the negroes. There were therefore more frequent marriages between white women of the lower classes and Negroes. Even today, the majority of black-white intermarriages are between white women and Negroes or mulattoes. Soon the planter aristocracy followed the example of this lower social class. While, out of self-preservation, white servants were forced over time to increase the distance between themselves and the slaves, the all-powerful slave-owner was able to maintain quiet relations with the coloured maids without fear that his rank or plantation discipline would suffer The coloured "mistress" and her mulatto children were a general institution on the plantations. "Many slave owners were the fathers or grandfathers of some of their slaves," said Reuter.[1] Later, when a mixed-race class with a majority of white blood—quarterons and octavos (one-quarter and one-eighth Negro blood), who were often well-to-do and whitened by Western civilisation—was born, the number of illegitimate liaisons between whites and free mulattoes expanded considerably in the large cities.

The political and social demands of the black population grew in proportion to its increase after the abolition of slavery—it must be remembered that its numbers have risen from one million in 1800 to twelve million today and are increasing by one million every decade. But the defence of whites was proportionate. The Southern states were the most ardent defenders of the colour line, and they were the first to erect a barrier between whites and coloureds in social and racial terms.

Before we turn to the measures taken to defend the States against racial mismatches, we must take a look at the sociological and racial relations

---

[1] Reuter, *The American race problem.*

between the "Negroes". It has already been said that pure Negroes constitute only a quarter of the population and that the majority is made up of half-breeds of all shades, from the half Negro to the octavo. The level of education, the social situation and the political demands are therefore also different.

The pure Negro is culturally and socially at the lowest level. The cultural and social position of the mestizo also increases with the higher proportion of white blood—and the rejection of blacks. The more white hereditary heritage a mestizo possesses, the more radically he distances himself from his racial fellow citizens. He looks at them with disdain, feels better than these 'negroes' and strives to find a woman who is preferably even whiter than he is. He finds himself placed between the races, denying the inferior race and not being accepted by the superior. From time to time he succeeds in penetrating the white race and if he does not succeed, then perhaps his children can. Thus, in spite of all the barriers, Negro blood enters the popular white body, even if it is diluted. Easy entry will be possible where the racial image is already coloured by Mediterranean or Oriental types.

The half-breed does not always aspire to be admitted into the white race. A number of intelligent mulattoes have sided with the negroes and become their leaders. Just as the former deny their Negro blood, so they deny their white blood heritage. They want to be Negroes, to preach the racial consciousness of the Negro man, and to attribute to the Negro the same intelligence that they possess—certainly by virtue of their white origin. This is their trump card: they claim that in spiritual performance, the Negro is capable of accomplishing the same things as the half-breed. It is an undisputed fact that more than four-fifths of all important "Negroes" had little Negro blood, and thus that the white blood heritage dominates in the Negro ruling class.

A large proportion of the Negroes emigrated to the north and to the big cities at a very early stage. In 1930, 43% of them were already there. New York was home to about 330,000, Chicago to more than 230,000 members and descendants of the Negro race. Living conditions were more favourable for the Negro in the north. He is not exposed to social banishment and restriction of his political rights as in the South (since the Civil War, he is an equal citizen on paper!) His life is also safer in the North than in the South. Between 1885 and 1924, 3,165 Negroes were lynched, more than nine-tenths of them in the southern states. Despite emigration to the north, the South is still extremely negrified today. Mississippi leads the way. More than half of its population (50.2% compared to 58.5% in 1900) is of Negro blood. Next comes South Carolina with 45.6% and the three states of Georgia, Alabama and Louisiana with an average of 30–40% Negroes or mulattoes. No state is without Negroes. Neither the Northeast nor the North Central still show the healthiest relations.

The United States of America has taken a stand against racial mixing. It did not want to absorb the Negroes and form a melting pot of races, as in South America. Measures were taken early on in the most dangerously threatened southern states. It is not necessary to discuss here the historical development of racial legislation, but only the law in force today.[2] Comparisons with the progressive racial legislation of the Germans are obvious.

Firstly, it must be said that this is not racial legislation in the German sense, which prevents the birth of half-breeds and thus the enlargement of the half-breed group in all cases. The prohibitions in force were not only aimed at *marital relationships between whites and coloureds*. Illegitimate sexual relations—the most common racial smear because it is the most difficult to control—are not legally prohibited. (As an opposite example, Italy prohibits sexual relations between Italians and natives, while mixed marriages are not punished for the sake of the Curia.) Similarly, marriage, and of course illegitimate relations between mestizos and various races of colour, are not prohibited. Some Indian tribes were an exception, as they were to be protected from interbreeding with Negroes.

Nor is there a uniform racial law across the Union. Out of forty-eight states, only thirty have enacted bans on mixed marriages. These are mainly the southern and western states. The Northeast remains passive in this area.

When we look closely at the relationship between the black population in each state and racial legislation, the following can be established:

Of eighteen states with more than 5% Negroes, seventeen have banned intermarriage (exception: New Jersey). It can therefore be said that here the racial-biological necessity has been taken into account. The remaining states with less than 5% Negroes do not show the same trend.

---

[2] Excellent research is presented by Krieger: *Racial Law in the United States*.

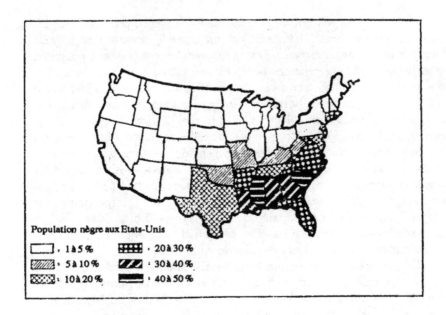

Population nègre aux Etats-Unis

☐ : 1 à 5 %   ▦ : 20 à 30 %
▨ : 5 à 10 %   ▨ : 30 à 40 %
▧ : 10 à 20 %   ▬ : 40 à 50 %

Of the fourteen states with a Negro population of 1–5%, only five prohibit intermarriage, while the remaining nine do not seem to be convinced of the need for such a measure.

In contrast, eight of the sixteen states with less than 1% Negroes voted against mixed marriage.

This lack of unity regarding the main conception of the racial question was also apparent when it came to defining the concept of "Negro" in the spirit of the marriage law. In one case, half-breeds, including up to a quarter, in ten cases half-breeds, including up to an eighth of blood, in three cases proof of a trace of Negro blood, and in sixteen cases people of "African origin" or "coloured race" are generally referred to as Negroes—the drawing of the borderline is left to the discretion of the courts.

An octavo can thus marry a white partner in the state where the boundary between white and black goes all the way down to the quarteron, and finally mixed marriages can be concluded between whites and coloureds of all kinds in states where there is no racial legislation. This shows that this barrier too can complicate legitimate racial mixing, but cannot prevent it.

Let's summarize again:

There is no legal way of preventing the racial mixing that takes place through *illegitimate* relations between the white civilised people and the negroids. Nor is there any way to stop the growth of the mulatto population through legitimate or illegitimate liaisons within it and with other coloured races. Nor do the intermarriage prohibition laws of a number of states provide sufficient protection against racial interbreeding.

North America will not be able to solve the Negro problem with the measures now in force. The mestizo population will increase year by year. Firstly from its own substance, and secondly from the constant possibility of existing and future relations between whites and coloureds. Added to this is the aggravating fact that the white ruling class, as elsewhere, is suffering from a declining birth rate. Finding a solution will be difficult. The old project of sending the Negroes back to their African homeland always resurfaces: but twelve million men do not allow themselves to be so easily removed from a civilised environment which, for them, has become a place of life, to return to the one from which their ancestors were torn three hundred years ago. And the unsuccessful experience in Liberia does not encourage repetition. Added to this is the fact that the transplantation, the "repair" would have to be carried out against the will of the vast majority of the Negro population. In addition, there is the influence, in Africa itself, of the natives and the holders of colonies and mandates.

Nor can we abandon to the Negroes the southern part of the Union invaded by them and settle further north in a defensive position. But we can—as a temporary measure—create a really general racial legislation which shows both the most enthusiastic white Democrat and the most ignorant Negro that it is not advisable to break down the barriers which nature has created. And, against the increase of the Negro and half-breed population, the will and vitality of the White race can at least be mobilised.

Apart from Negroes, the United States is home to other racial groups. There are the former masters of the country, the Indians, numbering 330,000; in addition, there are 1,400,000 Mexicans, 140,000 Japanese, 75,000 Chinese, about 50,000 Filipinos and a few thousand Hindus and Malays.

The fate of the Indians is well known. Their almost total extermination is a troubled chapter in the history of the white conquerors. If today their number has risen above 330,000 again, they are not all pure Indians and there are a number of half-breeds. The main areas of Indian expansion are the southwestern states of Arizona, New Mexico and Nevada where they represent between 5 and 10% of the total population. The smaller number of Indians and their descendants, the drastically smaller gap between whites and Indians and the deferential opinion of whites for North American Indians resulting from their courageous attitude at the time of the conquest did not create racial opposition and racist measures as it did with regard to Negroes.

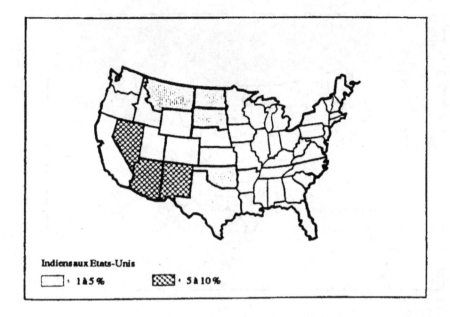

Indiens aux Etats-Unis

☐ · 1 à 5 %   ▨ · 5 à 10 %

There, only seven states prohibit intermarriage between whites and Indians and their descendants. Of these, some of the southern states have less than 1% Indian population, so relatively few, while the states with 1–10% Indians—with the exception of Arizona—have not banned intermarriage. The attitude of the southern states is explained by their unpleasant experiences with Negroes. They take precautions in all cases. In a certain State, only Indians and half-Indians are not allowed to marry; in two other States, Indians and half-breeds, including octavos, in the rest of the States, a trace of Indian blood is sufficient to exclude them, and generally they are referred to as Indians and descendants of Indians, and the decision is then left to the courts.

A special chapter should be devoted to the Jews of North America. About four and a half million Jews live in the United States—and they live perfectly well. Nowhere else in the world do Jews enjoy such a dominant position as in this democratic country. They did not participate in its discovery, they came later, when the age of fighting was over, replaced by the age of capital. It would have been difficult for them to integrate into the ruling classes earlier, but when a new world order was established, which classified people according to their money, the original restrained attitude of 'society' disappeared completely. The depraved hate campaign that could be (and still is) freely waged against National Socialist Germany shows how strong the influence of the Jewish element is on the other side of the ocean. Therefore, no one will expect to find racist measures against non-native Jewry. Nor are they subject to restrictions in the immigration law. They are listed as guests of their former nation, as "Germans", "English", "French"!

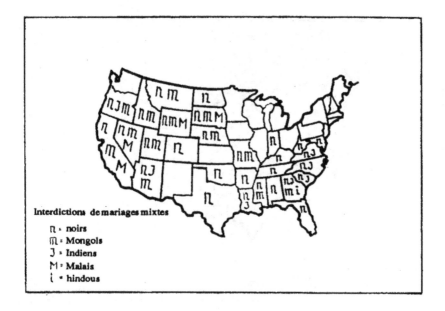

Interdictions de mariages mixtes

n · noirs
m · Mongols
J · Indiens
M · Malais
i · hindous

Finally, a word on the selective effect of immigration laws on European applicants. The current regulations (quota law of 1924) are intended to curb the influx of elements from southern and eastern Europe. This means a return to the Indo-Germanic forces that created the northern continent and which cannot be renounced in the future. America must not leave the group of great Nordic peoples. It follows from what we have just read that Americans today are not racially the same people as they were a hundred years ago or earlier. Madison Grant, the champion of the Nordic idea in America, estimates the present share of the Nordic race in the United States at 70%, compared with 90% at the time of the Revolution. This may be considered an exaggeration, since he underestimates the proportion of Nordic blood in the German people. But it is not a question of numbers, it is a question of ideas. It is a question of the importance of race for the life of the people. And it is good to see that voices that confirm our world view are crossing the oceans.

SS-Ustuf. Dr Karl

SS BOOKLET No. 4. 1938.

ROMAN CHURCH AND RACIOLOGY

In Italy an extraordinarily interesting discussion is taking place. For the first time since the existence of the Fascist Party, there is talk of the need to consider national and historical questions in a racial way.

The milieu that gave rise to this impulse and demand consisted of a group of prominent Italian university professors. Thus, this innovative ideological vision had already found some credit. It could not be ignored and it was not. Its importance was immediately recognized, as it allowed for a modification of the overall picture of the state that fascism had created for itself, or at least for a broadening of the essential points of view. While ideology, especially racial ideology, was the driving force of National Socialism from the very beginning, Fascism initially defended only state objectives and demands. The great Italian past, above all antiquity, had a major influence on its spiritual vision. Apart from that, it left a lot of room for the religious activity of Roman Catholicism, which held a predominant position in Italy. Seen in this light, Fascism's very recent stand for the Italian race and for the Aryan racial community signifies a revolutionary advance whose historical repercussions cannot yet be foreseen.

The Roman Church was quicker to react to the Fascist comments than the customs of Vatican politics would suggest—for one of its basic principles in politics is to wait. The Pope himself used an audience with students of the missionary congregation at his summer seat in Castel Gandolfo to speak out categorically against any racist remarks. It is often forgotten that he said, among other things, that *the whole human race forms one great universal human race*. He went so far as to suspect that Fascism was imitating German racology.

"One has to ask oneself", as he literally said in his speech, "why by misfortune Italy needed to imitate Germany".

The response to this aggressive warning was bound to come. While *Starace,* the Party Secretary, had admitted the validity of the racial demands to the university professors, none other than *Mussolini* himself approved their consideration. His brief and pithy reply to the Pope was soon known in Germany:

"Everyone must know that we too will walk into the future from the perspective of the race question. To say that fascism imitated anyone or anything is simply absurd."

The discussion in Italy is therefore not yet over, but it is nevertheless being conducted in a strict and direct manner, because the Church is continuing the fight against racology in a covert manner; with increased efforts, because no issue seems so dangerous as racology for the Roman Church, for its credit, its influence and its existence as a religious society, as we shall see.

At a time when these questions have taken on a particularly topical dimension, it seems quite justified to ask, through careful examination, what relationship the Roman Church has with racology. This attitude is not at all as clear as it seems at first sight if one considers the completely authentic statements of the pope. The ecclesiastical positions on raciology even reveal a rather confused view.

Certainly, the Church expresses in this way its constant biblical mission to preach Christianity to all peoples. This mission is the basis of the Roman Church's will to universal power, which can in no way tolerate a racial difference between peoples, especially in terms of religious feeling, and a difference in racial *value*. But on the other hand, the results of German racial research are of such scientific value that an unconditional refusal by the Roman Church would lead to a significant loss of prestige for the Church in Germany.

Copernicus also had to disprove religious dogma with his scientific results. It was Copernicus, not the Church, who was right in the eyes of history. The Roman Church is in danger of having to lower its voice in this matter one day because of its relentless struggle against racism.

It is thus faced with the choice of making itself laughable in the face of history by rejecting raciology, or of abandoning one of the most important conditions for its international effectiveness by recognising it. The *worldwide* Roman Church provisionally decided in favour of the first choice, which was only possible as long as raciology and its practical application remained more or less limited to the German area. The Roman Church in *Germany* has taken a different path.

But before we come to study the episcopal and therefore ecclesiastical positions, let us mention the publication of the Roman priest and university professor Wilhelm *Schmidt,* whose attempt to "refute" raciology from a scientific point of view is interesting in more than one way. Schmidt is the Roman scientist who dealt with raciology in a particularly detailed, if only superficial, way.

But the results he arrived at in his book *Race and People do* not correspond to those of racial science, nor to the fundamental principles of the National Socialist world view. The method he used is certainly extremely simple, scientifically not only criticizable but also perfectly condemnable. In particular, he seeks—albeit perfunctorily—to pit each representative of racism against each other. In this way he achieves the results he needs for his religious conviction.

On page 33 he comes to the conclusion that 'physical qualities have not been shown to be overt racial characteristics' and draws the conclusion that 'yet the racial doctrine defining everything spiritual as "racially determined" and based on physical qualities, totally collapses'.

When considering the relationship between moral qualities and race, Schmidt becomes even more superficial as he simply appeals to the Church's doctrine that 'the soul is a proper, autonomous substance, which in turn has no hereditary relationship, not only with any body but also with no other soul, nor with the souls of the parents, but each time God recreates it for each individual' (p. 41).

Schmidt concludes this passage of his book with the most simplistic statement:

"The soul as such is not bound to any race, nor does it have any earthly homeland.

Since, in Schmidt's view, there is therefore no hereditary transmission of psychic and physical qualities, he could have spared himself the trouble of giving these explanations. Instead, he has revealed through his sometimes extremely clear reasoning which particular points of raciology cause problems for the Roman Church. Schmidt defends himself against the fact: "that race determines *all* human experience; it could be that it embraces only specific areas and that there could even be a racial difference that is expressed in certain areas of one race as well as another" (p. 53).

And on page 56, it says:

"One must emphatically reject the conception ..., asserting that each of these (racial) types has its own sensitive faculty and its own morality appropriate to it, so that this morality entails, so to speak, duties ..., just as there are truths recognised by men of all species, so there are also general human standards of morality which result from human nature and can only disappear with humanity itself" (p. 56).

These positions are revealing, for they clearly show what gaps the Roman Church considers a threat to its own doctrine. If, as raciology asserts together with ethnology, proto-history, Germanistics etc., it should be true that each race can only have a morality adapted to its nature, that for example the Nordic race cannot observe the same moral laws as the Jewish race, if it is capable of the greatest creations, then there is no place and no justification "for general human norms of morality which result in their own right from human nature. By general human standards of morality Schmidt refers in particular to the morality of the Roman Christian doctrine.

Schmidt is aware of the impossibility of really wanting to refute raciology in a serious way. And so his own aim is not to deny raciology at all, but to tear its claws out and make it harmless. At a conference in Vienna, he made this clear:

"Race and people can only take their value from the deist faith in the One Creator who created all men from one origin. Both are further transfigured, purified and strengthened in the Christian-Catholic religion, which fully accepts the many duties arising from belonging to a race and a people, gives them moral character and gives men the strength and will to fulfil them.

This is the sound of the melody that is being sung in accordance with all ecclesiastical statements in Germany. This means that the Church deliberately claims to accept the values of race, people, nation and love as the highest "natural" values intended by God. Above these merely "natural" values, however, would rise the "supernatural" values of divine grace, etc., which are meant to diminish, polish and thus perfect the simplifications and exaggerations of natural values. A practical example of this view can be found in the "Catholic Missions", where it is stated in the booklet No. 3 of March 1938:

"She (the Church) accepts man as he is with his race, his people, his nation, his State, in the region where the creative will of God makes him grow, approves therefore all these creative forces stemming from blood and soil. But we cannot and will not forget one thing. The man of today, above all the delivered man, no longer lives in "pure nature". Redemption and supra-nature are a reality and through this reality nature has entered a new order. The consequence of original sin is that people exaggerate and defend natural values. Whether it is humanity, freedom, law or race; the Church will always contain these escalations in the place they occupy in the divine and absolute order of value. They are therefore in no way reprobated; they are merely given an exact place in everything that has value.

To show them their exact place is the watchword by which the Church achieves her greatest success, where she has the greatest, best, most skilful and most tried and tested experience. When, in all ages, the Church has not succeeded in spiritually suppressing these currents which are foreign or even hostile to her nature, because she neglected the right moment or did not have the strength to do so, she still has a means which almost always enables her to triumph: assimilation. It simply accepts values that are foreign to it, inverts and falsifies them until they fit its own system, gives them a place in its scale of values and renders them harmless, while at the same time being able to disseminate them as its spiritual property. A manifesto of the "Bavarian Clerical Leaf" of January 23, 1935, provides evidence of an unparalleled insight:

"The meeting of Revelation and race belongs precisely to the most attractive chapter in the history of the Church. The race was the instrument, Revelation was the melody, Christ the artist. And so, the Church, inflamed by Revelation, had from time immemorial the finest flair for perceiving all real biological values.

(Only his current pope seems to have lost this flair!) After reading this, one can only be amazed!

We do not wish to close these accounts without at least one more episcopal statement. On the occasion of the memorial speech of Bishop Bares in the Hedwig Church in Berlin, Bishop Machsen of Hildesheim said the following about the exact place of raciology:

"It is absolutely impossible for a Catholic bishop to deny all that relates to the notions of people and country, all the values of blood and soil. Religious knowledge gives us the certainty that the flesh rises again and thus confers on our body and its values a dignity that makes them approach the divine. According to the teaching of the Church, nature is the basis of faith—and so from supra-nature we lay the foundations not only for biological and ethnographic questions, but also for social ones... This view of faith thus provides us with an accurate view of the nobility and dignity of human nature. The notions of blood and soil find a hierarchical place and thus have the possibility to flourish organically.

All these examples clearly show that the Roman Church is unable to escape the influence of raciology in Germany. Outside Germany, in a world dominated by the Church itself, by liberalism, which is at least related in this respect by its egalitarian doctrine, or by Marxism, rejections of raciology are heard, even to the point of outright hatred, which testifies to a resentful impotence.

We do not quote articles from anti-German Catholic immigrant newspapers, but instead give two examples from a book published in Switzerland in 1935 in which, without concern for any facts, purely political demagoguery is expressed, although Roman bishops are among its contributors. In this article, the Bishop of Debreczen invites racial theory to "keep within the narrow limits of its childish nature", and in the article by N. Berdiajev, it is said:

"Both the racial and class theories—mean the intrusion of polytheism into social life; they—the racial theory to a greater degree than the class theory (!)—are incompatible with Christian doctrine and lead to confrontation with Christianity. Both theories are not scientific hypotheses but idolatrous myths within an atheistic and godless world."

We quote the following passage from this work mainly because of its unspeakable silliness and clumsiness, its pleasant humorous effect, rather than for its practical importance. The author draws the appalling conclusion from the erroneous assertion that Zoroaster was an Oriental prophet, to whom Nietzsche gives the famous words "I beseech you, my brothers, remain faithful to the earth..." in his work of the same name:

"Racial theories are therefore (!!!) only a phase of Orientalism; they must be seen as an attack on the heart of Western culture, on the belief in the power of the mind over the body, and must be fought.

In view of such enormities, which can only be interpreted as political and which are understandable on the part of the Roman supporters, one must state with astonishment that even the Vatican offices, which usually show some diplomatic skill, address and flexibility as soon as they feel prompted to speak out on raciology, adopt a tone that hardly differs from that of their emigrant colleagues outside Germany.

The Cardinal and Secretary of State of the Pope had the opportunity to speak twice in 1935 about raciology, once in his closing speech for the celebrations of Lourdes, the French pilgrimage site, and the other time in his congratulatory text addressed to Cardinal Schulte for his 25th episcopal anniversary. In Lourdes Pacelli explained:

"With their claim to proclaim a new wisdom, they are in reality only deplorable plagiarists who clothe ancient errors in new clothes... Whether they are obsessed with the superstition of blood or race, both philosophies are, however, based on principles which are contrary to the Christian faith."

And it says in the text of congratulations to Cardinal Schulte:

"When false prophets with Luciferian pride arise, claiming to be the bearers of a new faith and a new gospel that is not that of Christ, then the hour has come when the bishop, neither pastor nor mercenary, strengthened by his office and his oath that unites him since the day of his blessing to the faithful souls, must raise his voice and repeat fearlessly and inexorably the word of the apostle before the High Council:

"Judge for yourselves whether it is right to obey you more than God!

This tone betrays a nervousness that reflects a trait of character that is also found in the above-mentioned speech of the Pope; this nervousness stems from the fact that the Church suspects that the racial worldview is capable of changing the image of the world and of history even more strongly and radically than it did in the past through the results of Copernicus' research. In any case, it is thus affected more seriously and in depth.

In a letter from the Congregation of the Seminary and Universities of the Roman Curia in Rome to the rectors of the Catholic institutes subordinate to it, the Vatican returns to its old judicial and doctrinaire tone, but remains absolutely intractable in this matter. In this letter, which is a regulation inviting to fight against all doctrines of raciology and its applications, it is said:

"What touches our Holy Father in an extremely painful way is the fact that impudent blasphemies are reported to excuse this injustice, and that by the dissemination of very pernicious doctrines presented as science, although they wrongly bear this name, they seek to confuse minds and extirpate true religion from souls."

The following principles are particularly to be condemned:

2. The strength of the race and the purity of the blood must be preserved and maintained in every possible way; everything that leads to this goal is therefore good and worthwhile.

3. The blood containing the racial type delivers all the spiritual and moral qualities to man as its main source.

6. The first source and absolute measure of all legal rule is racial instinct.

The book dates from April of this year. Fascism's profession of faith in raciology has not yet been able to change this position. The Church still seeks to maintain its old position. It will seek to maintain it desperately until it has to move down one place. But there is no doubt that one day it will have to move backwards all the way.

SS-Schaf. Horst Pabel

IV. PEASANTRY, ECONOMY, SETTLEMENT

SS BOOKLET NO. 3. 1939.

THE BIG QUESTION FOR GERMAN YOUTH

It is a fact that all the achievements of a people, its culture and its works, will only benefit it and remain its own if the historical creators of these achievements remain. Works of art of a great civilisation can still exist: just think of the history of Egypt. It is then only a matter of chance that these historical documents are found a few centuries later. Even if the people, as such, concerned by these works of art are no longer alive because their blood has dried up, men populating the country and feeling themselves to be its heirs can still exist under its name. However, they are not the physical descendants of the original creators, but at best the bearers of a name; they no longer possess the creative power of the original blood and are therefore often no longer able to manage their traditions, let alone understand and perpetuate them.

The Hellenes are a good example. Of course, we still know them today through their works of art. We know from their works of art that the Hellenes were once a people, but despite perfect state institutions, they were unable to prevent their blood from drying up: the Hellenes of the classical era no longer exist today, their blood has disappeared or merged with foreign blood. Because the Hellenes began to despise procreation, they no longer have any descendants who bear witness to the actions of their carnal ancestors. Only the blood relatives of the German-German sphere have been able to rediscover the cultural documents of the Hellenes and understand their ancient meaning. *Without the sister blood of the German civilisation, the Helladia would have long since fallen into oblivion.*

The Chinese people give us the opposite example. *The religion of this people prescribes to preserve their blood by numerous descendants:* it is the very basis of their religiosity. In spite of all national and natural catastrophes, the Chinese people have survived the millennia and contradict by their very existence all the intellectual considerations of the West on the birth or disappearance of a nation. Any idea of fatal decadence, in the sense of Oswald Spengler, is shattered in the case of the Chinese fact and its vitality.

Perhaps we can better explain the opposition that exists in the evolution of these two peoples, Chinese and Hellenic, if we remember that Lycurgus, admittedly mythical but nonetheless brilliant creator of one of the most perfect Hellenic legislations, of the Spartan State, was unable to save Sparta and make it last until our days because the Spartan blood in the meantime ran dry. In contrast, the descendants of Confucius are still living today, and he can be considered a *contemporary of Lycurgus, and* has had a decisive influence on the spiritual and moral attitude of the Chinese. They live today in the same place, in the same court where Confucius lived and worked in his time. In the 77^e generation, the descendant of Confucius still bears witness to the exploits of his brilliant ancestor, while non-Hellenes—German researchers—are trying to recreate the legislation of a Lycurgus and its survivals with delicate and meticulous work. *Confucius did not understand state building, but he instilled in the souls of his people the will to live forever, proclaiming that the fulfilment of his religious faith lay in the child and that eternity would be his, not only in his works but in his living identity and descendants:* Lycurgus certainly built the state of Sparta, unique in history, but he forgot to impose on his people the will to eternal life through descendants and, as a consequence of this vital law, to perpetuate the creation of his state through the perpetuity of blood.

The question of the survival of a people by the laws of life is essentially whether a people has "the will to survive forever by giving life to a new generation and in its future descendants; it is also a question of whether the people submit to this vital law of blood or whether they no longer have the spiritual, moral or physical strength to do so.

It is remarkable, but historically irrefutable and conclusive, that all peoples of Indo-Germanic or Germanic character have survived only insofar as, in addition to their knowledge of the laws of blood, they have not neglected their ownership of their own land and property and have survived only as long as they could remain peasants and recognised themselves as such.

The Germans enter European history as peasants, and their peasant way of life is so characteristic that they avoided colonising the Roman cities and settled outside the cities in the open country. In the atheistic world of the decadent Roman Empire, which had fallen entirely under the control of a Jewish plutocracy, the Germans created a new peasant-like land law. If anything can prove the peasant origin of the Germans, it is this Germanic land law within the Roman Empire.

These considerations and observations show us our duty today. We Germans have entered history under the aegis of Germanic laws. We must therefore respect the laws of Germanic blood if we are to survive and not condemn ourselves to death. But the legitimacy of Germanness has its roots in the peasantry. At the dawn of history, Germanness was born of the peasantry, and it was from the peasantry that it drew the sacred power of eternal life. This is the fundamental law of Germanic legitimacy.

If we are now facing the problem of rural exodus, *it is not so much a question of our food policy.* Nor is it an agricultural issue. The rural exodus is simply the problem of *the existence and destiny of our nation.* For for the first time in its history, our people must decide whether they want to separate themselves from their peasantry or identify with it. The problem of the peasantry is not a social problem, nor even a corporate problem as many people think, but a question of blood and therefore of the continuity and future of our people. Only the youth will be able to solve this problem, because only they will face it and will have to decide whether they only want to profit from the present historical years or whether they want to be the faithful managers of them. *German youth must decide clearly what they want to do and what they can do in these circumstances. It must advance with inflexible rigour and determination along a clearly defined path. But Adolf Hitler's National Socialist youth has been accustomed to follow him so far in other matters of our national political existence.* This is all that can be said to German youth about the desertification of the countryside if one still wants to trust their soul and their dynamism.

(With the permission of the editors of *Volonté et puissance*, issue 6 of 15 March 1939).

SS-Obergruppenführer R. Walther Darré

SS BOOKLET NO. 3. 1939.

THE BASIC LAW OF THE GERMAN PEASANTRY

"The realisation of the fundamental thought of national politics awakened by National Socialism, which finds its expression in the theory of "Blood and Soil", will mean the most profound revolutionary transformation that has ever taken place! These were the words of the Führer a few weeks before the decisive victory of the National Socialist liberation movement, on 3 January 1933, in his speech to the NSDAP Agrarian Policy Congress. The first step in this direction was the implementation of the Hereditary Domain Law on the harvest day of the German people, reunited by National Socialism. The work had already been prepared in detail and in detail during the power struggle by R. Walther Darré and his colleagues in the NSDAP's National Agrarian Policy Department. Only two months after Darré's appointment to the ministry was it possible, in addition to the basic plans for the regulation of the market, to present the Hereditary Property Act to the Führer.

The day this law came into force is more important than one might think. On that day, the Führer told a delegation of farmers in Berlin: "The condition of German farmers is not only an occupation for us, but the representation of German vitality and thus also of the German future. These words are the key to understanding the Hereditary Domain Act. In order to give all those who have recourse to this fundamental agrarian law a clear picture of its aims and guiding ideas, the Reich Government prefaces this law with a foreword so impressive that it is worth any summary or exegesis. Here it is:

"In order to protect the old hereditary traditions, the Reich government wants to preserve the peasantry as the racial origin of the German people.

Farms will have to be protected from indebtedness and inheritance fragmentation, so that they always remain the heritage of the clan, in the hands of free peasants.

A fair division of the large estates will be necessary, for a large number of viable small and medium-sized farms, if possible spread throughout the country, will be the best defence of the health of the people and of the state.

The Reich government therefore enacted the following law. Its main idea is as follows:

An agricultural or forestry estate of the size of an acre and less than 125 ha is a hereditary farm if it is owned by a professional farmer.

The owner of a hereditary estate is called a peasant.

Only a German citizen (of German race or equivalent) of good character can be a peasant.

The hereditary estate is bequeathed without division to the principal heir. The rights of the co-heirs are limited to the peasant's other property.

Privileged non-heir descendants will receive vocational training and equipment commensurate with the size of the farm. If they were unjustifiably victims of fate, the state would come to their aid.

The birthright shall not be abolished or restricted by reason of death.

The family farm is fundamentally inalienable and cannot be mortgaged.

This foreword, together with Dr. Harald Hipfinger's remarkable, very clear and comprehensible introductory letter (Reichnährstand-Verlag, Berlin 1938) on *the law of inheritance of farmers in the Reich*, are more important than a programme proclamation. In accordance with the precise wording of the law on agricultural inheritance, and if there is any doubt as to the application of this law, they should serve as a guide for the conduct of important decisions.

It is clear from the foreword that the leaders of the National Socialist State consciously based the Reich Agricultural Heritage Act on the old hereditary right which has its origins in the law of the Odalic era. R. Walther Darré has shown in his seminal work *Peasantry as the Source of Life of the Nordic Race* that this ancestral hereditary right of the Nordic race provided a vital link between blood and soil, that it has always been the law of the peasant peoples of the North, and that its violation meant the death of the nation in the long run. This truth prevented the National Socialist government from merely generalising the inheritance customs still existing in many German districts. This would have been a dangerous half-measure, for these customs already meant, in a decisive area, a capitalist alteration of ancestral hereditary law.

The fundamental idea of hereditary law, the unique transmission of the agricultural farm as the very basis of the peasant family, from generation to generation, has often been maintained only arbitrarily in hereditary practices. In fact, the farm was regarded as a capital asset in the inheritance and divided among the heirs in such a way that the main heir who took charge of the farm had to pay substantial compensation to the other heirs, or else mortgage his farm heavily. It is typical that in regions with preferential heirship customs, more than a third of the farm debt was owed to liabilities arising from inheritance disputes. It was not uncommon for a conciliation to be impossible due to the excessive claims of the co-heirs at the time of the inheritance, forcing the farm to be overvalued. In other places, the peasantry tried to avoid the destructive effects of this alienation of land into capital by reverting more and more often to the system of double or even single offspring. The Reich Hereditary Estate Law did away with this possibility by ensuring an unencumbered, complete succession to the preferred heir, preventing other children from claiming compensation, in the form of land, mortgages, or money.

The firmness of this no-compromise solution was interpreted as unfair severity towards the co-heirs by those who did not understand the deeper meaning of the Reich Inheritance Law: the necessary assurance for the peasantry of a fundamental, strong and intangible reason for living as the racial source of the nation. A quick examination shows that this criticism is wrong. First of all, it must be recognised that in no case are the other children disenfranchised from the main heir, as these critics claim. On the contrary, the Reich Agrarian Law explicitly grants them the following important rights:

1. The right to a proper education and maintenance on the farm until the age of majority.

2. Right to vocational training in the farm's speciality.

3. Entitlement to furniture to be provided at the time of their settlement, especially for female descendants on the occasion of their marriage.

4. Right to recourse to the nation in case of undeserved distress.

These requirements are naturally limited by the size and production capacity of the inherited estate and therefore do not depend in any way on the arbitrariness of the principal heir. As a rule, it is not he, but the father himself who meets these requirements. The great improvement in the law of agricultural inheritance compared to the previous legislation is precisely the fact that the absence of any financial burden in the inheritance allows the farmer to work for his children from his earliest years. He is no longer obliged, as before, to spend his best creative years paying off inheritance debts. All his energy is freely used for the good of his children. It is nonsensical and malicious to claim that the Agrarian Inheritance Law, because of the alleged handicap it imposes on co-heirs, obliges the poor peasant to have an only child. On the contrary: only the agrarian inheritance law guarantees the peasantry the full affirmation of its vital energy.

Equally aberrant is the claim that appears from time to time that the Reich Agrarian Law prevents the allocation of the farm to the most deserving of the heirs. This law is by no means a rigid and schematic regulation. It consciously takes into account the various old customs of the land. In no case is the farmer's power of decision excluded if, after careful consideration, he is convinced that another son would be better suited to take over the farm than the legal heir. In regions where, according to old customs, the right of first-born or the right of the youngest child prevails, the farmer will in any case have to request the agreement of the probate court in order to designate a son other than the principal heir. If his plan is based on established facts, he will receive the full approval of the court, as it is composed of peasant judges like himself.

The other higher public authorities governing inheritance matters are also peasant courts. Thus, the application of agricultural inheritance law is, to a large extent, in the hands of the peasants themselves, especially since the agricultural leaders have been deliberately involved in the process. This ensures that the practical application of the law of succession will be in line with the farmers' sense of justice and will take into account the contingencies of peasant life. This is all the more important because the law of succession is not a rigid set of paragraphs, but merely lays the foundations according to which agrarian judges will define and shape the law and thus contribute to the creation of a realistic peasant status. In this respect, the law represents a revival of the old German legal concept of the reign of the dead letter and makes the judge entirely responsible for the application of the law to the letter.

The fact that the agrarian courts worked in coordination with the agricultural leaders to ensure that peasants who had forgotten their duties or who were incapable of doing so were brought back into line or sentenced, shows the extent to which the peasant judges were aware of their responsibility. The steely determination of the law of succession in this respect is characteristic of the National Socialist conception of property. The law of succession takes every conceivable measure to safeguard agricultural property. Therefore, if it is not to degenerate into the granting of privileges, it must firmly uphold the principle of right. Ownership entails a twofold obligation: the maintenance of the hereditary estate as a sufficient means of living for a large family, and its best use as a source of food for the German people. A peasant who abandons and allows his farm to wither away lacks loyalty both to his clan and to his people. It is not only those who complain about the restriction of property brought about by the agrarian law who overlook this fact, but also those who speak of a privilege granted to the peasantry. In the German conception of justice, right and duty are mutually dependent, so that the peasant right is inconceivable without its corollary, the peasant duty. The right of inheritance was established with due regard to the vital importance of the peasantry as the racial source of the nation. For this reason, a strong protection of the hereditary estates, the foundation of healthy peasant families, was established. The peasant who is unaware of his duty, or who is unable to do so, jeopardises this objective and is detrimental to his family and his people. That he neglects his duty to feed the nation at the same time makes his fault even worse. If, therefore, National Socialism does not wish to jeopardise its aim of protecting the agricultural racial source, it must, in such cases of dereliction of duty, concern itself with re-establishing the concept of right and duty. The way in which the Inheritance Act operated indicates that it was able to combine defence and creation in its punitive measures.

Thus, the State Inheritance Act appears to be the basic law of the German peasantry in every respect. The criticism that arose at the time of its introduction has become very muted. The common sense of the peasantry has long since understood what the law of inheritance means to them. It would have been astonishing, moreover, if the limited view and the ever-present misunderstanding had not sought to quarrel with a law as far-reaching and fundamental as this law on agrarian succession. After all, the chorus of critics has served, albeit unwittingly, to highlight the importance of this law. "The solid fund of small and medium-sized peasantry has always been the best protection against social diseases. So says the Führer in his book Mein Kampf. The law of inheritance established the principle of the development of the peasant force, whose characteristics Walther Darré underlined with these very apt words: "A peasant is one who, rooted hereditarily in the soil, cultivates his land and regards his activity as a duty to his generation and his people.

Günther Pacyna

SS NOTEBOOK NO. 5. 1942

PEASANTRY

Even if the peasant behaves outwardly like a city dweller, wears white linen every day, has a piano and furniture in a nice room, this does not change much in his innermost nature. He is still a peasant, he thinks like a peasant and acts like one. Even if he has relations with city dwellers, has relatives and friends in the city, he considers them all as men of a different species, of a different nature, not as neighbours. This notion only concerns men who are on the same soil, who think and live like him. In the best of cases he becomes a good friend, just as we may be with a particularly distinguished representative of a foreign race. But between him and all the fellow citizens who do not break the earth with the ploughshare, do not mow the stalks of wheat, there is always a wall that cannot be broken down.

Even where, as in the vicinity of the big cities, peasants and townspeople live together in villages, there is no relationship between the two. Peasant pride is too great; even the servant is prouder than the city dweller who lives in a colourful villa and owns a carriage and a car.

This pride is well-founded, because the peasant forms the people; he is the holder of civilisation and the guardian of the race. Before the city existed with its varnish, the peasant was there. His family tree goes back to the time when the stone pickaxe loosened the soil. The peasant brought about the first culture and established his customs where, until now, hordes of semi-wild hunters and fishermen led an existence comparable to that of the wolf and the otter.

Then came the peasant with his pastures, marking out the site of the house, driving posts into the ground, covering it and binding it with solid walls. As he drew the flames from the three sacred woods on the stone hearth, he took possession of the land in the name of civilisation. For it was first the peasant who created what we call this. The fishermen, hunters and wandering shepherds have no—or only a little—culture. He was precisely the holder of civilisation. The Edda, Tacitus, the rich apogee of architecture at the time of the great invasions teach us how great his civilisation was. The furniture of the ancestors, which once adorned the home of the German peasant and is now amassed in museums, is also a trace of this. The foundation of all culture lies in the peasantry.

The peasant knows this well, not just as an individual, but as a community. For the individual does not only have a memory; whole strata of the population also possess a faculty of recollection that is infallible, more faithful and more solid than inanimate objects such as stone, parchment and paper. The strength of this memory says:

"Before you were here, you people of the city, rich or poor, big or small, I was here. I broke up the earth, I sowed the seed, I created the field through which you can live and grow with your activity, your trade, your industry, your relationships. I invented the law, I gave the law, I repelled the enemy, I carried the burdens for millennia. I am the tree and you are the leaves, I am the spring and you are the stream, I am the fire and you are the glow. These were his thoughts, which he could rightly utter.

Where would we be if the peasant had not had strong bones, strong nerves and pure blood? Hunger, plague and war would have destroyed us. We would never have recovered from the Thirty Years' War. And who would retain our innermost essence? Would the German spirit have survived without the thatched roofs of the villages?

Hermann Löns

SS BOOKLET NO. 8. 1939.

CONVOY TO DEATH

Anyone who knows how to interpret the signs of the times can only see migration from the countryside as "the convoy to death". A German writer used this striking phrase as early as a century ago to describe the so-called "rural exodus ", to which the Minister of Agriculture, SS-Obergruppenführer R. Walther *Darré,* has recently drawn the attention of the *entire* German people. In his great speech on Reich Farmers' Day, he rightly addressed *all* German agricultural workers. In no way is the purely agricultural sector of the German political economy alone affected by this migration. On the contrary, it must be made very clear here that this *is a problem that will decide the fate of the whole of Europe.*

What exactly is a "rural exodus"?

For a long time now, science has been addressing this problem; experts in agricultural policy have been talking and writing about it. The question of what the rural exodus actually is has been answered in a variety of ways. Some saw it as migration, others as a *problem of agricultural labour.* The Minister took a firm stand against the latter view, pointing out that "the problem concerned the sons and daughters of peasants just as much". From 1885 to 1910, out of a migration of 3,578,000 peasants, 2,019,000, or 56.4%, were self-employed, while only 43.6% (1,559,000) were agricultural labourers.

To the assertion that *all* migration cannot be regarded as a rural exodus, we must oppose above all the mission that has been given to the peasantry to be the source of German blood. We have known for a long time that the cities are doomed to death without the uninterrupted flow of population from the countryside. Berlin provides only 43% of the births it needs to survive. The average for German cities is 58%, and even for small and medium-sized towns it is only 69%. In the countryside, only ten years ago, 13% *more* children were born than were needed for natural renewal. So only the countryside is really growing, and only the current from the countryside is keeping the cities from withering away and dying. Burgdorfer's calculation that after the fifth generation of Berlin's 4,000,000 inhabitants there would be barely 100,000 left in the capital of the Reich is well known. Less well known is the calculation that after five generations, only 20,400 of the 750,000 inhabitants would remain. The example of Vienna tells us nothing else. In the last five years (1933–1937) 58,000 children were born there, *but* 122,000 inhabitants died. Therefore, as long as we do not want to leave the cities to their own fate as far as their survival is concerned, we must allow some migration from the countryside.

One should be wary, moreover, of this idea of "flight" included in the word exodus, for exodus is understood as a disordered, aimless flight that should lead to defeat. The overflowing power of the rural birth rate can never be considered as fatal. The only thing that should be considered as rural exodus, which is harmful to both the political and the rural economy, and harmful to the entire population, is the *disproportionate* migration of the population from the countryside to the city, as long as it is not a question of the natural *overflow of the* rural population, but rather of a persistent amputation of this population.

A thousand-year-old history

Moreover, the rural exodus is by no means a product of modern times. Even in Rome there was a rural exodus in the past. The Middle Ages also suffered from it on several occasions. In any case, there is not a single region in Germany where "desertification", i.e. the gradual abandonment of estates, does not indicate a real abandonment of the peasantry from the end of the 14th century to the beginning of the 16th century. In Hesse, for example, around 40% of the rural settlements disappeared. On the other hand, ploughed land and grain land were reduced in favour of meadows and forests. Even a non-specialist expert knows that the "lack of profitability" of agriculture, higher taxes, the difference in price between agricultural and industrial products (today we would say the undervaluation of agriculture) were the cause of rural deprivation at that time. There was a rural exodus also in the following centuries. Thus, the records of the Prussian chambers of agriculture constantly mention the shortage of agricultural workers.

In Mecklenburg in the 17th and 18th centuries there were constant reports of the need for labour. However, it was not until the middle of the last century that the rural exodus became alarmingly widespread.

The deep roots

We must name here the root causes of the rural exodus in Germany which has never ceased since: the alteration of Stein's agrarian legislation by the Freemason and friend of the Jews, Hardenberg, an alteration which uprooted a large number of peasants from the land and turned them into a class of landless and propertyless agricultural workers; the fragmentation of the common property which took away from many small farmers their supplementary means of existence; the transformation of the farmer's share into payment in kind or in money, which could not compete with the general growth of trade; the new techniques of farming, the cultivation of sugar beet, the threshing machine, etc., The employment of foreign workers (437,000 in 1914) invaded entire regions, lowering the level of cultivation and remuneration of German farm workers. Mecklenburg worked with them for two thirds! But above all, it was the capitalist spirit, the liberal land laws, the fragmentation and consequent poor distribution of property in certain regions that were the primary cause of the rural exodus. The distress of agriculture, which often stemmed from the fact that it was devalued, and the prosperity (real or only apparent) of industry have always provoked a strong rural exodus because, in these cases, the demand for industrial workers swallows up the agricultural working class and, on the other hand, the development of the factories of large-scale industry forces peasants to leave their land. Thus, at all times, many conditions came together, varying according to place and time, or even the migrants themselves, to determine this exodus. When questioned, 50% of the migrants once gave low wages as the reason for the exodus, often due to a lack of money from employers. The rest of the respondents blamed the lack of opportunities for advancement, the increasing difficulty of creating a family, which often leads to forced celibacy, the long and irregular working hours, the hard work in the fields. In the end, the distractions of the big cities proved to be attractive here and there. Bismarck said it best: "It is the café-concert that eats away the earth".

Millions are lost

Having shed some light on the nature of the rural exodus itself, we can now give a numerical picture of it. There are no really irrefutable figures, either for the past or for the present. The fact is, however, that *millions of people have deserted the land* since this devastating human flood reached the peasants. A comparison between the 15.9 million farmers in 1882 and the 13.6 million at the time of the seizure of power in 1933 gives us, for this half-century, a *total loss of 2.25 million, which is in* fact much greater, since the natural growth of the population is not included. According to another estimate, 1.5 million agricultural workers have migrated to the city since 1907. That's more than the entire population of Thuringia. Since industrial regions are always very attractive and industry in north-east Germany has generally not developed very much, the rural exodus is often presented as an *east-west migration, which* is significant for the occasional figures on this exodus. East Germany lost 3.5 million people between 1840 and 1910:730,000 East Prussians, 600,000 West Prussians, 750,000

Pomeranians, 675,000 Silesians, 880,000 Posnians. Silesia lost more than 20%, East Prussia even more than 50% of its birth surplus and the loss due to the rural exodus in Eastern Pomerania was 378,000 people.

Similarly, a comparison of the percentages of our urban and rural populations in relation to the overall population gives us a shocking picture. The expansion of the "city, a sterile machine" shows better than any phraseology where the rural exodus of our people has led us and will lead us again. From the Middle Ages to modern times, 90% of the German people lived in the countryside, and in 1816 around 70%; in 1871, on the other hand, the urban population accounted for 14.8 million people, almost 36%, and in 1934, even 76.5% of our population! The number of people living in large cities rose from 5.5% in 1871 to 30.4% in 1932. In 1871, one in twenty Germans lived in a large city, in 1933, on the other hand, almost one in three.

The rural exodus since the takeover

The Minister of Agriculture, in his Goslar speech, again emphasised that the rural exodus persisted despite all the measures taken to combat it; he noted, in view of the figures given by the workers' book statistics: "There was, in 1938, an available agricultural workforce 400,000 workers less than in 1933. Taking into account that Darré estimated only 300,000 people for the workers' families not included in the statistics and the surplus due to population growth, he arrived at an estimate of *700,000 to 800,000 people for the labour force lost to agriculture.* The last of the citizens can therefore perfectly understand what the rural exodus means if one is willing to see the consequences.

The consequences for the household basket

The consequences of this rural exodus can be divided into two main categories, depending on the two tasks assigned to the peasantry. Since the peasantry was once entrusted with the task of feeding our people, the exodus poses a threat to our food policy. The peasantry has so far been able to avert this danger largely thanks to the unimaginable readiness of the rural population to do its part in this task. In fact, in the last two years, 21 million more working days have been provided for "pickaxe cultivation" alone, even though the labour force has decreased in number. However, a sensible person will see clearly that there are limits set by fate. Any setback in the area of "safeguarding German supplies" must grip every city dweller's stomach and, because of the lack of bread at breakfast, must remind him of the existence of the rural exodus, even if his own industrial enterprise and thus his labour force "intensifies". For, 'without work in the fields, the people end up starving'. Or, as the representative of the East Hanover district put it so well: "Every citizen, even if he is a millionaire, will starve if there is no one to plough, sow and harvest". If one accepts, as pointed out above, the impact of the rural exodus on the city dweller's shopping basket, the decrease in the agricultural labour force evokes the "*ghost of the regression of agricultural production".* The significant decline in milk production, for example, has shown the damaging force of the rural exodus. In any case, Darré sufficiently drew the attention of his audience in Goslar when he said: "If the permanent staff of the farmers were ever to be drawn away by the rural exodus, it would become difficult to train, even with the available volunteers, new qualified personnel".

Irreparable damage?

We will be forgiven for not continuing to describe the consequences of a rural exodus in the area of food. In particular, its increase would prevent the peasantry from being the lifeblood of the nation. The big cities are the cemeteries of the people and any migration towards them is basically a convoy to death. The average urban family dies within three generations. The rural exodus *indirectly* dries up the source of life for the peasantry in the cities, but it also constitutes a *direct* danger for them. The Minister of Agriculture has made our point quite clear: "The situation of the land workers, especially the lack of female labour on the farm, is now making it impossible for the German peasantry to have many children because of the increased workload. Although the countryside, and in particular the peasantry, is still ahead of the city in terms of the number of births, the situation created by the overwork of the peasant woman has made the real aim of our agricultural legislation, which is to guarantee many births in the countryside, barely achievable. It must be shown with the utmost rigour that the situation in the countryside is taking a turn in this direction which may cause irreparable damage to the people as a whole.

Just as the effects of the rural exodus from the point of view of national biology represent a danger that can hardly be overestimated, the same applies to a national policy for the border regions. For a stranglehold by foreigners only occurs where the human bulwark of the peasantry begins to break down. The great danger of a German exodus from the border areas is shown by the fact that the number of Poles, for example, in the minority villages of the former Posnian March in West Prussia increased by 7.9% between 1913 and 1937. On the other hand, it was calculated that five cantons in this former province had suffered a loss of about 12,000 people due to emigration. In the rural municipalities there was a 15% decrease in population. For the migrants themselves, the consequences of the exodus are harmful: the apparently higher salary in town is often not enough for the same food requirements and is largely squandered on expenses unknown to the farm worker (travel, entertainment, accommodation, etc.).

What needs to be done to combat this exodus?

It would be beyond the scope of this study to list all the measures taken by National Socialist agrarian policy against the rural exodus. The deep roots of this type of exodus were eradicated by means of a consolidation of the rural patrimony (hereditary farm law) and a modernisation of the peasantry. As the relationship between the problem of the agricultural worker and the rural exodus was also identified, the modernisation of German agriculture was largely directed towards agricultural workers, who were given 45% of the newly created farms. The improvement of living conditions through the construction of more sanitary workers' housing, the regulation of their working hours and minimum wages, the creation of opportunities for advancement, and the expansion of "seasonal employment" also contributed to combating the rural exodus. The Year of Agriculture, the National Agricultural Service, and the raising of cultural standards of living helped to counteract the rural exodus. If, in spite of everything, the call of the city was stronger, the fault does not lie with the agrarian policy of National Socialism. It must be attributed to the reasons mentioned above, which SS-Gruppenführer Dr. Reischle summed up in the short formula "that the rural exodus was caused by the current depreciation of agricultural labour".

The rural exodus, enemy of the Party

One thing is certain, and here too the Minister of Agriculture showed us the way: "The rural exodus cannot be stopped by economic or legislative measures alone, but only if the NSDAP, with its knowledge of blood and race, resolves unwaveringly to fight it under all circumstances! Darré further explained that victory over the rural exodus "would be a decisive test for the NSDAP" and, pointing to those in authority as "the real protagonists of the end of the very idea of the exodus", he called the rural exodus "an enemy of the Party" whose defeat could no longer be a matter of class or permanent organisation. This fight against the rural exodus is the business of the Party, as the Gauleiter of Eastern Hanover quoted above said, and must be led by it with great energy. This will be the fulfilment of the Führer's demand, which he formulated at the Party office demonstration on 6 March 1930: "The state has the duty to raise the economic and cultural level of the peasantry to a degree commensurate with its importance for the whole people and thus to remove one of the main causes of the rural exodus. Every SS man is called upon to fight in this direction, according to his means!

Jost Fritz

SS BOOKLET NO. 2. 1938.

ECONOMICS AND IDEOLOGY

The task of the economy is to support the state in its struggle to safeguard the vital principles of the people.

In the liberal age, no area of life has moved further away from our ideology than the economy. But since the economy is made up of human actions and results, and since any worthwhile action is only the result of a strong ideology and a responsible way of life, economic activity must also be the mark of a specific ideology and way of life. Even today, many 'practitioners' scoff at this requirement. It is seen as 'fuzzy idealism' or 'romanticism', when they demand harmony between economy and ideology and claim that the economy follows its 'internal law', which has very little to do with ideology.

The 'internal law' of the economy

National Socialism rejects such ideas because it has the good of the whole people constantly and everywhere in view. It clearly recognised that the term "internal law of the economy" was intended only to prevent the political management of the economic tasks of our time, which was regarded as an "unjustified encroachment of the state into the economy". *But it should not be forgotten that the consequences of this law were the absence of political authority, the collapse of the international economy, the misery of the peasantry, the scourge of unemployment and the annihilation of the people's purchasing power, thus the total destruction of the economy.*

When, on the other hand, National Socialism declared that the necessary political authority and control of the economy are the basic principles of all economic policy, it did away with the chimera of the internal law of *the economy. The economy, too, can know only one law: to serve the good of the people.* The more it follows this law, the more it submits to the vital needs of the people, and this makes it all the easier to establish a concordance between ideology and economy. *For serving the people is the supreme law of our ideology.*

When we try to outline in a few words the whole of our ideology, the following principles emerge: *we believe in the law of soil and blood, the law of duty and honour, and the law of the people and the community.* If we look at the past economic form and compare it with some of our fundamental laws, we must agree that practice and economic science have not recognised these laws. The dominant economic liberalism was much more in line with the English thinking of the eighteenth and nineteenth centuries and. The economic founder of this vision was *Adam Smith.* These ideas were as destructive in Germany as those of the French Revolution from the West. Even today, this English doctrine is often referred to as "classical" in Germany, which is more or less the same as calling parliamentary democracy a "classical" form of constitution. Today, this concept can no longer be considered to have any real value. Unfortunately, the ideas of the English school still prevail in the field of economics.

The pioneers of a German national economy

At the time, it was completely forgotten that a national and particular economic conception had also emerged in Germany. Friedrich List had disapproved of Adam Smith in the strongest terms. Gustav Ruhland had castigated the destructive consequences of the exploitative capitalist economy in his *System of Political*

Economy, previously published by R. Walther Darré. However, Ruhland was ignored. List was indeed favourably quoted, but his refutation of the English doctrine was not taken seriously. Finally, the great German philosopher Fichte, who had laid the foundations of patriotic liberation in his *Discourses to the German Nation* and who had presented important suggestions for economic policy in his "Autarkic Commercial State", was not taken into consideration.

But a wrong lifestyle necessarily develops from a wrong doctrine. *Foreign ideas can never produce a life-style that benefits the people.* This is shown by the economic development before 1933.

The decline of the German economy

It was precisely in the economy that the assimilation of the Jews had the most disastrous consequences. While the foundations of any truly characteristic form of life and economy should be the goal, pride and duty, the type of the honourable merchant was replaced by that of the cunning tradesman. The peasant, whose work feeds the people and thus represents the basis of all economy, was described as inferior and despised. The social situation of the worker, who was increasingly adopting the idea of class struggle, was getting worse by the day. It was crushed by the palaces of the big banks and department stores. Capital, whose task was to serve the economy, was entrusted to its masters and the management of capital itself was handed over to anonymous powers. People spoke of the "infinite extension of the economy" and neglected the large tenement buildings and the slums of the big cities that they had created. They spoke of the "international economy" and failed to see that the internal foundations of the economy, the peasantry and the working class were terribly affected economically. The basis of the German food and raw material economy abroad had been changed because import and export were not carried out according to national points of view, but remained subject to the arbitrariness of the individual. The fact that the international powers had got their hands on the most important raw materials was overlooked. But also overlooked was the fact that the economic war against Germany had begun in 1914—and was continued in a different form. Germany's tribute payments on the basis of the Dawe and Young plan, the private indebtedness of that country through a policy of foreign borrowing, the sudden deduction of short-term foreign credit in 1931 brought the whole front system crashing down. The boycott of Germany, but at the same time the entry of foreign capital, was in fact the most important economic struggle of all time.

National Socialism as the foundation of a new order

By saving the peasantry and the workers with the first four-year plan, the Führer thus laid the foundations for a new German economic order which could only be created on German soil by German labour. The second four-year plan logically continues this creative work: increasing efficiency in all areas of the economy, managing the foreign economy, organising work according to national goals, protecting and improving purchasing power and thus national power through responsible price management. All these measures are designed for the people and for the protection of the country. The second four-year plan encourages the people to work and express their determination, sets great goals that arouse the moral will of the individual and the creativity of the community in the service of the nation, and thus shows that the struggle is the origin of all that exists.

A new attitude, the result of a new worldview, is also beginning to emerge in Germany in the economic sphere.

SS-Hstuf. Dr Merkel

SS Booklet No. 2. 1939.

Underestimating the Agricultural Result, a Danger for the People!

The role and spirit of the SS is to take a clear and distinct stand on all decisive issues affecting the future of the people. This attitude is necessary, even though it might be convenient to "stick one's head in the sand" and ignore everything. The task of every SS person is not only to be aware of this stance, but also to argue for it at every opportunity.

When the propaganda chief and Party comrade Goebbels indicated that one of the most urgent tasks of the Party was to engage clearly in the fight against the "rural exodus" and the "undervaluation of the importance of the agricultural result", the SS thus received the signal to attack!

The question of rural exodus has already been studied. Measures such as the agreement between the Reichsführer SS and the Reichsjugendführer to promote *the establishment of peasant soldiers*, the implementation of the *HJ agricultural service*, the extension of the *women's labour service*, the appeals of the *Gauleiter of* Saxony and Brandenburg to industry, etc., are a start in the fight against the rural exodus, the results of which will gradually be seen. In the long run, *the ideological education of the German people, especially the young troops, will also contribute to the youth of Germany seeing the work of the land as a noble and very important service to the nation.*

Putting an end to the "undervaluation of the importance of the agricultural result" is of course the condition to solve the problem of rural exodus in a natural and appropriate way.

Already since the middle of the last century, i.e. with the increasing industrialisation of Germany, agriculture has had to deal with an underestimation of the importance of its results. Of course, without success. It was customary, according to liberal "economic principles", to "*estimate the importance of agriculture for the national economy on the basis of calculations"*! By this method, German agriculture would naturally decline, since foreign countries, favoured by a better climate, lower wages and land prices, could provide food at unbeatable prices! But in addition, long before the First World War, the opinion had been formed, thanks to authoritative opinions, that the German people's food supply did not need to be absolutely assured within its borders. The well-known phrase of the Munich "national agronomist" Lujo Brentano: "Our cows are grazing in La Plata", is typical of the former irresponsible attitude towards national agriculture, and thus also towards *one of the most important vital issues of the German people!* Because of the possibilities of cheap imports of foodstuffs from abroad, the German peasantry was prepared to be sacrificed to the export interests of industry. At *the outbreak of the First World War, the fatal consequence of this dependence on foreign countries was a totally inadequate economic preparation for food, which cost the German people more than 750,000 deaths from malnutrition during the war and, ultimately, the final victory!*

By refusing to consider the legitimate demands of the peasantry based on the *safeguarding of the* German *food supply, the political importance* of a numerically strong and successful peasantry *for settlement was completely overlooked.*

It is therefore not extraordinary that the National Socialist government, based on the knowledge that *without a healthy peasantry, the national future is seriously threatened,* studied the problem of undervaluation in a comprehensive way and had to take a stand against it.

Is this considered to be the notion of "undervaluing the importance of agricultural outcomes"?

Viewed coldly, the pricing of agricultural products in relation to the protection of labour and costs, which the production of agriculture required, is insufficient.

This underestimation, which results in an insufficient return on agricultural output, is also shown by calculations. If one chooses a type of *production balance* based on current mercantile views, the following table is obtained:

Production balance sheet for agriculture in 1936/37
(in millions of RM)

Allocation of money:

Personal use (cleaning, services and other)	3,033
Wages and salaries in kind	1,572
Social insurance (employer's contribution)	136
Compensation of the farm holder with staff	4,200
De facto economic expenditure	3,438
Flat rate for overheads	450
Professional representation	68
Taxes	480
Debt service	630

Payment of interest on equity capital   2,440

                                                       16,447

Productions

Total production: 11,894

Deficit   4,553

                                                       16,447

The "interest payment of equity capital" from agriculture (around RM54.3 billion) with a percentage of 4½% corresponds to the tax in use in the country. It is also important, since the farmer has to get the necessary means from it to develop the estate (yield battle!) for equipment and education of children, for old age pension insurance, etc. The "wage for the work of the farm owner with his family" corresponding to the guidelines of the tax legislation, with 700 RM in the year for good labour, is not too high. Agriculture waived the interest payment on its own capital—an unfair requirement that could lead to the closure of any professional farm for "non-existent profitability"—so the deficit amounted to about RM 2 billion.

On the same basis, when the production balance of German agriculture for the years 1929/30 to 1937/38 is calculated, the following product is obtained

The evolution of production in German agriculture from 1928–1938 (in millions of RM)

Year	Deficit
1929/30	4,894
1930/31	5,336
1931/32	5,853
1932/33	6,180
1933/34	5,252
1934/35	4,405
1935/36	4,481
1936/37	4,545
1937/38	4,372

Both *the* worst years of the agricultural crisis before the takeover and *the effectiveness of the agrarian policy measures taken by the Third Reich* can be clearly distinguished. The good harvest of 1937/38 can also be seen as a consequence, but also the fact that agriculture is once again falling behind because of the promotion of the industrial sector, which is necessary to ensure the security of the German living space, and *despite significant additional production achieved in the struggle for yield.*

This can also be seen from the following breakdown of the *annual per capita income of the agricultural and non-agricultural population*, as well as from the work done on other bases by the "Institute for Economic Research" on the subject of "agriculture and national income", which was published at the end of March this year.

	Annual per capita income		
	Agricultural population In RM	Non-agricultural population In RM	As a % of
1913/14	1,191	1,665	139.7
1924/25	813	1,953	240.2
1925/26	846	2,006	273.1
1926/27	976	2,058	210.8
1927/28	1,024	2,313	225.8
1928/29	1,171	2,404	205.2
1929/30	1,147	2,404	209.6
1930/31	1,021	2,206	216.0
1931/32	907	1,772	195.4
1932/33	782	1,364	174.4
1933/34	912	1,358	148.9
1934/35	1,084	1,510	139.3
1935/36	1,103	1,687	152.9
1936/37	1,136	1,871	164.7
1937/38	1,172	2,048	174.7

Already at the *Reich Farmers' Day in Goslar in 1938*, Reichsbauernführer and SS-Obergruppenführer R. Walther *Darré* drew attention to these facts. Conscious of his duty to the German people, he pointed out the dangers that had already arisen or might arise if German agriculture did not receive decisive help soon.

These dangers are of an economic and food-related nature, as well as of a population policy nature. For example, we cannot avoid the beginning of a decline in agricultural production, which is already evident here and there. It will become increasingly difficult for agriculture to make the *technical improvements* required by the battle for yield (construction of silos for fermenting fodder, purchase of tractors) on its own, which would increase its production capacity to an unimportant degree. The tense economic situation of the farms and the impossibility of paying wages as high as those paid in part by *industry (the depreciation of the usual wage in kind plays a significant role in agriculture!* The result is that, in addition to the excessive workload of peasant women in particular, which is not insignificant from the point of view of health and birth policy, there is also a *depopulation of the countryside.*

This *weakening of food resources* and *threat to the blood source of* our people forces them to devote all their attention not only to the problem of rural exodus but also to the devaluation of agriculture.

It is not the intention here to examine the means of eliminating this source of danger to the people. *A large number of measures have already been implemented by the Reich, the Party and the Reich Food Service (Reichsnährstand) or are in preparation* (e.g. incentives to build housing for farm workers, fermentation and fertiliser silos, provision of state allowances and credits for the most diverse purposes, tax exemption, substantial financial support for the farm worker on marriage as a sign of recognition for long years of faithful work, etc.). These are, of course, partial actions. *But as a whole, they contribute to the final result, which of course can only be achieved by a comprehensive and systematic action of the participating services and, ultimately, of the whole people!*

It is understandable that the agricultural economy, thanks to the *Hereditary Domain Act,* owes its consolidation to *the regulation of the agricultural market* and other agrarian policy measures of the Third Reich. It also knows *that it was saved from the total collapse that was likely to occur before the threatening chaos of 1932.* It is also understandable that the agricultural economy also recognises that an era governed by higher political views of a national nature makes it difficult to provide immediate assistance. *But the fact that important departments have recognised the existence of problems and taken a stand on them, gives it the legitimate belief that the Führer and his delegates will act in good time.* German agriculture today finds itself in the position of the soldier at the front who maintained extreme confidence in authority and also maintained comradeship under the terrible rolling fire of the Great War!

For 1 May 1936

"*1 May Spring Day of the Nation!*
Day of solidarity of a people in work!
This day must symbolically translate that we are not citizens of a city and a country, that we are not workers, employees, craftsmen, peasants, students, bourgeois, nor supporters of any ideologies, but that we are members of a people.
The greatest thing God has given me here on earth is my people. In them lies my faith. I serve them willingly and give them my life. Let this be our most sacred common oath on this German Labour Day, which is rightly the day of the German nation.

Adolf Hitler, 1 May 1935

SS Notebook No. 2b. 1941.

In the East a new people is growing up in a new land

Transplantation and installation accomplished together

Among all the current historical events, one process of a special character can be discerned: the Führer's great work of transplantation and colonisation! A year and a half has passed since Adolf Hitler announced it in his speech in the Reichstag on 6 October 1939. Half a million Germans returned home. This was not a migration of *peoples,* but rather of groups and small colonies whose situation had become untenable and who were reattached to the German people's body and soil. The possession of a new space was the condition for this repatriation. It was opened up to us by the reclamation of former German populated and cultivated lands. We were thus taking possession of the future settlement areas for hundreds of thousands of new settlers from the former Empire.

Lack of space always leads to misery for the people!

Over the centuries, our destiny has always been determined by the fact that too little living space drove thousands of Germans to emigrate abroad. The lack of space was always the cause of the people's misery!

For a thousand years now, men of our blood have been moving to the vast territories of the East to conquer a new living space through hard pioneering work.

Their fate teaches us that a large country populated by Germans can only survive through the healthy use of the soil by a strong peasantry with many children.

In the future, the reclaimed German living space in the East must be secured—firstly by the influx of German people from abroad, and secondly by settlement with Germans from the Reich. This can only be done centrally and through extensive planning, with the aim of completely reorganising the new living space according to national socialist principles.

When the Führer entrusted this task to the SS Reichsführer, who was appointed Commissioner for the Consolidation of Germanness, the SS was given a new task. Its racially oriented and natalist education offered such special conditions and opportunities that it was mainly SS officers and soldiers who worked on this task together with comrades from other associations and staff from various party and state departments.

Model farm for German immigrants in the East.

SS men perform their agricultural service by working in the fields.
The peasantry, the new nobility of blood and soil.

While the recovery of the population took place despite the war, the colonisation and organisation of the new settlements in the East did not begin until after the end of the war, in accordance with the Führer's order. The returning German soldier had to contribute his authority. The call from the East is addressed to the best people to secure and improve, by their work and actions, what is rightfully ours from an old heritage. In accordance with the lessons of history, the most important point will be achieved this time by a policy of rural development. The consolidation and growth of

Germanness is the key to this organisation, as well as to the general organisation policy in the East. Racial separation and selection, as well as the creation of a strong and healthy peasantry, are therefore central to this objective. From a territorial point of view, a healthy distribution of land should make it possible to attach as many Germans as possible to the land. The structure, size and location of family farms will provide a secure basis for the life and development of farming families with many children.

The settlement of the returned Volksdeutsche was carefully planned according to these principles. While the general organisation was carried out by the Commissioner's Higher Staff Office for the Consolidation of Germanness, special staffs were created to carry out the work on an individual scale and to make the practical study of the settlement, which was at the disposal of the Commissioner's representative in the eastern regions.

It is true that one needs in-depth data to develop a work plan. You need to know how much land, how many farms, how many villages are available, what is the general and regional structure of the country. Is the land good, average or bad? What are the farms and villages like? How big are they on average? Can Germans be settled there? Which districts are suitable for the settlement of German farmers? What are the traffic possibilities, in what condition are the roads? These are just some of the many questions that arose. It was often difficult to answer because the country had been under Polish rule. Either no information could be found anyway, or it was unusable. New data had to be created—it was a huge job! Also, a plan had to be drawn up for the settlement, distribution and transport of the settler groups. The peasants from the lowlands returned to the flat country, the miners to the mountains, the German miners from Galicia came to the Beskids of Upper Silesia.

Colonisation is a matter of the heart!

Since "transplanting" means "replanting", various things have to be taken into account for an organised planning work. However, one should aspire to create similar or equivalent living conditions for the transplanted people as in the old homeland! The community structure as well as the main villages must be preserved. Neighbourhood problems are therefore taken into account in the overall studies. Depending on the possibilities, horse breeders are given farms surrounded by meadows, gardeners are brought to suitable land near the towns.

Each future farm must be selected, as well as each village. The appropriate farmer can be selected for each available farm based on surveys in the migrant's former homeland that indicate what his or her farm looked like, and on the EWZ map (Immigrant Central Selection Result).

Once this detailed planning has been completed, the groups to be settled in the villages to be colonised are assembled. The transport study must then set a deadline for departure and the route to be followed, and ensure that the practical installation runs smoothly. The groups, gathered on paper, must be concentrated in camps in the East, examined again, transport lists drawn up; farm numbers must be assigned, the immigrant and his luggage taken on board, installed in safety in a new home and finally taken to a new farm in accordance with the village plans.

Once this service is set up, 180 families leave daily for the ultimate adventure!

In the first ten months, about 20,000 farms were allocated to peasants from Volynia and Galicia, mainly in the Wartheland and around Cholm and Lublin.

At the same time as this settlement was taking place in the cities (Baltic Germans were also in the majority in urban professions), the German administration began its general reconstruction enterprise. The appearance of the country, as experienced by the soldier in the Polish campaign, was completely transformed: the uncultivated disorder and the Polish economy gave way to strict order, dignity and an ever-expanding economic and cultural life. The East no longer looks like it did during the Polish campaign, a reflection of a degenerate, collapsing state and the incapacity of the Poles. There is certainly much to be done to finally overcome the Polish legacy and bring about a new, healthy and beautiful life in every constituency. Everywhere the impetus and rhythm of German work, of the energetic creative will, can be felt. To take one example, the work that was done in the field of road building alone, as well as in the field of bridge building, today exceeds the twenty-year activity of the Polish state. In the cities, new buildings have been and are being erected; the number of places of German culture is increasing. The Jews are being expelled from villages and towns on a large scale, and where they are still present in large numbers, they have been given their own residential areas.

A new-style village
Departing from the usual image of our villages in the Reich, this structure consists of a village centre surrounded by several hamlets, as shown in the sketch. The advantage is that every farmer lives on his own land. The path to the centre is only a few minutes walk away.

The creative work begun during the war will be continued, when peace comes, by a great restructuring. The settlement area has been completely redeveloped according to a plan which had to be established by careful scientific work. Questions such as the harmonisation of town and country, access to traffic and industrial centres, must be solved as organically as the problem of the intelligent insertion of the new villages into the overall programme—it makes no sense to simply "patch up" the consequences of the anarchy that prevailed in the East. The country must be seen as a new land. For the first time since the period of the great invasions, we have the opportunity to carry out a real German planning of the country in the East, this time according to the concepts of 1941. The villages that are and will be created will have new locations that are not determined at random but by a conscious choice taking into account all scientific laws.

This will be best achieved by adding to a group of villages a main village that is easily accessible on foot. While each village (300–400 inhabitants) is to be provided with community centres dealing with political, cultural and economic life, the main village will contain community and administrative establishments requiring greater co-operation. Each village will therefore have a Party house containing a small room for the ceremonies and administrative rooms of the Party and its associations, and will run a kindergarten and a health office. Educational and physical training buildings, a hostel with a hall and buildings for economic and community purposes already exist in each village. On the other hand, larger facilities, festival halls and squares, stadiums, warehouses, repair shops, a labour service camp, should be built in the main village. In addition, each village must have a beautiful bell tower.

The form and structure of the village should correspond to its size and location in the province. Great importance should be attached to the arrangement of the gardens and the appearance that the landscape acquires through the planting of trees, shrubs and hedges and through reforestation. The task and goal is to constantly imprint the villages with a German spirit in all areas; to provide the Germans with a beautiful homeland in a healthy, German cultural landscape and to combine both beauty and profitability.

In accordance with this, the farms were not only to meet practical requirements in the East, but also to be the visible mark of a new German farming culture. The most modern, labour-saving technology is used in their construction and they are built with the best building materials to ensure high durability. This does not mean that they are built without thinking, but that they are built to fit the landscape and the nature of their people.

There is also a special concern—and this is a new development—for the condition of the agricultural worker and the village craftsman. The distribution of jobs for agricultural workers must be carefully considered and they must be assured of a sustainable future. They also represent forms of social advancement to the status of peasant-owner, but the candidate must, as a matter of principle, have worked for several years on a foreign farm as a servant and married farm worker:

Village craftsmanship, which is inextricably linked to the peasant function, is all the more strongly linked to the village as the craftsman is rooted in the village community through a corresponding land allocation and a hereditary estate. Craftsmen's posts needed by the village community must be created in this spirit of general labour.

All these issues reveal the breadth and depth of the tasks in the East that we have been assigned, and make the nature of this high goal clear. First of all, it is a question of connecting the emigrants organically and sentimentally with the old German folk and cultural life. Their energy, dedication and skills have been put to use in the service of the German land in such an important way that a secure future is guaranteed. Their work will once again benefit our people and our country, and no longer a foreign people.

A greater task remains, however, which is to safeguard this area in the future by a comprehensive work of colonisation and construction carried out for the first time in a centralised manner and with the clear aim of strengthening and increasing the German people. What the German pioneers achieved and built over the centuries, what the German sword won, the plough will now conquer once and for all!

SS NOTEBOOK NO. 1. 1944.

OLD AND NEW VILLAGES

...What will the new villages and peasant farms of which there has been so much talk lately be like; how big will they be and how will the work begin?
...

These were the questions I was asked by the farmer I was helping last year at harvest time. I told him that we are first trying to understand the origin of our old villages and farms. In the course of this research we found that they have always been influenced by local conditions and have developed gradually. The tribe, the nature of the soil, the space and the climate have always been important in influencing their shape. Where, for example, the conditions for good grazing were present, isolated and self-sufficient farms, groups of farms and rare villages were created. In contrast, the mountain valleys only allowed for long stretches of land, and where larger areas could be ploughed, only isolated farmsteads were created. Later on, however, the expansion of the area under cultivation led to the formation of groups of farms and finally to the unaligned villages that we know so well today. On the other hand, there are still villages of various forms, those on flat land. Water or other conditions play a big role. Even though many of these village structures are still present today, many conditions have changed since their appearance, making it necessary to renovate them.

In Prussia, for example, the same soil had to feed a population that had doubled in the space of seventy-five years (1815 to 1898) compared to the 18th century. Ways had to be found to increase the production of the soil so that the supply of the people did not depend on foreign imports. We have succeeded to a point that would once have seemed impossible to achieve. A Pomeranian farm of 80 hectares with four agricultural workers provided, for example, in the 16th century: 9 large units of livestock and 21.6 tons of grain (the products of pickaxe cultivation are converted into grain value).

In contrast, today a farm of only 15 hectares in the same village also supplies 9 large livestock units and 35 tonnes of grain.

In addition to the increasing demands placed on the agricultural economy over the last few centuries, there have been major changes due to other circumstances. New industries and means of transport took over large areas of land, had negative side effects on whole territories due to poor management and unplanned developments, and particularly degraded the social order.

Farmers argue that it is difficult to do the necessary work on the farm today because of a lack of skilled labour. A regular working time comparable to that of a city business is not sufficient, and therefore farm work in general is not as sought after as in the past. I draw attention to the fact that since the use of machines, the purely mechanical labour force has increased so much that on average (worldwide) there are fifteen times more machines than manual workers.

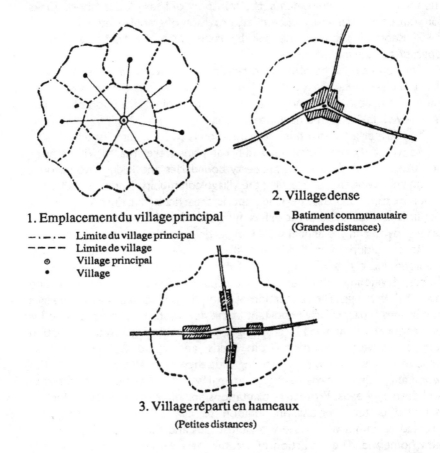

1. Emplacement du village principal

— . — . —   Limite du village principal
— — — —   Limite de village
⊙   Village principal
•   Village

2. Village dense

■   Batiment communautaire
(Grandes distances)

3. Village réparti en hameaux
(Petites distances)

This comparison shows particularly clearly that all companies that have to carry out many difficult physical tasks are at a disadvantage compared to the more mechanised workshops. The latter have the possibility to carry out work and projects relatively independently. Farmers' businesses have to make allowances for time and allocate working time appropriately.

When you consider that 70% of all farming work is done on the farm, it is a priority to build buildings and create tools to avoid unnecessary work as much as possible.

But the fields must also be well situated in relation to the farm. Detours and obstacles of any kind, such as uneven ground, poorly laid out boundaries, transport routes, etc., between the farm and the land must be removed.

Our new peasant farms and villages are also faced with two important demands:

1. Establishment of administrative buildings that facilitate, in addition to the most diverse requirements, the transport of heavy loads (short tracks for transporting fertiliser and fodder, provision of grapples, etc.).

2. Reorganisation of the soil by redesigning the fields to shorten operating distances.

The routes must be planned to facilitate good work with the machines. The old village, which is too dense, should be spaced out and the new village should be built in such a way that the best possible distribution of the soil is achieved, taking all the data into account.

The farmer asks how this reorganisation is to be accomplished.

As with the cities, economic and urban plans were created. Village plans are also created, setting out property boundaries and taking into account all the improvements concerning the village community, land use, traffic and other matters. Shaping the landscape is a particularly painstaking task. It requires consideration of the different relationships between soil, water, air, plant growth and the animal world. In particular tasks, one has to study:

Reforestation of badlands and steep slopes, improvement of water management, e.g. by storing water from melting snow, creation of snow fences, development of water banks, removal of cold and wet areas and many other things. The protection of plantations by creating forest hedges and bushes is particularly important in the new eastern districts. They offer protection from the wind by stopping it, protect against snow accumulation and excessive evaporation from fields and meadows, prevent soil impoverishment and wind scattering. But they must also provide us with wood and fruit, offer shelter to the animal world and serve to concentrate and destroy weeds. Protective plantations are of great importance for the deprived eastern regions. In addition to climatic improvements, they provide us with a wide variety of landscapes and thus shape the face of a new homeland. The attraction of creating new villages in the East for the planners lies in the fact that they can use all their experience and knowledge without being hampered by paralysing situations.

I would like to draw your attention to the directives of the Reichsführer SS, Commissioner for the Consolidation of Germanness, concerning the size of the new villages. They define the implementation procedures for their construction in the new eastern districts. A village with an area of 10 to 15 km^2 should have about 400 to 500 inhabitants. 30–40peasant farms of different sizes should make up a village, but these will mainly be family farms or holdings. These are about 25 to 40 hectares in size on light to medium soil. It is expected that there will be room for one family of farm workers for each farm. Approximately eight to ten villages form, together with the main village, a central village estate. In the main village, provision should be made for all the community and administrative institutions which cannot be provided in each of the smaller villages, for example the new large school (see Fig. 1).

The peasant woman wonders if the village will have a bell tower with a clock that strikes the hours.

In the centre of each village are the community buildings, which are clearly visible and easily accessible from all parts of the village: the village house with communal rooms, the school, the kindergarten and a bell tower, the community's economic buildings with a laundry, machines that the farmers cannot afford, a small workshop for mechanical repairs and other facilities. In the middle of the village there are also the shops and boutiques of the craftsmen. When all the necessary conditions governing the management of the farms and the shaping of the landscape are considered, the new village is better organised than the previous one. Soil, climate and other factors determine the shape of the village, and the following diagram can be sketched (see Fig. 2):

The strongly articulated structure of the new village facilitates a good reciprocal arrangement of farms and fields; allows for a slight widening and despite the spaced settlement, allows for a rich relationship with the community buildings in the centre. The distribution also corresponds to the methodical evolution and our current spatial representation, which encourages stronger contrasts between built and delimited hamlets, open fields with protective planting and the village centre. If the location is on a higher ground, its importance will be even more strongly felt. The cemetery should also be well located and visible in the landscape.

To conclude our discussion, the farmer and the farmer's wife ask themselves whether the standard planned for the farms will not involuntarily contribute to creating a monotonous and boring similarity in the village. I note that in all periods and in different regions the various types of houses that we know so well and hold so dear came into being through similarity of function: for example, the Lower Saxon farmhouse, the Alpine or Frankish farmhouse and other styles of farmhouse. We must also consider the fact that today we may produce fewer different styles in our homeland, which extends beyond the old and countless ethnic borders. It would even be a mistake to try to change architectural forms that have their raison d'être and thus risk creating buildings that are perhaps more inappropriate. Diversity should rather be reflected in the enhancement of craftsmanship in a typical spirit that has already produced things of indisputable value.

Alfred Roth

SS NOTEBOOK NO. 9. 1944.

CITIES AS FORTRESSES OF THE REICH

There is an old popular saying: "Nothing but walls separates the bourgeois from the peasants". There is undoubtedly a great deal of wisdom in this phrase. The character of the defensive fortress is determined by its walls. This is one of the essential features of the city. The other foundation of the German city is the fundamental peasant character of a large part of the agricultural bourgeoisie as well as the corporate spirit of the peasant regions.

The Germans could not integrate into the cities of the Roman Empire, as Tacitus reports. It did not matter how diverse the Roman character of these Rhine and Danube cities was at the time. They all bore the basic features of that urban lifestyle, which was by nature alien to the peasant colonies, produced by that particular class spirit. The legacy of the Greek city-state was passed on to Rome's sister cities. Thus, even the twelve great cities that fell into the hands of the Germanic tribes as remnants of colonisation along the old Roman borders from Cologne to Regensburg were rebuilt on the basis of new plans and a new mindset. These first city-like buildings, which were established on German soil, were the communities of German merchant guilds and had a greater range of action. A chain of towns and fortresses of other origins then developed on the Elbe and Ems rivers and on the eastern border of the German state. They were home to a merchant guild, but more important was the peasant garrison living in the large fortresses as a bulwark against enemy attacks from the east. This backbone of the defensive belt against the horsemen's hordes was at the same time the starting point for German penetration into the disorganised countries closest to it.

The history of the founding of these German cities is particularly linked to the personality of King Heinrich I. Magdeburg was the most successful of all, while Lübeck, Nuremberg and Vienna were the next to develop regions in the east. In the course of two centuries, the Saxon and Salian emperors succeeded in developing these burgher communities and establishing a municipal law on German soil, which seems to have originated in the German peasantry but was adapted to other uses. This medieval German town law was one of the most effective forces protecting the settlement of German citizens during the medieval migration to the East.

"Know that the Germans are free people", says the Duke of Bohemia in the charter of the German bourgeois commune in Prague in the heart of the Czech environment. The municipal law of Magdeburg, Nuremberg and Lübeck in the Hanseatic towns along the Baltic Sea coast and the Viennese municipal law in the south-east were the basis for elaborate legal relations. This law also created the order that not only allowed the peasant and mining regions of the former East Germanic tribes to flourish, but also enabled the Slavs and other peoples to acquire a state structure.

"The cities became the most fortified towns of old and the representatives of the idea of empire. From the very beginning, the Reichsführer SS adopted this position as Minister of the Interior to show his support for the mayors. Consider the immense result of the Hanseatic League and its repercussions in the Baltic Sea area, or the great work of the imperial merchants in the time of Emperor Maximilian I thanks to the southern German cities. The imperial eagle was always the heraldic animal whose wings housed the various ordinances. The Fuggers in Hungary, as well as in Spain, became the men of the Empire. Apart from peasant chiefs and knights of the calibre of Hutten and Sickingen, it was the burghers of the kind of a Tilman Riemenschneider in Würzburg, an Albrecht Dürer in Nuremberg, a Veit StoB in Krakow, who were the messengers of faith in the idea of the Empire. Countless mayors became rebels out of loyalty to the Empire against the princes.

During the centuries in which the German princely class gradually took over the royal rights of the Empire and gained privileges, the German cities did not become city-states, but imperial cities in the highest sense of the word. During the Hussite and Turkish attacks, and later during the Thirty Years' War, the German cities proved to be the armed guardians of German imperial soil and law right up to the present day. Freed from the old borders and the princely chains of small oppressive states, they fulfilled their mission and emerged as the holders of the German imperial idea.

"If the classes, the spiritual and secular princes represented regional or dynastic egoism and did their utmost to break up the Empire little by little over the centuries, unfortunately with success, the German cities—with certain exceptions—were the bulwark of the imperial idea and the representatives of loyalty to the Empire. From the ranks of the German mayors came countless great men who in many cases became the champions and defenders of the unity and greatness of the Empire at the cost of their blood and their lives."

In the words of the Reichsführer SS, this 'rich and glorious tradition' of German cities is the foundation of the will to resist that underpins the struggle in the heart of the homeland. It is precisely because the cities were the cement of the old imperial structure and not the products of narrow nationalistic plans that they possess this unifying force today. Neither houses nor factories and workshops survive the hail of bombs today. It is only this deep-rooted attachment to the city that has proved its worth. The cities that have remained healthy inwardly, as representatives of the Empire under attack and defence, find their destiny in this war by fulfilling their new tasks for the Empire.

V. GENERAL POLICY

"D'ESTOC ET DE TAILLE", BY GUNTHER D'ALQUEN, 1937.

THE IDEA OPPOSED TO THE SYSTEM

Since the German uprising under the sign of the swastika, the notion of revolution appears in a completely new light.

All the revolutions of modern times, the French Revolution of 1789, the Parisian revolution of July 1830, the insurrections of 1848, the days of terror from March to May 1871 of the Parisian communards, the Russian Revolution of March and October 1917 and the German revolt of November, but also all the revolutions of the previous centuries generally show the same disfigured face; they always end in a destructive rather than creative logic. They are social-revolutionary manifestations driven only by purely social or economic tendencies, born of a doctrine far removed from the earth and therefore hostile to life.

In all these revolutions, a cold system rebels against life. They are based, not on the landed classes, but on the city masses and on that spiritual decadence which already opposes all authentic life.

The rabble and an uprooted intelligence! Such are the groups with tainted blood that gather around the flag of destruction. The hatred of these degenerates is directed not only at this State, the existing social order, but at life itself. Hence also the orgies of bloody fury in which these rebels soiled themselves, for its real meaning lay in this stupid bloodshed: to sacrifice life to a doctrinaire idea.

The greatness of the German revolution can only be seen against this dark background. It differs from all revolutions in world history not only in the extreme discipline of its external course, but even more profoundly in its internal form, which is not the product of an inert thought pattern but of a living idea. It is not limited to achieving social and economic goals. It does not only aspire to make a revolution, it wants to create the *new revolution* of a whole world. The German revival did not choose the old Nordic sun symbol as its emblem by chance. It is because life itself marches under its flags. It is the blood of all the depths of the earth that thunders here and wants to abolish all systems in order to create forms of its own in the state, in law, in science, in art and in all areas of economic life.

It is not surprising that this revolution of blood and soil attracted the best racial forces, which, like a wave of red blood, is waving its flags over the country.

They are a symbol, but not a system; they shake and clatter like all living things. Life must no longer be transformed into a system in this people.

We want to sacrifice all doctrines to life, as rebels of the German land.

Anyone who considers that the German recovery follows the laws of logic has understood nothing. An internal revolution can only take place according to the laws of life. For as the failure of all doctrinaire attempts teaches, life does not organize itself under duress, and blood always takes its revenge.

In the past, the Movement conducted its struggle legally by following this great order of organic laws; it purified itself of barricade doctrinaires and remained on legal paths until the internal evolution of German life had matured into a historical turn.

And when persecution wrung the cry of bloody retribution from oppressed hearts, they forgave and forgot. But such moral strength is the hallmark of the victor who regards the dungeons and graves of heroes as an ultimately necessary fate. How could there be good swords if they were not soaked by fire and hammer blows?

But even the harmony of the great laws of life is reflected in the measured way in which the nation's victorious recovery is set on the road to construction. The upheaval was already rich in itself. During the revolutions of past eras, it was only spatially active. And while everything was being destroyed to build a new system on the drawing board, the effort to let things happen and bear fruit is noticeable. Because, like any harvest, creation does not happen all at once, but is reaped little by little.

Nothing is done in haste, nothing is done in artifice. The Führer had the great wisdom to tackle only those problems that had a solution, like ripe fruit.

Only a fool would point out that the banks and department stores have not been completely nationalised, that there are still remnants of the old world and that many questions have certainly not been resolved. Who would want to cut the wheat in the spring, to harvest in the summer, when it is done in the autumn? The doctrinaires are impatient. They eat the green fruit—and they die.

National Socialism does not express itself in the schematic execution of a programme, but rather strives to make us profit from the experiences of flourishing life. At present, the final objectives are still far from sight, or at any rate unattainable; only through gradual development will they be brought closer and closer.

In the field of domestic politics, developments had advanced to such an extent that the German recovery, seeing its time, fought the great battle of the historic breakthrough. It could and should therefore strike hard, as with a scythe in the ripe wheat. Only the stubble remained. And who could deny that the work had been done, that the outdated memories were gone, and that a high goal had been radically achieved? The harvest was done, and the next one was already being planned.

What can be done now and in the future does not need to be done in a big way. Doctrinaire measures and interventions achieve nothing, even if they seem desirable to many at the time. Today, only two objectives can remain: freedom outside, bread and constructive work inside the country. For the academic quarrel about currencies and the economic system is not important; only life is sacred, and 67 million people must have their lives assured and bread on their tables.

The wheat has now risen, but the time has not yet come to cut it. The farmer is sharpening his scythe for the harvest; he is not in a hurry, he is watching and waiting. When the time is right, the wheat will fall, but there is still time to go until then. Then he will plough, harrow and sow. Winter will come and then spring again, like a tide that comes and goes.

Blessed are the people who recognise the strength of the earth! Blessed is the man who knows how to act and decide at the right time. He honours the eternal law of life.

"D'ESTOC ET DE TAILLE", BY GUNTHER D'ALQUEN, 1937.

COMMUNITY OR COLLECTIVITY?

When the old National Socialists look back on the early years of the struggle, they see a beautiful picture of a true community. Unencumbered, the men of that time, who were of one mind, had come together and created a community such as the world has rarely seen. Despite the lack of external organisation, these men formed an incredibly strong force.

They accomplished great things that took on an almost mystical dimension, expressing the loyalty of the Germanic troop, and culminating in the supreme sacrifice. We see that this strength of the Movement comes directly from this voluntary fusion which nevertheless allows the individual to exist as a personality and thus to be an independent fighter.

This community of fighters was the first to give strength to the Movement. It is a matter of nurturing it in the future and of ensuring that, in an age when the Movement should use violence, there is never a danger of the community degenerating into a collective. For never can the organised mass gathering, by destroying the values of personality in the natural man, increase his strength.

On the contrary, a good dose of violence is needed to hold together such a fundamentally non-German formation. Anything that destroys the personality for the benefit of a mass is not German, and anyone who thinks only in terms of the mass does so in a Bolshevist way and must eventually come to that idea which a Marxist once expressed when he preferred "to be wrong with the mass than to be right as an individual".

But every community is spiritually based on the old Marxist fallacy of the equality of all men. This is not the case in nature. On the contrary, men are unequal. Some are good, some are bad, some are honest, some are dishonest, some are tall, some are short, some are fat, some are skinny. The spiritual defenders of the community were always faced with a desperate struggle, made all the more difficult by the fact that they had to constantly deny manifest reality.

There is no doubt that, apart from those who, as conscious enemies of National Socialism, defend the old error of equality, all those who, by nature and character, cannot understand National Socialism analogously are likely to act unconsciously in a collectivist spirit.

This type of man is both dangerous and comical when, in defence of the old Marxist egalitarian theory, he introduces the National Socialist notion of community, and suspects of professing class struggle anyone who notes that in a people there are intelligent people and their opposite.

No, it has nothing to do with a division of the people, for these are simply natural facts. But our old National Socialist view of the "decisive minority" is just as much a political translation of these natural facts as the "to each his own" demand that has always opposed National Socialism to the Marxist slogan "all equal".

A fundamental distinction between community and collectivity is also manifested in leadership. The community naturally and necessarily has a leader who holds power over the souls and hearts of his fellows. The despot of a community is the supreme master of the bodies of individuals. His position is based on fear, whereas the leader of a community is driven by the love of the men who follow him voluntarily.

It is no coincidence that real leaders see themselves as the servants of their community because of their wisdom and sense of human superiority. Frederick the Great saw himself as 'the first servant of the state'. Adolf Hitler saw himself as the 'agent of the nation', and the Führer's representative drew the attention of the political leaders at the swearing-in ceremony to their task of being the servants of the people's community.

We thus see that the supporters of the community see their ideal in 'domination'. Through their sense of human inadequacy they fall into the other excess and are as despotic towards their subordinates as they feign submission to the higher echelons. They do not know that the leader must have a superior faculty of understanding, but above all that superiority of soul and strength of heart of which Fichte tells us that it is these that bring victory.

Moreover, it can be seen that the head of a community calls to him the most capable and qualified men, and that the head of a community naturally has no need of independent collaborators, but only of creatures who are his blind instruments and who must constantly assure him of his worth. Thus it is clear what monstrous danger, arising from collectivist thought, could directly threaten our people in the time of their rebirth.

Here, too, the National Socialist Movement has given the nation a principle of inestimable value by presaging in exemplary form the notion of a community of loyal fellow workers. In this way it has set an example for all time of the true pooling of forces and has clearly rejected all collectivist ideas.

But the old soldiers of the Movement will never admit that the powerful human masses of our demonstrations and organisations can be wrongly regarded as a reign of the man-mass, and that the National Socialist notion of community is thus consciously or unconsciously distorted and transformed into collectivity.

The crowning achievement of any spirit of sacrifice is the dedication of one's own life for the existence of the community.

Adolf Hitler

"D'ESTOC ET DE TAILLE", BY GUNTHER D' ALQUEN. 1937.

REFLECTIONS ON THE LEADER PRINCIPLE

The greater the tasks that an age gives to men, the more distinctly the group of those who are only apparently qualified for those tasks manifests itself. Where the highest values are concerned, the inferiors will always try to drape themselves in the appearance and attitude of the superior men of the elite.

Let us imagine a good and totally insignificant fellow citizen whose ardent wish is to be able to command one day. He does not want to wait until he is finally given a mission that places great responsibility on his shoulders. For he will probably be able to wait a long time; if he has no ability, he has a consuming ambition and this alone would prevent him from achieving it. Let us assume: Little Moritz, with his power complexes, becomes a big Moritz, and the misfortune is that he first learns to simulate non-existent abilities.

Our friend becomes a leader in some capacity. He knows that the importance of his personality is now accepted (only for a while). Former comrades who have not risen in rank imagine themselves to be inferior to the above-mentioned figure. Emphatic speeches persuade the citizens of the authority of the great Moritz. In his new offices, the telephone facilities were transformed. A listening table was set up in the chief's room to 'deepen trust', the posts were reorganised and the first circular questioned the established competences.

Unfortunately, mastering the job is not so simple. The newly-qualified superior does not like to show that he is not yet fully qualified and that he has to be advised. He sees his authority wavering and does not want to show the same little weaknesses as everyone else, nor his lack of basic experience. The lack of internal self-confidence must be compensated for by an even greater external self-confidence. The distance to former comrades is growing by leaps and bounds. Who is his favourite now?

The 'subordinate' is his favourite, because he willingly and often publicly confirms that he, the 'superior', is a particularly deserving individual. In his stupidity he certainly does not notice that the 'subordinate' says exactly the opposite behind his back. But if he were to notice here and there realistic objections from one of these "subordinates" or even counter-proposals on any issue, then the "boss" would infallibly see that he has a dangerous opponent before him. So he is brought down and, if necessary, secretly plotted against, being convinced of his own undoubted worth and the other's ineptitude.

But this man is always on the brink. Woe to him when the moment comes when he needs his collaborators to correct his work, in a joyful collaboration, with a sense of absolute and resolute devotion to their leader! This ordeal can happen every day, by chance, when a mistake or an absolute task requires it. A painful situation arises when the superior no longer has the confidence of his men. His fall is therefore certain. Fate is fulfilled with an iron logic.

There is another kind, apart from the ambitious turned savage, pocket-sized tyrants, the fussy bureaucrats. They often have unquestionable knowledge. But what distinguishes them from real leaders is the fact that they are absolutely unwilling to accept any responsibility whatsoever. They accept everything patiently and carry out regulations and orders to the letter. They only see the apparatus, the organisation and its cells. The way a York acted in the wars of independence is an abomination to them. They would not have followed a Hitler, but a Kahr.

In both cases, these are caricatural distortions of the nature of the leader. The first sees only men. It sees leadership exclusively as a rank of precedence of persons. The century of democracies and parliamentarianism was totally successful in opposing this domination of men over men, and was quite right in the face of those leaders who see only personal preponderance in their rights.

The old authority had lost its internal legitimacy. The selfish and ambitious princes no longer had any right to power because they no longer saw themselves as servants of the state, but saw the state as a tool for personal power. When this false authority became a rule and a system, the time had come for a more structured organisation of the people. Thus, in our country, false authority is destroyed by internal logic, while education and selection produce a genuine elite that develops naturally. There is no question of abandoning this mission to the next millennium, for the creation of a new class of leaders was never in history a matter of a few years. What is important is the progress of our people in this history, not the little informers and undisciplined characters. In the end, they serve no purpose and do no harm; our strength lies in action, in creation and in the future. Sincere fighters in the service of an ideal always make history.

From character came action.

Darré

SS BOOKLET No. 10. 1937.

SS-Staf. Kinkelin: National Socialism creates a new world out of a new faith

With National Socialism, the Führer has given us a new world view. This means that the National Socialist teaching the Führer's doctrine sees himself and the world in a different light. He now has *his own way of seeing* and no longer looks through the distorting glasses that other powers representing a foreign ideology had put on him.

National Socialism sheds new light on the old system of values and power relations governing the world. When he looks back at the recent past, he sees that not only he himself—but also his people—have been dispossessed of their spiritual wealth, sidelined, but also reduced to pawns on the chessboard of foreign powers. Now it is learning to differentiate itself from others by defining what is its essence and what is alien. He is confronting the old values he was taught with the new, totally different and unknown values that emerge when he follows his *own rule*. The German has learnt to differentiate between *what is his own and what is foreign* because he has first become aware of his own inner nature, something that was previously denied to him. In the past, he was seen as just one of many sheep living in a large pen. He escaped. In this way he has regained his freedom by finding himself. Previously, he and his people were only components of a cultural world, a mental universe whose source, spirit and guiding principles were foreign to the German people.

It is clear, then, that the National Socialist sees the wider world, himself and his people, his destiny, in a completely new, rejuvenated light. Since then, he has been confronted with a totally different world which had long since ceased to be his own, of which he was no longer a part, and to which he could no longer belong.

He discovers a new system of values and assimilates it in order to reject, to abolish all the more easily the old values which are precisely those of the others, because they no longer suit him at all. He knows that he is part of a powerful group, of a great community whose scope is limitless: *He finally lives his people.* And he feels that he is an *element,* a link in this immense chain, in the national community.

A thousand ties bind him and tie him to this community. His future is inextricably linked to the powerful bloodstream of his people. For the first time he understands his people as a huge *racial community.* In the past, he was told that it was language, nationality, Christianity, etc. that determined membership of a community. Now he knows that these old considerations are all out of date, for he sees in his own home men who do not belong to his own people, and on the other side of these old boundaries men who belong to his own people just as much as he does. The old barriers are falling, the old frontiers, the old walls are no longer of value. Everywhere he looks, he sees a great renewal in progress.

A new and great unity has emerged from the collapse of the old systems: *the German people.* Old corruptors are trying to debauch it, but they have no power over it. Prayers and threats no longer have any effect. The National Socialist German has escaped their grasp, he has shed their pressure as easily, freely and naturally as an old garment. The recall is under way! By the thousands, by the millions, they are rallying to their people.

This is how the German citizen experienced the *mystery of blood.* But not only that. He sees this blood as the vehicle of his innermost essence. He recognises blood as the most precious heritage which his most distant ancestors have passed on to him and which binds him to them indissolubly. It is hard to imagine to what extent, in the past, he was taught to despise, disdain and scorn blood! To what extent he was educated to despise and deny his ancestors instead of venerating them! Many blinders fell from his eyes. The enemies of the people were even forced to demonise the doctrine of blood in order to be able to control this dangerous notion all the more easily and to destroy it. But now the pressures and threats no longer work.

Living in the heart of his people, the German feels differently: he feels that he is part of it and an active component of it. The divisions into classes and social strata of the past have disappeared. It is a living, immense, meaningfully ordered and structured unit, a giant army of free men: *the people;* a living whole based on duties and rights. This active, fervent profession of faith for the people today goes beyond the level of intellectual awareness, of unattached teaching, of a sense of selfish wealth. "*What does not serve my people harms them!*

Equipped with this new scale of values, which he has acquired by listening to the message of the blood, the German is now interested in all aspects of life. He is determined to ignore any value that is not his own, that does not embody his world view, to no longer attach importance to things that he himself does not consider important. No area is immune to this inversion of values and new considerations. The National Socialist German thus restructures his entire world.

This conscious, awake German turns his gaze inward. *A new faith* lives in him. He draws his greatest strength from it. But this faith is not a dogma, it is not a doctrine of foreign origin; it is the fruit of his ancient biological heritage. National Socialism finds itself in harmony with the inner world of its fathers and connects *directly* with the divine.

Our faith is the origin and measure of all things: all spiritual creations come from it and return to it. It is therefore understandable that we should make a general examination to see whether or not everything that comes from the spiritual creative fields of our people, philosophy, art, science etc., is in accordance with our new ideology, our new faith. The stricter and more consistent we are, the clearer our vision becomes. There is no doubt that we will clean up! We are determined not to leave any aspect of life untouched. We examine every single element from the old world with the utmost care. To our surprise, we find that many belong to us, which the old system, under the pretext that it is its property, has taken over. We are therefore reintegrating it into our system. If we still need the old elements, we keep them, but to create our own substitute. We get rid of everything that is foreign and even throw it in the garbage. We are determined to build a new world out of our blood and everything connected with it, under the victorious sign of the swastika.

In the past we were regarded as intellectually minor and our entire spiritual heritage was managed in a pretentious manner. Now we are letting all the enemy powers know that *the German people have come of age,* that they intend to take charge of all their spiritual property themselves without exception. We demand the return of our ancestral heritage, which was usurped by unworthy and unfaithful proxies. In this area, too, a four-year plan to rebuild the spirit of the people must be put into effect.

Nothing can prevent us from devising a new law, a new morality or any other rule of national life. Our worldview sees the economy as a component of the new order, which must serve the people, not enslave them.

Like the economy, many other old idols are subject to the law of renewal and the National Socialist order. No work, however threatening, monstrous or respectable it may seem, frightens us. Even if the defeated era continues to issue threatening warnings, these tables of the law no longer terrify any National Socialist. They have been exorcised. Not because a National Socialist would not respect anything, as is often lamented in bigoted offence. But simply because he has acquired a new faith, a new scale of values defining what is sacred to him and what is not, what is divine and what represents arrogant, alien idols. New foundations, an extreme sense of the divine felt in his people, in his blood, give him confidence and invincibility. The divine apprehension of his own people, of his blood and of this new faith, has developed in the National Socialist a sense of the sacred that makes him respectful. We know today that our blood, our country, is sacred to us, because these two names are of divine essence.

Considering this fact, the verbiage of "neo-paganism" or even "atheism" seems petty, false, misleading and, in the end, a dangerous illusion for our opponents. They will learn that it is our faith that enables us to bring down the old world and build a new and more beautiful world.

The German people have freed themselves politically from all their chains, from economic dictatorship, and have purified their race from invasion. In the future they will also put an end to those guardianship, suzerainty and spiritual authority which are alien to the people and do not serve them. The German people will soon regain their freedom in every respect. To serve the people in order to follow the divine law, to return to the original principles of our blood and the divine world, is the meaning of National Socialism.

He who is, is not concerned with appearances.

Rückert

SS Notebook No. 5. 1943.

Our revolutionary mission

We Germans have always played a special role in the world. We were the restless and tormented element among the peoples. Even in times of our greatest commercial prosperity we were dissatisfied with our fate. The outbreak of the First World War was felt as a liberation. The cause of this was not the fanatical warlike exaltation which has so often been imputed to us by our enemies, but the liberating feeling of having a new and decisive vocation. The German cannot live with the life of a shopkeeper. The state of rest and satiety is against his nature. He feels called to higher tasks than to engage in a lucrative trade in agricultural or industrial products. This way of being has been described as a Faustian characteristic of the German. It can be interpreted as a blessing or a curse; in any case it determines the reputation of Germanism for good or ill. It was the original fate of the entire Germanic world. Without this obsession to move, the Germans would have been an insignificant people of peasants in northern Europe. They shed their blood all over the West in constant battles, but they also shaped the face of this corner of the world. Even today, they seem to be called upon to fulfil the destiny of this century.

* * *

The gigantic battles of the Second World War marked the end of one of the great eras of humanity. The domination of gold is stopped, the people regain their rights, man once again measures the value of things. This war is being fought for reasons other than changes in borders and interests. It is about the fate of a thousand-year-old culture that has given the world the magnificent expressions of human genius. The greatest revolution of all time is being accomplished in the storm of battle: the revolt of the peasants against the merchants, of labour against the power of gold. The same process that we experienced years ago in the struggle for power in Germany is being repeated today on a world scale, and we are facing the same adversaries. We know their methods of struggle too well to be surprised anymore. We are now in the thick of the struggle, and this war will not end until the continent is rid of its executioners. Whatever the future may bring, it is our duty, for the sake of our dead comrades, to resist, to attack unceasingly, until the enemy force is destroyed. There can be no compromise in this struggle, for the continuation of the previous situation would result in terrible upheavals which would ultimately destroy the West. Germany has become the bulwark of European freedom. Our country's enemies are also Europe's enemies. It is no longer a question of a quarrel between peoples and states, but of various principles of configuration, the final realisation of which decides death or life. In this way, our struggle goes beyond the sphere of power and interests to that of the spirit. It is not primarily a question of oil sources or mineral deposits, but of maintaining all the spiritual values that allow the human presence to be magnificently realised. What do American railway magnates and Bolshevik despots have to do with Europe and its multi-millennial culture? England has long since turned to its overseas possessions and regards the continent only as the plaything of its interests. Germany, on the other hand, has remained tied to the West's destiny, however painful this may be. There is now no choice for the peoples of Europe if they want to believe in their destiny. The fronts are sharper than ever, the divinity itself judges nations on their strength and worth.

War is again revealed, as it was in the past, to be a judgment of God. In the clash of the battles of our time, the face of the world will be reshaped and no one will recognise its old face. Whatever the outcome of the battle, there will be nothing left of the old world. The old primordial forces of life are in motion and will not stop until the powers of degeneration and destruction are finally crushed. For the past thirty years, the most gigantic process of transmutation that the history of the world has ever seen has been unfolding. The living forces are demanding their rights. The peoples are rushing out of the atrocious confines of their living space towards the light and the sun. A new migration of peoples is underway. With the old powers, a whole spiritual world that has held Europe back for two thousand years is collapsing. The alliance of the democracies with the Kremlin has put an end to the last doubts about the necessity of our struggle. Truth, justice and life are with us.

* * *

The West is still engaged in a decisive struggle for its future. The horizon often seems obscured by terrible events, but at the height of danger the strength of the human heart proves itself. There are still large parts of Europe in a state of quiet contemplation, unaware of the threatening gravity of their situation. Blind madmen turn against the only power that can protect them from destruction and annihilation. These things no longer affect us. We are used to fighting alone, surrounded by hatred and contempt because we are aware of our mission. The destiny of the world is fulfilled by our action and by the will of the divinity. Even if thousands of men die, if tens of thousands return crippled, the Idea will live on as long as Germany sees the birth of men. We are invincible because we have an unshakeable faith. This faith has sustained us in all the circumstances of our existence; it has given us the precious moments of triumph and accompanied us in sorrow and misery; it will one day lead us to victory. The gods do not bestow their grace, they only grant their favours to the brave who resist all violence. Fate has given us special missions. It is up to us to fulfil them. In God's eyes, a people is only a tool of His almighty will. He mercilessly defeats that which proves to be unfit. We stand and fight, for the Empire, the strength and the splendour are ours.

Hans Henning Festge

Man is superior to matter when confronted with the necessity of a great attitude, and no external power of any kind can be conceived to which spiritual force is not superior. Therefore, he who is capable of this can draw the conclusion that in man, in real man, there live values which cannot be destroyed either by projectiles or by mountains of explosives.

Ernst Jünger

SS Notebook No. 7. 1943.

Idea and Appearance of the Empire

The idea of the nationalist state must be defeated

As clear as the struggle for the defence of our homeland against the onslaught from the East is, so clear are the outlines of a new organisation of Europe, outlines that no longer follow the borders assigned to them by a nationalist conception. What calls millions of men to arms in Europe today is not only the struggle for raw materials and living space, but also the will for a radical reorganisation of this continent for which it is worth living and dying. The fact that thousands of Norwegians, Dutchmen, Flemings and Walloons are fighting on the Eastern Front in the ranks of the Waffen SS can only be seen as a symptom of an awakening of energy among the Germanic peoples, who, beyond the boundaries of the political order in which they have lived up to now, are seeking the path to a new future. There can be no doubt that our vision of what Europe will be one day when this harsh and relentless struggle is over already takes us far beyond the limits of the old nationalistic conception. No thinking mind in Europe believes that at the end of this bitter struggle, as fate will decide for ever, the restoration of the old political order can take place. Just as the sacrifices of the present war legitimize, at its conclusion, the creation of an order which corresponds to the breadth and depth of the National Socialist revolution accomplished in the heart of the continent. This new order can only be established on the basis of the idea of *race*. The Dutch, the Flemings, the Walloons, the Scandinavians, who today are fighting alongside us in the ranks of the Waffen SS, are not only defending their homes against the Asian wave, they are also the pioneers of a *reorganisation of Europe on the foundations of the Germanic idea. In this way, a process similar to that which led to the creation of Bismarck's Reich seventy years ago is taking place on the European territory.*

On the left, a young Danish volunteer with the face of a child.
On the right, Heinrich Himmler visits his SS on the Eastern Front in 1941.

The SS unites many European nationalities under its runic emblem.

At that time, the German principalities, under the influence of the nationalist principle, joined together to form an Empire. The National Socialist revolution has absorbed the nationalist idea and replaced it with the idea of race. Therefore, at the end of this war, a new European order must be established on the basis of Germanic solidarity. The nationalist idea flourished in Bismarck's Reich. At the moment when the innumerable waves of Asia are attacking the borders of Europe, the continent is turning back to that great historical construction which it had already built centuries earlier on the basis of Germanness. We have reached a point in evolution where the concept of race begins to become a historical and political reality. The people and the nation appear more and more as particular expressions of this concept. The revolution in political thought which first took place within our Empire soon extended its effects beyond the borders of the old Reich. It can no longer be contained; it is sweeping away the old errors of the old liberal doctrine with the same unyielding rigour with which it is tearing down the small artificial states created by the English policy of balance. The test of the war against the Asiatic enemy no longer permits the survival of the system of States which was born at Versailles. And now we find ourselves in the hour of struggle and danger before a new European organisation; we are witnessing the *birth of a racial Empire*.

This is the aim of our struggle. All those are called who are influenced in their attitude by the same blood. The German feels, of course, that he is the heart of this Empire which must embrace the whole area of our race. But he must not regard this Empire as an extension of the nationalist idea. The German nationalist idea acquired a new dimension in 1938. *Our opponents want to persuade the peoples of Europe of the idea that everything that followed was only the consequence of German imperialism.* Here too they have failed to understand the National Socialist revolution. It could not lead to imperialism but must, according to its principles, integrate the national state of the Germans into a vast Germanic Empire. All attempts to define in legal-political terms the future relationship of the Germanic states to the Empire can only fail because existing concepts such as federation, federal system, federalism belong to the realm of the past and miss the revolution in our thinking brought about by the concept of race. The German revolution is becoming a Germanic revolution. On the battlefields of the most terrible war that has ever been waged against a hostile world trying to smother the germ of a new vital order accomplished by the German revolution, there is a powerful appeal to the Germanic peoples to form *a* Germanic Empire of their own.

THE ETERNAL EMPIRE

The idea of a Nordic Empire is not a product of our time. It accompanies our entire historical existence as the image of an ordered world which invites the man of our race, on the strength of his creative artistic power, his inventive gifts, and his ability to found a cohesive organic system on the model of the Empire. The proud centuries of the history of the German

Empire are still close enough to us to remind us that all states owe their foundation to the energy of Nordic leaders: the state of the Cheruscan Armin, of the Battalion Civilis, of Marbod, that of the Burgundians, of the Vandals, of Theodoric and Charlemagne, the creator of the Germanic West, the state of the Varegues which extended from the Baltic to the Black Sea, that of the Vikings and that of the Normans. The history of these Germanic peoples is our own history. We can experience today that in the ranks of the Waffen SS there are prominent representatives of the Germanic ethnic group who for centuries have waged a difficult and united struggle against the forces of the foreigner and who speak of the Empire as an idea which they have defended with arms and safeguarded. This is proof that the historical structures of the past still have an active influence and that the idea of empire outside the German state has been kept alive. It is now a matter of revising this historical image which hostile propaganda and false schooling have aroused in the Germanic populations of the West and the North and of re-establishing historical relationships such as those which conceded to the Dutch, Flemish, Walloons, and Scandinavians for centuries while they were members of the Reich, a civilised, free and flourishing life. We must think in terms of centuries. Enemy propaganda has profoundly changed the original face of these countries. The state organisations which the French Revolution and the English policy of equilibrium built up with such artifice and tenacity are condemned by the iron law of history. The political creations of the 19th century are now definitively collapsing. The idea of Empire, on the other hand, is being reborn, like the phoenix from its ashes; it is being reborn among all peoples of Germanic blood who no longer believe in the possibility of a political existence distinct from the Reich, if not directed against it. The idea of Empire is the strongest tradition on the continent and, therefore, the most decisive real force for a lasting historical order.

THE EMPIRE AND EUROPE

We agree today that the political creations of the Germans in the past could only be ephemeral, for the energy of the race, a feeling of inexhaustible wealth, was diluted in a foreign ethnic group. The idea of the race makes it our duty in the future to *preserve and concentrate our energy in the strictest possible way*. The tragic division that dominated the Middle Ages Empire arose from its dispersal and from an often deficient or too narrow consciousness. This alone explains why the Europe of the time, already structured according to the Germanic principle, succumbed to *the universalism of imperial Rome and Christianity*, and why precious blood was shed for ideas that were at odds with its history and way of thinking; it is necessary to acknowledge the faults of the past if the future is to take shape.

It must therefore be made clear that a lasting order in Europe can only be established by the Empire. The destiny of Europe in the future will be as it was in the past, determined by the destiny of the Empire. Europe was a unit, the centre of human civilisation, as long as the Empire was great and powerful. At the time when it reached the height of its power, the kings of England and France considered themselves vassals of the German Empire. But Europe was disturbed and left to the aggression of powers outside its area, when the Empire broke up. We must remember that the name as well as the historical reality we imply in the word "Europe" is a creation of the Nordic race. That is why the Empire is also in the future the *European heart and bridgehead,* the magnetic centre that attracts and holds together the Germanic peoples. It is not our task to define the *political structure* that the future holds for the community of European peoples. The answer to the question raised by the situation of the Dutch, Walloons and Scandinavians in relation to the Empire can only be given at the end of the war and in the light of the Führer's decision. It will certainly result from an examination of the participation of these peoples in the struggle for the regeneration of this continent. It will by no means be formed on the basis of a fixed scheme, valid for all; nor will it proceed from the methods and vocabulary of liberal nationalist and legal theories. What will emerge will be a *true community order,* within which each one will have a place and a rank according to *the results and sacrifices made for the whole* and the specificity and particularities of its own being. The position of a particular Germanic people's unit within this Empire will be determined in accordance with the political and spiritual energy which radiates from it. The ultimate decision will not be taken at a conference table, but on the battlefields where the Germanic peoples under German leadership are fighting for their future as equal members of the future Empire. The Waffen SS has been given the task by the Führer of cultivating the Germanic idea. It is its immediate duty to prepare the way for the new Reich, for which members of all Germanic peoples are fighting and dying in its ranks.

> *Any Empire that is divided weakens. So no Empire disappears without internal division. The building of a house and the creation of an Empire require the same unity.*

> Paracelsus

SS BOOKLET NO. 9/10. 1943.

EUROPE'S GERMANIC SOLIDARITY

A voice from Holland

When thinking about or writing about a topic, it is necessary to be clear about the objective. And it may be that you realise that you have not asked the right question and that you have strayed from the original objective.

This is what happened to me with this article. I had already chosen the title; I knew where I wanted to go and yet what I want to express goes beyond simple solidarity.

It is always useful to give an exact definition of a word. When, for example, we open the page of the Linguistic Brockhaus to the word "solidarity", we find: "A feeling of belonging together". Do we have to give a foreign name to what is the greatest ideal to be achieved? Is there no such thing as a Germanic word? You don't have to look hard: "Unity"! But what does unity mean? The Brockhaus says: "Something that is strongly joined, inseparable". So the difference is not great, yet the foreign word sounds different to our ears and therefore also has a different content. Let us now think of everyday language. We are talking about an organic unity, the unity of Germany. A living being is a solid unit; it is made up of organs, but these organs, however different they may be, are not 'united', they form a unit. An "organic solidarity" is an absurdity. So we are getting closer to the meaning of our question.

We clearly feel that we cannot consider Germany as a single unit. The word solidarity is appropriate for Europe. Europe is a whole, it has common enemies, it can only exist if there is a sense of cohesion and it starts to become a unit. The racial composition of southern Europe is different from that of northern Europe. On the other hand, the mutual enrichment is long-standing, we can even say as long-standing as European civilisation, and a whole has arisen from the geographical situation and history. But German unity is something different. It is really a question of an organic unity, of a form that is also a racial unity because the Nordic race has permeated the whole from the earliest times and left its mark on it.

So we have arrived precisely where we wanted to go. If Germany is something "strongly joined, inseparable" because it is racially homogeneous, then we can say that the unity of all European peoples should also be based on this principle. We Germans who do not belong to the German people can therefore have a different relationship to Germany than that of solidarity. And this other relationship, this organic unity, which for us represents the highest and most absolute thing, we call "the Empire".

Is this title incorrect? Yes and no. Yes, if we think of the solidarity of all the peoples of Europe, to which we, the Germanic peoples, also belong. No, if we understand that the unity of Germania is in solidarity with the rest of Europe. This is clearly expressed in politics. There are many people in the Germanic border regions who understand and loyally believe that solidarity is necessary. They also like to talk about a 'Europe'. They think like 'Europeans' and feel like 'nationalists', which is quite compatible. For them, this solidarity is the starting point and the end of all their thinking. There are others who rarely talk about "Europe", who are not even nationalists in the narrowest sense of the word! In saying this, I am aware that I am opening the door to some misunderstandings.

It is not true to say that these men are not strongly attached to their people, to its customs and art, to its country and way of life; but they aspire to something higher than this homeland, which is not the mere product of a vulgar feeling of solidarity, but has a deeper cause: the great Germanic awakening, the consciousness of the racial bond, the experience of what we call "the Empire". When we speak of Empire, we do not think primarily or secondarily of solidarity. The Empire represents for us the consciousness of an organic unity which is simply present, but which had disappeared from the horizon, from the consciousness of our people, and which is waiting to take shape. We are, of course, "nationalists" but in a different way from others.

Anything that is to become an organic unit must take time to grow and cannot be decreed. We cannot profess the idea of Empire without an ideological background, and a world view cannot be a matter of regulations. Only this created unity can be defined as "firmly coherent and indissoluble".

The road to this is long. We do not want to deny solidarity the character of a feeling of cohesion. It can also lead to Empire, but we must be clear that there is a big difference.

The SS was the first organisation that consciously tried to realise the idea of an 'Empire' based on this importance of unity, not on solidarity but on an internal racial consciousness.

We *have faith* in the Empire. We want to fight for it.

We know that it is more than just a state construct, that it embodies the whole of Germanic civilisation united in an external state form.

He who makes the heaviest sacrifice must have the top job, but not out of "nationalistic" sentiment, for "Empire" will exist wherever it is consciously experienced as being above all petty nationalisms, even if these might be estimable in themselves.

After a long historical division, the birth of the Empire is difficult. We can already say that it never existed because Germanic countries were never part of it. The Empire is therefore not a recovery from the past but a *future*, both for the central area and for the neighbouring peoples.

J. C. Nachenius, Holland

As National Socialists, we want to unite the other Germanic peoples with the strength of our hearts and make them our brothers.

Heinrich Himmler

(in front of the Junkers in Brunswick on 12 December 1940)

SS NOTEBOOK NO. 9. 1944.

THE AWAKENING OF OUR RACE

written by a Dutchman

The mission entrusted by history to the Germanic peoples is now inflexible. The Western world of ideas, in which we have lived for so long, has collapsed. New forces are at work. Europe is now being challenged by powers that want to reduce it to a colony. This Europe can only assert its autonomy, its space and its high culture if it fights together. It was from this continental thinking, from this awareness of the common character of the Germanic communities, that the first political alliances were born. The political consequences followed the awakening of the race. All the Germanic countries brought together a selection of their youth in the SS Order.

That Germany is ahead of us in fulfilling her mission of restoring political vigour to the Nordic race and spirit is due to the fact that we Germanic peoples have too long slumbered in the shadow of England.

Norway has its fleet, the Netherlands has its colonies, Lithuania, Estonia, Latvia, liberated with the help of Germany and England, are swinging between the two. Now, for all of us, the matter is serious. It is often said too easily that we are living through one of the greatest revolutions in the history of the world, a time at the end of many centuries. Generally speaking, people are not at all aware of the dimension of this era, which is not simply a change of governmental regime. The upheaval spans a century and what we are experiencing today is the succession of the French Revolution by the National Socialist Revolution. It is the beginning of an era in which the ideals of a so-called democracy dominated by international big business no longer prevail, but a turning point in history in which the renewal of our blood, the revolt of our race, influences our lives. Only in this way can we understand the superhuman performance of the German blood soldiers over the last four or five years. The men and women would not have endured the frightful bombardment of the cities with such greatness of spirit if they did not know that their very existence was at stake. All these millions of human beings act, fight, and die in a new religious upsurge. From their blood is born a new faith that enriches the natural and healthy forces of life. This law of blood is at the same time the law of the same race. He who betrays his blood betrays himself. All mixing leads to destruction. If a race is to survive, men must fight for the preservation of the species and women must be prepared to ensure the survival of the species for generations through their children.

We fight as National Socialists and SS men for a life in keeping with our species, against all foreign psychic intrusion and against race mixing. We seek to return to the sources of our life and our species. The law that the bloods of related peoples attract each other demands a fight against all the powers that want to bastardize and fragment us. These are the same powers for whom, in their plan for world domination, peoples and races are merely targets to be exploited. They are also the ones who want to prevent people of the same blood from coming together. It is the Bolshevik-Plutocratic power with its new agents throughout the world, international big capital, the power of Judaism, international Freemasonry and as a third power, the politicised Christian Church with its thirst for political power. At the other end of the spectrum is the slogan for the reunification of the Germanic world: the fight for the Great German Empire.

We are fighting today, often misunderstood by our own people and branded as traitors to our homeland. It seems as if these people have taken over the role of the Jews and the Freemasons in the 1930s and are acting in their place. Peoples and races do not die out in wars if they remain true to their blood, but through internal decomposition, in the course of a long peace.

Wars are always nothing more than trials that history imposes on people. In Adolf Hitler we honour the leader of all Germans, and when we Germanic volunteers speak of Germania, it is because we believe that in the future our own survival is guaranteed only in the interests of the Germanic world as a whole.

The small Germanic countries on the periphery of the Great German Empire wanted to work towards a general European goal. Blood calls for blood. We must contribute our strength and will to a great German Empire because, more than Germany, we have fallen into disunity and foreign domination. Even if there had been no German Empire in history, there would still be time to build one. Not only would we then be following a law of nature, but our survival and freedom threatened by the Soviet Union, the United States and the British would be assured.

We must join this future community of all Germanic peoples with equal rights, but one can only speak of equal rights if one has fulfilled equal duties. This is a National Socialist principle for the common life of the peoples. Equality of rights presupposes equality of duties and benefits. We are convinced that in ten, twenty or thirty years' time this great Germanic community will become a reality and that in the government of this great Germania there will sit men from the various Germanic regions who today fight in the SS. Just as today men from the Netherlands, Norway, Denmark and Sweden fight together, so they will work in the new community of peoples, supported by the loyalty of their fellow citizens, for the whole nation. The small disagreements that have arisen from time to time cannot destroy this great picture, this hopeful opening to the future. Adolf Hitler is its guide and guarantor.

Let's open an important parenthesis about the German Empire. My father served in the Dutch army but never had to risk his life, nor did my grandfather or great-grandfather. And then, suddenly, I myself am a soldier in the front line and this peaceful, middle-class clan life is interrupted for the first time by my going to the front. This act is an important contribution to the formation of the future German Empire. Moreover, for the first time in our clan, my son will have a father who was a soldier at the front. In this way we are entering the heroic tradition as it lives in Germany.

This new emerging tradition also includes a proud generation of soldiers' wives. Thus we are assured of the future, for National Socialism, in its warlike expression, can only be based on front-line soldiers.

In one of his last speeches, the Führer said: "No bourgeois state will survive this war". This was of great importance to many workers, but it must also be important to us. No bourgeois state will survive this war; this means that a totally revolutionary society will arise. The struggle will not end with our victory, and the men at the front in all the German-speaking countries must also set to work after the war to make National Socialism a reality. The SS must be the driving force behind the National Socialist Revolution. The SS is not the Party, but only the storm troop of National Socialist ideology.

It is, moreover, a community of the Order whose aim, after the battle, is to transmit the ideological heritage seamlessly from generation to generation.

As we can see, there is hardly anything that separates the Dutch from the German or the Norwegian. The greatness that we all share is the sublime heritage of the Nordic race and National Socialism as an ideology in keeping with our species. We consider the combination of these two things to be the most important, and we will overcome the small differences. In faith in our historic mission, we want to build the new Europe together with all Germanic people. We are not only soldiers, but also pioneers and as such the guarantors of the race and the future of Europe.

The reality of the heroic commitment of an elite of Germanic peoples on all the fronts of Europe is a striking proof of the value of Nordic blood in general.

"TO ARMS FOR EUROPE".
SPEECH GIVEN IN PARIS ON 5 MARCH 1944 AT THE PALAIS
DE CHAILLOT BY SS-STURMBANNFÜHRER LÉON DEGRELLE.

THE HEALTH OF THE PEOPLE

Unity there is made, and it is the only unity that will triumph. Europe is made not only because it is in danger, but because it has a soul. We are not only united by something negative, like saving our skin. What matters on earth is not so much to live as to live well. It is not to have dragged on fifty years of inactivity, it is, for one year, for eight days to have led a proud and triumphant life.

Intellectuals can develop their theories. They have to. These are innocent games, often games of decadence. How many French people take pleasure in these subtleties! *How many French people believe that they have made the revolution when they have written a fine article on the revolution!* Europe is the old country of intelligence, and the great laws of reason are indispensable to European harmony. But all the same, our century means something more than the awakening of the forces of intelligence alone. There have been so many intelligent people who were sterile beings. By awakening all the instinctive and rumbling forces of the human being, by recalling that there is a beauty of the body and a harmony, that one does not lead people with dwarfs, gringos and deformed beings, by reminding us that there is no action without joy, nor joy without health, racism, awakening those great forces that come from the depths of the world, brings back to the leadership of Europe a healthy and indomitable youth, a youth that loves, a youth that has an appetite. So when we look at the world, it is no longer to analyse it ... but to take it!

Germany will have done a priceless service to a decadent Europe by bringing it health. When we looked at pre-war Europe, when we went to the menageries that were the parliamentary assemblies, when we saw all those grinning faces, all those old, stultified gentlemen, their bellies falling out as if they had had too many pregnancies, their tired faces, their stained eyes, we wondered: "Is this our people? The French people still knew how to be witty, which was basically a form of sneer and revolt, but they no longer had this great innocent joy of strength, whereas Germany had this reservoir of limitless strength. What surprised you, men and women of France, when you saw them arrive in 1940? It was that they were beautiful as gods, with harmonious and supple bodies, that they were clean. You have never seen a young warrior, you don't see him yet in Russia, with a democratic beard. All of this is clean, all of this has allure, race, mouth.

With racism, with this awakening of healthy strength, Germany restored health to her people first, and then to the whole of Europe. When we left for Russia, we were told: "Ah, you will suffer over there, you will be prematurely aged men". When we came back from the front and looked at the others, we found them all to be old coils, while we felt in our veins a strength that nothing would stop.

People's revolution

Everywhere in Europe the people were unhappy, everywhere happiness was monopolised by a few dozen anonymous monsters—material happiness locked up in bank vaults, spiritual happiness smothered by all forms of corruption. Europe was old because it was not happy; the people were no longer smiling because they no longer felt alive.

At this very moment, what else is going on? Whether you look at Paris or Brussels, you find the same humiliated people in the suburbs, with starvation wages, with leper supplies. You arrive on the boulevards and find these big indolent pashas, larded with beefsteak and thousand-dollar notes, and who say to you: "It's practical, the war: before the war we were winning, during the war we are winning, after the war we will win. Oh, let them count in the end, they will win our machine-gun discharges, they will win the rope of the hangmen!

For what interests us most in the war is the revolution that will follow, it is to give back to these millions of working-class families the joy of living, it is that the millions of European workers should feel free, proud, respected beings, it is that throughout Europe capital should cease to be an instrument of domination of the peoples, to become an instrument in the service of the happiness of the peoples.

The war cannot end without the triumph of the socialist revolution, without the worker in the factories and the worker in the fields being saved by the revolutionary youth. It is the people who pay, it is the people who suffer. The great experience of the Russian front still proves this. The people have shown that they are capable of making their revolution without the intellectuals. In our ranks, eighty per cent of our volunteers are workers. They have shown that they have a clearer head and that they can see further than thousands of intellectuals who have nothing left but ink in their penholders, nothing left in their heads and above all nothing left in their hearts, intellectuals who claim to be the elite. That is all over.

The real elites are formed at the front, a chivalry is created at the front, young leaders are born at the front. The real elite of tomorrow is there, far from the gossip of the big cities, far from the hypocrisy and sterility of the masses who no longer understand. It is created during grandiose and tragic battles, like those of Cherkasy. It was a great joy for us to find ourselves there among young people from all corners of Europe. There were thousands of Germans from old Germany, men from the Baltic—and in particular the Narva Battalion with the Latvians—there were tall blond boys from the Scandinavian countries, the Danes, the Dutch, our brothers in arms the Flemings, Hungarians, Romanians. There were *also a few Frenchmen, who represented you in this scrum, while so many of your compatriots were engaged in other sectors of the Eastern Front. And there, between all of us, a complete fraternity was established, because everything has changed since the war. When we look at a slouching old bourgeois in our Fatherland, we do not consider that man to be of our race, but when we look at a young revolutionary from Germany, or from elsewhere, we consider him to be of our Fatherland, since we are with the youth and with the Revolution.*

We are political soldiers, the SS badge shows Europe where the political truth is, where the social truth is, and, joining this political army of the Führer from everywhere, we are preparing the political frameworks of the post-war period. Tomorrow Europe will have elites such as it has never known before. An army of young apostles, of young mystical men, stirred up by a faith that nothing will stop, will one day emerge from this great seminary at the front. *It is there too, Frenchmen, that we must be present.*

Every people must earn their place

In the national parties, there are now in France, men who have understood that it is necessary to work with the whole of Europe, who have understood above all that the revolutionary unity of Europe is the SS. The first, the SS, had the courage to go straight ahead, to hit hard and to want the real socialist revolution. For a year or two, at the front, we have seen France. And now inside, we see France: the France of the de Brinons, the Déats, the Doriots, the Darnands, and above all the France of the young. We see something other than little guys on the corner of bars, with a cigarette falling out and a pernod ready to be swallowed. We see big, well-built boys, capable of making the revolution and then choosing a beautiful girl in France to give her vigorous children.

For years, you have had proportionally three times fewer children than the Russians, twice as few as the Germans. One wonders why in this country of love. Love cannot go without children! Aren't they the poetry and the resurrection of love?

This denatality was one of the symptoms of the general impotence of democratic peoples, impotence to think far ahead, impotence to be bold, impotence in the face of revolutionary fervour and impotence in the face of privations, in the face of suffering itself. You must be told, Frenchmen, that you have lost fifty years in a Europe of soldiers, which is fighting, which is showing its courage, which needs to be heroic, but which is preparing a social revolution and a moral foundation for each people. It is no longer possible for these hundreds of thousands of men to have died, borne by the most sublime virtues, only to return to the dunghill of mediocrity, baseness and spinelessness. The front has created not only forces of salvation on the military field, revolutionary forces which tomorrow will pass through everything, but it is preparing the revolution which is most necessary for Europe: the spiritual revolution. We need upright and pure men, who know that the highest joys of man are in the soul. We will no longer admit the mediocrity of souls, we will no longer admit that men live for sordid joys, for their egotism, in a narrow atmosphere. We want to elevate the people, to give them back their appetite, their grandeur. We want people to have the sovereign joy of rising above everyday life.

That is why, my dear comrades, we must be united. Europe, standing up against Communism, in defence of our civilisation, our spiritual heritage and our ancient cities, must be united, and *each people must earn its place, not by adding up the past, but by giving the blood that washes and purifies. Europe must be united in order to carry out, under the sign of the SS, the National Socialist revolution, and to bring to souls, the revolution of souls.*

You don't beg for a right.
We fight for him.

Adolf Hitler

SS BOOKLET NO. 6. 1943.

RESPECT FOR THE INDIVIDUAL

The Movement must ensure by all means that the person is respected; it must never forget that the value of everything human lies in personal quality, that every idea and every result is the fruit of a man's creative force and that admiring its greatness is not only a right due to him but also unites him with those who benefit from it.

The person is irreplaceable. He or she must be because he or she embodies the creative cultural element of a non-mechanical nature. Just as a famous master cannot be replaced by another who takes over his unfinished canvas, so a great poet and thinker, a great soldier and a great statesman are unique. For their activity is always in the realm of art; it cannot be instilled mechanically and represents an innate divine grace.

The greatest upheavals and conquests of this earth, their greatest cultural results, immortal deeds in the field of state art etc., are indissolubly attached to a name that represents them. To forgo paying tribute to a great spirit is to lose an immense force derived from the names of all great men and women.

From *Mein Kampf* by Adolf Hitler

SS BOOKLET NO. 8. 1938.

THE BOOK, THIS SWORD OF THE MIND

There was probably a time in Germany when the importance of books was overestimated.

The bourgeoisie, increasingly uprooted and intellectualised, did not escape the danger of seeing it as a fetish to be worshipped, a magic key that opens all doors, especially those leading to a quick and successful career. Those were the days when gangly, four-eyed teenagers who could do nothing with their ten fingers, devoured books day and night, were pampered and adored because of their academic achievements. The attitude of the parents remained unchanged, although these highly educated prizewinners mostly ran away from the harshness of life. Most people overlook the fact that a pallid, home-bound generation grew up nourished by uninterrupted reading, that the mind was indulged and that the strengths and qualities of the body were neglected. The mind, or what was considered to be the mind, triumphed. German youth was increasingly in danger of ignoring what life was really like, and of forming second-hand ideas through instruments—or even more damagingly—through writers, through lives lived in literary works, or through simulated lives in superficial novels.

The general transformation of things also concerns this field. The danger of overvaluing the book has disappeared. Books and bookish knowledge are no longer an absolute goal. They must serve the rebirth of our German people through the harmonious training of the individual, through the definition and implementation of general tasks.

But since evolution never follows a straight line, the pendulum of the event swings all the more strongly in the other direction. And so the previous danger has been replaced by its opposite. Overvaluation is no longer to be feared. Rather, it is a matter of preventing an undervaluation of the book.

The book of value best defines the reality of life; it has the task of communicating new experiences to those who are willing through the spiritual vision it arouses in them and the emotions that arise from its art. A book truly worthy of the name must not distract man from what is proper to him, but uncover what is deepest in him, if he possesses the magical power to translate his will into action. Such a book survives the ephemeral moment and is today the ferment, the extremely important material for reflection.

Consequently, after years of overestimating the book, in times of real danger, it is necessary to prevent it from being sidelined by all means. In this respect, the book week, etc., is a great help. The individual who takes a book from his library and communicates his experience to the other members of the community, however, performs the most important action. Together with them, he or she wants to make concrete what he or she has read and to rediscover what inspires all important books: life lived in an exemplary way, rooted in the soil, rich.

Hans Franck

"D'ESTOC ET DE TAILLE", BY GUNTHER D'ALQUEN, 1937.

HUMOUR IS A NECESSITY!

Woe to the people who have no sense of humour!

Woe to him who cannot laugh heartily until he has tears in his eyes. Woe to him who fears humour, who detects it with a suspicious air in every distrustful brain and cannot have a spontaneous attitude because of a lack of inner confidence and control. Woe, thrice woe, for he shows that he is weak and self-righteous.

We receive many letters, hundreds of them, expressing great joy and telling us about the way we deal with the various problems of everyday life or issues that are not problems. And the ever-increasing daily mass of mail shows us that our people enthusiastically understand that we should not observe, with frowns, the occasional little grains of sand that slightly grind the giant machinery of our state.

We look down on them with a smile and do not magnify them to the point of suggesting that the little grains of sand could stop the machine.

A good friend advises us not to shoot sparrows with guns. We only "work" with heavy weapons in very rare cases that require it. The sparrows think that the threatening laughter is a barrage and they are already getting very angry, except when they notice that we don't take them for golden eagles! We won't shoot the sparrows with cannons but with crossbows because we don't want to dirty the facades of our buildings—more for aesthetic reasons than for fear of shaking the foundations of National Socialism.

No one can force us to take up arms with a serious face, even for small, insignificant things. But we do not tolerate seeing stains on a beautiful crystal glass. It is true that a simple wipe is enough to make it sparkle!

For us, humour has become one of the essential weapons in the fight for power. It must remain a weapon. We mocked a whole system with sonorous laughter, put every leader of the November clique under the microscope with terrible humour and removed the false nose of his 'dignity'. The sharp pencil of Mjölnir (the famous cartoonist of the SS newspaper *Das schwarze Korps*) mocked them and ridiculed an evil and dangerous police system. All of us who know Mjölnir appreciate and honour him for his humour, as a serious artist using this weapon in the service of the struggle.

The more confident our laughter, the harder the fight became. In the worst moments, the laughing faces of our fellow soldiers told the Führer that his troop was intact and filled with an indomitable faith in victory. For sceptics never laugh.

Should we put on a grim face when we are now in power and National Socialism has won its impregnable position because the people trust it?

National Socialism is not a medieval institution. It has captured the hearts of German youth. This youth, looking joyfully into the future with its indomitable and overflowing strength, embodied the new Reich. This conscious and proud confidence gives rise to a joyful, happy optimism. It is an inexhaustible source of contemplative humour.

One day, we would like to "make a fuss" and provoke the discontent of some and others. But we will do nothing more than frequently air the dust-filled rooms of the asthmatic bourgeoisie. It is not our dust that they breathe. For who is the one who feels insulted when attention is drawn to the black spot on his nose? Only petty bourgeois and Pharisees who believe that the time for German evolution has come to an end because they are blind, stupid and do not want to see anything.

But time moves on. Nothing can be done about it. A little more humour sweeps away serious thoughts and laughter relieves and liberates. A little more humour every day! Otherwise you will become cantankerous, old and grey and won't even be able to stand yourselves.

But we...

SS NOTEBOOK NO. 9. 1944.

TELL EVERYONE

Let everyone say to himself
in the depths of his heart,
every minute:
When I am weak, my people are weak.
When I am a hypocrite, my people are hypocrites.
When I fail, my people fail.
When I abandon my people, I abandon myself.
When I oppose my people, I oppose myself.
Losing courage and initiative
means losing your life,
means betraying your father and mother, your children and grandchildren.

There is only one way
against war: war!
against weapons: weapons!

against the enemy's bravery: his own bravery!
and against misfortune: the spirit of sacrifice.
Against the hatred of the world, the only help,
is the love of our people,
ready to make any sacrifice.

The weakness of the heart devours everything around it
like rot,
as among the fruits,
where one apple spoils the others.
What you allow yourself, your neighbour also allows himself.
When you cheat, he cheats too.
When you complain, he complains too.
When you gossip, he gossips about you too.
And when one of us finally betrays,
everyone betrays himself.

We call for justice.
But you have to earn your fate too.
He who is unworthy reaps indignity,
the one who is courageous the courage,
the best the best.
And even when the gods refuse their help,
the right man still gets their blessing.

All life is dangerous.
You don't just die in a fire.
Every mother risks her blood for the life of her child,
perpetuating his people.

To preserve life
all risk their lives,
some for themselves, their hunger,
their own necessity,
others for many,
and one man for all:
the hero on the battlefield.
He grants life to all. He lives in them.
By his death
eternal laurels crown his sleep
survives the homeland.

What has taken place, remains active,
the good and the bad.

Let no one believe
that he might be hiding something,
and secretly do evil.
What is healthy begets healthy,
the rotten the rotten.

Nothing can betray us—except our own mouth.
Nothing can lose us—except our own hearts.
Nothing can strike us—except our own hand.
No one can deliver us—except ourselves.

Wil Vesper

CHAPTER II

I. HISTORY

SS BOOKLET No. 8. 1938.

THE OATH OF THE ATHENIAN EPHEBES

"Whatever our objective may be, I do not want to defile the sacred weapons and abandon my comrades. I want to fight for what is great and sacred, alone or with many others. I do not want to betray my country for any advantage. I must constantly listen to the leaders and obey the present and future laws, for it is the people who create them. And if anyone undertakes to abolish the laws or not to obey them, I cannot admit it without intervening, alone or with all. I must honour the beliefs of the fathers. May the gods be witnesses to this![3]

SS BOOKLET No. 2. 1944.

THE BIRTH OF GERMANIC EUROPE AROUND 500 AD

When in the 5th century AD the Germanic tribes struck violent blows that caused the disintegration of the Roman Empire in Europe—in Italy, Gaul and Spain—they simultaneously created the foundations of present-day Europe. A new era began with them. The Imperium Romanum was already in a state of internal decay when, in January 406, the Germanic armies definitively destroyed its borders on the Rhine and in France. They not only expanded the Germanic territory through incessant colonisation, but also founded cities in bold expeditions of conquest. A few decades later, a Roman recounts:

"The officials, not only in the cities, but also in the rural communes and villages, are all tyrants. Everything is taken from the poor, widows groan, orphans are trampled underfoot. The pressure of taxes and extortion weighs terribly on everyone. Many of them, even men of noble origin and free people, flee to the Germans in order not to fall victim to the

---

[3] From the "Soldier's Breviary", edited by Bruno Brehm.

prosecution of the public power and be massacred by it. They therefore seek a Roman humanity among the barbarians because they can no longer bear the barbaric inhumanity of the Romans. They would rather be free under the guise of servitude than lead a slave's life under the guise of freedom. And even the Romans living under the rule of the Goths, Vandals and Franks have only one wish, and that is not to return to live under Roman rule. The entire Roman people beg the heavens that they may continue to live among the Germans.

Wherever the Germans established their rule, law and order replaced the despotism of the great landowners and financiers.

These new Germanic states established on the soil of the Imperium had a destiny rich in adventures. Most of them were East Germanic peoples who settled there in the south. They had come from Sweden and Denmark around the beginning of the Christian era and settled between the Oder and the Vistula—the Goths, Vandals and Burgundians, as well as many others such as the Roughs, Heruli and Gepids. They took over the homeland of the Bastarnes and Skires who had settled on the Pomeranian coast a thousand years earlier. From the 2nd century onwards, the conquering convoys of the East Germans set out from this East German area. While some of the Vandals took over Hungary, the Goths founded a powerful empire in southern Russia and Romania. From the 3rd century onwards, they simultaneously undertook constant warlike expeditions against the Roman Imperium. The Romans, so proud in the past, could only defend themselves with difficulty against the attacking troops, and then only with the help of Germanic auxiliary troops in the Roman army. But when, around 370, the Huns emerged from Asia and defeated the Goth Empire in Russia, the Visigoths left their homes. They devastated the Balkans, entered Italy in 410 under the leadership of their king Alaric, conquered Rome and consolidated their rule after the death of their glorious king in southern France, from where they reached Spain around 460.

In a similar way, the Vandals and Suebi had reached the Rhine in 406, attacking along the Danube; they had crossed Gaul and conquered Spain. While the Suevi remained in the north-west of the peninsula, the Vandals moved a little later towards North Africa and subdued this rich province. But their warrior strength soon weakened under the softening climate of the Mediterranean. And their numerical strength was not enough to establish a lasting supremacy over the locals from other peoples—the entire Vandal people consisted of only 85,000 men. There was no trace of them left when they were destroyed by the armies of the Byzantine emperor a century later.

Apparently, the fate of the Ostrogoths in Italy was similar. They had left Hungary around 470 under the reign of their great king Theodoric—where they had lived since the collapse of their southern Russian Empire—and had conquered the Italian peninsula with their swords in a short time. Theodoric surpassed all other Germanic kings of his time in power, fame and influence. Yet his people were not strong enough to hold on to power. After twenty years of fighting, they finally succumbed to the superiority of the Eastern Roman Empire in 553. The remnants of the people who remained in Upper Italy assimilated into the Lombards, who received their inheritance and built up a strong power in northern and central Italy that lasted for centuries.

Thus, in southern Europe, an area was created where Germanic peoples dominated the Roman population—in Spain, the Visigoths and Burgundians, then also the Franks, in Italy the Ostrogoths and, later, the Lombards.

In all these countries, the migrating Germanic people had settled with wives, children, servants and maids as a fighting nobility that exercised power over the natives they had defeated. The latter had to give up some of their property and slaves to the new lords so that each Germanic family could have its own domain. The Germanic men were therefore both peasants and warriors. In times of peace, they lived mostly as peasants scattered throughout the country, while many of the younger ones formed the king's retinue at his court or fought in grouped units that garrisoned border castles and towns to keep the peace with their weapons. But in case of danger, they rejoined the old military units and took up their swords with a cheerful heart.

The description given by a contemporary of the Goths reigning in Spain reveals the nature of the Germanic conquerors: "The Goths have agile and strong bodies, lively and self-confident minds. They are tall and slender, full of dignity in attitude and gesture, quick to action and insensitive to injury. They even boast of their injuries and despise death.

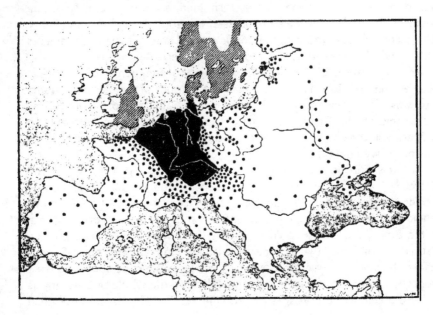

Germanic Europe around 900.
In the German area, the heart of Europe, the vital centre of Germanic Europe was born. The North Germans who founded states in southern Europe also allowed the Germanic blood to take hold among the Roman peoples. Around the year 1000, the North Germans also became part of the continental Germanic culture, of which the German Reich was the purest expression. In this way, the Germanic blood of all European peoples came together and gave rise to the common basic features of its culture at a time when the German Empire was the ruling power in Europe.

But in the long run, these many numerically weak tribes could not keep their distance from the dominated peoples. Over the centuries, they had to merge ever more closely with them. At first, the chiefs of the natives became rulers, and soon the Germanic lords also learned the language of their subjects and wore southern costumes. They gradually lost their Germanic character and thus gradually blended in with the indigenous peoples. It is regrettable that so much Germanic blood was lost. But this, on the other hand, was a precondition for the birth of a homogeneous Europe. For for centuries, even into modern times, the heritage of Germanic blood survived in the ruling classes of these Roman peoples.

The influence lasted a long time, even into the Middle Ages. The key figure of the Middle Ages, the knight, was totally animated in his attitude by the Germanic spirit. It was therefore also the heritage of Germanic blood that was reflected in the great works of these peoples in the following centuries. The Germanic heritage was perpetuated in the noble Spaniards who, from the 12th century onwards, drove the Arabs out of Spain and set off as conquerors towards America. It lived on in the Provençal knights who helped protect Europe on the eastern Mediterranean front from the onslaught of Islam. It was also expressed in Leonardo da Vinci and other Renaissance greats who, around 1500, created the cultural achievements without which our present life would be inconceivable.

The annexation of southern Europe to the community of Germanic peoples, this creation of a forward base in the south of the Germanic home area, was of the greatest importance for the overall future of Europe. It was only thanks to the Germanic ruling class that these peoples were able to cooperate in the chivalric civilisation of the Middle Ages—in which the first Europe, as we know it today, was revealed.

But this Europe 'ours' was only really founded by that part of the Germanic people who made Central Europe, the German heartland,— including the Netherlands, Belgium and northern France—a Germanic ethnic territory. The achievements of the Franks were at the origin of this. In the 8th century they could rightly say, and were clearly aware of its historical significance, that Europe is the land of the Frankish Empire. Shortly before the Christian era, the Germanic peoples had moved south and west from their former settlement area and colonised the whole of Germany as far as the Danube, the Vosges and the Meuse. The German territory had become a "Germania". For centuries the Roman Imperium had contained these peoples, mainly the Franks in the Lower Rhine, the Alamanni in the Upper Rhine and Danube, and the Bavarians in Bohemia, although it could not prevent the ever-increasing settlement of these Germanic colonists west of the Rhine. But after the collapse of the Imperium shortly after 400, these populations also advanced; however, they only subdued the country they could colonise completely. Thus, Germany became Germanic up to the crest of the Alps including Switzerland and Alsace, while the Franks crossed the Rhine from the Moselle to its mouth and within a century invaded the whole country extending to the Seine region (a little north of Paris) with dense Germanic settlements. At the same time, the Frisians and Saxons had occupied the Netherlands north of the mouth of the Rhine. Further north, the Angles and Saxons began to colonise England from the mouth of the Elbe.

Thus the Germanic living space in the centre of Europe had become a powerful block, stretching west and east from the Rhine to the English Channel and the Oder. Here now lived the majority of the Germanic peoples, who in the following centuries were to unite to form the Germanic people. And it was from here that the centre of Germanic Europe developed.

The Franks achieved a major feat by creating a homogeneous political power with the previously independent tribes of the Bavarians, Alamanni, Saxons and Thuringians. For centuries, they were the only truly dominant people in Europe. Their king Clovis founded this state when he took power around 500 A.D. He first of all united the various Frankish regions into a powerful Frankish state. This unification made the Franks so powerful that Clovis and his sons succeeded in integrating the other tribes—the Alamanni, Thuringians and Bavarians—into the Frankish state and thus creating a large Germanic bloc in the centre of Europe. This was later completed by Charlemagne, who attached the Saxons and Bavarians to the Reich. Charles thus completed the work of Clovis, who had already begun the integration of southern France after his triumph over the Visigoths and Burgundians: thus, after subduing Lombard Italy, the Roman peoples under Germanic rule—with the exception of the Spaniards—were closely linked politically to the powerful central Germanic Empire.

Just as King Clovis had expanded his power with an iron fist, Charlemagne also created the future basis for the internal structure of France. He broke down all resistance to him, and consolidated and extended his royal power. He gave special powers to chiefs of regions, tribes and judges—who depended on him and had to implement his decisions and not those of the popular assemblies. In this way, the king gained the power to lead the people and direct the state by his will.

Thanks to his capitularies, a class of Frankish chiefs bound to the king by the Germanic rule of troop loyalty gradually emerged under his successors, and whose values of honour and loyalty determined their actions. Concern for their subordinates, for those they had to protect, and the just application of law were their supreme law. They maintained order and justice in the name of the king.

The Frankish Empire thus created an internal national structure comparable to that which later existed in the German imperial era, where the values of the Germanic soul determined the life of the whole people as well as of each individual.

The marking of the basic features of national life gave rise to the principle of Germanic Europe, as this Empire comprised the largest part of the Germanic peoples and became a European political reality.

This Europe united the Germanic people between the English Channel and the Oder. The Germanic ruling classes of the Roman peoples in Italy, France and Spain were linked to it. The Germanic culture of the medieval imperial period was able to flourish and to permeate the Germanic peoples of the North and of England. Thus the Germanic blood unity of the European peoples, which was given a boost by the Germanic peoples around the year 500, was the basis for the development of present-day Europe and its culture.

Hans fürg Boecker

SS BOOKLET NO. 8. 1939.

MODERN ANTI-JEWISH LAWS, ALREADY EXISTING IN THE TIME OF THE GERMANS!

Levy on Jewish wealth, 1300 years ago

It is now universally known that the Jewish question has not only arisen since the birth of National Socialism, but that already in the Middle Ages German peasants and townspeople had to defend themselves against the destructive Judaism of the peoples. But very few people know that a *Germanic* tribe had to fight to the death against international Judaism over 1300 years ago.

Unfortunately, we have few records of this conflict between Germans and Jews. They are, however, sufficient to give us a picture of the events that took place in the Spanish Empire of the *Visigoths*. We are surprised to find that the laws and decrees against the Jews bear a striking resemblance to the anti-Jewish laws and decrees of the III Reich—especially the latest ones concerning the wealth tax.

How did the Visigoths come to enact these anti-Jewish laws? During the Roman Empire, Spain had been a citadel for the Jews. The Jewish octopus had stuck its suction cups on all commercial centres, communication routes and public offices. This preponderance had been abolished with the foundation of the Gothic Empire in Spain. The Visigoths themselves at first regarded the Jews as just one of many people living on the Iberian Peninsula. The Jews were therefore initially treated with great benevolence. The Visigothic kings soon realised, however, that they were dealing with a very special race of men who differed from the rest of the population not only in their beliefs, but above all in their criminal predispositions. For this reason, the Visigoth king *Rekkared I* was the first, in 590, to enact a law forbidding Jews to own slaves, to hold public office and to enter into mixed marriages with non-Jews. His successor, *Sisibut,* was even more severe. Of course, this was not, as Jews and Christians claim, the result of Christian religious zeal, but because this far-sighted Germanic ruler, described by his contemporaries as exceptionally learned, generous and tolerant, especially in the treatment of prisoners of war, was convinced of the danger of the Jews and their harmfulness. Sisibut issued two anti-Jewish decrees, of which the most important provisions are given below:

1. Jews must no longer hire servants or maids. If they still have them, they must be dismissed after a legal period.
2. The Jews should have only Jewish employees.
3. Marriages between Jews and Christians will be dissolved immediately.
4. Christians who convert to Judaism will be severely punished.
5. All political and public activities are forbidden for Jews.
6. Any Jew wishing to travel must obtain a pass which he must have stamped by a clergyman in all the towns where he has stayed and which he must return to his home.
7. It is forbidden for any Christian to buy medicine from a Jew or to be treated by a Jewish doctor.

In conclusion of this law, Sisibut, the king of the Visigoths, added: My successors on the Goth throne who lift these prohibitions will be condemned, along with the guilty Jews, to eternal damnation.

Sisibut reigned for only eight years. *He died suddenly in the year 620, poisoned* by an unknown person!

His son *Rekkared II* further reinforced his father's anti-Jewish laws. He reigned for only fourteen months, for on 16 April 621 he *too was* found *poisoned!* We who have lived through the murder of William Gustloff, Ernest von Rath, Codreanu and other opponents of Judaism, have no doubt who instigated the assassination of these two Visigothic kings. However, *Svintila,* who ascended the throne after Rekkared II, abolished the anti-Jewish laws of Sisibut!

It is true that some of the later Visigothic kings took severe measures against the Jews, especially against those who were baptised. It seems, however, that these prescriptions were not followed with the necessary rigour by the lower clergy responsible for their application. Indeed, the demoralising influence of Judaism did not weaken but, on the contrary, strengthened in the years that followed. During the internal disorders which shook the Visigothic Empire and undermined the authority of the kingdom at the expense of the Catholic clergy, the Jews were able to resume their subversive activities. However, resistance against the Jews also increased during the reign of the best Visigothic kings: King *Egika* (687–702) invited the Council of Toledo in 693, where he came in person, to *extirpate Judaism entirely!* He also asked for a new law *forbidding Jews to enter the ports to trade with Christians.* In another council (Toledo 694) he revealed the *high treasonous plan of the Jews against the Visigothic Empire: the Jews of the Visigothic Empire had entered into a relationship with the Jews of North Africa. The revolt hatched by the Jews broke out in 694. The North African Jews would land in Spain and this would be the signal for the attack on the small social class of the Germanic Visigoths!* After the discovery of this Jewish plot threatening the stability of the kingdom, King Egika adopted the conclusions of the council, namely that *the Jews, with their wives, children and all their possessions, would be considered part of the public treasury, stripped of their homes and dwellings and placed individually, as servants of the king, in the service of the Christians.*

We see here, with shocking precision, how the methods and aims of the Jews have remained the same, but also with what insight this Germanic king had seen through the Jewish plans and had knowingly taken measures, many of which today seem banal.

The oar of the Visigoth Empire was that the subversive agitation of the Jews had spread too far in a disorganised state and that the king lacked the authority to enforce his laws effectively. The fate of the state was tragic and inevitable. The Jews then began their vengeful work against the Germanic Empire, which had dared to raise its hand against "the chosen people". The first plan of high treason was discovered by Egika himself. The second plan for the annihilation of the Germanic Empire of the Visigoths succeeded: *The Jews called the Arabs of North Africa to Spain.* They flattered them with promises to convert to Islam. As the Arabs remained sceptical, they quoted to them old prophecies in which one could read that it was at this very time that the Jews were to return to Islam. *The Arabs landed in Spain and the Jews opened the gates of the strongholds to them. The capital Toledo itself fell to the Arabs in treason.* Everywhere the Jews welcomed the enemy as liberators. The enemy showed his gratitude by leaving the cities of Cordoba, Seville, Toledo and Gharnatta in their care. With the help of the Spanish Jews, the Muslim general Tarik landed in Andalusia and defeated Roderich, the anti-Semitic king of the Visigoths, with his army in Jerez de la Frontera in a seven-day battle in the year 711. The Visigothic Empire collapsed and the last Visigoths fled to the mountains of Asturias.

A passage from a work by the Jew Rosenstock written in 1879 shows us with what jubilation the Jews hail the "prowess" of their fathers: "The cruelty of the persecutions increased under Erwig and Egika, no less, however, than the resistance of the Jews and false converts (i.e. baptized Jews), and the Visigothic domination finally collapsed when the Jews welcomed the Arab invaders under Tarik as their liberators, made common cause with them, and helped them conquer the whole land. They fought for the conquest of the power of some as well as for the fall of others. The fall of the Visigoths made Spain a paradise for the Jews, who soon filled the highest positions at court and in public employment.

SS-Uscha. Büttner

SS NOTEBOOK NO. 6B. 1941.

THE GERMANIC BLACK SEA EMPIRE

Discussions under the Crimean sky

A soft September sun shines in a cloudless sky. Beneath it lie the vast steppes of the Black Sea, dotted endlessly with small hills. Our marching columns also seem to be endless and, stretching out into the distance, reach the nearby river crossing point. Not long ago, the skilful hands of the pioneers built a makeshift passage. Now the dusty grey columns gather ... machine guns and A.C.D. cannon fill the path. After the forced marches of the last few days, a rest, although brief, is doubly welcome.

"Just like in the great invasions ..., only we carry machine guns instead of spears ..., thinks a slender young soldier aloud.

—Are you still thinking about your Germans, especially your beloved Vandals?

—This time it was the Goths," laughed the apostrophist. They had built a powerful empire here in Ukraine almost two thousand years ago.

—But, a young Rottenführer interjects into the discussion, the Goths lived under the great Theodoric in Italy and sank into decadence after twenty years of heroic fighting.

—Naturally, you get that from your Frederick Dahn, *Fight for Rome!*

—Let's let our "prehistoric troubadour"—as our Silesian is called in his company—speak, says the amused Rhinelander, clapping the youngster on the shoulders. Soon, a few more interested comrades approach the group to listen too.

—I have often told you," begins the Silesian, "that long before the foundation of Rome (753 B.C.) our own ancestors, the Germanic people, reached a level of great cultural prosperity more than a thousand years ago. But towards the end of this era (around 800 BC) such a brutal climatic change occurred in our homeland that tribes were increasingly forced to leave their homeland in search of more favourable lands. They experienced the same catastrophe as we are experiencing now: a people without a territory!

Naturally, the farmers in the far north were particularly affected. For this reason, the huge emigration of land over many centuries was mainly the work of Scandinavian peoples. They were also called the "East Germans" because they initially settled in the eastern German lands and in the border regions of the Baltic Sea. The best known of these are the aforementioned *Vandals*, the *Burgundians*, who later established their empire near Worms on the Rhine—you all know them from our Nibelungen song!—and the *Ruges*, who gave their name to our beautiful Rugia.

Towards the beginning of our era, the *Goths* came last from Sweden via the Baltic Sea. There, the Swedish provinces are still called Gotland East and West, as well as the island of Gotland, after them. They took possession of the territory at the mouth of the Vistula River, and soon extended over the whole of western Prussia as far as Pomerania, and in the east to Ermland and Samland. Trade and transport flourished so much thanks to them that they soon dominated all the Baltic regions. Our Führer therefore named liberated Gdingen "Gotenhafen", in their honour and rightly so. Do any of you remember our dangerous campaign through the Tucheler? There I showed you the chalk stones and mounds near Odry, old Gothic sites from the first century AD.

A traveller's convoy left 2000 years ago

But the Vistula region soon became too narrow for the expanding Gothic people. Its tribal legend, later transcribed in Italy, tells that a large number of them set out again under King Filimer (II century), to seize land further south-east. This Gotthard legend also describes very precisely the difficulties encountered by the emigrants. We soldiers can understand them perfectly well. They also had to cross the terrible Pripet marshes, build bridges and lay down plank paths. And if it had only been men, soldiers! But no! Like our Volksdeutsche, the Germans of Russia, the Goth peasants set off with sacks and bundles, with women and children, wagons, harnesses and everything else they needed. In spite of everything they were creators. These damned fellows did more than we thought they could do. You know yourselves what education and discipline is needed to achieve this, but also what a sense of command and organisation!

—But what do you mean? Didn't the peasants emigrate blindly with all their harness? How did the Goths know these southern countries? Didn't they have maps, by any chance?

—Of course not! —The Goths did not leave by chance either. But three or four centuries before them, other eastern Germans, the Bastarnes and the Skires, had already reached the Black Sea. Of course, they were still in touch with their former northern homeland. Through them, the Goths learned about the fertile Ukraine. Many trade and amber routes also went south. When there were too many people again, some of them systematically settled in the rich fields of the southeast.

—But, tell me, how can you know all this so accurately? There are lots of old legends everywhere.

—Don't say that. They are authentic. As far as the Goths and their south-eastern expedition are concerned, our researchers have demonstrated their authenticity through their tireless work in uncovering hundreds of excavations. It is a pity that our offensive did not reach Kowel! Nearby, a superb spearhead was found with a runic inscription and swastika ornament. It was probably lost by a Goth leader. It is an indisputable proof of the route followed by our "precursors" in Ukraine.

—How about that? So all this was once German land?

—No, not exactly. The Goths only settled in this region as a rather scattered lordly class. But they became so powerful that around 200 AD they were able to found a real state. Their lord at that time was the legendary King Ostrogotha. He was the last leader of the entire Gothic people. In the west, his empire extended as far as Romania and Hungary, over the whole of today's Bessarabia, Moldavia, Wallachia and Transylvania, and in the east beyond the Ukraine to the Don.

—In the long run, this giant Empire had difficulty in maintaining itself because it was only sparsely populated by the Goths. Legend has it that Ostrogotha himself spread his people among the Visigoths or Terwingen (Western Goths) between the Dniester and the Danube and the Ostrogoths or Greutungen (Eastern Goths) between the Dniester and the Don, giving birth to the Ukraine. During his reign, the Crimean peninsula in the Black Sea was also annexed to the Gothic settlement area.

—But, tell me, was it that simple? Wasn't this country depopulated?

—Of course, during the 3rd century Gothia was still shaken by troubles. There were always clashes with the powerful southern neighbour, the Roman Empire. The new rulers also had to impose themselves on the natives. By the 4th century the height of power had been reached.

Under the leadership of its king Ermanaric of the glorious Amelungen lineage, which lasted for almost a generation, the Ostrogothic Empire embraced not only the vast region of southern Russia. The Slavic countries in the north and east, even the Aestis and Finns, had already been subdued beforehand, so that the Gothic domination finally included the enormous area from the Black Sea to the Baltic Sea. The Goth historiographer Jordanes proudly reports that Ermanaric was often compared to Alexander the Great.

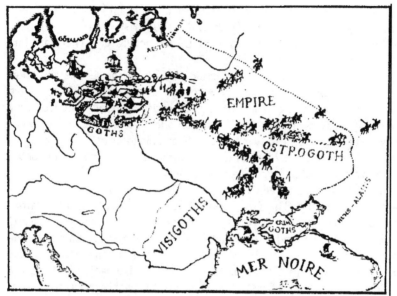

Coming from the north, from their homes in Sweden, the Goths crossed the Baltic Sea and settled in the Vistula territories. But they also migrated in convoys to the east and south-east. They founded a proud Empire in the regions where we are fighting today.

But this display of political power naturally went hand in hand with the cultural expansion of the Goths. The once famous Greek commercial and industrial centres at the mouth of the Dniester and Dnieper rivers, Tyras and Olbia, had fallen into their hands. Both sites experienced a new and constant boom as Gothic arts and crafts flourished. The Goths also proved to be incomparable masters of metallurgy, and particularly of goldsmithing. Stimulated by contact with the Greek and Scythian Aryan sister peoples, they developed a new kind of artistic style in southern Russia, which even had a strong influence on the rest of Germania and on the local decorative arts. The creations of this "coloured style", a gold cloisonné technique often complicated with multicoloured stone inlays, are the most beautiful creations of the human mind. Beautifully shaped garment clips and various other jewels came into being under their skilful hands.

Gothic art—proof of civilisation!

Gothic eagle buckles, the belt buckles worn by women, with fittings ending in an eagle's head are quite original. These buckles were elegantly decorated in an artistic way and also decorated with coloured stones. One of the most magnificent ones comes from Nokopol on the Dnieper. In fact, these eagle buckles date from a somewhat later period, around the 6th, 7th and 8th centuries.

In contrast, the technically famous crown of Kertsch in the Crimea seems to have been produced during the lifetime of the old Ermanaric. It is a gold diadem in the form of a band, richly decorated with stone inlays, with an arched central trim apparently formed by two eagles' heads, this time opposite each other. —The eagle once played an important role in Gothic craftsmanship. Even sword pommels were decorated with them, and later even beautiful eagle-shaped garment buckles were created. We must therefore recognise in the latter the Gothic heraldic animal which is today also the symbol of our own imperial unity. The Goths must have seen and hunted this royal bird in the great steppes of their empire—even today it is a frequent sight in these countries.

The unique cultural findings of the Goths in southern Russia are all the more significant because the discoveries of the excavations made so far are more or less the result of chance. Methodical work became more and more scarce. They were carried out by German researchers, especially in the Dnieper loop and the Crimea. In particular, walls and burial sites were uncovered. They show once again that the Gothic lords were able to assimilate foreign influences without ever denying their own creative ability and independence.

For the first time in history, the Goths created an organising force of the highest order in the previously impenetrable and untouched east of Europe. However, this peaceful and happy development fell victim to a brutal catastrophe from the east—as has so often been the case over the centuries: the attack of the Huns (375). These hordes of horsemen from the Asian steppes overwhelmed the Goth Empire, bringing murder and fire, and eventually destroying it. According to legend, the old Ermanaric did not survive the misfortune of his people and committed suicide after being severely wounded in battle. Subsequent Germanic singers composed a song about a tragic clan struggle that is among the precious treasures of the old Icelandic Sung Edda (Hamaismal).

The Germans—once the bulwark of Europe!

The collapse of the brilliant Gothic Empire in Russia had international historical consequences. The mighty bulwark stretching far to the east, which had protected a rich and thriving culture, was demolished. Europe lay under attack from the Asians. We, contemporaries of Adolf Hitler, are particularly well placed to know what this means!

For almost a century, the plundering expeditions and devastations of the Huns ravaged even remote Western Europe, spreading terror and dread everywhere. Naturally, the eastern Germanic tribes most severely affected tried to evade them. Europe thus experienced a fatal turning point in its destiny. Due to the subsequent decline of the Roman Imperium, the path of the conquering Germans was diverted from the east to the south and west of our continent.

Certainly, the discoveries of the aforementioned eagle loops still attest to the presence of considerable Ostrogothic remains in the Ukraine for a long time. However, the bulk of their army had left. Even larger groups must have returned to the Vistula and East Prussia, as the eagle buckle found in the Sensburg region proves.

In contrast, a Gentile population remained in the enclosed Crimean peninsula for well over a thousand years. Excavated objects date back to the year 1000. Oral and written traditions still exist until the 15th and 16th centuries, after which the name Goth is lost for good, here in southern Russia, just as it disappeared a thousand years earlier in Italy and Spain, often after heroic struggles against numerical superiority...

A comrade still wanted to ask some questions, but orders were given. The columns formed up and prepared to go to the opposite bank. But in more than one heart the words vibrated. Involuntarily, the men's busts stiffened, aware that they were the custodians of a heritage and that they were carrying out a great German-German mission in Europe.

G.M.

SS Notebook No. 2. 1943.

The Teutonic Order in Prussia

On 14 September 1772, the gates of Marienburg opened before the Prussian general Thadden who took possession of the fortress at the head of the Sydov regiment. Thus ended a foreign domination of more than 300 years. However, the appearance of the castle had changed! The light-coloured brick was hidden under a grey plaster, the overloads made by the Jesuits in an unwelcome baroque style disturbed the serious solemnity and the strict purity of the old building of the Order; filthy shacks were piled up at its feet. The Poles had built thin walls between the pillars of the castle because they doubted the boldness of the vault. Even the remains of the Jesuits had replaced those of the masters in their vaults!

However, with the arrival of the Prussian regiment, a new rule was established. After the Wars of Independence, work began on restoring the old castle, which lasted for a century. Today, it once again shines with its immortal beauty, a unique testimony to the spirit of the Order that made this country a German land.

It is remarkable how certain the Prussia of Frederick William I and Frederick the Great was that its destiny lay in the *Eastern mission!* The Elector of Prussia at that time, which did not completely include present-day East Prussia, had already overcome the Polish yoke. Frederick Wilhelm carried out a political and economic reorganisation and the great king unified the country with East Prussia. Prussia demonstrated its German vocation as much by this revival of the old German eastern policy as by its task of supervision on the Rhine! We know that the young Frederick was deeply concerned about the fate of the Order and that the decline of the Teutonic state upset him. It was not without reason that the Marienburg order of loyalty demanded unconditional loyalty to the re-established authority!

Marienburg Knights' Hall.

The Teutonic Order was one of the great historical references of the SS. Above, Hermann von Salza, Grand Master of the Teutonic Order.

The role of the SS was also to guard the symbols of the Empire.

Rarely has there been such deep satisfaction in considering German history as in seeing the reconquest of Prussian land for the benefit of the German people! For, as the history of the Teutonic State during the three hundred years of its existence has proved, this was a definite achievement! And, just as the name of the country of the Order, the spirit of the Teutonic State also put its mark on the great power that became German, as Brandenburg Prussia. It has been said of the Prussia of the Hohenzollerns that it had to be the hammer or the anvil; that is, it had to strike to prevail or be broken. The Prussian king had to be a soldier-king, for the happiness of his people lay at the point of his sword. The Order had therefore also chosen the warrior ideal of life and was governed by the *law of combat*.

Already in the West, the fraternity that had set itself the goal of caring for the sick had been transformed into a chivalric order. It was in the year 1198, the tragic year in which the German Emperor Henry IV died and lost his power. In the year 1230, the master of the country, Hermann Balk, travelled with seven brothers into the wilderness of Prussia, thus beginning the great chapter in the history of the Order that could only be written in blood. No sooner had the Prussians been defeated and joined the new Teutonic state than the Order came up against the Lithuanians, who blocked its path to Livonia. A similar order, the Order of the Glaive Bearers, had fought hard to gain sovereignty there: but in 1237 it was absorbed into the Teutonic Order. Thus the Order's claim to sovereignty now reached Narva. However, the Lithuanians were advancing between the western and eastern parts of the Order's territory, and the whole of the 14th century is filled with warlike incursions towards Schamaiten and the Memel, going into the heart of Lithuania. The Vistula branch could not remain within the western limits either. Eastern Pomerania and Danzig had to be returned to the Order. When Eastern Pomerania was conquered, it became clear that the Order was not pursuing the idea of an anti-pagan struggle but was fighting for *specific, perfectly legitimate claims.* Eastern Pomerania was of great importance as a bridgehead to the German heartland in the west. For the first time, the Order came into serious conflict with Polish politics, which only became dangerous in 1386 with the union of Poland and Lithuania. In the 14th century the Order fought alongside the Hanseatic League against Denmark to ensure that the Baltic remained a German sea. The Order thus also became a maritime power. In 1398, it took possession of the island of Gottland in the struggle against the Vitalian brothers.

The XV century was a time of battles and retreats in the face of the Polish-Lithuanian embrace. Abandoned by the Kaiser and the Empire, the Order lost the great battle of Tannenberg against the Poles in 1410 and after 1466, at the time of the second peace of Thorn, totally abandoned, it fought desperately to keep the rest of its state until the final battle in 1519. The last knights, under the leadership of a Brandenburger, once again faced the Poles. Franz von Sickingen's son Hans provided them with a small army on his father's orders, but this did not help them much either. The loss of this battle led to the transformation of the Teutonic state into a western duchy.

It is admirable to see all the solutions that the Order was able to find to its military problems. It is also astonishing to see that the conquest of Prussia was accomplished with few means, thanks to a methodical drive and timely action. With singular foresight and boldness, the Order exercised its limited power in the service of a policy of great sovereign power. It defended itself tenaciously and fiercely against the superiority of many external and internal adversaries! Only a German elite was capable of this. It is totally untrue that *the Order betrayed the law of combat,* and fell victim to internal slackness, even if some men wanted to distinguish themselves despite the pact of some with the Poles, 'which stopped Heinrich von Plauen cold.

The Order's fighting spirit was superior, as was its *sense of state authority.* And it is the latter that unites the new Prussia with the old. This Teutonic state was distinguished by its masterly administration, carefully thought out and controlled down to the smallest detail. While on the one hand all the forces of the country worked towards common goals, on the other hand taxes were distributed so flexibly to the individual that all classes flourished harmoniously in the country. The administration of the Teutonic State, in its rigour and justice, is one of the finest creations of the Nordic willful and structured spirit. We can still examine the accounts of the Order since all the documents of its financial management have been preserved until today. And we can see that there was no misappropriation until the end of the 15th century! This can only be the work of a selected order of men. The rule that the friars had given themselves not to lock the cupboards is an illustration of this! The life of this fighting community of Nordic men is based on unconditional mutual trust.

A third idea united the men of the Order, the kings and statesmen of the new Prussia: the *will to colonise*. Wherever the Order's banners flew, swamps were drained, almost impenetrable forests were cleared, dykes were built, roads were laid out and lush fields and meadows appeared where previously there had been deserts and swamps. The Order's land became a land of German farmers. His greatest success was to attract German peasants to the land. He gave his conquest stability and historical value. Then the German peasants were followed by craftsmen and merchants, and towns were born, protected by the Order's fortresses. By 1410, the Order had created 1400 villages and 93 towns! This work achieved through colonisation is the only possible but obvious justification for German intervention in the East!

The development of the Prussian land for the benefit of German culture is thus the work of the Teutonic Order, a community work in the best sense of the word. The Order certainly had a number of great minds in its ranks: outstanding personalities were mostly brothers of the Order. But history only records a few names. Everyone knows Hermann von Salza, the adviser and friend of Frederick II, who led the Order eastwards and influenced the German future. Perhaps we have heard of Winrich von Kniproche, who, as Grand Master, led the Order to its peak and under whom Marienburg was completed. Or perhaps Heinrich von Plauen who, after the defeat at Tannenberg, went with the rest of the Order to Marienburg and defended it victoriously. But apart from these three great names, knowing the others is a matter of scholarship. No one knows the names of the many knights of the Order who were left to fend for themselves in hard winter battles and who held the forward bases in Prussian country, miserable entrenchments made of wood and earth, facing the flood of attacking Prussia and who often fought for months. But all of them contributed to the union of forces that was achieved in the light of history, and the whole of the work done by their order made them immortal. It is in the nature of an order that the *community benefits from fame, not the individual.*

Let us briefly consider again the *reasons for the decadence.* The first is that the ideological objective of the Order was conditioned by *the idea of Christianisation.* When this idea lost its strength due to the voluntary conversion of Poland and Lithuania, the Order was faced with a completely new situation. But we have no doubt that it would have overcome this—the premises existed—if not for the second reason, which was *its form of monastic life*. And, as a negative consequence of the vow of chastity, the Order decided to fill its gaps by immigration from outside the Reich. With every Teutonic knight who died, a noble fruit of the great tree representing the German people, which was to germinate in this land, was lost. The order could not survive on its own strength, as it had no more sons. Secret sons born when the vow of chastity had been broken were not recognised either, and entry into the Order was also denied to Prussian nobility. A third reason was that the Order made its appearance in history at *the time of the decadence of the Empire*. The Emperor and the King had sponsored the creation of the Order, but the Papal Church soon abandoned it because it was too independent. Eventually, it even became involved with Poland. After the death of Frederick II, no emperor took any further interest in the Order. The political interests of the Habsburg house extended to the north-east of the Empire, and there was no one there to ally with. The Order therefore faced the Lithuanian-Polish attack alone, while the waves of the struggle of the states—also a consequence of the collapse of the Empire—undermined its foundations. If the Order had had sons, it would have broken its bonds without the emperor and without the Empire.

Although the order collapsed, its achievements are part of German history. After a long period of foreign domination, it was resurrected in the Prussia of Frederick the Great. The Emperor conferred on the Grand Master *the black eagle of the Reich* as his coat of arms, as a prince of the Empire, which Prussia has retained. And when the Hohenzollerns became kings, they received the black eagle, while the Habsburg eagle had become red. The black eagle also became the link to Frederick the Great's Prussia as the heraldic animal of the new German Reich. Could we see this as a symbol of the fact that the genuine work done is immortal?

Heinrich Gaese

SS Booklet No. 10. 1938.

THE GERMAN UNIVERSITY IN THE STRUGGLE AGAINST THE COUNTER-REFORM

(A chapter on the spiritual tragedy
of the Roman Catholic Church)

Although today we can no longer experience the religious revolution that the Reformation unleashed against Roman spiritual bondage, there remains the historical gain that *Luther* made when he urged people to free themselves from the spiritual grip of Rome. Luther's call was strongly echoed in Germany, for soon afterwards large areas were freed from the pope's rule, but it is true that they were later partially lost again. *The history of the German university* also shows us how cleverly the attempt at recovery was carried out by means of the Counter-Reformation.

At the end of the Middle Ages, German spiritual life was concentrated in the universities. The church and monastic schools had lost their importance and the castles—once the repositories of medieval culture—had mostly fallen into ruin; on the other hand, the cities were becoming prosperous and were home to the new centres of spiritual life, the universities.

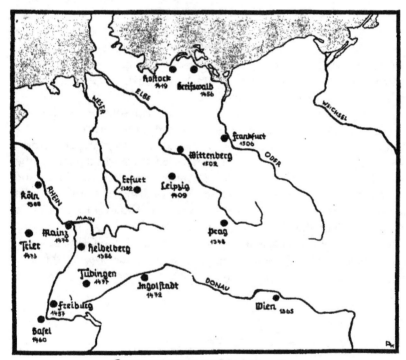

German universities until the Reformation

From the beginning, even if they still needed papal consent to open, the German universities were animated by a German-German spirit in opposition to the French Romanesque type, of which the Sorbonne in Paris was the typical example. Scholasticism still prevailed, a philosophy that saw its mission as being the tool of theology. Certainly, at the beginning, the first German universities could not yet free themselves from the influence of scholasticism. While the Sorbonne continued to follow the old pattern for centuries, the German universities followed their own evolution and, after Luther's call, almost all of them freed themselves from the Roman spiritual yoke, thus testifying to the magnificent refusal of the German soul to be enslaved. But the important thing about the creation of the German universities was that, thanks to the birth of these spiritual centres, science left the old ecclesiastical and monastic schools, numbed by scholastic pettiness and spiritual sterility, and went to these new universities.

At the beginning of the Reformation, we see a scattering of universities in Germany (see Map 1). When one considers that only a century and a half separates the foundation of the first German university (Prague 1348) from the Reformation, one sees the importance of this date. The Reformation itself led to a whole series of new institutions, such as Marburg (1529), Königsberg (1544), Jena (1558), Helmstedt (1576) and Altdorf (1578). Marburg was the first reform university to be established, as well as the first German institute, which no longer required papal consent, let alone that of the emperor, but began to offer courses. It took twelve years to obtain the emperor's consent. But the fact that the university flourished at this time sheds significant light on the reduced authority of the Empire.

Apart from these new Protestant centres, most of the existing universities were converted to the Reformation, with Luther's Wittenberg leading the way. These Reformation institutes became the most important centres of influence for non-Roman doctrine.

The Jesuits clearly perceived this danger and started the fight against the "Protestant decadence of Rome". Casinius, the most intelligent and important of the Jesuits, tried to influence these hotbeds of "heretical" thought with a "barrage plan" typical of the sophisticated Jesuit strategy.

One after another, opposing Catholic centres were established next to the regions that had gone over to the Reformation (see Map 2). A horseshoe-shaped belt of Jesuit universities surrounded the part of Germany that had become Protestant, stretching from Olmütz (1573) in the east, Graz (1585), Innsbrück (1606), Würzburg (1582), Paderborn (1614) to Osnabrück (1630). The Jesuit college founded in 1636 in Breslau became a university in 1702 and thus a cornerstone of the Jesuit attack.

The circle would not have been closed if one had forgotten Dillingen (near Augsburg), which was the first institute of the Counter-Reformation established as early as 1554—i.e. before the appearance of the Jesuits in Germany.

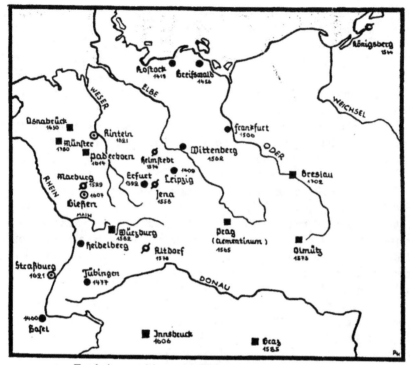

●· Fondations antérieures à la Réforme
ø· Fondations protestantes avant la Contre-réforme
■· Fondations adverses jésuitiques
◉· Fondations adverses protestantes

German universities in the fight for the Reformation.
The diagram shows how the region that went over to the Reformation was methodically encircled by a line of opposing Jesuit centres; one follows the line of universities indicated by a square from Osnabrück to Münster, Paderborn, Würzburg, Innsbrück, Graz, Prague and Olmütz to Breslau! Freiburg, Dillingen and Vienna were also added to the list, which were taken over by Casinius for the benefit of the Jesuit counter-reformation. The Protestant foundations in Rinteln, Giessen, Strasbourg and, to a certain extent, Altdorf, were politically important in the context of the Jesuitical blockade and encirclement policy: they constituted breakthroughs in this 'spiritual barrier'.

There is one more event that cannot be overlooked in this context! In Prague, whose first German university was at the forefront of the fight for freedom of research and conscience, the Jesuits counterattacked in a way that is still felt today and that destroyed the spiritual life of the city. From 1565 onwards, the Clementian academy began to be favoured in Prague. In 1618, the Jesuits won the dispute over this usurpation of rights and occupied the Faculty of Theology and Philosophy. Today we know that behind the quarrel of nations lies a battle of *racially* determined ideologies. In this respect, Prague provides us with an instructive example of the perpetual struggle of the German-German spirit against foreign imperialist pretensions.

This all-encompassing attack on the intellectual and spiritual life liberated by the Reformation had to be repelled. This was due to the strengthened struggle of the old universities and also of the new centres that had gone over to the Protestant side in opposition to the Jesuit foundations. The universities in Giessen (1607), Strasbourg (1621) and Rinteln (1621) owe their birth to this initiative.

When these last Protestant centres arose in response to the Jesuitical barrage policy, the Thirty Years' War had already been raging for three years in Germany. The battle was no longer fought with spiritual weapons. Germany was to be brought to its knees in a war; the seed of the Jesuits was to rise terribly! Two thirds of the German population were to lose their lives. The Treaty of Osnabrück sealed Germany's division and powerlessness.

Today's Catholic University in Salzburg proves that the "spiritual actions" of the Jesuits at the grassroots level always remained the same. Here, too, a centre of spiritual resistance, a Catholic stronghold, is to be created on the direct borders of the Reich. A glance at history explains the significance that Rome expects from this new "opposing Jesuit settlement" in the face of German liberation from the Roman spiritual yoke.

Dr. H. W. Hagen

SS BOOKLET NO. 10. 1936.

SS-OSTUF. DR. WALTER BOHM:
THE BELIEF IN WITCHES

Although the Inquisition was not able to cause too much damage in Germany—the worst promoter of the auto-da-fé, St. Conrad of Marburg, was killed in time by our ancestors—the Church was nevertheless responsible for another great misfortune in Germany, which was much, much worse than the auto-da-fé: the witch-hunt. The peremptory doctrine of the Church, both Catholic and Lutheran, states that the devil exists. He seduces men and women to practice lust with them and then confers on them the nature of a witch for women and a sorcerer for men as thanks. One should not smile at such stupidities.

Hundreds of thousands of the best blood, especially women and girls, perished on the rocks during the Renaissance, not the 'dark' Middle Ages. St Augustine, an African, and St Thomas Aquinas peddled the belief in witches for Catholics; for Lutherans it was Martin Luther, based on the Bible. He preached from the pulpit of the castle church in Wittenberg:

"Witches must be killed because they cause all kinds of nuisance. They should not only be killed because they are harmful, but first of all because they trade (which means: practice lust) with the devil.

Just as the council, and thus the new pope, holds the ultimate truth in the eyes of Catholics, so the Bible does for Lutherans. Neither the Pope nor Luther recognises freedom of belief. The Bible teaches that the woman is inferior, that her womb is insatiable (Proverbs 30:15-16), that she commiserates with the devil (Genesis 6:1-7). The Church teaches that the devil can also transform himself into a beautiful woman to seduce man. Martin Luther never abandoned his ideas from his time in the monastery, nor his literal belief in the Bible.

The Inquisition conducted the witch trials. The torture rack extracted any confession that lecherous calotins—think of the constant morality trials against the Franciscans in our time—put into the mouths of the poor victims. Fire was the conclusion. In witchcraft trials, it was impossible to obtain a pardon, which was commuted to imprisonment or a sentence of galleys as for heretics. A body that had given itself to the devil had to burn. Only the soul could be saved. The Jesuits and Lutheran pastors were then eagerly concerned with the eternal bliss of the victim.

The witch-hunts began around 1454 when, for the first time, it was claimed that there was a 'sect of witches', i.e. people who were allied with the devil in his fight against the teachings of the Church, and who were therefore considered 'heretics' to be prosecuted as such. Sprenger and Institor appeared in Germany as papal inquisitors to suppress these heretics. In all places they met with resistance, as the people did not understand their allegations and suspicions, and the secular authorities could not bear to have them conduct or even initiate trials. In particular, it is said that the bishop of Brixen expelled them from his diocese and maintained the opinion that they were mad.

In 1484, they obtained from Pope Innocent VIII the 'Witches' Bull', also known as the Summis Desiderantes Bull (the first words of this bull). The bull states that there are still witches in some parts of Germany—details are given—but that the clergy and the secular powers made difficulties for the inquisitors. The inquisitors were instructed to use whatever means they deemed appropriate, in particular to preach from the pulpits of all parish churches. No one was to hinder them in the exercise of this teaching or its application on pain of excommunication and severe penalties. An imperial edict by Maximilian I granted full validity to this bull in the face of the secular authorities.

In 1487, Sprenger and Institor's *Hammer of the Witches* appeared, which was reprinted in nine successive editions until 1500, followed by further editions in 1511, 1519, 1520, then a break in 1580, and then further editions at short intervals.

In order to give credit to The *Witches' Hammer* when it first appeared, Sprenger and Institor requested a report from the Cologne theological faculty, but did not receive it in the form they had hoped for. They only published excerpts from this report that referred to the Cologne edition. As far as the excerpts outside Cologne are concerned, the report is so falsified that it satisfies the papal magistrates and receives—thus distorted—the written approval of the entire faculty.

In 1487, the first large-scale witch burning took place in Strasbourg, where the first heretic bonfires had already taken place a century earlier under Conrad of Marburg (80–100 victims). In order to break the resistance of the law and secular authorities, Sprenger and Institor entrusted the local courts with the conduct of the witch trials so that the men of justice would bear the responsibility for the trial. As all the wealth of the condemned was seized, the witch trials were a source of unexpected revenue for the local authorities, which largely explains their scale: entire regions were burnt so that all the landed property would revert to the local lords! The number of witches burned in Strasbourg in 1489 was eighty-nine.

But Sprenger and Institor had their greatest 'success' when they spread this belief among the people with their *witch hammer* and thus facilitated the witch-hunt. From 1515 onwards, the bonfires burned every day: in the following twenty years, 5,000 people were burned in this place alone. The same thing happened wherever the witches' *hammer* began to work. We can see that the witch trials began at the same time as Columbus discovered

America (1492) and Dr Martin Luther sought to reform the church (1516). So the witch trials were not a fact of the Middle Ages, but started at the beginning of the period we usually call the Renaissance! This plague wreaked terrible havoc! The number of victims in Strasbourg says it all: 5,000 people in twenty years. No official figures are given for the region of Trier, but the *gesta Trevisorum* (history of Trier) tells us that in 1588 only two women were left in two places because the others had all been burned as witches. By "women" we mean all female persons over the age of eight. "There were no more peasants, no more winegrowers. No plague, no fierce enemy has devastated the region as much as the terrible Inquisition. Not one of the accused escaped death; the children of those executed were burned, the estates annexed...". In the princely bishopric of Breslau, the principality of NeiBe, more than 1,000 people were burned in nine years—among them children aged between 1 and 6 because their mothers had "confessed" on the torture rack that their children had been fathered by the devil. In 1539, in Zuchmantel, Freiwaldau, Niklasdorf, Ziegendals and NeiBe alone, two hundred and forty-two witches were actually burned, and in 1551 the religious foundation in Zuchmantel had eight active executioners. In the diocese of Bamberg, six hundred people were burnt to death between 1625 and 1630—one hundred years after the Reformation—and in 1659, one thousand two hundred. The diocese had only 100,000 inhabitants at the time, so in 1659 more than one percent of the population fell victim to the belief in witches. In the diocese of Würzburg, in Gerolzhofen, the number of witches burned in 1616 was ninety-nine, in 1617 eighty-eight, in 1623 ninety, and from 1627 to 1629, in Würzburg alone, one hundred and fifty-seven.

But it would be a mistake to believe that this horror was committed only by the Catholic authorities. Protestant regions were not spared. Witches were burned at the stake in Wittenberg before Luther's eyes. Luther gave the witch-hunt a particular impetus in his treatment of the witch issue, teaching that it is a just law to kill witches. In Mecklenburg, in 1532, the witch hunts began with the cremation of a woman and a man alleged to have practised magic to counteract the spread of the Reformation! There was such an increase—unfortunately little data can be verified—that according to contemporary historians, whole villages were depopulated because all inhabitants ended up at the stake. The Lutheran convent in Quedlinburg burned about sixty witches in 1570, forty in 1574, and one hundred and thirty-three in 1589, out of a population of about 11,000 to 12,000. So here too, in one year, more than one percent of the population was murdered because of this madness. From 1589 to 1613, the Duke of Brunswick-Wolfenbüttel became infamous as a witch-hunter: He used to attend the tortures and often burned more than ten witches in one day. In the end, there were so many bonfires at the place of torture opposite the Löcheln woods that it looked like a forest. The Calvinist Reformed regions experienced the same drama: In Geneva alone, between 1512 and 1546 Calvin had about nine hundred people arrested for witchcraft. Their fate remains a mystery, but there is no doubt that most of them were burned. But the worst happened in the home region of the Reformation itself, in East Saxony. Prince Elector Augustus was also involved in the tortures. He enacted a law that went beyond the insanity of what already existed: death penalty also for evil alliances that had not harmed anyone! In East Saxony lived the most "brilliant" witch judge, the famous jurist Carpzow, who, until his death in 1666, pronounced or confirmed, in a certified manner, about twenty thousand death sentences.

Witches' bonfires were widespread until the 18th century. Thereafter, they did not diminish because the Church or its priests and preachers demanded it, but because the absolute rulers could no longer admit that the men they needed as soldiers, or the women and girls who gave birth to them, were put to death. The last official burning, by trial and despite the protest of the government—five witches—took place on August 20, 1877—so barely sixty years ago—in San Jacob (Mexico) and there have been witch burnings in that country until today. Even today, illegal cremations of witches are known, for example in Italy and Ireland. Therefore, it cannot be said that the witch-hunt is definitely over.

Large areas of Germany were massacred and depopulated as a result of the burning.

But the Church has always held fast to its missionary vocation, which led to the Crusades, to its religious dictatorship, from which the Inquisition arose, to its belief in the devil and witches, for which millions of people were sacrificed throughout the world up to and including the 20th century.

SS BOOKLET NO. 5. 1938.

THE LANSQUENETS

Almost the entire Middle Ages were dominated by sword-carrying chivalry. Infantry played a secondary role in general: the nobility and their armoured equestrian troops dominated the battlefields and claimed the honour of being the only ones to bear arms.

Georg von Frundsberg.
Creator and organiser of the German lansquenets. 1473–1528.

With the beginning of the Renaissance, around the 16th century, their hegemony on the battlefield was definitively broken. The romantic period of chivalry ended not only because of the invention of gunpowder in the West by the monk Berthold Schwarz, but also because of the establishment of an army of peasants and craftsmen who were already aware of successfully defending themselves against the encroachments of a few domineering despots.

As this definitive restructuring took place precisely at a time when brilliant artists were flirting with antiquity and thus initiated an era we call Renaissance, we could also speak of a warrior renaissance. Indeed, the Roman infantry was taken as an example with some variations and proved once again the great value of the infantrymen in many battles to clear a path for the cavalry.

Different types of lansquenets. Lansquenet with an "estramaçon", on the right with a halberd, in the middle with a flute, a drum and a flag bearer (Drawing by Daniel Hopfer, middle of the XVI century).

Although art came close to matching that of antiquity, especially in painting, the new armies created did not succeed in their field; the *discipline* which made the Roman legions invincible was almost lacking in the whole. The striking power of the infantry, decisive in many battles, was maintained only because an ardent love of country animated each soldier; in this way, the absence of military discipline was compensated for by fighting spirit.

The tactical wisdom in building up troops was expressed mainly in the *square detachments*. 5,000 to 8,000 men were assembled in a compact square, in the front ranks of which were already experienced fighters. Pikes several metres long were the main weapons that were raised towards the enemy and before which the knights surrendered as they were unable to drive in these "hedgehogs". In the battle of *Granson* in 1476, the knight *Chateauguyon* made an immortal name for himself because he recklessly pushed his horse into a Swiss hedgehog and defeated this fighting formation. However, his daring did not essentially influence the course of the battle. He himself was killed by the infantry. This was the last successful "daring move" of the late Middle Ages.

Fighting lansquenets. From Frondsberg's war book of 1565.
Woodcut by the Swiss engraver Jost Amman.

The first form of combat used by the Swiss was soon adopted by the Spanish and Germans. In Italy an attempt was made at the same time to advance the infantry *in separate lines,* by which pits, walls and hedges were used as shelters, thus negating the supposition that the infantry line is an invention of the last century.

The constant wars of the olden days had as a consequence that many men, out of a taste for the art of war, abandoned their profession if they had one and devoted themselves entirely to this new branch of activity. Thus was born *the army of mercenaries* of which we now call every *lansquenet,* (i.e. servant of the country). It was not only greed, the prospect of making rich booty by pillaging cities, that was the main reason for joining these feared units. The taste for adventure, the joy of open combat with the enemy, the free and varied life were enough to drive thousands of men to follow the various warlords.

Procession of an army of lansquenets on the march. The lansquenets used to be accompanied by their wives and children. A particular official had to keep the various cantonments in order. (From Frondsberg's war book of 1565.) Engraving by Jost Amman.

The most renowned of the lansquenet leaders was undoubtedly *Georg von Frundsberg*. Experienced warriors proudly joined his army detachment, standing in the front line in more than one battle with the powerful spike and striking with Herculean force blows that broke through the spiky foreheads of their enemies. However, it was not so easy to be accepted into his small troop; Frundsberg preferred people who had already proven themselves in a few battles and made those who wanted to be recruited undergo a trial by arms.

It was also Frundsberg who, in his time, tried to solve the problem of breaking up enemy detachments in a new way.

He soon realised that victory in the fight depended solely on the first six rows of the "hedgehog" and the rest of the square did nothing but put the first fighting line in front. In this way, the lansquenets in the fight lost their freedom of movement and were thus prevented from parrying the spear blows usually delivered by the third row. When two "hedgehogs" had in fact entered each other, a powerful thrust began, the aim of which was to break up the opposing military detachment, which was then usually inexorably lost.

Frundsberg widened the rigorous square at the cost of depth in order to present the enemy with a *larger front*. This offered the possibility of reaching the enemy's flanks earlier, but at the same time also averted the danger of succumbing precisely to a flanking attack. He placed the few existing gun carriers at this sensitive point, since he could not exactly change the front quickly by movements with his lansquenets. The courageous Frundsberg could not realise his favourite ideas of long fronts with only a few ranks because his army *lacked the necessary discipline* and *individual training,* two conditions which only allowed modern soldiers to achieve results with dispersed lines of troops.

The fighting spirit of the lansquenets was therefore mainly based on their risk-taking and their ambition to fight in the front ranks of renowned military detachments. As they did not have to perform any weaponry, they had a lot of free time when they were not directly on the field. Their lifestyle was one of forced inactivity to a certain extent, since they could never stay long in a place that was razed to the ground by Frundsberg's troops a short time later, since Frundsberg was not able to forward the necessary supplies to the troops. In addition, the soldiers' salaries were too often delayed. For this reason, the rulers of the time also allowed them to plunder in order to calm their revolts.

However, the army itself did not constitute the main danger for the regions travelled through; clearly more dangerous was *the train of crews* that followed in its wake. It was not only the wives of the lansquenets who cooked for their husbands, kept the clothes in order and, in addition, looked after a family that was by nature nomadic. The pejorative meaning of the word "adjudant" in popular language comes from the latter's role of supervising the train of crews.

The lansquenet himself had the impression of being a lord in the land. He was the one who set the right tone in fashion and whom the bourgeois imitated, who indicated how the pourpoint should be cut and how the feathers should be worn on the toque. Radical changes in the cut of the costume did not always come about through the whims of mercenary taste, however. Tight-fitting clothing even became unfashionable in a single day.

When the fortress *Stuhlwei-Benburg was* stormed by lansquenets during the rule of Emperor Maximilian, they were unable to climb the high walls because of their tight clothing. Without hesitation, they slashed the trousers at the knees and the doublets at the elbows with their knives to give their limbs the necessary freedom of movement. And when the assault took place, the attackers put saffron-yellow silk on the slit places of their suits with proud satisfaction and thus laid the foundation stone for the "slit" fashion that soon reigned throughout Germany.

*Lansquenets seduced by voluptuousness and threatened by death.
Woodcut by the Swiss engraver Urs Graf around 1520.*

However, progress was also made at the military level, and real assault troops were formed. War experience had improved to the same degree on all sides and it became increasingly difficult to break the enemy's hedgehog. Here, too, it was Frundsberg's strategic science that engineered a dramatic transformation in the way the war was fought at the time.

He divided his ban into a 'lost' and a 'reserve' detachment and thus exhausted—except in the case of technical innovations—the attack possibilities of the infantry, which over the centuries had abandoned the type of combat of its ancestors. However, during the Great War, it was re-adopted and offered the only possibility of carrying out victorious attacks with a reduced number of human casualties.

The task of the 'lost detachment', whose mercenaries were called *'exchangers of blows'*, armed with short swords and strong sticks, was to assault the enemy 'hedgehog', to slip under the spears and to allow, by hand-to-hand combat, several fellow soldiers to push aside the unwieldy spears on both sides with clubs. When this trick was successful, the main body of the 'reserve detachment' arrived and entered the enemy square through the breach thus created to disperse it.

After the victory, the terrible danger to which a troop without discipline is exposed became apparent. Unable to regroup in a short time or to fight an orderly retreat, they all ran away and were pursued by the light cavalry and shot.

The experience of two years of war would not have been necessary to understand the importance of having storm troops if something had been learned from the history of the lansquenets. Thousands of Austria's best Germans would not be buried in the desert steppes of Russia for trying to break the enemy's resistance with suicidal mass attacks. Or perhaps our valiant shock troops were something else than "swingers" who in the Middle Ages penetrated the opponent's hole, equipped with the "modern technique" of attacking maces and daggers and preferred the dreaded field spades to the rifle in a melee? The company also followed them after successful surprises—the 'reserve detachment'—which attacked and held the position fully.

The lansquenets were rough companions; more than one town was pillaged by them and more than one peasant tortured. Their leaders were guilty of most of these excesses, hiring more mercenaries than their purses could support and thus abandoning whole tracts of country in compensation. But they were all brave fellows and fought well when things went wrong and put their honour in being entrusted with the fate of a battle, even if they had not received their pay for months.

V. J. Schuster

SS Booklet No. 2. 1939.

The Promised Land

Shadows are marked in this country: there is no intermediate state between blinding brightness and deep darkness at all; the day does not break, but bursts in, suddenly, radiantly. Evening does not fall slowly and gently as it does in Germany; the fireball descends rapidly behind the bare rocky mountains, the desert and the parched steppes plunge into bluish-purple hues, night suddenly bursts upon the dark landscape, stretching into the distance.

So this is the Promised Land, the promised land! Emperor Frederick II looked out at the deep night, over which the starry sky to the south stretched in sparkling diversity. Only Hermann von Salza, the faithful and discreet man, the master of the German court, was near him. The emperor has serious thoughts. Finally, he speaks, calmly and cautiously: "I trust the Egyptian Sultan: he is playing an honest game. He and I are a lonely couple in this world. We have understood that no one can be forced to adopt a belief that is not his own. He wants to leave Jerusalem and the tomb to me, free access and the pilgrimage route. What more do we want? If I take these achievements back to Germany, there will be no more crusades. The Holy Roman See will finally stop sending thousands of warriors to this country every year, forcing the princes to abandon their important tasks and seeking to liberate a tomb which in reality no one has disturbed.

Hermann von Salza nodded: "I don't think the Pope would like it at all if one day there were no longer any reason to crusade in Palestine. We Germans will no longer waste our strength in this foreign country, but will build a great Empire in the north and east, much greater than the Papists want. I have news that the Order of the Temple and the Johannine Order want to do everything to ensure that this imperial project fails and that the treaty with the Egyptian Sultan is not concluded."

The emperor says nothing; he spies on the night. In the distance, the sound of horses' hooves can be heard. A rider's form approaches the camp, crossing the lines of the outposts. Two men of war lead the rider on his small horse to the emperor's tent. The Arab jumps up, crosses his hands over his chest, touches his forehead and the ground with his right hand. He is a handsome, slender, young man with a fine nose and very large, almond-shaped eyes. He takes out of his colourfully embroidered jacket a roll of parchment and hands it to the emperor with a measured bow, then remains silent. Frederick responded to the greeting, formally, politely, but nevertheless with the attitude of one who stands in a higher rank, as is customary in the East. He opens the scroll—it contains a letter in Arabic, holds out a second letter in Latin characters.

The emperor reads the Arabic text first, then the Latin letter, spontaneously grabs the jewelled dagger at his side and holds it out to the Arab rider: 'Present Sultan Malik al Kamal with my imperial thanks—may the Lord grant him life for a hundred years! He has behaved with me as a chivalrous adversary. Take this dagger from me as a souvenir, for the message you brought me may have saved my life."

The messenger bows. Two of the youngest German knights lead him to a tent to quench his thirst.

But Frederick II, speaking jerkily with deep excitement, seized the hand of the master of the knights of the German house: "Hermann-do you know what this is? The superiors of the Order of the Temple and the Johannites have written jointly to the Sultan and informed him that on Sunday I intend to ride to the Jordan to make the customary pilgrimage to the water in which the Lord Jesus Christ was baptized. They advised the Sultan to suppress me on this pilgrimage and to leave me for dead. The Sultan sends me the letter and warns me personally This is the result of what Pope Gregory has plotted against me!"

The old caravanserai is crowded with German pilgrims going to Jerusalem. The Sultan has visited the Emperor. With only a few advisors, they have both been sitting for four hours already in the large carpeted room—but outside are waiting for the German knights, and are the Sultan's companions, his giant negroes, motionless in their Persian armour, elegant Arab lords with small pointed helmets, round shields, long white garments, Kurdish cavalry chiefs in their dark suits, with long drooping moustaches dyed red, sheiks with green turbans that distinguish them as distant descendants of the Prophet and venerable beards. Dominating them all, slender, ivory-faced, with a short jet-black pointed beard and large almond-shaped eyes, is the Sultan's general, Amir Said, whom they call "Rukned Din", "the pillar of the law".

The men of war of both lords quickly gathered. One of the German knights has sketched the plan of a castle on an old slab of sand, and now they are playing siege; they are examining how the towers could be destroyed, how fires could be lit under the walls and how counter-passages could be built. The great emir observes, interested.

From time to time, some of them look up to the window where the emperor is in talks with the sultan.

When an old Arab with a white head descends, the Emir stops him:

"Shall I go upstairs?

—Your presence is no longer necessary. The treaty has been ready for two hours; the emperor obtains Jerusalem without the mosque and, in addition, the pilgrimage route there. The city remains unfortified. The emperor will not put any men of war there.

Meanwhile, one of the German knights asks awkwardly in Arabic: If the treaty is already ready—what are they still doing up there?

The sheik laughs a little, partly out of politeness and partly out of joy at having unlocked the secrets of great men: "You won't believe it. They talk about mathematics and the deep meaning of numbers.

The Teutonic knight shakes his head.

At this moment there is a commotion at the door; Patriarch Gerold of Jerusalem enters surrounded by his clergymen and some armed men. The conversation then ceases as if on cue. It was as if a spirit had arrived to sow discord. The patriarch, a great man, goes among the men, distributes his blessing here and there. Some of the knights bow down, others act as if they did not see the blessing. They are the vassals of the emperor, and the patriarch is the representative of the pope who has banished him. The Arabs stand still; only one of them, a man with a long beard and a scarred face, makes the sign of defence against the "evil eye" during the patriarch's blessing and whispers: "I appeal to the one god against the lies of those who serve the three gods! Without the patriarch saying a word, it was as if the spirit of religious hatred, which has already drunk so much blood here on earth, was walking through the ranks. The patriarch crossed the narrow, vaulted entrance to the house where the emperor was still talking to the sultan. Only two of his priests followed him, the others stood close together at the entrance. In the courtyard, the discussions have fallen silent, including those of the knights about the game. The voices above can be heard growing louder—and then the figure of the patriarch appears at one of the windows. He is leaning against the rounded edge of the open window, talking to the emperor, but so loudly that everyone in the court can hear him:

" ... This peace, Emperor, is a betrayal of all Christendom, an insulting compromise, but what is more serious is a sale of the Holy Sepulchre to the infidels. You have tolerated with indifference that this city should remain unprotected. Without walls, without garrisons, only on the word of an unbelieving Sultan, you are willing to accept this city, for the ridiculous gift of this deceptive possession, to let yourself redeem the sacred privilege of Christendom to fight with the sword for the Holy Sepulchre and to glorify the name of Christ in the blood of the heathen!

The Patriarch marches on while the Emperor is already turning his back on him with contempt: "In the name of the Holy Father of Christendom I pronounce a ban on Jerusalem, no bell shall ring, no holy mass shall be held where the banished foot of this Emperor has landed, he who has made an insulting treaty with the unbelievers, who has stripped the Church of her illustrious privilege of calling to battle against the unbelievers in the cause of the Holy Sepulchre! Cursed be he who stands by the side of the banished emperor, cursed his every step, cursed his friendship with the unbelievers, with their false prophet!

The shrill voice echoes into the courtyard. It is the voice of the hatred that has devastated this country for over a century. All the horrible images of the peoples' struggles for this tomb resurface. Arab emirs and warriors have the awful memory passed down from generation to generation of the first crusader army attacking Jerusalem and slaughtering the Islamic population to such an extent that the blood in the alleys reached the joints of the horses' legs. The crusaders were reminded of all the frightening things they were told about the cruelty of the Mohammedans, the secret dungeons where prisoners were tortured, the bloody barbarity of the Turks. Naturally, the two groups separated. When the patriarch finished his venomous and piercing discussion, one of the Kurdish cavalry chiefs shouted towards the window one of the most vulgar Arab curses used by donkeys and camel drivers. Already here and there, hands are raised to arms. When the patriarch, followed by his clerics, advances towards the courtyard door, the warriors from the West and the East form a hedge, some on his left and others on his right. But the patriarch raises the cross on his chest in front of the emperor's warriors: "Blessed are those who never cease to raise their swords against the unbelievers!

A tiny spark would be enough at that moment to set the two troops at each other's throats. When one of the emperor's servants arrives unarmed, in his multicoloured silk garment, with only a small, light dagger at his side, the eyes of the people turn to him. Almost involuntarily, eyes turn to him. An Arab, the young messenger who brought the letter to the emperor, walks towards him. The two men greet each other, the German a little more awkward than the other who grew up in the climate of the East: "Do you remember that you gave me bread and water in your tent when I rode to your emperor!

—It was only a small thing, but may it be a sign of peace," said the other, quickly recovering his language skills.

So the tension has fallen. The hands leave the loves—as if the spirit of the two men who are talking up there, or perhaps who have been absorbed in a deep and friendly conversation for a long time, is being transmitted to the group.

The great Amir Said also turned to the valet: "I also want to thank you for receiving my son as a guest. My house is yours, it is open to you forever.

—I shall look forward to seeing it—the emperor says we can trust your friendship, despite differences of belief."

The emir raises his eyebrows a little, perhaps surprised that the young man would discuss such serious matters with him. Then he gestures to one of the older Teutonic knights and says, "This man in your army also says that the emperor wants to end the struggles of belief!"

The grey-haired German bows his head: "Without prejudice, of course, to the truth of our faith, which is revealed to us by Jesus Christ.

The Amir contemplates this and thinks for a moment: You know that our faith is also revealed to us, even if it was revealed many centuries after your Christ.

—You know," said the German, "that we have the word of God written in the Bible.

The Amir smiled slightly: You know that we have the word of God in writing in the Qur'an—how do you want to prove that your revelations and message are correct?

—We believe it, Amir! We believe that we have the exact message of God!

—We believe it too, only our divine message is more recent. You have lived long enough in this country and you know that everything your priests say about our prophet is a lie, that he was rather an estimable man who was really convinced at the time of his life that God spoke to him. How do you want to demonstrate that we do not have the right word?"

The old knight considered him thoughtfully. Yes, that was right—and one could not simply rebuff this objection with loud rebukes of "false prophets" as the preachers were wont to do, perhaps he was also right? So God had spoken twice? Finally, the old knight pulled himself together: "Then God must have spoken indeed, since you call on God and I on you, and we each have a holy book and a revelation of our own.

—God has spoken to the way I feel," said the Emir. You know this land. When a man is alone in the desert, he hears voices in the sand and the wind, he hears them in himself. And when a man is chosen, then God calls him to his sight and speaks to him from the solitude of the desert and makes him partake of its mysteries which otherwise he cannot discover. For you see, man is miniscule before God, a speck of dust in the hand of the Lord. He cannot know what is right or wrong. But in the solitude of the desert, in the great isolation, God calls him to himself, he who is a true prophet. And so he also gave his truth out of mercy to a Mohammedan—may his name be praised—who was a man like us. He revealed to him what man could not know; for no one is great except God."

There were many enthusiastic nods in the circle of Arab men-of-war, as if the tall emir had expressed what all felt.

The two men look at each other, the young Arab has an emotional expression on his face.

The old knight reflected: "We do not feel that way. We have no desert, nor do we hear voices in it; we have no dead sands, no dead wind. Everything lives in us. The seed lives in the earth, still under the snow, in spring the forest is green, in Germany the field is green, all the flowers bloom, in summer the wheat fields quiver, in autumn the forest is dark red, but everything lives in us. God is also in the smallest seed. God is in the forest and in the year, he is in all things that bear life. God is also in us. You see, I am not even a priest, I am just saying what I think. In every man there is a little spark of God. So man is not small at all, but small and big at the same time. He is a part of God... But how can I explain this to you? —God is precisely everything that lives, he is in our consciousness, in our heart.

The Emir considers him very thoughtfully: God is the creator of all things, so I could summarise your thoughts. But I know that I would be doing you a disservice. Further north, in Persia, I met many men who profess the faith of our prophet and yet think like you. There were many blonds among them; perhaps the fair-haired people all think like you. But is everything you have told me in the Bible, and what do the priests teach about it?

The old knight looked at him astonished, surprised and a little disconcerted. I have only expressed how I imagine God and how I feel about Him—no, our priests don't say much about that!

—So you have two times—on the one hand you are Christians; but if you want to be true to yourselves, you have to think quite differently and you have a second faith. See, that's the difference between you and us. You went to conquer the Holy Sepulchre and always wanted to believe in it in battle—but your heart always went to the other faith. We have a faith from the best man of our people in which God really speaks to us as we feel and understand Him; for this reason all your armies have been unable to take this land from us. One can only convince with one's own God.

At that moment, the emperor and the sultan pass through the door of the house—the discussions stop and the warriors greet them.

A light emanates from the faces of both sovereigns. Accompanying the Sultan to the door, Frederick II says once again: "There is more piety in mathematics than in all the patriarchs of Jerusalem and the dervishes who will now grumble against you. Mathematics is eternal and applies to all peoples—but God speaks to each people in its own language.

The Sultan nods: May I say something and know if it does not hurt you? Why do your priests speak to your people in Latin and why can the Pope never be a Ghibelline?

The emperor smiles: Yes, it's an upside down world. The priests should seek the peace of God and preach the war of religions, but the rulers who should lead the religious wars, conclude the peace in their place, deal with mathematics and wonder why there are so many different conceptions of God.

But in his room, the patriarch sits down and writes to the pope: "And from such a blasphemous relationship with the Saracens nothing can come out but doubt. It has already reached such a point—it is terrible to say!— that the men who went to liberate the Holy Sepulchre are now asking themselves whether the revelation of Mohammed is not preferable to that of Christ, or even whether the two revelations are right or wrong, or even—supreme horror—in battle they appeal to reason and let it decide which religion is better. Holy Father, I see with fear a nest of heresy springing up in this country, I can only imagine with fear what will happen to You, Your power and Your rents if this appeal to reason is propagated, and even the terrible erroneous doctrine that each people lives its god in its own way…"

A race is a unity of body and soul, of physical and spiritual qualities. A man's deepest religious feeling is ultimately conditioned by his race. It is for this reason, therefore, that the value of religions to members of different races cannot be disputed at all. It is simply that each people must live in accordance with its species. The danger lies only in the fact that a universalist religion claims the power to spiritually violate men of different races and to fanaticize an ambitious clergy for often very secular purposes.

SS-Stubaf. Dr Johann v. Leers

SS NOTEBOOK NO. 1. 1944.

THE COSSACKS

Germanic remains in the East

Russian history is often full of gaps because historians were bound by the orders and instructions of either the Tsarist masters or the Soviet tyrants. Thus, Russian historians claimed that the Ostrogoths went west after the death of Ermanerich. They do not know about the three battles of the Goths and Colches against the Huns in the Colchis region, the fact is that a large part of the Goths still remained far away in the North Caucasus region and in the Caucasus itself. They were so weakened that they no longer founded a state. A memoir of the Colches says that later a Goth became a bishop of the Orthodox Church of Colchis. Melanchton also reports that witnesses told him that the Turks found a Goth in the vicinity of Colchus during the conquest of the Crimea. He also says that the inhabitants of this country speak a Germanic language. Thus, it is proven that the Goths left only in small numbers to the west after the death of Ermanerich.

The Varegians and Vikings founded the Kiev Empire. Around the year 1000, some of them went south-east and probably created the principality of *Tumtarakan* on the Black Sea. These northerners forced their way into the Byzantine Empire. Prince Mistislav of Tumtarakan tells us that he subdued the Cosogues (Cossacks) around 1022 and that the Cossacks mixed with the Tumtarakan inhabitants. At that time, there was also the Kazar Empire in the region east of the Black Sea. In the vast spaces where the peoples of the Mongolian East often fought against the Aryan West, where the Nordic and Dinaric races met, the Russian thought he had erased all traces of Germanic peoples such as the Baskars, Skires, Russians, Goths and Normans. This was not the case.

In the 2nd century, the Cossacks appeared in the Zaporogue region and on the Don. Who were their ancestors? We do not know. Russian historiographers sometimes claim that they were a pure Slavic tribe, or that they were descendants of the Huns or the Pechens—but external racial characteristics tell us that we are dealing here with a mixed people of Norse and Dinaric. It is certain that these remnants of Germanic peoples who disappeared on the steppe, mixed with the Slavic Chechens and other Caucasian Aryan peoples. This people of fighting horsemen of the steppe, repelling all invaders, also willingly undertook raids in other countries.

The Cossacks had to suffer harsh reprisals after the Mongol assault. Some of them fled to the mountains, others went to the grand dukes in Moscow where they lived in fortresses (Gorodnoje) or as free Cossacks (Wolnje).

A Genoese author tells us that in the 15th century the Cossacks, called Brodnikis by the Turks, spoke a mixed language. This does not coincide with the fact that they had always spoken Ukrainian or Russian. In the disputes between Poland, Moscow and Turkey, they were sometimes on the side of

Moscow, sometimes on the side of Poland. Sometimes they also fight alone against the Turks.

In 1654, the tsar succeeded in winning over the Don Cossacks through a treaty of friendship. They were granted special rights and privileges and since then have led a life that has many similarities to that of the Germanic peasant soldier. These free peasant-soldiers of the steppe not only took more than one characteristic from the Western chivalry, but also from the Aryan princes of the Caucasus. They were always fighting against the invading peoples of eastern Inner Asia and protected Western Europe at a time when it was itself weakening in religious struggles (the Crusades, the Reformation, the Counter-Reformation).

Apart from the Zaporogues and the Don Cossacks, there are also the Kuban, Terek, Mountain, Orenburg, Semir, Sibier, Saheikul, Yenisei, Usur and Amur Cossacks.

The Cossacks live in closed villages and call them stanizas. A small colony is called a chuter, several chuters can join together in a staniza. At the top of a staniza is the ataman. He is chosen from an assembly of men. As a sign of his rank, on solemn occasions he carries a silver sceptre with a skull carved on it. In the time of the tsars, the following words were engraved on the sceptre: "For God, the tsar and the fatherland! As soon as the ataman raised his sceptre at a gathering, he thus gave the message that there should be silence. The Cossacks freely obeyed this elected ataman. The major decisions concerning the tribe were taken at the popular gatherings of the men. War and peace, land allocation, and judgements are discussed. Three Cossacks act as advisors, secretaries and treasurers alongside the ataman, and ten armed Cossacks form the police. He is also responsible for judging minor offences. Honour and fidelity are the fundamental principles, not only taught in the family, but also to the young soldier. Thieves are excluded from the community. Women are not allowed to attend popular meetings.

Women are in charge of the household and are highly regarded. A strict selection is made when choosing a wife. When a Cossack wants to marry, he can only marry a Cossack, or he has to steal pretty young girls from a neighbouring Caucasian people. When he takes a Cossack girl, the girl's father must give his consent to the marriage. There were no divorces. When a woman was unfaithful, she was punished by her own husband. In this case he had the right to beat her. The Cossack could not marry Mongolian women, but later also Jewish women. On celebrations such as weddings, one could drink for days on end. The couple was usually accompanied to the church by comrades on horseback.

After their conversion, they joined the Orthodox Church. They live strictly according to the rules of their faith; at Christmas and Easter they fast, i.e. they do not eat milk or meat for long periods. They are the defenders of the Church. At the age of 19, the Cossacks of the Zaporogue, Don and Terek rivers were gathered in a military camp on an island. Strict order and discipline prevailed there. The Zaporozo Cossacks had their military camp on the island of Kortiza, the Don Cossacks on the island of Don, near the town of Novotcherkask; the Terek Cossacks on the island of Tchetchen (mouth of the Terek in the Volga). The Norman Varegues were also found in these military camps. The family army of the Cossacks is also Germanic.

In the Tsar's time, the 19-year-old Cossack presented himself for military service. During the inspection, he was directed, depending on his degree of aptitude, either to the cavalry, the artillery or the infantry. He took part in a nine-month training course. In December of the same year, the rich young Cossack entered his regiment with a horse, a saddle and a sword. He had to provide these at his own expense. The poor Cossack entered either the infantry or a cavalry regiment with a sword. He also received a horse and saddle, a coat, two uniforms, three sets of linen, a cap, a rifle, a pistol and a sword.

Equipment was always checked by military commissions. Active service lasted three or four years. The regiment was divided into centuries (Germanic centuries). They were assembled according to the colours of the animals. Great importance was attached to discipline and comradeship. Prizes were awarded for performance in riding and shooting. The most deserving went to officer training schools. After the period of active service, the soldier returned home. After five years in the reserve, where he often had to report with his equipment, he went to the second reserve. Then he was allowed to sell his horse.

After military service, he had the right to appear armed at men's gatherings, and could also vote. He also had the right to apply for land and thus became an independent peasant. He could dispose of his surplus income as he wished. At popular gatherings, the ataman had to give an account of the common property of the village community. As with the Germanic tribes, there was also a community property: the pastures, the stallion, the village bull, fishing and hunting.

They also had a common school. Children of foreign peoples could not go to the Cossack school. The common property was administered by the ataman. In his spare time, the Cossack was happy to hunt and fish.

As mentioned above, the Zaporozo Cossacks had their military camp on the island of Kortiza. For political reasons, they were moved by Catherine II and established on the Black Sea, where they have since been called the Black Sea or Kuban Cossacks. Out of respect for this great empress, they founded the city of Ekatherinenburg (now Krasnodar), where they erected a monument in her honour. The Cossacks received not only economic privileges from the tsar, but also military ones. They were the tsar's bodyguard. The tallest, strongest and most handsome men were chosen for this unit. One of these faithful men was also ordered to guard the tsar's children. Even today the Cossacks proudly display a picture of a Kuban Cossack with the former son of the tsar.

The Don Cossacks had their military camp on the Don Island. It was not until 1624 that the Tsar concluded friendship contracts with the Don Cossacks, and later with the other Cossacks, about whom it can be noted that they are really peasants and free warriors. They became the most loyal defenders of the Tsarist Empire.

The Terek Cossacks lived on the Terek and had their military fortress on the island of Chechen. They did not want to submit to Tsar Ivan Net and were therefore attacked by him on their island. After hard fighting, they gave in to the superiority of the enemy. The survivors fled to the mountains and called themselves the Mountain Cossacks. Shortly afterwards, they recognised the Tsar who sent them to fight against the Tatars. After a victory over the Tatars, he gave them permission to return to the plains. To increase their numbers, he had a thousand families of Don Cossacks and five hundred families from the Volga regions settled on the Terek.

There is not much difference between the habits and customs and the way of life of each tribe. The customs are adapted to the provincial characteristics. Character traits include courage, bravery, a great sense of honour and pride. Excessiveness and inconsistency are the faults of the Cossacks. Great hospitality is a remarkable feature of the Cossacks. No one is turned away. If a visitor finds an extraordinarily beautiful object, it is given to him. The Cossacks of the mountains and the Urals have adapted to the living conditions of the mountains. All the tribes of the Cossacks come from the Don, Kuban and Terek Cossacks. The Tsars established Cossacks wherever the Empire was threatened by enemies or when conquests had to be made. The Cossacks played an important role in the conquest of East and West Asia. As shock troops, they invaded enemy countries, settled there and founded small fortresses, the "Ostrogi", and then pacified the country. These shock troops amounted to fifty to one hundred men and were called a centurie. The command of the foreigners was removed, the rest of the population was defeated and politically brought to heel. Apart from their warrior character, the Cossacks had their agricultural work done by the serfs they received from the tsar. At the height of serfdom, they welcomed an influx of peasants fleeing from all parts of the Empire. These were admitted into the tribal community after taking an oath. They were also given land at the Stanize gathering. The tsar had retired soldiers established in the Cossack regions to strengthen the Cossack settlement. In 1835, the Don Cossacks were forced to ask the tsar for a ukase that promulgated a ban on further settlement in the Don Cossack region.

After the collapse of the Tsarist Empire, the Cossacks fought for a free republic. In 1917, they proclaimed it in the northern Caucasus. The Bolsheviks tried by all means to destroy the newly founded empire. After four years of fighting, the

Cossacks were defeated by the Bolshevists. They say that the Jewish commissars treated the people cruelly. Those who survived were sent to the interior of the country or to prison. In 1929, the Cossacks rose up again and became counter-revolutionaries. They refused to accept kulakisation. The uprising was crushed. They had to give up their independence and their particularities to the Bolshevist state. The outbreak of war in 1941 prompted the Bolshevists to give the Cossacks back their independence. Now they could wear their costumes and weapons again, and they had a national personality. It was hoped to win over these brave warriors. But most of the Cossack regiments took the first opportunity to side with the Germans in the hope of winning with them. They also dreamed that after the war they would be allowed to build an independent state under German leadership.

It was Germanic blood that motivated the freedom-loving peasant-soldiers to take this step.

I have never heard of Slavic matriarchal law or Slavic or even Hunnic customs among the Cossacks. In none of the accounts do I find any foreign peculiarities.

Is there not an analogy between the description of the Germanic Cats and the Cossacks when Tacitus says of the latter: "In this nation, harder bodies, nervous limbs, threatening faces and greater vigour of soul. For Germans, a great deal of reasoning and skill: to take for leaders elite men, to listen to their leaders, to keep their ranks, to recognise opportunities, to defer their attacks, to order their days, to fortify their nights, to take luck for uncertain, virtue for sure, and finally, which is very rare and has only been granted to Roman discipline: to expect more from the leader than from the army.

ANNALS N° 1. JANUARY 1944.
EDITION OF THE SS WALLOON BRIGADE.

THE BURGUNDY STICKS

Long before their arrival in the Netherlands, the dukes of Burgundy had crossed sticks in the form of the Cross of St Andrew as their emblem. The choice of such a cross was not made lightly, but in contrast to the crosses of the French and English kings, the Cross of Saint Denis and the Cross of Saint George.

The dukes of Burgundy had a patron saint: Saint Andrew. Was this proof of clericalism? No. For every country has its patron saint.

It is with Philip the Bold that we first see the Burgundy staffs in our provinces, which became gnarled under John the Fearless. Since then they have remained the symbol of the western provinces, especially during the

Empire. Our first two pages of illustrations are an example of how the gnarled staffs were regarded. These pages, taken from the magnificent manuscript of the Golden Fleece, owned by Mr Léon Degrelle, show the arms of Charles V, in which the knotted staffs and lighters of the Golden Fleece can be distinguished four times, and a portrait of the same emperor. On his ceremonial garment, he wears the embroidered staffs; his collar is decorated with a garland of lighters and the Golden Fleece.

It is known that the towns of Wallonia were never easy to govern and often the dukes of Burgundy had to crack down on them. However, of their own free will, they inscribed the knotted sticks on their monuments. We cannot cite a better example than the one that can be seen in Liege, the unruly city par excellence. In the old chimney of the town hall, the old emblem of the dukes of Burgundy was proudly engraved.

During the Empire, many Walloons joined the armed service of the Emperor. Prince Eugene, glorious in more than one battle, was not a little proud to fight with the military flags with the Burgundy Cross at his side, mixed with the flags bearing the eagle. The Walloons always had the gnarled sticks on their military flags and on page 84 of the Battles of Prince Eugene, published in The Hague, there is a large plate showing the Prince in battle next to a flag with the Burgundy Cross at the battle of Audebarde.

On the other hand, the Empire's coins minted for the western provinces from Charles V to Joseph II were regularly marked with the gnarled staff along with the eagle.

During the French Revolution, thousands of Germans from our provinces revolted out of loyalty to the Empire against Jacobin France. Their banners bore the red Burgundy Cross on a white background.

Thus, the last Walloon soldiers loyal to the Germanic Community heroically resisted the French invasion under the folds of old flags with gnarled sticks.

Our provinces never had any other symbol. It took the relentless efforts of French propaganda to make some people forget the gnarled sticks and for a new emblem to appear: the cockerel, symbol of France's annexationist aims in Wallonia. It did not appear until around 1913 as an anti-Flemish and anti-German badge.

Even now, it is under the sign of the gnarled sticks of Burgundy that the best of the sons of Wallonia are fighting alongside the Germanic eagles.

Dp.

II. CULTURAL HISTORY

SS BOOKLET NO. 10. 1937.

FORMATION OF A WORKING GROUP ON NATIONAL ETHNOLOGY

Reichsleiter Darré, Hierl, Himmler, Rosenberg and v. Schirach formed a working group on German national ethnology at the beginning of January.

What are the aims of the formation of the National Ethnology Working Group?

Even today, our ideological opponents from the various camps of reaction and the churches are trying, both potentially and effectively, to destroy our work and denigrate it, just as the enemies of the people attacked their most sacred heritage during the last millennium.

This working group must act with the utmost energy to put these enemies out of action. It must, moreover, enable ethnological work to find applications within the Party and its associations because of its great importance for education and training.

What is national ethnology?

National ethnology is "the science of studying what constitutes the people". The way of life of the German people is therefore the focus of scientific national ethnology, e.g. folk beliefs, songs, dances, language, customs, symbols, the whole range of stories (tales, legends, funny stories, riddles, proverbs, etc.), handicrafts, clothing (costumes), furniture, construction, housing.

The recent National Socialist science of National Ethnology bases the protohistory of our people on the knowledge of racial psychology and raciology. It regards it as one of its main tasks to remove the traditional heritage from the foreign influences introduced in the last millennium.

How important is national ethnology to us?

In contrast to the "objective" and "absolute" science of the past, we regard national ethnology not as an end in itself and for its own sake, but from the point of view of the National Socialist world view, which is to serve the people. The exploitation of scientific findings serves to educate the people ideologically, because the traditional folk heritage expresses and makes perfectly clear the world view of our blood.

Germanic religiosity and belief in the Nordic God are as much to be found in the traditional world of stories, legends and songs as in the world of customs. They can be seen in the sacred signs and symbols that we find everywhere in our country houses and in our handicrafts.

It is not at all a question of elaborating a religious system from these remnants of a previous worldview by resorting to hasty interpretations. This would be to follow an inorganic process that would give rise to a new dogmatism. But knowing the history of the eventful evolution of the traditional spiritual and material world of our ancestors can sharpen our senses to enable us to discern what is ours and what is alien. In this way we can better grasp the interactions and effects of the spiritual forces of our people that have passed through the mists of time and that are expressed today in a pure way in the celebrations of the fighting organisations of the Movement and in the great festivals of the nation. The latter express the new unity recovered by our people.

The great words of Ernst Moritz Arndt express this desire for concreteness: "To be a people is the religion of our time; through this faith it must be united and strong, and through it defeat the devil and hell. Abandon all petty religions and follow the great message of the one who is superior to the Pope and Luther, unite in him in a new faith.

The practical tasks of a German national ethnology.

They are primarily concerned with the design of festivals and the daily lifestyle. The festivities that punctuated life, the year and the nation's great festivals were above all a wide field of activity for a science that was aware of the importance of its National Socialist work. The study of the preparation of festive evenings in all the major organisations of the movement and the state poses many questions for national ethnology. It therefore has a fundamental responsibility and must study the fields of architecture, clothing and creative craftsmanship.

SS-Ostuf. Ziegler,
Director of the specialised office of the Labour Commission.
SS-Hstuf. Strobel,
head of the office's education department.

SS Notebook No. 3. 1944.

Birth and End of the World in the Aryan Myth

Where do worlds, gods, men and all things between heaven and earth come from? And what is their destiny, above all that of the gods and worlds, even if they survive the earthly life of man and are subject to a great cosmic law?

These are the eternal questions that man has always asked himself, in all eras and among all peoples. The comparative study of myths and legends reveals an astonishing concordance, both in the questions and in the answers. But it is not simply a matter of noting a racial difference in the study of myths. The Aryan myth of the birth of the world is in principle different from the Chinese, Babylonian or Aztec myths. Although the representations of a cosmic order seem, at first sight, to be equally divergent in the Aryan racial area, there is, despite spatial and temporal differences, a common basic structure that is recognised. The same knowledge of an eternal universal law is discernible in the emerging experience of the Germanic North, in that of the thinkers of Vedic India and in the prayers of the great Aryan mystic Zarathustra.

The Rig-Veda and the Edda provide the most magnificent evidence of world-birth myths from the Aryan racial sphere. Almost two thousand years before the philosophical perception of the world began in Greece, the Indian Aryan wisdom reached the limits of human knowledge beyond which ignorance reigns. Today we cannot but have great respect for the compelling purity of Aryan wisdom which manifests its full depth in the tenth book of the Rig-Veda, chapter 129:

1 "In the past there was no non-being, nor was there being. There was no space and no sky above. What was moving? Where did it move? In what expanse? Was the water unfathomably deep?

2. In the past there was no death, no immortality, no difference between night and day. The One breathed without wind from its own power; there was nothing else but that.

6. Who knows with certainty, who can announce here where it was born, where it comes from, this creation? The gods are on this side of the creation of the universe. But who knows where it comes from?

7. Where did this creation come from; whether it is created or uncreated. He who watches over it from heaven. He knows it well! or does he not know it more?

In the eyes of Christian thought, this last question might seem to be a severe outrage and a denial of divine omnipotence. The Aryan mind of India knows no such fetters, nor any absolute divine revelation which curses a priori any human idea relating to it. Like the Greeks of Homer, like the Germans of the heroic songs of the Edda, the Indian presents himself to his gods with a proud self-consciousness and an almost serene calm. He also knows that the gods are 'on this side of the creation of the universe' and that, like man, they are subject to a higher world order. And, to understand this ultimate cause of the world verbatim, he invests himself entirely in himself, isolated in the attractive and promising fields of the mind. Nor was he able to define that which did not exist in the beginning. But like a wanderer who can no longer explain anything, he seeks and struggles for knowledge, explores the word in its deepest foundations and finds long before a Plato and an Aristotle the absolute fundamental notion: Atman and Brahman—the one and the all—sat and âsat—being and non-being. Thus, our text illustrates in an exemplary way the fact that Aryan India transformed the multiple and pictorial creation of poetic experience into a thinking reason, into an abstract notion.

In the Edda, the destiny of the worlds has remained a genuine, structured myth of the profound prediction of the Norns and the wise seers with their faces imbued with mystery. Where India already manifests the sacredness of abstract thought, the prediction of the Germanic Volva envelops the Nordic country with its whispering song, where every word reflects the earthly environment.

There are certainly multiple questions and answers, yet the 'seer's face' acts as a powerful music, roaring in fatal chords, then whispering again and speaking softly of eternal things—whereas in Aryan India, naked and raw language alone is explicit.

The Edda begins with the prediction of the seer. The importance that was once attributed to it can already be seen. Attempts to find in this poem of the fate of the worlds a religious purpose of an alien nature have always failed. The prediction of the Volva is not a religion and does not want to be. It is a vision of great style, mythical, of an era that still knew how to learn from the study of the outside world, that was intent on spying on the many secrets of the forests and the seas.

The seer expresses her mysterious science in a voice that makes all noise cease and imposes a solemn silence:

Silence I ask all
Sacred beings,
Young and old
Son of Heimdall;
Do you want me, Valfüdr, to
I reveal
The ancient stories of men,
The most remote I can remember,

I remember the giants
Originally born,
They who, a long time ago,
Gave birth to me;
Nine worlds I remember,
Nine huge expanses
And the glorious tree of the world

Buried under the earth.

It was in the first age
Where there was nothing,
Neither sand nor sea
Nor cold waves;
There was no land
Nor high skies,
The emptiness was gaping
And grass nowhere

What a gulf between the 'being and non-being' of the Rig-Veda and the 'Neither sand nor sea/ Nor cold waves' of our poem! Here are the limits of the mind's solitary reflections, here the lived features of the Nordic country! On the one hand, the first great attempt of Aryanity, which has always remained alien to this environment, to understand things in a purely rational way, is expressed; on the other hand, the seen and the experienced are transposed into mythical and also poetic words, which reveal an extremely lively relationship with this environment. One can see the particularly glaring gaps that have caused the Aryan mind to follow different paths during evolution.

The Germanic myth of the birth of the world is an immortal testimony to the living interaction between experience and creation. And when the seer first evokes the ancient times of mythical memory, she immediately unfolds before our eyes a grandiose image of the world that synthesises past, present and future with unyielding necessity. Gods and men are born, a creation, a construction, and 'war came into the world', a fact that must be faced heroically.

One has the impression of witnessing a process of world evolution presented as a great symphony in major keys, but the seer soon curses the first minor chords. She senses the doom that no one can avoid. The twilight of the gods and the worlds is taking shape. The gods are preparing themselves and men too. Inevitably, Volva interprets the infallible signs of the impending end:

The brothers will fight each other
And put themselves to death,
Parents will defile
Their own layer;
Rough weather in the world,
Universal adultery,
Time of the axes, time of the swords,
The shields are cracked,
Time of storms, time of wolves

Before the world collapses;
Person
Spare no one.

The sun is getting darker,
The land sinks into the sea,
The shining stars
Flicker in the sky;
Rage the fumes,
The flames are roaring.
An intense ardour
Play to the sky.

The twilight of the gods and worlds—this is the boldest Aryan thought. It concludes the myth of the birth of worlds and the grand beginning ends in an equally powerful ending. The Aryan mind knows no perfect world, born and then collapsing, nor a final judgment. Rather, the world is "a wheel turning on itself" symbolised by the swastika. Vedic texts often refer to the cosmic order as "the great wheel of becoming" which rolls irresistibly along with destiny. Nor is the decay of the gods and the world the ultimate end that continues with a life in an eternal afterlife.

Since Nietzsche, the notion of the "eternal return of all things" has been a great thought in the making. The teaching of the return finds its most sublime form in the Völuspa. Yes, the twilight of the gods is quite absurd without a new morning of the worlds in the Germanic perspective. The victorious transformation of the bad into the good will be accomplished when "the bad become better and Baldr returns". The most sacred Aryan certainty is that light will finally triumph over darkness, good over evil. It found its timeless manifestation in the teaching of the great Aryan Persian Zarathustra in an illustrious age.

Fritz Reich

SS Booklet No. 3. 1938.

Germanic vision of the sky

For millennia, the Earth has revolved around the Sun, the stars, and has carried humanity's self-awareness. And it will continue to do so for millions of years, but it is only in the last million years that human eyes have consciously turned towards the Sun and the stars closest to 'their sky'.

Apart from the adoption of an extremely simple way of life, we know nothing about the first human lineages developing hundreds of thousands of years ago. It is only around 100,000 BC that traces of their land migration become distinct, and around 30,000, 20,000 BC we start to find some details. However, it is only around 10,000 years ago that man appears in the *light of history*, and from that time onwards we begin to know more about him, his daily and spiritual life and also his relationship with the stars. For after the assurance of daily needs, there is nothing to which man would be more intimately and originally linked than to the Sun and the stars. The poets, who express the popular consciousness, always sing and speak of the stars. Man learned to know them better and better and created his own image of the world, his *image of the sky*.

Astronomers describe to us these terrestrial and celestial visions of the peoples—be it the Greeks, Romans, Egyptians and Babylonians. We find very detailed astronomical works from the last fifty years—the astronomy of the Arabs is not absent either—only there is nothing about the celestial vision of the Germans! There are a few remarks about the site of *Stonehenge,* because an English astronomer wrote something about it—but here too, scholars did not agree for long.

In the specialised literature, one finds a new and very thorough history of astronomy, which, in six hundred and fifty pages, devotes seven pages to the astronomy of the Germans. The author makes statements such as: "The Germans learned from the Romans the use of the month and the seven-day week", and otherwise cautiously provides little information. Works of young scholars contradict them, but one does not go far when, for example, one of them holds the following view:

"In the original sites of the Germanic peoples, in Northern Germany, Denmark and Southern Sweden, the weather has hardly changed from the Bronze Age, the Iron Age and later. Mostly, because of the overcast skies and frequent rainfall, it is exceptional to be able to observe the sky and its manifestations every night and to notice changes, except in a celestial body as clear and bright as the Moon."

No, this view cannot be accepted because the skies of the Copper Age (around 5000 to 2000 BC) and the Bronze Age (around 2000 to 500 BC) were different from the skies of the Iron Age (from 500 BC to the present day, when the light metal age has already begun). For a warmer, sunnier and less rainy era gradually gave way to a colder, rainier climate since 3000 BC.

It was precisely at the beginning of the Iron Age that the climatic changes disappeared and the situation that we still know today was established. This fact cannot be ignored. Thus, during the Bronze Age and long before, the Germanic area at the beginning of the Neolithic period had a much more favourable climate, especially for sky-watching.

The rock drawings in southern Sweden describe the rainfall during this period.

These engravings relate mainly to the observation of the sun and solar festivals. Their richness indicates that a meticulous and constant examination of the sky was carried out and does not only concern the daytime period. One cannot be interested in the solar year and its causes and ignore the night sky! Indeed, the traces of astronomical knowledge dating from this period confirm this.

If we go back eleven centuries, we can read the prayer of the cloister of Wessobrunn:

Dat gafregin ih mit firahim firiwizzö meistä,
da ëro ni was noh ufhimil...

This seemed to me to be the most profound wisdom of men,
That once there was neither earth nor sky above,
Still no trees, no mountains,
No shining star or shining sun
The moon did not shine, the sea did not exist.
Nothingness reigned-there was no end and no becoming...

Engraving from the Middle Ages
"That I know the world in its most intimate nature.
Goethe

There are three more verses in which 'the Almighty God is called the most merciful of men', a purely Germanic and totally unchristian attitude towards God! Here the prayer itself ends in prose. Despite the Christian reworking at the end of the prayer, a trace of tradition shines through in this first part in its spiritual description which leaves one wondering. This becomes even more striking when one compares it with *the Edda* and its *Völuspa,* which is three centuries later:

It was in the first age
Where there was nothing
Neither sand nor sea
Nor cold waves;
There was no land
Nor high skies,
The emptiness was gaping
And no grass anywhere.

In both poems the description is equivalent, that in the past "there was no earth, no sky above". Moreover, we also find the same thing in Wessobrunn's prayer when she says that there were no trees, while the Völuspa reports that green—literally grass—was nowhere to be seen. The Edda, as well as Wessobrunn's prayer, were transcribed by a Christian hand, and one might generally think that this concordance may derive from a

Christian conception. But we have other Indo-Germanic sources that are much older—almost 3000 years. Thus in the Rig-Veda it is said:

> Once it was (the universe),
> Neither non-being nor being;
> There was no space
> Nor the sky above...

In the second half of the lines of the Rig-Veda, there is an almost literal concordance with the other two texts. Thus, Germanic paganism is recognized. The Rig-Veda words of being and non-being are perfectly equivalent and analogous to the lines last quoted from the Wessobrunn prayer.

This prayer was written around 800 in a Bavarian cloister and the Edda dates from the 10th century. But the transition from the common Germanic worldview corresponds to the Germanic period and, as the Rig-Veda proves, goes back millennia. But even the tradition transcribed in the Rig-Veda was brought to India from the original homeland and does not seem to have been created in Germania immediately before the migrants left for India. So this idea of the creation of the world is certainly even older.

This is how our ancestors pictured the original state and birth of the universe and the Earth. Following this, we can also mention the later account of creation in the Edda. A stanza in the *Wafthrudnismal tells of the* fate of the original giant, *Ymir.* He had been killed by *Odin* and his brothers, the sons of *Burr,* and it is said further on:

> From the flesh of Ymir
> The earth was shaped,
> And from his bones, the mountains,
> The sky, from the skull
> A giant as cold as frost,
> And of his blood, lamer.

Thus, poor Ymir provides the raw material for world building with his body. Let us return to the Völuspa:

> Then Burr's sons stir up the mainland,
> They who created Midgard the glorious;
> From the south the sun shone
> On the pavement of the room,
> Then the earth was covered
> Green leaves.

> The southern sun,
> The companion of the moon

Extended the dexter
Towards the edge of the sky;
The sun did not know
Where it belonged,
The moon did not know
What strength she had,
The stars did not know
Where they had their site.

Then all the gods went up
On the seats of judgment,
Supreme deities,
And they consulted each other;
To the night and the absence of the moon
They gave a name, They gave the morning
And the middle of the day,
The fresh and the brown
And counted the time by years.

Creation is thus complete and has its laws. It is clear that the establishment of this mythical legislation could only take place after man had carefully observed these laws of nature. This further proves the antiquity of Germanic astronomical knowledge.

According to the evidence of the rock drawings in southern Sweden, our ancestors knew the course of the year perfectly, not only during the Bronze Age but also long before, during the Stone Age. This is also proven by their stone constructions, the huge sun worship places that date back to this time. There is no doubt that such knowledge was not amassed in two decades or even two centuries, and that it required a much longer period.

Moreover, we know that the acquisition of this knowledge did not happen by chance, but that our forefathers acted in an absolutely systematic way because they were already farmers in those remote times! All this knowledge flourished from the work of the peasant who cultivated his field, perhaps originally with a hoe on fertile soil.

SS NOTEBOOK No. 6. 1944.

TREE OF LIFE AND WORLD TREE

Transformation of an Aryan symbol

In various parts of Germany, there are stone memorials dating from the 17th century whose construction materializes the death of the recumbent in a characteristic and significant way.

For example, in the bas-relief of the funeral plaque, we see a bouquet of beautiful large roses. Death, represented by a skeleton, sits nonchalantly and ironically picks the most beautiful of them. No one can mistake the meaning of this image: the flower is suddenly cut off, the vital fluid no longer passes through it or the bouquet; such was the fate of the dead man in this tomb.

The gentle melancholy and subtle tone of this illustration has been replaced on other funerary monuments by a savage, haughty, almost brutal violence. Death, always represented by a horrible skeleton, is seen cutting down a tree with one sweeping gesture. The cut is already deep; the lightning result is distinct.

In other representations, the tree has already fallen under his blows; sometimes a destructive lightning bolt shoots up from the clouds. But everywhere one hears the words, with their very clear meaning: "As the tree falls, so shall you fall, O child of men! There is no doubt, then, that the tree represents the tree of life of the dead, that its life symbolises that of man.

Man and tree are presented here in deep inner symbiosis. The tree is not an image of reality, nor a reflection of nature, nor a work of art to be appreciated aesthetically. For the 17th century sculptor, there is a meaning, probably unconscious, rooted in the depth of our beliefs. We can only mention here the extent of the use of this "tree of life". The mythology of the ash tree has its roots in the early Indo-Aryan tradition. The tree lives on in legends as a house tree, a protective tree, a tree planted for a newborn child. It can be found in fairy tales such as the *Machandelboom* or the Apples of Life. It can be found in the songs and customs of the May tree and the Christmas tree, nailed to the top of houses and kept for a year. Everywhere, the life of a man or a family is secretly linked to the good health of this tree. It is therefore truly a "tree of life".

It would be an illusion to believe that these representations of a felled tree were born in the 17th century, that sad and painful century that was so often and so harshly marked by the axe of death. This is not the case. The idea of death felling the tree with an axe appeared much earlier. An engraved print in the songs of Sebastian Brant, published around 1500, already reproduces a comparable image. More significant, however, is the fact that it is not just one man but several sitting in the tree falling into a pit before it is felled.

Even more characteristic is the final scene of the Dance of Death by Nicolas Manuel Berner. In the tree attacked with an axe, we see many men whom death cuts down with arrows. As we have already suggested, this is not the tree of life of one man, but that of the whole human race. This is even clearer in an engraving by the master from the 1470s: the tree of life is really a tree of the world, because it shows people in good order and in three rows, symbolising a well-structured world.

Above us we see the clergy, below them the lords, emperors, kings, princes and counts, and below them the bourgeois and peasants. In the declining Middle Ages, we see the existence of this ancient subdivision of humanity into three different classes known from the poetry and philosophy of the Indo-Germans. The tree, however, is not notched; it is gnawed night and day by two beasts and placed in a boat that sails on the waves, symbolising the passing of time. Death raises his bow and shoots his arrow at the men sitting in the tree.

As individuals, we are nothing more than leaves on the tree; today they are green, one leaf is bigger, the other smaller. One wilts, then the other. All this is irrelevant as long as the tree remains alive.

Adolf Hitler

This tree is therefore much more than a tree of life, more than a "tree of classes" as it has been wrongly called; it is in fact the tree of the world that embraces all men in a precise order. We can refer to the Nordic ash tree that shelters gods and men in its branches and also to other trees of the Indo-Germanic world. They not only provide shelter but also give joy and happiness. Today we can only suspect what this great myth from the depths of our race was in the remote darkness of the past. We can, however, follow its evolution thanks to the few testimonies we have just given.

In this late medieval engraving, some traces of Nordic grandeur are still alive and one feels the mythical cosmology emanating from the representation of the sacred tree. The subsequent forms of Sebastian Brant's book and Berner's Dance of Death are simpler, more blatant and crude, but still full of symbolism. At this time the meaning changes a lot. The general gives way to the particular, which is rarely found in medieval representations of trees of life. Because of this particularism, the images become simpler and more understandable; they lose their hidden meaning and mythical grandeur; they become sensitive, even sentimental, and arouse emotion, melancholy and pity.

But in the end, the symbolic content disappears and the reader only considers these images as allegories or works of art whose beauty and aesthetic effectiveness he admires. Thus ends the evolution of the old symbol of the world tree and the tree of life. All that remains is for us to look carefully through the evidence to the depths of the past and feel this mark of majesty.

SS NOTEBOOK NO. 4. 1942.

MOUNDS AND ROCK DRAWINGS

A contribution to the Germanic faith

The most impressive cultural monuments of the Germanic people's distant past—dolmens and rock carvings—have been preserved in the region of origin of the Germanic people up to our times. Almost 4,000 years ago, a strong farming people honoured their dead in northern Germany and Scandinavia by erecting monumental burial sites to which prehistoric legends and customs that are strange to Christian thinking are still attached today. The graves bear witness to the moral strength of these people and their strong sense of community. At such an early time, we already encounter, not without emotion, the idea of the family, which acquired great importance in terms of the notion of duty of the living towards the dead. It had sanctified the eternal, unchanging vital rhythm of birth and death. They lived it in the inconceivable course of the stars and felt attached to it as peasants. They had an inner perception of the powers of life. This is how their sense of duty to life, to their moral world, came about. It was an absolute and homogeneous world that could only be conceived in a spiritual way.

The dead man leaves the life here below, yet he continues to live, not physically in an earthly way, but in a unity of soul and spirit similar to the body, like the descendants of his clan. He even needed his weapons, food, drink, the memory and care of humans. He became an example and certainly even a protector of his clan.

For our pagan ancestors, stones and trees expressed the power and wisdom of the gods.

Kivik's burial chamber.

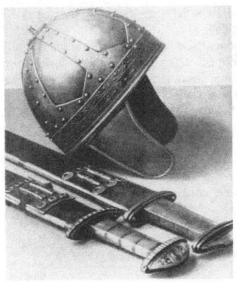

Germanic weapons from the cemetery of Gültlingen.

Under this severe appearance, he was in connection with the powers of fate and influenced the lives of the living.

The people of this mystical dolmen era expressed their religious feelings in symbols, just as the Germans do today. We find chiselled on tombstones the sun wheel and the sign of the axe as a sign of the life-giving powers. We find the axe hidden under the fireplace of the house. This was not magic, but only a belief in the strength of the powers that man needed.

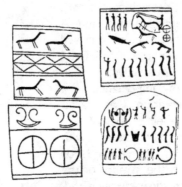

Symbolic representations of the powers of life (left) and the religious customs of ancestor worship (right) on the tombstones of Kivik's grave.

The religious universe and also the moral laws of the Nordic peasants were rooted in this world. The powers were accessible to their healthy religious feelings because they acted on life and did not retreat into a "substanceless afterlife".

In Kiwik-on-Schonen (southern Sweden) a stone tomb was discovered in 1748 under a dolmen, which gives us a new insight into the religious representation of our ancestors. It dates from the early Bronze Age (around 1800 BC) and is an advanced form of burial mound. The inner walls of the slabs of the chamber are decorated in different ways, artistically and ornamentally, partly with symbolic signs, partly with illustrated scenes that must surely relate cultural events. The relationship with the vital powers, the sun (the sun wheel), the lightning (the axe), the earth (the zig-zag band as a simplified sign of the snake) and the cult of the ancestors is quite clear here. They are always conceived as a unity—as the great unfathomable cosmos.

On the right:
Symbolic representations of the religious customs of our Germanic ancestors.
Above: sun wheel bearers, solar boats pulled by horses, the snake in the boat. In the middle: the god with axe and spear, symbol of the vital powers. The course of the year of the god with axe against the archer. The tree of life as a symbol of eternal life. Below: The sacred plough pulled by oxen. The god with the axe carrying the life-giving power (the sun wheel).

Scandinavian rock pictures speak of the religious representations of our Germanic ancestors in an even more penetrating way. Engraved on bare rocky protrusions, they are found in the middle of fertile arable land. A strange prehistoric custom has also survived to our time. These are symbols of belief and representations of religious custom. The people did not attach any importance to a hyper-realistic representation of what contained the essence of their beliefs. We are therefore dealing here with deities with multiple forms, whether personified or abstract: the sun through the symbol of the cross in the wheel or the spear-carrying god, which survived until the Christian era in the form of the mysterious Wotan-Odin, the lightning as the god with the axe, who was considered simultaneously as the giver of life and fertility and who appears in the guise of the late Germanic god Thor-Donar. The earth, and presumably also water, is also symbolised by a snake or a zig-zag. As a whole, the rock images illustrate the cultic celebrations of the passage from one year to the next. On a horse-drawn chariot, or on a boat, the Sun crosses the universe and fertilises the Earth with his rays. He is the centre of peasant thought. After the end of winter in the North, the day of his return was celebrated with religious festivals. The land was cleared with the sacred plough with the symbol of the Sun.

Life relates to the world of earthly representation and is not lost in 'transcendental speculation'.

Behind these symbols of the fundamental powers of life lies the awareness of the essence of the world. The consciousness of German man took a long time to travel this long road. But that is not what is important. What matters is the attitude to life. The roots of the moral strength of ancient Germany are not magic or any other primitive form of the mind or soul, but faith and worship.

Werner Mahling

A people lives happily in the present and in the future as long as it is aware of its past and the greatness of its ancestors.

Heinrich Himmler

SS NOTEBOOK NO. 4. 1942.

ON THE RELIGIOUS ORIGIN OF RUNES

Few people imagine that the language we speak every day is not only a means of communication in human relations, but is the expression of the soul in its deepest roots. The language of the poet expresses the greatest mysteries and always influences linguistic creation. The sound of a word, its nuance, its musical content, often expresses more than logical concepts. Finally, language and writing have a religious origin, just like art. Our ancestors were aware of this. In the Edda song about the awakening of the Valkyrie, the creation of the runes, i.e. the signs that our ancestors engraved in small characters, is attributed to Odin: "Interpreted them/ Engraved them/ Conceived them Hopt". But in Viking times, Odin was the god of warriors and scaldes and thus also the holder of the mysterious original wisdom. The myth of the essence of the runes is given to us in two verses of the Edda. Odin speaks about himself:

I know I'm hanging
Al 'arbre battu des vents

Nine full nights,
Sorry about a spear
And given to Odin,
I myself have given,

...

I looked underneath,
I picked up the runes,
Screaming I picked them up,
From there, I fell back.

In his extreme distress, Odin delivered himself by collecting the runic characters. In the sublime poem of the Edda, 'The Seer's Prediction', there is the verse 'The Aesir gather .../ Remembering/ The great events/ And the ancient runes/ Of Fimbultyr'. Fimbultyr is Odin.

The Nobely stone, dating from around 600, attests to the same conception of the origin of the runes through the inscription: "I painted the runes from the counsellor" (Odin). For the Germans, the runes are part of creation, part of the power guiding the world.

The words "runes" do not only refer to the characters of the runic script, but to the sacred, mysterious signs of strength, giving divine grace, protecting from all dangers threatening body and soul, and also being able to harm and destroy. The popular belief in the immense power of runic signs continued in the northern countries until modern times, especially in cases of illness or disappointment in love. But it also lived and reigned in ancient Germany. The verb "becheren" (to give a gift) tells us this. Its original meaning was: to create or make something for someone by cutting runes. The name of the magical mandrake root (Alraun), which is endowed with mysterious powers, is also related to this. The key to understanding this Germanic folk belief lies in the questioning of fate by throwing small pieces of wood, as mentioned by Tacitus. The marks made by the spell were so powerful that the gods themselves were subjected to them; they must therefore have been powerful, sacred and come precisely from the powers of fate.

The ancient runes used by the old Germanic tribes.

ᚠ	f	bétail, richesse	ᛈ	p	
ᚢ	ur	Auroch	ᛉ	z	élan, défense
ᚦ	th	Thurse, géant	ᛋ	s	Soleil
ᚨ	a	Ase, dieu	↑	t	Tiu, dieu de la victoire, la rune de la victoire la plus ancienne
ᚱ	r	course, mouvement continu	ᛒ	b	branche de bouleau, nouvelle vie
ᚲ	k	maladie	ᛖ	e	cheval (ehwaz nordique original)
ᚷ	g	cadeau	ᛗ	m	homme
ᚹ	w	joie, pâturage	ᛚ	l	poireau, prospérité
ᚺ	h	Hagel, corruption subite	ᛜ	ng	
ᛏ	n	nécessité	ᛟ	o	Odal
ᛁ	i	glace, corruption sournoise	ᛞ	d	jour

These characters will already command respect because of their great age. For research in the last decade has probably discovered that at least a quarter, if not half, of the runes in the Common Germanic Futhark can be traced back to prehistoric symbols that have disappeared.

The Futhark characters cited were derived from names embracing the entire conceptual world of the Germanic people: they reflected the world of the Germanic peasants in the Germanic-Nordic settlement area. Each mark therefore corresponded to a particular word, for example the fourth rune to the word 'anzuz', i.e. Ase. At the drawing of lots, three small sticks were collected and a verse was written by hand from the sign-words that represented the answer to fate. But this could only be done when the sign was considered both as a sign with an initial sound, and thus as a character, whose initial sound, for example 'anzuz', served as the letter 'a'. This dual aspect of the runes has only become clear in the last decade.

The Germans also possessed, through their predictive characters, a set of letters that could be used to communicate in writing. Who had the creative idea for this use and where did it take place are questions that remain unanswered for the time being. Some indications given by Roman authors lead to the conclusion that this art was practised very early by the spiritual leaders of the Germanic tribes.

However, it is clear from all this that our ancestors were aware of the religious origin of the runic script and thus also of the language. In 1938, research led to the conclusion that the runes were more than just a means of communication. Their engraving has a religious basis and a purpose similar to the ancient rock drawings: to strengthen and immortalise.

Edmund Weber

SS Booklet No. 2. 1939.

German-German authority

The destiny of a people is linked to the greatness and worth of its ruling class. In it is expressed the revolutionary power of courage, will and aspiration. The laws on which it depends, which govern its actions, are timeless and eternally valid. Only men who love risk and danger, its tireless promoters, are called to be leaders; they never lose the creative fever, put on their helmets after every victory and constantly seek out more difficult and more attractive tests in new battles. In the past, the history of our nation was shaped by these forces. Periods of weakness and historical emptiness for our people reigned when they failed and with them this courageous spirit. But after this decadence, and long before the popular force withered away in a desolate renunciation, the nation was taken in hand by a strong leader, straightened by a new will. The history of our people is the history of its leaders. Whoever wants to understand it and learn from it must go back to its sources.

The association of all popular forces and their coming together to serve a higher community based on the idea of a ruling class and a troop, are not inventions of National Socialist ideology, arising after the period of political impotence and internal fragmentation of the post-war period. Rather, it resurrected them. For the notion of the leader is an essential component of the nature of German-German man. It is, so to speak, an inherent law of the blood, a vital expression of the racial essence that aspires to order in the community and corresponds to the innermost need to commit one's life to a cause or a work. It gives meaning to the life of the individual only within the group and enables him or her, as part of the community, to put national values to work in a creative sense. Without the organic unity of leaders and troops, no national and social achievement on the part of the Germanic people could be expected, even in the past. All periods of national expansion found at their head those figures whom we can look upon with pride and admiration. But their achievement was always based on a voluntary and faithful recognition of their ability to lead the community.

Elite chefs

Every genuine ruling class in the German-German spirit has risen from the bottom, from the people, to the top, and this by force of personality, by its predispositions and worth. This natural selective process goes back a long way in the recent history of our people and corresponds to the political concept of the Germanic peasantry, from the individual and his economy to the community, extending in ever-widening circles to the peoples and ethnic groups. The intelligence of an organic interplay between all the forces present in the organised community blocks that arose from daily needs was aroused by the particularity of the peasant farm in which all members work together. Like the peasant leading the farm, which is part of a whole, a chief was at the head of larger communities and popular groups, concentrating all units on the basis of voluntary subordination. However, the will of the chief did not influence the communal order; only the autonomy of the free members was decisive. The people had all the rights, the chief had no legal power of his own. He was a mere delegate of the people and had duties to fulfil towards his group.

The choice or acceptance of the Germanic leader was based on his origin and personal worth. The Germanic man considered that his ability to lead the community came from the quality of his blood, the clan from which he came. To this racial selection was added the judgement of personality: what the racial origin promised in virtue, character and value of the individual, was valued in his achievements and its approval was made by the clan and the community. It was according to these two principles that Germanic men co-opted their leaders. It has been rightly said that Germanic life was a 'man evaluation' where aptitude and deeds were judged reciprocally in order to identify the best in the community. Only the best, noblest, bravest and proudest could be elected as chief, the first of all.

The leader and the troop

The Germanic ruler did not rule over subjects. His relationship was based on a faithful alliance and a pact of assistance between free men and equals in rights; this pact was established on a voluntary feeling, dignity, love of freedom, pride and a sense of responsibility. All rights and duties between the leader and the troop were reciprocal and determined by purely practical, legal, economic and political aspects of life, thus giving rise to a high moral standard. The leader saw his troop's right as his own, his distress as his own, and his honour and fame as his own, and his affront or outrage as that of the whole troop. "On the battlefield," wrote the Roman writer Tacitus in his Germania, "it is a shame for the leader to be defeated in courage, it is a shame for the companions not to match the courage of the leader. But above all it is a blight on one's life and a disgrace to have returned from a battle in which one's leader has perished; to defend him, to save him, to bring to his glory his own exploits, is the essence of their commitment: the leaders fight for victory, the companions for their leader."

The clan held the source of earthly life, which was fed by the hereditary position indissolubly linked to the lineage. The product of the field, the Odal, was the lifeblood of every legitimate Germanic man, chief and trooper alike. Since the ethnic communities consisted solely of peasants, the peasant chiefs were also chiefs of peoples. Neither the confrontation with the Roman world and the troubles of the great migrations, nor the glory and joy of battle destroyed the peasant roots of the Germans. Their aim was to preserve the freedom of the home and the land at all costs, to protect the work and effort of the peasants. When Bojokal, the leader of the Angrivarians, met the Roman monarchs with the intention of finding land, he spoke out, looking up at the sun with his arms raised: "As the sky is given to the gods, so is the earth given to mankind, and any land that is abandoned must become someone's possession. The Roman legate was mistaken about the legitimate request of the Angrivarians; he only wanted to give the arable land to their chief, with the intention of making him an ally. However, Bojokal refused such an absurdity, 'as a token of treason', saying: 'We may lack the land to live, but not to die'. The loyalty of the Germanic leader bound to his troop for better or for worse was expressed in this attitude, and he preferred death to accepting an advantage of which his people were to be deprived.

Sense of freedom

The names of the great Germanic leaders and their political deeds are unforgettable. The words of Hermann the Cheruscan express how strong their ethnic consciousness was: "If they (the Germans) preferred the fatherland, the ancestors and the ancient customs to the despots and the new Roman colonies, then they had to follow him as their leader to gain fame and freedom. And when he later met his brother Flavus (the fair-haired one), who had joined the Romans, he laughed at "the low reward for his servitude" and spoke of "the sacred rights of the fatherland which they inherited from their ancestors". The dignity and statesmanship with which Ariovistus, the Germanic leader, confronted Caesar's general-in-chief is exemplary: 'I do not dictate to the Roman people how they should use their right. If Caesar declares that he will not consider the hostility of the Aedui without reacting, then he must know: no one has yet fought with me without falling. If Caesar feels like it, he can fight: he will see that the invincible Germans are heroes. These words express the same nationalistic pride as the Führer's speech at Wilhelmshaven on the policy of insolent English interference in matters of German life and territory.

Although the Germanic state idea lacked a solid external framework—the concept of borders—and was thus deprived of a homogeneous strike force, it was distinguished by an elaborate justice and a good structure. The extension of the communal order to several tribes and peoples depended even more on the ability of the individual chieftain to create a state than on kinship. Thus, the Roman historiographer Velleius Paterculus reports that Marbod, the chief of the Marcomans, 'did not gain power among his countrymen by a coup de force or the favour of fate; after strongly consolidating his empire, he took the royal power and then brought his people out of the Roman sphere of influence. As some peoples had yielded to the superiority of arms, he decided instead to advance where he could enhance his personal power. He took possession of the ... fields surrounded by the Hercynian forest ... and subdued the whole neighbourhood by war or treaty. Under his authority, the mass of those who protected his Empire and who had almost acquired through constant training the strong structure of Roman military discipline, reached in a short time a great level of development, dangerous for our (Roman) Empire.

But when Marbod turned from an ethnic and peasant leader into a stubborn ruler and allied himself with the Romans 'to increase their tyranny', his proud Marcan Empire went to war with the Cheruscians fighting 'for their old fame and soon recovered freedom'. Tacitus tells us (Annals II): 'The strength of the two peoples, the worth of their chiefs were equal, but the title of king made those of Marbod odious, while Armin (Hermann) won all the favours as a freedom fighter'. The resistance of the people was not against kingship per se, which is a Germanic form of expression, but only against the abuses of royal power, and for this reason most of Marbod's troops went over to his enemy Hermann in order to fight under his command for their ancient right and freedom. Throughout the Germanic period and into the Middle Ages, there were uprisings led by the ruling class united with the people against rulers who were considered degenerate because they no longer wanted to be leaders of the people, the first of all, but masters of their subjects and thus muzzle the old order and freedom. Julius Civilis, the leader of the Batavians, expressed this feeling of Germanic freedom in these words: "May Syria, Asia Minor and the East, which have been won over to the king, remain in their servitude: in Gaul there are still many people who were born before a tribute was imposed on the country ... nature gives dumb animals a sense of freedom. On the other hand, virile virtue is the hallmark of the human race. And the gods are favourable to him who has the greatest courage. (Josephus, Bell. Jud. IV).

Example and attitude

The framework of the Germanic communal order only appeared in extraordinary events. It was most evident in external political events, colonisations and warlike expeditions. The tasks of the leader then went far beyond those of everyday life and, in addition to courage and bravery, required a special political skill, intelligence and prudence. In the national assemblies, the most worthy of the innumerable small tribal chiefs was raised to the podium. "Kings are chosen according to their nobility, chiefs according to their courage," reports Tacitus, "but the power of kings is not unlimited or arbitrary, and chiefs, by example more than by authority, if they have decision, if they attract attention, if they fight in front of the front, impose themselves by admiration."

In war as in peace, the Germanic leader was an example of valor and action. When his competence was tested in turbulent and battle-filled times, the troops closed ranks around him and demanded that he express his sense of duty unreservedly to the death. The sovereign power of the leader was not, however, unlimited; a higher right only implied greater duties. The man in the troop owed less obedience than loyalty to his leader. This was the bond, the basis of the relationship of mutual responsibility. If the leader betrayed, he lost the right to obedience of his troop, for the German-German man owes obedience only as long as loyalty demands it. Despotism and blind obedience are alien to him.

The purely human relationship between leader and troop is only healthy and natural when it is determined by friendship and comradeship and does not violate the natural distance conditioned by value and its respect. But it would be a mistake to confuse this distance from the troop by any true leader with a lack of comradeship. The lack of distance and the crude familiarity also exclude any notion of authority; the person in this position is an individual among others. The leader must share joys and sorrows with his troop in good times and bad, be one with them in prosperity and misfortune. He must, however, constantly maintain his dignity, be an example in the best sense, prevent excesses and outbursts, keep a sense of proportion and respect good morals. These qualities are a manifestation of the nature of the German-German man, especially of the peasant, who can only maintain his authority over the members and subordinates with whom he closely cohabits under one roof by means of distance, power and dignity. In a genuine ruling class, the feeling of distance reflects the living heritage of Germanic blood. It must not be lost under any circumstances and forbids even the display of emotions before the troops.

A genuine German-German legal community is characterised by the participation of the entire free people in political life and by the small social gap between the leaders and the people. The extension of this elementary principle is revealed today in the naturalness of our National Socialist state system, whose internal structure is based on the clear recognition of our particularity. When the Nordic peasant Aki replies to his king in the Heimskringla: "If I am your man, king, then you are also mine", he is expressing what we still feel today, namely that the relationship between leader and troop is based on the mutual duty of loyalty and assistance.

Peaceful missions

The Germanic ruling class not only participated effectively in war and combat, but also influenced the peace of the homeland, law and civility, honour, calm, order and prosperity. It still lacked an external framework at that time, for 'during peace', says Caesar (B. G. VI), 'there is no common authority, but the chiefs of the tribes of the provinces and districts discuss with their people, law and benign quarrels...'. The fact that these chiefs of small communities belonged to noble racial communities or that they were large free peasants determines in an essential way their peculiarities and their tasks. In the old Norse texts, they are all generally referred to as tribal or clan chiefs, 'the first of the region' or 'the ruler of the province', in contrast to their troop of 'Thing people'. Such Thing communities constituted legal and administrative units; their chiefs were considered 'the first of all' on the basis of their origin, achievements, and honourability, and formed the supporting pillar of the political order and community structure. This relationship between the Thing and the ruling class at the origin of the political order of the community can best be defined as a happy connection between a democratic (popular sovereignty) and an aristocratic (noble sovereignty) principle.

Apart from this military authority in war, the tasks of the Germanic leader extended to the exercise of religious faith, the safeguarding of law and administration. As a leader, the chief was also the one most entitled to perform religious ceremonies in public and in the community and to preside over the great cultural festivals. For the ruling class touched on all areas of life that still formed a whole, such as faith, morals and law. The knowledge of the sacred was not monopolised by wizards but was the common property of all, and the acts of consecration were performed both by each peasant in his own community and by the chief of the Thing.

As regards the safeguarding of law, the chief only had the power to practice the right of assembly, the calling and holding of the Thing Assembly. He had little influence on jurisprudence itself, for pronouncing, enacting law and making laws was the business of the Thing assembly. "Then the king or the chief," says Tacitus, "each according to his age, according to his nobility, according to the glory of his campaigns, according to his eloquence, make themselves heard by the ascendancy of persuasion rather than by virtue of their power to command. If the advice has been displeased, they reject it with murmurs; if it has pleased, they stir up their framées: the most honourable assent is praise with arms." Only his great legal knowledge enabled the chief to assert himself, to safeguard the rights of his Thing people and to guarantee their protection. In the old Norse texts, the emphasis is on knowledge of the law, for example in the Njala: "There was a man named Mörd ... a powerful tribal chief and a great legal adviser, so learned in the law that no judgement was considered lawful unless he attended it." "Skapti and his father were great tribal chiefs and great scholars of the law."

Legal knowledge, helpfulness, righteousness and insight were as valuable as warlike fame. At a time when there were no treaties and no neutral jurisdiction, but only self-defence and the law of the quarrel, they were the best instrument at the disposal of the chieftain to settle problems peacefully and to maintain the community order through honourable agreements and arbitration. The words of the great Nordic legal chief Njal express the importance attached to keeping the law and laws to ensure peace: "Our country is built by law, but devastated by lawlessness.

The Germanic people voluntarily placed themselves under the protection and authority of the chief; they looked to him for friendly help, not only in words and advice, but also for energetic social support when they suffered from bad harvests and old nuisances. In the Nordic sagas, the generous chief is referred to as 'the most beloved man in the region' or as 'one of the noblest of the pagan era'. The human relationship between the chief and the troop was a pact of assistance that was driven by a genuine spirit of comradeship and imposed on the first man in the community a sense of duty to help when misery struck. "It is customary," says Tacitus, "for the cities, by voluntary and individual contributions, to offer to the chiefs large cattle and wheat, which, received as a tribute, provides for their needs." The chief received as much as he gave; the gifts made to him were considered cooperative capital for the relief he distributed in a patriarchal manner. For the troop man, his contributions were voluntary, he provided the chief with no imposed services or contributions but with friendly help and gifts as is customary between free and equal men.

The law of honour

The Germanic ruling class was not only concerned with the 'leadership of the province', the legal order and administration on an external level, but also with the definition of morality. The laws that were generally recognised as moral values were the foundation. The supreme moral law was 'life with honour', to which the ruler was even more strongly bound than any other. For the man of the old Germanic period, honour was of decisive importance, enabling him to judge the value of his life and his character. At the level of public judgement, honour was also the proof of one's ability and value to the community. On honour depended the individual's self-esteem and commitment, the consciousness of his own worth. It determined his authority as well as his political and social position. It related to personal pride as well as to public judgement and was generally regarded as the recognised law governing human life and by which judgement was made.

The community felt it had a mandate as a judge to apply the law of honour to the chief. The latter had to prove his honourability and defend it. For the honour of the chief was also the honour of the troop. If a citizen's honour or his own was damaged, then so was that of the whole community, and everyone had a duty to clear it up. The leader displayed a sense of honour, an extreme virtue before the troop and exerted his moral influence on the community. These moral values included heroic attitude, bravery and self-assertion, sense of dignity, individual and community responsibility, unconditional fulfilment of duty to the community relying on him. Apart from this, other particular virtues of the leader were celebrated such as magnanimity, generosity, generosity and constant dedication to support in deed and word those who need help.

All these qualities and virtues of leadership are not exclusive to one era. They do not only characterise the internal community structure of our

Germanic ancestors, but also constantly determine the nature of the authentic, mainly Nordic ruling class. To participate in them, to emulate them, is for us the noblest action, for there is always a lack of leaders, of men who cannot live without a goal and a struggle, without the desire and the fever for action, men who are inhabited by a creative force and whose self-control calls them to lead others.

Our generation is alone in the fleeting present. We must learn again to know the laws of life most characteristic of our popular existence, which was denied us by the direct route of natural transmission. The recent past up to the outbreak of the Great War shows us only satisfied and softened generations who manifested their own lack of culture and participated from afar in the struggle. We cannot draw any strength from the emptiness of their existence because we are now on the threshold of a new world. We have to look for a virgin path and walk with courage in the darkness of the future. We must find our own scale of values in the untroubled source of our history, in ancient Germanic history, and choose the models of its fighters and leaders to guide our dangerous existence. We are an awakened and creative generation that cannot live without its historical ties and its brothers from the past.

He who today claims to lead, must know what was the origin of the ruling class in the course of history, must be aware of the great duties he has to fulfil at all levels, towards the past and the future. He must beware of the spirit of complacency and be filled with a fiery Germanic pride that overcomes and breaks down all obstacles.

SS-Hstuf. Ernst Schaper

SS NOTEBOOK NO. 11. 1943.

THE HONOUR OF THE GERMANIC WOMAN

The axis of Germanic morality and life has rightly been considered to be the sense and awareness of honour. For the ancient German, honour is the law governing his existence, the scale of values by which he judges himself. But it is also—insofar as he is constantly subject to external judgement— the touchstone of his confirmation, his merit and his value to the community. The social and political position also depends on the importance attached to the individual's observance of the law of honour.

Honour implies personal inner pride and drive and personal and community value. The sense of honour is proportional to the individual's self-respect. But honour also means consideration and social position. Because of its bilateral character, linked to pride as well as to the judgement of those around it, honour is the generally recognised law to which

Germanic human life is subject and which serves as a legal reference. But this means nothing other than that Germanic man subordinates himself completely to an idea, to a supra-material, spiritual value, which the Germanic mind has established. Honour is man's greatest asset. It is what first gives him authority, what makes him a man, so to speak. A man without honour does not count in the Germanic community. Honour is more important than life, which is so highly valued by the peasant. "I would rather die with honour than live in shame. "I would rather lose you than have a dishonoured son. "Goods disappear, clans disappear, you die too. I know only one thing that never perishes: the fame that the dead man has acquired.

The close union of all biological parents, involving duties and rights, means that what concerns the individual concerns the clan and vice versa. In principle, it acquires the character of a general law. The honour of the individual becomes that of the clan, just as the honour of the clan is also that of the individual. If the honour of any member of the clan is harmed, that of the others is also harmed and they all have a duty to clear themselves. The woman, too, who is recognised as a member of the clan as much as the man and whose personality is respected, is an integral part of this great heritage of Germanic man. However, we cannot be satisfied with this general statement, which is obvious to the man living in the ancient Germanic world but incomprehensible to the man hindered by an Eastern worldview. We are mainly interested in the extent to which women have contributed to the development of this Germanic law of life and principle of all morality, how they have concretised, defended and perpetuated it during their existence; how they have lived honour.

HONOUR IS THE COMMON IDEAL OF WOMEN AND MEN

Our texts speak as much of the woman's sense of honour as of the man's. It is significant that the same term is used for an honour-conscious woman as for a man, thus making no difference in kind between the honour of the man and that of the woman. Man and woman are referred to as 'drengr-godr', the 'man's honour' (literally an upright and proud individual) of the Old North. We can see that the drengr-godr ideal has deeper roots than the overvaluation of so-called 'masculine qualities'. But it seems important to us that this ideal of the sense of honour, the Being-in-possession-of-honour, which is necessary for both sexes, should be embodied in the two individuals who have valued it. To us, who strive to remove the allogeneic label classifying all vital manifestations as 'masculine' or 'feminine' from our linguistic usage as well as from our thinking, this formulation seems to be dangerous to say the least. It is our duty to act seriously and to put an end to this conception which considers bravery, discipline, selection and honour as "masculine" virtues. Only Eastern and

Western habits of thought have instilled this limited view in us. *Germanic antiquity shows that Germanic peasant women are driven by the same courage, bravery, love of freedom and self-discipline as their men*, and that they are prepared to stake their lives on these values.

It was not only the women of the Cimbers and Teutons, of the Ambrores and Tipurinians, whose fearless bravery in the Roman wars, a wild love of freedom and an ardent sense of honour were forever immortalised even by an enemy hand, who provided proof of their 'masculine' qualities. The Germanic peasant women, who remained in the shadow of the great political events, were in the same situation; their lifestyle, the indissoluble attachment to the community and the clan which knew no respite from war, drove them to think and act for the clan with bravery and firmness. They had to aspire only to the good of the clan and follow a discipline. We will not assert that bravery, discipline and a sense of honour are masculine or feminine virtues since they are strongly present in both sexes. Nor will we insult our old mothers by saying that they are not feminine if they possess these 'masculine' virtues. But neither can we give credence to those assertions which attribute the drengrgodr spirit solely to men. Knowing the Germanic worldview, the structure of the community, the evaluation of personality independently of gender, it is not surprising to see Germanic peasant women constantly rubbing shoulders with men dying for honour, and animated by the same sense of honour. It is natural that a people who consider their women to be 'sacred and mysterious' do not deny them what makes them fully human in Germanic eyes, namely honour. On the other hand, it seems important to us to note that in the course of evolution, an Eastern worldview gradually suppressed the Germanic character of women's sense of honour or substituted another content. Female honour becomes—in accordance with an Eastern way of life—solely and exclusively a physical-sexual matter and ultimately means only physical virginity and purity. Here the concepts are reversed.

A WOMAN'S GREATEST HONOUR LIES IN MOTHERHOOD

In Germania, too, chastity is naturally prescribed; but this requirement relates firstly to both sexes and secondly has a different motivation from that of the Eastern rule of life: 'To have intercourse with a woman before reaching the twentieth year was considered extremely shameful... Those who have remained chaste for a very long time receive the highest praise from their own people; they believe that this promotes good stature and increases strength and desire."

Caesar's text shows that the Norseman valued chastity in order to avoid the danger of sexual excesses—to which the Eastern mentality is more subject than the reserved nature of the North—and moreover, he did not confuse it with the idea of honour. Lack of chastity from a certain age, or more precisely, too early sexual intercourse, is regarded in Germania as a danger to the psyche and the body of the man. It signifies a disturbance of the ideal of human perfection and a threat to other Germanic principles of life. The demand for sexual purity of the physically and spiritually immature young man is based on the desire not to threaten the purity of the blood on the one hand, and on the other hand entails the general moral principle of self-discipline which governs the entire life of the German.

In Germania, chastity is demanded of immature men in order to preserve the blood which one must pass on intact to one's descendants and out of duty to oneself, from its value based on self-love and dignity. On the other hand, when Germanic man has become fully grown up physically and morally, it is natural that he should not, because of a sickly inversion due to deformed minds, contravene the law of creation and the dispositions which nature gave him, by hindering his fecundity and his will to reproduce by too prolonged chastity. The German does not live against nature and its laws but in harmony with it. He does not let the gifts she has given him to think wither away by debasing himself in a human way, but considers that man is fulfilled by putting them to good use; that nature wants men and women, not asexual and neutral beings. So the demand for too much chastity, the choice of a celibate and abstinent life that produces a 'superior' humanity, is not at all natural in Germania. They are even considered a contradiction and an offence to the law of eternal life itself. For the Germans, therefore, chastity is merely a necessity conditioned by the rule of life, not an absolute moral value that inflexibly governs man's conduct. *The virgin and the monk are not Germanic examples or superior beings, but rather the opposite, since they have not fully developed the forces within them.*

In Germania, this conception of the precise value of chastity imposed only on the immature being, applies equally to men and women. The ordinances prescribing penalties for concubinage and homicide of women show strikingly that the virginity, the purity of the woman is not at all fundamental, and not even taken into account in judging the value of the free German woman. Swabian folk law prescribes that concubinage with a married woman (mulier) is to be punished twice as severely as concubinage with a virgin (virgo). It is not virginity, chastity and purity that determine the value. The Salian, Ripuarian and Thuringian law books prescribe that the punishment for the homicide of a woman fit to bear children or who has already borne children is worth three times that of a virgin who has not yet borne children. This type of law marking a difference between virgin and woman (virgo and mulier) clearly shows that the notion of virginity is not fundamental in judging the value of women. It is simply ignored because the murder of a woman is considered three times more serious than that of a virgin! It is not chastity but the biological value which, unlike the condition of a virgin, is linked to the achievement of motherhood, and is fundamental to the appreciation of women. The Germanic idea of value determined solely by chastity cannot be clearer than here. The childbearing woman, the mother whose conception is never a defilement, is held in higher esteem in Germania because she follows the law of life, both individually and in the minds of the people. But the value of the woman depends, as has already been said, on her qualities, her achievements, her soul and heart, her mind and character.

How is it that chastity was considered a moral concept? How did purity come to be equated with 'woman's honour' in the moral conception? We recall that the Germanic feminine ideal, the 'Germanic saint', was always represented by mothers, the original mothers (Frigg, Lady Holle); that, according to Germanic sentiment, conception was not a blemish, a defilement and a degradation. On the contrary, such an idea would have been considered an offence to Germanic mothers. In the sagas, we see hundreds of times that widows are as coveted as virgins, and that no Germanic man would think that a widow is inferior because she is no longer pure.

The Judeo-Oriental mind, on the other hand, considers the virgin more desirable than the woman: the word "desirable" is intentionally chosen because there is hardly any question of a moral evaluation of chastity in the Oriental mind's valuation of the virgin. When the holy book of Islam, the Koran, promises the orthodox Muslim in the garden of paradise "young women whom no spirit or man has yet touched" as a reward for his personal use, we see that female chastity must indeed have a special value for the Oriental since it constitutes, so to speak, a reward and a paradisiacal joy.

Virginity and purity in the "Garden of Eden" could have absolutely no moral value, but instead a sensual value. For a woman's chastity only makes sense if she is promised to the man who destroys her in that paradisiacal life. The possession of "the virgin with eyes as black as pearls in a shell", the love of God of the paradise followers, clearly reveal that the chastity of the oriental woman is only demanded for the greater pleasure of man.

We have thus seen which race gives such an obvious role to the purity of the woman and what is really behind the requirement of chastity. The Germanic man could not have conceived of a virgin mother, nor would he have placed a higher value on her. His goddesses and the women dear to him have maternal traits and are mothers. Motherhood is their nature. Then the Virgin Mother of God replaced the maternal deity of Germania due to the intrusion of a foreign value system. Nuns were privileged over Germanic clan mothers, and a greater respect for virginity rather than motherhood was forced into the skull of Germanic man until he accepted it in his moral conception. We can therefore appreciate the depth of the violent upheaval that affected the Germanic worldview and the enormous shake-up of the Germanic instinct. The young girls of an entire village were proof of this.

They had all taken the veil, revealing how much this idea had disturbed their being by taking away the serenity of their healthy and pious worldview.

THE CONCEPT OF HONOUR SURVIVES IN PEASANT MORALITY

Even today, rural morality does not resemble what the new doctrine might wish. Even today, certain customs are still animated by an ancient force. A moral sense had established them, which no longer corresponded to the later foreign teaching. In spite of the threat of hellish torments and purgatory, "rendezvousing at the window" has survived among the South German tribes as the recognised right of young men, and no one would have thought of considering it a sin. Even the public authorities, believing themselves to be the guardians and judges of good morals, turn a helpless, if reluctant, blind eye. Despite the fact that Christianity stipulates an absolute requirement of chastity, which is hostile to motherhood, it is not uncommon for young peasant women to offer a child to their future husbands before the Christian blessing and the marriage. But they are not shamed and reviled by the peasants in whose homes they live, and the pre-marital children are not regarded as children of sin with a defect. This only happens when a girl shows weakness of character, when she is rejected by the moral spirit of the community, but not at all when she marries the father of her child just after its birth. The foreign, oriental appreciation of chastity has little to do with it, but rather the ancient Germanic moral law of blood preservation and inner discipline. Even today, losing chastity is not considered a loss of honour, any more than it was in ancient Germania. In Germania, the requirement of chastity is a value in itself, complementary to honour, a good whose loss may, in certain circumstances, devalue the woman, but which never amounts to the loss of her honour. Who would have thought of reprimanding a daughter of Thordis Sur for dishonouring herself? The judgement of the Germanic community is not so dogmatic but depends on particular circumstances. The legal books also attest to this fact when they only set penalties for concubinage when a woman has committed a sexual act with four or five men and her moral weakness is thus proven. In the same spirit, it can be seen that virginity in ancient times was never considered an ideal, not even a concept, as there is no word to define it. This is also another proof of the importance attached to a female life that is fulfilled in motherhood considered as a mission and an ideal. Above all, it is clear that the chastity of the immature man forms one of the many values that were held in Germania, but honour is the absolute law of life.

Chastity is not a woman's honour. This restriction, the consequence of a sense of values that is alien and harmful to Germanic femininity, produces those shocking visions of caning by husbands that haunt the ancient texts of the Middle Ages. But it also allows us to understand the signs of decadence in modern female life. For what is left of the woman if her personality is devalued from the outset, if as the instigator of sin, as the camel-like and material embodiment of the evil principle, she is opposed to the good spiritual male pole? What is left for her if, in addition, she is removed from the framework of the united clan and her ego is blamed for sins, or if she is enslaved to the man considered as her "master"? Is she still aware of herself, of her freedom and responsibility, the first conditions of all morality?

The phrase 'He must be your master' means nothing other than the destruction of all Germanic female values, of all possibilities of constant collaboration in the work of the community, and implies a pathological alteration of the community insofar as the woman is its other component. In particular, this means that the man also assumes the monopoly of morality, becomes the master of morality, so to speak. He has a decisive say in moral issues, in ethics, or as we used to say, he 'teaches' them according to written dogmatic principles. Now that women have been deprived of their sense of right and wrong, have been more or less convinced of their inferiority, and have been described as having a bad bloodline morality, it is obviously no longer very difficult to exclude them from moral issues.

Margarete Schaper-Haeckel

SS NOTEBOOK NO. 8. 1943.

LOVE AND MARRIAGE

"When I was young, I was given to Njal, and I promised him that we would have a similar fate.

The Bergthora peasant woman

When we wish to speak of love and marriage, we must flee from the spirit of the great cities to the north, to the mountains filled with clean, healthy air where the ancient lines live under the oaks and ash trees. From the homeland of the peasant Bergthora we look out upon the vast country, ancient and venerable, dignified and flourishing, in which the youth sings the old love songs again:

Do you want to give me your heart?
then it is done in secret,
and our common thought
no one can guess it
and

To know a faithful heart,
is worth the greatest treasure.
It is a pleasure to welcome him,
He who knows a faithful heart.

It is our homeland which, often soiled, constantly speaks of the purity of love and marriage in the magnificent works of its art. We see Njal and Bergthora again in Heinrich and Mathilde of Brunswick. But our parents at home are already giving us the example of a dignified life.

In this beautiful country, whose "virtue and pure courtly love" Walther von der Vogelweide once sang, the people are still fighting against the poison of Judeo-liberal shamelessness that has been debasing love and marriage for decades. In this area, a national ethic has not been established at all on a public level. It is not dignity and dress, nor a keen awareness of a sacred duty to our ancestors and the future of our people that influences love life, but rather the voice of the "light muse". We will always see the expression of superficial senses and hot blood. But we do not notice that the Jew can use them to influence our people, and thus reach us in our substance.

Love and marriage are the source of the cultural and popular life of our nation. Love between the sexes generates not only life but also art, true knowledge, religion and the order of society (morality). But if everything comes from love, the destiny of a people also depends on the love ethic that prevails in its state.

Let us consider two aspects in love and marriage: *the experience of love* and the *natural* law that governs love.

What is the experience of love? The two sexes are attracted to each other, moved by each other, inflamed by each other and moved by an abandonment such as is found nowhere else in life. This experience of love is general. But apart from that, we wonder about the how. How does the German love, how does the Nordic man love? What value does he attach to love? Or what does he consider to be the value of love? In each case, it depends very much on the personal value of the person seeking love or of the lover himself. His nature also influences the way he loves. He can sometimes completely forget his origin, consider the Judeo-American civilisation of tango (today we would say rock) as a Nordic cultural creation and not notice in which hands it has fallen. But he can also succeed in fully manifesting his personal racial value through his love. The value of a personality is revealed in his way of thinking, in his inclination and thus in his feelings. Each person expresses his true character in love, if he "lets himself go", if he is carried away, becomes a prisoner of the elementary sexual impulses and no longer considers the love union as anything other than the satisfaction of sensual pleasure. On the other hand, his character can retain its dignity in love. He then venerates the personal value of the loved partner. He may also seek the religious aspect of the love event, the experience of a divine will of creation. He is then able, through the pleasure and happiness of the love union, to experience the divine wish to see many children procreated. And then, for some people, the sense of honour is also related to love. When the sense of honour is linked to the sense of identity, then the noble man will feel a strong sense of honour in his love, for love is not this 'secret sin', but a personal relationship of mutual honour. Beyond the realm of love life, the male honour must also be aware that he must uphold the dignity and culture of love among the people as a whole. It is not the women who are guilty when their charm and grace are debased and made immodest. It is not the dancers who are guilty when they show off their legs in a performance, but the man who is responsible for leading the community where love life matters.

When we call *marriage* that connection between the sexes which is determined by value and not by sensual madness, and which wants to be embodied in children and is therefore virtuous, then we can say: the "love" of some does not deserve the name; all the less can it be considered a union, even if it were celebrated by ten priests. But the love of others is a love in the true sense of the word and constitutes a union, even if it had never been blessed and consecrated. Divorce then represents a great misfortune.

Let us now ask ourselves about the natural law governing love. What is at the origin of what we feel to be love, the attraction of the sexes, is quite subtle. This law only gives rise to love between specific beings. We then say that the spouses are equal. The loving spouses embrace each other in a creative act. A new life is born in the fertilised egg where the maternal and paternal parts "couple" in the embryo. They love each other even in their mutual tastes. Those who seek love therefore practice choice. They look for what will satisfy their eyes, their feelings and their critical minds. For the man—only a certain ratio of physical proportions in the woman and a certain type of form will please him. We all have a strong preference for a certain look, a particular gesture. The look, the strength of the facial features, the curvature of the lines of the mouth, nose and eyes, the chin, the ears, the temples and the forehead all contribute to forming an opinion. Already at this stage one feels affinity or antipathy. But it is first the qualities of character that are decisive, which are not manifested in pure appearance but only through a thorough knowledge of the person, placed in various circumstances of life or clan history: his sense of beauty and goodness, his judgments on important matters, his dignity, his consequence, his helpfulness and temperament, the proof of his unshakeable trust in a god, his faith and a pure and unselfish love of God. The values to which men seeking love "put a price" usually reveal, as was said before, something estimable. However, we are all more or less attracted to what is of unquestionable value, what is pure, even if we are not worth it. Most people will admire with respect a Greek Venus, a female statue of Kolbe, as well as their living incarnations. More than one of us would like to love a being who is close to perfection, even though he is inferior. He desires it even in case he should err and not be loved. Nature itself ensures that love is not based on reciprocity. Apart from this, the clan still influences the marital choice of its youth. A genuine love relationship only arises where decisive character-building qualities are matched by other people. Therefore, whoever 'looks like' himself 'loves' himself.

We must also see that this natural law of love is the one that governs marriage, because marriage is precisely about procreating hereditarily healthy children and about a good upbringing that creates a strong family feeling between similar characters. Consequently, it is hoped that the descendants will always like to get together. This is how the spirit of the lineage is born.

Today, love (most often confused with sex life, which is only the organic aspect of love) is considered a pleasant moment ("Love brings great joy, and everyone knows that…") as opposed to marriage, which is worthy of pity ("marriage = rope"). This is due to a general misunderstanding of the deeper nature of love which stems from the artificial, selfish and pleasure-seeking mindset of people today. The problem of "love and marriage" is also solved when we know what the ultimate goal of love is. All genuine love aspires to marriage. Marriages that respect the natural law are love marriages, which are consolidated by a good hereditary heritage. One can truly speak of heaven on earth. The combination of objectives is thus achieved: *The desired procreative event is united with the happy experience of love.*

Since, on the one hand, the happiness, peace and salvation of the people lie in as many marriages as possible, but on the other hand, it is extraordinarily difficult to find a good spouse in our modern life and in the mass of the people, the fundamental task of an ethnist state will be to create the conditions for finding a healthy spouse. This is also the most important practical goal of all our cultural work.

J. Mayerhofer

Absolute love resides only in absolute strength.

Hölderlin

SS NOTEBOOK No. 3. 1943.

SIGURD, THE KNIGHT GEORGE AND THE FIGHT WITH THE DRAGON

THE SS ORDER—ETHICS & IDEOLOGY

The struggle for the fatherland forces us all to return to a natural existence. All those who had lost their ties to the land, feel the call of the heritage of the past again, a peasant heritage that encourages love for the fatherland.

Outside, nature is still dormant. But the daylight is already growing, spring is not far away. This word moves all hearts because it means the end of the annual struggle for the rebirth of life.

The peasant mind has produced wonderful allegories of the struggle of the seasons, which are also symbols of a worldview characteristic of the race. These are symbols that cannot be perfectly defined by words and concepts, for they comprise the total world of existence. They are sometimes new, and yet they are connected, however they may appear, to a near or distant past, to the Germanic past of our people. Tales and legends, even Christian legends, contain symbols of ancient wisdom and knowledge. Which of our children, in the harsh winter weather, would not welcome guests from the land of legends? What genuine youthful heart would not beat proudly when hearing for the first time the story of a heroic battle?

Happy is the world whose customs and art have preserved symbols of the struggle for life. In many places, winter is still put to death in the form of a dragon, the gentle queen of spring freed and united with the king of May. Behind these pictorial figures lies the ancient myth of the renewal of life. Only the eternal vigil can overcome death. Everywhere fate, the monstrous dragon, stands in our way and denies us access to the fountain of youth, forbids us the conquest of the vital drink, the "glittering treasure".

The sun god Wotan.
Ornamental plate on a helmet from Vendel in Sweden.

The two aspects of life, birth and death, day and night, summer and winter, are found in various forms and our folk heritage has preserved them in its rich imagery, even under the Christian garment, which could not otherwise overcome the strength of the Germanic folk soul than by placing it in the service of the Church. Thus the dragon-slaying knight St. George has remained the most Germanic of all heroic figures. Bernd Notke derived his St. George from the Germanic fortitude. An old document says: "It is precisely at this time—Easter—that one must triumph with George when winter is driven away by the south wind, when the earth enters its adolescence and gives birth to plants and flowers.

And when we look to the Germanic past for symbols of this assured life, we are surprised by the abundance of evidence and the frankness of expression. First of all, let us look at the sublime symbol of life that is the Edda: "I know that an ash tree stands/ Is called Yggdrasill/ The high tree, sprinkled/ With white swirls/ From there comes the dew/ That in the valley falls/ Eternally green it stands/ Above the well of Urd." But in its depths dwells Nidhögrr, the horrible fate that guards the fountain of the drink of immortality and gnaws the roots of the tree of life. "Comes flying/The dark dragon/The glittering viper, descended/ From Nidafell; /He bears in his plumage/—Hovers over the plain-/ Dead bodies, Nidhôgg/ Now she will disappear." And the dragon says of himself, "I breathed venom/ When lying on my father's heritage/ Huge/ Stronger on my own/ I thought I was, than all/ Careless of the number of my enemies."

Ornament with a dragon and the sun wheel.
Design of an old Icelandic door.

Odin and Thor, the magnificent gods, are themselves involved in the fight against this dark dragon for the survival of the world. Their divine strength is perpetuated in heroes like Sigurd and Dietrich, whose feats of arms were sung in the Germanic royal courts. "O mighty serpent! / You made great spits / And hissed with a harsh heart; / Hate rises all the more / Among the sons of men / When one has this helmet on his head." Life could not be won without death: "I advise you now, Sigurdr/ And you take this advice:/ Get out of here! / The sound of gold / And the silver as red as brier / The rings, will lead you to death."

This Germanic attitude is already attested to by the oldest evidence we have dating from the 3rd millennium BC. On the engraved stones of Sweden—a symbol of ancient customs—appear the Midgard serpent, the tree of life, the fight of Thor and the dragon. But it was especially during the time of the great invasions, the time of the great political breakthrough of Germanicness, which was already known in the Bronze Age—that the spiritual forces of an untouched conception of life animated the craftsmanship. With the art of the northern Vikings, this force found a great revival and survived into the Christian era.

Sigurd's fight with the dragon.
Design on a doorpost in Hyllestad, Sweden.

The self-confident and self-controlled sun god depicted on the Homhausen horseman's stone rides through the world without fear of the evil powers of the abyss. The dragon motif appears in various forms even in the clothing and woodcuts of the early northern churches. Artists' hands have depicted Sigurd's fight with the dragon on the Hyllestad gate. A motif from Iceland beautifully illustrates the triumph of life over death. In this symbol, the two aspects of the universe are shown and the essence of the mythical god Odin is explained to us. In all these personifications it is constantly apparent that the Germanic people were aware that the divine destiny of life lay in themselves, in their faith, in their power of action. From time immemorial, its power was able to meet the divine challenges. Only the weak succumb to the dark forces.

Our stories, tales and legends, our folk art are symbols of the spiritual and moral life of our people's ancestors. We must not mistake the simplicity and clarity of these psychic representations for naivety. Do we not likewise aspire to recover that unity of life which radiates from the ancient tradition, from which even the medieval Church drew its energy to strengthen its alien doctrine? Are not the moral foundations of our will the same as in ancient times?

We do not yet know the deep forces that led Germanity to adopt a Christian thought that was alien to it. Perhaps it was at the dangerous moment when it was acquiring a new awareness of a higher life. It discovered attractive, almost similar concepts, but frozen in the formal perspective of a Roman-Christian life.

The knowledge of our identity has brought us back to the divine order of which we are a part, from which no spiritual transcendence can separate us. Body, soul and spirit are once again a unity. The eternal rhythm of life beats within us, now as before, and life appears to be the divine manifestation present in all things.

Dr Mähling

SS NOTEBOOK No. 3. 1944.

HOW LOKI AND HEIMDAL FOUGHT FOR FREYA'S NECKLACE

The Germanic legends have lost much of what they told of the actions and sufferings of the gods.

In a famous poem, the scalde Ulf Uggissohn sang of Heimdal's duel with Loki for the beautiful, sparkling necklace of the goddess Freya. Of this poem and the legend that celebrated the duel, only two lines remain that tell us that Heimdal won the duel with the evil companion of the gods. The

Icelandic sage Snorri also tells us that they both looked like seals during this fight.

Let us allow the poet the possibility of reconstructing a general view from these few scraps.

"Once, Loki, the unstable offspring of a giant whom the gods had unwisely accepted into their community, flew over the sea in the form of a hawk, and saw a large fish beneath the surface whose scales and fins glittered with gold.

In his lust for the jewel, Loki charged towards the waves, but as his talons plunged into the water to seize the precious fish, the invisible net of the sea giant Ran surrounded them. With cunning and illusions, she had lured the greedy being into this trap and then took him to the bottom of the sea to her dark kingdom.

She held him in prison for nine days among the drowned sailors in the dull depths until he promised by the most sacred oath on the head of his faithful wife Sigrun, to bring Freya's splendid necklace as a ransom to the dreadful ruler of the seas.

This necklace of stars of the goddess, which shines every clear night in the sky, was the pride of the gods and the happiness of men. Freya never took it off her neck. But Loki, the very clever son of the giant Laufey, knew what to say to her so that she would entrust him with the celestial ornament.

Freya, the radiant goddess of beauty who inflamed the hearts of gods and men, and whose grace made the heavy giants burn with desire, was herself unhappy in love. She had given her heart to a man named Od and married him, but he abandoned her and she searched in vain for him in all the lands. When Loki returned to Asgard, in the castle of the gods, he went to Freya and spoke to her: "I have found Od, whom you were asking for. Ran, the giant thief, has lured him into her deadly nest and is holding him prisoner at the bottom of the sea. However, she is willing to give him back to you if you give her your glittering necklace as ransom."

Freya would never have parted with her magnificent finery, but love demanded the highest price. Golden tears of joy streamed down her face. "Take the jewel!" she said. "No jewel is too precious to me for the life of Od, the beloved. Bring the bridegroom close to my heart and I will be eternally grateful!

Loki, exultant, untied the jewel from his neck and dived in the form of a seal into the depths of the sea to bring the ruthless Ran the extracted ornament.

But someone had heard the words of the deceiver, Heimdal, the great guardian of the sky, whose all-seeing eye day and night never slumbered and whose ear was so keen that he perceived every sound. He, who could see into the heart of the earth, knew of Loki's captivity at Ran and perceived the deception. With the speed of lightning he assumed the air of a seal and dived towards Loki.

In the sea waves, a furious battle ensued between the strength of Heimdal and the treacherous cunning of Loki, who always escaped the suffocating grip of the guardian of the heavenly castle. Ran, the horrible one, wanted to go to Loki's aid, but the nine wave-mothers of Heimdal, the child of the sea, seized her and prevented her. Gjalp, the roaring one, Greip, the seizing one, Eistha, the attacking one, Eyrgjafa, the sand maker, Ufrun, the wolf, Angeyfa, the oppressing one, Imd, the whispering one, Atal, the perishing one, Iarnsasea, the one with the iron knife, all of whom gave birth to Heimdal, rushed at the giant thief and prevented her from intervening in the fight.

So the waves rolled furiously, so angrily that white foam flew into the sky, men's boats smashed into the sea waves and even raised land around them.

Finally, Heimdal managed to grab Loki and take the shining jewel from him. Loki, without strength, sank under the water, but Heimdal lifted him up and flew as an eagle to the divine heights. "How could you trust the corruptor?" he chided Freya, handing back the sparkling jewel. "You know you will not see Od again until Ragnarök, the twilight of the gods, comes. You look in vain for him at Ran. Only Odin and I know the secret that hides him. But you will see it again on the day of the battle of the worlds, before the new world rises from the waves in tears and blood. And then Loki will receive his punishment, he whose malice has so often wronged us gods.

When the White Aesir returned to the celestial bridges, watching that the giants did not storm the castle of the gods before their time, he took the notched wooden staff and made a notch in it beside the many others that remembered the misdeeds of Loki, the villain. As he lay in his bed with a bitter smile on his face, he suddenly felt a pain in his chest and groaned in a torment he had foreseen; yet his wife, Sigrun, his faithful wife, comforted him."

Hermann Harder

III. Customs and Religion

"D'Estoc et de Taille",
by Gunther d'Alquen, 1937.

Form and Content

One of the most important questions of our time concerns the religious attitude. In the last few years, in the search for a path in accordance with the National Socialist conception, an extraordinary number of German citizens have spontaneously tackled this difficult problem by finding the most diverse solutions.

It is not our role to define ourselves for or against this or that type of solution. But it is our duty to provide clarification without taking sides on all these issues.

As always, in such an examination, our aim is not negative: A religious experience must never be based on a conflict with another religious conception. This would be in contradiction with the spirit of the Party programme, with our ethics. Therefore, when examining the problem, it must be repeated that as National Socialists we are not interested in the substance of any of these doctrines; but the important thing is only to what extent it corresponds to the principle of our world view, for religion is a private matter.

The new state has clearly defined its position on the religious question in two fundamental declarations. Article 24 of our programme guarantees: "the freedom of all religious denominations within the state, insofar as they do not endanger the stability of the state or contravene the moral sentiment and good morals of the Germanic race. Thus a racial instinct becomes the absolute criterion for religious conception.

In the so-called Freedom of Conscience Act, the National Socialist state has clearly defined how this feeling is to be interpreted: "Belief is the most personal matter and one is responsible only to one's conscience. The result is that:

The National Socialist state refused to interfere in religious matters as long as their representatives did not intervene in the political sphere.

This is the only way that a Christian, Catholic or Protestant, or a follower of another religion, can live his or her faith within the Party and Germany if he or she does so out of personal conviction and choice.

But this should not imply that this freedom can be interpreted in a negative and malicious way.

The Reichsführer SS made it clear in a speech about the tasks of the SS:

"But for this reason we do not tolerate being called atheists because of the misuse of the word pagan, because as a community we do not depend on this or that denomination, or on any dogma, or require our men to be attached to it."

We aspire to a religious feeling and renewal, and this means that we have nothing to do with that materialistic historical conception which rejects all religiosity on principle, because it denies the existence of the metaphysical because of its subjection to the earthly world. According to the Reichsführer SS, we regard those who do not believe in anything as "presumptuous, megalomaniac and stupid".

Consequently, our position has nothing to do with those who, devoid of any religion, are free of spiritual ties. The denominational churches are not entirely wrong when they observe that no awakening or renovation of a religious nature could be expected from these circles, for negation alone does not constitute a valid ground for the emergence of new ideas. A truly original religious experience can only come from a desire for positive concretisation, which leads to an attempt to create a new religious content.

But, according to natural laws, only an individual can do this work—a man who must have in him the makings of a reformer or a prophet, though it is not necessary for him to behave like one.

Nor do we understand why Germans who, for ideological reasons, want nothing to do with Christianity because they refuse to accept as moral law those elements of Christian morality which seem alien to them, should not organise themselves in the form of a public and legal community.

This in itself would be desirable, because it is the only way to treat people and their families equally, which is necessary and even urgent.

For these reasons, we also believe that in the long run it will not be possible to demand of all those of our fellow citizens who are faithfully and convincingly attached to the moral law of our race, that their descendants and betrotheds should be deprived of all public blessings and, in the end, their burials of all solemnity. But we also know that a new form of religion, if it is not to become a buffoonery, must be developed gradually and rooted organically in old authentic customs still existing today, and therefore cannot be "created" suddenly by any organisation.

However, we believe above all that these customs, which alone justify regulation, must never lead to an 'ideological-religious organisation'. For not to tolerate tutelage of any kind or a collective conception in this area is the typical sign of a truly Germanic religious attitude.

For the Germans, religion was and remained a private matter. The heads of Germanic families also acted as priests and did not tolerate any priestly class.

What we need is not a vague enthusiasm for a pseudo-religious secret or sectarian society, but an honest and good faith embrace of those religious and 'above all moral' conceptions of our ancestors.

This was one of the most disastrous mistakes made by those many little leagues that wanted to renew the religion of our race by linking up with the living tradition that violent Christianisation had once muzzled.

It is impossible to erase a thousand years of human and national evolution and consider it non-existent.

Wotan and Thor are dead—and those dreamy spirits who sacrificed a horse on an old sacrificial stone a dozen years ago were sad fools who needlessly compromised the good cause. Neither the pre-Christian religious custom nor the representations underlying it can be used. If one seeks to express one's own moral consciousness in external religious forms, one must try to refer to the sacred book of our ancestors, the Edda, as Christianity did with the books of the Old Testament. If we want to create a kind of moral law, we must take inspiration from the beautiful poetic passages, especially those that express the world view. But let us not try to go too far.

Religion is a spiritual matter and can only be based on the spiritual. Our task is only to act in such a way that we do not offend a German who has renounced Eastern doctrines and is striving on his own to reclaim the ancestral heritage.

"D'ESTOC ET DE TAILLE", BY GUNTHER D'ALQUEN, 1937.

THE SPIRITUAL CRISIS

When the opponents of National Socialism realise that overt or covert resistance on the political level is hopeless, they drape themselves in a suitable guise and reappear to try to put up an even more camouflaged front. This camouflage can be very different: it can be purely religious or tinged with 'science'. However, this does not make us lose sight of the fact that it is still the same circles which, as in the past, seek to hinder National Socialism in its development.

"In his new book, German Socialism, Werner Sombart has attempted to review the present situation in its entirety and thus to shed light on the causes of the crisis in which our fatherland and the entire civilised world find themselves. He rightly looks for the ultimate causes of the enormous chaos that is shaking and threatening our entire existence—in the realm of world view rather than in political and economic events.

With these words, the Deutsche Bergwerkszeitung in Dusseldorf begins its editorial with a clear statement. We are, of course, accustomed to all sorts of hateful attacks on our worldview—but rarely have we been told with such impertinence that we are not only responsible for the present weakening of Christianity, but also for the future decadence of the entire world.

The author, who calls himself Spitama, knows how far he can go without falling foul of the law with his pile of cleverly disguised insults against National Socialism. He forgets that we do not judge words but the spirit, and that, moreover, we are not so stupid as not to consider this "scientific discussion" for what it is, i.e. a political text.

But an authoritarian reaction on our part would serve both Mr. Spitama and the *Deutsche Bergwerkszeitung*, which has allowed this insolent contempt for the National Socialist vision to be expressed on its first two pages in eight columns. A spiritual sphere under attack cannot be cleansed by any coercive measures. We are determined to make it clear to those German citizens to whom the *Deutsche Bergwerkszeitung is* addressed that the "present spiritual crisis" is totally different from what Mr. Spitama presents, and in particular that what he regards as a "cause of illness" is the only remedy and the only way out for the German future.

We had no idea that we are living in a "frightening chaos, which threatens and undermines our whole existence". We were under the impression that citizens who do not yet share our ideals (in case there are still any among the readers of the *deutsche Bergwerkszeitung)* agree with us that National Socialism has put an end to precisely this "frightening chaos" and replaced it with an order that is as productive as it is fertile. But the developments of the last year have clearly not been perceived by Mr. Spitama and his colleague, for they assume that the German people are still living in the hell of destruction which they present—this is the real meaning of their article—as the inevitable result of an abandonment of Christianity.

By means of high-flying objective justifications, Mr. Spitama demonstrates in his article, which he calls "the cause of the disease", that Marxism has set itself the goal of destroying religiosity in Western thought. He proves with numerous quotations that the actual abandonment of Christianity, or rather of the Christian Church, especially in the last half of the previous century, was an obvious concomitant of the materialist world view.

There would be little to object to in the historical, religious and philosophical spheres if the point of the essay were not to attribute similar tendencies to National Socialism in precisely these areas. Mr. Spitama's wisdom culminates in his conclusion: "Salvation and deliverance for Germany can only lie in the return to Him who is the way, the truth and the life (i.e. Christ!) Only in this way can the West escape the predicted decadence.

So there we are! National Socialism, with its obvious hostility to the Church, is responsible for the eventual demise of the West. For de-Christianisation "is the disease with which we are afflicted and from which we must perish if we do not succeed in overcoming it.

This is demonstrated with the full range of clerical arguments. The naive and dusty Professor Sombart is quoted in a somewhat obscure sentence, which Mr Spitama considers to be "full of character":

"What we have experienced can only be explained as the work of the devil. We can clearly see the paths along which Satan has led men to himself: he has increasingly undermined faith in a world beyond and thus launched men into the perdition of this world."

If only Mr Spitama had called us great and small devils, he would have blamed us for the fact that today his 'belief in the afterlife' has effectively disappeared from the majority of our fellow citizens. For as the writer depicts it, it is the most horrible of terrors:

Modern people are no longer subject to the fear of threatening hells and the promise of reward in the afterlife no longer consoles them for the unpleasantness of this world.

There was certainly no need to set a trap for us by mobilising none other than Heinrich Heine in support of these theses, as if Jewish thought, which is therefore devious, had foreseen exactly the course of evolution by believing that we could willingly abandon heaven to the angels and the little birds.

Certainly, our religiosity, and therefore our faith in our people and its future, is firmly rooted in reality. But let it not be said that these visions "tried to replace the god present in the conscience".

We do not tolerate our most sacred belief being called a pseudo-religion because our faith is inferior to that of the denominational community. We believe in eternity in the same way as religious Christians. We believe that the forces that have enabled our people to escape death are just as "religious" as those very diverse representations which, almost buried under medieval dogmas, form the real core of current religious doctrine. If we can, it is precisely because we are able to see and experience eternity in this world—a faculty that Christianity, wherever it lived and lives, has cultivated and nurtured.

"Belief in God and the afterlife is in fact the foundation of morality, from which it draws its power of action. Autonomous morality, which no longer sees God as a legislator and judge, is the product of intellectual reflections. It cannot survive and resist the attacks of the great temptations of life. Moral autonomy, this product of modern subjectivism, leads to the adoration of man. Here it is, the sneaky stab!

For us, this morality which comes from above and is imposed on the people is as condemnable as those hypocritical ways which, for example, use the most understandable faults through the secrecy of confession to politically dominate the weak-minded.

The abstruse doctrine of original sin makes redemption necessary. The Fall, and even the notion of sin according to the Christian conception, with a reward and punishment in the afterlife, is unbearable for people of our race because it is not compatible with the worldview of our blood.

Overlooking all denominational controversies—and there can hardly be any debates in Germany about religious problems—we consider it unquestionably important for the future of our people that religion in the service of the State should create new and appropriate spiritual forms so that the heroic ideal of life of our race can be realised. Then—and only then—could Christianity, which is unfortunately still influenced by the South, really take root in our people, something which, as we know, it was not able to do at all a thousand years after the forced Christianisation.

This is why Spitama is insolent when he defines the dogmatic Catholic form of Christianity precisely as "the faith of our fathers"; as if it had not taken centuries of hard fighting to impose this religion of love on our fathers by sword and torture!

Moreover, we know today how strongly the religious feeling of Germanism permeates "German" Christianity, and that the social morality, which the Church would like to consider its most fundamental creation, is based more on the ethical qualities of our race than on the pulpit doctrine of the medieval centuries.

Finally, we must not forget that the last thousand years have been an alienation of the principle of our being and of our species in every respect. We certainly do not want to ignore them or eliminate them completely from our consciousness, but we do not want to forget that this millennium is but "a day and a night compared to God—to the eternity we feel in this world", which is the origin of our being and our religion.

In the face of the millennia of existence of our people and the tens of millennia of existence of our race, the proud errors of a false doctrine alien to the people do not count for much. This should be said to those who, with ill will and in borrowed garb, imagine they can slander our religious sensibilities with impunity.

"D'ESTOC ET DE TAILLE",
BY GUNTHER D'ALQUEN, 1937.

POWER AND HEART

The Trinity of body, mind and soul forms a harmonious and living unity in healthy people. But these three essences, which are perfectly equivalent for us, can be evaluated differently. In the course of history, this has always been detrimental to man.

For example, we are familiar with the medieval religious viewpoint that gave legitimacy only to a so-called "soul ", thus attempting to divert the intellectual spheres of man towards the afterlife and no longer taking an interest in the body. We are also familiar with those tendencies which only took into account the spirit, the ratio, and reduced everything to a pure mechanism, to a causality without a soul.

These partially false positions are unhealthy when they collide head-on with pure reality. It is a vision that is not as strong as reality and does not coincide with it. It is inadequate and unsustainable.

One can speak of an over-assertion of the 'moral' aspect with regard to the national principle. Where once liberalism emphasised only the material, we see the same opposite error arising as a reaction against liberalism, only more exclusive in concept and ideology. In this case, national reality, the racial idea and, in short, our love of this world become an illusion without foundation and give way to considerations that analyse the people in a metaphysical or scholastic way, chimerical speculations and a falsification of the mystical meaning of national reality.

We see this "nationalist" mysticism at work here and there. Their representatives are as calotinous and intolerant as the Dominicans of the Middle Ages; their conceptions deal with "custom", runic gymnastics and mysterious magic. They meet in sects and believe that fighting other calotines gives them an alibi. They hate clear concepts. Science and economics are for them a priori only liberalist domains and inventions of the devil.

Nationalism sees itself as a popular reality. It insists on the primacy of the worldview, but without neglecting other aspects of our existence.

The decomposition of the whole of humanity and the dissociation of the physical, spiritual and moral realms also manifested itself from the point of view of the state. It was not only the individual who was deceived and the essence of the people who was violated, but also the state and the authority that lacked genuine harmony. Moreover, art was forced to limit itself to the political needs of power, and the latter no longer possessed those spiritual and moral values that are the hallmark of true humanity.

Germany has thus found in our presence both power and spirit, power and soul. Thus art becomes independent and power does the same. The reason for this separation of the two domains lies ultimately in this hostility and alien nature. Art cannot thrive in the long term without political power, and a state will freeze and become reactionary if the spirit and soul do not provide it with an inner life.

We have gone beyond the ideal of a purely active state apparatus, for the whole people now influence the state and thus the spirit and soul of the nation. Therefore, German spirituality no longer evolves without positive contact with power. It is therefore no longer in danger of falling into the hands of the Jews as it once did. But, unlike in the past, the state no longer regards the spirit as a deliberate, undesirable and forbidden enemy, but as a vital manifestation of the nation.

Our task is to synthesise the power and spirit that reigned long ago. Art often found protection from small, powerful princes, but the great ones often remained silent. For this to happen, power and spirit must go hand in hand. The moral data which the German people have in abundance is mentioned. Thus the most serious problem is not only to create harmony between power and spirit, but to achieve a perpetual synthesis of power and soul.

The greatest task that has been given to our people today is to combine and continually maintain these principles. Then the power will not become fixed; it will never become a facade and will always be in close connection with the Germans.

But the German soul will look back on itself and free itself from these alien reveries because it will take reality as its starting point.

It will always strive to observe the highest reality that exists on this earth: a happy people and their continuity.

SS NOTEBOOK NO. 4. 1942.

GERMANIC PIETY

Through their religion, our ancestors honoured supernatural forces whose action and power they believed they could feel in the fields and the forest, in the sky and on the earth, certainly, but above all on their own existence. This was always the essential aspect. Man is also a child of nature, but as a being endowed with speech and spirit, his link with the community is totally different from that of the animal. The original relationship with the family, clan and people into which he was born influences his life on a much greater level than his relationship with 'nature' which is the field of his activity. The popular community also provides him with his religion—as well as his language! Through the cult and myth that he learns, it transmits to him the specificity of his relationship with the divinity. Better still, he distinguishes the will of the divinity itself, which is expressed in the action and motivation of this community, in the laws and rules that govern it, in the moral values that are inherent in it. He discerns it first in the community because these rules and relationships derive their sacred force from the fact that they are established, according to the ancient belief, by the gods themselves, are subject to their supervision and protection.

In this context, the Icelandic sagas describing the Norse sacrificial feast are particularly instructive. We learn that at the great annual festivals, sacrifices were made on the one hand 'for the harvest' (or a 'good year') and 'peace', and on the other for 'victory' and the king's reign. This shows that the sacrifice organised by the popular community represented by the community cult was linked to the life and destiny of that community. A good harvest and peace on the one hand, victory and sovereignty on the other; these are the two poles around which the life of a people moves: the natural biological aspect and the political-historical aspect. On the one hand, there is peace, which involves the work of the peasant and culminates in the harvest; on the other hand, there is war, which, crowned by victory, brings honour and power. The fact that the gods were asked for these things at the sacrificial festivals shows that they were regarded as the providers and protectors of these goods, i.e. of everything that constituted the soul and the raison d'être of the ethnic community. The Germanic man believed that the gods decided both the prosperity of his peaceful work—cultivating his field—and the conquest of victory in the war that ensured the survival of the people.

But the formula 'til ärs ok fridar' carries a greater lesson than the translation 'for a (good) year and peace'; for the word 'peace' characterises not only the state of peace, as opposed to war, but also the moral and legal order on which the peaceful common life of the human community rests. Nothing can better express the religious meaning of this old formula than Schiller's words:

"Sacred order, heavenly son bringing the blessing that unites the whole community in freedom and joy. The gods are the dispensers of good, of the goods of life; they are the masters of war, the rulers of victory and thus determine the destiny of peoples. They are also the guardians of the sacred peace which is based on law and law.

Compared to the knowledge of worship and the impact of religion on public life, it is difficult to imagine the inner religious attitude of the Germanic people, their piety. The sanctity and power of the deity give believers a sense of dependence. But for the Germanic man, this feeling of dependence on his god was free of any servile submission. Instead, it was supported by a strong, courageous trust. In the North, trua ('trust') is an expression of religious faith and the god on whom the Icelandic relied above all else in the miseries and difficulties of life. He called him his "Fultrui", i.e. the one who deserves full trust. Like the Norwegian Thorolf Mosterbart, many Germanic men sought salvation from their god when they had difficult decisions to make and sought his advice. Did they know they were safe under the protection of the powerful god, or was it just an instinctive reaction to see him as the safe 'friend'? There is ample evidence that Thor was the first to be so regarded. He is called Astvinr ("the kind friend"), in the saga. Such a beautiful and dignified relationship does not diminish the gap between man and God on which all pious belief rests; it resulted in a piety that gave man confidence and strength; it is the noblest characteristic present in the conception of Germanic religion.

Walter Baetke

Man must grasp God at the heart of things.

Master Eckhart

SS BOOKLET NO. 6. 1942.

BODY AND SOUL

The ancient conception of antiquity and Christianity establishes a difference in nature between the body and the soul. They both have a different origin: the body is of earthly and material origin, the soul of divine and spiritual essence. Each follows a different destiny: the body dies and decomposes, the soul is immortal and lives on after death. They also have a very contrasting value: the body is the source of instinct, baseness, inferiority and vileness; the soul is the support of what is great and beautiful, and therefore of absolute value. An impassable gulf separates them; hostile, they face each other. The body, profane, is the chain that holds the soul back from its immaterial and divine flight to the heights. It is the earthly, impure straitjacket.

Our worldview and ethnic beliefs contradict these principles of a decadent and dying world.

We know that these two aspects, soul and body, have been granted to us by the Creator. Both are for us the manifestation of the ever-creative, eternal and wonderfully active divine nature.

We know that our ancestors have passed them on to us and that they will live on in our children. We know that we ourselves are responsible for their survival or death. We are fully aware that our mission is to continue the work of the Creator and to enhance it over time.

We know that the nobility and purity of our body is also the nobility and purity of our soul, and conversely, he who corrupts his body also corrupts his soul. The education of our soul and the development of our body go hand in hand.

We know that our body and soul are ultimately one and that to honour one is to honour the other.

L.E.

SS NOTEBOOK NO. 8A. 1941.

WHAT DOES 'SOLSTICE' MEAN?

The Sun, father of the universe,

creates spring and winter, heat and cold

Being on guard duty far to the east has frankly nothing to do with astronomy. Yet the soldier who is there, facing the enemy, can become a 'confirmed expert in astronomical matters', especially if he observes the sunrise.

Sunrise over the vast eastern plains is an unforgettable sight for anyone who has seen it! A bright red announces the event in the morning sky, then the rays appear above the horizon; a pale winter Sun rises and prepares a new day. These are the things that everyone can see every day.

But now we would like to study this natural spectacle from an astronomical point of view. We don't need a telescope, a compass or a watch—just a fixed point for several days and some sticks. Each day, when the sun rises, we mark our mark at the rising point by sticking a stick a few dozen paces ahead of us in the snow.

The next day or a few days later we go to the same place. Sunrise is imminent—and this is where most people are surprised! It doesn't appear behind our stick as it used to, but a little further south, so to the right. As we started our observations at the beginning of December, the Sun will move further to the right each time it rises ... until December 22. On December 21, 22, and 23, even if you are not on duty, it is worthwhile to be awake before sunrise and to observe the sunrise in the east from a predetermined point.

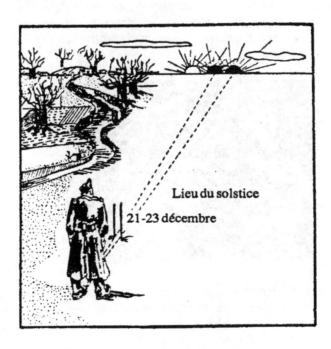

Lieu du solstice
21-23 décembre

What happens during these three days? The Sun, which is still moving southwards from the eastern point on the 21st, reaches its highest point of sunrise in the south on the 22nd and *moves* northwards again on the 23rd. The fact that we have dispensed with sleep allows us to actually witness the unfolding of the *solstice*. We have seen this event happen twice a year—with pious admiration—as our Germanic ancestors did, for they rose early, as did every peasant, and which determined their most sacred festivals. For the change in the course of the sun promised them—and us—increasing daylight and sunshine! It also indicates that the dark winter is over and that there will be spring again. Let us now consider our drawing which reflects this observation.

But one may wonder why the winter solstice indicates such a short day, while the summer solstice indicates precisely the longest day? For Berlin, the difference in day length is indeed 7 hours in winter and 17 hours in summer.

Our second drawing will explain why. Let's imagine that we could climb above the Earth in a stratospheric balloon, and let's also assume that what our eyes would see would be exact: the Earth's surface would be shaped like a disc and the sky like a half-ball... We could therefore follow the trajectory of the Sun on this half-sphere, because we would stay a whole day with the balloon at this height. If we ascended exactly on December 22, we would see the Sun appear in the south, skim the south during the day in a westward arc, and set again in the southwest. But on June 21 we would see the Sunrise high in the northeast, then the arc rising directly over the sky towards the west and the Sunset in the northwest. The drawing reveals that these daily arcs are of different lengths, and that the Sun's radiation can have a variable duration.

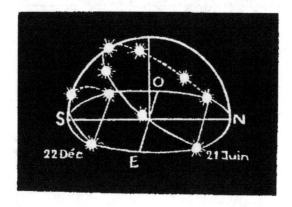

But perhaps this still does not answer our question. We rightly say to ourselves that the Earth is not a disc and that the Sun does not move in the sky in this way at all. So let's take our stratospheric balloon a few thousand kilometres into the universe and see what summer and winter look like in the universe from this enormous distance. We have to go away for a whole year, otherwise we would not be able to see the differences so clearly.

When we are far enough out in space, we can see the Sun. At the centre of the ellipses described by the planets of the solar system. Together with Mercury, Venus, Mars and the other planets, our Earth orbits the Sun, turns around its axis every day and, for a year, exactly once around the Sun. The icy poles of our Earth would appear to us as light-coloured caps, but curiously enough, the north and south poles are not at the highest and lowest points of the globe, but laterally offset, so that the Earth's axis is *oblique* in space.

This tilt of the earth's axis, or ecliptic, means that we experience mild heat in our temperate latitudes in summer, cold in winter, long days in summer, short days in winter. The tilted earth axis explains our seasons. Our third picture explains this.

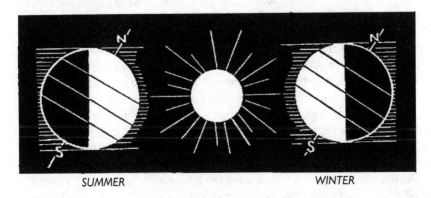

SUMMER   WINTER

In the middle is the Sun shining, on the right and left is our Earth at these two points which designate 21 June and 22 December. Now, with a torch and an apple or a round potato that you have pierced obliquely with a wire, you must imitate these two positions. The earth's axis constantly points to the same point in the sky (towards the North Star), and the Sun also remains constantly in the same place. Its rays therefore illuminate a larger area in the north, and six months later a larger area in the south. We can reproduce the whole phenomenon with the torch.

The middle part of the Earth, the area towards the equator, constantly receives the same amount of light. So each day lasts exactly twelve hours, and the Sun passes vertically over the heads of people living in the tropics every day. But during the summer, the Sun shines much brighter over the northern part of the globe. In the far north, the sun simply does not set and our comrades in Narvik even experience the midnight sun, the great wonder of this region. Further south, the sunrise rises high in the north, the day is long and the sunset is in the west. At the same time, the southern half of the Earth experiences shorter days and winter night reigns constantly at the South Pole. After a year, when the days have gradually become shorter for us, the southern half of the earth experiences exactly the opposite phenomena.

We humans are therefore subject, as are all the planets, the Earth and all living beings, to the great divine and solar law. This is also the idea that crosses our minds on the day of the solstice.

SS Booklet No. 7. 1938.

Solstice

The farmer walked with a heavy step in the deep snow. His tall, broad figure stood out, black, against the bluish white of the winter landscape and the starry night sky. The man who accompanied him was dry and gaunt. His fur coat fluttered in the wind and he walked with such gusto that he looked like he had just emerged from adolescence. The bitter cold that had hypnotised and petrified the moor and the forest did not seem to touch him, for his woollen waistcoat was half-open. From time to time, with his left hand, he scratched his grey beard in which his breath was constantly condensing into small crystals. Behind the two men, at a distance, as befits the respect due to age, followed Eib, the farmer's eldest son. Like the others, he carried his weapons: the long sword, the dagger and the spear. He had thrown his shield back and on his right hip hung an artfully crafted horn, preserved for generations and handed down from father to son.

The marchers passed in silence over the hills where their ancestors were buried. Here must have slept kings and princes who had once been mighty and whose warrior valour was celebrated in song. The gaunt elder before him on the father's right was also an initiate who wandered from farm to farm telling stories and who 'knew more than his breviary'. Eib saw that the grizzled man, when he passed a large mound, saluted him with his spear. During this solitary walk, he was probably secretly conversing with the dead?

The young peasant remembered the stories that the black-haired trader from the south had told, a few moons earlier. There would be people there who avoided the abodes of the dead because they were afraid of the dead. At this memory, Eib shook his head. Why fear the dead when they were still part of the clan? Didn't the ties that bound the generations go so far back in time that no one knew where they came from, and would they not continue through future generations in a future that no one knew how it would end? Had not the dead passed on their heritage to the living as a sacred legacy that demanded respect?

Ancient pagan symbols were revived by the SS. Here, the famous candlestick of him which was given to each new SS couple on the winter solstice.

The SS celebrates the winter solstice, the night that heralds the return of the Sun.

The man from the south had spoken of demons and ghosts, of disturbing beings in whose bodies the dead lived, beings who played a nasty game with men, intent only on harming them and bringing them misfortune. Could death have changed the fathers who lay under these hills so much? Incredible, no, impossible: the young peasant answered his own question.

He who had remained natural in life could not be different in death. He who had worked for the good and the future of his clan and his people could not, once his ashes were buried in the earth, become the enemy of his own race.

It is possible that among the southern peoples they frightened the living during the lonely nights. The black-haired men were of such a different nature, so dark in character; perhaps their dead were different from ours. The young peasant decided to ask the grey-haired elder, who had been his father's guest for some days, about this. He knew that this thin man had seen many countries and peoples.

The three men had now reached the central plateau of the moor which was the goal of their journey. The icy night seemed to have cleared. The circles of massive vertical blocks were clearly visible and the farmer and his guest approached them. He stopped in front of a block in the middle of the circle. This stone had a secant plane which seemed to be directed towards a point in the sky. With a quiet gesture of his hand, the farmer pushed back the layer of snow covering the point of the stone.

He knew what he had to do. Hadn't he been coming to this place for years with his father, at the time of the solstice, in summer and winter? He turned north, walked between two circles of stones to a third, in the centre of which two blocks stood close together. He carefully removed the snow that covered it like a cloak and returned to his father. In the meantime, his father had carefully inspected the starry sky and then turned towards the south-east where a faint light was shining, heralding the dawn of a new day. The south became brighter and brighter, while the north was still sleeping in the darkest blue.

Then the peasant raised his hand. "The time has come," he said solemnly. "The day star (Arktur) bows to the earth. He knelt behind the menhir so that the sharp edge of its flat surface was a line before his eye. This line seemed to pass through the narrow gap between two blocks of the other circle and reach the bright star twinkling just above the horizon. Then he stood up and made way for the old man, who just as carefully aimed through the gap at the star, which was disappearing more and more into the northern vapour as the sky cleared to the south.

"You're right," said the skinniest one, "the star of the day is setting in the direction that announces the festival: in three days' time we'll be celebrating the middle of winter.

The elder stood up and, at a sign from the father, took Eib's trunk, raised it to his lips and sounded the traditional signal over the moor. Three times he sounded and three times the call rang out. The men listened in the early morning. Shortly afterwards the call was answered. The sound of the trumpet had been heard in the villages along the moor, for it now seemed that on every horizon the trumpets were awakening and echoing the call from farm to farm, announcing the solstice festival at which the clans and people of the villages would gather in three days' time.

(These observatories, which were used to study the stars in order to determine the feast days, in particular the winter and summer solstices, were very numerous in the German regions. They were destroyed by monks and Christian zealots. However, we have preserved one of them. These are the stone circles on the Tuchel moor near the mouth of the Vistula. These rock circles with their sighting stones are partly oriented north-south and east-west, partly towards the two solstices. A fifth line points to the setting of the fixed star Arktur, called the "day star" by our ancestors, by which the solstice is announced three days in advance. This solar and star observatory of the ancient Germans was studied by Professor Rolf Müller of the Potsdam Institute of Astrophysics and scientifically certified as an observation post.)

Arranged by clan and village, the men well armed as if in battle, the women in their finest finery and jewels, they all surrounded the high hill of the Thing on which a great fire was burning. The flames rose into the night that enveloped the land. The clan elders approached the fire and listened, as did their clan mates, to the words spoken by the grizzled old man, again explaining the meaning of the ceremony.

The young Eib had often heard the father speak of this stone, but it seemed to him that he only now understood the meaning of these traditional words. Now the farmer's host, whom all the clans revered and whose wisdom they recognised, was talking about the eternal order that governs the sky and the earth, the sun and the stars, the trees, the animals and the people. The age-old symbol of this eternal order is the course of the sun. In winter, it sinks ever deeper into the bosom of the Earth. It returns to Mother Earth, which gives it life again, and rises higher and higher in the sky until the solstice. An eternal death and rebirth.

He heard the old one speak: "Death is not the end of life: it is the beginning of a new becoming. The Sun brings forth new life from the bosom of the earth. Grass and flowers, leaves and trees turn green and bloom again. The young seed is raised, the cattle are strengthened on the heath, a new generation grows on the farms. The year of men passes like the solar year of growth. The snow of hair weighs down on the old, like snow on the fields. But as light is reborn, so is generation after generation. The flame that we honour as an image of the Sun and to which we entrust the bodies of the dead, purifies and enlightens. It frees the soul from that which is mortal and leads it again to a rebirth in the eternal light. What comes out of the mother's womb never ceases, just as nature never stops and completes its cycle in the same way as the Sun.

Eib was still pondering these words while the elder had long since fallen silent. Around the luminous hearth, constantly fed by a few young men, the girls began their rounds. They would become mothers and give life, like the bosom of the earth to plants and animals. Three women stood out from the circle. They went from clan to clan, offering some gifts.

"Do you know what these three women mean," Eib whispered to him.

He looked around and gazed into the clear eyes of the grizzled old man.

"These three women are the Norns," said the voice of the elder. "Urd, Werdandi and Skuld. Urd, the ancient one, who lies in the earth, Werdandi, the present, the blood that beats in our arteries, Skuld, the duty, this destiny that every being carries within and which turns into a fault when we deviate and do not obey it."

The round of dancers had grown in size, their steps and gestures mimicking the game of good and right versus evil and wickedness. Then came cloaked figures symbolising the struggle between light and darkness, and behind them a boisterous troupe who, with every crack of the whip, din and din, chased away the winter so that the grain would become green grass and all earthly creatures would be healthy.

The strict order of the clans and villages was loosened; on the one hand the old, reserved and taciturn, on the other the young, playful, whose first couples, having become engaged during the warm summer nights, threw themselves and jumped over the flames.

When morning then came, the clans lined up again and lit their torches in the flame of the dying solstice fire, to revive the dead souls in their homes. The peasant, too, turned to his clan mates, carefully watching the holy flame he carried.

Eib knew that the companions would find the meal well prepared in the upper room. He went back behind his people, towards the farm, clutching the arm of the girl he had chosen long ago, with whom he had jumped over the flames and whom now, according to the old custom, he was leading to the farm of which he would one day be the heir. Bound to nature and to the land, like all the peasants of the North, he had united himself on this mother's night with the one who would bear his children and prolong the clan. What was only a symbol would soon be life, as the eternal order commanded. A great joy filled his heart when he thought that his promise of marriage would be validated by the clan members in the great hall, at home, before the new fire of the hearth and under the green bough, symbol of eternal life and of the immense trees that rise to the sky. The clan companions would not object to the happiness that the flame of the winter solstice had already blessed.

Attached to nature as were our ancestors, they saw in this winter solstice festival the divine law of death and birth.

Mother's Night, the holy night, was, more than any other holiday, the clan's holiday, just as it is still today the holiest and most majestic of family holidays. When we light the lights on the tree, do we still know that it is the symbol of light and life that is eternally renewed? When we gather around the evergreen tree, do we still suspect that our ancestors once saw it as a symbol of the continuity of our race? Do we still know that we have before us the great tree whose roots lie in the past, whose trunk represents intense life and whose branches reach towards the sky, towards the future?

The old tales and customs of all our Aryan peoples bear witness to what this festival meant to our ancestors. We must listen carefully to participate in this ancient wisdom.

Kurt Pasternaci

SS NOTEBOOK No. 3A. 1941.

SOLSTICE IN THE SACRED CIRCLE

Stone circles celebrate the Sun

Sunrise in the Odry sanctuary

Near the village of Odry in West Prussia, in the heart of the vast Tuchel moor, there are about ten stone circles which, despite repeated destruction, still have a perfect shape. It is true that the location of the circles seems to have been chosen in an anarchic and accidental manner. Some of them are aligned in one direction, but these directions intersect according to axes whose meaning is difficult to discern.

Perhaps this is just a burial site? We do indeed find tumuli that are surrounded by stone circles. The Odry sites have been described as burial grounds of Gothic tribes, without attributing any other role to them.

There are only two days in the year when Odry reveals his deepest meaning: it is the day of the summer solstice and its opposite—the winter solstice.

When, on 21 June, we look at the sunrise in the westernmost circle of stones in the northern group and look beyond the two circles to the easternmost one, with two massive boulders next to each other in the middle, then our gaze reaches the horizon. When the sun rises—this is a moment of great intensity—we see it appear exactly behind the two stones of the farthest circle. A direct angle of view thus crosses the four circles of stones until the rising Sun where, placed in the middle of the first circle, we form the "focus", the two central stones of the last circle forming the "focus".

Months later, on December 21, we can, placed in another circle, also look at the Sun on the winter solstice towards the southernmost circle. We conclude that Odry's stone circles were not placed by chance, but 'spotted' exactly on the summer and winter solstice.

Were the Germans bad observers?

But the critical observer will retort that on the morning of the solstice in Odry, the Sun does not quite rise behind our marker stones: the first rays of sunlight should appear exactly in the middle of the aperture, of the "double focal point" of the central stones.

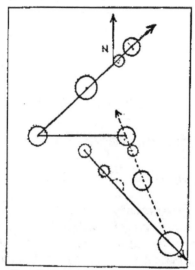

The orientation of the Odry stone circles
The lines connect the centres of the circles. The upper line to the right indicates exactly the summer solstice. The lower line to the left indicates the winter solstice. The dotted line may indicate the direction of a star.

This is not the case. They appear behind one of the two stones. And when we determine the exact angle to the north with a compass and pointing glasses, we get an angle of 48.1 degrees at the summer solstice, which in astronomy is called the "azimuth". Our ancestors or the Germanic stone circle builders seem to have made a mistake here. Or perhaps they were so poor observers that they could not place the stones exactly where the sun rises?

It is hardly conceivable that they made a "false location". People who were so close to nature, especially farmers, knew how to take perfectly accurate measurements. But there could be disagreement as to what was meant by 'sunrise' in the past: was it really the first rays of the sun, or the appearance of the entire solar disc, or even the moment when the sun completely leaves the horizon? It is clear that this results in already significant angular differences. When, for example, we consider in Odry the moment when the

When the sun reaches the top of the two marker stones, the line of sight seems rather accurate.

But astronomers are now interfering in our discussion and pointing out that the Sun does not rise in the same place today as it did at the solstice 2,000 or 3,000 years ago. They have made precise calculations and even if the differences are not huge, they are nevertheless measurable. For Odry, for example, the 'azimuth' for the year O is 47.4 degrees and for the year 1000 BC is 47.1 degrees. It is therefore no longer surprising that our angle of view does not match, but we are wondering what the date was that corresponds to the exact alignment. This will allow us to easily determine the date of the erection of these groups of stones. The Sun provides the answer when it rises!

This would certainly be possible if we only knew when the Odry astronomers took their landmark. We can establish an average value according to the different possibilities and we obtain approximately the year O as the date of the erection of the Odry sanctuary. Of course, it may also have been a few hundred years earlier, and excavations in the area of the stone circles do indicate 150 BC. This means that they are the work of the Gothic tribes that once populated East Prussia.

Stonehenge—solar sanctuary

From the knowledge provided by Odry, we could conclude that many—if not all—stone circles in the northern region were oriented to the Sun. But the impossibility of exact measurements, the confusions we have mentioned and the destruction of many stone circles make it difficult to confirm this. For example, the famous Externsteine and the cave there with a north-facing wall hole still pose many riddles to science, although it seems to be a clear solar cult shrine.

Things are quite clear about the magnificent site of Stonehenge in England. The site of the stones is circular and was surrounded on the outside by ramparts and ditches over a diameter of 100 metres. To the north, the ditches allow a straight road to pass through, 400 metres in length. The outer circle of the sanctuary once consisted of thirty giant stones, arranged in columns, which were connected at the top by brackets. Inside were five pairs of stones in the shape of an open horseshoe in the direction of the northeast path.

The road itself is man-made and beyond it, 33 kilometres away, are long linear land constructions placed exactly in line with a line running from the centre of the stone site to the centre of the stone gate and heading from the middle of the road to the north-east. The sun rises on this line on the solstice today, or at least varies by barely a degree. The 'azimuth' is 49.34.3 degrees today on this line, but the azimuth in the year 1900 was 50.30.9 degrees when Stonehenge was studied astronomically. The difference of 56 minutes and 6 seconds is due to the age of the site and indicates, with a variation of 200 years more or less, that it was built around 1700 BC.

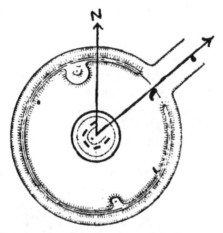

The orientation of the Stonehenge Solar Observatory

The majestic circles of the site open onto a central direction which is also reflected in a road and a landmark stone: the exact direction of the summer solstice.

Stonehenge is a huge site, built with rocks that took a lot of work and were transported over a hundred leagues. But even small sites like Odry were not built in two days. Northern Germany, which is "rich in stones", does not have such large boulders everywhere that ten stone circles could be built with an average of 178 stones of 80 centimetres in height. A strong will and an even greater faith are behind such an effort. The cult of the universal Sun is also something natural for us, today's men, as it was for our ancestors who erected their sanctuary...

W.J.

SS NOTEBOOK NO. 7. 1942.

MOTHER'S NIGHT

Wherever Germans live and put down roots on the vast earth, the Christmas tree is lit on the winter solstice. The evergreen tree, which blooms with lights in the middle of the holy night, has become the symbol of Germanness and the archetype of its presence. The settlement area extends far to the east and south-east of the Reich. The plough-holding Germans broke into the chaos of foreign tribes and peoples; but everywhere, in the Bohemian forest, in the Zips, in the scattered settlements of the Carpathians and far away in the blazing overseas, at Christmas, the lights on the tree that became the tree of the Germans.

When a people expand their living space, they take their household gods with them to remain true to themselves; it may be the soil of the sacred homeland, the columns of the great hall, or the solemn customs containing folk wisdom. Many precursors and equivalent traditions have adopted the symbol of the world tree. This is the tree-top that the valiant Vikings carried from their Nordic homeland to Iceland and across the oceans to distant Vinland. The blue flame that we light on the tree today for all the brothers near and far on Earth is closely related to the flame that was once lit for the "minne" of those who sojourned far away on dangerous voyages or who sought new lands beyond the Marches to bring forth the light of folk life.

It is the same event that is repeated today, as in ancient times. Joyful messengers from our ancient history, ancient authors speak to us of the customs and beliefs of our ancestors, which move us all because, over the millennia, the same blood, the same soul, lives on. The Germanic peoples travelled far and wide, and with their swords and ploughs had conquered new territories beyond the limits of the Roman Empire. But they faithfully preserved there what had once been born in their homeland. The Angles had left their homeland in Holstein to settle in Britain and eventually become Christians; but around the year 700, the Christian priest Beda still described their Christmas customs:

"They used to call the night that is so sacred to us the pagan word "Modranicht", which means "night of the mothers"; probably because of the blessing customs that were celebrated throughout the night.

Doesn't the name "Mother's Night" from the adolescence of our people touch us, reminding us of our own childhood? It is the night that is dedicated to the mystery of motherhood, hinting at that great experience of the rebirth of the Sun from the abyss of the world, from the maternal womb of every being. If the mother with child is today largely the object of the festival, it is also an ancient heritage, for the couple with child under the world tree is a representation that is certainly closely related to these customs of blessing on Mother's Night. But the name is even more significant: through the many works, (our folk customs and legends still testify to this today), we know that the three mothers are among the most familiar figures in our local beliefs. At that time, they travelled around the country, holding feminine wisdom and maternal goods, distributing gifts, giving good advice to men—especially where a child is sleeping in a cradle.

Two thousand years ago, this thought was already so deeply rooted in our people that even the Germans, who had become Roman employees governing the German Rhine, erected sacred stones in honour of these three mothers who protected newborn babies. The Romans gave way and new Germans arrived. Even a thousand years later, they too still knew the three mothers. On holy nights, housewives made a point of covering the table, putting food and drink on it and setting out three knives so that the three sisters, as they were called, could eat. Pious zealots castigated them; but the maternal sisters were too strongly present in the hearts of the people and a monument was even built for them in the cathedral of Worms, under the names of Einbede, Waebede and Willibede.

Germanic legends and tales have preserved their features even more faithfully. The holy nights when the new light and the new year are born are also dedicated to them; elves approach the cradle of the newborn and bring their gifts. In Bavaria, they are called the "great counsellors", even more frequently the "Perchten", which means the luminous ones because they accompany the light during its birth. They are invited by men and prove to be friendly and helpful to those who are good. They appear—certainly elsewhere too—in the tale of Sleeping Beauty to whom they give the gift of life. Despite the evil influence of the thirteenth fairy, they remain the strongest. In the old Norse tale of the "Host of the Norns", the nuns light the child's flame of life; the deep connection with our luminous Christmas festival is particularly clear. And since they have been manifesting themselves since ancient times in the form of the sacred ternary, bringing the child their gifts, full of wisdom, they may have passed on much of their character to the wise men of the East, whose number and names are unknown, and may even have been the origin of the innumerable games of the three kings.

The original myths and ageless legends tell us of the three mothers who sit at the foot of the world tree and spin all the futures. The night of Christmas, which we celebrate as our ancestors did, is dedicated to them. As a great poet expressed it, to provide for these mothers, we must return to ourselves, to the living roots of our popular existence, which today has found a universal symbol in the radiant world tree.

J.O. PlaBmann

SS NOTEBOOK No. 4. 1943.

SPRING CUSTOM AND ABUNDANCE OF CHILDREN

When the spring sun lights up the sky, when the days grow longer and warmer, when on the trees the buds swell and the first flowers appear timidly, the villages are crossed by joyful bands of children, bringing happiness, blessings and asking for presents from the peasants. By this time our Mardi Gras is long over; the carnival garment hangs quietly in the wardrobe again; the fires on the mountains are extinguished; the flaming wheels, with their gushing sparks, rolling down to the valley are but a familiar memory.

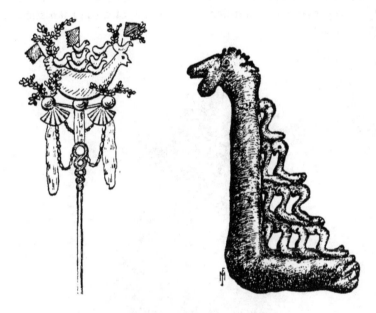

On the left, the Meppel staff in the Netherlands.
On the right, a swan with palms and many young, a symbol of fertility that is baked for Easter in the Netherlands.

But Easter is coming. The children's procession passes from house to house with a loud song and decorated spring sticks or bushes. This custom can be found throughout central Germany from Silesia to the Palatinate in the west and from the Netherlands southwards to the Alps. Of course, each region has its own way of expressing it; sometimes it is the Sunday of mid-Lent, "Laetare Sunday" or a Sunday close to it. The procession may also take place only at Easter or in the week before Easter, and Holy Sunday is also popular, but it is always the same custom. Tree tops decorated with multicoloured paper and cakes or, according to old customs, with painted snail shells, are carried as symbols of spring. The sticks are decorated with multicoloured pleated paper and fresh greenery. Large pretzels are hung on them as a sign of blessing, luck and fertility. These are often delicately garnished, embellished with braids and lovingly fixed with green boxwood twigs. Apples, the ancient symbol of fertility, are not absent either. Despite the extreme difference in character between the individuals, the palm leaves resemble each other, thus revealing their authentic popular and non-Christian origin. Whether large or small, modest or rich, they bear pastries and greenery, multicoloured chains and small flags, apples and a set of bright sequins. In Lower Germany and the Netherlands, these palm leaves are particularly meaningful. Wonderful wheel-shaped pastries, often richly and artistically woven, play an important role here. The baked birds, which vary greatly in size, that adorn and decorate the tips of these palm sticks are almost never absent.

Despite Christianity, many pagan customs were preserved in the peasant world. Above, decorative bread.

On the left, a symbol of fertility at the spring festival in Questenberg in the Harz. On the right, Hagal runes on a peasant chair.

Dances for the May Festival in the Bregenz Forest.

They are roosters or swans, animals that come from the myths of our prehistory and that have preserved an echo of their profound meaning in these pastries, but above all in the tales and legends. One species, the hen, is particularly amusing in its appearance, yet has a very deep and delicate meaning. The baker places three, four, even eight, nine, ten youngsters made of dough on the back of this bird, mixed together in a dense crowd, so pretty and lively that you think you can hear them chirping. Is there any more beautiful symbol of the abundance of joy, of the year full of wealth, of the great spring rich in fertility, than this representation of the mother and her young? Popular belief erects an obvious monument to her here. We see the symbol of the life that the German man carries within him. It is the belief that many offspring are a blessing, an asset and a blessing in disguise. Happy, life-loving, laughing children bring this happiness from house to house. Happy and smiling, they accept the gifts that are distributed to them willingly. The good old spirit of our people lives on in this modest spring custom.

What these Dutch bird-shaped pastries suggest is not a unique case, an exception or a rarity; other pastries express comparable ideas. In the Tyrol, at Christmas, a large baked hen is offered here and there as a Christmas present for young girls, with many snails on its broad wings like chicks. There can be up to thirty little shells. The child is proud to have this wealth, which is also seen as the happiness and luck of having many children. The hen, by the faithful attention she gives to her young, perfectly symbolises true motherhood. She walks her young, protects them from danger, takes them under her wings. In Sweden, the golden hen in the Christmas cakes is also surrounded by many yellow chicks, gathered around her like so many children. This event takes us far back in time. More than 1300 years ago, the Lombard queen Theudelinde had a golden hen with seven golden chicks sent to Monza Cathedral. The costly goldsmith's work required for this bird, which has been preserved for us, undoubtedly has a profound meaning. It can still be seen today, together with an ordination crown and other gifts, in the arch above the cathedral door. Considering the current custom, which is still alive in many regions, it is certain that the queen wanted to pass on something special and that she is following a Germanic custom. Another tradition that is still practised in Saxony today is that the godparents give their godchild a clay piggy bank in the shape of a hen carrying many chicks on its back. The symbolism is easy to understand, and the wish is that the money will be plentiful and prosperous in the long term. The bird with its young is therefore supposed to bring good luck, as in spring festivals. Having many children is a sign of immense happiness, which guarantees eternal life, a bud in the springtime of life. This is the meaning of the joyful procession of our children passing through at Easter time. Ribbons flutter in the wind, twigs crackle, pretzels, wheels and birds exhale a sweet fragrance. But the careful observer perceives a deeper, immemorial meaning behind these things.

Friedrich MöBinger

SS Notebook No. 5. 1943.

Bride of May—Queen of May

The sunny month of May awakens a whole range of beautiful customs in traditional Germany that have a deep meaning and are still perceptible today. The May tree rises into the blue sky, which the resurrected Reich still keeps beautiful and strong. At nightfall, Mayfires, the late cuttings of the spring fires, blaze in many regions and bring happiness. Wrapped in thick foliage, the "May man", the "Maimann", travels through the silent villages of our mountains from the Saar to the Bohemian Forest, and also a little in the north of Germany. It also has other names. The proud wrestlers of May and Whitsun and the many games of that period have become rare. With rustling and crackling noises, May and Whitsun wreaths swing from ropes in the streets of villages and small towns. During the day, children hold hands in their care and at night, boys and girls make merry rounds during which the elders stay in the joy of the home and exchange memories.

A custom of little girls still persists, often forgotten and neglected. They gather quietly and decorate one of their own with a crown of flowers in a multitude of bright and shimmering colours. It represents the May bride led by two young girls decorated in the same way and accompanied by many comrades, without ornaments, who start a round in the village. The procession goes from house to house. Everywhere the troupe sings a joyful song, and many presents are distributed to them. Often, during the song, the little May bride is surrounded by all the others in a solemn round and, as is the practice in Alsace, she often carries an elegantly decorated May tree around which three dances are performed.

The two girls in charge sometimes hold a bow decorated with many ribbons tied above the little bride, but very often the bride sits in a small, richly decorated cart. She is completely hidden under green foliage; the procession takes on a solemn and mysterious character. It is more than just a children's game. This is reflected in the songs. For example, in a rhyme from the Lower Rhine, a golden wagon and a silver whip handle are mentioned.

What the village girls do in all simplicity and fantasy seems to be a joyful distraction to the present observer, but it is in reality the meagre remnant of an ancient and meaningful custom, originally practised by adult boys and girls. Even today, the little bride is often not alone, but is accompanied by a boy who is May's fiancé. In the past, a boy and a girl played the role of the May couple. The youth would gather in a large and rich wedding procession through the whole village, with joyful dances performed under the tree for most of the night, when it was decorated with lights that made it shine with wonderful beauty. The Queen and King of May, the Countess and Count of May, often serve as models for the two young children who represent the springtime of the country, the new growth and prosperity, the rebirth of nature through their symbolic nuptial union. Just as the happy union of two beings produces many children, so the fullness of nature's gifts is brought about by the union of the two sexes. This gives us a deep and clear insight into the natural phenomena of the world, and we can see to what extent man is inscribed in nature, to what extent these representations are ancient and deep-rooted. As early as the 12th century there is talk of the tour of a richly decorated Pentecostal queen. Tacitus' account of the journey of the chariot of the goddess Nerthus of fertility and the earth undoubtedly stems from the same spirit. This old description and the one used in the North show that already among the Germans, the same thoughts animated men during springtime; those of concern for the future, the power of life, the strengths of the clan and also of the people.

In most cases, it is quite clear that today our May customs passed on to our children have no longer retained this old meaning, they alone perpetuate them. But those who know how to look at it, perceive the links that connect them to the past and to the beliefs of their forefathers.

Friedrich MöBinger

SS NOTEBOOK NO. 5. 1942.

HARVEST CUSTOMS

The harvest festival begins on the farms when in autumn the wind blows over the fresh stubble and carries strands of straw into the last potato fields. With it comes the end of a year of hard work and great joy, for the farmer is aware that through his work he is participating in the great natural cycle of life and death, growth and harvest.

This communion with the natural event characterises all the customs of peasant festivals and work. These traditions show us that the farmer is not only motivated by the desire to feed himself, thanks to the benefits of his work, but that he is intimately linked to the land he works. When he "crowns" the field at Easter with the branch of life and rides around it on horseback, he wishes the seed to be good. For this reason, a decorated shrub, a "tree of life", is often placed in the field, and for the same reason, "Hegel's fires" were once seen shining, bringing happiness to the land.

The peasant speaks of the wheat in bloom, says that it ' wodelt' in the fields, that the 'goat' or the 'boar' passes through the wheat. These curious expressions did not only reflect the image of the waving wheat field, whose ears are blown away by the wind, but were associated with the divine forces on which the fertility of the soil depends.

The farmer begins the harvest period, the culmination of his work, with the same sense of gratitude.

The harvesters come out decorated with flowers and the harvesting begins with the recitation of a saying or a song. Most often, the farmer of the estate cuts the first sprigs himself and distributes them to the audience. Sometimes a child also does this and gives the first spike to the farmer. These first sprigs are often saved and—like the grains of the 'last sheaf'— are mixed with the following year's seeds, as they symbolise the fertility of the land. They are also fed to the rooster in the house, or to the birds, as in Transylvania.

The hard work of harvesting that begins, however, is a joyful time. The reapers often exchange headbands and scarves before the harvesting begins, and in the evening, when the first task of the day is done, a solemn feast, the tasting of "crown beer" and a dance take place in Mecklenburg and Pomerania. The farmer or another acquaintance arrives unexpectedly in the field. He is then "tied" by surprise, nowadays usually with green ribbons and bows, originally with two ears of corn.

He is only released in exchange for a ransom for the reapers. This custom is meant to bring good luck, as reflected in several sayings of the reaper:

I attach the headband of ears of corn
The link that puts no one to shame.
You don't need to wear it for long,
I don't have to tell you to take it off either.
However, as is the old custom,
Listen first to my wish:
May heaven grant you happiness and joy
Throughout your life!

The same thought is expressed in the "Henseln" of newlyweds in Hesse, to whom an ear of corn is tied to the arms, or in the decoration of fruit trees with ears of corn at Christmas, so that they may bear beautiful fruit the following year.

The work of the following harvest weeks leaves no room for celebrations. There is only the Carinthian "night cup", to which an overworked farmer invites harvesters and gleaners, which also ends with a meal and solemn dances. This Carinthian custom has found its more serious counterpart in Swabia and Switzerland in the tradition of 'night boys' who secretly come to help with the harvest at night when a farmer has suffered a misfortune or a widow is unable to complete her work. This example *particularly illustrates* the community spirit of the peasant world.

The customs become richer and more diverse at the end of the harvest period. As the ears of corn fall on the last field, the "wolf" (or "goat", "boar" or "rooster") "is cornered". The sheaves are eagerly removed and the binder, which has finished the last sheaf, is tied to it as the "bride of the wheat". Apart from these amusing games, in other regions there is a great deal of popular piety when, even today, the harvester and the reaper dance around the last bound sheaf, which is particularly large, of the "harvest goat", the "harvest cock", the "elders" or the "straw man". They then bring it to the farm with the last cartload of the harvest.

The last wreath is decorated, covered with clothes. A green shrub, a stick decorated with flowers, is stuck into it. In its place, a decorated tree is sometimes placed, a walnut tree in Westphalia, a small fir tree on the banks of the Moselle. In more than one region, a bunch of ears of corn may also be made at the end of the harvest and placed in the sacred place of the house or farm.

Often the last sheaf is left in the field, sometimes also the "last wheat" that has not been cut, the "Waul-rye", as in the Schaumberg region, where a child plants a stick decorated with flowers or ribbons, the "Waul-stick". The harvesters then dance around the wheat, shouting "Wold" or "Wauld" nine times, or they tie it into a bunch and jump over it. Not only does the call to Wode or Wold show that this custom is a mark of respect and recognition of divine forces, but the traditional verses also show the same thing:

Wode, hal dynem Rosse nu voder (Futter),
Nu Distel und Dom,
Thom andern Jahr beter Korn.

(From Mecklenburg)

Fru Gode, haletju Feuer (Futter)
Dat Jahr upden Wagen,
Dat andre Jahr upde Karr (Karren).

(From Lower Saxony)

For this reason, it is also said that the last ears of corn are for the "Wode horse" (Wotan), for "Mrs. Gode" or "Mrs. Holle", for the "little birds of the Lord" or—in religious language—"for the poor souls". The fruits and flowers that decorate the altar room are also nothing other than gifts given in thanksgiving to the Lord, and are now taken up by the Church.

But the return of the last cart represents the climax and the solemn closing of the harvest: horses and carts are covered with flowers, the harvesters go to the farm singing, where the farmer or the heir of the estate awaits them. The peasant woman sprinkles water on the cart, in reference to the beneficial forces of the water of life. At the top of the cart is the artfully made harvest wreath, decorated with all kinds of grain. The garland or wreath that is given to the farmer again expresses the wish for happiness:

Now we wish the farmer happiness
And let's bring him the garland.
This is the reaper's masterpiece,
Which is more valuable than the shine of gold.

On the peasant farm, the work of the harvest weeks ends with a joyous celebration, which begins with a hearty feast and the "harvest beer, Wodel or oldtimer". Competitions and games, pot and cock fights, races, sack races, fishing in the Buntwater (Lower Germany), equestrian games such as the Silesian Goliath pike or the cock race in the Waldeck alternate with the harvest dance, which often lasts until the morning. The festival, which was once celebrated on a single farm, has developed into a village community festival, which begins with a joyous procession and the presentation of the harvest wreath to the village mayors. In spring, the inhabitants of the rural community ride around the fields, and the farming communities return once again to the fields where they have sown and harvested.

The war put an end to all these sonorous celebrations. But the union of the peasant with the powers is too deep to be prevented from thanking them. The whole German people are doing it with him. As in so many other areas of life, the war will also purify the harvest custom. Only those things that have a deep meaning can remain in the customs. What is most ancient can be revived through this necessary war, can be brought up to date. The great harvest festival, which was solemnly celebrated by the Führer on the Bückeberg, embodied this revival, as powerful as the popular community, as rich and varied as the flowers and fruits of the German soil, as the peculiarities of the German ethnic groups and landscapes.

J. Kern

(Author's note: the animals mentioned, such as the goat, boar and cock, are ancient pagan symbols of fertility that were cursed by the Christian Church. The terms Wode, wauld, or wodelt refer to the Norse god Wotan who presided over the destiny of the world. Hegel's fires are derived from the rune Hagal, a symbol of luck, happiness and world order).

SS Notebook No. 5. 1942.

THE SACRED BREAD

Our childhood was lulled by the old legend of the proud woman Hitt who despised bread, cursed it, and was punished by being turned into a giant stone. As in most German legends, a myth from the earliest times has also been perpetuated in this one. The bread of life and salvation was sacred in Mitgard, in the human world protected by the gods. Whoever raised his voice against it had to return to Udgard, the deserted world of the stone giants in spirit, a little wheat was put in the grave of the dead; the place in the house in which the wheat was kept was a sacred room, and the Germanic halls contained a shrine where the divine life itself dwelt. Very ancient myths of peoples related to us speak of the suffering and sacrifice experienced by the holder of divine salvation; one of our tales speaks of the king's daughter, the new life, who must be liberated by constantly suffering all injustices. The Greeks told that Dionysus, the son of Zeus, was torn apart and devoured by the Titans; but the shattered Titans begat the lineage of men, all of whom carry parts of Dionysus within them. The Germans created the myth of bread on a very similar basis; Wodan, who still lives among our peasants today, offers himself as a sacrifice, just as he also takes the lives of men when necessary. But he survives in different forms: in the sacred bread as well as in the intoxicating drink, being honoured as its inventor, and by which he transmutes and elevates man's spirit.

The old spirit of wheat still lives on in our folklore through various symbols; whether it is the straw man who chases children out of the wheat to protect the sacred fruit; whether it is the "rye cock" or the "rye pig" which represent images of the vital spirit and also give their name to the last sheaf. A very old mythical idea is embodied in the harvest cockerel, which decorates the last cart in many German regions and is placed on the barn door as a wooden symbol.

Bread and all cakes are therefore sacred; already in archaic times the bread was given the shape of the symbols of the circle representing the sacred world, the shape of the god of the year or his victims, but above all the sign of eternal rebirth and victorious life, the swastika. With each new year, these cakes were eaten in honour of the life-giving deity. The eating of the bread symbolically reunited God and man, so the dead of the clan and the people also participated. Even today, on the Feast of the Dead, the "bread of all souls" is distributed, for they too are subject to the great law of the universe.

The peasantry is therefore noble and does the most sacred work: it is the guardian and protector of the sacred bread in which the divine lives.

Respect for the sacred bread means respect for the laws of life, the sources of immortality.

J.O. PlaBmann

IV. Art

SS BOOKLET NO. 6. 1943.

THE SUPREME COMMAND IN ALL ARTISTIC APPRECIATION

Only that which is truly great is eternally preserved and guaranteed to find lasting consideration. The fact that great works are innumerable is not even a drawback!

It is a mistake to oppose the great cultural creations of eminent artistic heroes with the often time-conditioned barrage of dominant and ephemeral artistic conceptions. Only a nature that is totally insensitive to art could conceive of such a process. In truth, it is a mistake and a lack of respect for our great past and, moreover, a historical stupidity. Only a disrespectful person would condemn Mozart's "Magic Flute" because the text goes against his ideological conceptions. Similarly, only someone who is unfair would reject Richard Wagner's "Ring" because it does not correspond to his Christian vision; or Wagner's "Tannhauser", "Lohengrin" and "Parsifal" because he is not capable of appreciating them from a different angle. The great work has an absolute value in itself. This value cannot be judged on the basis of a conception outside the artistic work itself and conditioned by an era!

If, moreover, each generation claimed the right to get rid of artistic works from a different political, ideological or religious past, then each political upheaval would mean the destruction of the culture alien to the political environment of the moment.

It is for this reason that the supreme commandment in all artistic appreciation prescribes the greatest tolerance for the true cultural creations of the past. A great age can only afford to respect the work of its ancestors (which it also wants for itself) both politically and culturally, if its era finds credit with its descendants.

Adolf Hitler, at the Reichsparteitag of Labour in 1937.

"The Kiss", by Auguste Rodin.

"Screaming Warrior", sanguine by Leonardo da Vinci.

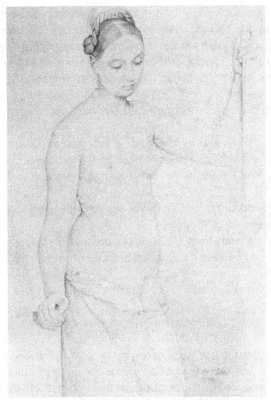

"Meditative girl", by Schnorr v. Carolsfeld.

Whoever wants to create must be joyful.

Goethe

SS NOTEBOOK NO. 1. 1943.

ARTIST AND SOLDIER

Each SS booklet is governed by a specific guiding idea. In this we have a clear intention.

Our aim is not only to make the notebooks interesting. Those who seek only entertainment will not find it in the SS Journals. The easy way out, i.e. to win the approval of everyone by writing articles that are easy to digest, would also be much easier and more enjoyable. But there are other books and notebooks for this purpose.

In the SS Notebooks we do not want to disperse and distract the reader, but rather to concentrate his best forces and make him reflect on himself, i.e. on his true substance. Only in this way can we help the comrades to realise themselves and to fulfil their mission within the clan community of the SS and the people. When we see the same sentence appearing again and again in letters in similar formulas: "For me the SS notebooks are a comfort before every new battle", or when a young artist writes to us: "... This article made me feel for the first time what I still have to find within myself to become an artist", such examples clearly indicate the path we are following.

This booklet is governed by the guiding principle of 'Toughness'. The soldier knows how much toughness is needed to hold on in battle and to endure setbacks. And he also feels that it is toughness that makes any job possible.

But it does not occur to him that in order to understand art, one must also cross the threshold of harshness.

Some take as art everything that pleases them at first sight. They think that they have already entered the sanctuary and often refer to the words of the great master: "Serious is life and joyful is art". They do not know that joyful art was often the result of a difficult struggle, such as that which Mozart gave us.

Others say, "I don't understand it," when it comes to art. Before they can learn the enrichment that art could bring to their lives, they close the door to its strengths. Instead, they settle for ersatz, more easily digestible food, insipid and superficial works of no value. They prefer a photograph to a work of art whose depth is not apparent at first glance. They swallow three-penny books by the dozen, while they supposedly have no time to read a valuable book. This cannot be our position.

He who took part in the harsh war in the East also knows that there are times of recollection when, precisely, one seeks simplicity in art and draws hidden forces from it.

Yet many say: "How can we compare our sense of combat and our artistic sense! Combat is work, fatigue, pain and sacrifice. But from art, we expect relaxation and distraction.

You say "relaxation and distraction"? Why are you so modest, you who can demand the greatest from it? Why do you ask so little of art? Why do you not demand from it creative force, eternal life and divine joy? Don't you know that art can give all this? But perhaps you do not know the true meaning of art. For too long it has lost its rightful place in life. It was, like religion, only a nice accessory for a party night and Sunday. It was a colourful bird, a luxury that could be dispensed with in times of need.

But what is true art? It is the purest embodiment of the apprehension of the world. By the gift of art, God has granted men the ability to represent His law.

An example: Through the observance of the racial laws we can, by the right choice of marriage, bring our race closer to the image that corresponds to the divine will. In sport we can work the body into the proper form for its predestined purpose. In art, however, genius can fashion an ideal human body in accordance with the natural law.

Another example: Originally, landscapes only roughly reflect the imprint of the Creator. Those modelled by pure breeds come close. However, to reflect the image of this landscape in all its splendour, it is to the artist that God has granted this gift, that is to say, to this artist (another does not deserve the name) who, himself, obliges the Creator to manifest himself to him.

The decisive fact is that the artist only manages to feel God by extreme work on himself. He restores His image in the human body or in the landscape he represents. Capturing this image in stone or on canvas is still a difficult task.

It is not possible to judge in the usual way how difficult it is for a creator to accomplish his great mission. Let us read the biographies of a Rembrandt, an Andreas Schlüter, a Tilman Riemenschneider, a Schiller, Mozart, Beethoven. They had to fight against themselves in order to get rid of all obstacles, all external or internal hindrances, in order to free the work, so that only the creative soul remained free to perceive and carry out the divine mission. There is only one comparison that can be made, and that is the toughness of the soldier who consciously risks his life.

In this field, soldier and artist are related in the success achieved through hard work.

In extreme danger, when all weaknesses are overcome, haven't many of you felt that moment when, suddenly, previously unknown forces are released? It is as if an envelope in which you have always been enclosed is bursting open. You burst out of it and feel like a god or a child. There is no longer any hesitation, reflection, doubt or consideration. One acts freely and justly, and can do whatever, in the moment, must be done. This is the feeling that Schiller spoke of when he wrote: "He who can look death in the face, the soldier alone is the free man".

A young poet of our time must have felt particularly clearly this creative kinship between the soldier and the artist. He wrote to us recently, in the midst of the fiercest fighting on the Eastern Front: "I cannot say what joy and pride I feel. I would like to tell a legend where a whole people would be born, would live for generations. I know that one day I will be able to express what my heart holds in this warlike hour. I want to become a gold digger in my own heart, to pass on all that I live and enrich all men.

Of course, toughness *alone* cannot bring knowledge to either the soldier or the artist. Other virtues and gifts are needed. Toughness is, however, a significant factor.

And this is the subject of my article. It is precisely this knowledge of the common character existing between artists and soldiers that must enable you, comrades, to enter into a new relationship with true art, which alone is worthy of you. The path is not easy. But who could achieve it if not you who have overcome the hardest fighting and the superiority of the Bolshevists? Understanding art is of course not what many of you still imagine. But it is not in conflict with the experience you had as soldiers and fighters. On the contrary, it is closely related.

In spite of everything, you got there more easily than the artists themselves. They precede you on the path; they look for the steep slope and point it out to you. But they themselves must follow it. It costs sweat and perseverance.

In return, the divine reward beckons you from the highest peak.

You will certainly find it because it is within you. Some people have already succeeded "by chance". Having exhausted everything, they have had to resort to reading 'serious stuff' out of desperation, first reluctantly, then enthusiastically. In the end, they realised that you can't swallow classical poetry like a Kolbenheyer novel, but that a real work of poetry can give you more strength and joie de vivre than a bunch of superficial literature. He who has been aware of this in a moment of clarity must also find the strength to emphasise the higher principles.

He will one day reap the fruitful fruits after having lived through the difficult moments when he was trying to understand great art, which are comparable to the most dangerous moments of combat. He will find treasures which he did not suspect until then and in front of which he passed blindly.

Hans Klöcker

SS Notebook No. 5. 1944.

German Artists and the SS

Art exhibition in Breslau

There was a time when military spirit and art were considered mutually incompatible. That was when the former was regarded as the business of a sabre-runner and the latter as the bohemian impulse of an attic dweller. In reality, these forms of expression of two worlds were merely their caricature. The true natures of the military and artistic worlds are totally different, for at heart they have much in common. They have the same origin, that is to say, the race that gave birth to soldiers and artists from its blood. The careful observer will not be surprised that our greatest soldiers have had an artist's nature and that our greatest artists have also had a soldier's nature. Frederick the Great not only created Sans-Souci, he also fertilised all the arts of his time with his own ideas. Let us also mention the great emperor Frederick II of Hohenstaufen. Prince Eugene did not advise the greatest artists and architects of his time by chance when he commissioned Lukas von Hildebrandt and Fischer von Erlach to build the Belvedere in Vienna. He himself was an artist. Leonardo da Vinci, the most versatile artist of all time, worked for his princes as an architect, inventor of weapons and adviser on new military plans as well as an artist. There are also many examples where a military talent was not directly visible. We cannot imagine the works of Goethe, Schiller, Lessing, Kleist, containing war scenes, without a keen interest in and genuine familiarity with the military world. However, in both cases, when great soldiers manifest artistic genius and when great artists turn out to be eminent soldiers, it was never the result of a one-sided special interest. For these creative men, these two worlds were merely different forms of expression of a great idea. Ideas are nothing more than reflections of the soul, the expression of an essence. The great idea that will govern the millennium that is now beginning is National Socialism. Its creator, the Führer Adolf Hitler, a soldier and an artist, has already etched its contours with a brass stylus at the threshold of the new era—the military and artistic spirit. The SS, the Führer's order which, as the Waffen SS, must represent the military aspect of our world view, also feels called upon to participate in an active and stimulating way in the artistic creation of the future era. The reason for this is that the nature of National Socialism is creative, and the nature of the SS is to spearhead this idea. The exhibition "Artists and the SS" in Breslau was only the beginning. The most important thing is that it takes place in the fifth year of the war. An appeal is made to all present and future artists in the Reich to choose the idea of empire and the ever more powerful order as the theme of their work, so that the military expression of the Reich on all fronts finds its equivalent in artistic form.

SS Notebook No. 2a. 1941.

Beauty under the sign of the SS runes

Allach, tasks and purpose

No people lives longer than the documents of its culture!

The Führer's words are a point of reference for all cultural matters concerning the German people and they govern the spirit of the Allach Porcelain Factory in Munich.

Many people will ask why the SS produces porcelain. The explanation is simple. The Reichsführer had already planned for a long time to intensify the SS spirit of cultural work, which was not really possible until after he took power. In 1935, he therefore founded the Allach Porcelain Factory in Munich, the main instrument of his will in this field.

For the Reichsführer, it was not a question of founding a new porcelain factory with the aim of producing economic value—i.e. to make money. From the outset, Allach's primary task was to use the most attractive material available, porcelain, to create artistic works of art and objects for everyday use that would reflect the spirit of the times and bear witness to the artistic feeling and creative will of our time for generations to come.

Each era produces its own forms of expression and adapts them to its cultural style. The same applies to our own. With the Führer's large-scale constructions, we are witnessing the birth of a new style—our style— whose decorative art also includes the development of new ceramic forms.

In this spirit, the Reichsführer SS charged Allach with setting an example in artistic creation, in the quality of the material, in execution and workmanship, and in pricing.

A retrospective can show what the spirit of porcelain production was: In the past, almost all porcelain factories were founded by princes (Berlin by Frederick the Great, MeiBen by Augustus the Strong, Sèvres by the Marquise de Pompadour, to name but a few). With a few exceptions, their mission was to produce noble porcelain of great artistic value for the glory of their founders, disregarding any economic benefits. Great artists were hired and were able to carry out their projects in peace and seclusion, free from all material worries. The result was wonderful porcelain that reflected the spirit of the age, the Rococo and the Empire—artistic works that have always retained their value and deserve the greatest admiration because they express the artistic feeling of their creators.

Single copies and mass-produced items

But times change. For almost all porcelain factories (note the significant name "manufacture" [manu= with the hand], whose work still today requires the artistic hand of man), financial and economic issues became increasingly important. Soon profit was the decisive factor. Patrons of the arts and princely commission agents gave way to merchants. All too often, art was considered to be of little value. In this period of artistic decline, a few renowned manufactures managed to remain true to their spirit.

Aryanity as a representative of a certain type of values becomes the absolute reference in art.
Porcelain from the SS factory in Allach.

Different porcelains from Allach: On the left, a vase with protohistoric motifs. On the right, a
candlestick given to every child born to SS families.

Amazon.

First, there is sculpture. It often gave rise to domestic horrors due to a lack of artistic spirit or sloppy workmanship. Allach therefore saw his first task as helping to bring the true national artistic sense to life. To be honest, this was not easy and not all projects could yet be realised. First of all, artists had to be found and hired who would create artistic works with their inspirational genius and creative talent.

But the Reichsführer said: *Art must be present in every house, but above all in the house of my SS!* Every table must be furnished with elegant dishes, not only in the living quarters but also—and primarily—in the canteens, so that the German worker and the combatant can draw new strength from the harmony of their surroundings in their hours of rest. There is no doubt that the simplest dish in a beautiful dish tastes better than the most expensive roast in a canteen! Allach wants to serve the Reichsführer's plan as well as possible.

In the few years since the Allach factory was founded, it has acquired a privileged position in the field of porcelain production. *Figures of heroic young men* from the Wehrmacht or party associations, astonishingly authentic *peasant folk figures* and, above all, *noble animal sculptures* which show the animal in all its beauty, were produced with our present-day sensitivity. These are works that must be seen as evidence of a naturally strong artistic feeling and a creative will aware of its duty.

Ceramics, jugs, vases, candlesticks contain a beauty that benefits every German household. Thus the Reichsführer SS's aim that every utilitarian object—even the simplest water jug—should be of impeccable beauty was magnificently achieved. The great cultural treasures discovered in numerous excavations provided inspiration for design and decoration translated into the style of our time. A bridge was thus built, linking the natural creations of our ancestors with the artistic feeling of today.

Utilitarian objects were created—and will be created—which already sweep away all criticism by their beauty and utility. In the course of time, all the ugly and unsuitable forms will have to be eliminated and replaced by beautiful and utilitarian tableware.

Aware of the fact that the environment has an enormous influence on human well-being and attitude, the Reichsführer ordered his porcelain factory in Allach to act in this spirit. The home of every SS man, or simply of every German, should contain only artistic objects and tableware of the best taste. In this way, Allach offers the man working in his daily environment the beauty that regenerates him and makes him worthy of the great tasks given to him by our heroic age.

W.

SS Booklet No. 4. 1938.

THE LAW OF BEAUTY

Everything that is of eternal value to us is subject to laws of iron. Even if we wanted to stop the course of the stars, they would continue their course according to eternal laws, just as nature also follows the rhythmic law of birth and death. The eternal laws reject chaos, decay and the destruction of all values.

Long before man recognised the rightness of things, he was already obeying its law in his creative activity. He who has wandered through our rich art galleries with contemplation understands why the classical marble statues of the ancient Greeks strike him with their charm as much as the most beautiful contemporary works. Three thousand years have passed without marring the ideal of beauty that animated the Greeks and for which we also have a deep admiration.

There was a time when it was fashionable to consider art as something dead, which is still being peddled today in those dull circles that are interested in things of the 'beautiful mind'. They are very concerned about the alleged lack of new creative ideas and thus seek to demonstrate that the artists of our time can only copy the antique.

But no creative artist can truly create by deviating from the classical law of beauty. As in the past, the Venus de Milo remains an ideal of form, and the immortal works of a Michelangelo do not seek to imitate those of the great Greek masters Polyclitus or Lysippus, but are intuitive creations made according to the eternal laws of beauty.

Leonardo da Vinci was the first to recognise the principle of beauty. The formula of the "golden ratio" is attributed to him: a: b = b: (a+b). This means that the human body, from the top of the head to the navel, is subject to the same ratio of proportion as the other lower parts, and vice versa with the whole body. Neglecting the rule of the "golden ratio" does not lead to a new art form but to the negation of the law of beauty and thus to chaos.

Sculpture from the exhibition "Degenerate Art".

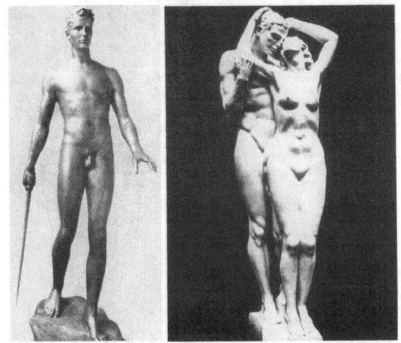

Artistic sensitivity reflects the incompatibility of certain conceptions of man. On the left, "Young Boy" by Fritz von Grävenitz.
On the right, Josef Thorak's "couple".

Let's just remember those "revolutionaries" who enjoyed denying the "golden ratio". They were the Dadaist artists and all those who rightly counted themselves among the "primitives", and who thought they were the precursors of a new era. What they have left us are monsters, not human portraits, the sight of which should uplift us, not horrify us. What painter can disregard the rules of perspective with impunity without producing factitious works that we rightly regard as degenerate art? The architect must always take into account two fundamental elements, the load-bearing and load-bearing parts, in order to assemble them into a harmonious whole.

In architecture, too, it was felt that the classical examples should be contradicted by noting that the facade should be adapted to the organisation of the space and not the other way round. The building was divided into two opposing and incompatible parts. But the art of architecture lies in combining these two elements in a harmonious way. The degeneration of the golden rules is expressed in those houses whose walls have asymmetrical windows of different sizes, which only proves the incapacity of this style of architecture that believes it can omit the laws of beauty.

Not long ago, our art galleries were enriched by a unique piece acquired by the Führer: Myron's discobolus. In it we see the presence of all the laws of beauty, including the perfect harmony of the body. He is represented at the precise moment when he swings the discus and then throws it. This is the moment when two different movements take over; the swing of the arm, the "dead centre" before the actual throw.

One cannot randomly choose any moment that is circumscribed in the movement. Whether it is a horse jumping or a man running, one can always find a "dead point" within the movements that make up the action.

"Sankt Georg", woodcut by Lucas Cranach (1472–1555).

Today we know the rule of beauty governing artistic works, their construction and composition. Ancient artists did not know anything about the "golden ratio" formula, but they were guided by a healthy artistic feeling.

For a long time, it was thought that no absolute and eternal law governed art. People thought of the taste of the time and believed that everyone had their own ideal of beauty. Art was thus confused with fashion. If you visit an art gallery with the most beautiful works of the last few centuries, you will find that not one of them corresponds to the "public taste", i.e. is "fashionable". Today we are confronted with this type of work, without understanding them, because the viewer must feel through the creation the feeling that animated the artist when he created it. Indeed, no work of art can be understood if it has to be explained in an intellectual way beforehand. A work of art speaks for itself, otherwise it is not a work of art. And it is remarkable that all the "artists" who, in order to conceal their incapacity, follow new paths in the belief that they can thus evade the laws of beauty, are hostile to all true art, which they regard as dusty. They try to dismiss anyone who respects the eternal laws of beauty as a vulgar imitator of the antique.

Art gives everything to him who respects its laws. When we look today at a man who hardens and toughens his body by physical exercises, he can approach the ideal and resemble Myron's discobolus.

Beauty is a well-defined concept that has proved its worth over the centuries. Each race may have its own ideal of beauty, but it remains unique and absolute for that race.

We can see that the artist is also bound by iron laws in his creative freedom, which he cannot circumvent if he does not want to sink into chaos, decomposition and nihilistic cultural Bolshevism.

SS-Ustuf. V. J. Schuster.

The work of art is religion materialised.

Wagner

SS Booklet No. 3. 1938.

Architecture as an Expression of Community

People always try to divide architecture into two forms of expression: sacred and secular architecture, confusing the object and the end it can serve. A Gothic cathedral is not an expression of Christian culture because masses are said there. Otherwise the Gothic style would only be expressed in the construction of churches. But if you go around Germany today, you will see town halls and Gothic city towers with equal admiration. All these buildings were built *by the community for the community. They* served as places of assembly, administration or defence. They stand before us as monuments to the greatness of the community.

Whoever looks at the temple of Athena, the Parthenon on the Acropolis in Athens, today feels a deep admiration for the architecture of the Greeks and surely does not think of the religious rite that gathered the community in its halls. In many cases, we are not at all sure what purpose a monument may have served. Scholars have not yet unanimously decided whether the largest pyramid at Giza was designed as a *tomb* for King *Cheops* or was built at his behest to pass on *mathematical formulae and rules* to subsequent generations through a monument that defies the millennia, even though most scholars consider it a giant burial site.

Only people who are short-sighted or speculative speak of "Christian" architecture and consider the cultural asset of our people, which is expressed in cathedrals, as the most inherent style of a denomination. On this basis, the West should have been frankly poor in architectural monuments before Christianity spread to Europe.

But it is precisely the "eternal city" near the Tiber that contains a large number of "pagan" buildings, and the Colosseum is at least equal in architectural beauty to St. Peter's; although it would be inappropriate to compare two buildings of different periods, one of which was erected 1500 years later than the other.

In any case, both buildings had *only one* purpose: to serve the popular community as a meeting place. But when we talk about "Christian art", we see that it was extremely primitive, as evidenced by the excavations that extracted from the "catacombs" various utensils belonging to the first Christians.

The popes themselves, who enjoyed building, were not good builders. *Bramante,* who was entrusted with the construction of St. Peter's Basilica, planned the Greek shape of the cross to give the most powerful cathedral in the world the imposing mass that it was also intended to have in perspective. After the death of Bramante and his successors, the old *Michelangelo* took over the direction of the work.

This brilliant man wanted to improve on Bramante's plans and thus give more strength to the overall impression that was to be obtained. He raised the dome to emphasise it, simplified the plan by shortening the arms of the cross.

However, his plan was not followed. After his death, the pope demanded of *Maderna,* his successor, despite various objections, that he extend the western arm into a long nave that was a little too reminiscent of the plan of eastern Rome, Byzantium.

The result was that Michelangelo's unique design lost all its effect. The architect Maderna tried to "save" what could be saved. But it was only Bernini, the creator of the colonnade, who gave the façade its full meaning, and this by using a perspective effect that deliberately created an oval square that the viewer thinks is round. It is hard to believe that the Pope, his financial backer at the time, was aware of this optical trick. In any case, three generations of architects were forced to correct the architectural desires of the popes with constructions not originally planned.

The majority of architectural monuments have served and still serve 'secular' purposes. This is demonstrated by the town hall of Alstadt in Brunswick: this Gothic building has nothing to envy to any cathedral. The community built an 'administrative house' that corresponded to its sense of self and its cultural will. It should also be borne in mind that the members of the council did not have unlimited powers, but that they had been given the task of building a town hall by the inhabitants, so to speak, through their representatives, which was to symbolise the community outwardly.

There is not enough space here to mention the names of the many town halls, warehouses, clothmakers' houses, weigh houses, etc. It is certain that church buildings are not superior to public buildings either in architectural art or in the type of execution. On the contrary: only "master cathedral builders" who had *already made* a name for themselves through their work were commissioned. It was therefore the *national community* that employed the master builders, whose representatives had enough sense of style to distribute large architectural contracts with the help of plans.

There is no man among the builders of cathedrals who has not proved himself before, and no pope and bishop builder can claim to have *discovered* an architect.

Michelangelo was at the height of his fame when he was commissioned to build St. Peter's, and Fischer von Erlach would have gone down in architectural history if it had not been for the Karlskirche in Vienna, although we are fortunate to have this Baroque building, one of the most beautiful of its time.

Among the monuments, we also find many 'gates'. These are fortifications, "strategic points of support" in the usual city walls, which had no other purpose than to protect the community. Most of them are now in the heart of a city that has outgrown its old walls and no longer builds them because they would have no reason to exist in our time (!)

Indeed, no building has ever been built for its own sake and almost none has entered the history of architecture by serving only the individual and not the community. If one thinks one can object that there were castles and burgs, it should be noted here that all emperors, kings, princes and knights symbolically personified a community and that no proud people would have suffered their representative to live in a place that did not conform to what the dignity and cultural level of the people demanded of him. And when the community angrily protested against a ruler, it was not because he had erected too many 'ceremonial buildings' for his use, but because he was *not worthy of* representing the *people*.

It was the cheap propaganda argument of Marxism to compare the architectural magnificence of the ruling classes to the 'barrack housing' of the workers. It is precisely the workers who show a desire to create lasting cultural values in the history of architecture, which is best expressed in the magnificent guild houses in Ghent, Bruges and Memel.

The tailors, blacksmiths, butchers, fishmongers and weavers were, however, only *workers* who had joined together in guilds and had paid for the construction of the guild houses out of their own pockets. They were the representative building of their guild, the home of their professional community where they gathered to spend evenings together and cultivate camaraderie. In these buildings, their class consciousness was enhanced, their sense of union and mutual aid knew only one law, that of "all for one, one for all" which governed their actions and conduct. Their sense of community was so strong that in times of war, they participated as a *corporation* in battle, more than once winning the day.

Architecture is not only music turned to stone, it also reflects the spirit of the popular community. Even the most talented builder cannot realise his boldest dreams without the community that provides the manual labourers who carry out his plans. And when we look with respect at our cathedrals today, they are not the result of "Christian art" but of the cultural performance of the thousands of hands that created them. The stonemasons were not always "God-fearing Christians", as many of the gargoyles, which are frankly compromising for the monks, still testify today.

Nor were the cities with the most cathedrals 'the most Christian'. In fact, there was a time when rich cities, to show Rome that it was neither envy nor avarice that led them to refuse to pay tribute to the pope, generously provided mendicant monks with the means to build churches, as was the case at the end of the 12th century. A large part of "Franciscan" architecture owes its birth to this. When the pope wanted to build as the "representative of Christianity", the cities refused to allow him to do so because they did not consider him worthy of speaking for "their"

Christianity. Even cathedrals are nothing more than the expression of the will of the people's community, which has become stone.

The architectural history of all civilised peoples teaches us that architecture, as a form of expression of a value-creating people, was neglected or even extinguished when the community itself degenerated and disappeared from history. In truth, we ourselves experienced architectural chaos when the popular community was torn apart. Powerless and lacking in vitality, it has thus watched helplessly as non-native elements have attempted to monopolise the form of artistic expression as a selfish means of making money.

But art can only come from the community and from a creative style that embraces the universe. That is why architecture is also a reflection of a homogeneous people, of the popular community.

SS-Ustuf. V. J. Schuster

SS BOOKLET NO. 2. 1938.

NOTES ON STYLE

Two men stood in front of one of our new buildings and talked thoughtfully about the cultural values of our new style. They wondered whether it could really be called a *German style that was in* keeping with the nature of our people and had deep roots in it.

These were two criticisms.

The critic is used to looking at the world openly and with a sound opinion. But judgements made at first glance can only be prejudices, which the superficial critic will resolutely contest. Nevertheless, there are hardly any areas in art and history that have not yet been judged by critics. No critic has yet complained that there are more critics than artists. In addition, it is precisely the creative artist who asks the critic to make a judgement. For it is a fact that the critic's activity encourages the work.

We are not saying that one should accept all the explanatory arguments that are put forward without a word. It is undoubtedly much more difficult to create a work than to criticise it. Since art needs time, it is tragic that critics never have any.

In the land of 'classical criticism' in Paris, art critics take the liberty of visiting painters in their studios to contemplate the work they then propose to exhibit in the salons. The artist will object in vain that it is not completely finished. The critic reassures him; he is satisfied with it and tries to express in a rational way what it already evokes. His mind was already made up when he descended the stairs, even though the painter was still working behind his easel for three weeks.

Above, the rose window of Strasbourg Cathedral.

Central nave of the Chorin cloister.

The Chancellery in Berlin. When sacred and secular art come together in the same aspiration to elevation.

Let it not be said that this example is excessive. The two men standing in front of the new building do the same when, after one day of analysis, they cannot define that the style is German. Their judgement has not improved at all when they submit it to us after three months of more reflection.

Baroque reigned two hundred years ago and we have experienced it as a style. Art connoisseurs speak of sacred and secular baroque buildings, baroque furniture, vases, wooden sculptures, baroque crockery and fire-rails. It is unthinkable that a silversmith at that time would have sat at his work table with the intention of working on a fruit bowl in the Baroque style. Nor was he aware that he was sitting on a Baroque chair. However, the expert who now holds this fruit bowl would date it to the Baroque period.

Style expresses the spiritual attitude of a people at a particular time in their history. We are only at the beginning of *our* new era, and we must give future generations the opportunity to appreciate the cultural assets we have created. National Socialism would not be a worldview if it believed that it had achieved its goal by taking power. Our task is to fight for all people and to educate a people who no longer need an ideological line simply because they have internalized the National Socialist worldview. If they express themselves artistically, these men will create values that are typically German and personal because that is their nature and that is precisely their style.

We find everywhere traces of a style that have linked it to another cultural period. It is therefore impossible to speak of a significant influence when brilliant architects personalise and influence it. It is therefore impossible to judge an architectural style solely on its creative values without taking into account the forces that gave rise to it. The history of peoples clearly shows that the great periods of architecture coincide with the level of evolution of peoples. The *degenerating* peoples have left us no style. What expresses their greatness are the results of their ancestors, whose legacy they scatter.

Artistic history is inextricably linked to world history, architecture to the powerful development of a people. In ancient times, war values determined the fate and future of a popular community. We know of no people who left us a classical architectural style and who played a secondary role on the battlefield. This is the best proof that people of soldiers are in no way hostile to culture, but rather appear in history as elements of civilisation.

Style is also an asset that our ancestors pass on to us to manage. And we will leave an architectural style to our descendants. We must therefore educate the youth in the spirit of creating a new style. They will take care of it because it will represent for them a sign of their union with their people throughout history.

The cars drive noisily through the cities of Germany. Winches creak and scrape the stone. Buildings are being erected whose purpose and size are not only dictated by the demands of the moment, but which must bear witness to future generations of our desire to create lasting values, even if we cannot enjoy their fruits. Later, we should not be reproached for having had the best *intentions* but never having been able to realise them. Posterity is merciless and only accepts what *lasts*. Giving good advice means nothing more than making descendants responsible for our sins of omission.

We know even today what this means. Architecture has not been spared. Large arteries are proof of what the builders were designing when they were only trying to satisfy the taste of *the individual* and were building these individual houses. They were not trying to impose themselves on others, but rather to *surprise* themselves. This is the only thing that can explain the rows of houses built during the sad years when the Empire was founded. Dominated by the ephemeral, the "personal touch" was given precedence, and what we now call style was curiously avoided. Instead, they were 'modern', 'moving with the times' and innocently imagined that the next generation would also follow this spirit.

Now this generation is tearing down soulless stucco and plaster with a pickaxe, and no one feels any disrespect for our ancestors. We need space for those tasks that history has entrusted to us. What is valuable, because we *feel* it to be so, we preserve as part of the cultural heritage with which we have a sentimental and ideological relationship. And that is why the man who gives our people this awareness of a national identity is also our first master builder.

V. J. Sch.

"D'ESTOC ET DE TAILLE", BY GUNTHER D'ALQUEN, 1937.

HOMOSEXUALITY AND ART

It is not necessary to demonstrate that homosexuality played an important role in the German artistic life of the last decade. For those who do not know, suffice it to say that there were theatre scenes where more than 50% of the artists claimed the "right to lead this singular existence". On the other hand, there is total silence about women. Unfortunately these were not isolated cases.

For National Socialism, the manifestations of life are not regarded as a problem with its own laws. Every 'problem' of the past enters the realm of political decision through its organic relationship to the community. National Socialism has restored politics to its original meaning; it is therefore not a limited work in itself that can stand alongside other equal or higher values. The conclusion must be drawn that in all areas of life only its values are subject to political realisation. Any other scale of values can only logically lead to the notion of liberalism, i.e. to the recognition of the anarchist character.

Our current policy is clearly based on these fundamental findings and art has its rightful place in it. When today's pack of émigré writers rant against the alleged "political violation of art" in Germany, these howls show the hard of hearing how important the new National Socialist orientation is.

There is no longer any reason to complain that police intervention threatens the existence of art. On the other hand, the destruction of an artistic principle of international significance will always make much more noise. We will certainly not calm the hysteria of the literary barricade fighters on the Kurfürstendamm, but they do show us that we are on the right track.

The basic findings of National Socialist cultural policy are simple. They have that timeless simplicity which is typical of all National Socialist demands. They reduced art to a creative process and placed artists back into the legitimacy of the divine order, which alone concretises the meaning of life, preserves it and transmits it into the future.

Seen in this way, art rediscovers in our people what has given it its dynamism at all times and among all peoples, that is, the natural, and therefore divine, polarity of creation.

If National Socialism claimed to have discovered this fundamental law, it would be denying the eternal creations of past generations. No, they have passed this indestructible law on to it directly. But it can rightly claim to have discovered an artistic—one might almost say systematic—determination. And thanks to this, he can claim to have made a one-sided interpretation of all artistic creations and to have defined their unique scale of value.

Thus, the eternal notion of the freedom of art was found by National Socialism. For our artistic concept has definitely liberated art. It has triumphed over the concept of individuality.

Later generations will judge what this event means for artistic creation.

An art is governed by the original law of creation, but this impulse must not be restrained by limiting itself to an individual form or valuation. Nor should it be isolated from a realm of authentic artistic achievement, nor from the area of the national community, and thus from the divine order, because of the instability of an individual will representing both the taste of the time and a solitary character. Such art unconditionally expresses the artist's own personality in the creation of the purest eternal values. For the artist's "ego" is translated into the meaningful (not exceptional and transient) experience of the male-female creative polarity in the interpretation of the divine order, and this fundamental experience becomes the starting point for all communal creation beyond the individual.

Thus art has been purified from pure instinctive impulses, from a perfectly sterile erotic problematic, from all ideologies of self-satisfaction and self-release. It is resolutely based on the experience of love, which is not an end in itself, but apprehends the divine order through its creative and life-protecting forces.

Man is not violated by such art, nor by an ideology hostile to life or by instinctive and anarchic forms. He is liberated because he takes in what is the fulfilment of his destiny in its divine grandeur.

Only that which makes sense speaks the language of eternity. Incoherence is a source of unrest caused by all asocial and destructive forces. The Führer defined the foundations of art when he said that health is the only terrain that can produce true art.

National health is the only guarantee of the life of the people. This is the aim of National Socialist hygiene and racial policy. It alone can ensure the survival of the people through all the vicissitudes of history. This is the profound meaning of German defence policy. Vital principles are served by economy and industry, not by selfish aims. This is the heritage for which every young generation is responsible and which represents the greatest national wealth from the past.

German art is immutably embedded in this programme, which is a creator of German culture.

For it is only meaningful if it reflects an era whose goal has broken down all the temporal barriers of the old political factions; but it is only tolerated if it has perceived and realised in its creations the greatness of this goal and if it serves an eternal world order through its moral principle. The meaning of art, the meaning of cultural creation in the New Reich expresses the will to shape this future. It has thus become a historic rejection of individualism, liberalism and internationalism, a total rejection of all ideologies hostile to life.

The superficial reader, attracted by the title of the article, will have seen with a certain astonishment that so far only art has been discussed, and not homosexuality at all, although this was the theme.

But now we are the ones who are embarrassed to criticise for the sake of criticising, but we arrogate this right to ourselves because we consider that it allows us to put aside everything that might hinder our will and our creativity. We want to define what art and culture mean to us. In this way, we fight against the dissolving forces on the basis that the knowledge of the true is the best way to destroy the false.

The reader who is annoyed and weary because he has already understood that such art cannot produce anything pathological or abnormal is our best friend. One thing must be added, however. Just as the question of homosexuality can be approached from the criminal angle but above all from the political angle, so the question of homosexuality and art constitutes a clear problem for us.

It has two aspects from which the same conclusion is drawn.

When we consider the evolution of art in the 19th and 20th centuries, we can say that the progression of homosexuals in the field of art and artistic creation certainly belongs to the chapter of the Jewish question.

After the Jewish takeover of German culture, propaganda was also made for homosexuals. This is a very useful instrument in this work, because insofar as it includes gifted people, it represents an asocial character; just as the Jew does in the field of German culture.

The homosexual can never be a creator or convey art from creative abilities because these people of another species lack the creative experience of a pure biological nature. A homosexual is thus excluded from the eternal laws of life. It is therefore no coincidence that the principle of 'art for art's sake' and its aesthetics become the domain of homosexuals. Nor is it by chance that the degenerate logically adopts the Jewish ideology of the destruction of life, Bolshevism; more than one present-day emigrant is living testimony to this.

We see that the management of art by homosexuals can only result in a strict rejection of the natural community of life.

But these findings are purely political in their effect, for they reveal consequences that are counter to the community by the very basis of this 'art'. For our healthy sensibilities, there is unfortunately no degree in the concept of hostility to the state; all those who intend to speak in this area must come to terms with the facts. The divine order of unchanging nature proceeds with the same rigour and we do not allow ourselves to judge the Creator and His laws.

It is precisely because we consider art to be an overcoming of reality and the expression of timeless ideals that we must vigorously reject works by human beings who are incapable of adapting to the laws of life and yet want to violate the laws of the people as critics or creators. They will produce the same process of degeneration as the results of the Jewish Bolshevist artists whose works became the formal and thematic elements of decomposition.

The other aspect of the problem is typically individualistic. Originating from the spirit of independence of the individual, it manifests itself in the field of homosexuality as an unconditional recognition of the different nature.

One can simply say that it is a crime of intellectual individualism which, through its fundamental conceptions of homosexuality, has produced the best incentive in this direction. For from the claim to the right to unfettered individuality, the path to "being different" is not far. It is therefore not difficult to understand the establishment of the notion of the "artist man", which represents the sum of individualistic specialisations. The "collective man", the mass that is "characteristic" in its legitimacy, is opposed to the artist who must be different in order to be able to truly create. It will be seen that many German artists adopt this type of cynical discourse of artistic masters:

"Are you Jewish, homosexual or Viennese (i.e. a special variety of Jewish artists)? Then what are you doing at the daitsche theatre? (Author's note, Yiddish distortion of deutsch).

Our ideological assertions are thus demonstrated. The different being, both in terms of race and sexual disposition, becomes the starting point of the artistic fact. The strong smell of the strange animals that make up the bestiary of Judeo-Bolshevik artistic production is enough to attract the curiosity of the masses.

The concept of difference connects with the notion of the artist and finally breaks away from it. The primitive instincts of the fair directors, who show hunchbacked dwarfs and a bearded woman, had been completely liberated in the field of artistic creation. As a result, the attractions had to be renewed to maintain a positive turnover. For this artefact is alien to any popular feeling.

That which is hostile to the community, and therefore asocial, became the archetype! The Bolshevisation of concepts culminated in the notion of the 'third sex'.

But this direct consequence has a second, no less dangerous inversion. The existence of women could not be totally disavowed within the framework of this "cultural-political" line. Recalling that the homosexual is a stranger to woman, whose essence he does not by nature grasp, allows us to understand the emergence of a new feminine type and its affirmation. It is not only the "lesbian" who corresponds to the homosexual taste, but also all those female natures that are fundamentally incapable of following their authentic vocation. Let us not focus on this category; we have a clear-cut conception of women by National Socialism. Without showing narrow-mindedness and prudery, we must disregard in this chapter the masculinisation of women as it has occurred in past years. For the notion of the comradeship between man and woman becomes evident if between these two beings a child symbolises the ultimate self-sacrifice in love, duty and sacrifice.

Human destinies are therefore tragic when they cannot or will not meet with the desire to found a natural life; when this great experience is denied the couple.

The right to existence of the historical community of our people requires the removal of all elements that disturb this community. This is the policy of hygiene.

This fundamental law spares no area.

Neither is art!

V. NATURAL AND PHYSICAL SCIENCES

SS BOOKLET NO. 8. 1939.

THE ETERNAL LAWS OF LIFE

As the Führer said, "National Socialism rigorously teaches the reality of the most precise scientific knowledge and expresses it clearly. Our piety bows unconditionally to the greatness of the divine laws of life. We have only one prayer: to courageously carry out the duties that flow from them.

National Socialism derives its truth from observation of the world. It is therefore a true philosophy. But to have a philosophy also means to behave towards life and the values of life in a way that is in harmony with one's view of the world. Every human being sees the world through *his own* eyes and lives the world to the rhythm of *his own* blood. The world view is therefore always specific to each people.

How do we Germans see the world?

When a German walks through the fields on a fine summer day or a white winter night, he contemplates with reverence the beauty of the world: the clarity of the blue sky and the sun, or the legion of eternally twinkling stars, the dark course of the clouds, around him the ripening harvests and the vast meadows of grasses and flowers, the shining lake, the gentle fall of the snowflakes. And when he hears, during the autumn nights, the drumming of the rain, the forests in the storms, the struggle of the dunes against the waves along the sea, he understands then that the world is a place of beauty, at the same time as the immense battlefield of the eternal struggle.

The strong man takes the world as it is.

The thought that the earth is nothing but a "valley of tears" would never occur to a German. The divine power of creation in this world is, according to our belief, too noble and too rich to have created a "valley of tears".

The German who walks along the flowery paths in springtime and hears the sweet song of a bird nestling in the boughs where five chicks are about to follow their destiny, could never imagine that these chicks would be hatched with the curse of original sin. But as he listens to the bird's beautiful song, he feels the joy of nature proclaiming that procreation and birth are applications of divine laws. In our people, does not a mother also obey a divine law when she gives children to the nation? No parents could ever believe that paternal or maternal happiness is tainted by the curse of original sin. Never have children come into the world so tainted!

The things of life are born of procreation and childbirth and pass away with death. When the leaves fall in autumn, when the old tree falls in the wind, this is fate. The death of the living being is not, however, the "ransom of sin".

The observation of the world thus provides us with the certainty that the environment in which we live is not a vale of tears, it is the land of our homeland. Procreation and birth are neither sin nor fault, but the fulfilment of the divine will. Death is not the consequence of sin, but the law of life, necessity and destiny. The Führer once said:

"At the head of our programme is not mysterious intuition but lucid knowledge. There were times when darkness was the necessary condition for the effectiveness of certain doctrines; we now live in an age when light is the foundation of our successful business."

The light of science thus illuminates the eternal truths of National Socialist ideology. It is the culmination of the struggle for science and the affirmation of our specific nature.

To fight for knowledge, for light and truth has always been considered by the obscurantist world as heresy. Thus knowledge and respect for the laws of the universe has suffered the curse of the priests and even today the Church's anathema does not spare them.

Giordano Bruno was burnt alive as a heretic for proclaiming with heroic passion, totally in the spirit of our faith: "We seek God in the unalterable and inflexible law of nature, in the respectful harmony of a soul submitting to that law. We seek Him in a ray of sunlight, in the beauty of the things that come from the bosom of our mother earth, in the true reflection of His creation, in the contemplation of the countless stars twinkling in the immense sky…"

From the very beginning, the German soul had a direct approach to God: reverent and pious, this soul delighted in the law of the land, in the rustling of the forests, the roar of the seas and storms, the contemplation of the starry sky. It was this respect that prompted him to follow the natural laws. To respect them was to affirm God. To transgress them was to distance oneself from the divine.

Today we know again that the law of the world is also the law of our human life. As the Earth remains in the orbit of the Sun, so we men must remain true to the laws of life. Just as our ancestors with the wonderful instincts of our race lived in unison with the laws of nature, so can we, enriched by experience and science, consciously bring our lives into accord with the laws of the world.

Respect for life is always the foundation of a living faith and true piety. He to whom the world appears divine because it is created by God, will never lose his respect for life and its laws. The separation of God and the world comes from an alien way of thinking. To deny the divine character of nature is to despise the world and life on Earth. Whereas primitive man, aware of being the holder of divine life, respects himself and life, the man who represents God only in the hereafter, knows neither true respect for his own person, nor respect for what grows and flourishes on Earth. He respects only what he imagines to be above the world and himself, only through the feeling of being a creature, that is, a creation of God.

We see paradise in the beauty of the blessed and sacred Earth. At the dawn of the year, millions of flowers, the quivering gold of the cornfields, the brilliance of the snow and the purity of the flakes at Christmas, the birth of life in the womb, are for us a manifestation of heaven.

This is where Rosenberg's words apply: "If one considers this great veneration as ungodly and atheistic, one may reply to this groundless assertion that if, indeed, one teaches the existence of a Creator and celebrates Him in hymns and prayers, one cannot then consider the observance and enforcement of His laws as sacrilegious and their transgression as a sacred duty."

If we look at the history of all the peoples of the Earth, we see that every people has the destiny it deserves. Since people were born by the will of life, they have been responsible for their destiny. This is why the following adage is so true: There is no God who decides what is right and wrong in history: people are masters of themselves.

The end of a people is the natural conclusion of its reckless transgression of natural laws. Only the respectful acceptance and conscious observance of the divine laws of existence ensures the continuance of a people. The eternal life of our people is the objective of our work and of all our struggles. Indeed, "the victory of life is the reason for the universe".

Wherever we see the presence of life, we recognise the will to maintain and conserve the essence of the species. "The sacred law of every being is to safeguard and defend its own character" (H. St. Chamberlain). Every organism therefore fights for its life and the world becomes a place of perpetual struggle. Struggle is nature's way of maintaining a vigorous life. It ensures the world's "Great Health", for that which cannot win must necessarily perish.

"To the initiated eye, everything indicates the trace of a god.
Schiller

The "House of Nature" in Salzburg had the task of acquiring and developing a better knowledge of nature, which today would be called "ecology". It studied the origin and essence of the natural environment in its many forms, the interactions in the life of man, his position in nature and also in relation to it.

Nature is the eternal teacher of people, constantly teaching the ephemeral nature of the individual but also the durability of the group and the eternity of life's relationships. It also shows how to ensure survival.

Nature is infinitely varied and presents itself uniquely in millions of different aspects, but every organism and every event in nature involves specific laws. They are necessary because without this legitimacy, nature would not be structured. Order is part of the essence of life. It is the duty of humans to understand the order of nature and to recognise its legitimacy.

The Germanic respect for life was revived through National Socialism. Struggling for our own world view, we have come to realise that we honour God only by respecting the eternal laws which, from His will, govern the world.

SS-Hscha. Dr Schinke

SS BOOKLET NO. 10. 1938.

COMRADE AT MY SIDE...

When walking in the snow one feels—depending on the individual—either pain in walking or joy in contemplating the wonderful winter landscape.

We do not know that there is also a logic in the structure of snow. But when you look at snowflakes under high magnification, you can see what a great artist nature is.

Here, comrade, are some illustrations showing the beauty with which the snow crystals are branched, worthy of an embroidery pattern. The structure is always in six parts. In all the illustrations we find the rune Hagal, the rune of the world, the symbol of the organisation of the world, the wheel with six spokes. These crystals are so beautiful that they could be used as models for lace, ornaments, etc. Imagine wrought iron like the first illustration. And isn't the second picture in the shape of a rose-the third one six little Christmas trees?

Why are we interested in these things?

Because you, comrade, must learn that a *divine order,* which we can also call *world law,* governs even the smallest natural things—which we consider as insignificant as a snowflake.

Everything has its rule. Everything has its law that determines its essence, its existence,—like you! We recognise the greatness of creation through the order, purpose and beauty of the nature that surrounds us.

SS-Standartenführer Dr J. Caesar

SS Booklet No. 4.1938.

Our modern knowledge
of the structure of the universe

The science that studies the structure of the universe is a branch of astronomy. It is that part which is concerned with the organisation of matter in the immense space we call the universe, the location of stars, the size and distance of celestial bodies. In the following, we will present in a concise form what we currently know about this construction of the universe.

Everyone knows that our narrow habitat in cosmic space is the *planetary system* consisting of the central body, the *Sun*, and nine large planets orbiting it: *Mercury, Venus, Earth, Mars, Jupiter, Saturn, Uranus, Neptune and Pluto*.

The last one, Pluto, was recently estimated in theoretical calculations made by the Americans and actually discovered by them. Mercury is the closest to the Sun, Pluto the furthest of the nine planets. The size of the planets varies greatly. The smaller planets, Mercury to Mars included, would fit largely into the larger planets Jupiter to Neptune. Jupiter, for example, is more than ten times as big as the Earth, which has a diameter of almost 13,000 km.

Even though it has become smaller due to technology and traffic, the globe is already an enormous figure for us humans; however, it is nothing compared to the central body of our system, the Sun. Its diameter is 1.3 million kilometres. This can be imagined if we consider that the celestial body closest to our Earth, the Moon, is on average 384,500 kilometres away from it. The Sun is so large that the entire Earth-Moon system would easily fit within it. When we imagine the Earth with the Moon transposed into the Sun, with the centre of the Earth coinciding with the centre of the Sun, the Sun's area far exceeds the Moon's orbit. The size of our solar system itself is characterised by the fact that, for example, Neptune, the second-to-last of the nine planets from the Sun, is on average 4.5 billion kilometres from our central star, whereas the Earth is on average only 149 million kilometres from the Sun.

If we leave the solar system to go into *space*, the measurement in km adapted to our human scale is already no longer sufficient to define the environment near the Sun. If we wanted to express the present dimensions in kilometres, this would create an insurmountable handicap preventing the communication of astronomical and scientific information because of the number of digits. Astronomers have therefore adopted another unit of measurement, the light year. As we know, light travels 300,000 km/sec. A light year therefore means the distance travelled in one year by light at 300,000 km per second. Expressed in kilometres, the light year corresponds to a distance of 9.4 trillion kilometres (a trillion is a million times a million).

The nearest fixed star to our Sun is four light years away; its light needs four years to reach us. We can conceive of such a distance by making the following comparison. Let us imagine all the distances and ratios in the universe so small that the diameter of the Sun, which in reality is 1.3 million km, is *40 m;* in this case, this fixed star would be even further away from the Sun than the effective distance between the Earth and the Moon, i.e. it would be 380,000 km further away. And the same applies to the nearest fixed stars to us!

It follows that the stars are so sparsely distributed that it is virtually impossible for the Sun to collide with other stars. This is confirmed by the fact that what we call the 'nearest' environment to the Sun is that part of the universe that light travels from the Sun in 70 years on all sides, i.e. a ball with a radius of 70 light years. *In this enormous part of space there are only two hundred stars.* If we imagine this reduced in size so that the stars form pinheads, they would still be 60 to 100 km apart in real distance. The stars and all the matter in space are so sparse that they spread out like pinheads over distances of 60 and 100 km. As a result, a collision between two stars in the universe is very rare or even impossible.

The size of stars, which are nothing more than distant Suns, huge balls of matter in an extremely high temperature state, varies greatly. There are stars that are much smaller than the Sun and others in which the entire Earth-Sun system enters and which are therefore so large that their surface area would exceed its orbit if their centre could be made to coincide with that of the Sun. As a result, stars are divided into *giants* and *dwarfs*. In spite of this, the Sun is already something of a giant compared to our narrow living space, the solar system. However, it belongs to the group of *dwarf stars*. In the universe there are completely different dimensions to those in the large planetary system, which is already enormous compared to the Earth.

Our solar system and its immediate surroundings mentioned above are themselves only a small part of a larger star system, namely *the Milky Way*. It manifests itself indirectly to us through the flaky, wispy light that crosses the sky on clear nights. This band is produced by an almost infinite number of stars, i.e. luminous Suns that are so far apart that only the largest telescope is able to break up the clouds of the Milky Way into a host of luminous points. Many stars are clustered in space around a flat surface and are very far apart, whose light adds to that of the Milky Way as we see it with the naked eye. The total number of stars in the Milky Way can be estimated at ten billion, but this is still less than the actual number. The extent of our Milky Way is 60,000 light years. It therefore takes 60,000 years for light to reach the other end.

The boundaries of our own Milky Way are not yet the limits that can be reached by modern science. Outside our own Milky Way, there are many others that cluster together as an almost infinite number of stars. This extragalactic system—i.e. outside the Milky Way—is called a nebula, although this type of designation does not correspond to the true nature of this image. It dates back to the time when it was not known that these images are actually *conglomerates of stars*.

To date, approximately two million 'Milky Ways' are known. The one closest to us is *the Andromeda galaxy, which is* one million light years away. Extra-galactic nebulae are very disproportionately distributed in the universe. It is not yet known whether these Milky Way systems, these islands of worlds, are interconnected or scattered randomly through space. What is certain is that the nebula is a conglomerate. The most distant of these nebulae, which represents the limit reached by the human mind, is

180 million light years away. The light we perceive today left when our Earth was at the height of the saurian age and man did not yet exist.

This is what the universe looks like as far as we know at present. Let's try to reduce it to a human scale again to make it more concrete. The dimensions are so small that the distance from the Sun to the Earth, which in reality is 149 million kilometres, is one millimetre large. The Sun should have a diameter of $/^1{}_{100}$ mm, our Earth $/^1{}_{10,000}$. They would no longer be visible to the naked eye. How small man would be on this scale! —The solar system, our home, would be six centimetres large. The nearest fixed star would be 260 m away, the clouds of the Milky Way between 80 and 100 km (!). The furthest point of our own Milky Way would be 13,000 km away, i.e. at the other end of the Earth. Since the Milky Way is so close to us, the galaxy mentioned above would be more than 20 million km away—and all this on a scale where the distance between the Sun and Earth is 1 mm.

So this is what we know today about the nature of the universe, and no doubt future research will reveal things we never imagined.

But all that remains is for us to bow with respect to this prodigious work and its creator.

Joseph Meurers

SS NOTEBOOK No. 4. 1943.

FIGHTING IN THE WILD

Apart from all the other dubious gifts offered by the almost two-thousand-year enslavement of the Near East, the Nordic man has also inherited the forced representation of an imaginary country with a world called "paradise" that has never existed and will never exist. Blandness and softening are the major chords in this set of Semitic ideas that speak of love, of the indolence proper to the weakness of the Southern man, and that brings together fierce lions full of gentleness and a patient donkey.

Such chimeras are the expression of an alien and decadent character. The healthy and lively intelligence of a German could never have invented such nonsense, for he is still too close to nature, standing with both feet on the ground in the struggle with—and in—raw reality. We are therefore living in a time when we are finally ridding ourselves of the foreign burdens that hinder our Aryan spirituality and are rediscovering the truth of our soul.

On this Earth, all events and all forces of nature are based on pros and cons. Every push meets an opposite reaction, every evolution requires a corresponding decline. The life of one often means the death of the other. It has always been so and will always be so, at least as long as the Earth carries life. Because of this natural law, every living thing must constantly fight for its existence, whether it is a plant, an animal or a man. This struggle can vary greatly, as can the weapons of attack and defence. One could almost say that there are as many methods of fighting as there are life forms and species. Moreover, the struggle for life of an evolved nature is harder than that of a single cell. A good man has more opponents than an insignificant being. There is no man without an enemy; otherwise, he is a nullity who must be put aside. Consequently: the greater a people is, the more numerous are its envious and therefore its enemies.

The natural struggle extends to all phases of life. The first moment of a creature's life is already a form of struggle for air and food. The search for food will continue throughout its life until its last breath. But there follows a whole series of other struggles that are expressed both in attack and in defence; the struggle against the environment, against bad weather, heat and cold, against drought and humidity, shadow and light or for light. In addition, there is the struggle for a sexual partner, for reproduction, for the child, the home, the living space and finally against the personal enemy. The forms of struggle can be direct or indirect. They may be in the physical strength and form of the body, in colour, speed, type of movement, endurance, size or smallness, number of offspring or innumerable special forms, but also in the spiritual faculties.

In the body of every living being, whether it is a single-celled amoeba or a multi-celled plant, or whether it is an animal or a human being, there is a continuous assimilation of air, soil or food, which is returned as energetic matter. Moreover, every living being is subject to a process of constant evolution. There is no dead time. It grows from birth to maturity; but it also changes continuously, in a retrograde way. It withers, grows old, one function dies out after another, and finally it offers no more nourishing soil for the driving force of life and dies out.

And so the community is continually changing, just like the individual. The only major difference is that the life span of the community is much longer than that of the individual. A people, for example, is capable of living for millennia, even if its members, the fellow citizens, live only for the time of their brief existence. But as they are constantly replaced by newcomers, popular stability and homogeneity is guaranteed over an immense period of time. The life span of a generation, an ethnic group or a people depends primarily on internal and external circumstances, which are largely related to vital principles. A people clearly aware of the natural human bond, which does not excessively abuse its possibilities of civilising evolution, never grows old or weakens. But by the exact application of the laws of nature, and thus of Blood and Soil, it is continually renewing itself and is vastly superior in value and life span to the people who do not fulfil these preconditions. Indeed, this rule requires a perpetual struggle in many forms.

Above all, it is the fight for the preservation of the race, for the territory and for survival.

The struggle for reproduction is the climax of the natural struggle. It also exists in the world of plants. The magnificence of flowers is one element. One flower outshines another in terms of colour beauty, bizarre shape or fragrance in order to induce fertilisation and thus ensure multiplication. The colourful family of butterflies, but also countless other insects, perform this task, albeit involuntarily, but by natural instinct. In the tropics, there are also many birds, such as the small balls of feathers known as hummingbirds, the beautifully coloured hummingbirds and many others. Mammals can also be ambassadors between male and female flowers.

However, the most beautiful form of love struggle takes place during rutting or courtship periods, when fierce fights often take place. They take place in mammals as well as in birds, reptiles and even insects. Let us remember, during our childhood, the fights between male lucanus and also the duels between deer.

This fight is the most obvious expression of the powerful instinct to reproduce. Those who have heard it will never forget the bellowing of the deer in the fog-shrouded autumn forest. It is a call. Two mighty warriors meet, and all around them the clash of mighty antlers resounds. Two old fighters, full of strength and experience, measure themselves in a chivalrous duel. For a long time, the fight remains undecided, the female standing aside and following the virile action of her suitors with sharpened senses. Finally, the fight is over. The defeated one withdraws and leaves the victor to carry out his supreme duty. But that is not all, for the natural feminine also exists in the game. The fight for the female is followed by the fight to win her docility. The life of animals is very similar to that of human beings. The behaviour of the female praying mantis after the act of love is puzzling but nevertheless meaningful. It is a cousin of our grasshopper that lives in the South but also in some warmer parts of our Empire. After fertilisation, it murders its male. Having sufficiently fulfilled her procreative duty and purpose, he is then seized by the larger female and properly devoured. This is a good example of how nature tends to conserve the species and not the individual.

The survival of the species depends on the rate of increase. The lower the number of offspring, the more the existence of the species is endangered. This is why animal species whose young live in particularly dangerous conditions produce a large number of offspring. It is not only fish that lay hundreds of thousands or even more than a million eggs. This is a form of defence against the countless dangers that threaten offspring in the water. On the other hand, there are animals such as the lammergeier or the bearded vulture that only mate every two years and produce one chick. In such a species, the danger of extinction is naturally great, especially when another danger arises in the life of the animal. This was the case with the bearded vulture, whose survival was threatened by the long-range guns of man. As a result, this powerful bird unfortunately disappeared from all parts of the Alps about fifty years ago. Man has destroyed all kinds of animals, not only for reasons of conservation or use, but often out of carelessness. In these sad cases, the struggle for life has far exceeded its natural limit. Moreover, man is constantly confronted with his living and non-living environment. Just think of the fight against pests. But the proliferation of so-called pests, be they mice, rats or insects of all possible kinds, is almost always the result of unilateral human action. Most insects multiply and become pests precisely because humans cultivate their nutritious plants in unnatural enclosed fields. The same applies to voles living in grain fields. City mice and rats, on the other hand, owe their overpopulation to human food stocks. But rats are not only economically damaging, they also carry bacteria. Man's struggle against the microscopic living world is simply frightening. Many small creatures that are invisible to the naked eye are a constant danger to plants, animals and humans. As a result, many researchers are exclusively concerned with the fight against pathogenic bacteria.

These few examples show us how much existence depends on struggle and that a life without struggle is absolutely inconceivable.

SS NOTEBOOK No. 8. 1944.

THE FOREST AS A COMMUNITY OF LIFE

The Germanic peoples have a strong and deep love for the forest. As a reminder of the ancient forest environment in which their ancestors lived, it still resonates in songs and legends, myths and tales. The Nordic man has an innate sense to grasp the essence and the particularity of nature and also to understand in a pure and direct way the miracle of life that reveals itself to the one who is given to perceive it. We see in it a living whole, even if we do not discern every particular aspect of the harmony with this great vital hymn. In his regional and traditional songs, the Nordic man has always tried to define how he feels the mystery of the "forest". Whether he speaks of the "eternally singing forests", tells of his "forest homeland" or sings of the "sacred forests and lakes", "which stretch beyond the borders of the quiet heights to the green sea", one constantly perceives the same characteristic expression of union with nature. Nowhere does the Nordic man experience the sacred better than in the forests of his homeland.

A keen awareness of the nature of the forest, its changing composition and its local structure permeates whoever leaves the lowlands for the mountains, or climbs from the lower reaches of the earth to the higher ground. The soil is generally suitable for sustaining a forest. Two particular factors contribute to the birth of forests under natural circumstances: temperature and humidity. Heat and rainfall influence the growth and life of a forest. When the Earth was in warmer periods of its history, the forest had a number of species but was not dense. It only became dense when the polished stone and bronze ages cooled and moistened as time went on, and the *northern forest was* born. In the past, there were red beeches and hornbeams, and in the highest places firs and spruces; they made the forest denser and more impenetrable than before. The Nordic forest develops its full strength and magnificent beauty in favourable weather. This is how it came into being in our era.

The forest floor prevents rainwater runoff, maintains and preserves the fertility of these areas and forms the natural plant mats. The forest's crown of trees collects the rain so that it falls sparsely, does not wash away and does not silt up the soil. The foliage itself promotes the formation of dew and frost. Storms and wind are stopped by the forest, their drying and soon to be damaging effects on the landscape are reduced. The forest floor drinks up water from melting snow, rain and other precipitation like a sponge and can receive a huge amount of it without it running off. Fluid water can either run off or stagnate on the hard surface of the forest floor. Even when it is standing, the flow of water in the forest is very much hindered. The soil is constantly flowing with springs and groundwater in order to provide life and growth. The upper layers of the irrigated soil are retained widely and deeply by the forest through the roots of its plants. The trees move at the junction of the soil, which rises and falls under the effect of the great lever formed by the trunk and the roots. This is how the forest carries out its own unique "soil work".

The top life-rich layer of the forest floor, which we call the mother earth or humus, is formed by the foliage of the forest falling to the ground each year. Thus the mother earth, the humus-rich, living layer, is the source of life in the forest floor. When the farmer turns a piece of forest into a field, as was the rule in the old days in the peasant regions of Central Europe, this humus produces the harvest. The farmer considers it his present. In general, the forest is not turned into a field and the farmer himself carries out the fertilisation of the soil that was once obtained by the forest.

It is easy to forget that the vast majority of soils in Germany used for agricultural purposes are originally former forest soils. Only the black soils or loess soils are grain soils and not forest soils. But on all the remaining soils, the forest once produced the mother earth and thus gave them life and fertility. The farmer has respected this and all living things to this day. We are therefore also a forest people!

At present, the forest is being pushed heavily out of the habitat of the northern peoples, usually on those areas that can only be made profitable by the forestry economy. At the end of the 19th century, the creation of a forest right to maintain the site-dependent characteristic of its species and strength was barely considered. It was a low-interest investment. This was the way of thinking at the time, and a forest was ended with a light heart—often to reinvest the proceeds in other operations. In this way, large areas of land lost their forests for good, including their fertility and ultimately also the possibility of life for large human settlements.

Above, 'The Forest', by Fr. Karl.

Opposite, "Escherndorf on the Main", by Bodo Zimmermann.

"German Spring", engraving by Hennemann.

The profoundly ecological position of National Socialist Germany puts everything at stake to enable the maintenance of a healthy forest. In the previous era, measures for the creation and renewal of forests were only considered for the purpose of timber production, according to the expectations of these areas, and only took into account the benefits of forestry investments. Although wood production is also essential for our economy and especially for the war economy, it is only a secondary manifestation in the life of the forest. In the natural system, the forest does not only have the task of providing wood for humans. We need it much more to develop and maintain a rich and healthy life. A forest that only partially covers the country fulfils this purpose in our latitudes. All that is needed is an extensive network of areas with well-distributed forests. Then the forest and its richness will persist, remain fertile and dense. With a vast network of wooded areas, such as there are today in the Central European area, the country also has the character of a forest landscape and thus harmonises with the nature of the Nordic man.

SS BOOKLET NO. 5. 1938.

ETERNAL CYCLE

We stand on the bank of a river and watch the play of the whirlpools, rejoicing in the blue of the sky reflected in the water. We are proud that man has recognised the greatness of nature, that he is able to drive ships on the broad backs of the waves, that his strength drives mills. Let us think of the distant times when our ancestors stood on the bank of this river in which they fished and sailed upstream in their boats.

For centuries, for millennia, this flow stretches through its valley, carrying away a piece of land here, another there, and changing its face almost from second to second.

An eternal river? —Yes, as far as we can speak of an eternity, it is an eternal river. It pours its water downstream into the sea and is lost there. But the sea returns the water to the air, which, saturated, rises again over the seas. This is called clouds in the sky! They carry the water-filled air above us and move far inland—producing fog.

And then, somewhere above the earth, the clouds encounter colder layers of air, or they hit the snow-covered mountain tops. They can no longer carry their load of water and leave it behind. And it snows when in winter the air is cold, or rains in summer.

The water that made its way down from the high mountain peaks, first as a small stream, then as streams, rivers and seas, and finally as the sea, returned to its starting point.

This *is one of* the water cycles.

Another is more modest, yet just as important.

When it rains, the thirsty earth eagerly drinks up the water and stores it in its bosom. Plants absorb what they need to live, and so does man via a spring. The water then diffuses into the body of the animal, man or plant. It brings nutrients to the leaves of the plant and then evaporates and returns to the atmosphere, rising into the warm air or falling as dew.

It is constantly flowing out of all the pores of animals and plants and back to the earth. We could not live without water. Without the perpetual cycle of water, there would soon be nothing but a great ocean and barren, infertile land like the Sahara or other places around the world where it rains so little that no living thing would survive.

When man foolishly disturbs this earthly order, disasters can only occur which inevitably destroy all life. He who clears the mountains whose trees hold the water should not be surprised if the springs cease to flow. Life is extinguished because the water washes away the soil that the forest once held and leaves the rocks bare. When the snow melts, floods ravage the plain. The mountain has disappeared from the water cycle. It no longer stores water, it no longer releases it slowly; it is now only a precipitation zone.

So we protect the mountain forest because we don't want to follow the path that other people have followed. Their land has become barren, destroyed because of the stupid intrusion into the cycle of life (of nature).

He who recklessly disturbs the natural order perishes by the original power of nature.

SS-Staf. Dr Caesar

SS NOTEBOOK NO. 1. 1943.

THE LIMITS OF LIFE

Until recently, bacteria were considered to be the smallest living things known. Consisting of a single cell, they grow to sizes that make them invisible to the naked eye. Only the world of the microscope gives us a glimpse into the life processes of these microorganisms. The groundbreaking discoveries of a Pasteur and a Robert Koch proved that an immense number of these small living beings are the cause of terrible epidemics and serious diseases. But today we know that there are also many useful bacteria without their existence damaging the process necessary for the preservation of life.

According to the latest research results, there seem to be even smaller life forms in parallel with these bacteria. The conclusion is that, despite the great success of bacteriological research, almost all human, animal and plant diseases are caused by these "microbes". In many cases, however, no positive results were obtained, although the contagious nature of the disease was undeniable. Thus, the assumption that only the incredible smallness of these living creatures hindered research was further reinforced.

Only in recent years has some light been shed on this darkness. The "mosaic disease" became a dreaded disease for farmers, as it attacks many plants such as potatoes, turnips, tomatoes, tobacco, etc. In addition to the enormous reduction in yield, the leaves of the attacked plants are coloured like a mosaic and covered with white and yellow spots. Aphids proved to be the vehicles of this disease. Sucking the microbe with the plant sap, they transport it to another healthy plant. The microbe of this disease remains invisible. Science gave it the name 'ultravisible virus', which means 'poison beyond the limits of visibility'.

In the meantime, in a few decades, virus research has become a very broad science. Today, more than two hundred species of virus are known.

But it is above all by knowing the nature of the microbe that the researcher acquires the possibility of discovering the means and methods of combating its destructive action acting in a living organism. Thus the dreaded polio, smallpox, rabies, measles, parrot disease and many other very serious diseases are caused by species of virus, and the fight against them is gaining ground every year.

In a few cases, the mystery of the invisibility of viruses has been solved. The German researcher Paschen succeeded in discovering the smallpox microbe, which is one of the largest of its kind and reaches the size of about one hundred and fifty millionths of a millimetre. Bacteria seem to be gigantic to us, whereas until now they have seemed to be the smallest known units of life, and, to give just one example, the tuberculosis microbe reaches 1.3 to 3.5 thousandths of a millimetre. By way of comparison, the difference in size between viruses and bacteria is the same as that between a flea and an elephant.

The virus species only parasitise living cells. They multiply enormously and destroy certain tissues or cause swelling. It is very difficult to develop a serum for human viral diseases. For example, the treatment of polio is successful with a serum extracted from human blood that defeated the disease and therefore had the appropriate 'antibody'.

Viral research has not only brought to light completely new considerations in the fight against certain diseases, it is also in the process of profoundly expanding our vision of the nature of life. One researcher has even succeeded in preserving the microbe of monarchic disease in crystal form. Other results show that in more than one species of virus we are dealing with forms that are thousands of times smaller than bacteria. The old concept of the cell as the smallest component of life is therefore outdated.

As with so many other things, man finds himself particularly embarrassed when he stands on the threshold between the inanimate and the animate. Moving from the study of a cluster of the smallest particles, molecules, to the study of the whole organism holds many surprises. It shows us the metabolism and development of life forms that we humans can hardly suspect. The human mind will succeed in broadening and deepening its discovery of the mysteries of nature. But when, through his understanding of life, he succeeds in surprising one of its eternal laws, he feels all the more respect for the greatness of creation.

Karl Weiß

SS NOTEBOOK NO. 11A/B. 1941.

LIFE IN THE BUD

A chapter dealing with the beginning of spring

Each year, it would be impossible to predict the arrival of spring according to the calendar if it were as rare as an eclipse of the Sun or the appearance of a large comet. People would gather and marvel at this wonder!

Is it not a miracle? Through the white of the snow and the black of the thawed earth grow green spikes that spread flower buds towards the light. From the lifeless bark of the branches, seemingly lifeless balls that we call buds point towards the light after many months spent in the winter calm under the harsh frost and the icy wind. Tender greenery and various leaves full of flowers are blooming. But where does this greenery come from, where does it form, how can it grow so quickly, where do the colours come from and—a difficult question—how does the tree know that winter is over, when the March sleet is raging?

For those of you who are Cartesian and do not fully realise how amazing this process is, let us quote some figures as established by our scientists on flowering cherry trees. A medium-sized cherry tree has about 40,000 to 50,000 buds on its branches, some for flowers and some for leaves. The cherry tree flowers before the leaves develop, so we can count about 20,000 to 30,000 flowers. The maturation time from the bud in its closed capsule to the resplendent flower takes an average of three to four days. In terms of growth time, this means a segment of about 2 cm per day, i.e. the growth of billions of cells, which must also divide into stem cells, sepals, petals: stamens. And even if these Cartesians were not convinced by the splendid whiteness of the cherry blossoms, they will at least be admiring the number of these flowers born in three days in thirty thousand places at once: that's almost 50 kilos, half a quintal of flowers!

How does the tree achieve this? Nature uses the same processes for plants as it does for animals and humans, which also have an impact on the spiritual realm—the processes of selection by value and evolution. The buds that the tree creates slowly and carefully during the previous summer are not dead balls but a collection of cells that initially have no purpose but are structured in accordance with the nature of the parent species. It is this tiny assembly that constitutes the bud. In spring, a natural law causes the sap to rise in all the buds, which then undergo their development: the cells multiply thanks to the stored nourishing sap that flows in.

The plant has thus overcome the difficult period of our climate by hibernating the buds, but has lost none of its strength and vitality during the winter. This also teaches us that we must often "put to rest" our desires and need for action so that they can blossom with strength in more favourable times.

SS Notebook No. 1. 1944.

THE EARTH HOLDS THE FORCES OF SALVATION AND DEATH

The farmers in the small villages in the Swabian Alb had always thought that a bee sting was a harmless thing. A teacher who had two hives in his garden was often stung without anything happening to him. But there was the story of young Stiegele—a swarm of bees had attacked his car and made the horses so sick that one of them died. Some bees stung him too, and he was found panting and convulsing beside the overturned carriage, lying on the edge of a field. When the doctor arrived, he found that he was dead A respiratory paralysis had ended his life. —

The local farmers nodded their heads. If bees can kill people, people must be protected from their venom. Could the fact that the heir to the Stiegele estate had lost his life be compensated for by the usefulness of fertilising the flowers and harvesting the nectar? What is poisonous must be eliminated, said the farmers. And the previous day's accident had proved to them that bees are sometimes diabolically poisonous.

*

Another story from the Swabian countries is worth mentioning. In long lines, young girls sit in front of specially constructed hives, grabbing the bees with tweezers and stinging them with a specially prepared paper. They take the venom—the same venom that killed the young peasant in the Swabian Alb. People are treated with this venom, mainly rheumatic patients. It is both beneficial and harmful.

Paracelsus said that there is no such thing as poison per se, that only the dose is dangerous. Is this not also true of bees? The teacher in this Swabian village had rheumatism before he bought a hive and was stung. Now they have disappeared—a "dosage" of occasional bee stings had shown its benign effect. However, two bees had stung the farmer Stiegele directly in the arteries, the venom being carried by the bloodstream to the nerves. The dose had been too strong.

Things are not dangerous in themselves. Two German scholars, Arndt and Schultz, established a law many years ago that clarifies Paracelsus' formula. They say that all irritations, and therefore also poisons, stimulate vital activities, in medium quantities they promote them, in large quantities they paralyse them and the strongest ones interrupt them. As far as poisons are concerned, it must be said that the word poison in the strict sense should only be used above a certain dose.

*

In fact, this dose is often small. However, the venom that the cobra injects into a bite through its fangs is enough to kill a man. In a roundabout way, the snake's venom can be used for the good of man. Lepers often suffer excruciating pain which can only be relieved by morphine. A leper was bitten by a tropical spider, the mining spider, about fifteen years ago. The remarkable result was that the patient's severe nerve pain ceased quickly and for a long time. The doctors who discovered this case followed up the case and conducted trials. It was known that the venom of the cobra and the rattlesnake should produce the same effect as that of the mining spider. Since snakes were easier to obtain, they were preferred to spiders.

In the meantime, snake venom has been collected in many parts of the world. In Germany, too, there was a particularly intensive interest in this. Snake venom was used in very small quantities mainly for pain relief and not directly as a remedy. Nevertheless, there have been recent reports of improvements in certain conditions, although no definite conclusions can be drawn. The greatest success has so far been achieved in the fight against painful conditions, such as Pott's disease—known as "tabes"—and certain cancerous cases.

However, we can see with much more interest that the venom of the ominous spectacle snake can be a blessing to some patients. A spectacle snake is placed in a laboratory, which bites furiously into a muslin-covered glass in place of the victim's flesh, and the deadly juice is allowed to drip for a long time. The animal's jaws are carefully loosened so as not to break the venom fangs and, to the delight of the martyred reptile, it is left alone for a period of two weeks to reconstitute its venom.

*

The pharmacies of ancient and modern times are full of these venoms that have been transformed into benefits through wise dosage restriction. The great medical garden of nature is rich in healing poisons: belladonna, lily of the valley, foxglove, henbane and many others. Among them, the heart-healing substances found in foxglove, lily of the valley, Adonis roses, oleander, giant African onion and many others have yielded new insights. We owe them to a cardiologist, IY Karl Fahrenkamp. His patients enabled him to discover a completely new type of solution.

After thousands of experiments, he knew, like all cardiologists, what benefit foxglove can bring to prevent a dangerous attack of heart weakness. The pulse returns to its natural rhythm, the strength of the heartbeat responds again to the body's demands. The heart is said to be "compensated". This is an old clinical experience which is the basis of all our knowledge of foxglove and its comparably acting variants, such as the lily of the valley, the giant African onion and the tropical strophantus species. Strophantus or foxglove has become an indispensable tool for the modern physician, enabling him to temporarily avert a life-threatening danger for countless people. But the duration of this compensation, and thus of the balance between cardiac force and effort, remains uncertain. The only thing that could be done was to take foxglove again when a new heart attack occurred. Could it not be possible to prevent the attack? Karl Fahrenkamp followed this path and tackled a vast and fundamental biological problem. He found that there are fundamental differences between solutions produced from the whole plant or its active part and the purified, crystalline 'poison'. In some cases the poison was more effective, in other cases of heart disease it was again the solution.

He therefore gave his already compensated patients some low-dose solutions as a preventive measure. He obtained good results and concluded that he was obviously dealing with a deficiency that could be remedied in the same way as a lack of vitamins or hormones. His results were not believed, so he looked for a test, a proof. Animal research, as had been tried up to now with substances that were active on the heart, was not successful. Fahrenkamp then began to experiment with plants. The results, which have now been obtained after many years of tenacious work, are so important that they will be extended to a hitherto unforeseen extent. Their real importance is revealed especially since the experiments have been carried out on a large scale during the last four years. It lies in the following:

When, in autumn, countless foxgloves, lilies of the valley and Adonis roses, washed by the rain, return their heart-healthy substances to the earth, their career is not over. On the contrary, it has only just begun. The remaining plants, which are affected by the flow of substances, receive some of them and are activated. If you artificially activate vegetables, flowers, cereals with these plant juices, you can simply observe the difference. We have seen this hundreds of times in fields and test beds: in short, the plants become healthier. They can withstand wind and weather better, they keep longer, they stay—like potatoes and carrots—fresher longer. Many are more succulent, others are stronger. In short, the impression gained from this research is that the substance produced by these heart-active plants strengthens the state of health. Some animal experiments also came to the same conclusion.

Fahrenkamp called this substance the function. He was right in thinking that genuine vital substances are present here, which play a decisive role in the development of life. Humans also need them, as his patients prove, to prevent circulation disorders. However, as these plants do not grow in intensively cultivated areas, they must be classified as medicinal plants. These substances also have the particularity of slowing down the ageing process. The extent to which this can have important consequences for the preservation of the freshness of vegetables and meat is not yet fully understood. Our intensive scientific work shows that this vast problem will be studied with greater intensity and acuity in the midst of the war. But the most important thing is to proceed cautiously in the field of national health, i.e. from food substances, until all the preliminary practical and theoretical work is completed. Then poisons will become benefits.

*

Mastering a poison does not mean extrapolating directly to health. The purple calyxes of the colchicum can also perform unexpected tasks on a scientific level. The poison has been tested on plants and the results are remarkable and promising.

As is well known, each cell of an organism has a nucleus which contains chromosomes that are constantly present in a certain number, specific to animal and plant species. In humans, there are 48 chromosomes, in the midge 8. With the help of colchicine, the poison extracted from the colchicum, the number of chromosomes in plants can be doubled. This is also accompanied by an increase in growth, which can often result in a giant form. This means that, if necessary, we can obtain new, larger and also higher-yielding plants from medicinal plants. Practical trials, especially on trees, look very promising.

But colchicine has also taken on another, admittedly provisional and still theoretical, importance. We are indebted to the Göttingen oncologist Lettré for this research. At a certain dose, colchicine slows down the cell division that science calls mitosis. This process of retarding cell division is clearly demonstrated in animal tissue cultures. A large number of such mitosis poisons have been discovered from related chemical substances, and a search has been made for the one that uniquely prevents the partition of cancer cells. The universal importance of such a discovery—which is still hypothetical—is clear to everyone.

In the presence of these clarifications that we could make about the role of poisons and their variants in nature, it is obvious that what Paracelsus says, that nothing is a poison in itself, seems to acquire great significance for the new research that is of the utmost importance for the destiny of the human race. War should not oblige us to close the laboratories and wait for the days of peace. The general health, which is the object of most of this research, therefore also requires the researcher to work hard in the midst of international conflict.

Heinz Graupner

SS NOTEBOOK NO. 8. 1944.

THE ORIGIN OF ALL THINGS

Under the sky lies the blue mountain range, and the familiar homeland also lies at the edge of the year. The faces of youth face it, it emanates from the bark of the banks.

The stars rise above the fields, in the thickness of the forests the legend still breathes, from the mouths of the springs the spirits speak: the path ends in an ancient enchantment.

The cities become denser, but over the mountains thunder the waves of storms, the plains lie rich in lagging rivers.

Man sings of his roots everywhere, but the homeland is his most precious possession. It is the chalice of the centuries and the origin of all things.

Kurt Heynicke

CHAPTER III

I. BIOGRAPHIES

REICH HISTORY" MAGAZINE.

CHARLEMAGNE, THE FOUNDER OF THE EMPIRE

In the chaos of the great migrations, only one western Germanic tribe, the *Franks,* had been able to develop its own state structure. The Franks had not migrated very far and were constantly receiving reinforcements from the mother country. Under *Charles Martel,* the Frankish Empire still had a strong northern influence and had reached the major cultural centres of the Rhine and its tributaries. He protected the West from *Moorish* attacks at the Battle of *Poitiers* in 732. His son *Pepin*'s donation to the Pope, by which he confirmed the possession of the regions of Rome, Ravenna and Ancona, established the *Church States and* thus justified the Pope's secular claim, and had the most harmful consequences for German religious policy.

The Frankish kingdom reached the height of its power under *Charles I*, the grandson of Charles Martel. He succeeded in unifying the German tribes of Bavaria, Saxony, Thuringia and the Alamanni, uniting them in the Frankish kingdom and thus creating a great power. But his empire did not achieve unity between people and territory. In essence, he was no longer ruling a Frankish kingdom but a Franco-German Empire, as his residence in Aachen showed.

CHARLES AND WIDUKIND

However, this great Empire was to acquire Germanic features mainly through the will of Charles, and indeed Charlemagne was for the first time the master of a great Empire of the Germanic type. He also organised the first measures of expansion towards the east.

In pursuing his imperialist political plans, he did not shy away from forcing the restive tribes to gather. And the Saxon duke Widukind, Charles' greatest adversary, had to bow to this harsh fate. As much as we disapprove of his violent methods, we must recognise that Charlemagne made Europe a powerful unit. *Widukind,* the defender of the Germanic soul, and Charles, the great creator of states, bear witness to the greatness and atrocity of early Germanic and German history.

All the regions of the Carolingian Empire, united and centrally managed, flourished. Thanks to his eminent personality, Charles held the Empire together and dictated to the Church. Under his successors, however, the powers that be tended to divide the Empire became more and more dominant. The state-subordinate Church gave way to the political Roman Church, and Charles's son, Louis the Pious, became the docile instrument of this new power. In time, the Roman parts of the Empire became increasingly separated from the Germanic regions. The incompetent heirs to the throne followed the worst policy and the Empire was divided in the treaties of Verdun in 843 and Mersen in 870.

In Niedersachsenhain, near Verden, a monument erected by the SS in memory of the 4,500 Saxons beheaded by order of Charlemagne.

SS on guard at the tomb of King Heinrich I.

Reichsführer Himmler places a wreath on the grave of Queen Matilda for the ceremony in honour of Heinrich I.

Speech by Reichsführer SS Himmler in Quedlinburg Cathedral, 2 July 1936.

Heinrich I

It is often said in the history of peoples that one should honour the ancestors, the great men and never forget their legacy, but this wisdom is too rarely respected. Today, July 2, 1936, we stand before the grave of German King Heinrich I, who died exactly one thousand years ago. We can say in advance that he was one of the greatest founders of the German Empire, and at the same time one of the most forgotten.

When the 43-year-old Heinrich, Duke of the Saxons from the Ludolfinger peasantry, became king in the year 919, the most terrible inheritance of all was passed on to him. He became king of a German Empire in name only. Over the past three centuries, and particularly during the decade of Charlemagne's weak successor, the whole of eastern Germany had been abandoned to the Slavs. The former Germanic settlements on which the largest Germanic tribes had lived for centuries were occupied by Slavic peoples fighting the German Empire and challenging its authority. The North was taken over by the Danes. In the west, Alsace-Lorraine broke away from the Empire and became part of the West Frankish Empire. For a generation, the duchies of Swabia and Bavaria had fought and challenged the lazy German kings—especially Ludwig the Puerile and Conrad Ide Franconia.

The wounds caused by the brutal and bloody introduction of Christianity were still open everywhere. The Empire was weakened from within by the perennial claims of the prince-bishops and the interference of the Church in international affairs.

The historical event of Charlemagne's creation of an imperial power uniting rival Germanic tribes was close to total failure, and this through his own fault, since the system of this purely administrative and non-German central power was no longer morally and biologically based on the Germanic peasants of Saxony, Bavaria, Swabia, Thuringia and the Frankish Empire.

This was the situation when Heinrich I was given the heavy burden of becoming king. Heinrich was the true son of his Saxon peasant homeland.

As a duke, he had already shown a tenacious and energetic character, but it was not until he became king that this was confirmed.

At his royal investiture in Fritzlar in May 919, he refused—albeit without using offensive words—to be anointed by the Church, and thus demonstrated to all Germans that he had a correct perception of the political situation at the time and would not tolerate any interference in German political affairs by ecclesiastical power during his reign.

In the year 919, the Swabian duke Burkhart submitted to King Heinrich, who united Swabia with the German Empire.

In the year 921 he went to Bavaria with an army and there too he did not impose himself by the power of arms but by the persuasive force of his personality, and Duke Heinrich of Bavaria recognised him as King of the Germans. Bavaria and Swabia, which were in danger of being lost at the time, were thus annexed to the German Empire by King Heinrich and have remained there to this day and, we are sure, will remain there in the future.

The year 921 brought Heinrich, the experienced, cautious and tenacious politician, recognition of the now French West Frankish Empire, still ruled by a Carolingian. Alsace-Lorraine returned to the Empire in the years 923 and 925.

But let us not imagine that this reconstruction of Germany was done easily and without obstacles from outside. Every year for a generation, the hitherto weak German nation was constantly the victim of the almost always successful and victorious raids of *the Hungarians*. All over Germany, I would say all over Europe, regions and people were subjected to robbery by these remarkably politically and strategically directed hordes and armies of horsemen. The annals and chronicles of the time tell us of the attack on Venice and the plundering of Upper Italy, the attack on Cambrai, the burning of Bremen, and the repeated destruction of the Bavarian, Frankish, Thuringian and Saxon regions. As a clear-sighted soldier, Heinrich realised that the type of army that existed among the German-German tribes and duchies, as well as the tactics used at the time, were not suitable for defending against these enemies or even for destroying them. Luck came to his aid. In the year 924, he succeeded in capturing an important Hungarian army leader during a Hungarian invasion of the Saxon areas around Werla near Goslar. The Hungarians offered fabulous sums of gold and treasure to redeem their leader. Despite the opinions of the stupid and narrow-minded contemporaries, who were already numerous at the time, the proud king exchanged the Hungarian army leader for a nine-year armistice on the part of the Hungarians, first for Saxony and then for the entire Empire, and undertook to pay modest tributes to the Hungarians during these nine years.

He had the courage to adopt an unpopular policy, having the prestige and power to do so. He then began his great creative work, which consisted of raising an army and enabling the country to defend itself by creating fortresses and cities to risk a definitive battle with the previously invincible adversary.

At that time, there were two kinds of military units: on the one hand, the Germanic ban of the tribal duchies, which was called up in times of crisis, and on the other hand, the first German military unit consisting of professional warriors and mobilised men, which had been created by the Carolingians. Heinrich I united these two units into a German military organisation. He also decided that every ninth man should be sent to the fortresses to form part of a garrison from the mobilised men of the royal and ducal courts. For the first time in Germania, he really trained his mobilised units and made the warriors lose their habit of fighting in isolation. He organised the cavalry in a tactical manner and the troops were structured and disciplined.

In less than a year, an infinite number of small and large fortresses surrounded by ramparts and ditches, partly with stone walls and partly with palisades, sprang up on the eastern German border of the time, along the line of the Elbe and in particular in the entire Harz region. They contained arsenals and supply houses in which a third of the country's harvest had to be stored according to a royal order. Already at the time of Heinrich I, these fortresses gave rise to the *later famous German cities* of Merseburg, Hersfeld, Brunswick, Gandersheim, Halle, Nordhausen, etc.

After these preparations, Heinrich I began to create the conditions for a final battle with the Hungarians. From 928 to 929, he undertook *major expeditions against the Slavs*. On the one hand, he wanted to train his young army and harden it for the great battle, and on the other hand, he wanted to take away from the Hungarians their allies and the war resources mobilised against Germany in order to destroy them.

During these two years of war, which allowed him to subject his young army to the most difficult tests, he defeated the Havolans, Redarians, Abodrites, Daleminzes, Milzes and Wilzes. In the middle of winter he conquered the apparently impregnable town of Brennabor, now Brandenburg; after a three-week winter siege, he conquered the fortress of Gana and in the same year built the town of Meissen, which remained of great strategic importance in the following years.

In the year 932, when the king, pursuing his goal unyieldingly, considered that all the conditions had been fulfilled, he summoned the *prince-bishops to a synod* in Erfurt, and the people to a national assembly, in which he urged them in a persuasive speech to refuse to pay tribute to the Hungarians from now on and to accept national warfare in order to free themselves once and for all from the Hungarian peril.

In the year 933 the *Hungarians attacked* and suffered a crushing defeat at Riade on the Unstrut due to a strategically masterful German counter-offensive.

The year 934 found Heinrich campaigning against Denmark to defend the northern frontier against Danish and Slavic attack and to reattach to the Empire the northern territories lost in the past through the fault of his predecessors. The then internationally important trading town of Haitabu in the former Schleswig was annexed to the Empire.

From 935 to 936, Heinrich I, who was a famous and highly esteemed European ruler, especially in his *Saxon homeland,* true to his peasant nature and feeling that his end was near, wrote his will and recommended his son

Otto to the dukes and lords of the Empire as his successor at the Diet of Erfurt.

On 2 July, he died at the age of 60 in his imperial castle of Memleben in the Unstrut valley. He was buried in Quedlinburg, in this crypt of the present cathedral.

This busy life is full of lessons. Many others have reigned longer and cannot boast of having done such a great work for their country as Heinrich I did. And now we, the men of the 20th century, who live in the era of the great German reconstruction led by Adolf Hitler after a period of terrible collapse, would like to know what made it possible for Heinrich I to accomplish what he did The answer is given to us if we try to know Heinrich I as a Germanic personality. As his contemporaries recounted, he was a ruler who surpassed his court in strength, grandeur and wisdom. He ruled by the power of his strong and generous heart and the obedience he received was absolutely sincere. He reintroduced the ancient but eternal Germanic principle of loyalty between duke and man in violent opposition to the Christian religious methods of government of the Carolingians. He was as intractable to his enemies as he was faithful and grateful to his comrades and friends.

He was one of the greatest leaders in German history and he knew perfectly well that, despite the strength and sharpness of the sword, victory is greater and more lasting when other Germans are integrated into the community through frank discussion rather than petty prejudice and the killing of men who are valuable to the whole of Germanity.

For him, the word given and the handshake were sacred. He faithfully honoured the treaties he had made and enjoyed the respectful loyalty of his grateful followers during the long years of his life. He respected all that is sacred to other men, and he knew so well the principles of the Church, even resorting to murder, that he therefore contemptuously refused to interfere in the affairs of the Empire and did not intervene in religious matters. He curbed the devout tendency of his beloved wife who accompanied him throughout his life, Queen Matilda, the great-granddaughter of Widukind. At no time in his life did he forget that the strength of the German people depends on the purity of its blood and that the odalic peasantry is linked to the freedom of the soil. He knew that the German people, if they wanted to live, had to remain true to their origins and expand their living space. However, he was aware of the laws of life and knew that the ruler of a duchy could not be expected to repel attacks on the borders of the Empire on the one hand, if on the other hand he was deprived of all his rights and sovereignty, as the Carolingian administration wanted. He thought big, built up the Empire and never forgot that the great Germanic tribes had a strength that was based on a thousand-year-old tradition.

He exercised his authority so wisely that the natural qualities of the tribes and regions became faithful and docile helpers in unifying the Empire. He created a powerful imperial power and intelligently safeguarded the independence of the provinces.

We must be deeply grateful to him for never having committed the mistake that German and also European statesmen have made over the centuries up to our time: considering the destiny of his people outside their living space—we say today the geopolitical space. It has never succumbed to the temptation to cross the limits set by the destiny of the living and expansion areas of the Baltic Sea in the east, the Mediterranean in the south and to cross the Alps. As we can well imagine, he thus consciously renounced the sonorous title of "Emperor of the Holy Roman Empire".

He was a noble peasant from the people. He was always freely received in his home and saw the measures of state administration with him in person.

He was the first among his fellows and was shown greater humane and sincere respect than emperors, princes and other kings requiring foreign Byzantine ceremonial. He called himself duke and king and was a leader a thousand years ago.

I must now reveal a humiliating and deeply saddening fact for our people: the bones of the great German leader no longer lie in their burial place. Where they are, we do not know. We can only make guesses. It may be that loyal partisans buried his body, which they considered sacred, in a safe place, in a dignified but secret manner; it may be that, driven by resentful hatred, an enemy dignitary scattered his ashes to the winds. In the same way, the miserable bones of the most faithful men tortured to death were buried just outside this crypt, as the excavations in front of the cathedral prove, and which we make it our duty to bury with dignity. Today, in front of the empty tomb, we represent the entire German people, the Movement and the State, by delegation of our Führer Adolf Hitler, and we have brought wreaths as symbols of respect and remembrance. We also lay a wreath on the tomb of Queen Matilda, the noble companion of the great king who was buried next to her husband more than nine and a half centuries ago. We believe that we are also honouring the great King by thinking of Queen Matilda, that great example of German female dignity.

Situated on the hill inhabited for millennia by men of our blood, this ancient tomb with its splendid Germanic-style religious hall should be a place of remembrance where we Germans come to make a pilgrimage to remember King Heinrich, to honour his memory and to pledge ourselves on this sacred spot to follow the human and leadership virtues with which he made our people happy a thousand years ago; And to recommit ourselves to honouring in this way to the utmost, to serving faithfully in thought, word and deed, for Germany and Germania, the man who, after a thousand years, has taken over the human and political legacy of King Heinrich, our Führer Adolf Hitler.

> *He who wants to save his people*
> *can only have a heroic mentality.*

Adolf Hitler

SS BOOKLET NO. 4. 1938.

JOHANN GUTENBERG

The era of great upheaval in which we live would hardly be possible without the operation of broadcasting. It enabled one man to speak to millions of others and to share the great events that make up his destiny. Without radio, we would certainly not have become aware *in so few years* of being a people, and our people would certainly not have matured so quickly. On the other hand, radio would have remained a toy for the wealthy if it had not developed at a time when people wanted to become real communities.

The progress of the human mind is not a product of chance. The *need* always precedes it. That is when we feel, consciously or unconsciously, the need for progress, for invention, and then a gifted man—an inventor—comes out of our people and fulfils our desires.

"Black art" Printing workshop in the 17th century.
(Woodcut by Abraham von Werbt, 1676).

Benz and Daimler invented the automobile when existing means of transport *were no longer sufficient* to satisfy our desire to travel. *Lilienthal* took to the air when whole generations had already *attempted* human flight. *Marconi* created the principles of radio when it was already clear that the method of transmitting news by telegraphic cables *no longer satisfied* the demands. Today, we *need* a car that is accessible to all—and the manufacturer *Porsche* achieved what was impossible yesterday. Human genius is the best motivation for those who say to themselves: "*I must create this because my people demand it*".

We must therefore see in every inventor an *executor of the will of his contemporaries*. Only in this way can we understand him, his struggle, his superhuman sacrifices and the obsession with which he pursues his goal.

Johann Gutenberg. Black chalk, XVI century.

This is *Johann Gensfleisch zu Gutenberg, or* Johann Gutenberg for short, the inventor of *the printing press*. He also lived in a time of great upheaval and had to cope with its demands. The 15th century, during which he lived in Mainz (he was born in 1400 and died in 1468), saw the "dark" Middle Ages rapidly disappear, as the Church viewed spiritual life with suspicion as its monopoly and tried to prevent people from having their own spirituality, folk identity and culture.

In the XV century, daring *sailors* discovered the New World, thus overturning the dogma of biblical science. In the East, Islam knocked on the door of autocratic Christianity. People questioned the omnipotence of the pope, the absolute moral doctrines and scientific visions of the churches. Everywhere there was a desire for knowledge and *the exchange of news and knowledge*. Oral transmission had long ceased to be sufficient. People had to have access to knowledge—something that until now had been reserved for a few monks and great clerics. But what kind of man will use reading if *there is nothing to read* and if Fon only has a few handwritten copies of books and pamphlets, which are naturally expensive?

Johann Fust, who took the fruits of his brilliant invention from Gutenberg.

Gutenberg, a small craftsman whom we would today call a technician, lived in this time and in the world of his needs. He was working on a printing process that would satisfy the longing of Germans emerging from the slumber of the late Middle Ages. He wanted to print *books* and *brochures*—as *many as* possible and as *quickly as possible*.

The concept of printing already existed. Illustrations were carved out of wooden tables, coated with colour and printed (pressed) onto paper. Letters, words, sentences, whole pages of books were also made from wood and entire books were produced, but how long and how expensive! A skilled woodcarver needed two weeks to make a single page! It was an art that could only be enjoyed by a privileged few.

Gutenberg had two tasks to accomplish—we would say today: two technical problems to solve. Firstly, instead of whole pages of books, he had to use small blocks made up *of a single letter* which could then be assembled as he wished. Then to make these small blocks so strong that they can be reused. He found the solution to both problems. He developed a process for casting *lead* letters and a printing press with all the necessary tools so perfectly that the principles of his "black art" have remained unchanged over the centuries, and even today they can be seen under the magical cloak of modern technology.

Printing workshop dating from 1440.

One might think that this is all very simple. And yet, this invention required Gutenberg's unstinting self-sacrifice, all his labour, his joy of living and his hopes. Like all great men, and like most inventors, he encountered the misunderstanding, stupidity and malice of his fellow men. A miserable shopkeeper named Fust, who had "financed" him, frustrated him with the fruits of his labour, crowned himself with usurped glory and forced the man who had forged *the weapon of spiritual liberation* for the next generations to lead a poor and miserable life until his death; a life which, however, was devoted to the perfection of his art until the last day.

The true greatness of important inventors is revealed in their destiny, in their unyielding tenacity, their faith in their vocation, their contempt for all material things.

A page from the Gutenberg Bible with 42 lines.

We are easily led to judge them only by their inventions and what good and useful things they have passed on to us. But it is not only this that constitutes their genius, and we would underestimate them if we only saw this aspect. For it is certain that a progress which—as they say—"is in the air" will be achieved in every case, if not by one of them, then by another. In the XV century, the printing press was invented because a people wanted to see words reproduced in written form. And if Gutenberg had not done so, two decades later, a man of another name would have appeared. We would also drive without Benz and Daimler, we would fly without Lilienthal. And if we were to confine ourselves to the strict result, we could rightly say: A Gutenberg, a Benz, a Lilienthal only did what others would have done in their place if they had not been there!

But these men are superior to their actions, because they had the courage to be the *first*. They were more visionary than others. They had a higher calling than others. They did not follow paths that were already laid out, but entered a *no-man's land. They struggled under such difficult conditions that most of them had to make an act of self-sacrifice for the sake of their work.* They sacrificed their happiness and quiet existence to their faith so that future generations could live off their work. Thus, they did not become immortal only by their deeds, but on a higher level by the recognition that the people owe them from all eternity.

SS Notebook No. 7b. 1941.

Albrecht Dürer, 'sports correspondent

Or how the great artist valued the law of combat

Albrecht Dürer—a genius who outshines the mass of German artists! The mention of his name evokes before our eyes superb paintings of noble, sublime forms, in praise of the Madonna, the saints or other religious figures. We, the people of today, who are no longer sensitive to Christianity and the doctrine of the afterlife, nevertheless admire the noble features of Dürer's works, intentionally expressed by this Renaissance man who was already distant from religion. But in the past, all art had to do with the Church or God, and here too Albrecht Dürer created figures of unforgettable grandeur.

If we were to picture the life of the man Albrecht Dürer in terms of his 'official works', then, as the books teach, we would see him as the victorious genius, the aspiring transcendent, the pampered prince, the painter who, ignoring the miseries and sufferings of his people, lives and creates in an illustrious circle of emperors, princes, knights and bishops, in order to perpetuate their fame.

However, some of Dürer's simple, modest works, which do not fit completely into this framework, often touch us more than monumental creations. These are watercolours depicting Dürer's homeland, the surroundings of Nuremberg and the peaceful valleys of Franconia. They are drawings such as the 'little blade of grass', the 'hare' and the 'bunch of violets'. In the past, they were dismissed as "studies" of the painter and were never considered as representative of his personality.

A NEW DÜRER IS DISCOVERED IN VIENNA

Thus the years and centuries passed. Dürer, who was born in 1471, remained present in the hearts of the Germans as a genius dominating religious and courtly art, but they knew nothing of the man's real nature. However, something happened in early 1800, three hundred years after Dürer's time. The archives of the libraries and offices were turned upside down in the course of exhibitions and alterations to glorify the Habsburgs. In the library of the trust administration, the dust rises in thick clouds, and among the piled-up treasures and pandects, the Austrian archive advisors extract cards filled with strange old drawings—illustrations and series of drawings of men fighting and battling with different types of weapons, and also handwritten texts written in the characteristic curved characters of the late Gothic style, from Dürer's time.

This has caused some astonishment in Vienna, but even more so among scientists and art specialists who examine these Habsburg heritage cards with expert eyes. The significance of this set of drawings of fencers and wrestlers, and the identity of the commissioners and the creator, are being questioned at length. Even the light sketches on these sheets, which depict hundreds of figures and postures, bear the imprint of a master's hand, himself an expert in fencing and wrestling.

ALBRECHT DÜRER—IMPOSSIBLE! AND YET!

A murmur arose in the mass of art criticism journals. They assumed this or that, reviewed all the artists who lived before and after 1500, and also dwelt on Albrecht Dürer. The date and the genius of his pencil stroke could give him away. But was it possible to attribute these everyday, vulgar images, smelling of sweat and dust in the armoury, to the ascetic creator, lover of Madonnas and little Jesus? No, to even imagine such a thing seemed degrading to the art critics alive three, four, five decades ago. Dürer certainly had nothing in common with "the people" and especially such a quarrelsome, fighting and punching people!

And yet—experts and researchers bringing in other arms books from a slightly later period proved that bad draughtsmen and imitators had been inspired by these Viennese drawings. Historians also established that in 1500 Dürer's great patron, the "last knight", Emperor Maximilian I'", commissioned Albrecht Dürer to make a series of woodcuts on the knightly arts, which the master produced around 1502 in the treatise "Freydal". Was it inconceivable that this emperor, the last scion of a great civilised era, also wanted a master's hand to depict the chivalric arts of fencing and wrestling? Dürer carried out this task, but the work did not make much of an impression, so the master's drawings were left in the archives, and some of the leaves even appear to have been copied into other books.

But how—and this was the important question—was Dürer able to produce these "obviously sporting illustrations"? He shows people of his own time, even though the figures in the Bible were once painted in period costume, and only living models could provide him with examples of precise wrestling postures. Did such perfect fencing and wrestling exist at that time?

On this question too, we have been totally mistaken for a long time and until the most recent times. The Middle Ages were seen as a dark age of religious wars, of the persecution of everything secular, and especially of everything physical. The twilight of the gothic windows seemed to cover those centuries and all the peoples of the Middle Ages. It is only recently that we know that Christianity and the Church, from the dawn of Germanic times to the time of the Wars of Religion, were only a superficial covering for a free national lifestyle deeply influenced by the Germanic-Nordic soul. The Church's hostility to the body could never be imposed, not only on the hard-working peasants, but also on the knights who had to fight physically in battle. Thus, for example, games, dancing, bathing and physical exercise always had their place in medieval German society—even in Dürer's time.

It is quite conceivable that Emperor Maximilian wanted to produce a manual on these chivalric arts because he felt that the threatening times of the Wars of Religion were proving to be dangerous.

But it is possible that Albrecht Dürer himself observed in the new city of Nuremberg and in the emerging bourgeoisie the practice of these chivalrous arts which they used to defend their cities. In all German cities at that time, there were fencing schools, fencing masters, palm houses and bathing places. Albrecht Dürer did not have far to go to find suitable models for his drawings. Today, other sources have also confirmed that it was Albrecht Dürer who created these "sportsmen's drawings".

JIU-JITSU—NOT JUST A JAPANESE INVENTION!

We are very happy to be able to leaf through this book on fencing and wrestling by the great master. But there are also surprises in store.

In the field of fencing, the large estramaçons and curved swords, the small shield that we see in many drawings, have certainly disappeared. But these illustrations show us many things that have always been preserved in our fencing schools. What we used to call the illustrations of wrestlers are, however, the most surprising for us.

This is not wrestling as we know it. The holds in our sport come from the Greco-Roman school of wrestling, based on classical examples. It takes only the upper body as the point of attack and rejects "vulgar" holds such as the arm lock and the leg lock.

The latter are precisely very abundant in Dürer's drawings. One grabs, one reverses, the leg is interposed and the opponent is duped, as in all the holds we know in jiujitsu. A drawing with a description of the hold in Dürer's own hand is exemplary in this respect. "Item so du mit einem ringst, so prich aus mit der rechten hant und far zu stunt damit deinen arm in sein rechten elpogen und fas im den arm starck in dein peid hend und flaipf an seinen arm pis an das gelenk und zuck in starck an dich und ker den dein lingke seiten gegen im an sein rechte seite, als hie stett, und prich im dem arm..." In our language it means something like :

"When you wrestle with someone, throw your right hand violently and throw yourself at him by putting your arm at his right elbow. Grab his arm strongly with both hands and pull him to the shoulder joint, turn your left side against his right side in the manner here indicated and break his arm."

It is definitely jiu-jitsu, used to defend against a dangerous attack. To use modern language, it is a defensive sport used in case of last necessity!

These defensive arts were introduced only a few decades ago in Europe through the Japanese defensive arts of judo and jiu-jitsu. The incredible thing is that they were described by a German who lived 400 years ago, and by a German artist who has been regarded until now as a poet and painter of Madonnas.

This discovery in a Viennese storage room thus had a doubly positive consequence: Albrecht Dürer was found to be a sturdy fellow living among the community of his time, and our 'recent' art of defence was revealed to be an old German-German sport that does not concern the 'vulgum pecus' because it teaches important things.

THE OLD GERMAN ART OF DEFENCE ACCORDING TO ALBRECHT DÜRER'S MANUAL

N°19

Albrecht Dürer writes: If someone has grabbed you, turned around and grabbed you on the shoulder, then bend forward strongly, grab him with your left hand behind the leg and lift him up as shown in the drawing. Throw him face down or kick him with your knees.

N°20

Dürer writes: When you wrestle with someone, throw your right hand violently and throw yourself at him, putting your arm at his right elbow. Grab his arm strongly with both hands and pull him to the shoulder joint, turn your left side against his right side in the manner here indicated and break his arm.

N°21

Dürer describes this grip as follows: If you want to wrestle with someone who is very strong, grasp him boldly as if you wanted to wrestle with him with all your strength. But when he puts pressure on you with his strength, place your foot on his stomach, let yourself fall on your back and throw him over you, holding him firmly by the hands. He will then fall face down on the ground.

This is what Dürer's fencing book teaches us. But Dürer also confirms that the physically healthy people are the holders of a good race and pure blood, even if professions and vocations lead in another direction, into the realm of the spirit and art. Man is not only what his profession makes him— he must seek to become what the race and the people have passed on to him and what the race, the clan and the people demand of him.

SS Booklet No. 2. 1939.

The work of the Brothers Grimm

"The children's stories and legends of the Grimm brothers"—a magic formula for every German whose childhood links the first pure notions of storytelling and experience to this name.

In the various regions of our homeland and everywhere in the vast world where a man of our blood and language lives, the name of the Brothers Grimm is respected, and the book of tales that expresses the nostalgia and dreams of the German soul is generally regarded as a national work. It is characteristic and at the same time significant that "their international fame and the interest of many generations are not linked to the mere artistic or intellectual product but to the love put into the meticulous collection and preservation of a discrete and almost despised, anonymous folk heritage". For the work of the brothers Jacob and Wilhelm Grimm is more than just a fervent compilation of old German folk tales: with bee-like diligence, *they* went in search of the forgotten, largely neglected treasures of folk tales and legends, children's games, folk songs, beliefs and national law, because they saw in them the living, rigorous evidence of a vanished world. These forms, which came into being centuries ago, are pure products of German folk culture and art, and are for them the authentic sources of the history of this people, but above all they bear witness to the evolution of our beloved German mother tongue.

Jacob Grimm was born on 4 January 1785, and a year later, on 24 February 1786, Wilhelm Grimm in Hanau. In a speech he gave shortly after Wilhelm's death in 1859, Jacob spoke of the close, faithful, fervent and fertile understanding between the two brothers, which ended with the death of one of them: "After the school years, we moved into a small room with a bed, often working at the same table. Then, still with two work tables, we lived in two rooms side by side, faithfully sharing our possessions and books, except only when we had to have the same work on hand, which was therefore in duplicate. Surely our beds for the last journey will also be next to each other. Four years later this melancholy wish was also fulfilled.

The two brothers devoted themselves at first to the study of law, out of respect for their father who had practised that profession. Savigny was their professor of law in Marburg, and in 1805 Jacob collaborated in the great task of *writing the history of Roman law* that Savigny had previously dealt with. Jacob Grimm himself tells of his interest in studying Roman law: 'I studied law at a time when the monotonous grey of opprobrium and humiliation hung heavily over the German sky. For all its richness, Roman law left a noticeable gap in my expectations and I regretted that German law was not taught as much as I would have liked. The richness that it (Roman law) contained was not stimulating and attractive enough to teach me. So I sought compensation and consolation in the history of German literature and language. The fact that simple but unalterable things contained qualities and wisdom that our consciousness could rediscover was an invincible weapon that protected us from enemy pride. Abandoning grammar and its poor fruits, I studied in depth the *poetry, legends and customs of the country;* they could only lead me to the *national law!* All things are linked by visible or invisible threads that enable us either to explain them or to understand them. *The antiquity of law and religion* is still impregnated with the vestiges of paganism; the *language* has an even more pronounced pagan aspect which cannot be understood without its intermediary. From these lines, we can already perceive what the Grimm brothers' objective was and also the essential feature of their working method.

In 1812, the first volume of the "Children's Stories" was published, which the Grimm brothers had compiled during thirteen years of research into oral transmissions from the Main and Kinzig regions, the former county of Hanau. The second volume was published in 1815 and contained all the regional stories from Hesse. The researchers did not originally set out to transcribe heartfelt discussions in order to make them understandable to adults and children. Their intention was higher and was indeed to make the soul of the folk tales and legends still alive but threatening to die out, in order to perceive the laws governing the evolution of our people.

In fact, today's national ethnology no longer takes into account Wilhelm Grimm's opinion that in fairy tales (in which he also classified sagas, jokes, animal stories and legends in 1812 and 1815) "perceptible original German myths, which were thought to be dead but which still survive in this form". As science has shown, the storytelling that has been handed down to our German people for centuries is "surely a remnant of what they have created or inherited from their Germanic or Indo-Germanic past. The German story heritage is a collection of stories from which—especially during the crusades in the early Middle Ages—stories from all over the world have been added" (Friedrich Ranke). And yet! "Even though they have come to us from abroad at all times, they have long since lost their foreign character in Germany: our people have assimilated them over the centuries by means of multiple transmissions and have adapted them to their own way of seeing and understanding. For when we said earlier that the same tales are passed on among the most different peoples, the psychologist knows that a German tale is different from a French, Russian or even Turkish tale. *Each people has its own way of telling legends.* But even taking into account this readjustment of science and its scale of values, the work done by the Grimm brothers to collect tales and legends retains a value of unprecedented importance for the future.

The tales in the first volume (from 1812) come mainly from oral traditions in the Hessian homeland of the Grimm brothers. Their storytellers were members of the bourgeoisie—for example, a tale from Dortchen Wild: "The Clever People" and from Marie (Müller) of the Wildschen household: "Little Red Riding Hood", "The Frog King", "Little Brother and Little Sister", "Snow White", "Sleeping Beauty", "Tom Thumb", "The Girl without Hands", "The Thief Bridegroom", "The Undine in the Pond", "The Golden Bird" (Wilhelm Schoof). However, in the second volume (from 1815) we meet for the first time an "authentic" village storyteller, the lady "Viehmannin" from Zwehren near Cassel. In the preface to his "Children's Stories" Wilhelm Grimm says of her: "But it was one of those fortunate coincidences that we met a peasant woman in the village of Niederzwehrn near Kassel who told us most of the stories in the second volume, and also the most beautiful ones. She remembered the old legends and said herself that this was not everyone's lot. She spoke in a calm, confident tone, using alert language, and clearly enjoyed it. At first she let her spontaneity speak for itself and then, when asked, she repeated more slowly, so that with a little practice it was possible to write under her dictation. Many stories were thus preserved literally and lost none of their authenticity. Among the nineteen tales quoted by the "Viehmannin" are some of the best known and most beautiful of the whole, e.g. "The Faithful John", "The Twelve Brothers", "The Devil with Three Golden Hairs", "The

Six Who Can Do Anything", "The Goose Keeper", "The All-Knowing Doctor", "The Devil's Brother Covered in Soot", "Hans, My Hedgehog".

The Grimm brothers worked on their memoirs with constant attention. "In the way in which we have proceeded to assemble these tales, we have been guided above all by the criteria of fidelity and truth. We have not added anything of our own invention, nor have we embellished any circumstance or feature of the legend; we have merely reproduced its content as it was communicated to us. It is quite evident that the style and treatment of details are due for the most part to our intervention, but we have endeavoured to preserve every detail encountered in order to retain the natural richness of the story. The tales in the simple edition were transcribed in an ever more intuitive, simpler way. The tales in the simple edition were always transcribed in a more intuitive, simpler way, but they reflected the soul of the people because the Grimm brothers were the holders of a national knowledge.

At the time of the Hessian Wars of Independence, the Napoleonic legal code became the absolute standard, which meant that the jurisprudence no longer had any connection with traditional legal practice. This alien change in legal life led the Grimm brothers to abandon their legal career for good and to turn all the more enthusiastically to the study of the ancient wisdom that still harboured national folk values. Jacob Grimm wrote *The Antiquity of German Law*, distancing himself from the usual bookish erudition, taking an interest in all that is noble and great, and understanding the organic relationships of Germanic law. He showed that poetry is present in law, he considered the 'marvellous' and the 'trustworthy' as its foundations.

While Jacob's work concerned the study of law, Wilhelm's energy was devoted to the collection and selection of stories and legends; but the mission of both brothers was *to explore the German language*. In the context of a single article, it is impossible to evaluate their brilliant and tireless work in this field. Let us just mention that their main result was the "German grammar", "in which the whole culture of the people and its age-old development in all its various manifestations", and the "German dictionary", which is still being worked on today. However, the German language alone was not something inanimate governed by dead theories and rules, but a "living nature in which the subtlest movements and vibrations of the historical and moral German folk life of past centuries are imprinted". Jacob Grimm also interrogated language in his 'German mythology'. The names of the days of the week, plants, animals, mountains, places, sayings and legends as well as customs and superstitions—but above all on a grammatical level— were the carriers of the mythology of the German people. What Nordic poetry has preserved as a treasure trove of knowledge about Germanic religion was brought together with some beautiful finds from German literature and legends to create "mythology".

Jacob Grimm thus became the father of those sciences that we now call "Germanistics", "national ethnology". They were also a shining example: The Grimm brothers belonged to the fearless and loyal "Göttingen Seven", i.e. those university professors who courageously opposed the reactionary constitutional action of the King of Hannover.

"All Germans are free and German soil does not tolerate slavery" (Jacob Grimm).

Will Erich Peuckert has perfectly defined the importance of the Grimm brothers for us Germans of the 20th century: "In a silent era—and a hundred years before ours—they were the first to speak of the German people. They depicted the past greatness of this people and saw the present greatness that called for the liberation of the country. They did not impose anything. For the first time, they rediscovered the beauty of the things produced by the old times. *The Germany of the future is the Germany of the Brothers Grimm!*

Walther Ohlgart

SS NOTEBOOK NO. 11A/B.1941.

THE WEDDING OF PRINCE BISMARCK

The 'Iron Chancellor' is also an example here

They don't see what this woman has done to me.

Otto von Bismarck

Bismarck symbolises for us all the "Iron Chancellor". Iron in his work, iron in his determination, iron in his actions, he was above all iron in his belief in the Reich.

We know so much about this great man, but so little about his intimate personality.

Bismarck built his life around one axis, perhaps the most unexpected one, which allowed us to judge his actions: his marriage!

Bismarck himself wrote to his young wife Johanna: 'I married you to love you in God, out of emotional need and so that my heart could find a place in this foreign world. I find in you the warmth of a fireplace, by which I stand when it blows and freezes outside. I want to tend my fireplace, put wood in it, blow on the fire and protect it from evil people and strangers, for there are no things nearer, dearer, more pleasing and more necessary to me, after the mercy of God, than your love and the home of my birth." With these words worthy of a great poet, Bismarck shows that his genial nature was looking for its authentically feminine complement.

Our Führer and the Reichsführer SS taught us to think racially. Not only on a political level, but also in our personal life, in the choice of marriage. In this context, studying the nature of Bismarckian marriage is typical and enlightening for us.

What are the reasons that contributed to the happiness of this marriage, to its harmony, its stability, which triumphed over all the trials?

Bismarck and Johanna both came from the same class—the Prussian nobility. Their way of life was a perfect match. Although their lives took a great turn as a result of his political activity, they always remained what they were: simple, natural people from their rural homeland, living in an environment slightly tinged with courtly manners. Even when he was Chancellor, Bismarck preferred to speak Low German whenever he felt himself among the people in his circle. Adolf Willbrandt testified during a visit to the Friedrichsruhr estate: "Everything here is wonderfully Prussian. Nothing ostentatious, nothing overdone. And another, a man of the court, complained with a sigh: "The Bismarcks will never get rid of the look of provincial noblemen of small fortune!"

It is admirable how well Johanna adapted to her husband's changing circumstances. When Bismarck became Minister and Prussian representative in Frankfurt in 1851, she was confronted with these needs for the first time. While still staying with his children at his parents' home, he warned Johanna of her future duties in letters. "My poor child will now have to sit rigidly and respectably in the drawing room, say "excellence", be wise and wise with the excellences. Johanna was at first disconcerted by these obligations. However, her natural adaptability as a loving woman came to the fore again. However, there was another question that was more difficult to resolve than the external attitude. Bismarck knew his wife's horror of the French and how difficult it was for her to learn the languages. But he had to beg her to learn French. The warmth of his nature is expressed in the form his attempt took: "In the first place, you are my wife and not that of other diplomats who can learn German as well as you can learn French. Only, if you have leisure time or want to read, take a French novel. But if you find no pleasure in it, forget it. Could Johanna refuse such an affectionate request?

"MY HUSBAND IS CERTAINLY IN BOHEMIA ... BUT..."

Here's another typical anecdote: In Petersburg, Bismarck was telling a story and, as in his speeches to parliament, he made a deliberate pause.

Johanna, who was always on call, was worried. In the morning, her husband had suffered from foot pain and she thought that the pause was due to this. "But, Otto, why are you wearing your patent leather boots, we are in private! Bismarck realised that Johanna had not understood him. However, his face lit up with a serene glow. Calmly he said: "You are right, my love, other shoes would have been better. And he continued. When you think of those arguments between spouses that are provoked by biting words or allusions, it shows the great inner unity of the couple.

Johanna became more and more accustomed to the role that fate had given her: to be the wife of the great statesman, to have no ambitions of her own, but to do everything in keeping with his greatness. Bismarck enjoyed the serene family life, he loved the sociability of his small circle more than anything. Johanna also enjoyed it very much, but her activity only extended to purely domestic duties. She had to keep a firm grip on the household and all that depended on it. Thus, despite her modesty, she thought of nothing else but social life with Bismarck.

Thanks to these natural qualities, the man and the woman complemented each other both in their marriage and in their personalities. Bismarck's great foresight, his dignity, his penchant for independence went hand in hand with the kindness and love of his wife. The freshness and frankness of his nature, his total lack of sentimentality, were a compensation for him, the strong man, for he had so often to suffer from sentimental weakness, and as he said, found himself immersed in a "sea of tears". Thus, during the war years, the Prime Minister's wife, the 'manless' and extremely delicate woman, was never weak. A touching adventure is proof of this: One evening she sat alone on a bench in the garden. One evening she sat alone on a bench in the garden and suddenly saw a dark-looking man jumping over the wall of the park. Shortly afterwards she resolutely grabbed a spade from the flower bed and put the intruder to flight with this raised "weapon", saying: "My husband is certainly in Bohemia, but...". A real woman has no reason to be afraid.

THE DEEPEST LINK:
BISMARCK'S CHILDREN

But one of the strongest feelings that united the couple was the love for their children. The relationship with the three children, Maria, Herbert and Wilhelm, was purely affectionate, especially as they grew up. Bismarck himself, who, following the premature death of his mother, had had a sad childhood and a boarding school education, held the view that his children never received enough love and affection. So, from the beginning, he decided to adopt a tone of camaraderie rather than authority. He could think of no greater joy than to make his oldest son his collaborator. Johanna was exhausted in her motherhood. She saw in her children the meaning of her life and work, in whom she rediscovered the nature of her husband. Her natural maternal strength was so strong that she easily overcame the hardest physical strain of a child. Her daughter Maria was her "most sincere friend" and her joy when she married was seriously tarnished when Maria moved to Italy.

The two spouses only felt particularly comfortable when the whole family gathered around them. They suffered all the more from the obligatory separations in their midst. The children therefore became the strongest natural bond. In his private life, the Grand Chancellor was a caring and exemplary father. He always felt the separations in his family very cruelly. He wrote moving letters to his family between sessions of Parliament, between important reports and on the battlefield. When, during the military campaign of 1870n1, she nursed one of her wounded sons, a visitor described it as follows: 'Countess Bismarck spoke as the wives of the gods might speak when the war horn sounded against the enemy; by her son's bed she seemed to me to embody the old legend: Kriemhild on the field of her heroes.

But in this context one of their relationships could not be ignored: that with God and religion. Bismarck had a deep and natural faith, but he had little interest in the Church and its function. Johanna, on the other hand, came from a very religious family. So Bismarck began to lead his future wife in his direction as soon as he became engaged. He did this with humour, knowledge and skill, never forgetting to respect her faith and never offending her piety. He really did 'diplomatically' comfort her with the feeling that she had transformed him, the extravagant and carefree junker, when in reality he was educating her according to her wishes.

There was a constant exchange between them throughout their lives. Their moral instincts were expressed in a harmonious lifestyle because of their common origin. This is one of the causes of the "happiness" of this marriage. On the other hand, their spiritual and psychic qualities complemented each other so much, in small as well as in big things, that they achieved perfect harmony *with each other* without knowing it.

Bismarck felt it perfectly.

SS Notebook No. 7. 1943.

"Everything has an order".

On the work and life of the physician and mystic Paracelsus

Paracelsus was one of the most ardent and genial guides of the German people, and that is why he moves us so much. He followed his destiny, experiencing in turn vicissitudes and greatness, joy and sorrow, affront, defamation and misery, but also power and fame. However, he remained solitary. Nowhere could he find a home, beginning to travel at an early age and thus fulfilling his destiny.

As a wanderer, he travels the world and almost all of Europe, searching with a valiant heart for the last secrets of nature. He relies on the advice of the simple folk: he spies on the knowledge of the forest peasant, the coalman and the old woman. He sits with the shepherds and the bonesetter who teach him so much. He works out his ideas in the storm and hail. He crossed the German countryside in rain and snow, a restless traveller accompanied only by his art, medicine. But this was both his fate and his mission. Only in death did this "country traveller and wanderer", as he called himself, find rest. He died in 1541 in Salzburg at the age of 48, far too early. The common people did not want to come to terms with the fact that this great physician was no longer alive, that they could no longer come to him for help in their distress and illness. However, his thoughts and ideas have survived the centuries and are now more alive than ever.

The knowledge acquired by Paracelsus, the Swabian physician and mystic, is manifold. His decisive principle is that only nature can provide an answer to the many questions of the human heart. He despised the petty bourgeois and the 'infatuated doctors' who sought their wisdom in books covered by the dust of the centuries. "Creatures are like letters, and he who wishes to explore nature must read his books while walking. One studies writing through the alphabet, but nature from region to region. His clear eyes are his most powerful weapons.

Paracelsus broke with the old methods of science. His approach to natural science was completely new. Until then, God had been the origin of all creations; now it was nature and, with it, man. He is full of respect for the latter, which is the holding power of all life. It manifested itself everywhere to him in the form of measure, order and law, and he discovered that the same divine power lives and acts in the stones of the stream as in the stars of the sky, in the plant of the meadow as in man. But man is nothing other than the world in a smaller form, the microcosm. He is therefore also subject to the same divine and eternal laws as nature. The same laws that govern the course of the stars, that make plants grow and animals struggle for life, also govern man. Every man is therefore subject to the inexorable analogies and laws of life. Human and natural laws are identical. But he who deviates from these eternal rules of life perishes, as the tree that man uproots perishes. Often Paracelsus, full of pain and hope, looked to the stars for answers to his questions. The greatness and eternity of God are so clearly expressed in them, lonely travellers far from all humanity. He feels bound to the stars by fate. For the microcosmic man, the destiny of the worlds also becomes his own. The laws of the universe become the laws of the ego.

This new attitude towards nature and the cosmos also conditions his relationship with religion and God. Life is full of surprises for the mind. Everything is in motion, everything is an eternal change because everything is alive. But life is the creative activity of God. So the world is God's great gift, and this earth is also animated by God. He worships his Creator in the beauty and splendour of nature. He performs the divine service by understanding its deeper meaning through this fidelity to nature. Nature expresses itself in a sacred way and with it man. For Paracelsus nature is the absolute and profound rule. The law that God has placed in nature, he has also placed in man, and he who lives according to these natural laws lives morally. Thus, to be faithful is a sacred requirement and duty for us. It means understanding the richness of one's inner essence. "He who remains faithful to himself does not fail. This is the great moral law that Paracelsus gave us. He had the instinctive certainty that the voice of the heart is that of God. He felt himself inscribed in the universe, in God and at one with nature.

In essence, Paracelsus experienced his worldview as a heroic and positive outburst of the divine reality that he carried within him, which is present in nature and even in the whole world. God is not only the creator of the world, he is also the origin of the essence of the world, the power that breathes life and structure. "All things have order. The world is therefore good, as is man, and "we come forth pure and chaste from the mother's body. The earth does not deserve to be despised, precisely because everything is divine. He is therefore constantly in sharp opposition to the Christianity of his time.

Paracelsus follows the laws of life, but he also recognises that the struggle reflects the selfishness of life that is everywhere. That which opposes life does not deserve to live and must be constantly eliminated. He therefore launched an assault on weakness and decadence. He was the first to challenge the Christian disregard for the body, and was already drawing attention to the danger of hereditary diseases.

But in what does the meaning of life lie for Paracelsus, and what is the vocation of man? No one is exempt from work, no one is ennobled by idleness." "The hands were created for work, not for blessing." He therefore disapproves of priests and monks. "They preach for money, they fast for money." "The house of prayer is in the hearts." He wants productive work to be done in the service of the people and the state. Paracelsus sees work as the meaning of life and seeks a concrete socialism, not empty words.

Paracelsus was interested in almost all areas of human life. He called for the establishment of a law rooted in the people and derived from the living order.

He took a stand against celibacy in strong and harsh terms. Marriage is also a natural law; it is also part of the divine order of the world. "The fruit of your body is blessed, not your virginity. Marriage allows the community's wish to be fulfilled. We must bow with respect to motherhood.

He stood up to Judaism, knowing full well that an alien culture and spirit are harmful to the people, claiming that only the connection to the land is fertile. But what is the homeland of the Jew?

What helped Paracelsus to make his great medical discoveries was the realisation of the close and special relationship between man and nature and the cosmos. The vital rhythm of the universe and that of man follow the same course. Like nature, man also has seasonal rhythms, he also has his seasons in the literal sense of the word. Therefore, each disease must be treated for itself because it has a unique character. The great physician refused any generalisation in the treatment of patients. The psychic forces, the human relationship between doctor and patient and the will to recover have a decisive influence. The knowledge of the disease and the type of treatment are closely related not only to the structure of the body, to its form and appearance, but also to the environment—and not only the earthly environment, but also the cosmic environment—in which the patient lives. Paracelsus went so far as to seek the origin of disease in the spiritual-psychic character. But love had become for him the best way to communicate with the patient and thus to heal him.

Paracelsus remained a loner until his death. He always believed that petty minds could be overcome by generosity and benevolence, but this was only a belief. Silently he held his sorrow inside. He surrendered to his fate willingly and humbly. Yes, he loved it because he was in harmony with the laws of life, for birth and death also form the great natural law to which man is subject. He was in harmony with the eternal cosmic order, wanting all beings to have their harvest and their autumn. Man takes leave of life only when his work is done. "Nothing dies until it bears fruit. This was his conviction.

And yet, although his life was one of loneliness, struggle and hope, Paracelsus loved life with all the strength of his great heart. He was in the heart of life. He recognised himself in this beautiful, flourishing land, and accepted it despite all the hardships.

Paracelsus too was a son of his time—he could not free himself from the many superstitions. He also integrated magic and cabbala, astrology and alchemy into his great orderly system. Paracelsus was always whole, even in his contradictions. He lived and suffered for his science and with the people of his century.

He was not a spectator of his time; he was a fighter and a creator, and he was German. Here too he was whole and direct. He was the first professor to teach in German in 1525 at a university. He proudly confessed: "I am a German philosopher with a German mind. But his profession of faith was not only German, but also the Faustian inclination towards truth, the deep thirst for knowledge of the world, the desire and aspiration to understand the infinite and the passion with which he explores the depths of being. His life and work were German, German was the insatiable spirit that travelled constantly to gather new experiences, German was his fighting attitude. He was one of those who sail in the storm and are disturbed by the calm.

The driving forces behind his fertile creation were respect for the eternal laws of life, love of nature and of man.

When Paracelsus has been forgotten for a very long time, we will wonder why this solitary 'preacher of existence' led a rich and nostalgic life of constant struggle. We are left with his call to remain true to oneself and to recognise the truth of the natural order. This knowledge is best expressed in his words: "Everything has an order.

Friedrich Oesterle

Thoughts of Paracelsus

Is there any greater joy than to feel oneself living in harmony with the knowledge of nature? Is there any other misfortune than an intrusion against the natural order? We have our place in nature.

Hippocrates gave two examples that allow us to understand what disharmonies are, namely: too much and too little, exceeding nature by too much or exceeding nature by less. This is not good, because one must keep measure in everything; emptiness must be equivalent to abundance. When the balance is broken, nature is harmed, and it will not tolerate it. For when we consider nature as it is in its essence, then we must order all things, in number, weight, measure, circumference etc., and nothing outside of that, neither less nor more. Everything is vain if we do not take this into account.

Happy and more is the one who has the right measure and does not need the help of men but follows the path that God shows him.

The history of humanity is the history of a few men.
The others had no more part in it than the fish in the sea.

René Quinton

SS NOTEBOOK NO. 5. 1942.

NIETZSCHE, THE PROPHET

Born in Röcken, near Leipzig, on 15 October 1844, Friedrich Nietzsche belonged to that generation for whom the outbreak of the wars of independence was now only a childhood memory. But the death of his father drove the five-year-old boy from the village rectory to the city, and the fourteen-year-old from the home of his mother and sister to the circle of friends at the village school in Pforta. His university years were spent mainly in the cultural environment of Leipzig and in the circle of friends there. At the age of twenty-four, he was accepted as a professor of classical philology at the University of Basel, and thus Switzerland became his professional home for ten years. He was only able to take part in the Franco-Prussian War as a volunteer nurse, especially as a wound had prematurely ended his first year of service.

In the midst of the competitive spirit and the valorisation of industrial success by his contemporaries, the twenty-eight-year-old began to fight ruthlessly for the right to life of the German soul for fifteen years in increasing solitude. After ten years, the common front of the backward bourgeoisie and liberal materialism, opposed to his doctrine of the proud and dangerous life, finally overcame his physical resistance. In the Alps and in Italy, the solitary man meditated, in constant struggle with the pain that triumphed in 1889. On August 25, 1900, he was released after years of insanity, cared for by his mother and sister.

A stranger in a century that he disowned, an enemy of those around him who disliked him because they saw his lack of value and expressed it bluntly, Nietzsche lived the life of a voluntary outlaw, scanning the horizon in search of better times in the isolation of the high mountains. From the rocks of the Engadine, where he had retreated, he watched with concern the hurricane of civilisation, democracy and material conquests in which Europe was threatening to sink. What his contemporaries took to be perpetual expansion, he discerned in it a growing decadence beginning to dissolve all noble existences into the most harmful materialism. Closer to the stars than to the hustle and bustle of the city, the inhabitant of Sils Maria turned his visionary gaze towards a future with a higher type of man, towards an age dominated by a new ideal and new values, which could only be achieved by a voluntary detachment from the excesses of the 19th century. Nietzsche saw the most fatal sign in the general lack of motivation, in the increasing slackness, in the inertia of soul, mind and will, in the gregarious happiness of bourgeois ease.

"I welcome all the signs of the beginning of a virile and warlike age which will restore the honour of bravery! For it must pave the way for an even greater age and reap the strength it will need—that age which expresses heroism and incites to war by its warrior ideal and logic. Men who, silently, solitarily, resolutely, understand that they must accomplish themselves by working quietly. Men who, by nature, aspire to everything that constitutes a test. Men who animate with their spirit the festivals, the work and the days of mourning, being solid leaders and ready when necessary to obey, proudly in one case as in the other, equal to themselves: dangerous, productive, happy men. Because, believe me! The secret of a truly rich and profitable life is to live dangerously!

A critic and prophet at the same time, Nietzsche shows the threatening decadence to his contemporaries seized by the intoxication of progress, but at the same time he rebukes the pessimists who desperately allow themselves to believe in decline, because of their overwhelmed resignation, while he presents them with his brightly coloured vision of the future. We are not the victims of an inevitable fate, but only the will decides on recovery or decline. "To want is to liberate, for to want is to create. The creation of a great culture and the realisation of the aspirations of mankind are the mission of the Germans. Towards this goal, our endeavour must be "to restore the supreme unity between the nature and soul of our people. It is this German unity that we are striving for, even more ardently than political reunification: the unity of the German spirit and life." Nietzsche noted the gaps in Bismarck's work. The inner unity of the people, the harmony between their thoughts and deeds, had to be found again. "Form in yourselves an image that corresponds to the future and no longer be superstitious beings, epigones." Nietzsche spoke the decisive word. He invites people to get rid of fear, since they are only epigones, weak descendants of a great past that darkens the whole future because it is an unattainable example. It is not as epigones whose existence serves as a measure, but as precursors whose greatness is yet to come, that we must live. To begin a new age, an age of greatness and sovereignty, without looking back to the past, is courage. For this, Nietzsche favours courage as the source of all virtues.

"Courage and adventure, the desire for the uncertain, for risk,—courage seems to me to be the prehistory of man. War is also endorsed by Nietzsche. "War and courage have done greater things than love of neighbour. It was not your compassion, but your bravery that saved the victims. What is good? you ask. Being brave is good... You must go out to meet your enemies, you must fight your war for your ideas! So live your life in obedience and war! What does a long life matter! What warrior wants to be spared? I do not spare you. I love you dearly, my brothers in war!

The leader goes to the head of his warriors in a heroic renunciation, sacrificed to himself. "What does it matter what the lord, the prince, the individualist sacrifices? It is not the danger but what we strive for that must unite us as a warrior people fighting to the death for its ideal. "We must have a goal, and through it we love each other! All other goals are good only to be abandoned! The soldier spirit must penetrate all the working classes, all the professions, for it is this spirit which abolishes class differences and bases political action on attitude. "Workers must learn to feel things like soldiers. A fee, a salary, but no reward. No relation between payment and result! But only value the individual according to what he can achieve most in his field. One day the workers will live like the bourgeois; but above them, signalled by their lack of need; the upper caste: therefore poorer and simpler, but holders of power."

Nietzsche presents himself as the messenger of life with an enthusiasm for everything that makes man worthy of living, that makes him strong and proud, that is, that makes him aristocratic. In the hands of nature, war is a means of preserving the aristocratic vital order.

"A society which ultimately refuses both its instinct for war and conquest is in decadence: it is ripe for democracy and shopkeeper power. For this reason, too, he had a fanatical aversion to the democracy expressed in Western European parliamentarianism. "European democracy is not an unleashing of forces. It is above all an outburst of laziness, fatigue, weakness. Democracy has always been the decadent form of organising force. Nietzsche expresses the purpose of existence in this way: Man does not seek his own happiness at all—he wants something totally different. "One can only be an Englishman to believe that man is always seeking an advantage. It is not liberalism—German mass dumbing down as Nietzsche said—but war that makes man free. "For what is freedom?

It is to have the will to be responsible. That we maintain the distance that separates us. That we become indifferent to the fatigue, the harshness, the very deprivation of life. That one is ready to sacrifice men to one's ideal, including oneself. Freedom means that the virile, warlike and victorious instincts have supremacy over other instincts, for example, the instinct to seek happiness. The man who has become free, and even more so the spirit who has become free, tramples on the contemptible kind dreamed of by shopkeepers, Christians, sheep, women, Englishmen and other democrats. The free man is a warrior. By what is freedom measured in individuals as well as in peoples? By the test that must be overcome, by the effort required to stay ahead. One must look for the superior type of the free man where the greatest challenge is presented. Nietzsche talks about philosophy like no other thinker before him, and he knows why. He says prophetically in one of his last aphorisms: "The present war has turned into a war of ideologies. Our superiority is not only based on German weapons, it is also based on the German spirit.

Claus Schrempf

SS NOTEBOOK NO. 3. 1942.

RICHARD WAGNER

The Führer's relationship with the Grand Master

It is no accident or whim that, of all the great masters of German music, Hitler had a special respect and admiration for Richard Wagner. He also had a prince-like regard for the German cultural jewel of Bayreuth. The Master was deprived of it during his lifetime by the rulers of the German Reich under Prussian rule at the time.

From the very beginning, the members of the Bayreuth Master's family have shown the deepest understanding and the most faithful hope.

The Grimm brothers were able to revive the spirit of the old legends of our ancestors. "Tale", woodcut by Switbert Zobisser.

In an open letter dated January 1, 1924, in the darkest of times, Richard Wagner's son-in-law, H.-St. Chamberlain, the husband of his recently deceased youngest daughter Eva, praised Adolf Hitler's personality and work in a most prophetic way and to the great comfort of thousands of Germans. He relied on the strong kinship of the great men, Wagner and Hitler, when he said in this letter that the heart is the focus of the enthusiasm that forges Hitler's thoughts, and that the German leader loves his people with an ardent passion. Wagner, too, loved the German people passionately and asked for nothing more than his "sincere love" for what he was giving them. He was rewarded in return, but perhaps not in such an extreme and overwhelming way as the Führer. The people could only thank him with his constant and passionate love.

Meeting of two great artists: Richard Wagner by Arno Breker.

But the fact that the Führer remembers the sympathy and loyalty shown by the House of Wahnfried long before 1933 does not yet explain his passion and respect for the Master of Bayreuth: in the same way that he maintains Bayreuth, the Führer wants to enable thousands of his countrymen to enjoy humanity's greatest cultural assets not by paying large sums of money, but free of charge, as Richard Wagner wished to do from the very beginning. In this way, Adolf Hitler is also paying off this old debt to the Master of German music; for none of the great German composers was so obviously concerned about Germany. None fought so tirelessly with his works throughout his life for the dominance of Germany, and none saw so clearly and plainly as Richard Wagner "where the real enemies of Germanness are hiding".

The Führer knows that the magnificent and profound art of Richard Wagner means above all for the visitor to the Bayreuth Festival an enhancement of dynamism, an elevation of vitality necessary to him and providing a joy of living, an "entertainment of existence always based on the beautiful illustrations of the ideal forces of human nature". The Führer was a faithful and enthusiastic visitor to the Bayreuth Festival, admiring the purity and freedom of this ideal art. In the third year of this terrible struggle for the freedom of Germany and the whole world, the great solemn art of Richard Wagner fills thousands of people with creative hope, that son of eternal love which gives strength to struggling men.

One can compare the eventful experience of the first performance of Lohengrin attended by the twelve-year-old Adolf Hitler in Linz with the day when the Chancellor, now the leader of all Germans, raises his protective hand over the work of the Bayreuth Master! The description in *Mein Kampf* shows the impact that this performance of Lohengrin had on Hitler. The Führer recalls the glowing evocations in these words: "I was bewitched by this song. My youthful enthusiasm for the Bayreuth master knew no bounds. His works were the absolute reference for me, and I consider it a special opportunity to have been able to sustain a growing passion because of the simplicity of the local representation. The action of mysterious forces can be seen when we think of the prediction made to King Heinrich and put into the mouth of Lohengrin by the poet Richard Wagner:

"To you, the Pure, a great victory is granted. To Germany in the distant days the Eastern troops shall never go victorious.

Now our difficult times profess this grandiose confession: *The mighty fighter* who as a child kept these verses in his heart will walk this planet as long as it exists!

Hans Gansser

SS BOOKLET NO. 7. 1938.

GUSTAVE KOSSINNA

The old master of German prehistoric research

German prehistory, viewed from the point of view of race, forms the keystone of our National Socialist ideology today, and we have a duty to know the cultural level reached by our Germanic ancestors. We learn about our racial past not only in all schools, but also through the education of all our citizens by the Party and its organisations. While other nations have long been teaching their young people about their most ancient past, under the influence of a "one-sided humanistic cultural ideal", a preference has developed in Germany for the study of foreign peoples and cultures, especially the classical cultures of the Mediterranean countries. This narrow view has led our textbooks to neglect our own past!

The culture of the ancient Egyptians, Greeks and Romans is given pride of place, and our Germanic past is presented as that of a crude and barbaric civilisation. The Germans were only liberated from their barbarism and brought to a higher level of civilisation through contact with the currents coming from the south; this was particularly marked in the west of our homeland at the time of the Roman conquest and domination.

While considerable resources were spent every year on the study of foreign cultures, only very modest budgets were available for the study of German prehistory. This sheds light on the meaning of the words left to us by a poet: "In Rome and among the Lapps they dig in every corner, while we grope our way through the house of our own fathers.

We are solely indebted to Gustav Kossinna, the old master of German prehistory, for the fact that a turning point has been reached in this respect and that the true value of our past has been brought to light. Kossinna taught us: "We would be nothing like we are today if we did not have the immense heritage of our ancestors.

Gustav Kossinna was born on 28 September 1858 in Tilsitt in the East German March. Like his ancestors, who also came from East Prussia, he kept deep roots in his homeland all his life. His love for his homeland is constantly evident in a series of major works that he dedicated exclusively to it. His parents were strictly conservative; hence his strong nationalistic feeling from his early youth.

From 1876 to 1881 he devoted himself to philology in Göttingen, Leipzig and Strasbourg and later, more generally, to the study of German antiquity.

In Berlin, his teacher, the famous Müllenhoff, had a decisive influence on him and steered his studies in a new direction. Working on the basis of his master's research, Kossinna soon realised that linguistic science had much less to contribute to sociology, anthropology and the history of German colonisation than the exploration of the concrete cultural heritage of its past.

After completing his studies in Strasbourg, he was awarded a doctorate in philology in 1881 and turned to the profession of librarian to earn a quick living. A long career as a librarian took him from Halle to Bonn and Berlin. During all these years he devoted himself ardently to the study of German prehistory, acquiring through innumerable visits to museums all the knowledge necessary to approach the racial questions of antiquity with remarkable ease. We know that he often escaped from the narrow sphere of his profession to devote himself to his scientific research. This is evidenced by the fact that his superiors accused him of abandoning his professional work for his scientific studies.

When he gained notoriety at a meeting of anthropologists in Kassel in 1895 with a treatise on the "Prehistoric Expansion of the Germanic People in Germany", the direction of his future work was well established. In this treatise, which was a milestone in his research career, Kossinna presented his new archaeological settlement method, which was to be the key to understanding the spread of prehistoric tribes.

We must quickly recall the moment when national prehistoric investigation was born, heralding a revolutionary science.

To show the importance of this upheaval, we need to describe the situation of prehistory at that time. It was not represented in higher education and was only an accessory science in all branches. Historians, archaeologists, anthropologists and ethnologists adopted it into their sphere of work. Only many tyrannical local societies were interested in it, and German antiquity had been branded a second-rate science. Only the Anthropological Society, as a large scientific association, made a remarkable effort to study the past. Moreover, the whole of the research was influenced by the spirit of 'Romanism', a one-sided view from the South which left no room for northern insights.

At that time Kossinna's words resounded: "If I dare to relate the archaeology of the homeland to history and consider the lack of report of the rich finds gathered by our present work in the native soil…" words that opened his statement in Cassel and sounded like a revolutionary trumpet announcing a shattering study of national prehistoric research.

The deep love of the ardent and patriotic forerunner of Germanic antiquity is expressed in his conclusion at the time: "The German nationalist character and German civilisation, in its vigorous supremacy, have no need, in order to sustain their future expansion or even for the security of their existence, to refer to titles of ownership from past millennia, as other nations have done not without doing violence to the historical facts. We Germans, and with us all other members of the Germanic families, can only be proud and admire the strength of the little Nordic people, seeing how their sons conquered, in prehistory and antiquity, the whole of Scandinavia and Germany, spread in the Middle Ages throughout Europe and, in our own time, to the most distant parts of the globe."

His use in this treatise of a new research method invented by him was decisive, "the method of archaeological colonisation", which opened the way to new discoveries. He later summarised this method of work in one sentence: "Strictly limited archaeological regions have always corresponded to well-defined peoples or ethnic groups.

Although this new method of investigation met with much hostility, its accuracy became increasingly apparent, so that today it still forms the basis for the study of our prehistory.

After many efforts, in 1902, thanks to the support of many friends who had clearly recognised in Kossinna an outstanding researcher, he was able to obtain the first chair of archaeology at the University of Berlin, where he was able to develop a wide-ranging teaching activity over a period of twenty-three years.

We do not understand that he had to work all his life as a professor, certainly a remarkable one, and that he was never able to obtain a suitable university chair. This can only be explained by the great difficulties he encountered during his career. The strong 'nationalistic' connotation of all his work made him many enemies, but won him many enthusiastic friends. On the other hand, he stood up against a certain 'objective' science by emphasising in all his research the imposing power of races in the past.

Only those who know the obstacles he faced, who realise how this researcher, full of ardent nationalist feeling, one of the greatest of our people, fought for the development of his science, can fully understand his life's work.

It was not only a question of putting an end to the lie about the barbarity of our ancestors, but first of all of exorcising the optics which, under cover of the fetish word "ex oriente lux" (light comes from the East) sought the starting point of any cultural development. Moreover, the proof was there: these oriental cultures had often taken their inspiration from the North. Moreover, this innovative branch had to be freed from the harmful grip of neighbouring disciplines before it could develop.

Kossinna knowingly led this fight to a successful conclusion, a fight in which he found himself alone many times against many opponents. It is understandable that he has made many enemies on all sides. We are astonished to see a single individual, lacking the great means available to his opponents, in the midst of the worst trials of war and national decadence, bring his work to a successful conclusion and, at the same time, found the society for German prehistory that is linked to it.

It was clear to him that, in addition to teaching his students, who would then fight for the true value of their own past, he had to lead an important society that would spread the discoveries made about the German past to the widest popular spheres.

For this reason he founded the "Society of German Prehistory" in 1909, which had the journal Mannus as its press organ. Up to the time of his death, he was able to publish twenty-three volumes of this journal. This society is now the core of the National Socialist "Reichsbund für deutsche Vorgeschichte" (League for German Prehistory).

His opponents have often reproached Kossinna for presenting the Germanic aspect of his findings too one-sidedly and thus for overshooting his goal. To this we must reply that the old master was the first to enable us to appreciate our own culture in the face of foreign European cultures. Germany's awareness of the achievements and accomplishments of its own ancestors can be attributed solely to Kossinna's constant struggle against the old German science routine, which was enthusiastic about the "classical peoples of the South" and incomprehensibly opposed to the "barbarism" of our own ancestors.

His numerous writings, published in journal articles, in his periodical *Mannus* and in his collection, the "Mannus Library", had the most successful effects. The fifty-one volumes of the collection published before the author's death bear eloquent witness to Kossinna's creative spirit.

His books: *German Prehistory, an astonishing national science* (1st ed. in 1912), *The Germanic Golden Age in the Bronze Age* (1913), *The Indo-Germans* (1921), *The High Germanic Civilisation* (1927), *The Rise and Expansion of the Germans* (1928), *The Germanic Culture of the First Century A.D.*

When Kossinna died after a short illness at the age of seventy-three on 20 December 1931, nationalist Germany lost in this remarkable man a pioneer in the exploration of German antiquity who never, even in the darkest days of our homeland, hid his convictions.

His life was poor in honours; his professorship was refused and attempts were often made to silence him. His work was not honoured until shortly before his death, when a large delegation from the University of Berlin, led by the Rector, came to congratulate him on the golden jubilee of his doctorate.

If the value of his work had been recognised earlier and the state had given him the necessary assistance, the discovery of German antiquity could have developed in a completely different framework. We can only thank him for his magnificent work by continuing the work he started in the direction he wanted.

(See also R. StampfuB: *Gustave Kossinna, une vie consacrée à la préhistoire allemande.* Kurt Kabitsch, Leipzig 1935, and the catalogue *L'antiquité vue sous l'optique nationaliste*, published by the same publisher).

II. Geopolitics

SS Troop House No. 3 special. 1940.

SS-Ustuf. Dr Julius Schmidt, Paris: France

When Laval met the Feldmarschall General von Brauchitsch, he made the comparison with General Gamelin; *he then understood, as he says, why France had lost the war.*

Laval thus showed that he had discerned the causes of France's monstrous military and moral collapse: *At the decisive hour, the country did not possess men with a personality and an idea, a well-defined conception of order.*

The French intellect was only ready to accept this truth in the early days of the collapse. Today it is not. At that time, when the German armies were rushing in a victorious race from the Moselle to beyond the Garonne, when in Bordeaux the politicians were feverishly preparing their escape, when the cadets of the cavalry school at Saumur were throwing themselves desperately against the Germans along the Loire, the French intellect, under the pressure of events, was ready to admit the failure of France's human qualities. But now that the roads are again empty of thousands of sweaty refugees, of wandering mothers and children, of horses exhausted on their stretchers, that in Paris one can again drink one's familiar aperitif and that one can again dip one's fishing rod for hours on end in the rivers without being disturbed, one no longer wants to believe it. *We have found the time to study the problem from another angle since life has returned to normal.*

Now we judge events rationally, as befits a Frenchman. If you ask an officer the reasons for the defeat, he answers: we were not motorised enough. If you ask a civilian, he will tell you that the politicians had long since underestimated the fabrications of war. If you ask an intelligent man, he answers: our politicians were *stupid*.

This is the characteristic of current opinion as it stands on the French side. It is believed that on the German side, good equipment and pure intelligence won the day, but it is forgotten that equipment remains a dead thing if it is not used by men of heart, and also that where intellect fails, faith alone can force fate. *If the French had been aware of this truth, they would not be wondering today why their 32-ton tanks, the steel monsters on which the French command had placed its decisive hopes, could not hold back the Arras breakthrough.*

The importance of *French* sentiment and *tradition was* restored. Intellectuals seek new strength in a history glorified by its monuments on the banks of the Seine, but they forget what they could learn from it. Many

Frenchmen today read the names chiselled in stone on the Arc de Triomphe in memory of the army of the great Corsican and make sad comparisons with the present time. *In their comments, however, they forget that this army carried its ideology in its canteens, that Napoleon did not set out on his march across Europe with only his equipment and his new line of fusiliers voltigeurs,* but that his soldiers—one can argue about the following implementation—had faith. They overlook the fact that, for this army, "Long live the Emperor" and "War on the palaces, peace to the cottages" were more than just lip service.

The Frenchman who sketches a portrait of France refuses to accept this evidence. National Socialism is beyond his Cartesian thinking. He does not want to understand that he went into this war without ideas and was overwhelmed by a new ideology.

Against this spiritual background, the announcement of a Franco-German collaboration began. The French accepted this for their own benefit. The people, whose leaders were mainly lawyers and whose politics of the previous years had been marked by the "collective contract", immediately began to think like lawyers: a work contract with precise paragraphs was to be born in the near future. Marshal Pétain recently spoke out against the opinion of his compatriots when he pointed out that the era of lawyers was over and that "collaboration" should be considered as being in the process of development.

Old ideas and chaotic opinions are abandoned in search of a new direction. Groups which base their programme on the National Socialist or Fascist example believe that a national revolution is achieved by uniformity alone. The leaders of these groups come to German offices to receive National Socialist literature and then use it for training purposes. *In their eagerness they forget one thing: revolutions are closely related to the race and type of life of the people.*

Thus there are parties like the "Parti Français National Collectiviste" which have created a "Garde Française", a "Garde Spéciale" and a "Jeune Front" in the spirit of the SA, SS or HJ. There is a "Parti Français National-Socialiste" which has created "Troupes d'Assaut" and a "État-Major". These groups again have in their ranks an opposition which claims to have understood National Socialism in its purest form.

Doriot writes in *Le cri du peuple*. A former communist, he has moved to the nationalist camp. He asserts that, as in the past in Germany, the communists must be converted to nationalism. He adheres to the policy of Marshal Pétain, the "Grand Vieux". It is worth noting how much he would like to draw a parallel between his position and that of the old man on the one hand and the event of 30 January 1933 in Germany on the other.

Powers are proposing to rebuild France, which will hardly play their old role in the coming revolutions. The *royalists* announced their claims and believed they could gain access to the new European order through a

Restoration. They had placed their trusted men in Vichy who were to prepare the ground for the future kingdom of France, for the Count of Paris. The "high society" in the châteaux of the Loire, in the occupied zone, seemed outwardly apolitical. *In reality, the idea of the Restoration was so strong that politicians had to take it into account and did so.*

The Church offered its services, the development of which kept secularism and freemasonry at bay. In Vichy, it had a dominant influence and expected special protection from the Marshal. It had never hoped to strengthen its position as it does today. The *communists* also had their place in this struggle. It is true that they are acting illegally, but they know well who their allies are: *the tense social situation that follows a lost war.* Their appeal is addressed to the masses, who suffer most from the daily restrictions. One wonders about the *peasant.* The answer is found when we see that most of the *teachers* have not learned or forgotten anything either.

Beyond the seemingly normal course of daily events, many people get their information from a so-called "reliable source" and peddle it in their family discussions, offices or Parisian salons. The theme of this information is always the same: *Roosevelt and America.* They were trying to boost their morale since the final blow had not been struck against England. Here, in these salons, ideas are circulating that were equally valid in 1900 and 1918. The analysis of the German character is confined to the "winter tales" of Björn or Heine, an analysis which does not even bother to distinguish between "Prussians" and "Germans" in the year 1940. Also, Daladier's worn-out slogan, according to which we were fighting not against Goethe's Germany but against Hitler's Germany, still haunts people's minds. This is called having "spirit".

The old *self-love* is embedded in the political combinations. It does not want to recognise that the lack of men, in the true sense of the word, men of quality, was the essential cause of the defeat. *Thus, for example, there was a tendency to interpret the Franco-German colloquia as a request for French support.*

France has always been known as an old nation of rentiers and has not lost, even today in times of distress, this mentality of bourgeois tranquillity and daily comfort. Of course, we are willing to learn the lessons of the war, but not to pay the price. Thus it was believed that after the first contact between the Reich Führer and Pétain, a mass of benefits would pour into France. As this did not happen, disappointment followed. People only want to look at Germany's recovery at its climax, but they do not want to consider that this recovery was achieved through the occupation of the Ruhr, through the misery of the unemployed and through enormous personal and political sacrifices. *France believes that fate will make an exception for her; she does not want to believe, in her painful hours, that her rebirth will only be achieved through pain.*

Perhaps this will change somewhat when the life of France is no longer influenced by the 'hidden' intellectuals, but when the best of her sons who recently defended the Weygand Line with stubborn courage on the Aisne and the Somme have returned from their stalags. However, the human losses cannot be made up for, which is very worrying for France, a country lacking in children.

The attempt to find a new Franco-German relationship based on the generation of veterans of 14–18 failed. The symbol of this tragic failure was the death of Professor von Arnim, president of the Franco-German Society, who had devoted many years to Franco-German reconciliation; he fell at the head of his regiment in June 1940.

One wonders what will become of the young men of 39–40 who held a gun again. Nothing can be said today.

The tomb of Marshal Foch is located at Les Invalides in Paris. Poilus carry their commander-in-chief on a stretcher. The tomb is treated with the respect that a soldier owes to his adversary. But one wonders whether we Germans should regard this memorial as a symbol: Did we bury certain principles with Foch?

A leaflet gives the answer: distributed recently in Paris, it evokes the Riom trial. In a drawing, the old Clemenceau advances towards the judge's table and, pointing to himself, says: "and me?

The spirit that emerges from this leaflet teaches us that we must keep our eyes open. Behind the polite face that the French show us every day, there may be hidden the cruelty that we experienced on Good Friday in Essen in 1923.

This teaches us not to take a sentimental view of the Franco-German problem; we must keep our cool, remain *totally objective, purely political!*

POLITICAL SERVICE FOR THE SS AND POLICE.

GUIDELINES FOR THE IDEOLOGICAL EDUCATION OF ALSATIANS

History of Alsace
in the context of the history of the Reich and Europe

a) The landscape of Alsace, that blessed garden between the Rhine and the Vosges, corresponds in every respect to the Baden landscape. Nature has created two absolutely similar regions on either side of the Upper Rhine. The character of this landscape of rivers and mountains transformed by man into fields and vineyards, towns and villages, is identical in both regions.

It is true that Alsace and its towns are still more imbued with historical dreams, closer to the Middle Ages and its sovereignty than to Baden, which is more open to traffic and industry. Yet the unity of the area remains. The age-old efforts of the French to annex this rural and "geopolitical" region were therefore clearly unnatural. Memorable testimonies of the Reich and its culture, in southern Baden, the magnificent Freiburg Cathedral, in northern Alsace, Erwin von Steinbach's unique masterpiece, Strasbourg Cathedral, face each other.

Great works of German art were born in Alsace (Mathias Grünewald, Martin Schongauer, Baldung Grien).

b) The people of Alsace, like those of Baden, are of the same Alemannic stock. Alsatians speak one of the oldest German dialects, the "Elslisser Ditsch". On the other hand, one should not overlook the fact that the Alsatian character has been shaped by history, by centuries-old storms of its truly European destiny, differently from that of the Baden. Fate has been more lenient for the latter; he is calmer, more self-confident than the more original, often more discontented and chauvinistic Alsatian, who has been able to preserve his particularism for centuries but has also developed a natural contradiction bordering on *opposition on principle*. This is how we must understand, at least in part, the contrasts with its Baden cousins that are still alive today. It is understandable that the Alsatian is proud of and loves his beautiful homeland and its rich cultural traditions. Alsace has been in the Germanic sphere for 2000 years. In 58 BC, the fertile country was already claimed by the Suevi, whose remarkable general *Ariovistus* was defeated by *Caesar* in front of Mulhouse. Later, Alsace became part of the Roman province of *Upper Germania*. At the time of the great invasions, Alsace was almost continuously occupied by the Alamanni.

After *Clovis'* victory over the Alamanni at Tolbiac in 496, Alsace became a regional centre of the Frankish Empire. After the collapse of Charlemagne's Empire, the country was first attached to the kingdom of *Lotharingia* in 843, at the time of the division of Verdun, and then in 870 to the Franco-German Eastern Empire, at the *treaty of Mersen*.

Since Heinrich I, the true founder of the German Empire, and his powerful son Otto I the Great, who made the Empire a European power, France has been pushed back to the border of the four rivers, the Scheldt, the Meuse, the Saône and the Rhone. Alsace experienced its cultural and religious boom already before the year 900. After the Saxon emperors, the new merger of the Alamans with the lineage of the dukes of Swabia and Alsace and the promotion of the Swabian Hohenstaufen to the imperial dignity were the beginning of a brilliant era for the country. Frederick Barbarossa resided in his imperial castle in *Haguenau* and his brilliant grandson Frederick II considered Alsace to be his "most precious hereditary possession".

Now, situated almost at the centre of the Empire, Alsace represents the axis of a united Europe within it. Great historians and poets were born here (Gottfried of Strasbourg, the author of "Tristan and Yseult", Reimar von Haguenau).

After the fall of the Staufen, the border region passed into the hands of the Habsburg counts of the next generation of emperors in 1268. Soon afterwards, however, in the course of the following centuries, increasing pressure from France began to be exerted on the western borders of the Reich. The more the German unity declined in the course of these centuries, the more Alsace, which lacked a parent dynasty, broke up into a mosaic of small principalities. The labyrinth of small free towns, principalities, imperial cities, chapters and monasteries resembles in a smaller way the decay of the Empire itself.

In the XV century, a first French attack was bravely repelled. A century later, in 1552, the treachery of Elector *Moritz of Saxony*, who handed over the *bishoprics of* Metz, Toul and Verdun to the King of France, heralded the greatest dangers for the region, while from the 15th century onwards the whole of Alsace's spiritual life reached its peak. (1439, completion of Strasbourg Cathedral, 1440, invention of the movable-letter printing press by the Mayençais *Gutenberg,* in Strasbourg).

The country experienced the Reformation while still under German sovereignty and at the same time a powerful scientific (Upper Rhine humanism) and literary revolution. (Butzer and Jacob Sturm, Strasbourg reformers, confront the great Catholic satirical poet Thomas Murner). The imperial and social-revolutionary reformist efforts of the peasant movement, which began in Alsace with a strong anti-Jewish tendency, set the country abuzz; in Alsace, too, the spiritual and worldly particularism of the secular and religious princes overcame the knights loyal to the peasant and city empire. The situation was ripe for France, and Alsace became the hotbed of European politics.

The 16th century saw extreme poverty affecting the Reich and the German people. The Thirty Years' War sealed the triumph of feudalism and religious and local divisions. The Catholic Habsburg dynasty, increasingly distant from Germany, had to fight a war on two fronts, in the west and in the east (Turkey, Hungary, Bohemia) and was bogged down with Spain in an unfortunate supranational policy. But France, whose royal regime controlled partisan tensions and founded the absolutist administrative state, used the political and religious opposition in the Empire, and in the 18th century the Prussia-Austria dualism, to achieve its goal: *hegemony in Europe.* Alsace, at the central point, will be the key position for all his efforts.

In 1629, the great Cardinal de Richelieu wrote his famous programme which, despite the changing forms of political regimes, remained the foundation of French foreign policy until 1940. Richelieu appreciates with a sharp eye the crucial position of Alsace "… to conquer with Strasbourg an invasion route to Germany, slowly, discreetly, prudently".

France had already succeeded in gaining a foothold in Alsace during the Thirty Years' War. *The Treaty of Westphalia in 1648,* which is still for French historians of the 20th century the great charter of French foreign policy, transfers to France (in very ambiguous legal terminology) the possessions and rights of the House of Habsburg.

Louis XIV, the "Sun King", annexed the German land of Alsace piece by piece through the edicts of his famous "parliaments" under the guise of a shameless legal procedure.

The Empire succeeded in gathering an army on the left bank of the Rhine against the brigandage of Louis XIV, with the help of the *Great Elector* of Brandenburg. The superior French diplomacy played its cards against Habsburg and Brandenburg Austria in Sweden and Poland (and later with the Turks against Vienna) to protect its thieving policy. The Great Elector left Alsace at the end of 1674. In 1675, a brilliant victory was won at Fehrbellin against the Swedes, but France had achieved its goal: in 1681, in the middle of the peace, a strong French army captured the free German city of Strasbourg. The loss of Alsace was thus sealed for 189 years. The great indignation felt by the German people at this infamy was of no avail, although the *Great Elector* and other important German personalities such as Margrave Ludwig of Baden spoke out against the outrage against the Reich. In 1684, the Reich had to conclude a twenty-year armistice with Louis XIV in Regensburg, according to which it retained all the regions it had possessed until 1 August 1681, including Strasbourg (stolen on 30 September).

Incidentally, *the local bishop, Franz Egon von Fürstenberg,* played the pitiful role of a traitor in the capture of Strasbourg. The coup de force was prepared and carried out in agreement with him, and when Louis XIV made his solemn entry into the former imperial city, the German-born prince of the Church greeted him in repulsive blasphemy, and began his address with the biblical words: 'Lord, now let Thy servant go in peace, for my eyes have seen Thy anointed.

Towards the end of the century, Prussia also selfishly betrayed the higher interests of the Empire in the Treaty of Basel (1795) and handed over Alsace to France. Under the Bourbon monarchy, there was no Romanisation until the great Revolution. Politically, it is indeed a property of France, but it is treated as a foreign province. In any case, culturally, the link with Germanism was maintained. When Goethe studied in Strasbourg, it was still a fundamentally German city.

But the French Revolution directly manifested in Alsace, as in the rest of Europe, its centralizing force over the people in the sense of a total Frenchization. The waves of the greatest upheaval in European history also flooded Alsace, and revolutionary propaganda was carried out with great insistence not only in the political and social sphere, but also on a cultural level. Since that time, the French cultural influence in Alsace has been exemplary in that the anthem of the new France, the Marseillaise, was sung by its enthusiastic poet, *Dietrich,* for the first time in the salon of the burgomaster of Strasbourg (the fact that Dietrich had to go to the scaffold a year later did not harm this memory). Thus, the fact that Germans from Alsace rose to the highest positions in the revolutionary wars and Napoleon's campaigns contributed to the francisation.

During the revolutionary period and the Napoleonic era, a complete political overhaul took place in the new centralised system of France.

Culturally and politically, the Alsatian bourgeoisie became increasingly established in Paris, and this development became constant until 1870. The ruling class was thus largely Romanised, while the peasantry and middle classes remained faithful to their language and customs under the influence of courageous leaders.

After 1870, when Bismarck fulfilled the old dream of most Germans and reinstated Alsace-Lorraine as an "imperial province" in the new Empire, this upper class emigrated to France or followed the problematic path of the "protesters".

The period from 1870 to 1918 unfortunately reveals, apart from the brilliant results obtained in administration and economic management, a series of political mistakes. Already the establishment of an imperial region, additionally linked to Lorraine, was considered a bad solution by the Alsatians, who saw it as a kind of colonial status. The Prussian high officials did not always show the necessary psychological skills, which also applied to the education of Alsatians in the army. There were no far-reaching German cultural and political proposals; the imperial university town of Strasbourg was the source of some remarkable scientific work, but it had little impact. One of the greatest dangers lay in the fact that the German administration generally relied on this Francophile upper class of notables, instead of taking root in the broad popular strata, which had largely been won over to the German conscience.

One is sometimes too weak towards enemies and public traitors, while one lacks the necessary tact when confronted with the simple man, with his original qualities, his chauvinism. Unfortunately, these errors and these often simple misconceptions discredit in the popular consciousness the great result achieved by the Empire in the political and economic sphere, being' the cause of an unsuspected expansion of the country.

When the battle-weary but undefeated German army had to evacuate the country in 1918, the French were initially greeted with shouts of joy as "liberators". However, this attitude did not last long and soon loyalty to the fatherland and to the German conscience was once again heard among the peasantry. The unease caused by the administrative and political mismanagement of the Third Republic spread. The 'autonomists' at least aspired—and this is another proof of their lack of political culture—to a kind of independent status in administration, jurisprudence and culture. More than one Alsatian would have approved of full state independence like that of Switzerland.

The champions of freedom were condemned in the great trials (in winter 1939, the old Karl Roos fell as a martyr in Nanzig [Nancy] for his loyalty to German blood).

Despite this, it cannot be denied that French influence was strong on a large part of the intellectual and economic ruling classes. However, in 1940, after the total collapse of the Jewish Third Republic, the moment arrived when a large part of the Alsatian groups became aware of their identity again. In the meantime German administration and authority had established order in the region. It is only too understandable that now, in the trials of war, the "parochialism" of the Alsatians is once again making itself felt. This can be explained by the peculiarity of their character which, as in 1870, once again shows sympathy for France. It is the opposition of principle, always against the dominant power! One can also cite psychological errors in human relations. But Alsace once again belongs—and this time definitively—to the Empire. It must become a conscious member of the German people's community and of the order of the new Europe.

ALSACE AND THE EMPIRE

In the above historical sketch, you will find sufficient elements to reinforce and provoke in Alsatians the awakening of both German sentiment and European consciousness. The appeal to national pride will be the prologue to the new Europe.

Alsace has more than once been the focal point of great European politics, and in the heyday of the Empire, the country formed the centre of European unity in the Holy Roman Empire, with its fortresses, its imperial castles, its cities, its spirit of loyalty to the emperor and its very western mentality. It can be seen very clearly from its future history that the disintegration of the Empire is comparable to that of an organism losing its head and limbs. The period of French foreign domination proves the impossibility of hegemony on the part of the continental extremity. The period following the French Revolution leads to the great fragmentation of economic and political unity, through the intermediary of the grand bourgeois ideology and the idea of the nationalist state, which is becoming more and more prevalent. It should be noted that French 'civilisation', despite an outward veneer of 'European society', was not a truly unifying idea, nor was it sufficient to form the basis for European reunification.

The Bismarckian Empire, as a great power in the heart of the continent, must also be seen as the first step towards a new order, which is proven by

Bismarck's peace and alliance policy after 1870. England was to be seen as the enemy of a stable European society, France as its continental weapon threatening the Empire and its European mission.

The First and Second World Wars must be seen as a whole, the attempt to achieve the final liberation and independence of a Europe threatened by overpopulated powers. The new Europe was born in the midst of the storms of the Second World War and found its first expression in the combat comradeship of the Waffen SS.

It is precisely among the Alsatians that the pride of fraternity of arms with the best youth of Europe must be born and strengthened. The Waffen SS, the vanguard of the free peoples against Bolshevism (see also the book "Europe and Bolshevism"), fights for the vital centre of the continent, the Empire, but also for the life of all the European peoples. The new Europe will preserve and strengthen the rich culture of its peoples and races, their thousand-year-old traditions, their diversity and individuality, as long as they are strong and alive, for a better future. The Alsatian must not be hurt in his love for his homeland, his ethnic consciousness and his pride in life. He must not be "standardized", but he must understand that this international struggle is not being waged to preserve certain traditions or to regain material and spiritual ease, but for the very existence of Europe. This existence can only be prolonged in a new and better order of life, a true and strong community of peoples under the leadership of the Empire. Originality and provincial particularism at any price would be grotesque in the face of the terrible reality of foreign world powers, of Bolshevism and Americanism, the enslavement of humanity under the ferocious rule of the world Jewish power.

The common life of men and peoples will have to be founded on new foundations. The new Europe will be forged under the banner of revolutionary socialism. The importance of German socialism in its European extension will be understood by reading contemporary literature. Our position on private property will have to be examined more closely. The basic lines for the future organisation of the continent in the social sphere were provided by the great socialist achievements of National Socialism between 1933 and 1939.

Furthermore, it must be emphasised that the alliance between the plutocracy and Bolshevism and the underlying Judaism took place as a result of the fear provoked by the revolutionary will of the new Europe and Adolf Hitler's *true socialism* (compare with the first edition of "Political Service for SS Officers", pp. 13, 21 and the book "Europe and Bolshevism")

Alsatians also need to be told about the concept of Blood and Soil, the high value of peasant life and agriculture as the source of biological life for people, a concept advocated by National Socialism.

The concept of Empire and the idea of European identity should be treated from the beginning to the end of the instruction in a spirit of practice as well as knowledge and will formation.

ANNALS No. 2. 1944.
EDITION OF THE SS BRIGADE WALLONIA.

GERMANS AND GERMANS

Among contemporary German historians there is a clear tendency to broaden the historical view.

And this trend is by no means what one might call an "annexationist" trend based on narrow German nationalist sentiment.

In the past, German historians have tended to confuse the history of the Germans with that of the Germans.

Some very useful clarifications are now being made, as they provide a great deal of clarity in German intentions from the point of view of European policy.

In his remarkable book *The Great Eras of German History,* the German historian Johannes Haller makes the following curious comments on this subject

"Such is the force of habit, even among scholars, that they pay no attention to this confusion of terms: they equate Germans with Germans. By what right? Unquestionably, the Scandinavian peoples are Germans, and it has never occurred to anyone to incorporate their history into our own. The English are also Germanic, whether they want to be or not—in modern times they don't want to be, but that doesn't make any difference. To be honest, one should even say that, in history, the most influential representatives of Germanism have been the English...".

Germans and Germans are not synonymous. All Germans are Germans, but not all Germans are Germans. Among the Germanic peoples, the Germans form a special group, and—of crucial importance—an originally fragmented group. They did not live together originally, not at all, and it was only with the passage of time that they came together and developed together. In short: the German people are not the result of a natural union, but their unity has been forged by history. A great deal of trouble has been taken to determine the degree of kinship between the various Germanic peoples, in the hope of proving that some of them were, by nature, close to each other; in particular, it has been tried to prove that the tribes whose later union formed the German people constituted, precisely by nature, a coherent group, a special family among the tribes.

These efforts are doomed to failure. If there was a greater or lesser degree of kinship between the Germanic tribes, the same cannot be said of the later Germanic tribes, as they appear in history: there is no natural community between them. This can be easily understood by a very simple observation. All those who have had occasion to compare Hanoverians, Hamburgers or Bremeners with Englishmen, know that they are very close, extraordinarily similar in many respects, in short, almost alike. Is it possible to discern the same degree of natural kinship between a Hamburger and a Swabian, between an Oldenburger and a Bavarian, when one sees and hears them speaking their dialect?

I have my doubts.

We can therefore establish the following: the German tribes did not develop into a German people because they were united by natural ties, but they were brought together by destiny, in other words, by history.

We know these tribes; they still exist today, they are alive and recognisable: Franks, Swabians, Bavarians, Thuringians, Saxons, Frisians. Their common destiny and their exploits constitute German history. Consequently, German history can only begin when the six tribes are united.

This happened relatively late, and in stages. This reunion was the work of one of these peoples, the Franks. The Frankish kings brought the other peoples under their rule, one after the other. Clovis and his sons, in the first half of the 6th century, subdued the Swabians, who were then called Alamanni, Thuringians and Bavarians. After that, it was all over. There was even a regression in the VII century: the defeated regained their independence. It was not until the VIII century that a new Frankish dynasty succeeded in completing the interrupted work. Charles Martel defeated the Thuringians and Frisians; his sons defeated the Swabians; Charlemagne defeated the Bavarians (788) and finally the Saxons after a thirty-year struggle. By 804, the process was complete. About a century later, German history proper began. And all this history, over the course of a thousand years, will be one long process of national unification, with alternations of progress, backward steps, integration and disintegration.

It fell to Adolf Hitler to crown this great historical achievement by establishing the Great German Reich.

But we must already look higher and further afield. This German unification, which was not the result of historical determinism but of historical will, is in a way the prefiguration of the great Germanic and European unification.

What the Franks did in the VI and VIII centuries, because they were the bearers of a historical will, the Germans can do in the XX century because they too are bearers of a historical will and because they are the strongest and most powerful Germanic people.

The pace of history is accelerating, and it is no longer a question of establishing the supremacy of the German Empire, but of building a new German Empire bringing together all the peoples of Germanic blood.

The German Empire is not just an extension of the German Empire. It is something else that is being established on a higher plane. What this great German Empire of the new age will be, no one, not even in Germany, can yet say with any precision, for it is not a question here of an architectural construction according to theoretically predetermined plans. It is the development of a living organism driven by the common will of all the peoples of Germanic blood.

However, the fact that the distinction between Germans and Germanic peoples is already being made so clearly today is a valuable guide to what the new Germanic Empire will not be.

Thus we can already see that, in this great Empire, all the Germans will be able to enter not as conquerors, but as free men.

SS BOOKLET NO. 3. 1938.

SS-USTUF. DR KARL VIERERBL: CZECHOSLOVAKIA

Historical summary of the country and its political structure

More than 2,000 kilometres of German border, from the Oder over the Sudeten Mountains, the Erzgebirge and the Bohemian Forest to the Danube near Preburg, separate the German and Czech states. The *state border* is not *the border of the people,* it cuts right through the living flesh of the German people and makes three and a half million Germans Czech citizens.

The history of the Sudetenland, the western part of the Czech state, shows that this country has been inhabited for centuries by Germans.

However, *the policy of Czechoslovakia* indicates that it was created *to fulfil an anti-German mission.*

Viel lieber gestritten
und ehrlich gestorben,
als Freiheit verloren
und Seele verdorben,

BANNERSPRUCH DER FREIEN REICHSSTADT STRASSBURG

Rather struggle
And die honourably,
That losing freedom
And corrupt his soul.

Motto of the Free City of Strasbourg

Prague Castle, a testament to German engineering.

Viking grave found in the area.
The Vikings were the founders of the city of Prague

HISTORY OF THE SUDETENLAND

The Sudetenland was once part of the sphere of influence of the Nordic culture. The first known population, the *Boian* Celts, gave their name to Bohemia.

The Germanic branches of the *Marcomans* and *Quads* immigrated to the Sudetenland in the last century BC. Under the reign of *Marbod,* a great German Empire was born which challenged the power of Rome. After their departure into the mountains between the Lech and Enns rivers, other Germanic branches followed them into the abandoned settlement area, such as the *Lombards, Hermundurs, Ruges, Thuringians and others.*

It is only at the beginning of the 7th century that we learn of the settlement of the Slavic branches in the Sudetenland. They were not free men, but *subject to the Avars,* from whom they were freed by the Frankish merchant *Samo,* who took up their cause and supported them in their struggle. They elected him king at the end of the war, but after his death the Empire broke up again and the *Avars* resumed their dominance over the Slavic branches.

For the second time, it was the *Franks* who freed the Slavs from their subjugation by the *Avars.* It was under Charlemagne that the Sudetenland was incorporated into the German sphere as a vassal country. The unification of the Slavic branches and the birth of the Czech people on German territory took place under the rule of the *Przemysl* family. Just as the country and its people had flourished in Samo's time, so they experienced an unhoped-for era of close union with the German Empire.

The arrival of German princesses at the Przemysl court brought German noblemen, monks, burghers and peasants into the country, and with them *German art.* Not only did German immigration rekindle the fire of German tradition in Bohemia and Moravia, which had been smouldering uninterruptedly since the Germanic era, but it also influenced the behaviour of the Czech people by its *model* and *example* and narrowed the gap between Germans and Czechs.

The first bishops of Prague were German. German monks and nuns in the monasteries were not only ambassadors of the new faith but also heralds of German technical culture. They cleared forests, drained marshes and founded farms. The monasteries also became centres of spiritual and political culture, and the local castles competed with them. German troubadours sang their songs here. The Przemysl court was modelled on a German one, and King Wenceslas himself played the lyre.

However, in the towns that sprang up in the country, all inspired by the German model, crafts flourished. *Nuremberg* and *Magdeburg law* was introduced. The German tradition and national character soon had a major influence on the country and the Czech people. This was recognised by the Bohemian dukes and kings, who granted the Germans great privileges in the country. In the revealing historical document in which Duke *Vratislas* (1061–1062) granted the Germans certain privileges in the country in general and in Prague in particular, a document renewed a hundred years later by Duke *Sobieslas,* we read verbatim

"I take the Germans ... under my grace and protection and, as they are different as a people from the Czechs, I want them to be different also in their rights and customs. I therefore grant them to live according to the law and right of the Germans, which have been theirs since the time of my grandfather. Know that the Germans are free people.

The flow of German immigrants called into the country by kings and nobles increased at the beginning of the 12th and during the 13th century. More than 700 villages were founded at that time.

The Przemysl line died out in 1306. The most energetic personality was Ottokar II who, in an unmeasured blindness, attacked the German royal crown. The crown and the country then fell to the German-Luxembourg dynasty. In 1310, *John of Luxembourg* ascended the Bohemian throne. His son *Charles IV* fulfilled the dream of Ottokar I Przemysl and made *Prague* the centre of the great German Empire. The emblems of the Empire were kept for decades in the town of Karlsburg, which Charles IV had founded.

Under this king, Prague experienced its *greatest development* and even today, the buildings from this period bear witness to the prosperity of the country at that time. German architects and craftsmen shaped the city's appearance. In 1348, the *first German university* was founded in Prague.

The interior of the country also bears witness to the prosperity of this period. Charles IV, who had devoted all his love to Bohemia, was rightly called the "founding father" of the Reich.

After this period, the country entered a turbulent era. Czech forces rose up in the country and resisted German influence. Under the weak King Wenceslas IV, who also lost the German throne, they regained the upper hand. Their spokesman was the Prague university professor *John Hus,* who embraced the national and social religious trends of the time and, following the example of the Englishman *Wycliffe,* began to preach his own gospel.

When, in 1415, he was sentenced to death and burned alive as a heretic by the Council of Constance, the Czech people had their martyr. The storm was then unleashed during the Hussite wars against everything German in the country, which was identified with Catholicism. By the end of the wars, the prosperity of the country had disappeared, the towns and cities were impoverished, the fields and pastures deserted, and industry and commerce destroyed. This was a great loss for the Germans.

But it was the latter who brought the country back to life and prosperity in the 16th century and healed the wounds caused by the Hussite wars. After the Hussite wars, the Czechs placed the most powerful Bohemian gentleman, *George of Podiébrad, on* the Bohemian throne and thus founded a national kingdom. However, the expected recovery of the country did not take place.

In 1526 the Sudetenland, after a period of economic and cultural disaster, returned to the Habsburgs. In the following years, its development was halted by the religious unrest of the time, but thanks to German influence, it developed strongly and became an independent state.

The Czech states reserved the most terrible difficulties for the Habsburg government. Relations between the *Hradcany* and the *Hofburg were* further strained by religious opposition. When the Bohemian nobility, after the death of Emperor *Matthias,* declared the Habsburgs to be deprived of the throne of the Bohemian States, a pitched battle ensued. On 6 November 1620, at Weillen Berg, near Prague, the imperialists defeated the Protestants. The Czechs, in view of the aftermath of this battle, regarded this defeat as a victory of the Germans against the Czechs. In reality, it was a victory of the imperial central power against class domination in Bohemia and, if you like, a victory of Rome over Wittenberg. The property of the insurgents was confiscated; the entire population had to become Catholics. Anyone who did not want to recant lost all his property. The estates confiscated from the German and Czech nobility were given to the Catholic nobility who were faithful to the Church. Their nationality played no role. The new landowners were Italian, Spanish, French, German or Czech, because, as we have said, the criteria for the allocation of land were the Catholic faith and loyalty to the Habsburgs.

After the Battle of Weillen Berg, the Bohemian nobility changed their attitude. The rebels became courtiers who transferred their residence to the imperial court and led a brilliant life, which the mass of the Czech people had to pay for through drudgery and serfdom. The Bohemian nobles thus became the oppressors of the Czech people, who were liberated by the German prince *Joseph II* and the German peasant Hans *Kudlich* through the abolition of serfdom. The Czechs do not want to admit this reality. It does not fit in with their historical myth of the oppression of the Czechs by the Germans, and yet it is the historical truth.

THE FIGHT FOR THE INDEPENDENCE
OF THE CZECH STATE

The awakening of the Czechs to national consciousness at the end of the 18th century led to their aspiration for an independent state. When *Napoleon* entered Vienna, a Czech delegation paid homage to him and handed him a *memorandum* which demonstrated that the creation of an independent Czech state in the heart of Europe would be *the best guarantee for his sovereignty in Central Europe.*

This memoir was considered a burst of romantic enthusiasm, and the talks at the first Panslave Congress in Prague, which took place at the same time as the re-entry of the German parliament in Frankfurt, announced the political reality of the Czech struggle for independence. In domestic politics, it was a fight against the centralisation of the state on a federal basis, which was to give *the Czechs autonomy in their own area.* At the same time, the Czechs established ties with *Paris* and *St. Petersburg.* However, they did not yet imagine the destruction of the old Danube monarchy, but counted on its weakening, from which they hoped to realise their hopes in domestic politics. Their foreign policy calculations were as follows: Austria-Hungary's alliance with the German Empire meant a strengthening of the government in Vienna and its centralisation. Any weakening of German power would also mean a weakening of Habsburg policy. Thus they welcomed the Franco-Russian rapprochement against Germany which led to a military alliance, because they expected it to weaken the German Empire and consequently Austria-Hungary. At the end of a lost war, it would come to a social or national revolution. In one case the result would be a federal reorganisation of Austria-Hungary, in the other the birth of an independent Czech state.

The Great War broke out for the Reich on two fronts, against France and Russia; the Czechs saw that their time had come. Czech domestic politics began its *work of sabotage* and worked to weaken the Danube monarchy. Czech politicians abroad, especially *Masaryk* and *Benès,* tried to persuade the world that the liberation of the smaller peoples and thus the solution of the problem of nationalities in Europe *should be the objective of the Great War.* This would not be possible, however, without the destruction of the Habsburg Empire. The World War would be the great war of demoralisation of Europe, the war of freedom against the oppression of the Habsburgs, the Hohenzollerns and the Romanovs. These were the arguments of the Czechs.

When the American president published his famous 14 points at the beginning of 1918, in which he built the future Europe on the basis of the right of peoples and ethnic groups to determine their own political destiny, the fate of Austria-Hungary was decided.

The Czechs made known their designs on the Sudetenland, Bohemia, Moravia, Silesia, the Carpathians, Slovakia and Ruthenia. They explained that this was the only way they could fulfil their anti-German function: the wall against the 'Drang nach Osten'. The right to self-determination is not given to everyone. Moreover, it would be *"unjust for a few hundred thousand Czechs to be sacrificed to Pangermanism",* wrote Masaryk in his book presented at the Peace Conference: *The New Europe,* in which he gave the reasons for building a new independent Czech state. That more than three million Germans were sacrificed to the Czechs did not seem unfair to the humanitarian philosopher Masaryk. As compensation for their deprivation of self-determination, the ethnic groups incorporated *against their will* were to be given the widest possible *administrative autonomy.* A *"new Greater Switzerland"* was even to be born, in which the specificity of the ethnic groups would be guaranteed.

The Czechs and Slovaks, who had already decided in *Paris in 1915* and later in *Moscow* and *Cleveland* to form a state together, signed a treaty in *Pittsburgh* on 30 May 1918 in which they reaffirmed their desire to found a state. This treaty promised the Slovaks *full autonomy and an independent parliament.*

THE INDEPENDENT CZECHOSLOVAK STATE

The Czechoslovak Republic was proclaimed on 28 October 1918 in *Prague*. The old Danube monarchy was in its death throes. The Habsburg Empire, on which the sun never set, was crumbling. The Austrian front gave way. Two days later, the deputies of the old Danube monarchy met and proclaimed the Austro-German Republic, which was joined by the Sudetenland region of Germany. A few days later, they made their final decision: *German Austria is part of the German Empire.*

In Prague, the declaration of intent of the Germans and the Sudetenlanders was not recognised. Czech military hordes invaded both Slovakia and the Sudetenland region and occupied the territory. When the Sudeten Germans demonstrated again on 4 March 1919 for their right to self-determination, the Czech soldiery killed the unarmed demonstrators.

In Paris, people turned a deaf ear to the shooting and the cries of the victims. They were only Germans! The creation of the Czechoslovak state was ratified on 10 September 1919 in Versailles. Taken from the rich heritage of the old Danube monarchy, it was given a territory of 140,493 square kilometres, including the rich region of the Bohemian Forest up to the area of the Theiss springs, forests interspersed with cereal lands, even coal and mineral deposits, the chain of metal-bearing mountains, the world-famous thermal springs, Karlsbad, Frauzenbad, Klösterle, Giesshuebel etc.

Within the borders of the Czechoslovak state, live:

3,235,000	Germans
7,406,000	Czechs
2,230,000	Slovaks
700,000	Hungarian
550,000	Ukrainians
82,000	Polish
187,000	Jews
50,000	various

While the Sudeten Germans occupied the border regions of the Sudetenland, the Czechs inhabited *the interior of* the country. Exactly 27,000 square kilometres of German living area are concentrated in Czechoslovakia. Slovaks, Hungarians, Ukrainians and Poles inhabit the Carpathian region and its northern and southern borders. The Jews live mainly in the large cities and are spread throughout the country. In the eastern part of the state, they even form the majority of the population. It is in these more monolithic areas of settlement that Bolshevism receives the most votes!

The present borders of the Czech state did not satisfy the wishes of the Czechs. They presented the Peace Conference with a map by an officer named Hanush *Kuffer* that extended the borders of the Czech state to the *gates of Berlin, Nuremberg* and the *Danube*. This map again reflects the aspirations of Czech imperialism, which are still alive today.

THE CONSTITUTION

Czechoslovakia is a democratic republic based on the highest degree of centralisation. The promises of autonomy made to the Slovaks, Sudeten Germans and Hungarians *have not been fulfilled*. It does provide for an autonomous solution of state administration for the *Ukrainians,* but decrees on this have not yet been issued. The Constitution was created without the participation of Slovaks and other nationals and was granted to them.

According to the Constitution, all power is in the hands of the "Czechoslovak people" who exercise their sovereignty through the elected deputies in the Chamber of Deputies and the Senate. Parliamentary elections are held every six years. The Chamber of Deputies has 300 members, the Senate 150. Both chambers elect the president, who serves for seven years.

CZECH DOMESTIC POLICY

Domestic policy is based on the fiction of a Czech national state. It does not recognise the rights of ethnic groups to national identity and tries, by all means available to the government, to denationalise them in various ways, for example

By means of an "agrarian reform", the German Sudetenland *was stripped of one third of its forests and arable land*. The large *German* landholding was dismembered and divided among Czech settlers. But the forest was placed under state management and forestry workers and lumberjacks were dismissed from their jobs and replaced by Czechs.

A law on civil servants replaced more than *40,000 German servants* with as many Czechs. The remaining civil servants are constantly moved around the region so that their children are forced to attend a Czech school.

Sudeten German industry was forced by a series of measures to invest in *Czech* capital. The trust administrations took advantage of their situation to place Czech civil servants and workers in German private industry. Thus, German companies had to give priority to the *Czechs when hiring* and to the *Germans when they had to lay off workers*.

By means of the above-mentioned measures, the Sudetenland region was nucleated with Czech elements. At the same time, however, the mass of the unemployed in the Sudetenland grew to gigantic proportions as a result of the trade crisis.

At the same time as the denationalisation of the territory, *the denationalisation of the people took place*. German schools were closed. *More than 19,000 German schoolchildren had to attend Czech schools*. But in these schools, where the language of instruction was German, education was carried out in a Czech spirit. German youth had to be shown a disfigured history of the German people. On the other hand, they must be shown the brightest colours of Czech history. The most striking feature of Czech education in German schools is the disappearance from the books of the pictures of Sans-Souci Castle and the Battle of the Nations monument in Leipzig.

As a result of these attempts at denationalisation, *a ban on* the import of *German books and newspapers from the Reich was* introduced in recent years. In this way, the Sudeten Germans were to be spiritually cut off from the German people and made ready for 'Czechoslovakisation'.

CZECH FOREIGN POLICY

Just as the Czechs had expected the creation of an independent state from the Franco-Russian alliance, so they saw in this alliance the guarantee of their independence. The conclusion of a *military pact with France* was the first result of this policy. The then Foreign Minister Beneš would have concluded a treaty with the Soviets at the same time, had he not been prevented from doing so by the opposition of a parliamentary majority, but he persisted in this aim and achieved it in 1935, thus handing Czechoslovakia over to Bolshevism. The Little Entente was the hope of the Czechs to prevent the *strengthening of Hungary and the joining of Austria to the German Reich.*

THE STRUGGLE OF NATIONALITIES AGAINST THE CENTRALISATION OF PRAGUE

The Sudeten Germans responded to the constitution granted from Prague with the most vigorous obstruction, but the majority in the Prague parliament could override all the protests of the Sudeten German parties and ignore them. All these *legal measures aimed at the denationalisation of the territory and the people* followed one another at that time. These serious prejudices caused a certain nervousness in the politics of the Sudeten Germans and made them give in to the deceptive proposals from Prague. The German parties were told that the hard-line orientation of the Prague government would be changed if the Sudeten German parties ended their obstruction. Soon there was a conflict of opinion in the heart of Sudeten Germanism about the future attitude to the government. Some were prepared to join the Prague government to repel the planned attacks. The others remained suspicious and were wary of taking this step without assurance from the government, since experience had shown that Czech promises could not be trusted.

Despite this, in 1926 the *Farmers' League* and the representative of *political Catholicism* entered the Prague government. The governmental participation of the German parties lasted until March 1938. The German entry into Austria in the spring swept away Schu8nig and thus caused the failure of this German action in the Czech government. Even the Sudeten German Marxists were forced to recall their representatives from the government to which they had returned in 1929.

During the days of the public opinion struggle between the Sudeten German opposition and the government parties, the Sudeten National Socialists unfurled the flags of the Sudeten autonomy movement and raised the slogan: "The Sudeten region to the Sudeten Germans" even in the last village and the last factory. Under these flags the unification of Sudeten Germanism began. When the elections for municipal delegates in 1931 showed that the National Socialist Workers' Party of Sudetenland was becoming a popular movement, the Czechs thought that they could stop the development by dissolving the party. The measures taken in the autumn of 1933, in which the Metternich police spirit celebrated a joyful resurrection, made it clear to the Sudeten Germans that they would not back down from a major persecution. Gloom and despair were already threatening to creep into its ranks when one of its members stepped out of line and raised the wavering flag once again: *Konrad Henlein*.

He called for the formation of a Sudeten patriotic front, which was soon to be called the Sudeten German Party. Under his leadership, the work of unifying Sudeten Germanism was accomplished, which was confirmed in the municipal elections in May and June of that year. Konrad Henlein was legitimised as the spokesman for Sudeten Germanism and made his demand for equal rights and autonomy. The government in Prague thought that it would intimidate the German popular groups by *a military occupation of the Sudeten areas* and make them withdraw their demands. The opposite was true. Unity was strengthened precisely in these days.

The *Slovaks* followed the same path. The Czechs also did not think that they could keep the promises they had made in the Treaty of Pittsburgh and grant them autonomy. They too tried, first by obstruction and then by government participation, to induce the Czechs to keep their promises and force them to transform Czechoslovakia into a federation. The events of the last few months have shaken the Slovak people, who are now vigorously demanding compliance with the Treaty of Pittsburgh.

The same fate was shared by other popular groups in the state who today adopt the same attitude towards the Prague government as the Sudeten Germans and Slovaks.

*

The united front of the nationalists towards the government in Prague shows that it alone is responsible for the tensions in the state today, which are troubling the whole of Europe. The divided attitude of Czech politics, announcing the principles it thought it would not respect in reality, characterises the Czech people, who have shown throughout their history neither a legal nor a state sense.

The twentieth anniversary of the founding of the state, which the Czechs wanted to commemorate this year, was marked by a *state crisis*. A Hungarian newspaper wrote at the time that "the death knell has sounded for the great European sinner". In Prague, it seems that no one wants to hear this.

The President of the Czech Republic has said that democracies tend towards anarchy and decay if their bourgeoisie is not ripe for it. The reports in his own state show him how right he is. And yet all the conditions for a flourishing within the state existed precisely in Czechoslovakia. For a *philosopher* had been at its head for more than 17 years. A Greek philosopher like Plato favoured a state led by a philosopher.

The realities in Czechoslovakia refute the ancient Greeks.

SS NOTEBOOK No. 5. 1944.

SAXONY, LAND OF WORK AND ART

The spirit of Saxony is perfectly understandable if one considers this region as a point of intersection of German cultural currents and if one attributes to it an intermediate position.

Saxony expresses first of all a surprising diversity and a significant variety. The Saxon landscape resembles a highly animated and expressive game of mimics. Saxony looks like Vogtland, Erz or Lausitz, depending on which parts of these mountainous and rugged regions it encompasses within its borders. It is the agricultural world with its vast plains, the commercial and economic region along the waterways, in the ports of the Elbe and the bustling fairs of Leipzig. This is the land of home-based crafts, where for centuries the hands of women and girls have been producing artificial flowers or bobbin lace. Wooden toys are made thanks to the creative and tinkering genius of the people, strong musical gifts and other favourable external factors have allowed the production of local musical instruments. In noisy centres, coal and lignite are mined, textiles and metals are processed; mechanical engineering, clothing industries and hundreds of other branches of industry provide bread and work for the great mass of citizens near the large cities such as Chemnitz, Zwickau, Plauen and in the remote villages of the Erzgebirge, Vogtland and Upper Luzace. This physiognomic variety of the Saxon landscape corresponds to the variety with which Saxony participates in the history of the nation and the development of the German spirit. In countless cases, a combination of multiple forces and a broad range of influence can be seen.

When there were still prehistoric settlement areas, the battle for supremacy in Germania between Hermann the Cheruscan, and Marbod the Marcoman, was probably fought on one of its plains or near one of its rivers. Those western Germanic peasants, the Hermundures, who once lived in the Saxon area, were on Marbod's side. After his defeat, they built a powerful kingdom. The battle between Hermann and Marbod decided the fate of the countless armed struggles, battles, encounters, surprise attacks and battles that took place in the heart of Saxon territory and which were of major importance to some or all of the nation. Later, the other such battle, the Battle of the Magyars in 933, where King Heinrich I defeated bands of Hungarian horsemen who had been robbers after founding the MeiBen March four years earlier, allowed the German settlement policy to continue eastwards for years. The Hungarians had been called to help by a tribe of Slavs who had entered the desolate German homeland, the Daleminzes, who wanted to break free from Germanic rule. In the following centuries, the young East March had to struggle with these Slavs from the east—Sorbs, Poles or Czechs. Its Germanisation around 1089, caused by the appointment of the Wettin Heinrich von Eilenburg as margrave by Emperor Heinrich N, which lasted until 1423, when the MeiBen March was attached to the electorate of Saxony, was an important act on the part of the regents of Wettin lineage. In the following period, the country became a stronghold against the turbulent and rapacious neighbourhood of the Czechs; it overcame the misery caused by the Hussite expeditions with exemplary tenacity. Before the brother electors Ernst and Albrecht, who were well known because of the "kidnapping" by the knight Kunz von Kaufungen, made the mistake of dividing their estates in 1485, the whole of central Germany was dominated directly or indirectly by the Electorate of Saxony. Nevertheless, despite the Leipzig division, the Erz region experienced its great historical destiny at the time of the Reformation. During the turmoil of the Wars of Religion, the figure of Elector Moritz was clearly in evidence, for he was a far-sighted man who, with the forces of his country, resisted the voracious Catholic dominator Karl V and thus saved the cause of Protestantism. Under "Father Augustus", Saxony became the protectorate of orthodox Lutheranism, a position it soon lost in the Thirty Years' War because of the selfishness and political narrowness of its princes. It lost its leading position in the heart of the Brandenburg Empire because it became intransigent in religious matters. The handicap was compensated for by the Polish policy of Augustus the Strong. In the past, this policy and the means used by Augustus the Strong were strongly criticised, but today's political sense perceives that the choice of the Saxon Elector as the Polish king meant a Polish victory of Germanism over the eastern policy of intrigue of France. The Empire was strengthened by the desirable expansion of the German economic area.

The Seven Years' War caused Saxony a misfortune which was repeated in the Napoleonic Wars. It became a regular deployment centre and the preferred base of operations for enemy armies. But at that time the German regions showed great tenacity and astonishing vitality, and what it had lost as a great political power it sought to regain in all areas of cultural life. It thus became a field of experimentation and application mainly in the field of industry. It made an essential contribution to the development of the Second Reich. Here, as everywhere, it could not be prevented that the increase in population and industry in a very limited space, the concentration of manual workers in the cities and the consequent uprooting of their roots, constituted a dangerous breeding ground for corrupting, anti-people and anti-state ideas. But this was also the main reason why Saxony developed the great idea of National Socialism before many other German regions and became a major asset for Adolf Hitler's forces.

When considering Saxony's role as a point of intersection in the development of German civilisation, the flowering of troubadour poetry at the court of Meißner was followed by the development of the region as a result of the establishment of the University of Leipzig in 1409. Margrave Friedrich the Belligerent was far-sighted enough to offer protection and security in his country to the spirituality threatened in Prague by the Czechs. He therefore founded the University of Leipzig, which, together with the Vienna Institute, became a breeding ground for German culture in the East and an institute that still works with scientific seriousness and objective zeal in the field of Germanism and many other fields.

It has already been mentioned that Saxony acquired an unparalleled historical importance for the whole of the West as the centre of the Reformation and the scene of a spiritual revolution. In the course of this cultural-political mission, it acquired an unusual strength and significance: The poetic aspect of Lutheranism was enriched by the first artistic touch from the magically enveloped Erzgebirge. In the cities of Zwickau and Joachimsthal, which represent crossroads of exchange, a mysticism coupled with social aspirations flourished that was fruitful in many ways. Georg Agricola, the Glauchau-born rector of Zwickau, became the first mining engineer writer in the West. The nationalisation of all clerical property by Elector Moritz had the notable consequence of founding the later famous princely schools Schulpforta, Grimma and Meißen. Many Germanic pioneers were sent to the four cardinal points during the activity of these three schools! The same applies (in addition to the universities in the Upper Saxon region being built in parallel to Leipzig, such as Wittenberg, Jena, Halle) to the State Mining School and the Forestry School in Tharandt, and show that the country became a "pedagogical region" especially in this period. It is known that the language of the Meißen chancelleries flourished thanks to Luther's translation of the Bible into academic German; as a result of the line received, the region became a centre for linguistic and German education.

A similar influence was exerted on the whole of German civilisation by the second rise of the Saxon spirit, the period associated with the exuberant Baroque of Augustus the Strong and the period immediately following the Enlightenment. Under Augustus, who loved pomp, Böttger from Meißen discovered porcelain, Bach from Leipzig enchanted us with his wonderful oratorios, passions and cantatas. The unusual prince, who understood the importance of putting the Baroque stamp of his mind not only on his Saxon capital, but also on his Polish residence, allowed the talent of sculptors and decorators such as Permoser and Pöppelmann to flourish. Silbermann of Erz found churches worthy of his organs. The keep, the Catholic Hofkirche of Chaiveri, and an incomparable collection of rare porcelain were created by this prince, and the magnificent painting gallery by his son. The roads were completed; the Saxon roads were already well known at the time.

During the Enlightenment, a number of great Saxon intellectual figures emerged: Leibniz, who defined the entire scientific research of an era as a philosophy and envisaged nothing less than a fusion of the Catholic and Protestant religious movements; Thomasius, the first institute professor who held his lectures in German; Lessing, the great poet, animator, critic, researcher and defender of truth who lit new and brilliant torches before the altar of humanity. These were some of the spiritual figures who came only from the cities of Dresden and Leipzig! Baroque painting, which filled the galleries of Augustus and his successors and was based above all on the intense expression of ardent feelings, experienced a new prosperity in Saxony thanks to Romanticism and, above all, an internal transformation; it is linked to the names of Philipp Otto Runge, Caspar David Friedrich, Carl Carus, Ludwig Richter and appears to be inseparably linked to certain parts of the Elbe Valley landscape. In addition to Dresden, the old town of Meißen and its surroundings are not to be outdone when it comes to the influence of spiritual events in the background. The barons of Miltitz auf Siebeneiche and Schafenberg played an important role. The first of these made the poor son of a day labourer, Fichte, a student from the village of Rammenau in Upper Luzace, who was later to have a profound effect on the conscience of the nation; the same Miltitz was a friend of the poet Friedrich von Hardenberg (Novalis), who was a student of the mines in Freiberg (as was the nationalist hero Theodor Korner) and who was later to reveal the final mysteries of German mysticism as a poet.

Even today, a romantic maverick echo can be heard from more than one wild ravine in the Elbe Sandstone Mountains. Many places in Saxony still experienced extraordinary musical events. The memorable first performance of "Rienzi" took place in the Dresden opera house and lasted until midnight. Many performances of important works followed! And what a credit the Leipzig Tapestry House has earned in the field of national music!

Leipzig, a city of music, a city of bookshops, a city of national exhibitions, is a chapter in the history of German cultural trends! This city inspired the eastern Prussian Gottsched in his aesthetic concerns. The theatrical art of the Neuberïn, Germany's first great actress, gave him an impetuous impetus that was rich in perspectives. Booksellers, printers and publishers such as Johann Gottlob Immanuel Breitkopf, Karl Christoph Traugott Tauchnitz, Benedictus Gotthelf Teubner, Anton Philipp Reclam, created the nuclei of their international firms.

The Battle of the Nations in 1813, which led to Napoleon's defeat and swept the city into its vortex, could not hinder the powerful development of all the spiritual and economic forces concentrated here; but for the first time, it revealed to the German world a community of struggle and destiny made up of most of the German ethnic groups. Since 1833, Friedrich List has been living in Leipzig and sketching out a large-scale railway network with PleiBestadt as its centre. Germany's first major railway route began here; two years later the Leipzig-Dresden line was opened to the public. A further decisive step was taken to connect the German regions.

"Education makes you free. Spirit gives life!" These mottos illuminate and embellish the whole country with a frankness all the more important because it can claim a venerable tradition.

Kurt Arnold Findeisen

Only courageous people have a secure existence, a future, an evolution. Weak peoples perish, and rightly so.

Heinrich von Treitschke

THE SS TROOP HOUSE SPECIAL ISSUE. 1940.

NORWAY

Germany partly lacks the desirable clarity about the actual relationships in the North; instead, idealised conceptions and an optimistic illusion about the victory of the Nordic idea in the other Germanic peoples so closely related to us often prevail. The strong expression of this ideal very unintentionally led to the mistake of believing that relations in the North are better and healthier than ours and that these countries are simply ripe for a new order. It was believed that the same feeling that animated us should also dominate others.

For the first time since the time of the Hanseatic League, the German occupation brought the German and Norwegian people into close contact. The preconceived opinions that the Germans had were quite friendly. However, since they did not correspond to reality, disappointment was not long in coming.

That a conflict could arise between the two countries was already an indication that the spiritual basis for joint work was quite lacking on the Norwegian side. The second disappointment, which every German must have felt personally and which had the effect of dampening his feelings, was caused by the hostile mood of the population towards him. Only recently has this improved. The third and perhaps the greatest disappointment was that the exaggerated hopes which the Germans had brought with them to Norway were not fulfilled. The Norwegians did not correspond to the ideal representations imagined. They were also men with major flaws, whose outward appearance only partially matched the Nordic ideal. Even when the external image seemed to correspond to expectations, the spiritual attitude and the clear expression of the good characteristics that are characteristic of the Nordic race were again missing.

The prejudices on the Norwegian side were totally different. One must first take into account the lost geographical character and decades of isolation from the rest of Europe. We arrived in a country where liberalism was in full swing, where the long peace and dependence on the world economy had turned pacifism into an almost natural basic view. There were no acute problems that required immediate solution, except perhaps the social problem. There was no critical economic misery and unemployment, no direct political threat from outside, no racial issue of its own, no religious problem. Unlike Germany, Norway is a 'country without people'. All the external elements that could have brought about a change in the spirit of National Socialism were more or less missing; for this reason, there was no intelligence of the German processes. In reality, this is certainly a sham, for many of the issues mentioned do exist. But since they do not manifest themselves so openly, they could be overlooked until now. To all this was added the impression of the constantly increasing German power and the systematic excitement of the people made at home and abroad. The Norwegian people, whom we met in April of this year, had aims and also forms of life totally different from our own; no one will be able to demand of a German that he should regard the Norwegian development and attitude as right, but one must at least understand the conditions which gave rise to them.

For us Germans, Norway is not directly an economic problem or a question of space, but above all a question of the racial value of its men. It would be extraordinarily deplorable if, through false visions of this elementary point, the greater part of the Germans now engaged in Norway were to become disappointed and prejudiced. The image that will be formed in the Reich about Norway will not so much be marked by any publication, but by the reports of those who return from it. If misunderstandings arise, the understanding of the internal legitimacy of our work and also of the future creation of the Empire will be very much damaged. On the other hand, the reality of such misunderstandings is also proof of the ideological clarity that is still often lacking.

One only needs to take a few points from the National Socialist racial doctrine to immediately come to essentially different judgements about the Norwegian reports.

1. The Führer also mentioned the great importance of the diverse composition of the related races of our people and spoke of a happy mixture. No doubt the variety of our people's achievements in all fields must be attributed to this influence. The claim of the Nordic race to political leadership remained intact.

2. In racial doctrine, the difference between appearance and self-image is constantly pointed out. This refers not only to the different external characteristics, but above all to those peculiarities which have their origin in purely spiritual transformations and in this sense also in certain manifestations connected with each generation.

3. Closely related to this is the relationship between heritage and education. One cannot ignore the reality that a generation currently living is not only the result of the existing hereditary character, but that its attitude and all its ways are also very essentially determined by educational factors, educational factors which may change in the course of time. But the heritage is not affected.

4. As is well known, every breed has characteristics that are both good and bad. Throughout history, the Nordic breed has consistently shown that it only demonstrates its most valuable characteristics when confronted with difficult conditions or harsh tasks. On the other hand, it has the unfortunate characteristic of becoming languid in quiet times. Not only Norway, but also

the whole of the Germanic North is currently experiencing such a period of languor.

5. According to the National Socialist conception, the racial substance of a people is the only decisive factor in judging its value. But this racial substance proves, after all the careful examinations on it, to be absolutely sound in Norway. The proportion of Nordic blood is extraordinarily high among the Norwegian people. If the present generation has an attitude that only partly corresponds to the image of the Nordic man, the next generation may already have a totally different appearance.

In order to appreciate the current political situation of the country, one must also remember the conditions that have influenced its development so far. The strong alignment with England, which did not even start yesterday, was the result of a number of factors. The geographical situation, historical traditions going back a long way and finally political experiences rooted for generations, have played a great role. On the last point, let's just mention that several times in history, terrible famines overwhelmed Norway because of an English blockade. For example, the blockade during the Napoleonic Wars had such devastating consequences that it has remained in the popular consciousness even today. The blockade of the Great War was not nearly as serious, but had quite unfortunate consequences. Other events that contributed to the continued favouring of Anglophile policy were the many affinities, personal relationships and English propaganda methods that adapted to the environment. Moreover, after all the calculations of military estimation, a German intervention in Norway seemed so unthinkable, but a British intervention so conceivable, that the corresponding political decisions were taken all the more easily.

The question concerning the future form of German-Norwegian relations, which is constantly raised by the Norwegians as they begin to understand the development, is the question concerning the principle of creation or the idea of the order of the future Empire: Imperialism or racial association? From the German point of view, it is clear that there is no particular Norwegian problem, but that Norway can only be seen as a part of the Nordic whole, the starting point of the new political and spiritual order also in this part of Europe. From these points of view, the German mission in Norway takes on its real significance. The most decisive fact is whether the Norwegians realise that Germany does not want them to be oppressed or economically exploited, but that they should be encouraged to cooperate responsibly in order to build the new Europe. With the installation of the new government and the transfer of the country's political leadership to the Quisling movement, Germany tried to give Norway the necessary possibilities for this. It is still too early to assess the outcome of this development.

Through what has been said, the political situation in Norway and the spiritual situation at the present time have been briefly sketched out. The many internal problems in Norway and the immense tasks facing the new government have not been touched upon. Finally, they can only be mentioned briefly. In the cultural sector, they boil down to rehabilitation and renovation. I would like to take the word culture in a broad sense here and refer to ideological principles and the general feeling of life as well as to art and science. I would like to choose only three particularly salient issues: The creation of healthy spiritual conditions for a new population policy, the reform of science including the planned use of the large surplus of students and, for the first time, the adoption of a clear architectural style adapted to the landscape. In the social sphere, the tasks are to balance the existing contrasts. In the economic field, a total reorganisation is necessary. The main industries of the past, shipping and fishing, may lose their importance, but they will have to be completely overhauled anyway. The development of the country is shaped by settlement and the resolution of the traffic problem. Norway has three sources of wealth which it has so far hardly exploited and which promise new prosperity: electricity, the forest and its underground riches.

However, the path to further political expansion and the use of existing economic opportunities, and thus to Norway's participation in the construction of the new Europe, can only be followed in close cooperation with Germany.

H.H.

SS BOOKLET NO. 8. 1938.

ENGLAND—IRELAND

International interest has recently focused on the Czechoslovak question and in particular on the sending of the English Lord *Runciman* to Prague. It would be interesting, however, to consider an internal problem of the British Empire which has some analogy with what is happening in Czechoslovakia. When we think of European Britain, we are inclined to think of it as a unified entity. We too easily forget that there is a nationality problem for England on European soil, particularly in Ireland, which has been the subject of constant fighting and bloodshed for four hundred years.

Apart from economic interests, it is the community of blood that holds the British alliance—the British Commonwealth of Nations—together. The administration of the Dominions is in the hands of English immigrants who have been able to establish themselves everywhere in control and to anglicise immigrants from other nations to the maximum. In this way, a kind of community of destiny was forged over the centuries, which extended to the whole world and which, based on the community of blood and lifestyle, formed the basis of English domination in the world.

Only the Irish Free State occupies a special position in this respect. The Irish are the only true nation, apart from the English, within the British Empire. Their demand for independence is distinctly different from the aspirations of the other Dominions. Australia, for example, increasingly rejected London's overly insistent paternalism and, feeling itself to be a major nation, demanded the right to autonomy, naturally within the constitutional framework of the British Empire. Ireland, on the other hand, relied on the awareness of its strong national originality to demand absolute independence. The statements of its political leaders show that they are prepared to maintain this claim to independence even at the expense of the interests of the British Empire.

To understand the deep opposition between the English and the Irish, one has to consider three things: first, the strong ethnic difference, second, the denominational difference, and third, the different historical development of the two nations. Despite common general economic interests, these differences have never led to the unification of the two islands.

In the early historical period, England and Ireland were populated by Celts. With the invasion of the Roman legions the separate development of the two islands began. While Ireland remained uninvaded until the mid-medieval period, the English Celts mixed over the centuries with Roman legionnaires, Saxons, Angles and Latinised Normans. The subsequent English conquest of Ireland was merely a military event. The contrasts were initially so great that no amalgamation could be made.

Religious difference was the second factor which prevented the joint development of the two islands8. Because of their strong predisposition to mysticism, which must be attributed to their Celtic origin, they were from the beginning very open to Catholicism. From the first decades, monasteries flourished in Ireland with great variety. Irish monks played an important part in the Christianisation of Europe. At the time of the Reformation, the English tried on several occasions to turn the Irish away from their Catholic faith. They opposed this in bloody revolts. The religious question still separates the English and the Irish today, and this is not the least reason why a final compromise between the two countries is not possible.

England's hold on Ireland dates back to the 12th century, but the first invasion failed as the few English lords were absorbed into the Irish community. England did not take the conquest of Ireland seriously until it became a maritime power. In its quest to become a world power and the leading maritime power, it could no longer afford to neglect this geographically important island.

Ireland was a bridgehead for all sea routes to overseas possessions and protected the west coast of England from enemy enterprise. In the possession of the enemy, on the other hand, Ireland would threaten the English lifeline and be an outstanding base for an invasion of England. The support the Irish received, directly or indirectly from Spain, and later from France, led to harsh war measures on the part of the English, and later, when they finally won, Ireland had to pay all the harder.

These harsh actions of England, especially in her eagerness to wrest the Catholic faith from the Irish, made it impossible for the two peoples to come together. England's greatest fault was to punish very severely any marriage between Englishmen and Irishmen and to treat the latter as second-class citizens. This pernicious policy and religious pressure was the reason why Irish Catholics were unable to merge with the English community, despite the great advantages they could have gained from unification.

The English colonisation of the Green Isle remained, except for Ulster, the work of a thin layer of nobles, agricultural landlords, who always imposed their domination on the Irish. This colonisation continued to the extent that the soil and land was confiscated by the English king and given in fee to retired servants of the state. The retired servants leased their fee to the real owners, the Irish peasants. The latter were thus economically subjugated to their new lords.

The inability and unwillingness of this upper class of Englishmen to understand the Irish people went so far in the 18th and 19th centuries that not only were the leases not eased in any way despite catastrophic harvests, but no supplies were allowed to enter Ireland, so that the Irish were forced to leave their homeland. This was the beginning of the great wave of Irish emigration. In 1846-51 the population fell from 8.5 million to 6.5 million. Most of them emigrated to the United States of America. In 1846, a severe famine saw about half a million Irish people die of starvation or malnutrition. From that time onwards the population always declined until 1871, when it reached its lowest level of 4 million, a figure which is now slowly rising again.

Britain recognised the injustice of wiping out the Irish economy and tried to make up for it. It encouraged land redemption through the provision of credit, so that by 1914 the Irish had regained two-thirds of their former, but still mortgaged, property. It took all this time for the Irish economy to rebuild, at least as far as the supplementary agricultural economy was concerned.

England had achieved its goal after its long years of war: to assign Ireland's role in the English market to that of a breeding country and to bring its earlier considerable autarky within the bounds of the general programme.

Apart from the England-Ireland opposition, the Southern Ireland-Ulster behaviour further aggravates the history of Eire. The origin of the aggravation of this old opposition was the creation of the 'Ulster Volunteers' in 1912, a fighting troop of the evangelical population of Ulster against the Irish southerners. The latter founded the 'Irish Volunteers' in retaliation and only the outbreak of war in 1914 prevented a bloody settlement.

It was not until 1916 that the infamous Irish Nationalist Easter Rising took place, which cost the Irish 450 dead and 2,600 injured. The British government obviously seized the opportunity: they shot 15 Irish leaders but the British could not control the situation.

The guerrilla war lasted until 1921. Although England was able to reduce the Irish militarily, the sanctimonious pressure from America was felt. The right to self-determination of small peoples had been proclaimed loud and clear in order to bring down the powers of Central Europe, and the several million Irish-Americans turned American public opinion against England. Britain finally gave in and the Irish were granted a somewhat acceptable treaty in 1921 which gave them the status of a 'self-governing dominion' within the British Empire, excluding the six northern provinces around Ulster.

Sinn-Fein, the Irish nationalist party which had led the liberation struggle alone, fell at this hurdle. *Cosgrave*, its leader, was satisfied with the compromise of 1921, while *de Valera*, the party's second-in-command, went into opposition. The fighting resumed immediately. His aim was—and still is—a free, united Ireland (including Ulster), on equal terms with England and freely united with her. He succeeded in overthrowing Cosgrave in

Parliament in 1932, and from that time on he steered Irish politics in the direction of his main objective, and his achievement is clearly reflected in the new Constitution and the Treaty with England.

The main political problem for de Valera today is the management of Ulster, which he has not yet been able to resolve in the new Anglo-Irish treaty. His goal is the reunification of the whole island under one government. The people of Ulster, like the English government, are opposed to this. The six northern provinces of Ulster are the only territory in Ireland where Anglo-Scottish settlement has been firmly established. This settlement was not, however, deep enough for the English noble upper class to have succeeded in eliminating the Irish labourers.

This area with its disparate population has always been a difficult region, and to this day denominational antagonisms clash sharply: for example, in the summer of 1935, on the day of remembrance of the Battle of the River Boyne, eight people were killed and 75 injured. The Ulster Unionists commemorated the battle in July 1680 when William of Orange defeated James II and saved the colony of Ulster.

However, the antagonism is not only historical and confessional. There are now primarily economic reasons for the Anglo-Irish to reject Irish unification.

The noble landowners, merchants and industrialists of Belfast defended their religious security, commercial independence and political freedom along with the nationality of their six provinces. The secession of Northern Ireland at the time of the foundation of the Free State was the only way for the Protestant North to protect itself against the Catholic majority in the South. At least in the North, where the total population is two-thirds Protestant (compared to 8% in the whole of Ireland), they were left with the social pre-eminence and political dominance they had previously exercised over the whole island.

In a reunited Ireland, the Ulster Unionists would no longer be the ruling people, but a popular denominational minority to whom the small island cannot remotely afford the benefits of the great Empire in which careers are offered to them in the Army, the administration and the government, as citizens of that Empire. Attachment to England was also beneficial to Northern Irish trade. Belfast industry lost its hinterland in secession, of course, but it was compensated by the fact that the whole of the British market remained open to it without any tariffs. Its industry was essential to complement its agrarian economy, and it had to fight hard in competition with England from 1932 to 1937.

De Valéra had, shortly after entering the government, suspended the payment of the so-called agricultural annuities.[4] England retaliated with an economic war supported by all modern means. This economic war and

---

[4] Payment to dispossessed English landowners.

de Valera's subsequent economic nationalism became yet another reason for the Ulster Unionists to protest out of sheer selfishness to protect their commercial welfare against reunification. In this Anglo-Irish economic struggle of recent years, Ireland would have had the upper hand in the long run. So in the agreement reached in May this year, De Valera put aside his demand for Northern Ireland's reunification with Eire and settled for the return of commercial peace and full national independence for Southern Ireland. Thus ended the economic war between England and Ireland. The great dispute over agricultural annuities ended when de Valera cut off English demands with a one-off payment of £10 million. The cause of the economic war since 1932 was thus no longer present. A revival of Irish trade emerged, freely complementing English trade.

Ireland also gained full military sovereignty. The previous bases of the British fleet were ceded in return for a guarantee that the British fleet would be considered a threat to Ireland. Thus, military and political cooperation is mandatory between Ireland and England. England has thus added an element to the overall diplomatic-military equipment it has been building up by all means since the defeat in the Abyssinian conflict.

But it is easy to see how the unresolved Ulster question will again damage the Anglo-Irish union. De Valera declared again on his return from London to Dublin that he would never give up the fight for Ulster. The Irish press, despite de Valera's statement about a joint Anglo-Irish defence, went so far as to demand recognition of Ireland as a neutral state as the next step. On the other hand, the Northern Irish Prime Minister, Lord Craigavon, declared on the occasion of the National Day in July this year that Ulster will never bow to the Dublin Parliament and betray England. Ulster wants nothing more from Ireland than to be left alone. These words of the two statesmen and the repeated disturbances on this year's national day show how much opposition is operating among the people after as before despite the treaties.

The Anglo-Irish problem once again provides proof that old treaties are just useless and empty papers if they do not express the will of the peoples concerned.

SS BOOKLET No. 1. 1939.

GERMANS IN SOUTH WEST AFRICA

In German history, there are countless examples of Germans leaving the forested regions of Germany for the dry, hot lands of the South. Like water that evaporates in the sun, Germans gradually lost their identity in hot countries. This was already the fate of the Germanic tribes who, at the time of the great invasions, set out to build new towns in the southern regions.

After a short period of prosperity, these creations disappeared and a little later Germanism was diluted in the dark blood of the South. This has happened in many ways over the last 1500 years. The descendants of the German emigrants were often the bravest soldiers in the fight against Germany and thus hindered its struggle for life.

Knowing that in the past Germans had lost their national character quite easily, the Union of South Africa had refrained, unlike other conquerors of German colonies, from completely expelling German residents in South West Africa. 7,000 out of 13,000 residents were expelled in 1919–1920. Of the remaining 6,000 who were 'generously' allowed to remain on this piece of land torn from the desert at the cost of their blood and sweat, it was expected that they would gradually be assimilated by the Boers. This hope was believed to be all the more justified because the Boers themselves were mainly of Low German origin. In South-West Africa, as in other parts of the world, it was customary to compensate for the insufficient local demography by the immigration of good Germans. A South African politician once declared that the white population of South Africa could not be sustained without permanent immigration of Europeans. Talks were still going on in the autumn of 1932 for the settlement of more German residents.

How did South Africa's hopes for Germanism in the South West come about? The first generation of South West Africans, i.e. the soldiers and settlers who settled there during the German period and in some cases even later, resolutely defended their Germanness, even if not always in an appropriate manner. While in Germany the party feud was raging, in the South West they joined forces and did not allow anyone to become affiliated with one of the many German parties. Opinion remained conservative as it had been in German times, i.e. most Germans hoped for a restoration of the monarchy in Germany and, as a result, a 'return to colonial Germany'. There was little rejoicing in South Africa about this position of the German population, but it was believed that German youth, who had grown up in the meantime, were more amenable to racial mixing with the Boers. It was thought that, in view of the contradictions that had arisen during the Great War, the disappearance of Germanness in the South West would only gradually take place. This was the view of the Boer community, which was then in power in South Africa. For the Anglican and liberal circles, on the other hand, this slow development would come at the right time, since there would be no need to fear a too rapid awakening of the Boer national community through the influx of valuable German population groups. However, it was a great disappointment for both sides when it became clear, especially after the National Socialists took power, that the younger generation of Germans was even more attached to their Germanness than their parents and enthusiastically professed their National Socialism. The consequences of this were to be seen in the fact that the arrival of new German immigrants was prevented by decrees banning immigration.

KHORAB—SOUTH WEST AFRICA—JULY 1915

South African troops 'won'. 70,000 men conquered the country defended by 5,000 Germans. The peace was concluded after the Germans had fired their last shots. 3,000 reservists, farmers, tradesmen or artisans returned to their occupations and 2,000 professional soldiers were interned. The war was over, the resistance began.

WINDHURK 1924

The German community in South West Africa protests against the violence of the victors and the lack of principles of the German monks. It protests against the fact that it has been sold out. In 1923, the South African government represented by General Smits had concluded the 'Treaty of London' under which the Germans in the South West were to be naturalised, i.e. become South Africans (Boers). To make this pill less bitter for the Germans, they were granted the option of retaining their German citizenship in addition to their South African citizenship. This was demeaning and humiliating.

1932

The Boer invasion was over. So many Boers had arrived from South Africa and Angola that the immigration from Germany, which increased the German community from 7,000 to 13,000, could not compete with the Boer community: 17,000 to 18,000 Boers lived alongside 13,000 Reich Germans in South West Africa.

The year 1932 was a year of utter despair for the German community. The world economic crisis, a period of drought lasting several years and the catastrophic consequences of South Africa's colonial policy brought South West Africa to the brink of ruin. At the moment of greatest distress, the Boer community declared its willingness to act in conjunction with the Germans on the South African government to ensure that the destiny of South West Africa would be handed over to the whites of that country to a greater extent than before. The German language would also be made an official language and automatic citizenship would be sought for post-war German emigrants.

Germanism turned anxiously to Germany; it no longer understood the political process of its homeland. By-elections, Hitler against Hindenburg, German nationalism against National Socialism. One no longer understands anything. Only one thing is clear: an unprecedented event is brewing. 1932, the year of the suffocating storm.

SPRING 1933

The third year of drought in South West Africa, and yet a new year. The country's youth rallied to Adolf Hitler's flag. In Windhuk, a regional NSDAP cell was born and grew rapidly; the German youth organisation, like the German Scouts, came under the control of the Hitlerjugend.

1934

The Hitlerjugend and the NSDAP are banned in South West Africa. German youth begin to emigrate to Germany, a movement that continues until 1937.

At the same time, the Africans of the South West General Council passed a motion proposing that the Union of South Africa administer South West Africa as a fifth province. However, the Union of South Africa did not change the terms of its mandate.

1935

In Germany, 600 young Germans from the South-West amalgamate into the South-West African National Troop. This South-West African troop quickly brought order and discipline to the ranks of the South-Western youth and led them ideologically.

1936–1937

In December 1936, the Union government announced harsh measures against the South West African population. In a statement, the Union announced that it had expected that after the granting of citizenship to the Germans in 1925, they would flourish in the community, i.e. become Boers. Further measures by the agent forced the Germans in South West Africa to dissolve their single organisation, the 'German Alliance'.

SPRING 1939

A few years ago, a new scouting organisation was established in South West Africa, whose activities are restricted by very strict decrees. In addition, a new party, the "South-West Alliance", to which only naturalized Germans can belong, has taken over the political destiny of the German community in the South-West. For about a year now, the young Germans who had joined the South-West German National Troop have been retreating to the South-West, either individually or in small groups. After having trained themselves ideologically and professionally, they come to take over the defence of the German ethnic group in South West Africa. They want to assert themselves in spite of all foreign influences. They were all driven by the hope that South West Africa would return to Germany.

***

The German community has now achieved that inner unity which is necessary in order not to be brought down by the political and economic reprisals of the Mandatory Government. It is a well-known fact that those German popular groups which have attained such a state of unity and internal harmony cannot but grow stronger in the face of every external attempt to put pressure on them. Looking back on the development of the German people as a whole, one can speak of an enormous change, i.e., the birth of a new ruling class with the youth of the nation behind it, has erased the past and created new times. This development of the German nation as a whole can be found in a smaller way in the national groups of the South West. From the ranks of the younger generation came a number of capable men who, together with the leaders of the first generation, took over the leadership of the entire German community in the South West. Since then, the community has overcome its internal disunity and is now ready to defy any attack.

SS-Uscha. Kurt P. Klein

Saxon landscape.

The Grand Mufti of Jerusalem reviews the Bosnian volunteers of the Waffen-SS.

SS BOOKLET NO. 2. 1939.

ISLAM, THE GREAT POWER OF TOMORROW

The sudden death of the young King Ghazi I of Iraq, who about a month ago crashed his car into a tree and died after a few hours from severe injuries, brought the entire Arab world together again in a spirit of community and solidarity. The first spontaneous response to this event was the assassination of the British consul in Mosul who was stoned to death by the Arabs. The reason: in Arab circles, whose instincts had been honed by years of defensive fighting, the young king was not believed to be an accident, but was seen as a new victim of the British secret service, which was also responsible for the death of Ghazi's father, King Feyçal I. King Feyçal died suddenly and unexpectedly in 1933 in Bern. At first, his death was attributed to some oil tycoons. Today, it is known for certain that Feyçal was poisoned by the British.

But Ghazi's death once again draws attention to the backdrop against which events of great importance in the Arab world have played out in recent years. The attentive political observer will therefore inevitably ask himself the question: What connections exist here and to what extent is it possible to link a political, religious or ideological phenomenon with these events? However, one must avoid the mistake of considering the notions of the "Arab world" as something completely homogeneous in itself, because Arabism in French North Africa obeys completely different laws from Egypt, and the forms of religious expression among Ibn Saud's Wahabites diverge completely from those of the Arabs of Transjordan. Nationalistic demands determined by the tribe as well as cultural and religious differences create such a complex and turbulent picture, dynastic interests and political ties with some major European powers have such different repercussions that it is difficult to speak simply of a single, organised lifestyle based on established laws. And yet such a way of life exists. Not in a state sense. Not in the sense of total similarity of religious beliefs—just think of the many sects within Islam—but this high community is based on a reality that is very difficult for the European to understand.

What unites the Arabs to a certain extent in their struggle for liberation from British foreign rule is the ardent nationalism and the desire for freedom and an independent state. At the root of this is the religion which, as the doctrine of the Prophet Mohammed, has become an international power of the first order, which wishes to manifest itself under completely new conditions and which is currently proving itself to be a world political power, although it differs from tribe to tribe but ultimately forms a unity. However, when considering the nature of what constitutes these forces drawing their vitality from this inexhaustible source, one must go back to the time when Islam first came into contact with the Western world. In these confrontations between the Western-Christian and Eastern-Islamic worlds, which have had a decisive influence on the entire evolution of Islam, the East was the active element until the end of the 17th century. Then there was a temporary pause in the fighting until Napoleon, for his part, extended the warlike ardour of the West to the East and thus initiated a development characterised by a constant struggle between East and West which culminated in the Great War with the decadence of the Turkish Empire of Osman. For the first time in the history of the Arab community, the following years have perhaps brought the problem so much into focus that it is now possible to define more realistically the nature of the multiple forces of this movement and its dynamic emanations.

It is an established fact that Islam has ceased to be a mere religious doctrine and has instead represented a liaison between pure nationalism and religious fanaticism. But today, the common universe of Islam is shaped more vividly than ever by the sense of an Eastern-Islamic community of destiny naturally hostile to all that is Western. It finds its strongest and most powerful expression in this opposition to the West and to Christianity. However, we must make a parenthesis: this community of destiny of the Arab world with an Islamic background has nothing to do with the so-called pan-Islamic idea as it was propagated in the past by the Turkish caliphs and which aimed at the creation of a great united Islamic Empire. Especially in the pre-war period, this movement was an element to be reckoned with politically, since it was the result of political necessity. But it broke down with the fall of the Osman Empire, when tribal demands and multiple national movements were revived among the Arabs, with Muslims fighting each other when it served their political purposes. The memory of the 'holy war', to which the penultimate Sultan called the believers in Mohammed against the Allies, is still vivid everywhere and was a poor testimony to a pan-Islamic idea. It would be much better today, instead of a pan-Islamic movement in the spirit of the Sultan's, to speak of an Islamic nationalism which, admittedly, has origins as different as those of each tribe, but which everywhere—and in this lies its decisive importance—represents the same alliance between national and religious forces. But this correlation is probably best expressed in that part of the Islamic world which also became the starting point of Mohammed's doctrine: in the Arab living space of the Middle East. (In this context, it should not be forgotten that the followers of Islam are not only Arabs, but also in India, Japan, the Dutch East Indies, the Balkans, etc, And here, in the exclusively Arab world, Islam created a movement linked to national ideas, which was called Pan-Arabism, and in which the strongest defensive front, or more precisely the most violent hostility towards Europe and Christianity, was expressed, which had been launched in this territory since the advance of the Moors into Spain. (For that matter, let us compare the admirable cultural monuments and artistic treasures that the Moors produced in Spain with the wretched traces left by Christianity, the fruit of an artistic-cultural will from totally deranged minds and sensibilities!) This opposition is particularly evident where the forms of political life are still visibly imbued with the spirit of combat, as in Palestine, Algeria and other centres of the struggle for power. And here, in the heart of this combat zone, is also the place that is the driving force of the pan-Arab movement and represents both the spiritual and religious heart of this gigantic struggle, i.e. the centuries-old famous Cairo University El-Ashar. From this point of enormous concentration of religious and political energy, countless professors and leaders go annually to all parts of the Arab world to preach the hatred of all foreign domination. The remaining Muslim institutes in Damascus or Fez are also gathering points of the Islamic ruling elite, from where the Muslim professors, called "ulama", go to the battle front and create a new warlike impulse in small mosques and remote Bedouin villages.

In connection with the pan-Islamic efforts of the Turkish caliphate, it is important to mention the following: The abolition of the caliphate by Kemal Ataturk, the creator of the new Turkey, who passed away a few months ago, was in no way directed against Islam as such. In essence, it was imperative to remove the young Turkey from the problems of the remaining Arab states that had left the old Osman Empire, thereby ensuring the assured building of the young Turkish state that hard sacrifices had made possible. This is what determined the separation of the Sultanate and the Caliphate, which was followed later in the course of evolution by the complete but not totally definitive abolition of the Caliphate (and thus of the religious authority of all Mohammedans). The fact that the caliphate itself was then abolished should not be attributed to determined Arab personalities who wanted to destroy definitively at the source all reactionary hopes of a rebirth of the old Osmanic Empire. As a result of particular events, which cannot be elaborated on, the subsequent development of Turkey led to a definite separation between the state and Islam, so that Turkey today occupies a kind of special position in relation to the remaining Arab states.

But moreover, the enormous force of attraction that the holy place of Islam, the pilgrimage city of Mecca, exerts on all believers today, as it did in the past, demonstrates the strength of the sense of common belonging of all Muslims. Every year pilgrims from all parts of the world gather here. They receive new strength for their religious and political struggle and the Muslims, numbering about 250 million worldwide, constantly feel the deep sense of an indissoluble community. It is certainly a religious community with obvious anti-western features and is therefore the basis for a political struggle.

One of the most notable differences in nature between Christianity and Islam is also evident here. In all the dreams of power and especially in the imperialist lusts constantly expressed, for example, by the Catholic Church in the course of history, Christianity has been largely excluded from the latest political decision-making in all Western countries. This is not to say that it did not participate in the conflicts of the past: but when decisions and imperatives were made, it acted against the state and thus against the political development of the West. On the other hand, Islam was able to motivate and influence political decisions to a large extent from a religious point of view, again in contrast to Christianity—this is because, for both Arabs and Muslims, religion is simply the expression of their natural way of life, so that a clash of the two powers comparable to the clash of the emperor and the pope in the Western world could not possibly take place. But in the Arab world, as we have already seen, there are also oppositions which are exploited today mainly by the British to prevent a fusion of all Arabs. But all these divisions are secondary, even if they persist, while Islam unites with nationalism in that synthesis which we have called pan-Arabism, and which, as a future great power, will face the European powers still unable to take a clear stand.

In this context, one man deserves special attention. One of the Arab leaders who will play a decisive role is Ibn Saud, the king of Saudi Arabia, the largest Arab state today. This fearless warrior and diplomat, barely 20 years old and from the Persian Gulf port city of Kuwait, forced his way into Er Riad, the capital of the Arab Empire, in 1901 with a handful of reckless Bedouins and thus reconquered the land of his fathers. In 1924, he drove King Hussein out of the Hijaz when the latter wanted to appoint himself caliph, quickly conquered the whole of the Hijaz with his well-equipped soldiers and annexed it to his domain, which today indirectly includes Yemen, after forcing the Imam of Yemen to submit. This orthodox Arab of the Wahabi sect is today one of the figures on the Arab chessboard on whom many Muslims hope for a restoration of the caliphate. The Wahabi sect differs from the rest of the Islamic sects in that it purifies the Mohametan faith from all additions and expresses it through an almost puritanical rule of life. The liberation from theological dogmatism and the return to the doctrine as announced by the Prophet are the main characteristics of this community of the extraordinarily moral Wahabites.

It is not yet known whether Ibn Seoub will tackle the problem of the caliphate. For the political struggle is still too much at the forefront of the necessities for this more religious question to have been resolved yet. But when the decision has to be made, Ibn Saud will in any case put the weight of his strong personality and the power of his state in the balance if it is also a question of crowning the new creation of the Arab world from a purely religious point of view.

Perhaps then this new Arab leader will personify, in the sense of a strengthened pan-Arabism, that alliance between nationalism and Islam that is characteristic of the evolution that has taken place. The "holy war" of the past was a beautiful formula, but in reality it was totally meaningless. Tomorrow's "holy war" will be placed under the green flag of the Prophet and the banner of pan-Arabism, but also of the Western world, thus forcing the Arab world to clearly define its spheres of interest.

Alfred Pilllmann

SS Booklet No. 1. 1939.

The Empire of Ataturk

It is a curious coincidence that destiny would have people who are completely foreign to each other and who live in very different areas follow parallel developments, and moreover, at exactly the same time and under the same conditions.

We can also see this development in the history of Italy and Germany, both of which, after a great past, fell into political and national impotence due to their internal disunity. But in the second half of the 19th century, thanks to statesmen of genius (Bismarck, Cavour), they took the first step towards unity and recovery and then became great powers led by soldiers from the front after the war. We all have the unexpected chance to live and see that our countries have become world powers.

Turkey has experienced a similar development. The old nomadic Turkish people appeared at about the same time as the German people in international history. Towards the beginning of the Christian era, at the time of droughts, the Asian peoples of the steppe moved every year to the more fertile regions, sometimes as invaders such as the Huns of Attila or the Mongols of Tamerlane and Genghis Khan. The Turkic tribes went every year to the regions between the Black Sea and the Mediterranean Sea, mainly Anatolia, Mesopotamia, Syria and Iran.

The great miracle of Islam was that it was accepted voluntarily by the Turks, who until then had practised the cult of the stars from which their present coat of arms is still derived: the half-moon and the star. The Turks, who had now become sedentary, were so important that in the 8th century they became the driving force in all areas of life and by the 9th century they dominated practically the entire Muslim world, even though the kings and caliphs were Arab. They became the elite of the Mohammedan army, but remained faithful to their national character and language: this is one of the reasons for their invincible strength and faith in themselves despite long and bloody wars.

In these circumstances, it is not surprising that they gradually took over the leadership of the Muslim world, which in fact happened at the end of the 13th century. It was a Seljuk tribal leader, Osman, a great warlord of the time, who gave his name to the "Osmanli" dynasty.

His successors ruled Turkey until 1924.

The power of the Osmanli rulers lay in the fact that, unlike most potentates in Europe and Asia, they had a well-defined objective, obvious to the nation, which enabled them to achieve the supreme goal1: the unification and reunion of all Turkic tribes into a central Empire of the Turkish type. This was to be an Empire of born lords and masters who forged the unity of the Islamic world, a totally divided world united only by the teachings of the Prophet, clearly aware of the danger that would one day come from the West.

The weakness of the Osmanis lay in their establishment in old Europe, although the reason for this was a Greek emperor's call for help in settling an internal quarrel. While the Turks were a racially pure state in the 14th century capable of competing with any nation in the world, possessing one of the first regular armies, they exhausted their national forces all over Europe from that time until the 17th century. It is only thanks to the German armies and their leaders—in particular Prince Eugene—that they stopped in front of Vienna and gradually left Europe.

Selim I, who ruled from 1512 to 1520, was one of the wisest princes who ever reigned. His closest associates were not representatives of the nobility or the higher social classes but often sons of peasants and cowherds and they were proud of this fact. Writers of that time mention this fact as something unheard of and unknown in Europe. Selim recognised only ability and value. He was indifferent to extraction and origin. After the conquest of Iran, Egypt, Arabia and Syria he was, since 1517, not only Sultan, but also

Caliph, i.e. he was both temporal and religious ruler, and his successors remained so until Atatürk, before the complete ousting of the Sultans, separated the temporal and religious power.

The successor and son of Selim I, Suleiman II, was the most brilliant of the Osman rulers, but also the last of these great rulers. His successors degenerated more and more, provoked quarrels and intrigues, disorder and discontent. It was the time when Europe was awakening thanks to the initiative of Germany, despite the intrigues of France against European stability, and this was the end of the power of the Osmanli Empire. Prince Eugene drove the Turks east, but they remained in the Balkans for a long time. Napoleon inflicted heavy defeats on them in Egypt, and Turkish dominance would have ended much sooner had the European powers not been disunited as England and France were during the Egyptian campaign.

However, Napoleon provoked the awakening of the Serbs, Bulgarians and Greeks still under Turkish rule. The latter declared their independence in 1829 at the Peace of Andrinople and, soon after, the Russians began to take a keen interest in the Balkans, the Bosphorus and the Dardanelles. Their pan-Slavism made them outspoken opponents of the Turks. However, they were unable to get closer to their goals in the Russian-Turkish Crimean War.

We must thank Bismarck for finally bringing peace and tranquillity after these interminable disputes: it was he who, in 1878, at the Congress of Berlin, obtained that the suzerainty of the Turks over most of the Balkan states be abolished but that, on the other hand, the stability of the Osmanli Empire remain untouched, which, as we all know, led to Russian resentment.

In 1908, the Turkish revolution was born, led by Enver Pada, who wanted to turn the "sick state of the Bosphorus" into a structured state, which required, above all, comprehensive reforms. Turkey was still medieval, and cruel and despotic sultans were strongly opposed to any development.

The young Turks failed, however, because they too did not come from the people, but were recruited from the intelligentsia and the bourgeoisie of the country and therefore had no influence on the peasant masses. The decline became more pronounced. Bulgaria declared its independence, Italy seized Libya and Atatürk won almost the only victory of the war in the battle of Tobruk.

The Balkan peoples declared a war on Turkey that ended with major losses of territory but could have ended even worse, even with the end of the Turkish Empire, if the courage of the Anatolian soldiers had not broken the enemy's assault on Andrinople. 1913 saw the end of the Second Balkan War after two years of bloody fighting; the peace of Constantinople pushed Turkey almost completely out of Europe.

When the First World War broke out, it was clear to all that Russia saw its chance to finally bring Turkey down. As a result, Turkey was forced to take a stand against Russia, and thus with Germany and the central powers. When the Russian war archives were later examined, it became clear that Russia's intentions had been duly recorded.

One of the Turks' greatest feats of war was the defence of the straits, to which German officers contributed. Here we should mention General von der Goltz, the renovator and reorganiser of the Turkish army. During the Great War, von der Goltz was first a general aide-de-camp to the Sultan and later commander-in-chief of the First Turkish Army. The Anafarta Army Group bore the brunt of the battle; its leader, Mustapha Kemal Pasha, covered himself in glory for the second time in his life and ultimately contributed to the Allies' retreat. He also commanded the Seventh Army, which covered the retreat of the Turks in the rear and thus won the esteem of all his enemies.

However, for a bloodless Turkey, the war did not end with the armistice of 18 October 1918. At the instigation of France and Britain, Greek troops landed in Smyrna and began a cruel war that lasted three years and would have quickly spelled the end of Turkey had it not been for the intervention of Atatürk.

The real instigators of these deadly battles were not the Greeks, who thought they were doing the West and Christian culture a great service, but the two eternal fools, Lloyd George and Winston Churchill, who wanted to annex a land route to India by reducing Turkey to a conglomerate of small, miniature states that they would have put under Greek, English and French tutelage. The Greeks, on the other hand, were to get the lion's share of the credit.

Much of Turkey was occupied by the Armenians, the British, the French, the Greeks and the Italians under the armistice in question. When the Greeks, under the protection of the British and French fleets, went on the attack, the situation of the Turks was desperate. The nation, completely exhausted by eight years of war, was demoralised. The Sultan was pandering to the Western powers; he turned out to be an orderly politician, of the kind we knew in Germany at the same time.

Then Mustapha Kemal appeared. He did not worry about the sultan or the institutions, he gathered the Turkish armies, reorganised them and armed them with Russian help. The Soviets were happy to do this, as they knew that the Western powers would not stop at Turkey. Near the border were Baku and Batum, Tiflis, the oil wells whose shares Sir Henry Deterding had already cautiously bought, thus making the biggest blunder of his life.

Kemal Pasha was, however, shrewd enough to free himself from the noose in which the Soviets were gradually trying to entangle Turkey. While his foreign policy later cultivated friendship with Soviet Russia first and foremost, he ruthlessly suppressed all communists within the country. In the meantime he needed help. With poor means and in pitiful circumstances, he began to fight against an opponent three times his size, lost a few battles and then, as a born military genius, drove the Greeks back, battle after battle. When the Allies saw that the plan was failing because of unexpected Turkish resistance, they invited the Turks to a conference in 1921 in London, although Lloyd George had described the Turkish forces as a band of looters and Kemal as a rebel general, just as General Franco had recently done.

This conference did not produce any results. The battle continued. In August and September 1921, Kemal crowned his warrior glory by leading his poor troops to victory after long and hard fighting with numerous tactical manoeuvres, but above all with a passionate impulse against an enemy that was far superior in numbers and weaponry. The national assembly awarded him the title of "El Gasi", the victorious.

Within a few months, the enemy was definitively defeated, especially at the memorable battles of Afion, Karahissar and Inonu. The victor at Inonu was Kemal's chief of staff and his successor as president. The Sultan had to go into exile, accused of high treason and Lloyd George had to resign. This time he had been totally wrong. King Constantine of Greece abdicated, and Kemal began to educate his people, not without difficulty, to slowly but surely become a modern great power. On 24 July 1923, after about twelve years of war, peace was reached at the Treaty of Lausanne. The Greeks had to surrender the European part of Turkey and Eastern Thrace: the country was saved.

After the separation of spiritual and temporal powers, the heir to the throne was proclaimed caliph. When the clergy later proved to be totally reactionary and conspiratorial, Kemal abolished the caliphate and all that went with it without further ado. The people had little attachment to their church and did not move when the abolition came. However, the banning of the fez and the introduction of the hat caused unrest.

Apart from the fact that the people, completely exhausted, had to regain their strength, Kemal had a lot to do because of the illiteracy of 90% of the population and all the outdated institutions. He set an example, introducing the Latin script into the spoken language, abolishing the veil and the fez, travelling the country and teaching the peasants to read and write.

He was aided in his enterprise by the natural wealth of the country. For a surface area about twice that of Germany, Turkey has only 16 million inhabitants, nine-tenths of whom are of Turkish race and two-thirds of whom are peasants. The fertility rate is remarkable: 23 births per 1,000 inhabitants. This trend is reinforced by the return of Turkish emigrants living abroad who come to settle at the initiative of the state.

The new Turkey has already been self-sufficient for ten years. It no longer depends on foreign supplies, even in years of crop failure. The country is recovering visibly from the state of a medieval Empire of the

Thousand and One Nights to that of a modern state in a period of time hitherto unknown in the East. The Germans have contributed greatly to all these transformations and achievements. Once again, it turns out that here, as everywhere, the Germans are the only civilised people on earth capable of helping other developing peoples without exploiting them.

Our sympathy went to the Turks and the Japanese because in both cases we were dealing with chivalrous, hard-working and courageous people who, moreover, like us, experience a national communion from which they draw their strength. Like Adolf Hitler, Kemal Pasha, who after the creation of his family name was called Kemal Atatürk, abolished the social classes in his country and brought the sovereignty of the people in the person of the elected leader to the highest degree.

From then on, Germany became Turkey's most important trading partner. In 1937, Turkey bought 48,132,000 Turkish Liras worth of goods from Germany and exported 50,412,000 Turkish Liras to Germany. America followed at a very distant third, England at one-sixth and France at one-tenth. The most important Turkish export is tobacco. The main imports are fabrics, steel and machinery.

Politically, under Ataturk, Turkey became a leading power and master of the passage from the Black Sea to the Mediterranean Sea, a possession which was sovereignly confirmed to it in the Treaty of Montreux in 1936. This passage has always been of great importance as a link between the West and the East, between Europe and Asia.

For centuries Constantinople has been the major transhipment point for goods traffic between Asia and Europe. With this in mind, Germany wanted to build the Berlin-Baghdad railway line before the war, a project that was thwarted by England, until today, when the old dream has become reality: it will soon be possible to travel by rail from Berlin to Baghdad and Tehran.

In Turkey there is a very strong feeling of guardianship and a strong aversion to it. There is no trace of this in the case of Germany. Germany has always cooperated unselfishly in the development of the country. Germans have been working in Turkey for many years as soldiers, technicians, architects and teachers, the only foreigners who are supported there and even sought out.

In recent years, huge deposits of ore and oil have been discovered. Turkey is immensely rich. Germany only wants trade between friends. The proof of this is the 150 million marks of credit on goods which the Reich Trade Minister Funk has granted to Turkey. If now, all of a sudden, England is interested in Turkey commercially, the last person in that country knows what that means: precaution against the growing German influence in the Middle East.

And every Turk also knows that England will not change anything, that Turkey will not take orders from anyone anymore; it declared this in Montreux. The Soviets were furious because they had believed that Turkey would sail in their wake. Strategically, this country fears nothing. A powerful army, a good war fleet and 4,000 kilometres of coastline for 6,000 kilometres of border, apart from the fact that the "straits" are impregnable.

The Turks are a people with whom the world must reckon. We Germans have the advantage of old friendship, comradeship in arms and frank sympathy. Now that Germany has become the greatest power in the Danube, it will not be long before an intensive river trade is established between our two states. We export cloth and machinery. We need each other and will remain united despite the low blows of third parties.

SS-Ustuf. Lorenz

III. ADVERSARIES

SS BOOKLET NO. 3. 1936.

SS-OSTUF. HEINRICH BAUER:
THE OLD TESTAMENT, SELF-PORTRAIT OF THE JEWS

The history of the patriarchs and kings of the Old Testament is certainly a bad historical source, for it is full of tales, legends and falsifications; truth and poetry, the richness of the spirit of the Aryan peoples, Jewish distortions and additions follow one another in a jumble. But for us, the Old Testament has a fundamental value because it is the self-portrait of the Jews. An Aryan brain could not imagine stories comparable to those of Abraham, Isaac, Jacob and Joseph.

The figures of Abraham and Joseph are imaginary, but Abraham's journey and Joseph's life are based on historical facts.

The Jews were a tiny minority within the population of Palestine. In this territory of passage, of combat and of colonization of tribes of the most diverse types, racial chaos reigned, marked first by a Negro influence, then by an oriental influence from Asia Minor. The Jews assimilated the blood of the most different African, Asian and European peoples.

Between 450 and 400 BC, the prophets Ezra and Nehemiah established strict racial laws that forbade any further interbreeding with foreign tribes. It is significant that these racial laws of the eastern Jews have been preserved to this day and that the desire for separation persists in authentic Jewry. Thanks to this separation, which has been present for about 2,000 years and is fixed by religious law, the Jewish people have created a more or less homogeneous community in itself.

Miscegenation and the absence of an ancestral homeland have caused the Jew to spread throughout the world in the course of history, but he has always retained his ethnic characteristic.

From Ezra onwards, Jewry was built up gradually from the remaining population of Palestine and grew constantly. Like a spider's web, it spread throughout the Old World. The Jews settled in the major cities of the Mediterranean area and formed isolated settlements which were permanently reinforced by massive and voluntary emigration from Palestine.

The same process then occurred in all countries:

The Jews were at first tolerated by the population, then even favoured by the rulers, until the disgust and hatred of the population towards them reached its boiling point because of their arrogance, pretension and usury, and the Jews were expelled or protective laws were passed against them. This happened in Egypt, Babylonia and Persia, in Greece and Italy, in Spain and England. We had the same thing in Germany.

Like the figures of Abraham and Joseph, the figure of Esther is also legendary. But the story of Esther also has a historical background. The same principle has governed Jewish politics from the earliest times: The sensual woman serves as a weapon in the struggle for life of individuals and peoples. From time immemorial, the politics of Esther played a great role in the Jewish people's aspiration to world domination: beautiful and intelligent Jewish women became the mistresses of kings, princes and influential men; they chained them to themselves with their sensual charm and used them for the benefit of their people. In this way, they obtained advantages for their countrymen, learned the most secret plans, etc.

The "Jewess of Toledo", the mistress of the Spanish king Alfonso I, Is well known for having granted the Jews such unheard-of favours that the people resorted to violence.

In the salons, or rather in the brothels of high society, the beautiful Jewish women Henriette Herz, Dorothea Veit (later married to Friedrich Schlegel) and Rachel Varnhagen entertained statesmen and princes, poets and scholars at the end of the 18th century.

During the Congress of Vienna in 1814/15, the daughters of the wealthy Berlin Jew Itzig, who had married the bankers von Arnstein and Eskeles in Vienna, ensured that Jewish interests were defended after the War of Independence against Napoleon: politicians, including Hardenberg and Wilhelm von Humboldt, discussed the most secret political issues in their salons.

Chancellor Caprivi was a frequent guest in the political salon of the Jewish woman von Lebbin, and the later imprisoned Countess Fischler-Treubner of Berlin, a member of the Kaufmann-Asser family, was a meeting place for leading figures from the Foreign Office, politics and economics, as well as Erzberger, Maximilian Harden, Georg Bernhard, Friedrich Stampfer and other leading Jewish figures.

This presentation from Genesis, written by Jewish historians, and the Book of Esther, also written by a Jewish chronicler, should show the insurmountable opposition between the ideas, feelings and actions of Germans and Jews.

The history of the Jews begins with the call of the Jewish national god Yahweh to Abram, the forefather of the Jewish people: "Leave your country, your kindred, and your father's house, for the land that I will show you. I will make you a great people, I will bless you, I will magnify your name; be a blessing! I will bless those who bless you, I will reprove those who curse you. In you all the clans of the earth will be blessed" (Genesis, chap. 12, v. 1–3).

The departure of Abram and his family from Chaldea between the Tigris and Euphrates rivers to the fertile land of the Jordan River, Canaan, located west of the Mediterranean, later called Palestine, i.e. the land of the Philistines, was the beginning of the offensive of the Jewish people, travellers and idlers, to the countries surrounding Asia Minor and later to the other countries of the world. Dominating this convoy is the word of Yahweh that justified the claim and demand of the Jews to this day: "I will bless those who bless you, I will reprove those who curse you!

A famine drove Abram from Canaan to Egypt (another typical Jewish trait: where I feel good is my home!). But so that the Egyptians would not treacherously kill him because of his beautiful wife Sarai, whom they wanted to keep alive, he orders his wife (v. 13): "Say, I pray thee, that thou art my sister, that I may be treated well for thy sake, and that I may be left alive for thy sake. As a result, the Egyptian king welcomes the physically desirable prostitute wife into his house and bed and fills the supposed brother Abram with flocks and slaves, on top of everything else, because of her kindness. But this Sarai is precisely at the origin of the plagues that Yahweh inflicts on Pharaoh in an astonishing way until the latter recognises the state of things. The latter reproaches Abram severely: "What have you done to me? Why did you not tell me that she was your wife? Why did you say, 'She is my sister', so that I took her as my wife? With incomprehensible forbearance, the king lets Abram, the deceiver and matchmaker, peacefully leave Egypt with his wife Sarai and all the wealth he has obtained.

So he renewed his evil dealings with Sarai, mocking the most sacred and inviolable things. When Sarai learned that she was barren, she offered her own Egyptian servant Hagar to bear her a child, as if children were a commodity to be bought, a bargain to be purchased. But when the servant girl became pregnant, the hatred of the barren woman erupted and Abram retaliated to her accusation by abandoning the pregnant servant girl at this critical moment: "Well, your servant girl is in your hands, do with her as it seems good to you. (Sarai) now wanting to humiliate Hagar, she abandoned her (chap. 16, v. 6). Since the first Hagar affair, the Jew has constantly sacrificed the impure goy, especially a member of the nobler races, without scruples, when he had achieved his goal.

Shortly afterwards, Abram, the Jewish herder and trader, went to Gerar with his flocks (Genesis, chap. 20). Again, he passed Sarai off as his sister so that Abimelech, the chief of Gerar, would welcome the still beautiful and sensual woman into his house like all his fellow citizens, without knowing of their marriage. But Yahweh calls him back in a dream and orders him: "Now give back this man's wife: he is a prophet and he will intercede for you so that you may live. Through his unbridled immoral deception, Abram becomes Abimelech's saviour and apologises to the gullible Abimelech with characteristic Jewish cowardice and effrontery (v. 11): "I said to myself, 'Surely there is no fear of God in this place, and they will kill me for my wife's sake. Thereupon, with suicidal indulgence and philanthropy, Abimelech replies to the Jew: "See my land that is open before you. Settle wherever you like.

The son of the grandfather Jacob, Joseph, the intriguer and divider hated by his brothers, was sold into Egypt. By interpreting dreams and making prodigious calculations, he rose to the position of general administrator and vizier of the pharaoh of the time and made himself indispensable by his cunning economic and taxation policy. When poverty struck the land of Canaan, the Jews among Joseph's brothers—about seventy men—left for rich Egypt and found a hospitable home with the Pharaoh through Joseph. As they grew in numbers and wealth, Joseph put the hitherto free Egyptian people completely at the mercy of Pharaoh and facilitated the government's takeover of Egyptian land ownership. He thus took advantage of the poverty in Egypt, gathered much grain in the state granaries and exchanged all their livestock for grain (Genesis 47, v. 15ff.). But the famine persisted and the Egyptians, who were totally at the mercy of the cruel vizier Joseph, went to him again, pleading (vv. 19–20): 'Why should we die before your eyes, we and our land? So buy our people and our land for bread, and we will be Pharaoh's serfs with our land. But give us something to sow, so that we may stay alive and not die and our land be desolate."

So Joseph bought all of Egypt for Pharaoh. For the Egyptians sold all their fields since the famine was too much for them. The country was thus the exclusive property of Pharaoh. Only the land of the powerful priests was spared from the forced liquidation by the clever Joseph. But! History barely mentions this exploitation of the Egyptian people. When the Egyptians returned to work, reduced to the rank of serfs doing chores, he demanded of them (vv. 23–24): "So now I have bought you for Pharaoh, with your land. But of the harvest you must give one fifth to Pharaoh, and the other four shares are yours, for the seed of the field, for your food and that of your family, for the food of your dependents." Thus a fifth of all the revenue taken from the people stripped of their land is assured to the king thanks to Joseph, who with his position as grand vizier and his fame, acquires immense power and wealth. But after centuries of exploitation, the Egyptian people rose up against these parasitic Jewish hosts who had become rich and powerful in number, overthrew them and finally reduced them to servitude until they left Egypt for good.

The same thing happened in Babylonia. Under Nebuchadnezzar, the Jews were privileged and received, as always, wealth and high positions among the people who welcomed them. But here too, with their unbridled selfishness as bestowed by Yahweh, they exploited the people so much that the latter rose up against them and oppressed them. When the victorious Persian king Cyrus marched against the capital city of Babylon in revenge, the Jews betrayed and secretly opened the gates to the besieger so that the city would fall.

The Jews obtained great privileges from the state in the new Persian Empire. They knew how to make themselves useful to the king, as Joseph had done to the Pharaoh. The princes sided with the immigrant exploiter, while the people, at first defenceless, had to suffer their power.

The book of Esther (I, v. I) tells us that Ahasuerus—historically Xerxes—was the king of Persia, which included the borders from India to Africa—this was the time when the Persian Empire was at its peak. He wanted to show off the beauty of his wife Vashti to the great men of his empire with a festival that lasted 180 days in Susa, his capital. However, the princess, an Aryan woman, refused to reveal herself, considering that her chastity would be outraged. The king then repudiated her, a victim of intoxication of power and possession. And when young girls were sought for the harem of Xerxes, the Jew Mordecai saw the time to gain influence over the powerful Persian king through his beautiful ward Esther. She went to the king's house, was given the most beautiful toilet by the keeper of the women and placed herself and some others in the best place in the women's house—the place where the king would first see her. It is said further: "Esther had not revealed either her relatives or her people, as Mordecai had commanded her, and she continued to observe his instructions as in the days when she was under his guardianship. Chastity plays no role for the Jews (Judith also infiltrated the camp of General Holofernes as a prostitute to murder him on his bed at night, rather than the Jewish men attacking him in battle) but she could not reveal her origin if she wanted to win the game in a covert way. Soon Esther, the beautiful prostitute, stood before the king who succumbed to her sensuality and preferred her to the chaste Vashti who had been repudiated. Shortly afterwards, the game of intrigue began: two of the king's chamberlains were executed, because Mordecai had informed the king, through his soon-to-be powerful instrument Esther, that they had planned an attack against him. Xerxes was thus obliged to the Jews and two inconvenient opponents were removed. By the time of this expansion of the Jews, their arrogance had become intolerable and their influence a danger to the state. Xerxes did not notice this, but his faithful minister Aman did. Aman saw that the Jew Mordecai, who was on the daily prowl around the royal castle in Susa, and his fellow Jews living in the Persian Empire were not obeying the king and his orders. He also knew how much anger there was among the people against the exploiter. He made himself the executor of the popular will and explained to Xerxes the following (chap. 3, v. 8–9): "Aman said to King Ahasuerus: 'In the midst of the people, in all the provinces of your kingdom, there is scattered a people apart. Their laws are not like those of any other, and the royal laws are a dead letter to them. The interests of the king do not allow them to be left alone. Therefore let his doom be signed, if the king thinks it good, and I will pay to his officials, to the account of the royal treasury, ten thousand talents of silver."

"The king took his ring off his hand and gave it to Aman, son of Hamdata the Agagite, the persecutor of the Jews. He said to him, "Keep your money. As for this people, I give it to you, do with it what you will" ... (v. 13) and letters were sent to all the provinces of the kingdom with the command to destroy, kill and exterminate all the Jews, from the youngest to the oldest, including children and women, on the same day, namely the thirteenth of the twelfth month, which is Adar, and to sack their goods" (obtained by usury and fraud).

Mordecai and Esther immediately prepared a response so that the impending extermination would turn into a complete victory of the Jews over the hated Persians (Esther, chap. 5). Esther begged the king and Aman to come to a meal and the drunken king granted her everything she wanted. In the meantime, Aman had a gallows set up in his house from which the troublesome Mordecai was to be hanged. Shortly before the meal, Xerxes was reminded that he had been saved from the conspirators by Mordecai. When Esther told him at the meal that Aman had planned the death of all the Jews, Xerxes went away upset into the garden and Aman, seeing the catastrophe coming, prayed on his knees to Esther for his life. Xerxes returned and misinterpreted this attitude. In a fit of angry jealousy, disturbed as he was by the wine and the woman, he had his faithful minister hanged from the tree in his house.

The Jews took revenge on the Persians in a terrible way. Xerxes gave Mordecai the house and the ring of Aman, thus all the power. Immediately new orders were given to the 127 provinces of Persia in the following language (v. 10-17): "These letters, written in the name of the king Ahasuerus and sealed with his seal, were carried by couriers mounted on horses from the king's studs. The king granted to the Jews, in whatever city they were, the right to assemble for safety, with permission to exterminate, slaughter and destroy all the armed people of the peoples or provinces who wanted to attack them, with their wives and children, as well as to plunder their goods. This was to be done on the same day in all the provinces of king Ahasuerus, on the thirteenth day of the twelfth month, which is Adar.

"The copy of this edict, intended to be promulgated as a law in every province, was published among all the people so that the Jews would be ready on the day in question to take revenge on their enemies. The couriers, riding on royal horses, set out with great haste and diligence at the king's command. The decree was also published in the citadel of Susa. Mordecai came out of the king's house dressed in a princely garment of purple and white linen, crowned with a great golden diadem and wearing a cloak of byssus and red purple. The whole city of Susa rang with joy. It was a day of light, joy, exultation and triumph for the Jews. In all the provinces, in all the cities, everywhere where the orders of the royal decree reached, it was for the Jews, only gladness, jubilation, banquets and festivals. Among the population of the country many people became Jews, because the fear of the Jews fell upon them.

On the appointed day, the bloody tragedy was carried out (chap. 9, v. 5): "So the Jews struck all their enemies with the sword. It was a massacre, an extermination, and they did what they wanted with their adversaries (v. 16). For their part, the Jews of the royal provinces also gathered to make their lives safe. They got rid of their enemies by slaughtering seventy-five thousand of their adversaries, without plundering." At Esther's special wish, Xerxes had the ten sons of Aman hanged on the same tree, and the Jews made that day "a day of feasting and rejoicing. And in remembrance of the day of vengeance, they established the festival of Purim, which they still celebrate today.

SS BOOKLET NO. 3. 1936.

E. BRANDT: JEWISH RITUAL MURDER

Ritual murder or sacrifice is a very special aspect of the larger Jewish question. Most educated men do not want to believe such "stories". Official science found it unworthy of itself to examine the matter thoroughly and merely declared the "reports" of the Jew Chwolson and especially of the infamous Berlin professor Hermann Strack to be fundamental and authoritative, even though these examinations had nothing to do with scientific research worthy of the name and are merely misleading and biased apologetic writings of Jewry. For most scientists, therefore, the ritual murder case must be considered closed; in their opinion, it is only the product of the diseased brains of anti-Semites.

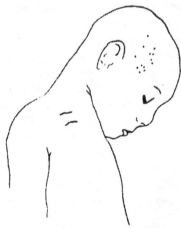

Schoolboy Andrej Juchchinskij murdered by means of thirteen ritual slashes during his sleep in 1911 in Kiev (Beili trial).

But the raw facts are quite different!

There are many Jewish ritual murders in history, starting from the 5th century of the Christian era. In my Russian-language book, I examined three hundred and twenty cases and four hundred and twenty in the existing German manuscript. The Catholic Church also counts among its martyred saints and beatified many victims of Jewish ritual murder, among them St. Werner, who is still venerated today by the Catholic population of Oberwesel on the Rhine and is the patron saint of the town. Let us mention only three ritual murders:

1. 1475, in Trent. The ritual murder, on the 28th of the month, of the boy Simon Gerber, who was beatified by the Catholic Church; the records of the trial still exist today, even in Trent, in the Vatican and in copies in Vienna.
2. 1840, in Damascus, on the Catholic Capuchin Father Thomas and his servant Ibrahim Amarah.
3. 1852/53, in Saratov, on Theophan Scherstobitov, aged 10, and on Michael Maslov, aged 12.

In the first and last of these cases, the victims had been circumcised before the blood was drawn.

These three cases are indisputably proven on a legal level. In the first two trials the Jews also made full confessions. They are disturbed by this, but their defenders have no qualms about claiming that this, as in all other similar cases, is the conviction of an innocent person. When one reads the records of the pleas in these trials, one can legitimately be surprised: minutes, depositions, even historical documents and pieces such as papal bulls are falsified in a very clever way. In many documents, certain things are distorted or simply omitted. Thus, the facts take on a completely different face. This demonstration only shows that the claim that there was no ritual murder does not hold water; for to prove the truth one does not use lies. It is also striking to see how the Jews make every effort to have the cases dismissed in all trials concerning ritual murders. False witnesses, the judicial authorities and the police are bought. In vain, because public opinion all over the world is moved; in Parliament, various regions have made proposals. Finally, even diplomatic representations were made. But it was also in vain because the Jews threatened reprisals, as they did in 1882 at the Tsza-Eszlar trial. The Parisian Rothschild had the nerve to send a telegram to the government of Austria-Hungary with the following postface

"If the government does not comply with my summons (to stop the trial and free all the Jews), I will do everything I can to ruin Hungary's credit.

It is not surprising that, under such conditions, most of the ritual murder trials were buried…

Let us mention only one of the many legally indisputable ritual murders: 1840, in Damascus.

On Wednesday 5 February 1840, Capuchin Father Thomas and his servant Ibrahim Amarah were victims of a ritual murder in the Jewish quarter of Damascus.

All the records of the examination and proceedings were published in 1846 in a book written by a member of the 'Oriental Society', Achille Laurant. Needless to say, this book is one of the greatest bibliographic rarities and can only be found in very few libraries. The original trial files are to be found in the archives of the Ministry of Foreign Affairs in Paris. The French specialist on ritual murders, Abbé Henri Desportes, claimed that all these documents disappeared under the ministry of the Jew Crémieux in 1870, while the defender of the Jews, Abbé Vacandard, assures that the French Ministry of Foreign Affairs must have officially certified on August 5, 1892 that all the documents are in perfect condition at the Ministry. Which of the two is right, one cannot say with certainty, apparently Desportes, because the Minister of the Exterior of the time, Pichon, refused a new examination of the original documents, on June 6, 1913, to the editor of the " Libre Parole", Albert Monniot!

Either these documents were destroyed by Crémieux, or they contain details so damning to the Jews that Brother Pichon thought it best to keep them secret. Yet it is obvious that if the documents could demonstrate the innocence of the Jews, as they always claim, they would have already been published officially long ago, and by the Cremieux Jew himself.

What did this trial reveal? Under the pretext that he had to vaccinate a Jewish child against smallpox, Father Thomas was locked up in a Jewish house, assaulted, stripped naked and had his throat slit by eight Jews, among whom were two rabbis. His blood was collected in a basin, bottled and given to the Chacham (rabbi) Abu-el-Afiè. After the murder, the father's clothes were burnt and the body was cut into pieces, all the bones of which were crushed with a pestle. They were put in a coffee bag and thrown into a sewer, which was quite far from the house.

The authorities obtained these confessions from two Jews, the barber Soliman and the servant Marad-el-Fattal, with the promise to pardon them if they told the whole truth. The two Jews were interrogated separately. Their statements coincided in every detail. Everything was checked on the spot. Even though a month had already passed since the murder, distinct traces of blood could be seen on the walls of the room where the father's throat had been cut. And at the place indicated by the Jews where the bones and the skull had been crushed, one could see obvious hollows in the ground. Traces of blood and pieces of flesh were found in the opening of the sewer. In the canal itself, the following body parts were found: foot bones with joints, a kneecap, parts of a skull, a part of the heart, a vertebra, a piece of nerve, a piece of the skin of the skull on which part of the tonsure could be seen (the remaining surface was covered with hair), and finally two shreds of a black woolen cap.

All the objects found were sent to the French consul Ratti Menton (Father Thomas was under French protection) with the intention of carrying out a medical examination. The French consul had the remains examined by two commissions and even by four European and six French doctors. The conclusions of both commissions showed that the remains presented were of human origin. The Austrian consul G. G. Merlato also assisted the Mohammedan doctors in their work. For his part, he submitted a certificate stating that he had learned that doctors certified the human origin of the remains cited. In addition, Ratti Menton succeeded in obtaining a statement from Father Yussuf's hairdresser that the pieces of the skullcap found could only be those of the father's skullcap.

When the results of the interrogation of the other defendants were known, they realised that persistent denial was useless and all confessed.

The father's servant, Ibrahim Amarah, searching for the missing father in the Jewish quarter, was locked up in another house by the Jews and had his throat cut in the same way as the father. Eight Jews also participated in his murder.

Of the sixteen Jews accused, four were amnestied against the promise of the Cherif-Pacha for their full confessions, two died during the hearing, the other six were sentenced to death.

But the execution of the death sentence did not take place because the Jews of Europe came to the rescue of their brethren. The famous founder of the "Alliance Israélite Universelle", the future French Prime Minister Crémieux, went to Egypt with his fellow Londoner Moses Montéfiore (Blumberg) to ask the Egyptian Khediv Mehemet-Ali to pardon the murderers. The Khediv published a firmàn in which he wrote that he was pardoning the condemned Jews at the request of Crémieux and Montéfiore, the representatives of the entire Jewish people. The word "pardon" displeased the Jews, because it confirmed their guilt. Crémieux and Montéfiore demanded that the Khediv change the term. Despite the discontent of the Jews, Mehemet-Ali struck out the word and replaced it with "liberated", which has the same meaning.

Here too, as in all ritual murder trials, the Jews did everything possible to obtain an acquittal. They bribed the witnesses and the authorities, but to no avail; attempts by the Jews to prevent the trial were met with the integrity of Ratti Menton. The trial went ahead to the end. It is therefore not surprising that the

The Jews did not shy away from any means to discredit the honest, courageous and hated French consul. The Austrian consul Merlato helped them in this. The Jews succeeded in buying him off. He suddenly changed his mind and claimed (in contradiction to his Christian statement of 3 March 1840) that the pieces of flesh and bones found in the canal were those of a dog! And the Austrian government went to King Louis Philippe to complain about Ratti Menton's 'illegal' actions. This went as far as the Chamber of

Deputies where the Prime Minister declared that he believed Ratti Menton's actions were justified, corroborated by the English consul, which was confirmed in London, and that he did not intend to sacrifice the two French consuls in Damascus and Egypt solely on the basis of a claim by the Austrian consul. He said among other things:

"I think I know better than you (the MPs) in this matter... I have carefully studied all the files on this case—it was transcribed—and let me say that they (the Jews) are much more powerful in the whole world than you want to admit; at the moment they have issued protests in every state... The Minister must have the courage to protect his civil servants in the face of such attacks... A French civil servant within his rights will always be protected from this kind of protest, wherever it may come from" (Monit. Univ. 3 June 1840p. 1258).

We can conclude on the ritual murder in Damascus with the words of the former Rabbi Drach:

"The murderers of Father Thomas, convinced of their crime, were only able to escape the rigours of the law thanks to the joint efforts of Jews in all countries... Money played a major role. (Drach, *Harmonie entre l'Église et la Synagogue*, vol.1, p. 79, Paris 1844).

What led the Jews to perform ritual murders? The Old Testament law of atonement: According to Jewish beliefs, atonement can only be made by blood. Thus, it is said in the Old Testament, Leviticus 17:11: "It is blood that atones for a life." And the Talmud, Joma 5a, says even more precisely: "Atonement results only from blood."

The Christian Church, which is based on the Old Testament, has accepted this rule. The Apostle Paul said in his *Letter to the Hebrews* 9:22:

"Besides, according to the Law, almost everything is cleansed by blood, and without the shedding of blood there is no remission. But the Christian Church teaches that Jesus Christ abolished this commandment by His sacrifice. The Church therefore introduced the bloodless sacrifice by the doctrine of the sacrament of the transubstantiation of Christ's blood in wine.

And the Jew? Without bloodshed, without bloody sacrifice, there is no atonement for him: since the destruction of the temple in Jerusalem, there is no place for sacrifice. There is no bloodless sacrifice like Christ's. What should he do? How can all his prayers and careful prescriptions for daily life help him if he cannot follow the main commandment of his religion? We note that the Talmud says, "Atonement comes only from blood." For an Orthodox Jew, however, this is appalling. This dread is expressed in the speech of an old Jew in San Francisco in 1922, which was published in The Friends of Israel. His conclusion reads:

"And it was clear to me that I had broken the Law. I had to atone, but that could only be done with blood, and there was no blood. Nothing but blood can purify the soul. In my grief, I went to the rabbis. I had only one question: "Where can I find blood for atonement?"

So these are not the musings of a madman, but the words of a true believing Jew. It would not have occurred to any Jew to call this man crazy. However, if he had acted like the candidate for the rabbinate, Max Bernstein, in 1888 in Breslau (he had indeed procured blood) and this act had become known to non-Jews as it did in the case of Bernstein, then the Jews and their press would have cried insanity. In his voluntary confession at his trial in Breslau in 1888, the candidate for the rabbinate, Max Bernstein, stated:

"The performance of the acts of atonement relieved my heavy heart and I determined to deliver myself from sin. Since, according to Bible doctrine, the soul resides in the blood of man, and since my sinful soul *could only find atonement through an innocent man, I had to obtain usable blood from a man who was still innocent.* Since I knew that the boy Hacke was suitable, that his soul was still pure, I decided to take some of his blood... *With the blood I accomplished my atonement.* He himself became a sinner by taking my sins.

The madness therefore lies not so much in the religious representations of the two Jews mentioned, but rather in the religious laws themselves.

The sacrifice of Kapores (the slaughter of a rooster or a hen) is performed as an expiation on the day before the coronation feast.

SS Booklet No. 3. 1936.

What Jews say about Jews

Benjamin Disraeli (Lord Beaconsfield):

> "No one can treat the racial principle with indifference: it is the key to world history. Language and religion are not the origin of any race—blood is!

Dr Jakob Klatzkin:

> "We are not Germans, French, etc., and Jews to boot, our Jewishness is not the superstructure of a Germanness, nor is it its infrastructure. We are simply of an alien nature; we must constantly repeat that we are an alien people in their midst and that we want to remain so. An insurmountable chasm is opening up between us and them.

Sir Alfred Mond:

"A Japanese born in Germany does not become a German. And a Jew who is born in Germany does not become a German either. Such are the questions of blood and race.

Prof. Eduard Gans:

"Baptism and even crossbreeding are of no use at all. —Even in the hundredth generation, we remain Jews as we were 3,000 years ago. We do not lose the fragrance of our race, even after dozens of crossbreedings. Our race is dominant in any sexual dealings with women; young Jews are born of it."

Walter Rathenau:

"A bizarre vision! At the heart of German life is a foreign tribe, apart, brilliantly and singularly endowed with a mobile and lively attitude. An Asiatic horde on the Brandenburg sand... Of close cohesion among themselves, of strict distrust of outsiders: they live thus in a semi-voluntary ghetto, not a living member of the people, but a foreign organism in its body..."

Arnold Zweig:

"The child of a Jewish mother is a Jew, no matter who the father is.

Dr Bernhard Cohn:

"When we see that the alliances of noble houses with rich Jewish families are multiplying, then, in spite of our liberal conceptions, we must consider this as the beginning of a moral decadence of the nobility..."

Dr Kurt Münzer:

"We have corrupted the blood of all the races of Europe. In general, today, everything is enjuvenated. Our thoughts live in everything, our minds rule the world. We are the masters. We are no longer hunted. We have implanted ourselves in the peoples, impregnated, defiled the races, broken the forces, everything has been spoiled and rotten by our vitiated culture. Our spirit can no longer be extirpated.

Jakob Wasserman:

"We know them and we bear them, those thousands of modern Jews who gnaw away at all the foundations because they themselves are without foundation; who disown today what they valued yesterday; who sully what they loved yesterday; whose betrayal is a pleasure, whose lack of dignity an ornament and whose denial a goal.

Dr Arthur Brünn:

"By Jewish national consciousness I understand the living consciousness of a common origin, the feeling of solidarity of Jews of all countries and the firm will to live a common future.

Chaim Weitzmann:

"Every country has a saturation point as far as Jews are concerned; it can only support a certain number of Jews if it does not want to get indigestion. Germany already has too many Jews... Jews know no political or geographical boundaries.

Baruch Levi:

"The Jewish people will be their own messiah. Its domination of the world will be achieved by the union of the remaining human races, the abolition of frontiers and monarchies ... and by the establishment of a world republic which will give the Jews the right of citizenship everywhere. In this new organisation of mankind, the sons of Israel, who are now scattered over the face of the earth, will unquestionably be the leading element, especially if they succeed in placing the masses of workers under the firm authority of a few of their number."

Karl Marx:

"Exchange is the real god of the Jews...

Moritz Rappaport:

"The Jew is the representative of the materialistic world view. They do not admit decisions coming from the heart, they destroy in themselves and in others the beliefs in the supernatural meaning of life, undermine religion and thus become ... strangers to all the peoples among whom they live."

Moritz Goldstein (March 1912):

"Jews suddenly find themselves in positions from which they have not been violently removed. It is becoming more and more apparent that it is as if German cultural life has fallen into Jewish hands. We Jews are managing the spiritual property of a people who are contesting our right and ability to do so.

Konrad Alberti Sittenfeld:

"Unfortunately, it cannot be denied that modern art, especially theatre, has been corrupted only by the Jews.

The Jew is the demon materialising the fall of humanity.

Richard Wagner

SS BOOKLET NO. 10. 1937.

IMPORTANT FACTS ABOUT FREEMASONRY

(Additional data for a conference with projection on Freemasonry)

The Blood Rite

At the solemn reception into the 9 degree in the Swedish system, blood is poured into a cup from a small bottle in which, since the time of the foundation of the lodge, blood mixed with wine has been contained. The bottle thus contains the blood of the brothers—also Jews—up to the oldest.

The National Grand Master Müllendorf of the National Grand Lodge of German Freemasons confirmed the blood rite during the trial against the lawyer Schneider on 15 March 1932:

"It is true that at the reception of the rank of Grand Chosen, the impetrant drinks of the blood of those brethren who have been accepted before him to that rank. It is also true that a few drops of the impetrant's blood are collected in the bottle and kept with those of the FFs, who have been part of this chapter until now."

Text of the Oath of Apprenticeship:

"I, N. R., do solemnly and sincerely swear in the presence of Almighty God and of this venerable lodge dedicated to St. John that I will preserve and conceal the secret usages of Freemasonry and that I will never disclose what is entrusted to me now or hereafter, except to the authentic and entitled brethren and in an authentic and legitimate lodge of FF, and companions whom I shall recognize after due and severe examination. I further swear that I myself will not write, print, carve, paint, draw, conceal, or engrave anything on any movable or immovable thing under the sky that is legible or comprehensible, or has the slightest resemblance to a letter or sign so that the secret art may be unlawfully perceived. I swear all this with a firm and unshakeable resolve to abide by it, without secret reserve or inner hesitation, on pain of having my throat cut, my tongue cut out, and being buried in the sand far from the shore as the low tide changes twice in 24 hours. May God assist me and sustain me in my commitments as an accepted apprentice."

(FF. Fischer *Explanations of the Catechism of Johannite Freemasonry* I. Catechism, p. 38).

The oaths of journeymen and masters say the same thing.

In the *Manual for the Brethren of the Grand National Lodge of Freemasonry in Germany*, 6th ed. Berlin 1912, p. 82, it is written about the separation of a brother from the lodge:

" § 171. Each brother is free to leave his lodge; this is called "covering the lodge". The explanation of the covering of lodges must be made in writing. By covering, the brother does not lose the character of a Freemason, he becomes a separate brother; but he loses the right to participate in lodge functions of any kind.

The rights which the brother has acquired as an effective, honorary or visiting member of lower lodges are not lost by covering a lodge of higher rank. But his rights in the higher grades are dormant.

The brothers' duty of silence:

" § 306. The duty of discretion demands the utmost care that not only Masonic knowledge, techniques and debates remain hidden from the uninitiated, but also that which is higher for the brethren in a lower rank. (Statute of the Grand Mother Lodge of Kurhessen at the friendly meeting with the Royal Grand Mother Lodge of York in Berlin in 1815).

Camouflaging Freemasonry as a charity:

"If a lodge ever practises charity, it is not out of pity for the needy, but as a temporary utilitarian means or form of legitimation." (*Bauhütte*, 1872, p. 140).

Similarly, the Masonic journal *Latomia* wrote in July 1865: "The pretext of charity used only serves the Masons to conceal another.

The "German League of Grand Lodges", which unites all German Grand Lodges in common work and maintains the alliance with non-German Lodges, was of particular importance, as can be seen from the words of Freemason *Kneifner* in "Communication of the Association of German Freemasonry", 1917/18, p. 54:

"The German League of Grand Lodges ensured that no one of the eight Grand Lodges would overpower the others. Its law prevents arbitrariness and the possible ambition for domination of each grand lodge."

The Old Prussian Lodges left the League of Grand Lodges in 1922, but reaffiliated in 1927.

Freemasonry's position on nation and race:

"There is no such thing as nationalistic or religiously inclined Freemasonry, but only pure, indivisible Freemasonry. Whoever preaches the opposite is in total error. Let us be a human league and not a sect. (The Freemason's newspaper *Auf der Worte* of 1. 03. 1925).

Similarly, the Mason Neumann (Association of German Freemasons) says to the Mason Eskau in a letter of 31 March 24:

"When you deny Freemasonry with its message of the equality of all that has a human face, you are not—forgive me a Freemason."

The Freemason Horneffer writes in *National Freemasonry Education in* 1919/20, p. 66:

"The struggle of the supporters of the idea of humanism (i.e. Freemasonry) must be a struggle against all nationalism.

In *the laws of the German Grand Lodge League* (published after the creation of the new legislation on 01.08. 1911, p. 16), it is stated:

"The German League of Grand Lodges declares that differences in skin colour and race are no obstacle to the recognition of a Grand Lodge or a Lodge.

Position of the Old Prussian Grand Lodges towards Judaism:

"We have been accused of being anti-Semitic and of not accepting Jews out of racial hatred. This is the greatest affront that has ever been made to us. The teacher taught us to love all men as brothers, and the Jew is as much a child of the eternal God who created us as we are of all men. If we do not allow Jews as well as members of other non-Christian religious societies into our close community, it does not follow that we hate them. We could also be rightly told that we hate women and children as well as people of low education because we do not accept them. But when a Jewish member wishes to be admitted as a guest to our work, then we welcome him to our house if he belongs to a recognised lodge; we welcome him cordially and are glad that he has no prejudice that there can be any barrier between him and us. We know that we owe it to him, and shall owe it to him, to act constantly in this way towards him as a brother. *(Manual on the "Doctrine of the Order of the National Grand Lodge of Freemasonry in Germany").*

International constitution of the three great old Prussian lodges

Structure of the National Grand Lodge of Germany. The constituency of the national grand lodge forms the seventh province of the order in the Swedish system, just as Denmark represents the eighth and Sweden is the ninth province of the order. At the top of each province is a vicar salomonis, a regent. The regent of the German province of the order was, for example, the infamous Friedrich Leopold of Prussia, who on 9 November 1918 was the first to raise the red flag on his castle in Klein-Glienicke near Potsdam. Prince Friedrich Leopold was an honorary member of all German Grand Lodges and patron of the three Old Prussian Grand Lodges.

Since Frederick the Great, the Prussian kings became the protectors of the great Old Prussian lodges, except for William II. The words of the Freemason Dr. Schletter in *Latomia*, 1865, p. 65 explain the aims of Freemasonry as follows:

"It was only in appearance that princes were given the direction of lodge affairs and the "delegates" cover their own actions with the princely name."

The princes had a special ritual so that they would not know the unworthy nature of the Masonic ritual.

Freemasonry was the driving force behind the French Revolution in 1789

This fact is confirmed by the report of the plenary session of the lodges concerned, "Paix et Union" and "La libre Conscience" in the Orient de Nantes of 23 April 1883, p.8:

"From 1772 to 1789, Masonry set in motion the great revolution that was to give the world a different face. Then the Freemasons spread the guiding ideas they had espoused among the popular masses.

GERMANIC SS BOOKLET NO. 1 AND 2. 1943.

1789

The United States of America faces a much greater danger than the one concealed by the Roman Church...

That danger, gentlemen, is the Jew!

In every country where Jews settled in large numbers, they constantly debased its moral grandeur and depreciated its commercial integrity. They have stood aside but never assimilated. They have mocked the Christian religion on which the nation is built and have tried to undermine it by opposing its prescriptions. They built a state within a state. But when they were thwarted, they used every possible means to strangle this country financially, as they did in the case of Spain and Portugal.

For more than seventeen centuries the Jews have wept over their sad fate because they were driven out of their homeland, which they called Palestine. But I assure you, gentlemen, that if today the civilised world would give them back Palestine as their property, they would at once find a pressing reason not to return there. Why should they do so? Because they are vampires and vampires cannot live on the backs of other vampires. They cannot exist on their own, they must vegetate by taking advantage of Christians and other people who are not of their race.

If you do not exclude these people from the United States by using the existing Constitution, then in less than two hundred years they will have multiplied so much that they will dominate and devour the country and change even our form of government for which we Americans have spilled our blood, given our lives, given our best, gambled away our liberty, and sacrificed our greatest ideas.

If you do not exclude these people, it is your descendants who will have to work in the fields to give the benefits to others, while these others will sit behind the desks and rub their hands happily.

I warn you, gentlemen: if you do not exclude the Jews forever, when it is possible to do so, they will never change, despite the generations. Their ideas will never match those of an American, even if they lived among us for ten generations. A leopard cannot change its spots. The Jews mean a threat to this country if they are allowed in, and they should be excluded by our Constitution."

American statesman Benjamin Franklin in 1789 before the US Congress.

WAKE UP AMERICANS!
DO YOU WANT THIS?

Clean up America! Break the Red Plague!

BOYCOTT the JEW!

SS Notebook No. 1 a/b. 1941.

"America" in Europe

Zeichnung: Erik

A front that crosses hearts and minds...

An artfully drawn world map from 1551 was found, showing everything that was known about the world at that time from the great voyages of discovery. On the new country of North America—not South America—the word "cannibals" is written. This means: man-eaters!

Then came the first white immigrants. They were the "Pilgrim Fathers", escaped from Europe, mostly from England, who left their homeland because of their Puritan religion. These Puritans were a special kind of saint who saw grace and divine favour in the fact that God had to fill their purses if He found advantage in their business affairs. In the logic of this faith, the good pilgrims were prepared to swindle, and above all to renounce all the goods and pleasures of this life. So they took no books with them to America other than the Bible and the prayer book, leaving the song books, texts, illustrations, dances and all the other beautiful things that Europe had. What distinguished these Puritans was the law that governed their actions, the culture they brought with them. It was not a real culture but a religious barbarism. The prayer book and the purse were the basis of all their thoughts and aspirations. The real Yankees still think like that today.

It must be said that the weakening of the faith led to a decrease in the importance of the prayer book. The purse grew ever heavier, was privileged and the prayer book became thinner, becoming more superficial—in Lutheran parlance—a dustbin lid for hiding a multitude of infamies.

The third wave of immigrants were the Negroes. They came from Africa in irons, taken as slaves on English ships. They came as poor devils and remained so. But at least, as natural creatures from their forest and savannah, they brought with them a kind of culture, works of song, dance, joy and suffering marked by their own blood—even if it was only Negro blood. But this sensibility was soon denatured on the plantations under the whips of the foremen, in the cold of the North and in the slums of New York.

Jews develop US 'cosmopolitan culture' for export

But it was this form that interested the last wave of immigrants still missing from this cosmopolitan country—the Jews. They heard the strange and exciting rhythms of the Negroes, they saw the secret jealousy of the Puritans for the light-hearted exuberance of these forest children, and they sensed the bargain and the possibility of paralysing the racial resistance of these "willing barbarians" by using this foreign magic.

Thus was born at the beginning of our century and year after year what is called "Americanism". It is a nonsensical joy of primitive excitement of the senses, whether it is loud sounds and colours, bloody films and stories, tense shootings, murders, kidnappings, sports exploits, dance marathons, swimming, poetry or prayer, "world records" in all fields, or the most important events in the world, swimming, poetry or prayer, 'world records' in every field, the adoration of gigantism and the 'biggest of the world', the assessment of women according to 'beauty standards' or childish arrogance.

When this country of old Puritans, which had become rich and therefore thirsty for joie de vivre, sank into this decadence, community life was transformed into "business", festivals into fairs—this Americanism became an export item. The joke turned into reality: the uncultured immigrants of old wanted to compete with the old civilised European country by showing it that their creations were more beautiful and new. One should say offer, because it was a cash transaction for the Jews in the film industry, the Jews in the record industry, the Judeo-Negro jazz singers and dancers, the hook-nosed newspaper editors and impresarios.

It was really a good deal and a success. For at that time, the Europe of 1918 was bled dry, starving, psychically exhausted by four years of war and sacrifice in every country. Europe had mainly collapsed into itself, both as an individual and as a nation. People were no longer sure of anything, neither of the state nor of their well-being. Everyone wanted above all a simple, natural world, and for want of anything better, the superficial, entertainment, and escape from the emerging misery.

The Jewish manager takes advantage of the weakness of Germany and Europe

It was at this point that the Jew and the Negro left America.

In that precarious moment, the peoples of the old civilised continent would grab any buoy, however pierced, thrown by an attractive new world in order not to drown psychically. The new music was so easy to understand, the new movements, called dances, so easy to learn. Life was so simple in the movies: the hero, the scoundrel, the sweet girl, the rich stepfather, and always the happy ending! And then there are the great beauty contests! Many girls are asked to undress—naturally for the sole purpose of being measured, weighed, photographed... They roar in the crowd, determine an 'ideal' type, distribute ballots (very democratically) and elect Miss Europe, Miss Berlin, Miss Petawank ... etc.

The poison brewed in the Jewish shop, the negroid sensibility and the colonial anti-culture eventually seeped into the gullible and defenceless hearts of Europeans and also of many Germans. It is a moral law that the habits of man that make him act "without thinking" attach themselves very strongly to him, so that he can only get rid of them with the utmost evil. That is why the "pleasure of the people" met with so little resistance, as well as that vulgarity in dances, songs, films, sports and love, and why there was rarely any attempt to oppose something personal, something better, to this foreign spirit.

It was really not easy to revive old feelings in a morally decomposed, nationally broken and economically decayed Germany. The opportunities that arose were missed, because the mass of the people could not seize them. Only when the Party was able to reach the hearts of the Germans after 1933 was the threat to our cultural heritage removed and a firm foundation laid. National films and strict controls on film imports improved the situation of German cinema. German poets appeared on the German stage, as did many young people whose early works still needed to be accepted. A German press was created, headed by German editors who knew how to distinguish between novelty and sensation. German sport was purified, our entertainment was influenced by our humour and gaiety, in accordance with the laws of our blood.

MUSIC EXPRESSES THE SOUL OF A PEOPLE...

The only exceptions are dancing and light music. It must be said openly here that any non-German feeling can be subject to a ban. But what use would that be if it caused a vacuum that many of the countrymen could not understand? Many of them would probably no longer be able to distinguish what is bad and pernicious in this forbidden music.

Schopenhauer and Richard Wagner once said the following about the spirit of music: "Music expresses what is essential", i.e. the soul of men, of peoples and of an era.

One can only understand this essential point of view if one is a musicologist and a creator oneself. If you are not, you cannot conceive of authentic music. Of course, rhythm is also an important component of music because it is fundamentally present, especially in our contemporary life. The noisy traffic of machines, the marching of thousands of soldiers' boots have left their mark on our flesh and blood. That is why the marches and soldiers' songs of this great wartime era bring them back to us. One thing is certain: Beethoven and Brahms, Bach and Reger, Mozart and Bruckner have created music that will continue to delight and satisfy our musical senses for centuries to come. When we have recovered from the overwhelming experience of this war, the day will come when German composers will follow a new path.

The victory of our weapons will also involve the victorious eruption of a new culture driven by the German cultural will. North America must also be defeated on this front, and this by means of a small, tenacious and daily internal war. We must also be victorious on the cultural front that runs through hearts and minds!

SS BOOKLET No. 10. 1938.

"LENINISM" AND "STALINISM"?

"If the Jews were alone in this world, they would suffocate so much in mud and filth that they would try to exploit and exterminate each other in hateful fights; provided that the fight does not turn into a theatre because of the lack of any spirit of sacrifice expressed in their cowardice. These words of Hitler are not recent but were written fourteen years earlier in *Mein Kampf.* Even so, this simple sentence allows us to appreciate and judge accurately this criminal jurisdiction that is currently operating in Moscow. Any observer who believes that he can detect in this massacre a struggle for influence between various ideologies, even if it is bloody, will find his attempts at clarification doomed to failure without further ado. It is not a question of ideas or ideologies, but of the consolidation and bloody safeguarding of the personal regime of Stalin and his Kaganovich group. Of all the commentators in the press, Count Reventlov has perhaps best grasped the situation as it is when he says in his "Observation of the Empire": "We are sufficiently distant to observe and consider with equanimity the Moscow trials past, present and future. It is not innocence, it is not a divine condemnor of evil and protector of good who sits with his angels in court. Nor are the accused innocent victims and martyrs of a noble conviction, idealists who are ready to die voluntarily for their people and their ideal. A criminal in power wants to get rid of two dozen other criminals who have been his accomplices until now. That is all. The set of accusations put together by Prosecutor Vychinsky is monstrous and so senseless that it refutes itself by its own lack of logic.

The criminal court accused the twenty-one defendants of espionage, sabotage and the commission of terrorist acts. They must, "on the orders of foreign powers, have attempted to provoke uprisings in the Soviet Union in order to separate the Ukraine, White Russia, the coastal provinces of the Far East, Georgia, Armenia and Azerbaijan from the USSR. The foreign powers were supposed to wait for the accused and their accomplices to support them in ending the communist system in the Soviet Union and reintroducing capitalism and the bourgeoisie. To this end, they were to join the Trotskyites (Trotsky, "who hid in the doghouses of the capitalists" as they say in the jargon of the Soviet press, is also the big villain in this trial because when he was commissar he must have had liaisons with agents of foreign powers), in addition to the Zinovievists, Menshevists, social-revolutionaries, and bourgeois nationalists of the Ukraine, White Russia, Georgia, Armenia, and Azerbaijan. Bukharin is accused of plotting with Trotsky to thwart the Brest-Litovsk peace negotiations, with the aim of bringing down the Soviet government and arresting and assassinating Lenin, Stalin and Sverdlov, the last presidents of the Soviet Union. Furthermore, we learn with surprise that the writer Maxim Gorky did not die a natural death, as has been generally admitted up to now, but that he was suppressed by Professors Pletnov, Levin and some other doctors with the participation of Iagoda.

But the horrors of this accusation are only brought to light by the people in question and who are usually the old Bolshevists renowned and emphatically celebrated for years by the Soviet press. First there is Bukharin, the former chairman of the Comintern, then Iagoda, the former head of the GPU and once the most powerful man in the Soviet Union after Stalin, Rakovsky, the former chairman of the Council of People's Commissars of Ukraine, thus the head of the Ukrainian government, then Rosenholtz, also known in Berlin, Minister of Foreign Trade, to speak in our terminology, Grinko, Minister of Finance, Kreskinski, representing the Minister of Foreign Affairs, Chernov, Minister of Economy, Rykov, Minister of Transport, Mendechinsky, former head of the secret police, in addition, among the doctors, Professor Pletnov, the heart specialist and Levin.

This so-called trial caused the world, which had been weary in the extreme of the bloody news repeating itself for twenty years, to turn its attention to Moscow with dismay and to express its disgust and repugnance even in the ranks of the friends of the Soviet Union. Léon Blum and Reynaud were upset, many Social Democratic newspapers were full of cries of indignation; England and France protested against the charges which implicated these two countries in the dubious relations maintained by the accused. When in France they wept over Chukachevsky, we deduced that this grief was perfectly selfish, even when one speaks of humanitarianism, all the more so because France is in touch with the Red Army. And the latter, we also believe, will not be strengthened by executions of this kind in its highest ranks.

National Socialism regarded Judeo-Bolshevism as the absolute enemy of civilisation. Above, for these Soviet soldiers with Mongoloid faces, the fighting is over. Below, a small group of partisans, dirty and ragged, were taken prisoner. Among them are two rabbis (the two bearded ones in the centre).

"Nun sind sie wieder da, die Hunnen. Zerrbilder menschlicher Gesichter. Wirklichkeit gewordene Angstträume, Faustschlag in das Gesicht alles Guten..."

"Here they are again, the Huns, caricatures of human faces; reality turned nightmare, a punch in the face of all good men...". Illustration taken from a propaganda magazine.

Presenting the situation in the Moscow trial was necessary to highlight the political and ideological problematic of this momentary theatre. The initial voices that believed that these questions would be resolved as "world revolutionary politics" or "national politics", "international Marxism" or "national Marxism", "integral Marxism" or "moderate Marxism", were beginning to be heard. Faced with such a confusion of ideas with regard to the facts, one is unfortunately not sufficiently warned. So we come to the proper exposition of our subject. Various notions such as "Leninism" and "Stalinism" have already been mentioned. This abstract division of Bolshevism must give rise to the assumption that Stalinist Bolshevism is different from Leninism. It must also give rise to the illusion that Bolshevism has changed, and we even hear some say that "Stalinism" is a transformation into nationalism, into social nationalism, into national socialism. "Do we not also call Stalin the guide?" these ideologues ask. Some even conclude that Jewish Bolshevism there is "a National Socialism from the depths of the Russian soul", and so there is every reason to tap the shoulder of this victorious branch of the Third Reich and exchange a friendly handshake! We can see how far this kind of confusion can go. Thank God, "Little Father Stalin" himself was keen from time to time to lift the veil and reveal the true nature of Bolshevism. As the Führer said in his last speech in the Reichstag, in these matters we must not concern ourselves with a foreign minister, with ultra-intelligent treaties or with oriental ideological strategies, but only with the Moscow hero with the moustache. Thus, Stalin was personally answering the open letter published in "Pravda" on February 14, 1938 from a young komsomol boy who was asking about the fate of the international revolution. Here is the brief meaning of the very long speech in his also open letter: The world revolution is growing, expanding and prospering. The journal "Contra Komintern" summarises the contents of the letter as follows:

"As long as there are non-Bolshevist states in the world, Stalin has not yet achieved his goal." Stalin publicly declares that the victory of the workers, at least in some countries, i.e. revolution and civil wars as in Spain, are necessary. This letter is clear proof of the aggressive attitude of communism.

This is the strict reality, and any realistic policy, if it wants to succeed, must see that world revolution is the sole and sine qua non of Bolshevism. It is the turn which Bolshevism must and will take if no comparable power stands in its way. According to its own definition, the Soviet Union is only the core which will become the "state" representing the world union of the socialist Soviet republics only through the destruction and incorporation of the existing states. The organs of this "state" are the sections of the Comintern, which are far more important for the Soviet Union than the immediate government of the Union itself, i.e. the Council of People's Commissars. As has been shown clearly enough, the Council of People's Commissars is led solely by the Party, and the Party, in turn, represents the leading and determining section of the Comintern.

A new "right" of the peoples is thus being born, which is nothing of the kind but rather a voluntary destruction of law. The national emblem affixed to the embassies of the USSR bears the inscription: "Proletarians of all countries, unite!" This is a flagrant attack on our domestic political interests! For this means that all workers are incited to commit illegal actions of high treason, sabotage, desertion, etc. Every individual who joins the Communist Party denies the sovereignty of his country and places himself under the exclusive sovereignty of Moscow. This appeal, hiding behind the extraterritorial protection of Soviet diplomatic representations, is already considered an official declaration of war to all countries. In its plans of action, the Red Army considers the communist sections of other countries as stable bases, pontoons, its auxiliary sections. It becomes necessary, therefore, in view of such signs, to revise the liberal law of nations and adapt it to the international situation so that Judeo-international Bolshevism can be fought with the means which its criminal tactics require.

"Leninism? "Stalinism"? There is only Judeo-international Bolshevism!

Wolfgang Fehrmann

POLITICAL SERVICE FOR THE SS AND POLICE.

THE CURRENT POLITICAL IMPORTANCE OF CULTS

All religions evolve, develop and gradually reach characteristic stages of expression and lifestyle. That religions evolve and must evolve is a scientifically accepted fact, but one that is contested by all orthodoxies that fight for the primacy of an 'absolute revelation', i.e. that claim an immutable legitimacy 'from the beginning'. This view can be defended in theory and theology as well, but the characteristics of all religions tell us something else.

Before defining the notion of only partial or constant evolution, it is necessary to make a brief remark on the "biological function" of religion. It must be established as a matter of principle that there is no more "religion per se" than there is "man per se", but only a concrete manifestation that has come into being and developed under the influence of racial, ethnic and historical data. Every religion has, by its very nature, unpredictable possibilities of development, comparable to those of biological organisms. Religions must therefore be deliberately regarded as units that are susceptible to bad developments and degeneration.

Evolution itself can be seen in a double sense and applied to historical religions. First, it must be understood simply as a successive or periodic manifestation of historical transformations in the course of which exchanges of reciprocal influences are possible. It must therefore be defined as a higher evolution in the spirit of a historically conditioned value experience; without doubt the historical-religious unity can never "progress" but only degenerate. Secondly, evolution can be seen as the manifestation of existing dispositions and possibilities in the unity; manifestation understood here in a double sense: as the continuous dynamic transformation of a determined faith or as the accentuation of existing essential character traits reaching the stage of dogmatic rigidity.

Historical-religious research has already noted the existence of several stages of evolution generally common to most religions. These are above all the various forms of protest (either through an active and aggressive prophetism or through the 'silent protest' of a mysticism removed from the world), Protestantism and the Reformation. It is as if there were a law of parallelism in the history of religions, which demonstrates a comparable development, *independent of* time and space, of different religions (one can see in an exemplary way the astonishing similarity existing between the religious background themes of the great Japanese reformers Honen—Shonin and Shinran—Shonin and the Reformation of Martin Luther existing almost at the same time).

If Protestantism and other religious protests must be considered as developments from the same origin, on the other hand, many religions have seen the birth of *sects* completely alien to their original religion.

While the evolutionary event cited first depends on the original religious starting point, the sect itself is always the product of a secondary manifestation. (The particular evolution of Buddhism in Japan and China, which leads to the fusion of various religious conceptions, is an exceptional form in its own right).

In every religion, there are degrees of "primary" and "secondary" piety. Primary piety is dynamic, original, concerns the content of the faith and is constantly opposed to abstraction, religious rigidity and all forms of dogmatism which are the marks of secondary piety. And it is clear that sectarian protest comes almost exclusively from a background of secondary piety, i.e. that a form of ultimate specialisation has been found and thus determines religious degeneration. In other words, it is not fundamental epochs of religious protest that lead to the formation of a sect (such as Luther's and Honen's and Shinran-Shonin's protest against good works in favour of "only faith"—sola fide), but almost without exception objects of secondary piety quarrel.

The observation of the immense number of sects provides us with proof of this. It is the increase in the number of acceptances and refusals of baptisms, the refusal of the vow, the denial of war, the refusal of the State, etc., things which are no longer in any causal connection with the faith demanded. On the one hand, the return of Christ is expected, on the other hand, priesthood and ceremonial are rejected, others preach abstinence again, demand a vegetarian way of life, reinstate the old Jewish tithe, or consider that showing Christian concern for antisocial elements is a salutary work. Who is the person who can find his way between the Baptists, the Methodists, the Sabbatarians, the Adventists, the Mennonites, the Salvation Army, the Unitarians, the Chileans, the Jehovah's Witnesses, who are all pretty much the same?

The phenomenon of sects is not a new feature or a reaction to the desperate religious situation of our century. The fanatical struggles of the Hussite spirit, the prevailing prudery of the "pious sisters", the begines and beghardes, the noisy penitential gatherings of the "flagellants" overwhelming

Europe and whipping each other to blood are the shocking testimonies of a human misguidance coming from an ancient time but unfortunately not completely over nowadays.

The political-ideological revolutions directly bring in their wake essential changes in the religious and moral field. When the great religious systems and their churches are not able to keep up with the process of political evolution, then sectarian attempts to amalgamate and synthesise immediately arise. Undoubtedly, efforts of this kind are mainly detrimental to the new political order and either fail in the face of a new overall political will or fall victim to compromise.

Here, too, Germany has never ceased to be a singular stage on which the *most savage aberrations* are manifested. The constant internal struggle enabled the people to become mature and to acquire an exclusively political will, i.e., to become aware, through concrete experience, of the dangers conveyed by foreign-minded sects. The latter do not primarily attack religious traditions, but rather the social life of the community they endanger, regardless of their intentions and types of marginalisation.

Whoever writes the history of our century and brings out the deepest elements of the most serious crisis of all times, must also reveal what was the not inconsiderable contribution to this world catastrophe, which is taking place for the benefit of an aberration of Judeo-Oriental-Christian mentality that exceeds the limits of what is tolerable. Perhaps it was Providence that in the course of history the national evolutionary process in Germany had to undergo every conceivable spiritual and moral purification because of the political situation, so that at the decisive moment the people could hold up the torch of a new order of ideas in the moral struggle of the world. The foundations of this order are the living expression of a community that knows the eternal laws governing natural events. In our field, this means that genuine faith and fundamental religious thinking will always be worthy of respect and understanding. The religious principles of this order of thought even outline the contours of a consciousness deeply penetrated by the eternal dynamics flowing from the specific divine faith of our people. But the rejection of any sclerosis or strangeness, of any aberration is all the more energetic when these pathological apparitions threaten the foundations of our new order.

Today's war contributes even more than many previous wars to differentiating between the essential and the accessory. This also explains why it has a totalitarian character in the ideological conflict. The *unbridgeable gulf* between our religious values and those of our enemies becomes obvious when they always emphasise the religious aspect. The enemy camp believes it is winning propaganda battles by gratuitously accusing us of religious desecration and crimes. They act in a spirit of complacency that is bound to remain so, since they ignore *any other* scale of values. What is very interesting and remarkable about this kind of enemy propaganda is that it is extremely versatile and allows the judicious observer to understand that a characteristic, truly pious religious attitude is missing. On the strength of an alleged faith, of the consciousness of being chosen by God, an attempt is made to unleash a holy war with the slogan: "*Forward, soldiers of Christ*". One can therefore understand all the religious motivations behind the enemy's propaganda presented in the international press and radio, and which will always be used.

The authentic British mentality is openly expressed in the preaching of the German Protestant office on London radio. In British religious broadcasts, the raging message of faith takes such a turn to implore God's blessing "and smash our enemies allo ver the world" that it is not at all taken as a joke, even though a bigoted, honeyed voice spares potential German listeners by asking for forgiveness of sins, redemption and the obtaining of grace. The impression becomes clearer when an equivalent service is performed in German. This state of mind explains these intentions to pacify the world. When American Baptist chaplains declare that the superhuman acts of American airmen could not have been done without divine help, they acknowledge the legitimacy of the American soldier to determine the Christian life in the United States through his war experiences. This is typical of a religious mindset with the same roots. *But if one could still doubt the true nature of the American-British religious attitude, one gains certainty when one notes that it fraternises with Bolshevism,* the third enemy which represents the true personification of *the Antichrist* constantly prophesied in the history of the European West. A priori, it does not enter into the framework of our consideration since it manifests itself, after all, as the product and the ultimate runt of a religious anarchy.

Today, it can be seen that Puritanism and Quakerism are fundamental components of the American-British mentality and thus also influence both world wars. Both sects are, at their peak, typical examples of a particular development. This is primarily due to the development of Puritanism, the "fighting association for evangelical purity". These are political and economic events of great importance. This precedent shows the interaction between political, economic and imperialist interests on the one hand and religious themes on the other. In addition, religious reforms were not undertaken in England or in the 'New World', and spiritual discussions were restricted to Europe.

It is not difficult for an enlightened observer to recognise the mark of the Jewish intellect, accustomed to theological quarrels, on the formation of that sectarian mentality which permeated the following centuries. The great creative and fertile impulses are lacking, whereas precisely at that time Europe was particularly prodigious in creations in all fields, be it art or science. Puritanism and Quakerism, however, were at the root of a process among their people that represented a unique synthesis of religious obsession and economic and imperialist endeavour. *Logic thus supersedes genuinely religious thinking and dynamic faith.* The entire structure of thought, will and feeling is permeated by the ideological influences of Puritanism and Quakerism. The European has great difficulty in understanding the self-righteous, arrogant, business-intractable, cagot, superstitious and mocking lifestyle that is the hallmark of the British-American mind. In this respect, bigotry and hypocrisy are the most significant and constant distinguishing features of the British attitude, which are expressed in the notion of "cant". The methodical education carried out in this spirit has undoubtedly forged the English and American type, much more than it has acted on all the European people. This conservative factor is in any case also a testimony to the development of a failed existence. *Intellectualised and specialised to the extreme, the British and American way of life is no longer capable of producing creative, organic and dynamic impulses; it is totally sclerotic because it is no longer linked to a living organism and cannot be confronted with Europe, which has, in the meantime, evolved positively, without causing disasters. The Anglo-Americans have to follow Europe's evolutionary path in their own way if they do not want to fall victim to permanent sterility.* Even now, it can be seen that a dramatic factor in international history is inherent in this process. Defining the nature and course of this process is by no means an idle or premature speculation. Rather, the history of religious movements or organisations teaches us that harmful developments or deviations have always been avoided, if not by rethinking, then after following a catastrophic direction. The deep religious implantation which is the result of this particular development in England and the United States, already shows that without an extremely strict reorganisation work which is not only the result of internal action, it is and will be impossible to recover the general common foundations of European evolution. It is also an elementary law that no one in the world benefits from achievements obtained at the cost of the blood and tears of others. In such cases, nature itself rectifies the matter in an infinitely harsh but fair way, and at such times it is only applying its simplest laws, which are both a warning and a caution to all future generations.

This present war is the ultimate clash between a disintegrated, decadent and practically frozen rule of life and a way of life that is the product of the spiritual torments and moral storms of the European West. The process that led to the birth of Europe is slow but organic, constantly correcting itself, acting through and within itself. The common character of the European struggle, however, allowed for the manifestation of many particular developments and mistakes were made, some of which were paid for with rivers of blood. But men rose up and stepped out of the ranks to show that a solution can always be found. A new stage was reached, a new step was taken which led to the creation of the European Community as such. The upheavals on the European continent were not, however, able to thwart this independently pursued development, which would one day lead to necessary and decisive confrontations with the continent.

It is totally wrong to say that the constellation of forces expressed in the present struggle of the peoples is the product of fate. We must become convinced, painfully but absolutely correctly, that the present war is the most natural and logical event in history. A Nietzsche gave another fifty years' delay and "the time will come when we shall have to *pay* for having been Christians for two thousand years. We will lose the burden that has weighed on our lives and influenced them—for a time we will be disoriented. We will suddenly adopt *opposing* value judgements with the same degree of energy that produced this overvaluation of man by man. The notion of politics has thus taken a back seat in this spiritual war. All the old society's concepts of power have exploded—they were all based on lies: *there will be wars like there have never been before on Earth.* Only this time will be the beginning of a great politics on this Earth.

Nowadays, history corrects itself. It urges the holders of the new order born before its eyes to prove their worth in a manly way. On the battlefields of Europe, they are the ones who defend the heritage of Pericles and Augustus as well as that of Goethe, Bach and Beethoven; who even include the cultural testimony of *Shakespeare* in what is called Europe, and thus fight against a world that has nothing to oppose them but a very Jewish hatred and a diabolical will to destroy, the last symptom of a dead-end anarchy.

IV. ART OF WAR

THE HOUSE OF SS TROOP NO. 4. 1939.

MILITARY SCIENCE

Tölz, a practical example

The political signs were pointing to great events when we parted this time. We had read the latest news at Munich station, which was now our final stop. This, together with an account of a comrade's experience from Slovakia, suggested that the Reich was determined to take the necessary steps.

As politicians, we were directly confronted with these events. We could not simply take note of them and, after our training course, return to our daily routine.

It was then that we felt the first doubts. Already, many comrades on their way home were asking themselves during the night, to the monotonous sound of the wheels on the rails: are our activity, our mission, so fundamental that they can survive the importance of the present times? It was not a sickly scepticism that inspired these thoughts, no apprehension about the mission assigned. It is this generous doubt, creator of progress and evolution, that spurs you on and does not leave you on the back foot, but prevents you from drawing too hasty conclusions and following the wrong path. Some people have kept their doubts to themselves, others have tackled the question in pairs or threes.

Were we really just on the edge of events? Did it make sense, in an era that gives you so much if you know how to take advantage of it? Was it reasonable to sit behind your books when the levers of history were elsewhere?

It was clear that every study was a step on the road to slow maturity; but would its fruits still be good? In view of the results, could we say that we had followed the best path; did that make us right?

These questions were swirling around in our heads as young intellectuals and we wanted to find an answer. Because, as scientists, we were in a field where, according to many people, the concepts remained particularly unclear. Many people do not believe that political and intellectual activity can solve these questions, or do not even ask about them.

The more we asked ourselves this question, the more we could tell ourselves that we believed we had found the answer, because experience from practice had forged our conviction. Looking back at Tölz, which had made further progress this year, we felt that our path had been the right one so far and would continue to be so in the future.

BEING A SOLDIER, A CONDITION

How should we understand our history?

If the results of the long discussions had been awaited in the scientific arena where so much has been debated, the present generation would still not have made any progress. It would be exhausted in sterile debates and the value of all its activity would be unconvinced. There was therefore only one solution for the young group: individual initiative.

There were soldiers in this intellectual field. As they had the profession in their blood, they felt the warlike character of this time very early on and grew up in it. Without worrying about skirmishes, they set themselves a number of milestones that seemed right to them. The motto they gave themselves was: *Military Science*.

Under this motto, they brought together those who thought like them. They both outlined a science and associated it with a new form of education. It need not be emphasised that they were not considering the kind of education that is carried out in the barracks yard, and that it *should* be, but an education that conforms to a certain attitude generally adopted in work and in life. It is indeed obvious that the limits of a soldier's liberties are not those of a man in an intellectual team.

Our team also adopted this view. As warrior education cannot be carried out in the form of pedagogical discussions, *practical application was made* in our troop through the warrior virtues such as *rigour, frankness, team spirit, chivalry, honesty, obedience* and, most importantly, *the dignity of the healthy man.* These qualities have proven themselves in conjunction with the political and scientific components, both for the troop as a whole and for each individual.

Based on this experience, we went to the SS Junkerschule in Tölz for the fourth time. For the fourth time we put the motto "art of war" into *practice.*

The necessary condition for teaching a truly warlike science is not only to be healthy, but also to belong to a valorous race. Both conditions are present in the men of the SS. For the art of war gives priority to man; it is essential. How one approaches knowledge also depends on the kind of man one wants to be. The way in which we see science is a fundamental question for us. This was the clear premise of the Tölz team: to *bring together warriors,* because we know that this is the weak point of our university. After all, programmes only make sense if there are people to embody them. *It is the precious warrior and racial humanity that will realise' and make necessary the union of the art of war and knowledge.*

We asked for military training during these camp days precisely because physical fitness helps to strengthen the spiritual attitude. This was not only a necessity resulting from our stay in an SS Junkerschule, but the voluntary proof that one can from time to time behave in a different way, not as an end in itself, but as an exercise.

Rigour and courage were expressed in the beautiful competitions between the cadets of the school. The cadets won in athletics and handball, the troop houses in swimming. These were chivalrous battles.

REAL MEN ALWAYS BEGET
THEIR FELLOW MEN

These exercises allowed contact with military personalities. Perhaps no phrase is more accurate than this: real men always beget their fellows. The impression they make means a lot to a young team that still has to take care of its attitude. Thus we heard Dr SS-Untersturmführer v. *Kraus* speak about the Nanga-Parbat expedition. We felt the strength of a warrior personality who fears no obstacle and sees an unsolved problem as a challenge to be overcome. Then Colonel *Rommel, an* infantryman decorated with the Cross of Merit, told us about the hardest selection test a soldier can face, the war during the breakthrough at Tolmein and Karfreit, in which he played a decisive role. What a great time we had with SS-Brigadeführer *Börger!* He had a manly and simple way of thinking, but he had the ability to move us with his depth and power of persuasion. Did we not sense in him the old revolutionary strength, some of the faith of the period of the power struggle and the realism of the battle of the Saale? It is good from time to time to feel this breath, for times of victory sometimes make us forget it. Didn't the old friend of the troop houses, who unfortunately had to leave the Führer's guard a short time ago, Reichsamtsleiter Bernhard *Kohler*, also enthuse us again? We remembered Austria when SS-Obergruppenführer *Heifmeyer* returned to our ranks and participated with us in the vigil for the war dead. With the same seriousness he drew our attention to the questions concerning the continuity of the people. We were no longer strangers to him.

DISCUSSIONS WITHOUT QUARRELLING

This time too, the focus of the course was on the seminar, as the warlike *character of the* team had to be demonstrated. There was a lot of discussion, especially about the problems of exact science. The excitement caused by the lively, contradictory discussions at the end of the lectures—freedom of research, technical and intellectual education, intuition and science—was enriching for the subsequent work. What do we take from the warrior spirit of the seminar? Here, too, the rigour and courage of discussion, never evasion, were the hallmark of *the chivalric spirit.* This is the criterion that is most important for the intellectual warrior because he appreciates frank discussion, never quarrelling. He respects the personality of the other and does not consider him a personal adversary. He 'grapples' with the other in a courteous discussion when quarrelling would separate them. What are academic discussions and faculty quarrels? If a team knows how to make a difference, then it has gained much in its intellectual work.

Discipline is also a component of the spirit of chivalry, which does not make a seminar a debating club. There is also the loyalty that forbids "strutting" to adorn oneself with the prestige of a scholar, which makes one acknowledge one's wrongs if the other is right. We disavow the principle of "winning at all costs" in scientific discussion. We experience the atmosphere of a sporting competition. We lose and we reach out to our opponent. The motto of Obersturmbannführer *Ellersieck,* which he so often repeated to us, applies here: *Know how to lose while laughing!*

But our greatest joy lay in the fact that we all had a common denominator, however different our tastes, however different our views on this or that point, however bitter the intellectual discussion: to be *an SS man.* This is and will remain for each of us the main point, the epicentre. It is with fidelity and unreservedness, with rigour and strength, with consequence in conception, as the SS expresses it, that these men approach their scientific work, today at the beginning of their career and later in their profession and their life.

In this seminar, scholars also added to our knowledge. Professor Karl *Vogt* from the University of Munich gave us an insight into his field of work: embryology. Professor *Esau* from Jena showed us the problems that physicists face today. The old precursor of racial thought, Professor *H. F. K. Günther,* of the University of Berlin, explained to us the necessity of creating a new nobility of leaders. As a criterion of this nobility he gave us: *heroic distinction.*

Of course, our troupe was interested in all aspects of life. Musical art is very much in the spotlight in every house. It could not be otherwise in this camp either. We were delighted to see the well-known poet Hans Friedrich *Blunck* again. One evening we had Gottfried *Rothacker* and Professor *Lampe* from Munich to share the pleasure of music with us.

Training men. All the valuable films show how true this is. They express the character of the people and their spirit. "The Sovereign" showed a type of man of action who can reveal the greatest violence and yet remain true to himself. "The king" sparkled with French "spirit". "L'escadron blanc" expressed the colonisation drive of a young Empire, "La fleur écarlate" the ideal of an English gentleman... The Way of Life" described the Russian proletarian and his belief in the equality of all men. Perhaps most instructive was the Jewish film "Tibuck". The actors, the setting and the theme were Jewish. For us, the best propaganda. The bearded characters in caftans were monologuing and the action showed moods bordering on the pathological.

*

When, after an address by SS-Obersturmführer *Ellersieck* and the loyalty song, the study cycle was over, we again had the feeling of having experienced something exceptional. The reward for a year's work. For this practical example of military science could never have been achieved if it had not been for the annual work of each troop house. In the end, Tölz shows in high magnification what took place in these houses. The real significance of this training camp is this: the removal of imperfections, the progress of scientific work, the improvement of the soldier's attitude. And all the more so because our relations with the cadets and their school, whose commander had received us so well, allowed us to reflect more deeply. These reports could only strengthen our certainty that we ultimately had the same goal and that only the means to achieve it differed.

We met many people who generally agreed but asked: "Where is your freedom? Freedom is the hallmark of knowledge, otherwise its system is flawed. It is precisely in *exact* science that the decisive importance of this freedom lies.

What do chemical formulas have to do with the world view?

We have always said that we consider *man* to be the essential factor, not science. Doesn't the intellectual history of peoples confirm this? Although the objects and results of the experiments carried out by the natural sciences were once the same, some of them became materialistic and mechanical, others on the contrary acquired under the same conditions a faith in the divine power. It depended on how the scientists as men looked at the course of things and what spiritual and ideological consequences they drew from it.

To be a scientist means to feel that you have a mission, to feel that you are not working in an empty space but in a community. Apart from electrons and atoms, there is also a living people who are more than an aggregate of physics devices.

We want warriors to feel that they have a mission as scientists. They owe it to themselves to do so. But before them lies the *open* field of science.

Julius Schmidt

(Author's note: the "SS troop houses" were a branch of the SS that brought together university students who wished to take up liberal, scientific, legal, etc., professions, i.e. not police, administrative or military).

Fighting is everywhere; without fighting, there is no life. And if we want to survive, we must also expect new battles.

Otto von Bismarck

SS Booklet No. 3. 1938.

A passage from the book of a front-line fighter, the Frenchman René Quinton, is intentionally reproduced here to show how much our National Socialist attitude is that of the Nordic man. Nordic blood flows as much in the veins of the fighters from Germany as from France, from Nordic states like England and from other countries; some countries have many of these fighters, others have only a few.

Maxims on war

The warlike idea is always the characteristic of the best elements of a people. The warrior idea and the action it implies, *the attitude*, are by no means arbitrary notions and have the same ethical basis in all strong races.

René *Quinton,* a French wartime biologist and physician, left notes that were not published until after his death. Quinton himself, in the hours when he put his observations on paper, did not think he would gain notoriety from them. Diary entries briefly written under fire; drawings sketching the sediments of laminating waiting on reserve positions. A man who became a *soldier* and *a warrior* with every fibre of his heart, a *thinker* whose profession as a doctor sharpened his eye and gift for observation, touches with his *Maxims on War* on the ultimate things of being or non-being, recognises the innermost relations of war as a natural law, and teaches us what is at the origin of courage and heroism, sketching the stature of the leader with unparalleled penetration.

René Quinton is not the first Frenchman who also has something to say to us National Socialists. Let us think of Count Arthur *Gobineau,* whom we also count among the precursors of a racial science of biological laws related to the earth.

We are all the more pleased to take this little book into our hands because its author was a committed Frenchman, a nationalist who wrote with the spirit of a soldier and a warrior and had to make these observations which are also decisive for us.

We thus deliver a quintessence of the chapter *The leader* honouring ourselves by showing to the adversary and to the soldier René Quinton that mutual respect which warriors feel. For war is more than a succession of battles, but, beyond that, the foundation that allows the best men of a people to test their heroic virtues.

*

The natural leader is the bravest.

It is a mistake to reproach a leader for his heroism, when it only involves him. It is because there are leaders who expose themselves that there are men who die.

A leader who is not exalted by the braves he commands is ripe for the rear.

The boldness of the leaders is made up of the joy of obedience of the troops.

The leader without courage annihilates a troop, bullies the courageous subordinates, creates a freemasonry, a chapel of cowards. He derides everything that is heroic, bold, difficult, praises prudence, the absence of joy, receives his best officers with a frozen face, pushes the bad ones, twists the promotion by secret, uncorrectable notes that he gives.

The heroic leader loves and rewards the brave, rejoices in a courageous act as if it were a gift, and creates around him the true spirit of war, made up of drive, initiative, joy, self-sacrifice, daring and sacrifice.

There is no such thing as fatigue in war. Man's resources are infinite. Fatigue is a weakness of the soul.

A body without a soul, a troop without a leader, always needs rest.

There are leaderless troops, there are no tired troops.

Tired troops are the preserve of inert leaders.

Fatigue begins when passion wanes.
Get your men excited, they will never need rest.

The brave is not the one who fears nothing, but the one who has overcome his fear.

Old saying

SS Notebook No. 12. 1943.

The war without mercy

We have entered the arena of a ruthless battle. The men who fight here are of two types, forming mortal enemies. On a higher level, the war waged here is truly the mother of all things. Its outcome will decide the face of the future world, which must emerge transformed by the fervour of this battle. The marks of hatred and satanic barbarism that have no place in the new world must disappear. The sword alone is decisive in this struggle which has destroyed all exchanges.

During the military campaign, the soldier on the Eastern Front found himself eye to eye with this adversary many times. Even in the heat and fury of modern battle, the moment when men face each other, weapon in hand, rage shining in their eyes, the will to destroy in their hearts, will always be the most important and the hardest. One must fall to make way for the other in a new battle. It will always be like this. Hand-to-hand combat is merciless! You or me, nothing else exists in the world. He who has not felt the burning breath of the enemy on his face, who has not seen the murderous look in his eyes, does not know the deepest mystery of war that is manifested at this moment. Man masters things by his will. His hands contain the power of the world. Only he who has lived through it, who has endured and been purified by this merciless struggle, even more hardened, knowing his own strength and the limitlessness of the human will, has passed through a thousand deaths through the door of life.

For a long time now, we have not been fighting for victory and success as we have in other battles. The whole of the West is fighting its ultimate and decisive battle through us, in each individual. Two worlds are in conflict, one of which must and will win, otherwise history would have lost its meaning. Each individual feels, in full consciousness, the power of this struggle as a battle in which all that a thousand years of history has bequeathed to us is expressed. The good spirits of our comrades in the Russian land live on in us day after day and urge us not to become complacent. Bolshevism has taught us that no weakness of character must prevail in this conflict. We have become as hard as steel through our will and determination. We know that we are masters of destiny and that we will force it.

Never again will man have an opportunity to live and see what we will endure in this terrible ordeal until the final victory. An army of soldiers was born in this war where each one fights with a clear conscience, with a deep faith and a spirit of absolute sacrifice. We have all been through all the challenges hundreds of times and we have understood their message.

Faith and knowledge have given life to the true revolutionary soldier. He fights for all that was sacred to past generations, for the protection of his home by defending the nation, for the lives of his children in a world that looms on the horizon of the West. Death, heat, cold and all the hardships of a difficult struggle do not count against the strength and confidence that the soldier derives from his daily experience and his conviction that this battle is of absolute necessity. His ancestors and fathers fight through him as the conscious heir to a thousand-year-old history. Their virtues are his. He adds new forces to the creative power of his time. The destructive powers of war are only a necessary means for it, in this international struggle, to manifest its deepest meaning in the creation of a future Empire. Together with his allies, the German soldier will win the victory that is his due through his faith and strength, for he has recognised the deeper meaning of his struggle. The day of victory will be his triumph because he knows that thus begins a new era.

New battles will be unleashed. Hundreds of kilometres of Russian roads will hurt our feet. We have already seen and experienced everything. We will no longer go up to the attack with the fiery enthusiasm of the teenagers we were when we faced this great challenge. We have become wise men—calm, reserved and serious.

All the fires of hell have consumed us, the blazing sun and the icy breath of the snowy steppes have burnt us. The images of an existence under the illusion of the most diabolical idea that mankind has ever had, live in us, just as we are aware that this fight will end as it began, that is to say, in harshness and lack of mercy.

The sun wheel is rolling over the Soviet Union. In flames and blood, a world is born that will give our sons space and peace for a happy future. We will be its builders. We have been through hell and burned ourselves to the point of acute awareness and extreme hardness. Our faith is more solid and stronger than ever. Death and the devil are already behind us—a new death and new hells cannot terrify us. Victory is ours!

Horst Slesina

The celebration of the authentic man is in action!

Goethe

A new warrior elite was trained at the SS officers' school in Bad Tölz.

Swearing-in of new recruits.

Sennheim, European SS training school.

Sennheim

A Fleming writes:

"I live in a community of men who outwardly aspire to the same goal, endure the same hardships and have a duty to perform. There is no room here for intrigue or the precedence of money. In principle, we are all the same. Who I was and what I was is in the past and does not matter. It doesn't matter whether I was a scoundrel or a saint; we are all born again here, from the beginning.

The era

The 20th century was marked by the rejection of the alien and the return to oneself; in short, by Germanic awareness, the desire to live in the homeland of one's ancestors, to fight with one's fellow human beings to rebuild one's world, and finally, to search for and discover oneself. Men of the same race want to follow the same path which, through struggle and defence, leads to the reunion of all Germanic peoples in the Empire. For some, this path passes through Sennheim.

THE LANDSCAPE

It seems to be made for hard work. To the north is the "Hartsmannsweiler". It still bears the traces of the Great War. It is an authentic example of unchanging loyalty and sacrifice. The line of bunkers from 1916/18 stretches along the edge of the school. To the east flows the Rhine, which is, today as in the past, the river that influences the fate of Germania. And to the south lies fertile Burgundy, at times a staging post for warlike expeditions, at others the homeland of the Germanic tribes, which died out or merged into the Roman world. The echo of their victories over the Romans and the Huns resounds so proudly in our ears; the figures of the Nibelungen legend are so magnificent.

THE MISSION

As the first German training school, the Sennheim camp has the task of imparting to the young volunteer the principles that constitute the military and political spirit; to make him a man in the spirit of what makes the National Socialist volunteer personality.

This mission is carried out with the awareness that it is above all unwritten moral laws that distinguish the value of each soldier and thus that of the fighting army. Priority is given to the absolute value and personal rigour of the volunteer, as well as to the observation of unconditional discipline. But loyalty to the leader, to the race and to the country, a virtue that consolidates the community, must be the foundation.

THE VOLUNTEER

The volunteers show more or less visibly the traits of the Germanic species; despite the interference of a foreign spirit, the natural character and the will to fight are the strongest. A healthy, discreet inner self-confidence, animated by the spirit of chivalrous competition, is harmoniously combined with a spontaneous sincerity towards others.

Idealism, i.e. in this case being prepared in spirit and deed to fight for the Reich to the end, is often combined with a lively originality, an aptitude for enthusiasm, and is counterbalanced by a healthy inclination for reflection.

The 'sacred spontaneity'—as Ludendorff calls it—coupled with the above-mentioned characteristic, makes it possible to acquire a heroic state of mind, to become a leader of great stature within the army and the state.

THE AUTHORITY

The reason for this is that the religious duty of the Germanic leader was to act faithfully and circumspectly. What characterises the entire life of the leader is the ideal. All great deeds, all forms of greatness, are based on total altruism. Following a great example leads to victory.

Constant exercise and the study of historical, cultural and literary matters maintain a good general condition. Sustained psychological work, a true science of character and soul, combined with a knowledge of man and qualities of the heart, are the necessary conditions for a fruitful life. Every leader must be broad-minded in the right sense of the word, because of his personal assurance.

The utmost frankness between leaders and troops is a basic principle. No barriers should imprison the mind. Obedience results more from an inner predisposition than from slavish fear. The community of combat and comradeship must radiate everywhere by their rigour. But the baseline of the camp is determined by the atmosphere of trust between the leader and the troop.

Raciology course in Sennheim.

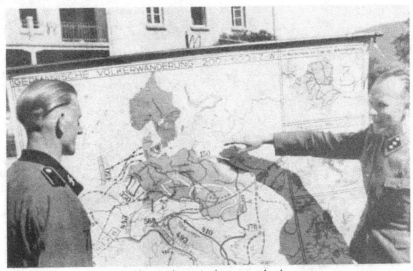

History classes in the same school.

Various weapons training courses.
Above, shooting practice.

Above, the use of mortar.

THE FUTURE

The nature of the soldier is one of frugal, Prussian rigour and duty, culminating in the glorious attitude of the leader who has distinguished himself in battle. His titanic strength, combined with an iron will and great valour, triumphs over the enormous difficulties of war. Strength of character and soul are the cause. But one must have gone through the trials of physical exertion, discipline, self-control and arduous spiritual combat.

A constant education of the will reduces internal inhibitions and, together with total physical control, transforms courage into valour, inner strength into toughness and constancy. In the troop, enthusiasm and camaraderie are transformed into a warrior spirit. The demand for good name and honour drives a hard breed of men to a strict conception of duty; willpower is transformed into heroism by the consciousness of doing one's duty and by the strength of determination.

The history of their ancestors teaches volunteers to understand the meaning of their time and mission.

Faith in one's own strength, in esprit de corps and in the certainty of the invincibility of the Germanic world form the basis of a general line of conduct.

THE FUTURE

The laws of the species and of life intended by God cannot be restricted for very long. An illusory despot who distorts the meaning and purpose of existence is always on the run.

Whoever wants to establish order must serve life if he wants to keep relations between the Germanic peoples healthy.

"Recognising that each people is an end in itself puts us in line with the laws of life. (Dr. Best). A future order must be established according to this principle. It allows each people as well as the whole of Europe to follow its evolution.

We know that a sower gets a good harvest if he takes into account the nature of the seed, the soil and the growing season. It is the same for people.

If today, following eternal truths, we sow the fields of destiny, the harvest of future generations will be rich. But, as Fichte says, this harvest will be that of the whole world.

SS NOTEBOOK NO. 4. 1943.

DUTY TAKES PRECEDENCE OVER LIFE AND DEATH

The crackling fire in front of us drew elusive lights and shadows on the faces of our little circle. Its warm colour reflected our fiery (enthusiastic) life and was reflected in the eyes of the men. Around the wooden walls of our shelter, the snowstorm is already swirling in the dark night and erasing road and path. To the monotonous rhythm of the shots and explosions of impact, the glass of the small window vibrates as if the iron chime of the war clock wanted to prevent us from forgetting what time we were living in at that moment.

However, the notion of time is variable for all those outside in the East who do not experience winter as a season but as a decisive event. Since the beginning of the war against Bolshevism, the great battles have become the means of testing a virile existence that has never been subjected to a more difficult test. In the meantime come the furloughs, like a silent pause in breathing, those days which everyone talks about as something quite singular and special, to give the comrade a piece of unknown, unimaginable joy. Under the deadly fire of this winter battle, the soldier's mission knows no limits, even those of the ultimate sacrifice.

These men seem to have forgotten what peace is and all that it entails. The future only makes sense in the mission they are given and will carry out, as long as their hearts are still beating.

They are aware of the hardships imposed by this inflexible duty, by this community of combat. Some speak of the fighting near Luga, in Volchov or now south of Lake Ladoga.

This image then brings back the moments of the battle. Memories of great events, but also of those who are no longer with us, come back into our minds.

We talk with our guest, Hauptsturmführer O., about the heroic engagement of his battalion, which a few days ago was still in the thick of the fight, having to hold an important point in the face of overwhelming Bolshevist superiority. It was surrounded and again broke through the enemy lines.

In the past, when war was still something new for all of us, we asked questions and knew how to give answers; the experience could be put into words, but today we no longer need to express our experience. It is like a secret agreement between those who have lived through these moments. They understand each other in a few words that let a feverish joy burst forth.

"I don't even need to describe the arrival of the tanks, you know that...
—And how the move achieved its goal!

Then there is silence again. They think of the moments when they were counting and distributing the last of the ammunition, when the radio link with the troops was cut off. They think of the order they received to rejoin their line.

But now a new thought assailed them, one they had not had last night: that this could have been their last battle. They thought about it but did not talk about it. For the sense of duty is stronger than they are.

Being a soldier means knowing how to accept death, but being a soldier also means never wondering when it will come. Suddenly, the discussion turns to this question. Only the devil knows how it appeared, prompted by the dying heat of the fire, the effect of the night, or the short pause after the battle. Foreboding, fate, destiny? Let us leave these questions to the philosophers living in quieter times!

The Hauptsturmführer sweeps them away with a word.

"I must do my duty! All reasoning, all speculation is vain and wrong. Chance and foreboding do not cost much. But it is necessary to keep a will of steel to accomplish one's duty.

Sports training as part of military training.

A path of struggle.

Boxing classes.

"I must do my duty! This inner call is stronger than all others, for it overcomes any spirit of fatalistic renunciation. It implies the will and strength to face everything and to be master of oneself.

Only the soldier is capable of experiencing the meaning of life which is at the origin of all things. It is the mark of a youth that wants to assert itself, that suddenly bursts into laughter, that blossoms into a song, that recognises, must recognise its destiny at the heart of this battle for life or death!

The logs in the fire are extinguished. The conversation has stopped. The morning turns grey behind the falling snow.

Army Correspondent, SS Dr Walter Best

War and courage have achieved greater things than love of neighbour.

Nietzsche

SS NOTEBOOK NO. 3. 1943.

A HOME WAR EXPERIENCE

In the delivery centre of the SS hospital my wife gave birth to twins, the third and fourth child born during the war. Today our grandmother arrived by train. So I can leave the two "big ones" to visit the good mother. My wife is in a nice clean room with three other women in labour. The minutes pass too quickly and the sister, pointing to the door, already indicates that the evening's visiting time is over. We decide to take our leave when the siren goes off: Air raid alert!

At present, there is a great deal of excitement in the ward, but no rush. The maternity ward and the entire hospital were repeatedly confronted with the need to get everyone down to the cellar. The nuns, the ever-present visitors and the SS men on duty then grabbed the baskets containing the fragile infants and took them down in the lift. Soon the precious treasure was secured in the well-equipped shelters. Then the mothers arrive. Two of the women, visibly happy in their maternal bliss, are placed in beds which, one after the other, slide down on rubber wheels to the shelter. In the deserted rooms, the lights go out, but life is concentrated in the basement in a narrow space, which one contemplates with all the more pleasure. The station staff, experts in anti-aircraft defence, take the initiative to ensure that there are always free passages and that coffee, bread and milk are ready to satisfy a sudden hunger. The doctors are there and exchange cordial and reassuring words with the women. The alert has concerned their department.

The first anti-aircraft gunfire can already be heard. The Tommy is here. The enemy is in the immediate vicinity of the building which has become the symbol of the vitality and confidence of our people. It is surrounded by houses in which our convalescent SS comrades are recovering from their wounds and awaiting their recovery. This moment makes us realise once again that this war is a total war.

The women are calm and confident. My wife says to me, pointing to the head of the department in his steel helmet, who is now walking through the cellar rooms: "It is so nice to know that you are close to the military protection of our men. A woman can feel what it means to belong to the SS through her husband. I have never experienced the spirit of the SS community as intensely as I do here in this house.

Regular heavy gunfire rang out in the vicinity, with brief pauses. However, the attempted breakthrough is reversed without causing any damage.

But something happens in the cellar. The sister asks the men to stand aside in a corner. Without questioning for a long time, they obey, and while walking, they already understand. Then, some time later, calm is restored. The sisters bring the swaddled babies to their mother. They are all in a jumble and it is often difficult to tell them apart. Everyone is soon satisfied. The cries, previously limited to one room, have spread all around and express a powerful will to live. Their intensity grips me, especially in such circumstances. I now hear two different kinds of sounds: on the one hand, inside, the small, piercing voices of children, and outside, the near and far clatter of the D.C.A. I stand next to my wife, who is carrying her twins and giving them her best.

In the evening I had another interesting experience with the entire staff, which I could see at a glance. I was struck by the fact that this group of women also constituted a real elite, visibly demonstrating the requirements set by the SS for being able to marry. The thoughts kept running through my mind. Our people will become healthy when this selection will become widespread.

The D.C.A. puts me out of my misery. Hungry infants, on the other hand, do not care about her. They don't know how their lives are already threatened at this moment, even though they are only one or two weeks old. Outside, four bright searchlights scan the sky. An attack is expected every second. Then there is a loud bang that shakes the whole house. The door, only pushed open, is torn off, and from outside you can hear the tinkling of shattered windows. A bomb had fallen about a hundred metres from us. The D.C.A. fired frantically.

The women, happy though they are, have to make an inner effort, but no one betrays the slightest trace of the anguish that such a situation can cause. We are all sustained by the spirit of the community we are forming at this moment and of which we are aware.

This terrible fear ends as evening sets in. The enemy air attack gradually subsides. After the alert is over, we help to take our most precious possession, our wives and children, back to their rooms for the night.

I have not experienced such a *beautiful* evening for a long time.

M.

SS Notebook No. 3. 1942.

Yamato

Yamato is the name of a Japanese region that gave birth to great Japanese soldiers. The name Yamato has become a symbol of bravery and duty. There is no trace of the spirit of a foreign people. The Japanese example teaches us that bravery and courage are based on religious spirit.

In the year 1932 of Western chronology, a commander-in-chief who had been severely wounded in the fighting for Shanghai lost consciousness and had the misfortune to fall into enemy hands. He was later freed again and brought back by the advancing Japanese troops. One day, the press reported that this commander had killed himself at the very spot of the fighting during which he had been taken prisoner.

What does this event teach us? The officer was taken prisoner only because he was lying wounded and unconscious; was this a shame for a warrior? Why did he end his life instead of serving his country with his knowledge, experience, courage and intelligence? His attitude can only be explained by the Yamato spirit, the spirit of Japanese men.

The tradition of the valiant knightly spirit has remained particularly alive in the legends of Western Japan; the principles of the legendary knight's spiritual education are contained in the book "Hagakure", a work on chivalric morality in which it is written: "If you have to choose two paths—life or death—then choose the latter. The Commander-in-Chief, deeply influenced by this teaching, followed the path of death. However, why should one seek it? :

It is said in the chivalric code of today's Japanese warriors, the "Senjinkun" or teaching in the warrior camp: "You must not suffer the dishonour of prisoners; after death, you must not leave behind a bad reputation of fault and misfortune." In Japan, it has always been considered a great dishonour to survive in captivity; it is better to die.

In today's war—unlike in ancient times—one cannot avoid being taken prisoner in some cases; one may think that it is not absolutely necessary to die as soon as one has done one's duty with the most modern weapons and that one is much more useful to one's country by staying alive and fulfilling one's vocation—whether in war or in peace. If he survives in the shame of captivity, it means that he did not fight to the death, that he did not have the opportunity to continue the struggle and deeply regrets that he did not fight to the death for the Tenno, the fatherland and the people.

Let it be in the sea where the water baptizes my body,

Whether in the countryside where my bones
are covered by the moss of the mountains—
I only want to fight for the great lord.
Without ever thinking about me.

This ancient song, which we still sing, expresses that the survival of the soldier is simply inconceivable. Lord Nelson said just before he died: "Thank God I did my duty". The Japanese, on the other hand, do not fight because of duty, but to sacrifice his life. Erwin Bälz, one of the leading experts on Japan, recounts a personal experience he had during the Russo-Japanese War:

"Once the young man had taken his leave, Dr. Bälz talked to the Japanese about the war; the old man told him that he had lost his eldest son four years earlier in the Boxer uprising and was now sending the second son to war. He went on to say that his family coat of arms, worn with honour, would now have no representative as he had no more sons. Bälz said to him consolingly: "Not everyone who goes to the front is destined to fall; I believe that your son will return with a great military reputation." The old father shook his head and replied, "No, my son is going into battle to find a heroic death, not to return alive." Erwin Bälz concluded that this was a wise statement, worthy of a philosopher.

This attitude alone explains why Japan has not lost a single war so far, and has achieved prodigious success in the current Greater East Asia War. To approach the United States fleet in tiny war submarines and sink its ships is an act of contempt for death. By self-destruction, Japanese airmen see themselves as part of their charge and rush to the enemy to become true to their calling. It is this spirit that protects the Japanese Empire. Already in 1274 and 1281, this heroic spirit enabled the Japanese army of only 50,000 men to defeat the vastly superior Mongols, who numbered 150,000 men. It was also the spirit that led to stunning victories in the Russo-Japanese War. Soldiers fighting today in the great Pacific, on land, at sea and in the air are all dominated by the idea of sacrificing themselves for the fatherland and joining the ranks of the gods.

Those who call this spirit "fatalism" and see in it an unconscious disregard for precious human life are very far from understanding the Japanese military spirit. The daring acts of Japanese soldiers are precisely manifestations of this energetic spirit fighting for the existence and honour of the Empire, for justice and true peace.

It would also be an unforgivable mistake to see it as a mark of original brutality. We know the Japanese love of flowers; his aesthetic sense does not make him look only for the flower, but he appreciates it much more in its organic relationship with the leaves and branches. Therefore, he never cuts it but leaves it on its branch. Japanese civilisation has developed in its people not only a high spirit of sacrifice but also a compassionate feeling.

The latter is manifested in the attitude of Japanese soldiers towards the enemy, especially towards prisoners. Let us give a significant testimony from the Middle Ages: In 1184, during a fierce civil war, the famous warrior Kumagai defeated a knight from the enemy camp, Atsumori, and cut off his head in accordance with ancient war customs. Atsumori was not yet twenty years old and, affected by his early death, Kumagai put down the sword, left the knighthood and became a priest to spend his life praying for the salvation of the soul of the deceased.

During the Great War, Japanese volunteers serving in the Canadian Army made it to the Western Front; among them was the volunteer Isomura who came upon a wounded German during an attack. The wounded man made it known to Isomura with faint movements that he was suffering from excruciating thirst and Isomura promptly gave him a drink from his canister in which there was still some precious water. Meanwhile, a British soldier had approached and attacked the German with a bayonet; Isomura objected and called out to him, "Can't you see that this man is badly wounded? —"Well then," replied the Briton, "wounded or not— every extra enemy killed is an advantage to us." "Where is your Christian love of neighbour? "I left it at home when I went to war," replied the Briton.

Similarly, the Japanese volunteer Morooka, who was bayoneting a very young opponent, heard him shout 'Mummy'. At that moment, having recognised the word he knew, it was impossible for him to attack the enemy for the second time and the latter, although wounded, was saved and brought back to his homeland.

The Japanese considered it an indignity to be taken prisoner; however, they have deep compassion for the prisoners they themselves take. During the Russo-Japanese War, many Russian prisoners were sent to Japan and they all remembered with gratitude the generous treatment they were given. In Japan, it has always been considered a virtue to adopt this attitude towards the wounded enemy. History tells us that the enemy Koreans involved in the Mongol invasion fell into Japanese hands and deserved no special treatment. They were, however, well received; the Korean emperor was even obliged to express his thanks for this conduct in a letter. Moreover, it must be considered that this Mongolian attack represented a great danger to Japan and its people. In the Russo-Japanese War, the Japanese First Division and Second Army had to take care of the first Russian prisoners; Japanese soldiers were ordered to visit the prisoners in order to familiarise them with the uniforms, insignia and characteristics of the enemy. However, some men from a particular company did not show up for the inspection, for the following reason: It is a shame to be taken prisoner as a soldier and it is unbearable to have to show oneself to the enemy in this way. The samurai understands the feeling of another samurai and spares him this humiliation. For this reason the soldiers did not participate in the inspection of the Russian prisoners. The enemy officers who gave the order to kill all Japanese, even the prisoners, could not understand the attitude of the Japanese soldiers.

In one of the scenes of the current Greater East Asia War, the Philippines, in early January, a number of Japanese civilians were massacred by American troops; such atrocities do not exist in Japanese history.

The Japanese are fighting today for their homeland and for all the peoples of Greater East Asia. They are fighting a hard and sacrificial battle, demanding the maximum of themselves. Nevertheless, they have a deep compassion for their fellow man and this attitude in battle will give rise to many characteristic and striking war events that will go down in the history of warfare, bearing witness to the spirit of Japan, the Yamato Tamashii.

Kazuichi Miura

Everywhere and always, the living example will be the best education.

Adolf Hitler

THE HOUSE OF SS TROOP NO. 4. 1939.

OUR LIFE!

Living means fighting. We are confronted with this principle inexorably and harshly; like a military order, brief and concise, from which no one can escape. One either accepts this order, improving oneself through it until one achieves the best, or one deserts—one perishes—in a vile and pitiful way. There is no other way.

To live means to struggle. This order that Providence has given us, differentiates the lord from the slave, the hero from the coward, the man of action from the talker, character from weakness—defines the good and the bad, the just and the unjust, and allows us to measure our daily work.

There have always been times in history when people thought they could evade this commandment; when they lulled themselves into the assumption that fighting is an abomination and that life is a perpetual state of peace; where attempts were made to transfer the struggle from this world to another; where good was measured by the degree of baseness, cowardice, servility, and evil by the degree of heroism; where treachery and lies were advocated in every way as a means of pressure in the face of struggle.

And again there were times when the heroic spirit celebrated its greatest triumph; when the creative force pointed out new goals and new paths to men; when the struggle had the greatest impact because of the original strength of the will to live, and when man, with his divine strength, gave life its proper meaning.

We find ourselves in this time of gathered energies, of fighting and creative spirit, and of unprecedented will to live.

We approve of life because we love the struggle and we approve of the struggle because we love life. For us, life is not a valley of tears over which unknown gods stand and rejoice to see us crawling on our knees in humility. For us, life is a battlefield that Providence has given us and that we want to conquer by fighting. Our prayer is the struggle, and our life is the prayer. Providence has given us life in the struggle and we want to dominate life in the struggle.

We fight and we are a strong link in the chain formed by our ancestors and our descendants. Through us, life from the earliest times must be passed on in struggle to the future.

This is how Providence wants it—this is how we want it. The will of Providence and ours will shape the age of today, tomorrow, and the day after tomorrow, just as they shaped the age of yesterday and the day before.

A healthy mind in a healthy body.

Living means fighting. Through centuries of struggle, our ancestors have trained us, enabled our people and clans to triumph over cowardice and baseness, servility and the denial of the world until today. It is a monument of heroic struggle and unshakeable will to live.

There would be nothing left of us, of the people and the clans, of the tribes and the blood, if our ancestors had not loved the fight as we do.

There would be no culture, no imperishable monuments of literature, music, painting, architecture, if they had not approved of life and thus of struggle.

Our people would have nothing left of the sacred land of Germany if millions of our ancestors had not risked fighting with victorious laughter to ensure the lives of their descendants. The blood and race of our people would have dried up if our mothers had not given birth to us in battle.

Our existence—our people—gave us the will to live and therefore to fight.

Living means fighting!

The fight of the grey armies in the Great War, the heroic death of two million soldiers, alone ensured the dawn of our people. It is not cowardice and baseness, nor servile moaning, that will ensure the existence and rebirth of the German Reich.

The barrage hit the trenches hour after hour. Heavy calibre fire erupted against the dugouts with an infernal roar and the attack was carried out in smoke and gas under machine-gun fire. Out of the dawn fog, the monstrous tanks raced to crush everything in their path. It was not because of plaintive humility that the positions were held, but because of the unbridled will to live and the imperious desire to win in battle and overcome all hardships.

The good comrade disappeared from the ranks and the friend fell to his death.

The terrors of war threatened to take over. But it was also the struggle for life which, beyond the tragic and horrible nature of the fates, triumphed over all other motivations. Only those who fight can triumph and understand the bliss of victory or the heroic end. But he who refuses to fight, and therefore to live, misunderstands their spirit. He will never understand the joyful feeling that Providence bestows on the fighter who dominates life—surrender is cowardice and God only helps the brave.

In this way we understand the greatness of the struggle of the soldiers in the Great War, and we salute the men who, by persisting in the fight, redirected the destiny of our people. The spirit of combat sponsored the birth of our new world of ideas—National Socialism—and overcame the terrors of the greatest of wars for four years. Only this fighting spirit preserves the life of our nation.

Living means fighting!

Under the hissing and splashing, the steel is poured into the moulds. Under the sound of hammers, in a constant din, iron takes shape to be used by men. In dark shafts full of dusty air and under constant threat, coal is sucked out and uncovered. On high scaffolding, between heaven and earth, men put their lives on the line in creative work. On the raging sea the struggle with the original element becomes the visible expression of life. Under a scorching sun, the rising wheat bends under the scythe. In hospitals and laboratories the human spirit struggles with death. All this is not the expression of a fatalistic and superfluous necessity impressed by alien gods, but constitutes a fighting life, a hard will to select and to win. In every place a decisive battle is fought which determines man's position in relation to

God. The creator man conceives his relationship with his god in combat, in battle. He does not see his struggle as a shame, as damnation, as a sin, but he sees himself as a lord, vividly demonstrating the order given by Providence: "To live means to struggle". For him, the sweat is not the wages of sinful action but the reward for his masterful creative power and joy.

Living means fighting!

In thousands of rallies and street battles, the political soldier puts his mark on his contemporaries. Despite heaps of rubbish, insidious attacks and slander, the Movement achieved victory. In spite of physical and spiritual terror, National Socialism today flies its victorious banner over Germany. It was the manifestation of the courage to live in defiance of death, of the sacred joy of battle that triumphed over all. It was the stream of the healthy and uninterrupted blood of our people that put an end to the actions of an international pacifist hypocrisy with the colours black, red and gold, to clear the way for a new heroic generation. And this is the only way to understand the greatness of the martyrs of the Movement. They are the symbol of the life of our people; the most worthy sons of the ancestors, who appear in the most distant future as the living priests of a heroic conception and civility.

Living means fighting!

In everyday life, the mercantile spirit takes hold like a poisonous snake. The day's work weighs on the body and mind like an almost insurmountable burden. Insanity and lack of character compete with each other. Vanity and pleasure apparently celebrate their triumph and human weaknesses are praised. It is never the servile mentality of the knaves that puts an end to all this, but always and only the fighting man feeling solidarity as a soldier on the battlefield of life, ignoring class and birth, wealth and poverty—only responsible to his people and his noble blood, from the ancestors, to whom the descendants will call to account.

We stand in the midst of the struggle and before our god, knowing that all creative power lies within us, and that it depends on us to dominate life. The daily chores—the small daily duties—are seemingly a burden, but even so, we do not want to do without them. For the greatness that distinguishes the work within the mass, that survives the centuries, is first of all made up of details. Just as the clockwork is made up of large and small wheels, just as the orchestra is made up of instruments, and just as the rhythmic steps of hundreds of people make the earth tremble, so we too, each in our own place, as wheels, as instruments and as walkers, have to carry out our duties and our struggle so that the work can come into being.

Monument in memory of the martyrs of the 1923 putsch.

"Having faith is the greatest strength there is.
Adolf Hitler

It is the work that will reveal the greatness of a generation even after centuries and that must show the way to descendants after millennia as a heroic epic.

We have the will to record ourselves and our actions in history with styli of brass. We have the will to measure our strength at every moment, and apart from the will, we have the power to surpass ourselves, as a memorial of fighting attitude.

Is it not deplorable to confuse errors of character with a brazenly servile attitude, instead of countering them victoriously in a daily struggle? Is it not disgusting when men with melodramatic suffering faces try to define life as a black infamy because they do not have the courage to draw the consequence of Providence's command and admit the struggle?

Is it not a mockery of God when, because of whining creatures, he is held responsible for their failure in life through lack of fighting spirit? Is it not a pernicious mercantile spirit when, because of this moaning, they deny the sentence of God which rewards their desertion of the life which God entrusted to them to dominate?

We have no understanding for such a stupid act.

Until now, such creatures have never been guides for men who, like granite cornerstones, survive the millennia.

For this reason, we do not want to spend our life, which Providence has given us, in damnation, contemplating it as a quagmire from which no one escapes; for our life is not a sin since it comes to us from God, and our struggle is not damnation since it is a heroic prayer.

We leave the cowardly and the wretched to crawl on their knees, the faint-hearted to groan in despair; for God is with us because God is with the believers.

We salute the heroic spirits of the distant past as the comrades-in-arms of our lives because we know that an eternal truth comes out of Nietzsche's mouth when he says:

"War and courage have done greater things than love of neighbour. It is not your pity but your bravery that has so far saved the unfortunate.

Kurt Ellersieck

We must bring a new and more honest faith, not only to Germany but to the world; not only for the sake of Germany but also for the sake of the world, which will perish from auto-poisoning if it does not overcome its present opinion of Germany.

Adolf Hitler

BIBLIOGRAPHY

The translations of the Nordic poems *of* the Edda are taken from Régis Boyer's *Les religions de l'Europe du Nord*, published by Fayard-Denoël, 1974. The texts by Tacitus are taken from the book *La Germanie*, by Tacitus, translated by Jacques Perret, published by *Les belles lettres*, 1983.

Sources published before 1945:
RuSHA and SS-Hauptamt publications:
SS-Leithefte
Germanische SS-Leithefte
Annals
Das SS-Mannschaftshaus
Politischer Dienst für SS und Polizei
Der Weg zum Reich
Glauben und Kämpfen.

From the SS *Nordland* publishing house:
Speech by the Reichsführer SS in Quedlinburg Cathedral on 6 July 1936.

Other:
Auf Hieb und Stich, a collection of editorials by Gunther d'Alquen that appeared in the SS newspaper *Das Schwarze Korps* between 1935 and 1937.
Organisationsbuchder NSDAP, 1938.
Die SS, Geschichte und Aufgabe, by Gunther d'Alquen, 1939.
Die Gestaltung der Feste im Jahres- und Lebenslauf in der SS-Familie, SS-Oberabschnitt West.
Prüfungsfragen für SS-Führer und SS-Unterführer, SS-Abschnitt VIII, 1 November 1938.
Aux armes pour l'Europe, text of the speech made by Léon Degrelle at the Palais de Chaillot in 1944.
SS Almanac 1944, last edition.
Devenir, newspaper for the French SS.

Works published after 1945not translated into French:
Ackermann Josef, *Himmler als Ideologe*, Müsterschmidt, Göttingen, 1970.
Hausser Paul, *Soldaten wie andere auch*, Munin Verlag, Osnabrück, 1966.
Wegner Bemdt, *Hitlers politischen Soldaten: Die Waffen-SS 1933–1945*, Schöningh, 1988.
These books are among the most important and well-documented works published on this subject in Germany.

The photographs and illustrations are all from the author's personal collection.

ALREADY PUBLISHED

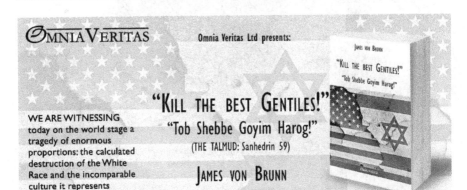

Omnia Veritas Ltd presents:

Fatima
and the
GREAT CONSPIRACY

This meant creating, or making, money out of nothing, being allowed to call it money, and to lend it to the public at a high interest rate.

This private syndicate acquiring a cast-iron monopoly over the supply and circulation of the money not just of England, but of the whole world...

Omnia Veritas Ltd presents:

The BabylonianWoe
by
DAVID ASTLE

"There was a class of persons who very well understood each other's interests, who very likely were related by racial and religious custom, and whose supra-nationalism transcended all city boundaries and borders of states."

"Yesterday it was a *conspiracy against the men of a city*, or a relatively small state; today a *conspiracy against the whole world*."

David Astle's masterpiece in a brand new edition!

Omnia Veritas Ltd presents:

FREDERICK SODDY
THE ROLE OF MONEY
WHAT IT SHOULD BE CONTRASTED WITH WHAT IT HAS BECOME

This book attempts to clear up the mystery of money in its social aspect

This, surely, is what the public really wants to know about money

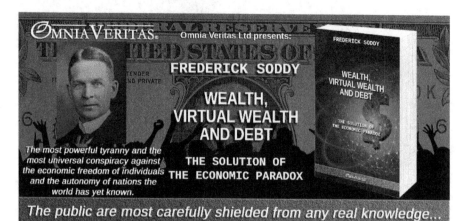

Printed in the USA
CPSIA information can be obtained
at www.ICGtesting.com
CBHW070315180724
11678CB00003B/150